THE
RELIGION OF ISLĀM

A COMPREHENSIVE DISCUSSION
OF THE SOURCES, PRINCIPLES
AND PRACTICES OF ISLĀM

BY
MAULĀNĀ MUḤAMMAD ‘ALĪ

1 9 9 0

THE AḤMADIYYA ANJUMAN IS<u>H</u>Ā‘AT ISLĀM (LAHORE)
U.S.A.

AḤMADIYYA ANJUMAN IS̲H̲Ā'AT ISLĀM LAHORE USA
P. O. Box 3370
Dublin, Ohio
43016, U.S.A.
Ph. 614-873-1030
Fax 614-873-1022
email: aaiil@aol.com
Website: www.muslim.org

FIRST EDITION 1936
SECOND EDITION 1950
THIRD EDITION (Revised) 1971
FOURTH EDITION 1973
FIFTH EDITION 1983
SIXTH EDITION (Revised) 1990
SEVENTH EDITION 1995
EIGHTH EDITION 2005

Library of Congress Catalog Card Number: 89-084 398

ISBN 0-913321-23-0 — Paperback

ISBN 0-913321-32-X— Hardcover

Typography: CompuType, Vancouver, B.C., Canada

PRINTED IN THE UNITED STATES

AL - AZHAR AL - SHARIF
ISLAMIC RESEARCH ACADEMY
GENERAL DEPARTMENT
For Research, Writting & Translation

الأزهر الشريف
مجمع البحوث الاسلامية
الادارة العامة
للبحوث والتأليف والترجمة

بناء على الطلب المقدم من السيدة سمينا مالك إلى الإدارة العامة للبحوث والتأليف والترجمة بمجمع البحوث الإسلامية بالأزهر الشريف بشأن الإطلاع وابداء الرأى فى مدى صلاحية كتاب بعنوان "الدين الاسلامى" The Religion of Islam تأليف مولانا محمد على باللغة الانجليزية .

تفيد الإدارة بأنه الكتاب المذكور يحتوى على معلومات مفيدة ونافعة ويستفيد منه القارئ المسلم الناطق بالإنجليزية .

والسلام عليكم ورحمة الله وبركاته

تحريرا فى :-
١٤٢٣/٤/٢٠ هـ
٢٠٠٢/٧/١ م

ع . أبو عليوه

مدير عام
البحوث والتأليف والترجمة

"السيد أحمد على مصباح"

إدارة الترجمة
ضياء الدين محمد محمد إ

Al-Azhar Al-Sharif
Islamic Research Academy
General Department for
Research, Writing and Translation

Book Review

Referring to the request submitted by Mrs Samina Malik to the General Administration of Publication, Research and Translation, Islamic Research Academy, Al- Azhar Al-Sharif regarding the opinion concerning the Book:

The Religion of Islam

written by Maulana Muhammad Ali in English, to review the book regarding its correctness.

The Department hereby informs that the above mentioned book contains beneficial and helpful information, and the Muslim reader whose native language is English will benefit from this book.

Assalaamu Alaikum wa Rahmatullahi wa Barakaatahu

1/7/02

General Director
Department of Research,
Writing and Translation
Ali Abdel Baky

Department of Translation
Ziauddin Muhammad Muhammad

SOME OTHER BOOKS BY THE AUTHOR

English

Translation of the Holy Qur'ān (with commentary and Arabic text).
Translation of the Holy Qur'ān (with abridged commentary and without Arabic text).
Muhammad the Prophet.
Muhammad and Christ.
Early Caliphate.
Introduction to the Study of the Ḥadīth.
Selections from the Holy Qur'ān.
Introduction to the Study of the Holy Qur'ān.
The Muslim Prayer Book.
Prayers of the Holy Qur'ān.
Antichrist, Gog and Magog.
History of the Prophets.
The New World Order.
A Manual of Ḥadīth.
Living Thoughts of the Prophet Muḥammad.

Urdu

Bayān al-Qur'ān, translation and commentary of the Holy Qur'ān, in three volumes.
Ḥamā'il Sharīf, translation of the Holy Qur'ān with abridged commentary.
Faḍl al-Bārī, commentary of Ṣaḥīḥ al-Bukhārī, in 2 volumes.
Al-Nubuwwat fil Islām, proof of the finality of prophethood.
Sīrat Khair al-Bashar, biography of the Holy Prophet.
Tārīkh Khilāfat Rāshidah, history of the first four Caliphs.
Maqām-i-Ḥadīth, the place of Tradition in Islām.
Zinda Nabī kī Zinda Ta'līm, the living thoughts of the Prophet Muḥammad.
Jama' al-Qur'ān, Collection and arrangement of the Qur'ān.

PREFACE TO THE THIRD EDITION

This edition of Maulānā Muḥammad 'Alī's famous book, *The Religion of Islām,* is the first to appear after the author's death. The first thought which comes to mind is to acknowledge the very great service which the Maulānā has rendered to the cause of Islām. Born in 1876, he acquired three University degrees in Literature and Law and, at a time when the prospects of a bright worldly career were wide open to him, he dedicated his life to the service of Islām. And what a dedication! He took up the pen in that cause in 1901, as a young man in his twenties, wielded it incessantly, untiringly and devotedly for half a century and did not lay it down until it was snatched from him by the hand of death.[1]

His English Translation of the Holy Qur'ān, a product of seven long years[2] of laborious and original research, not only marked an epoch in the understanding of Islām by Muslim intelligentsia but also made an impact on Western scholarship, an impact which is noticeable in the changed outlook on Islām and the changed tone of literature about Islām which has since appeared. The popularity and widespread acclaim commanded by this English Translation — the first ever by a Muslim — was due not only to the tremendous research carried out by the Maulānā, the tracing of the authentic meaning of words and verses, the detailed references to acknowledged works of lexicology and standard commentaries, the emphasis on the underlying significance of Sections and Chapters and on the continuity of the theme linking them one with another; nor was it due solely to the scrupulously honest and faithful rendering, without literary flourishes and without any attempt to pander to preconceived or popular notions; nor yet was it entirely on account of the enlightened and rational approach and the answers to all criticism against the Qur'ān; but was also the result of something much more which no scholarship can offer — the gift of inner purity. Maulāna Muḥammad 'Alī wielded a scholar's pen with a saint's hand, and therein lay the secret of his Translation becoming a spiritual force for the seeker after the truth. His work was a pioneer venture, breaking altogether new ground, and the pattern set was followed by all subsequent translations of the Qur'ān by Muslims. The Maulānā's Translation, which ran into several editions, was extensively revised by him in the closing years of his life.[3] Some of his other works are listed elsewhere.

1. 13 October, 1951. 2. 1909-1916. 3. 1946-1951

The Religion of Islām, originally published in 1936 with only slight alterations by the author, contains over 2,500 quotations from original sources,most of them from the Qur'ān. These quotations followed the translation adopted in the 1917 edition of the author's English Translation of the Holy Qur'ān. All of these have now been revised in accordance with the 1951 (fourth) edition of the Translation which, as already stated, had been extensively revised by the Maulānā. In a few cases, explanatory footnotes have been added or amended in accordance with the footnotes given in the revised edition of the English Translation. These changes represent the major revision carried out in this edition of *The Religion of Islām*. Certain other portions of the book have also been edited and brought up to date. The author intended to add two more chapters to the book on the *Muslim State* and the *Ethics of Islām*, but could not do so himself. Both subjects were, however, dealt with by him, though briefly, in two subsequent works, *The New World Order* and *Living Thoughts of the Prophet Muhammad,* and the material from these sources, with necessary editing, has been included in the two additional chapters at the end of this book. The treatment of these subjects is, however, not as detailed as that of the other subjects which originally formed a part of this book.

We are grateful to Mr. Muhammad Ahmad, M.A., son of the author, for having undertaken the revision of this book on the above lines, and for having gone through the proofs.

— THE PUBLISHERS

1. 1946-1951.

PREFACE TO THE SIXTH EDITION

This edition goes to press with corrections in the Holy Qur'ān and Hadīth references.

—THE PUBLISHERS

PREFACE

There could be no better comment on the prevalent Muslim lethargy towards Islām than the fact that non-Muslim contributions to Islamic religious literature in English are by far in excess of the Muslim. It is true that much of this literature draws a distorted picture of Islām, but even here the Muslim is more to blame than the non-Muslim, for it is his duty to place the right kind of material before a world whose thirst for knowledge is insatiable. But whatever may be said as to the superficiality of one part of this literature and the prejudicial tenor of another, it cannot be denied that Europe has made a very valuable contribution to research on the religion of Islām and the history of the Muslims. The Muslims are also turning their attention to the producing of religious literature in English, but the attempt is, as yet, a very weak one, directed more to appealing to the market than to serious efforts based on hard work and critical acumen.

"The Religion of Islam" is the name of a book written by the Rev. F.A. Klein and published in 1906. It was through the courtesy of a friend that this book fell into my hands in the year 1928. He had read it with pain, he said, on account of the distorted picture of Islām that it contained, and he suggested that I should write a comprehensive work containing a true picture of Islām and dealing in detail with its teachings. More than twenty years before this, and just about the time when this book had been published in London, on the 13th of February 1907 to be exact, the Founder of the Aḥmadiyyah Movement, Ḥaḍrat Mirzā Ghulām Aḥmad of Qādiān, had charged me with the writing of an English book which should contain all that was necessary for a Muslim, or a non-Muslim, to know about the religion of Islām, and to give a true picture of the religion which was largely misrepresented. The multifarious duties which I had to perform as President of the Aḥmadiyyah Anjuman Ishā'at Islām were a great hindrance, but the call of duty overcame these difficulties, and I set to work immediately, after going through Klein's book, and the work is now being published under the same name.

Had I been able to devote myself entirely to this task, it should not have taken more than three years. But seven years have passed, and still I am not satisfied that the book is as complete a picture as I had wished it to be. It has been my good fortune, from one point of view, to contribute to the literary activities of Islām and to be the head of a society which aims at the propagation of Islām, as the two works are so closely associated, but from another point of view it is a misfortune, since each of these works requires entire devotion to itself, to the exclusion of the other. I turned to the author's work again and again, amidst the many duties which I was required to perform as the head of a newly established society, but always to be recalled to some other task which the urgency of the moment forced on my attention. An author's singleness of purpose was not vouchsafed to me, and I have to confess that the work may, perhaps, suffer somewhat from this handicap.

There is yet another circumstance which may detract from the value of the book. I fell ill, rather seriously, in March 1935, and my medical advisers ordered complete rest for some time. Even after convalescence, I was advised to give up hard work, a direction which, to be candid, I have not been able to carry out, since the publication could not be delayed any longer. So I had to hurry the work; and, more than that, I had to relinquish two chapters which I originally intended to include.* Besides, the concluding chapters have not been dealt with as exhaustively as I had wished. I only hope that these and other deficiencies will be removed if I am spared to bring out a second edition.

Islām, as I have pointed out in the Introduction to this book, is a religion which deals not only with the ways of devotion and the means which make man attain communion with God, but also with a vast variety of problems relating to the world around us and questions that pertain to the social and political life of man. In a treatise which aims at giving a true picture of Islām, it was necessary not only to discuss all the laws and regulations of the system but also to throw full light on the principles on which it is based, and even upon the sources from which its teachings, principles and laws are derived. I have, therefore divided this book into three parts. The first part deals with the sources from which the teachings of Islām are drawn, and which can serve the purpose of guiding the Muslim world in its present and future needs; the second describes the creed of Islām or the fundamental doctrines of the religion; while the third treats of the laws and regulations of Islām which govern not only a Muslim's domestic, social and international relations but also his relations with God, which are the mainspring of the development of his faculties. An introduction has been added dealing with some questions relating to religion in general and Islām in particular.

A work of this nature would have carried little weight if it did not give full references to original authorities, and this had made the work laborious, for it contains over 2,500 references and quotations. The Holy Qur'ān, being the original source on which all principles and laws of Islam are based, occupies the first place in this list, and next to it comes Bukhārī, the most reliable book of Ḥadīth. It is on these two authorities that the present work is chiefly based, but others, besides these, have been freely quoted and referred to where necessary.

MUḤAMMAD 'ALĪ
PRESIDENT
Aḥmadiyyah Anjuman Isha'āt Islām
Lahore

LAHORE
Ahmadiyyah Buildings
21st November, 1935.

The Ethics of Islam and *The Muslim State*.

PREFACE TO THE SECOND EDITION

Owing to a heavy demand of the book all of a sudden, I was called upon to send this Second Edition to the press urgently and could not find time for the two chapters which I had promised to add to the second edition. I have, however, dealt with these two subjects, Ethics and State, in a later work, *A Manual of Ḥadīth*, and have also included a chapter on State in another work of mine, *The New World Order,* and I would refer the reader to these two books for necessary information on these subjects. The book is therefore going to the press as it was printed first with very insignificant changes only.

MUḤAMMAD 'ALI
PRESIDENT
Aḥmadiyyah Anjuman Ishā'at Islām
Lahore

LAHORE
Muslim Town
1949

LIST OF CONTENTS

INTRODUCTION

PART ONE

THE SOURCES OF ISLĀM

PART TWO

THE PRINCIPLES OF ISLAM

PART THREE

LAWS AND REGULATIONS OF ISLAM

TRANSLITERATION

In this book I have adopted the most recent rules of transliteration recognized by European Orientalists, with very slight variations, as explained below, but no transliteration can exactly express the vocalic differences of two languages, and the Roman characters in which Arabic words and phrases have been spelt give the sound of the original only approximately. Besides the inability of the characters of one language to represent the exact pronunciation of the words of another, there is another difficulty in romanizing Arabic words, *viz.*, that in certain combinations the pronunciation does not follow the written characters; for example, al-Raḥmān is pronounced ar-Raḥmān, the sound *l* merging in that of the next letter *r*. To this category belong all the letters which are known by the name of *al-ḥurūf al-shamsiyya* (lit., *solar letters*), and they are as follows: tā, thā, dāl, dhāl, rā, zā, sīn, shīn, ṣād, dzād, ṭā, zā, lām, nūn (dentals, sibilants, and liquids). Whenever a word beginning with one of these letters has the prefix *al* (representing the article *the*), the *lām* is passed over in pronunciation and assimilated to the following consonant; in the case of all other letters, *al* is pronounced fully. This merging of one letter in another occurs also in certain other cases, for which a grammar of the Arabic language should be referred to. I have followed the written form but in transliterating the adhān (call to prayer) and prayer recital, I have followed the pronunciation, for the facility of the lay reader, writing ar-Raḥmān instead of al-Raḥmān, and so on.

The system adopted in this work is as follows:

CONSONANTS

Arabic letters	*Sounds*	*Represented by*
ء	hamza (sounds like *h* in *hour* = a sort of catch in the voice)	'
ب	bā (same as *b*)	b
ت	tā (the Italian dental, softer than *t*)	t
ث	thā (between *th* in *thing* and *s*)	th
	jīm (like *g* in *gem*)	j
ج	ḥā (very sharp but smooth guttural	
ح	aspirate)	ḥ
خ	khā (like *ch* in the Scotch word *loch*)	kh
د	dāl (Italian dental, softer than *d*)	d
ذ	dhāl (sounds between *z* and *th* in *that*)	dh
ر	rā (same as *r*)	r

Arabic letters	*Sounds*	*Represented by*
ز	*zā (same as z)*	z
س	sīn (same as *s*)	s
ش	shīn (same as *sh* in *she*)	sh
ص	ṣād (strongly articulated *s*, like *ss* in *hiss*)	ṣ
ض	dzād (aspirated *d*, between *d* and *z*)	dz
ط	ṭā (strongly articulated palatal *t*)	ṭ
ظ	zā (strongly articulated palatal *z*)	z
ع	‘ain (somewhat like a strong guttural *hamza*, not a mere vowel)	‘
غ	ghain (guttural *g*, but soft)	gh
ف	fā (same as *f*)	f
ق	qāf (strongly articulated guttural *k*)	q
ك	kāf (same as *k*)	k
ل	lām (same as *l*)	l
م	Mīm (same as *m*)	m
ن	nūn (same as *n*)	n
ه	hā (same as *h*)	h
و	wāo (same as *w*)	w
ى	yā (same as *y*)	y

VOWELS

The vowels are represented as follows:

Short vowels	*fatḥah*, as *u* in *tub*	a
	kasrah, as *i* in *pin*	i
	*dzammah,*as *u* in *pull*	u
Long vowels	long *fatḥah*, as *a* in *father*	ā
	long *kasrah*, as *ee* in *deep*	ī
	long *dzammah*, as *oo* in *moot*	ū
	fatḥah before *wāo*	au
	fatḥah before *yā*	ai

Tanwīn ,, ″ ‘’ is represented by *in,an,un,* respectively. The short and long vowels at the end of a word are shown as parts of the words, as *qāla* where the final *a* stands for the *fatḥah* on *lām*, but the *tanwīn* is shown as a separate syllable, as *Muḥammad-in*.

LIST OF AUTHORITIES
AND
KEY TO REFERENCES

The Holy Qur'ān. — All references given without an indication of name are to the Holy Book, the first figure representing the number of the chapter, and the second figure the number of the verse.

AA. . .	Amīr 'Alī's *Muhammadan Law.*
'Abd al-Aziz, Shāh, of Delhi	*'Ujāla Nāfi'a.*
AD.* . .	*Sunan*, of Abū Dāwūd.
AH. . .	*Tafsir al-Baḥr al-Muḥīt*,by Abū 'Abd Allāh Muḥammad ibn Yūsuf, generally known as Abū Ḥayyān, according to the edition published by the Sa'āda Press, Cairo, in 4 volumes.
Ah. . .	*Musnad*, of al-Imām Aḥmad ibn Muḥammad ibn Ḥanbal, according to the edition printed at al-Maimana Press, Cairo, 6 volumes, 1306 A.H.
Ai. . .	*'Umdat al-Qārī* by Badr al-Dīn Maḥmūd ibn Aḥmad, Al-'Ainī, Ḥanafī, according to the edition printed at al-'Āmira Press, Cairo.
AM-AD. . .	*'Aun al-Ma'būd 'alā Sunani Abī Dāwūd*, by Abū 'Abd al-Raḥmān Sharf al-Ḥaq, commonly known as Muḥammad Ashraf, according to the edition printed at Anṣārī Press, Delhi, 4 volumes, 1318 A.H.
Amīr 'Alī . .	*The Spirit of Islām*, published by S.K. Lahiri & Co., Calcutta, 1902 A. D.
AR . .	*The Principles of the Muhammadan Jurisprudence*, by (Sir) 'Abd al-Raḥīm, printed at the S.P.C.K. Press, Madras, 1911.

*In the references to collections of Tradition, the first figure represents the number of the *kitāb* and the second the number of the *bāb*. In the case of collections which are not divided into *kitābs* and *bābs*, as also in the case of commentaries and other books, the reference is given to pages, the Roman figure representing the volume when a book has more volumes than one.

ASh	*The Muhammadan Law of Marriage and Divorce,* by Aḥmad Shukrī.
Bai	*Tafsīr al-Baidzāwī*, by Qādzī Baidzāwī, according to the edition of Mujtabā'ī Press, Delhi, 2 volumes, 1326 A.H.
Bible	the Holy; references to different books are indicated in the usual way.
Bosworth Smith, R.	*Mohammed and Mohammedanism*, 3rd edition, printed and published by John Murray, Albemarle Street, London, 1889.
Bq.*	*Kitāb al-Sunan* of Abū Bakr Aḥmad ibn al-Ḥusain commonly known as Baihāqī.
Bu.	*al-Ṣaḥīḥ al-Bukhārī* by al-Ḥāfiz, Abū 'Abd Allāh Muḥammad ibn Ismā'īl al-Bukhārī.
D.	*Al-Musnad*, of Abū Muḥammad 'Abd Allāh ibn 'Abd al-Raḥmān, commonly known as al-Dārimī.
Denison, J.H.	*Emotion as the Basis of Civilization,* New York, London, 1928 A.D.
DI.	Hughes' *Dictionary of Islam.*
Dm	*The One Volume Bible Commentary,* edited by J.R. Dummelow, printed by Macmillan and Co. Ltd., 1913 A.D
En. Br.	*Encyclopaedia Britannica*, 11th edition.
En. Is.	*The Encyclopaedia of Islam*, printed and published by E.T. Brill Leyden, Luzac & Co. London.
En. J.	*The Jewish Encyclopaedia*, published by Funk & Wagnalls Co. (New York and London), 1904 A.D.
FA	*Fiqh Akbar*, by al-Imām al-A'zam Abū Ḥanīfah al-Nu'mān ibn Thābit al-Kūfī, published by the Dār al-Kutub al-'Arabiyyat al-Kubrā, Cairo.
FB.	*Fatḥ al-Bārī*, by al-Ḥāfiz, Abu-l-Fadzl Shahāb al-Dīn Aḥmad ibn 'Alī, according to the edition printed at al-Mīrīya Press, Cairo, 13 vols.

*Books marked with an asterisk have been drawn upon through other authorities.

FBn. . . *Fatḥ al-Bayān fī Maqāṣid al-Qur'ān*, by Ṣiddīq ibn Ḥasan ibn 'Alī al-Bukhārī according to the edition printed at al-Mīrīya Press, Cairo, 10 vols., 1301 A.H.

Ft. A. . . *Fatāwā 'Ālamgīrī*, printed at the Nawal Kishore Press, Cawnpore, in 4 volumes.

Gibb. . . Prof. H.A.R. — *Whither Islam?* London, 1932

H. . . *al-Hidāya*, by Abū al-Ḥasan 'Alī ibn Abī Bakr al-Marghinānī, according to the edition printed, vol. I at the Curzon Press, Delhi, and vol. II at the Mujtabā'ī Press, Delhi, 2 vols., 1914 A.D.

Hirschfeld, H. . . *New Researches into the Composition and Exegesis of the Qoran*, published by the Royal Asiatic Society, London, 1902

Hj. . . *Ḥujjat-Allāh al-Bālighah*, by Shāh Walī Allāh, Muḥaddath, Dehlvī, Ṣiddīqī Press, Brailey, 1286 A.H.

Ibn Hajar . . *Nazhat al-Naẓar Sharḥ Nukhbat al-Fikr.*

Ibn Jauzī . . *Fatḥ al-Mughīth*.

IH. . . *alSīrat al-Nabawiyyah*, by Abū Muḥammad 'Abd al-Malik ibn Muḥammad ibn Hishām.

IJ-C. . . *Jāmi' al-Bayān fī Tafsīr al-Qur'ān*, by al-Imām Abū Ja'far Muḥammad ibn Jarīr Ṭabarī, according to the edition printed in al-Maimana Press, Cairo, 30 volumes.

IJ-H. . . *Tārīkh al-Umami wa-l-Mulūk*, by Abū Ja'far Muḥammad ibn Jarīr Ṭabarī, according to the edition printed in al-Ḥusainiyyah Press, Cairo, 12 vols.

IK. . . *Tafsīr Ibn Kathīr*, by al-Ḥafiz, 'Imād al-Dīn Abū-l-Fidā Ismā'īl ibn 'Umar ibn Kathīr Qarshī, according to the edition printed in Mīrīyyah Press, Cairo, 10 vols., 1300 A.H.

IM. . . *Sunan*, of Abū 'Abd Allāh Muḥammad ibn Yazīd ibn Māja Qazwīnī.

Is. . . *Iṣābah fī Tamyīz al-Ṣaḥābah*, by Shahāb al-Dīn Abu-l-Fadzl Aḥmad ibn 'Alī according to the edition printed in al-Sa'ādah Press, Cairo, 4 vols., 1323 A.H.

IS. T.	. .	*Kitāb al-Ṭabaqāt al-Kubrā*, by Muhammad ibn Sa'd, according to the edition printed in London, 8 vols., 1322 A.H. The small Roman figure indicates the part.
It.	. .	*Itqān fi 'Ulūm al-Qur'ān*, by al-Imām Jalāl al-Dīn Suyūṭī, according to the edition published by Azhariyya Press, Cairo, 2 vols., 1318 A.H.
JJ.*	. .	*Jam' al-Jawāmi'*, by Imām al-Ḥafiz Jalāl al-Dīn Suyūṭī.
JS.	. .	*Jāmi' al-Ṣaghīr*, by Imām al-Ḥafiz Jalāl al-Dīn Suyūṭī, according to the edition printed in the Khairiyya Press, Cairo, 2 vols.
KA.	. .	*Kashf al-Asrār*, 'Abd al-'Azīz al-Bukhārī.
KU.	. .	*Kanz al-'Ummāl fi Sunani-l-Aqwāl wa-l-Af'āl*, by Shaikh 'Alā' al-Dīn al-Muttaqī ibn Ḥisām al-Dīn; the second figure represents the number of the ḥadīth, according to the edition printed at Hyderabad Deccan, 1312 A.H. *The Ins and Outs of Mesopotamia.*
LA.	. .	*Lisān al-'Arab*, by Imām 'Allāma Abū-l-Fadzl Jamāl al-Dīn Muḥammad ibn Mukarram.
Lane, E.W.	. .	*Selections from the Holy Qur'ān.*
LL.	. .	Lane's *Arabic-English Lexicon.*
M.	. .	*al-Ṣaḥīḥ al-Muslim,* by Imām Abū Ḥusain Muslim ibn al-Ḥajjāj.
Ma.	. .	*Mu'aṭṭā*, by Imām Mālik Abū 'Abd Allāh Mālik ibn Anas ibn 'Āmir, printed at the Mujtabā'ī Press, Delhi, 1320 A.H.
Mau	. .	*Maudzū'āt*, by Mullā 'Alī Qārī, printed at the Mujtabā'ī Press, Delhi, 1315 A.H.
MD.	. .	*Miftāḥ al-Sa'ādah*, by Maulā Aḥmad ibn Muṣṭafā, printed at Dā'irat al-Ma'ārif al-Nizāmiyya, Hyderabad Deccan.
Mf.	. .	*al-Mawāqif*, by al-Qādzī 'Adzud al-Dīn 'Abd al-Raḥmān ibn Aḥmad, printed at al-Sa'āda Press, Cairo, 8 vols.

MI. . . *Maqālāt al-Islāmiyyīn*, by Abū-Ḥasan Ismā'īl ibn 'Alī al-Ash'arī.

MK . . *Mustadrak*, of Ḥākim.

MM. . . *Al-Mishkāt al-Maṣābīḥ*, by Shaikh Walī al-Dīn Muḥammad ibn 'Abd Allāh. The 3rd number (in small Roman figures) represents the *faṣl* (section).

Mq. . . *Muqaddamah*, by 'Allāmah ibn Khaldūn 'Abd al-Raḥmān, printed at al-Taqaddum Press, Cairo, 1329 A.H.

Muir, Sir W. . . *Life of Mahomet*, published by Smith Elder & Co., 1894.

-do- . . *The Caliphate*.

N. . . *al-Nihāyah fi Gharībi-l-Ḥadīthi wa-l-Āthār*, by al-Mubārak ibn Muḥammad ibn Muḥammad Jazrī, commonly called Ibn Athīr.

NA. . . *Nūr al-Anwār*, by Ḥāfiz Shaikh Aḥmad, printed at the Mujtabā'ī Press, Delhi, 1331 A.H.

Ns. . . *Sunan*, of Abū 'Abd al-Raḥmān Aḥmad ibn 'Alī al-Nasā'ī.

Palmer, E.H. . . *The Qur'ān*.

Q. . . *Qāmūs*, by 'Allāmah Shaikh Naṣr al-Ḥurainī, printed at the Maimana Press, Cairo.

Qs. . . *Irshād al-Sari*, of Aḥmad ibn Muḥammad al-Khaṭīb al-Qasṭalānī, printed at the Nawal Kishore Press, Cawnpore, 1284 A.H., 10 volumes.

R. . . *Al-Mufridāt fi Gharībi-l-Qur'ān*, of Imām Abū-l-Qāsim al-Ḥusain ibn Abu-l-Fadzl al-Rāghib.

Rd. . . *Radd al-Muḥtār*, by Shaikh Muḥammad Amīn, generally known as Ibn 'Ābidīn.

RI. . . *The Religion of Islām*, by F.A. Klein, printed at the S.P.C.K. Press, Madras, 1906.

Rz. . . *Al-Tafsīr al-Kabīr*, by Muḥammad Fakhr al-Dīn Rāzī, printed at al-'Āmira Press, 1307 A.H., 8 volumes.

Sale, G. . . *Al-Koran*.

Sell, The Rev. . . *The Faith of Islām*.

TA. . . *Tāj al-'Arūs*, by Abu-l-Faidz Sayyid Muḥammad Murtadzā al-Husainī.

SH. . . *Sharḥ Dīwān Ḥamāsah*, by Shaikh Abū Zakariyya Yaḥyā ibn 'Alī al-Tabrezī, 4 volumes.

Tkh. . . *Tārīkh al-Khulafā'*, by Shaikh Jalāl al-Dīn al-Suyūṭī, printed at the Government Press, Lahore, 1870 A.D.

Torrey, C.C. . . *The Jewish Foundations of Islām,* New York, 1933.

Tr. . . *al-Jāmi' al-Tirmidhī*, by al-Imām al-Ḥāfiz Abū 'Isā Muḥammad Ibn 'Isā.

Tr.Is. . . *Traditions of Islām*, by Alfred Guillaume, printed at the Clarendon Press, Oxford, 1924 A.D.

Z. . . *Al-Sharḥ 'ala-l-Mawāhib al-laduniyya*, by 'Allāma Muḥammad ibn 'Abd al-Bāqī al-Zurqānī, 8 vols.

ZM. . . *Zād al-Ma'ād*, by 'Allāma Shams al-Dīn Abū 'Abd al-Mālik, generally known as Ibn Qayyim, printed at the Maimaniyyah Press, Cairo, 1300 A.H.

INTRODUCTION

INTRODUCTION

Islām, not Muhammadanism

The first point to be noted in a discussion on the religion[1] of Islām is that the name of the system is not Muhammadanism, as is generally supposed in the west, but Islām. Muḥammad was the name of the Holy Prophet through whom this religion was revealed, and European writers call it Muhammadanism after him, on the analogy of such names as Buddhism, Confucianism, Christianity, and the like, but the name Muhammadanism was absolutely unknown to the followers of Islām. It is neither to be found in the Qur'ān nor in the Sayings of the Prophet. The name of the system as stated in the Qur'ān is Islām,[2] and he who follows it is called a Muslim.[3] So far from the system being named after its founder, prophet Muḥammad is himself called a Muslim.[4] In fact, every prophet of God is spoken of in the Qur'ān as being a Muslim[5] thus showing that Islām is the true religion for the whole of humanity, the various prophets being the preachers of that religion among different nations in different times, and Prophet Muḥammad its last and most perfect exponent.

[1] The Arabic word for *religion* is *din* or *milla*, the root-meaning of the former being *obedience* and *requital*, and that of the latter to dictate. *Milla* has special reference to the prophet through whom the religion is revealed, and *din* to the individual who follows it (R.). Another word for religion is *madhhab* which is not used in the Qur'ān. It is derived from the root *dhahaba* meaning *he went*, and *madhhab* signifies *a way that one pursues in respect of doctrines and practices* in religion, or *an opinion respecting religion* (L.L.). According to some authorities, the distinction between the three words is thus expressed: *din* in relation to God Who reveals it, *milla* in relation to the Prophet through whom it is revealed and *madhhab* in relation to the *mujtahid* who expounds it. The word *madhhab* as used in Urdu or Persian carries, however, the wider significance of religion.

[2] "This day have I perfected for you your religion and completed My favour on you, and chosen for you Islām as a religion" (5 : 3). "Surely the true religion with Allāh is Islām" (3 : 18).

[3] "He named you Muslims before and in this" (22 : 78), where *before* refers to the Prophecies, and *this* to the Holy Qur'ān.

[4] "And I am the first of the Muslims" (6 : 164).

[5] "And the same did Abraham enjoin on his sons and so did Jacob: O my sons, Allāh has chosen the religion for you, so die not unless you are Muslims" (2 : 132); "We revealed the Torah, in which was guidance and light; with it the prophets who submitted themselves (*aslamū*) judged matters for those who were Jews" (5 : 44).

Significance of the name Islām

Among the great religions of the world, Islām enjoys the distinction of bearing a significant name, a name that points to its very essence. The root-meaning of the word *Islām* is *to enter into peace*,[6] and a *Muslim* is *one who makes his peace with God and man.* Peace with God implies complete submission to His will, and peace with man is not only to refrain from evil or injury to another but also to do good to him; and both these ideas find expression in the Qur'ān as the true essence of the religion of Islām: "Nay: whoever submits (*aslama*) himself entirely to Allāh and he is the doer of good to others, he has his reward from his Lord, and there is no fear for such, nor shall they grieve" (2 : 112). Islām is thus, in its very inception, the religion of *peace*, and its two basic doctrines, the Unity of God and the unity or brotherhood of the human race, afford positive proof of its being true to its name. Not only is Islām stated to be the true religion of all the prophets of God, as pointed out above, but even the involuntary though complete submission to Divine laws, which is witnessed in nature, is indicated by the same word *aslama*. This wider significance is also retained in the strictly legal usage of the word, for, in law, Islām has a two-fold significance: a simple profession of faith — a declaration that "there is no god but Allāh and Muḥammad is His Messenger" (*Kalimah*) and a complete submission to the Divine will which is only attainable through spiritual perfection.[7] Thus, he who simply accepts the religion of Islām, the mere novice, is a Muslim, as well as he who completely submits himself to the Divine will and practises all the Divine commandments.

Place of Islām among the religions of the world

Islām is the last of the great religions — those mighty movements which have revolutionized the world and changed the destinies of nations. But it is not only the last, it is an all-inclusive religion which contains

[6] *Islām* means *entering into salm,* and *silm* and *salm* both signify peace (R.). Both these words are used in the sense of *peace* in the Qur'ān.

[7] "Islam in law is of two kinds; one is a simple confession with the tongue ... whether accompanied with belief (*īmān* or *real change*) in the heart or not... The other is about belief (*īmān*), and it means that along with confession, there is belief (*īmān*) or *real change* in the heart and a fulfilment in practice, and resignation to God in whatever He brings to pass or decrees" (R.).

within itself all religions which came before it. One of its most striking characteristics is that it requires its followers to believe that all the great religions of the world that preceded it have been revealed by God: "And who believe in that which has been revealed to thee and that which was revealed before thee" (2 : 4).

"Say: We believe in Allāh and (in) that which has been revealed to us, and (in) that which was revealed to Abraham and Ishmael and Isaac and Jacob and the tribes, and (in) that which was given to Moses and Jesus, and (in) that which was given to the prophets from their Lord; we do not make any distinction between any of them" (2 : 136).

"The Messenger believes in what has been revealed to him from his Lord, and so do the believers; they all believe in Allāh and His angels and His books and His messengers. We make no distinction between any of His messengers" (2 : 285).

Thus a Muslim believes not only in the Prophet Muḥammad but in all other prohets as well. And prophets were, according to the teachings of the Qurān, sent to all the nations: "And there is not a people but a warner has gone among them" (35 : 24). A Jew believes only in the prophets of Israel; a Christian believes in Jesus Christ and, in a lesser degree, in the prophets of Israel; a Buddhist in Buddha; a Zoroastrian in Zoroaster; a Hindu in the prophets who appeared in India; a Confucian in Confucius; but a Muslim believes in all these and in Muḥammad also, the last of the prophets. Islām is, therefore, an all-comprehensive religion within which are included all the religions of the world; and similarly, its sacred Book, the Holy Qur'ān, is spoken of as a combination of all the sacred scriptures of the world: "Pure pages, wherein are all right books" (98 : 2, 3).

There is yet one more characteristic of Islām which gives it a special place among religions. In addition to being the last and an all-inclusive religion, it is the perfect expression of the Divine will. Thus the Qur'ān says: "This day have I perfected for you your religion and completed My favour to you, and chosen for you Islām as a religion" (5 : 3). Like every other form of consciousness, the religious consciousness of man has developed slowly and gradually down the ages, and the revelation of the great Truth from on High was thus brought to perfection in Islām. It is to this great truth that the words of Jesus Christ allude: "I have yet many things to say unto you but ye cannot bear them now. Howbeit when he, the spirit of truth, is come, he will guide you unto all truth" (Jn. 16 : 12, 13). Thus it is the great mission of Islām to bring about peace in the world by establishing a brotherhood of all the religions, to bring together all the religious truths contained in previous religions, to correct their errors and sift the true from the false, to preach the eternal verities which had not been preached before on account of the special circumstances of any race or society in the early stages of its development and, last of all, to meet all the moral and spiritual requirements of an ever-advancing humanity.

New meaning introduced into religion

With the advent of Islām, the concept of religion received a new significance. Firstly, it is to be treated not as a dogma, which a man must accept if he must escape everlasting damnation, but as a science based on the universal experience of humanity. It is not a particular nation that becomes the favourite of God and the recipient of Divine revelation; on the contrary, revelation is recognized as a necessary factor in the evolution of man; hence, while in its crudest form it is the universal experience of humanity, in its highest, that of prophetical revelation, it has been a Divine gift bestowed upon all nations of the world. And the idea of the scientific in religion has been further strengthened by presenting its doctrines as principles of human conduct and action. There is not a single religious doctrine which is not made the basis of action for the development of man to higher and yet higher stages of life. Secondly, the sphere of religion is not confined to the next world; its primary concern is rather with this life, that man, through a righteous life here on earth, may attain to the consciousness of a higher existence. And so it is that the Qur'ān deals with a vast variety of subjects which affect man's life in this world. It deals not only with the ways of devotion, the forms of worship, and the means which make man attain communion with God, but also, and in richer detail, with the problems of the world around us, with questions pertaining to relations between man and man, his social and political life, institutions of marriage, divorce and inheritance, division of wealth and relations of labour and capital, administration of justice, military organization, peace and war, national finances, debts and contracts, rules for the service of humanity and even treatment of animals, laws for the help of the poor, the orphan and the widow, and hundreds of other questions the proper understanding of which enables man to lead a happy life. It lays down rules not only for individual progress but also for the advancement of society as a whole, of the nation and even of humanity. It throws light on problems regarding relations not only between individuals but also among different tribes and nations into which humanity is divided. It prepares man for another life, it is true, but only through making him capable of holding his own in the present one.

Religion is a force in the moral development of man

The question which perturbs every mind today is whether religion is, when all is said and done, necessary to humanity. Now a cursory glance at the history of human civilization will show that religion has been the supreme force in the development of mankind to its present condition. That all that is good and noble in man has been inspired by faith in God is a truth at which perhaps even an atheist would not cavil. One Abraham, one Moses, one Krishna, one Buddha, one Christ, one Muḥammad has, each in his turn and his degree, changed the whole history of the human race and raised it from the depths of degradation to moral heights undreamed of. It is through the teachings of this or that prophet that man has been able to conquer his lower nature and to set before himself the noblest ideals of selflessness and the service of humanity. A study of the noble sentiments that inspire man today will show their origin in the teachings and examples of some great sage who had deep faith in God and through whom was sown the seed of faith in other human hearts. The moral and ethical development of man to his present state, if due to any one cause, is due to religion. Humanity has yet to find out whether the lofty emotions which inspire man today will survive after a generation or two of Godlessness, and what sentiments materialism will bring in its train. To all appearance, the reign of materialism must need entail the rule of selfishness for a cut and dried scheme for the equal division of wealth will not inspire the noble sentiments which are today the pride of man and which centuries of religion have instilled into his very being. If the sanction of religion were withdrawn today, the ignorant masses — and the masses will always remain ignorant though they may be able to read and write — will sink back, gradually of course, into a state of savagery, while even those who reckon themselves above the common level will no longer feel the inspiration to noble and high ideals which only faith in God can give.

Islām as the basis of a lasting civilization

As a matter of fact, human civilization, as we have it today, is whether it likes the idea or not, based on religion. Religion has made possible a state of civilization which has again and again saved human society from disruption. If its history is traced back anywhere, it will be seen that whenever it has begun to totter, a new religious impulse has always been at hand to save it from complete extinction. Not only that civilization, with any pretence to endurance, can rest solely on a moral basis, and that true and lofty morals are inspired only by faith in God, but even the unity and cohesion of jarring human elements, without which it is impossible for any civilization to survive, is best brought about by the unifying force of religion. It is often said that religion is responsible for much of the hatred and bloodshed in the world, but a glance at the history of religion will show that this is a monstrous misconception. Love, concord, sympathy, kindness to one's fellow-man, have been the message of every religion, and every nation has learnt these essential lessons in their true purity only through the spirit of selflessness and service which a faith in God has inspired. If there have been selfishness and hatred and bloodshed, those have been there in spite of religion, not as a consequence of the message of love which religion has brought. They have been there because human nature is too prone to these things; and their presence only shows that a still greater religious awakening is required, that a truer faith in God is yet the crying need of humanity. That man sometimes turns to low and unworthy things does not show that the nobler sentiments are worthless, but only that their development has become a more urgent necessity.

Islām as the greatest unifying force in the world

If unification be the true basis of human civilization, by which phrase is meant the civilization not of one nation or of one country but of humanity as a whole, then Islām is undoubtedly the greatest civilizing force the world has ever known or is likely to know. Fourteen hundred years ago it was Islām that saved it from crashing into an abyss of savagery, that came to the help of a civilization whose very foundations had collapsed, and that set about laying a new foundation of rearing an entirely new edifice of culture and ethics. A new idea of the unity of human race as a whole, not of the unity of this or that nation, was introduced into the world — an idea so mighty that it welded together nations which had warred with one another since the world began. It was not only in Arabia, among the ever-bickering tribes of a single peninsula, that this great "miracle", as an English writer terms it, was wrought[8] — a miracle before the magnitude of which everything dwindles into insignificance. It not only cemented

[8] "A more disunited people it would be hard to find till suddenly the miracle took place. A man arose who, by his personality and by his claim to direct Divine guidance, actually brought about the impossible — namely the union of all those warring factions" (*The Ins and Outs of Mesopotamia*, p.99).

together the warring tribes of one country but also established a brotherhood of all nations of the world, even uniting those which had nothing in common except their common humanity. It obliterated differences of colour, race, language, geographical boundaries and even of culture. It united man with man as such, and the hearts of those in the far east began to beat in unison with those in the farthest west. Indeed, it proved to be not only the greatest but the only force unifying man, because, whereas other religions had succeeded merely in unifying the different elements of a single race, Islām actually achieved the unification of many races and harmonized the jarring and discordant elements of humanity. How great a force it was in bringing back his lost civilization to man, is attested by a European writer[9]:

"In the fifth and sixth centuries,the civilized world stood on the verge of chaos. The old emotional cultures that had made civilization possible, since they had given to men a sense of unity and of reverence for their rulers, had broken down, and nothing had been found adequate to take their place...

"It seemed then that the great civilization which it had taken four thousand years to construct was on the verge of disintegration, and that mankind was likely to return to that condition of barbarism where every tribe and sect was against the next and law and order were unknown... The old tribal sanctions had lost their power... The new sanctions created by Christianity were working division and destruction instead of unity and order... Civilization like a gigantic tree whose foliage had over-reached the world ... stood tottering ... rotted to the core... Was there any emotional culture that could be brought in to gather mankind once more into unity and to save civilization?"

And speaking of Arabia, the learned author adds that "it was among these people that the man was born who was to unite the whole known world of the east and south".[10]

Islām as the greatest spiritual force of the world

Thus Islām laid the basis of a unification of humanity of which no other reformer or religion has ever dreamed of; a brotherhood of man which knows no bounds of colour, race, country, language or even of rank;

[9] J.H. Denison, *Emotion as the Basis of Civilization,* pp. 265-268.

[10] J.H. Denison, *Emotion as the Basis of Civilization,* p. 296.

of a unity of the human race beyond which human conception cannot go. It recognizes the equality not only of the civil and political rights of men but also of their spiritual rights. "All men are a single nation" (2 : 213) is the fundamental doctrine of Islām, and for that reason every nation is recognized as having received the spiritual gift of revelation. But the establishment of a vast brotherhood of all men is not the only achievement of Islām. Equally great is the unparalleled transformation which it has brought about in the world; for it has proved itself to be a spiritual force the equal of which the human race has never known. Its miraculous transformation of world conditions was brought about in an incredibly short time. It swept away the vile superstitions, the crass ignorance, the rank immorality, the old evil habits of centuries, in about two decades. That its spiritual conquests are without parallel in history is an undeniable fact, and it is because of the unparalleled spiritual transformation effected by him that Prophet Muḥammad is admitted to be the "most successful of all prophets and religious personalities" (En. Br., art. Koran).

Islām offers a solution of the great world problems

Islām has a claim upon the attention of every thinker, not only because it is the most civilizing and the greatest spiritual force of the world but also because it offers a solution of the most baffling problems which confront mankind to-day. Materialism, which has become humanity's ideal in modern times, can never bring about peace and mutual trust among the nations of the world. Christianity has failed to do away with race and colour prejudices. Islām is the only force which has already succeeded in blotting out these distinctions and it is through Islām only that this great problem of the modern world can be solved. Islām is, first and foremost, an international religion, and it is only before its grand international ideal — the ideal of the equality of all races and of the unity of the human race — that the curse of nationalism, which has been and is responsible for the troubles of the ancient and the modern worlds, can be swept away. But even within the boundaries of a nation or a country there can be no peace as long as a just solution of the two great problems of wealth and sex cannot be found. Europe has gone to two extremes on the wealth question — capitalism and Bolshevism. There is either the tendency to concentrate wealth among the great capitalists, or by community of wealth, to bring the indolent and the industrious to one level. Islām offers the true solution by ensuring to the worker the reward of his work, great or small, in accordance with the merit of the work, and also by allotting to the poor a share in the wealth of the rich. Thus, while the rights of property are maintained in their true sense, an arrangement is made for equalizing conditions by taking a part of the wealth of the rich and distributing it among the poor according to the principle of *zakāt* (or *poor-rate,* an obligatory charity) and also by a more or less equal division of property among heirs on the death of an owner. Thus, writing towards the close of his book, a European orientalist remarks:

"Within the Western world Islām still maintains the balance between exaggerated opposites. Opposed equally to the anarchy of European nationalism and the regimentation of Russian communism, it has not yet succumbed to that obsession with the economic side of life which is characteristic of present-day Europe and present-day Russia alike. Its social ethic has been admirably summed up by Professor Massignon: 'Islām has the merit of standing for a very equalitarian conception of the contribution of each citizen by the tithe to the resources of the community; it is hostile to unrestricted exchange, to banking capital, to state loans, to indirect taxes on objects of prime necessity, but it holds to the rights of the father and the husband, to private property, and to commercial capital. Here again it occupies intermediate position between the doctrines of bourgeois capitalism and Bolshevist communism.'"[11]

Similarly Islām's solution of the sex question is the only one that can ensure ultimate peace to the family. There is neither the free-love which would loosen all ties of social relations, nor the indissoluble binding of man and woman which turns many a home into a veritable hell. And, by solving these and a hundred other problems, Islām — as its very name indicates — can bring true happiness to the human race.

Misconceptions underlying anti-religious movement

The anti-religious movement which has taken root in Russia is based on a misconception as to the nature of Islām. The three chief objections to religion are:

—That religion helps in the maintenance of the present social system, which has borne the fruit of capitalism with the consequent crushing of the aspirations of the poor.

—That it keeps the people subject to superstition and thus hinders the advance of sciences.

[11] H.A.R. Gibb, *Whither Islam,* pp. 378-379.

—That it teaches them to pray for their needs instead of working for them and thus it makes them indolent.[12]

So far as Islām is concerned, the facts are entirely contrary to these allegations. It came as the friend of the poor and the destitute, and as a matter of fact it has accomplished an upliftment of the poor to which history affords no parallel. It raised men from the lowest rung of the social ladder to the highest positions of life, it made of slaves not only leaders in thought and intellect but actual kings. Its social system is one of an equality which is quite unthinkable in any other nation or society. It lays down as one of the fundamental principles of religion that the poor have a right in the wealth of the rich, a right exercised through the state which collects annually a fortieth of the wealth amassed by the rich, to be distributed among the poor.

The second allegation that religion discourages the advancement of science and learning is equally devoid of truth. Islām gave an impetus to learning in a country which had never been a seat of learning and was sunk in the depths of superstition. Even as far back as the caliphate of 'Umar (634-644 A.D.), the Islamic state undertook the education of the masses, while the Muslims carried the torch of learning to every country where they gained political ascendancy; schools, colleges and universities sprang up everywhere as a result of the Muslim conquest. It is no exaggeration to say that it was through Islām that the Renaissance came about in Europe.

The third allegation that religion makes people idle by teaching them to pray is also belied by the history of Islām. Not only does the Qur'ān teach men to work hard for success in life, and lays down, in plain words, that "man can have nothing but what he strives for" (53 : 39), but it actually made the Arabs — the then most backward nation in the world — a nation of great leaders in all phases of life. And this great revolution was brought about only by awakening in them a desire for work and a zest for hard striving. Islām does teach man to pray, but prayer, instead of making him idle, is intended to fit him for a still harder struggle, and to carry on that struggle in the face of failure and disappointment, by turning to God who is the Source of all strength. Thus prayer in Islām is only an incentive for work, and not a hindrance.

[12] As summed up in *Emotion as the Basis of Civilizations,* p. 506.

PART ONE

THE SOURCES OF ISLĀM

Chapter I

THE HOLY QUR'ĀN

How and when the Qur'ān was revealed

The original source[1] from which all principles and ordinances of Islām are drawn is the Holy Book called *al-Qur'ān.*[2] The name *Qur'ān* is frequently mentioned in the book itself [3] which also states to whom, how, why, when, and in what language, it was delivered. It was revealed to

[1] Generally the sources are said to be four, the Qur'ān, the Sunnah or Ḥadith (Doings and Sayings of the Prophet Muḥammad as preserved in collections of Tradition), *Ijmā'* or *unanimous agreement* of the Muslim community and *Qiyās* or *reasoning*. The former two are called *al-adilat al-qaṭ'īyya* or *absolutely sure arguments*, and the latter two as *al-adilat al-ijtihādiyya* or *agruments obtained by exertion*. But as *ijmā'* and *qiyās* are admittedly based on the Qur'ān and the Ḥadith (Tradition), the latter itself being only an explanation of the Qur'ān, as will be shown later on, the Qur'ān is actually the real foundation on which the whole superstructure of Islām rests, and being the only, absolute and final authority in every discussion relating to the principles and laws of Islām, it is perfectly right to say that the Qur'ān is the sole source from which all the teachings and practices of Islām are drawn.

[2] The word *Qur'ān* is an infinitive noun from the root *qara'a* which signifies primarily *he collected together things* (LA.). It also signifies: *he read* or *recited*, because in reading or reciting, letters and words are joined to each other in a certain order (R.). "According to some authorities, the name of this book al-Qur'ān from among the world Divine books is due to its gathering together in itself the fruits of all His books, rather its being a collection of the fruits of all the sciences, a reference to which is contained in the words, 'an explanation of all things' " (R.). It also means *a book that is or should be read,* containing a prophetical reference to its being "the most widely read book" (En. Br.) in the whole world. The Qur'ān speaks of itself under various other names. It is called *al-Kitāb* (2 : 2) meaning *the Writing which is complete in itself; al-Furqān* (25 : 1) or the Distinction *between right and wrong and between truth and falsehood; al-Dhikrā, al-Tadhkira* (15 : 9) or *the Reminder or a source of eminence and glory to man; al-Tanzīl* (26 : 192) or the *Revelation from on High; Aḥsan al-Ḥadith* (39 : 23) or *the Best Saying; al-Mau'iẓa* (10 : 57) or *the Admonition; al-Ḥukm* (13 : 37) or *the Judgment; al-Ḥikma* (17 : 39) or *the Wisdom; al-Shifā* (10 : 57) or *the Healing; al-Hudā* (72 : 13) or *the Guidance; al-Raḥma* (17 : 82) or *the Mercy; al-Khair* (3 : 103) or *the Goodness; al-Rūḥ* (42 : 52) or *the Spirit* or *the Life; al-Bayān* (3 : 137) or *the Explanation; al-Ni'ma* (93 : 11) or *the Blessing; al-Burhān* (4 : 175) or *the Argument; al-Qayyim* (18 : 2) or *the Maintainer; al-Muhaimin* (5 : 48) or *the Guardian; al-Nūr* (7 : 157) or *the Light; al-Ḥaqq* (17 : 81) or *the Truth.* Besides these it is mentioned by several other names; and there is also a large number of qualifying words applied to it. For instance, it is called *Karīm* (56 : 77) or *Honourable; Majīd* (85 : 21) or *Glorious; Ḥakim* (36 : 2) or *Wise; Mubārak* (21 : 50) or *Blessed* (lit. *a thing the goodness of which shall never be intercepted*)*; Mubīn* (12 : 1) or *the one making things manifest; 'Aliyy* (43 : 4) or *Elevated; Faṣl* (86 : 13) or *Decisive; 'Azīm* (39 : 67) or *of great importance; Mukarram* or *Honoured. Marfū'* or *Exalted, Muṭahharah* or *Purified* (80 : 13, 14)*; Mutashābih* (39 : 23) or *conformable in its various parts.*

[3] 2 : 185; 10 : 37, 61; 17 : 106, etc.

Muḥammad: "And (who) believe in that which has been revealed to Muḥammad — and it is the Truth from their Lord" (47 : 2). It was revealed in the month of Ramadzān on a certain night which thenceforward received the name of the *Night of Majesty*[4] *(Lailat al-Qadr):* "The month of Ramadzān is that in which the Qur'ān was revealed" (2 : 185); "We revealed it on a blessed night" (44 : 3); "Surely We revealed it on the Night of Majesty" (97 : 1). It was revealed in Arabic language: "So We have made it easy in thy tongue that they may be mindful" (44 : 58); "Surely We have made it an Arabic Qur'ān that you may understand" (43 : 3). It was revealed in portions, every portion being written and committed to memory as soon as it was revealed, and the revelation was spread over twenty-three years of the Prophet's life, during which time he was occupied solely with the reformation of a benighted world: "And it is a Qur'ān which we made distinct, so that thou mayest read it to the people by slow degrees, and We have revealed it in portions" (17 : 106). It was not the Prophet who spoke under influence of the Holy Spirit; it was a Divine Message brought by the angel Gabriel,[5] and delivered in words

[4] The *Lailat al-Qadr* or the Night of Majesty is one of the three nights in the month of Ramadzān, 25th, 27th, or 29th, *i.e.*, the night preceding any of these dates (Bu.32 : 4). The Prophet was, at the time when revelation first came to him, forty years of age.

[5] It should be noted that the Qur'ān uses the words Holy Spirit and Gabriel interchangeably. In one of the reports speaking of the first revelation to the Prophet the angel who brought the revelation is called *al-Nāmūs al-Akbar,* or the great *Nāmūs,* and *Nāmūs* means *the angel who is entrusted with Divine secrets* (N.); the Divine secrets, of course, being the Divine messages to humanity sent through the prophets of God. The same report adds that it was the same angel that brought revelation to Moses. Thus both the Qur'ān and the reports make it clear that Divine revelation was brought to the Prophet, as well as to the prophets before him, by the angel Gabriel who is also called the Holy Spirit or the Faithful Spirit or the great *Nāmūs.* This clears up all doubts as to what is meant by the Holy Spirit in Islām; and in the mouths of the Old Testament prophets, as well as Jesus Christ, it carried exactly the same significance. It is true that there is not the same clarity here as in Islām, but it is equally true that the orthodox Christian conception of the Holy Spirit was quite unknown to the Jewish mind, and in this respect Jesus Christ was a staunch Jew, his terminology being taken in its entirety from the Jews. In the Old Testament terminology, the form used is the Spirit or the Spirit of God. In Ps. 51 : 11 and Is. 63 :10,11 the form used is Holy Spirit which is also the form adopted in the Tālmūd and Midrāsh. The Holy Ghost is peculiar to the New Testament writers. The Jews looked upon it as one of the created things; it was among the ten things that were created on the first day (En.J.). The function of the Holy Spirit is described thus:

"The visible results of the activity of the Holy Spirit, according to the Jewish conception, are the books of the Bible, all of which have been composed under its inspiration. All the prophets spoke "in the Holy Spirit"; and the most characteristic sign of the presence of the Holy Spirit is the gift of Prophecy,in the sense that the person upon whom it rests beholds the past and the future. With the death of the last three prophets, Haggai, Zechariah and Malachi, the Holy Spirit ceased to manifest itself in Israel" (En.J.).

to the Prophet who communicated it to mankind: "And surely this is a revelation from the Lord of the worlds. The Faithful Spirit has brought it on thy heart that thou mayest be a warner, in plain Arabic language" (26 : 192 - 195); "Whoever is an enemy to Gabriel — for surely he revealed it to thy heart by Allāh's command" (2 : 97); "The Holy Spirit has revealed it from thy Lord with the truth" (16 : 102).

It is the highest form of revelation

Though the Qur'ān was revealed piecemeal through Gabriel, yet the entire revelation is one whole, delivered in one and the same manner. Revelation, we are told in the Qur'ān, is granted to man in three forms: "And it is not vouchsafed to any mortal that Allāh should speak to him, except by revelation (*waḥy)* or from behind a veil, or by sending a messenger and revealing by His permission what He pleases" (42 : 51). The first of these three modes is called *waḥy*, which is generally translated as meaning *revelation.* Since the different kinds of revelation are spoken of here, the word *waḥy* is obviously used in its literal sense, its primary significance being a hasty suggestion (*al-ishārat al-sarī'ah*) (R.). Hence the inspired word, which enters the hearts of the prophets and of the righteous, is called *waḥy* because it is like a sudden suggestion made directly to the heart of the inspired one (*ilqā-'un fi'l-rau'*). It is not a message in words but simply an idea which comes like a flash and clears up a doubt

It is clear from this that the Jewish idea was that the Holy Spirit brought inspiration to the prophets, the only difference between this and the Islamic conception being that the latter looks upon the very words of revelation as proceeding from a Divine source, while the former apparently regards the words as being those of the prophet speaking under the influence of the Holy Spirit.

Jesus Christ and his disciples used the word in exactly the same sense. Jesus' first experience of the Holy Spirit in the form of a dove was the result of his baptism by John (Mt. 3 : 16) which seems to indicate its association with a certain stage in the spiritual development of man. The Holy Spirit did not descend upon him until he was baptised. The idea of a dove-like form is also met with in the Jewish literature. Moreover, Jesus speaks of the Holy Spirit as inspiring the righteous servants of God: "How then doth David in spirit call him Lord?" (Mt. 22 : 43); "For David himself said by the Holy Ghost" (Mk. 12 : 36); the Holy Spirit is given to them that ask Him (Lk. 11 : 13). Even the disciples' first experience of the Holy Spirit is a repetition of the old Jewish tradition. As there we find the Spirit coming with "a voice of a great rushing" (Ezk. 3 : 12), so in the case of the disciples of Jesus "there came a sound from heaven as of a rushing mighty wind" (Acts, 2 : 2). Thus the Holy Spirit as conceived by Jesus and his disciples was the same as in the Old Testament prophets, which again is almost identical with its conception in Islām, and the orthodox Christian view of the spirit as one of the three persons of the Godhead, co-eternal with God, is of later growth.

or difficulty, and it is not the result of meditation.[6] The second mode is described as speaking from behind a veil — a scene, carrying a deeper significance, is shown as in a vision (*kashf*), or in a dream (*ru'yā*), or words are heard by the person spoken to, as if coming from behind a veil. The third mode is that in which the angel bearing the message is sent to the recipient of the Divine revelation, and the message is delivered in words, and this is the highest form of revelation. As already stated, the angel entrusted with Divine message in words is Gabriel or the Holy Spirit, and this third mode of revelation is limited to the prophets of God only — to men entrusted with important Divine messages to humanity — while the first two lower forms of revelation are common to prophets as well as those who are not prophets. For the delivery of the higher message which relates to the welfare of mankind, a higher form of revelation is chosen, a form in which the message is not simply an idea but is clothed in actual words. The Prophet's faculty of being spoken to by God is so highly developed that he receives the messages, not only as ideas instilled into the mind or in the form of words uttered or heard under the influence of the Holy Spirit, but actually as Divine messages in words delivered

[6] Rāghib suggests a slightly different interpretation. He makes *waḥy* include not only an inspiration or a suggestion thrown into the mind but also *taskhīr, i.e.,* making a certain thing follow a certain course in obedience to the laws of nature, an example of which is the revelation to the bee (16 : 68), and *manām,i.e.,* dreams. And the second form, *from behind a veil,* he looks upon as applying to the case of Moses to whom, it is thought, God spoke in a manner different from that in which He spoke to the other prophets, that is to say, He spoke to him being invisible to him. Now, as regards the revelation to the bee, it is a clear mistake, as the verse states only how God speaks to men. And the statement regarding the mode of revelation to Moses is also a mistake, for the Qur'ān lays it down in plain words that revelation was granted to the Prophet Muḥammad in the same form as it had been granted to the prophets before him including Moses: "Surely We have revealed to thee as We revealed to Noah and the prophets after him" (4 : 163); and Moses is specially mentioned in this connection in v.164. Hence the second mode, from behind a veil, refers to *ru'yā* or dreams and *kashf* or visions, because a certain sight is shown in this case which has a deeper meaning than that which appears on the surface. The dream or the vision carries with it a certain meaning, but that meaning is, as it were, under a veil and must be sought for behind that veil. The dreams mentioned in the Qur'ān (ch.12) are an illustration of this. Joseph saw the sun and the moon and the eleven stars making obeisance to him, and this signified his greatness and his insight into things. A king saw seven lean kine eat up seven fat ones, and the meaning was that seven years of famine and hardship would follow seven years of plenty and eat away the hoarded corn of the country. Hence God's speaking from behind a veil means His revealing certain truths in dreams or visions. In a saying of the Prophet these are called *mubashshrāt*: "Nothing has remained of *nubuwwah, i.e., receiving news from God,* except *mubashshrāt.*" Being asked "what was meant by *mubashshrāt*," the Prophet replied, "good visions" (Bu. 92 : 5). In this category are also included words which some righteous servants of God are made to utter or which they hear under the influence of the Holy Spirit.

through the latter. In the terminology of Islām this is called "*revelation that is recited*" (*waḥy matluww*) and the Qur'ān was, from beginning to end, delivered in this form to the Prophet, as the quotations earlier given from the Book itself make it abundantly clear. It does not contain any other form of revelation. It is in its entirety *waḥy matluww* or revelation recited to the Prophet distinctly in words, and is thus wholly the highest form of Divine revelation.

Other forms of Divine revelation to men

As stated above, prophets also received the lower forms of Divine revelation. For example, we are told in reports that before the higher message came to the Prophet Muḥammad — *i.e.*, before he received the first Quranic revelation — he used to have clear and true visions. "The first of revelations that came to the Messenger of Allāh were good visions so that he did not see a vision but it came out true as the dawn of the day" (Bu. 1 : 1). The Prophet's hearing of certain voices as mentioned in the traditions[7] belongs to the same category, while the details of laws as expounded by him, and as met with in his practice,[8] belong to the first form of revelation, an idea instilled into the mind. This is called "*inner revelation*" (*waḥy khafiyy*). In the lower forms, revelation is still granted to the righteous from among the followers of the Prophet and even to others, for, as will be shown later, in the lowest form revelation is the universal experience of humanity. There is also a difference as to the method in which the different kinds of revelation are received. While the two lower forms of revelation involve but little change in the normal condition of a man, whether awake or asleep, and he is only occasionally transported to a state of trance, the highest form, which is that peculiar to the prophets, brings with it a violent change; it does, in fact, require a real passing from one world to the other, while the recipient is in a state of perfect wakefulness, and the burden of revelation is not only felt by him but is also visible to those who see him.

The Prophet's experience of revelation

The Prophet first experienced the higher revelation while he was alone in the cave of Ḥirā. Before this he had, from time to time, seen visions,

[7] Tradition — *Ḥadīth*, Sayings of the Prophet.
[8] Practice — *Sunnah*, Doings of the Prophet.

but when the angel came with the higher message, he found himself quite exhausted: "He (Gabriel) seized me and squeezed me to such an extent that I was quite exhausted", and this was repeated thrice (Bu. 1 : 1). And even after he reached home, the effect of exhaustion was still upon him and he had to lie down covered over before he could relate what had befallen. It was an equally hard experience when the second message came to him after an interval of some months. And even afterwards, the effect of the Spirit upon him was so great that on the coldest of days perspiration would run down his forehead: "I saw", says 'Ā'ishah, his wife, "revelation coming down upon him in the severest cold, and when that condition was over, perspiration ran down his forehead"[9] (Bu. 1 : 1). A

[9] Some misdirected critics have represented this extraordinary experience of the coming of the revelation as an epileptic fit. The question is whether an epileptic could, when the fit came on, utter those grand religious truths which are met with in the Qur'ān, or indeed make any coherent statement at all; whether he could have the strong will which made the whole of Arabia at last bow down to the Prophet, or possess the unparalleled energy which we witness in every phase of his life, or the high morals which were his, or be the master of that magnetic virtue under whose influence a whole country could be purified of the grossest idolatry and superstition; whether hundreds of thousands of men possessing the Arabs' independence of character would have taken him for a leader whose orders were obeyed in the minutest details of life; or whether he could produce men of the will and character of Abū Bakr and 'Umar and thousands of others, before whom mighty empires crumbled? The story of froth appearing from his mouth at the time of revelation is pure invention. Klein, writing in *The Religion of Islam* (p.8), makes the following statement on the authority of Bukhārī : "Another tradition says that froth appeared before his mouth and he roared like a young camel." Bukhārī makes no such statement, in the place referred to (Bu. 1 : 2). Elsewhere he says: "The face of the Messenger of Allāh was red and he was snoring" (Bu. 25 : 17). Statements met with in traditions are similar to those quoted from Bukhārī. For instance, we have in *Muslim* : "When revelation came to the Holy Prophet, he appeared to be as it were in distress and turned pale in the face." And according to one report, "when revelation came to the Prophet, he would hang his head and his Companions would do the same; and when that condition was over, he would raise up his head." All these and other similar statements contained in other collections of traditions, only show that the coming of the revelation brought a real change in the Prophet which others also witnessed.

Another misconception may also be removed here. When the Prophet related his first experience to his wife Khadījah, he added the words: "Surely I have fear regarding myself, *laqad khashitu 'alā nafsī*" (Bu. 1 : 1). Some critics have misunderstood these words as meaning that the Prophet feared he was possessed by an evil spirit; and a rather foolish story from Ibn Hishām as to Khadījah's taking off the veil and the angel disappearing (which is without the least foundation and against all historical facts of the Prophet's life) is narrated in support of it. The story seems foolish inasmuch as the angel appeared to the Prophet in the solitude of Ḥirā, and not in the presence of Khadījah. A cursory glance at the words quoted above would show that they could not possibly bear any such interpretation. The Prophet knew for certain that he had a message from on High for the reformation of the fallen humanity; all that he feared was lest he should fail in bringing about the desired reformation. That was how Khadījah understood it, as she immediately com-

Companion also relates that "he was sitting with his leg under that of the Prophet when revelation came down upon him, and he felt as if his leg would be crushed under the weight" (Bu. 8 : 12).

Nature of the Prophet's revelation

The next question is about the nature of the revelation itself. When Ḥārith, son of Hishām, once enquired of the Prophet how revelation came to him, he replied: "It comes to me sometimes as the ringing of a bell and this is hardest on me, then he (the angel) leaves me and I remember from him what he says; and sometimes the angel comes in the shape of a man and he talks to me and I remember what he says" (Bu. 1 :1). These are the only two forms in which the Quranic revelation came to the Prophet. In both cases, the angel came to him and was seen by him; in both cases a certain message was delivered in words which he at once committed to memory. That is the essence of the whole question. The only difference between the two cases was that in one case the angel appeared in the shape of a human being and uttered the words in a soft tone as a man talks to another; in the other case, it is not stated in what form he came, but we are told that the words were uttered like the ringing of a bell, that is to say, in a harsh, hard tone, which made it a heavier task for the Prophet to receive them. But still it was the angel who brought the message, as is shown by the use of the personal pronoun *he* in the first part of the report. In both cases the Prophet was transported, as it were, to another world, and this transportation caused him to go through a severe experience which made him perspire even on a cold day, but this experience was harder still when the deliverer of the message did not appear in human shape and there remained no affinity between the deliverer and the recipient. But whether the angel appeared in human shape or not, whether the message was delivered in a hard or soft tone, the one thing certain is that it was a message delivered in words; and the Quranic revelation is thus entirely one message delivered in one form. It should be noted that the Prophet often received the message while sitting with his

forted him: "Nay, by Allāh, Allāh will never bring thee to grief; surely thou dost good to thy relatives, and bearest the burden of the weak, and earnest for others that which they have not got, and art hospitable to guests and givest help when there is real distress" (Bu. 1 : 1). The faithful wife who had known him intimately for fifteen years enumerated these great virtues in him, as a testimony that a man of such a high character could not fail in accomplishing the task which was entrusted to him — the task of uplifting a fallen humanity.

companions, but the latter never saw the angel nor ever heard the words of revelation.[10] It was, therefore, with other than the normal human senses that the Prophet saw the angel and heard his words, and it was really the granting of these other senses that is called transportation to another world.

Arrangement of the Qur'ān

Though the Qur'ān was revealed in portions, yet it is a mistake to suppose that it remained long in that fragmentary condition. As its name implies, it was a book from the first, and though it could not be complete until the last verse was revealed, it was never without some form of arrangement. There is the clearest testimony, internal as well as external, that every single verse or part of a verse and every chapter that was revealed had its own definite place in the Book.[11] The Qur'ān is itself clear on this point: "And those who disbelieve say: Why has not the Qur'ān been revealed to him all at once? Thus (it is) that We may strengthen thy heart by it, and We have arranged it well in arranging" (25 : 32). The arrangement of the Qur'ān was thus a part of the Divine scheme. Another verse showing that the collection of the Book was a part of the Divine scheme runs thus: "Surely on Us rests the collecting of it and the reciting of it" (75 : 17). It appears from this that just as the Qur'ān was recited by Gabriel to the Prophet, in like manner, the collecting of its various parts was effected by the Prophet under the guidance of the Holy Spirit. History also bears testimony to the truth of this statement, for not only are there numerous anecdotes showing that this or that portion of the Qur'ān was put to writing under the orders of the Prophet, but we are clearly told by 'Uthmān, the third Caliph, that every portion of the Book was written and given its specified place, at the bidding of the Prophet: "It was customary with the Messenger of Allāh (may peace and the blessings of Allāh be upon him) that when portions of different chapters

[10] There is only one report which seems to convey the idea that the Companions who were sitting with the Prophet once saw Gabriel in human shape, but that incident is not related in connection with a Quranic revelation. A certain man, according to that report, whom no one recognized, came to the Prophet and asked him several questions about *īmān, Islām* and *iḥsān,* and lastly, when the Hour would come. He then disappeared and the Prophet is reported to have said: "That was Gabriel who came to teach you your religion" (Bu. 2 : 37). These words might mean that the answers given by him were of Gabriel's teachings, not that the man who put the questions was Gabriel.

[11] This subject has been fully dealt with in a separate booklet, in the Holy Qur'ān series, *Collection and Arrangement of the Holy Qur'ān.*

were revealed to him, and when any verse was revealed, he called one of those persons who used to write the Qur'ān[12] and said to him: Write this verse in the chapter where such and such verses occur'' (Ah. 1 : 57, 69).

Arrangement in oral recitation

In fact, if we bear in mind the use that was made of the Qur'ān, we cannot for an instant entertain the idea that the Book existed without any arrangements of its verses and chapters in the lifetime of the Prophet. It was not only recited in prayers but committed to memory and regularly recited to keep it fresh in the mind. Now if an arrangement of verses and chapters had not existed, it would have been impossible either to recite it in public prayers or to commit it to memory. The slightest change in the place of a verse by a person leading the prayers (*Imām*) would at once call forth a correction from the audience, as it does at the present day. Since no one could take the liberty of changing a word or the place of a word in a verse, no one could change a verse or the place of a verse in a chapter; and so the committing of the Qur'ān to memory by so many of the Companions of the Prophet, and their constant recitation of it, would have been impossible unless a known order was followed. The Prophet could not teach the Qur'ān to his companions nor the companions to each other, nor could he or anyone else lead the public prayers, in which long portions of the Book were recited, without following a known and accepted order.

Complete written copies of the Qur'ān

The Qur'ān thus existed in a complete and ordered form in the memories of men, but no complete written copy of it existed at the time,

[12] Among those whom the Prophet used to summon to write down portions of the Qur'ān immediately after their revelation are mentioned the names of Zaid ibn T͟hābit, Abū Bakr, 'Umar, 'Ut͟hmān, 'Alī, Zubair, Ubayy, Ḥanẓala, 'Abd Allāh ibn Sa'd, 'Abd Allāh ibn Arqam, 'Abd Allāh ibn Rawāḥa, S͟harḥubail, K͟hālid and Abān, sons of Sa'īd, and Mu'aiqab (FB. IX, p. 18). At Madīnah, Zaid ibn T͟hābit was chiefly called upon to do this work, and in his absence any of the other amanuenses would take his place, and this was the reason why Zaid was chosen to collect the Quranic writings in the time of Abū Bakr, and again to do the work of transcription in the time of 'Ut͟hmān. At Makkah, in the earliest days, there were Abū Bakr, 'Ali, K͟hādījah, wife of the Prophet, and others who wrote down the portions revealed. The Prophet took the greatest care to have a writer and writing materials with him under all conditions, and even when he had to fly for his life to Madīnah, he still had writing material with him (Bu. 63 : 45).

nor could such a copy be made while the Prophet was alive, and still receiving revelations. But the whole of the Qur'ān in one arrangement was safely preserved in the memories of reciters (*qurrā'*). It happened, however, that many of the reciters fell in the famous battle of Yamāma, in the caliphate of Abū Bakr,[13] and it was then that 'Umar[14] urged upon him the necessity of compiling a standard written copy, so that no portion of the Qur'ān should be lost even if all the reciters were to die. And this copy was compiled, not from the hundreds of copies that had been made by individual Companions for their own use but from the manuscripts written under the direction of the Prophet himself, and the arrangement adopted was that of the oral recitation as followed in his time. Thus a standard written copy was prepared, which was entrusted to the care of Ḥafṣah, wife of the Prophet.[15] But still no arrangement had been made for securing the accuracy of the numerous copies that were in circulation. This was done by 'Uthmān[16] who ordered several copies to be made of the copy prepared in the time of the first Caliph, and these were then sent to the different Islamic centres so that all copies made by individuals should be compared with the standard copy at each centre.

Standardization of the Qur'ān

Thus Abū Bakr ordered a standard copy to be prepared from the manuscripts written in the presence of the Prophet, following the order of chapters which was followed by the reciters under the directions of the Prophet, and 'Uthmān ordered copies to be made from this standard copy. If there was any variation from that standard copy, it went no further than this that where the Quraish[17] wrote a word in one way and Zaid wrote it in another way, 'Uthmān's order was to write it in the manner of the Quraish. This was because Zaid was a Madinite while his colleagues were Quraish.[18]

13 First Caliph of Islām, 11-13 A.H., 632-634 A.D.

14 'Umar became the second Caliph, (13-23 A.H. 634-644 A.D.).

15 *Bukhāri*, 66 : 3.

16 'Uthmān succeeded 'Umar as the third Caliph (23-35 A.H., 644-656 A.D.).

17 Quraish: the leading tribe of Makkah, Prophet Muḥammad belonged to the Banū Hāshim branch of this tribe.

18 Here is an account of what took place: "Anas son of Mālik relates that Ḥudhaifah came to 'Uthmān, and he had been fighting along with the people of Syria in the con-

As to what these differences were, some light is thrown on the point by Tirmidhī, one of the collectors of traditions, making the following addition to this report: "And they differed on that occasion as to *tābūt* and *tābūh*. The Quraish members said that it was *tābūt* and Zaid said that it was *tābūh*. The difference was reported to 'Uthmān and he directed them to write it *tābūt*, adding that the Qur'ān was revealed in the dialect of the Quraish." It would be seen from this that these differences of reading or writing were very insignificant, but as the Companions of the prophet believed every word and letter of the Qur'ān to be the revealed word of God, they gave importance even to a slight difference in writing and referred it to the Caliph. It may be added here that Zaid was chiefly called upon by the Prophet at Madīnah to write down the Quranic revelations, and the word *tābūt* occurs in a Madīnah chapter (2 : 248). Zaid had written it *tābūh* as the Madinites did, but as the Quraish wrote it *tābūt*, 'Uthmān restored the Quraishite form. This incident further shows that Ḥafṣah's copy contained the manuscripts written in the presence of the Prophet. These two reports furnish conclusive proof that if there was any difference between 'Uthmān's standard copy and the collection made by Abū Bakr, it was a difference only as to the mode of writing certain words. In short, there was no change of words, no change of verses and no change in the order of chapters.

Differences of readings

A few words may be added as to the so-called differences of readings in the Qur'ān. There were slight differences in the spoken language of different tribes, that of the Quraish being the model for the literary

quest of Armenia and along with the people of 'Irāq in Azerbaijan, and was alarmed at their variations in the mode of reading (the Qur'ān), and said to him, O Commander of the Faithful, stop the people before they differ in the Holy Book as the Jews and the Christians differ in their scriptures. So 'Uthmān sent word to Ḥafṣah, asking her to send him the Qur'ān in her possession so that they might make other copies of it and then send the original copy back to her. Thereupon Ḥafṣah sent the copy to 'Uthmān, and he ordered Zaid ibn Thābit and 'Abd Allāh ibn Zubair and Sa'īd ibn al-'Āṣ and 'Abd al-Raḥmān ibn Ḥārith ibn Hishām, and they made copies from the original copy. 'Uthmān also said to the three men who belonged to the Quraish (Zaid only being a Madinite), 'Where you differ with Zaid in anything concerning the Qur'ān write it in the manner of the Quraish, for it is in their language that it was revealed.' They obeyed these instructions, and when they had made the required number of copies from the original copy, 'Uthmān returned the original to Ḥafṣah, and sent to every quarter one of the copies thus made, and ordered all other copies or leaves on which the Qur'ān was written to be burned" (Bu. 66 : 3).

language. The Qur'ān was revealed in the dialect of the Quraish, the literary language of Arabia. But when, towards the close of the Prophet's life, people from different Arabian tribes accepted Islām in large numbers, it was found that they could not pronounce certain words in the idiom of the Quraish, being habituated from childhood to their own idiom, and it was then that the Prophet allowed them to pronounce a word according to their own peculiar idiom. This permission was given only to facilitate the recitation of the Qur'ān. The written Qur'ān was one; it was all in the chaste idiom of the Quraish, but people belonging to other tribes were allowed to pronounce it in their own way.[19]

There may have been certain revelations in which an optional reading was permitted. Readings belonging to this class can only be accepted on the most unimpeachable evidence, and the trustworthiness of the traditions containing such reading must be established beyond all doubt. But even these readings do not find their way into the written text, which remains permanently one and the same. Their value is only explanatory: they only show what significance is to be attached to the word used in the text; they are never at variance with the text. They are known to very few even of the learned, to say nothing of the general readers of the Holy Book, and are considered to have the value of an authentic tradition in explaining the meaning of a certain word occurring in the text. Thus, the so-called different readings were either dialectic variations, which were never meant to be permanent and, intended only to facilitate the reading of the Qur'ān in individual cases, or explanatory variations meant to throw light on the text. The former ceased to exist with the spread of education in Arabia, and the latter have still the same explanatory value as they originally had.

Collective testimony of the purity of the Quranic text

Random reports that a certain verse or chapter, not to be met with in the Qur'ān, was part of the text, have no value at all as against the conclusive and collective testimony which establishes the purity of the text of the Qur'ān. These reports were in some cases fabricated by enemies

[19] Some examples of these variations may be given here, *Ḥattā* (meaning *until*) was pronounced *'attā*by the Hudhail; *ta'lamūn* (meaning *you know*) was pronounced *ti'lamūn* by the Asad; the Tamīm read *hamzah* one of the letters, whereas the Quraish did not. In one report the meaning is made clear, where the following words are added from the lips of the Prophet: "Therefore recite it in the manner in which you find it easy to do so" (Bu. 66 : 5). In other words, the Prophet allowed a reader to pronounce a word in

who sought to undermine the authority of the religion of Islām.[20] In other cases, they may have been the mistaken conception of some narrator. However that may be, it is necessary to weigh the evidence as to whether or not a certain verse formed part of the Quranic text. It is a fact that every verse of the Qur'ān was, when revealed, promulgated and made public; it became a part of the public prayer and was repeated day and night to be listened to by an audience of hundreds. When the written manuscripts of the Qur'ān were first collected into one volume in the time of the first caliph, and later on when copies were made from that original in the time of the third caliph, there was the unanimous testimony of all the Companions that every verse that found a place in that collection was part of the Divine revelation. Such testimony of overwhelming numbers cannot be set aside by the evidence of one or two, but, as a matter of fact, all reports quoted as affecting the purity of the text ascribe a certain statement to only one man, and in not a single case is there a second man to support that assertion. Thus when Ibn Mas'ūd[21] makes an assertion to this effect, Ubayy's[22] evidence, along with that of the whole body of Companions, goes against him; and when Ubayy makes a like assertion, Ibn Mas'ūd's evidence along with that of the rest of the Companions goes against him. Thus there is not a single assertion impugning the purity of the Quranic text for which even one supporting witness can be produced.[23]

the way he found it easiest. In the proper sense of the word, these dialectic variations would not be readings at all. In exceptional cases, a person who could not pronounce a certain word, may have been allowed to substitute its equivalent. But even that would not be a case of a variant reading, since it was merely a permission granted to a particular individual, and such variations never found their way into the written text of the Qur'ān.

[20] For instance, *Muslim* mentions a report ascribing to Abū Mūsā the statement that there was a certain chapter of the Qur'ān, similar in length and force to the 9th chapter, of which only a single passage was all that he remembered. Now the *Mīzān al-I'tidāl*, a critical inquiry about the narrators of the reports, shows that Suwaid, the immediate informer of *Muslim*, was a *Zindeeq* (*i.e.* one who conceals unbelief and makes an outward show of belief), and, therefore, the report, as its very subject-matter shows, is a clear invention. The four other reports speaking of similar passages, not met with in the text of the Qur'ān, may be relegated to the same class.

[21 & 22] Two of the persons to whom such reports are ascribed.

[23] In many cases even internal evidence would show that the report was not credible. For example, one report ascribes the following statement to 'Ā'ishah: "The chapter of the Confederates (ch. 33) consisted, at the time of the Prophet, of two hundred verses: when 'Uthmān wrote the *Muṣḥaf*, he was only able to collect of it what it contains."

The theory of abrogation

That certain verses of the Qur'ān are abrogated by others is now an exploded theory. The two passages on which it was supposed to rest, refer, really, to the abrogation, not of the passages of the Qur'ān but of the previous revelations whose place the Holy Book had taken. The first verse is contained in the sixteenth chapter (*al-Naḥl*) — a Makkah revelation — and runs thus: "And when We change a message for a message,[24] — and Allāh knows best what He reveals — they say: Thou art only a forger" (16 : 101). It is a fact that details of the Islamic law were revealed at Madīnah and it is in relation to these details that the theory of abrogation has been broached. Therefore, a Makkah revelation would not speak of abrogation. But the reference in the above verse is to the abrogation, not of the Quranic verses but of the previous Divine messages or revelations, consequent upon revelation of the Qur'ān. The context shows this clearly to be the case, for the opponents are here made to say that the Prophet was a forger. He was so accused by the opponents not because he announced the abrogation of certain verses of the Qur'ān but because he claimed that the Qur'ān was a Divine revelation which had taken the place of previous revelations. They argued that it was not a revelation at all: "Only a mortal teaches him" (16 : 103). According to them the whole of the Qur'ān, and not merely a particular verse of it, was a forgery. The theory of abrogation, therefore, cannot be based on this verse which speaks only of one revelation or one law taking the place of another.

The other verse which is supposed to lend support to the theory runs thus: "Whatever message We abrogate or cause to be forgotten, We bring one better than it or one like it" (2 : 106). A reference to the context

'Ā'ishah could never have spoken these words, as she knew too well that 'Uthmān never collected the *Muṣḥaf*; he had only directed the making of copies from Ḥafṣah's *Muṣḥaf*. The false notion that 'Uthmān collected the Qur'ān is of later growth, and this affords the surest testimony that this report is a mere invention. Similarly, the words ascribed to 'Umar regarding the stoning of the adulterer are a fabrication. He is reported to have said: "If I were not afraid that people would say 'Umar has added something to the Book of God, I should write it down in the Qur'ān" (A.D. 37 : 23). This assertion is self-contradictory. If it was really part of the Qur'ān, why should people say that 'Umar had added to the Book of God?

[24] The word *āya* occurring here means originally a sign, and hence it comes to signify *an indication* or *evidence* or *proof*, and is used in the sense of a *miracle*. It also signifies *risāla* or *a Divine message* (TA.). The word is frequently used in the Qur'ān in its general sense of a Divine message or a Divine communication, and is, therefore, applicable to a portion of the Qur'ān or to any previous revelation. It carries the latter significance here as the context clearly shows.

will show that the Jews or the followers of previous revelations are here addressed. Of these it is said: "they say: We believe in that which was revealed to us; and they deny what is besides that" (2 : 91). So they were told that if a certain revelation was abrogated, it was only to give place to a better one. And there is mention not only of abrogation but also of something that was forgotten. The words "or cause to be forgotten"[25] cannot refer to the Qur'ān at all because no portion of it could be said to have been forgotten so as to require a new revelation in its place. There is no point in supposing that God should first make the Prophet forget a verse and then reveal a new one in its place. Why not, if he really had forgotten a verse, remind him of the one forgotten? But even if it is supposed that his memory ever failed in retaining a certain verse (which really never happened), that verse was quite safely preserved in writing, and the mere failure of the memory could not necessitate a new revelation. That the Prophet never forgot what was recited to him by the Holy Spirit is plainly stated in the Qur'ān: "We shall make thee recite, so thou shalt not forget" (87 : 6). History also bears out the fact that he never forgot any portion of the Quranic revelation. Sometimes the whole of a very long chapter would be revealed to him in one portion, as in the case of the sixth chapter which extends over twenty sections, but he would cause it to be written down without delay, and make his Companions learn it by heart, and recite it in public prayers, and that without the change of even a letter, notwithstanding the fact that he himself could not read from a written copy, nor did the written copies, as a rule, remain in his possession. It was a miracle indeed that he never forgot any portion of the Qur'ān, though other things he might forget, and it is to his forgetfulness in other things that the words *except what Allāh pleases*, in the next verse (87 : 7), refer.[26] On the other hand, it is a fact that parts of the older revelations had been utterly lost and forgotten, and thus the Qur'ān was needed to take the place of that which was abrogated, and that which had been forgotten by the world.

[25] Sale's translation of the words is misleading and has actually deceived many writers on Islām who had no access to the original. He translates the words *nunsi-hā* as meaning *We cause thee to forget*. Now the text does not contain any word meaning *thee*. The slight error makes the verse mean that Almighty God had caused the Prophet to forget certain Quranic verses; whereas the original does not say that the Prophet was made to forget anything but clearly implies that the world was made to forget.

[26] The word "*except*" (*illā*) is sometimes used in Arabic to indicate *istithnā' munqaṭi'*, lit. *an exception which is cut off*, the thing excepted being disunited in kind from that from which an exception is made.

Traditions on abrogation

"The traditions speaking of abrogation are all weak", says Ṭabraṣī. But it is stranger still that the theory of abrogation has been accepted by writer after writer without ever thinking that not a single tradition, however weak, touching on the aborgation of a verse, was traceable to the Prophet. It never occurred to the upholders of this theory that the Quranic verses were promulgated by the Prophet, and that it was he whose authority was necessary for the abrogation of any Quranic verse; no Companion, not even Abū Bakr or 'Alī,[27] could say that a verse was abrogated. The Prophet alone was entitled to say so, and there is not a single tradition to the effect that he ever said so; it is always some Companion or a later authority to whom such views are to be traced. In most cases, where a report is traceable to one Companion who held a certain verse to have been abrogated, there is another report traceable to another Companion to the effect that the verse was not abrogated.[28] Even among later writers we find that there is not a single verse on which the verdict of abrogation has been passed by one without being questioned by another; and while there are writers who would lightly pass the verdict of aborgation on hundreds of verses, there are others who consider not more than five to be abrogated, and even in the case of these five the verdict of abrogation has been seriously impugned by earlier writers.

Use of the word naskh

The theory of abrogation has in fact arisen from a misunderstanding of the use of the word *naskh* (abrogation), by the Companions of the Prophet. When the significance of one verse was limited by another, the former was sometimes spoken of as having been "abrogated" (*nusikhat*) by the latter. Similarly when the words of a verse gave rise to a misconception, and a later revelation cleared up that misconception, the word "abrogation" was metaphorically used in connection with it, the idea underlying its use being not that the first verse was abrogated but that a

[27] Cousin and son-in-law of the Prophet. He succeeded 'Uthmān as fourth Caliph.

[28] Some examples may be noted here — 2 : 180 is held by some to have been abrogated while othes have denied it (IJ-C.); 2 : 184 is considered by Ibn 'Umar as having been abrogated while Ibn 'Abbās says it was not (Bu.); 2 : 240 was abrogated according to Ibn Zubair while Mujāhid says it was not (Bu.). I have taken these examples only from the second chapter of the Qur'ān.

certain conception to which it had given rise was abrogated.[29] Earlier authorities admit this use of the word: "Those who accept abrogation (*naskh* here (2 : 109) take it as meaning *explanation* metaphorically"[30]; and again: "By abrogation is meant, metaphorically, explaining and making clear the significance".[31] It is an abrogation, but not an abrogation of the words of the Qur'ān; rather it is the abrogation of a misconception of their meaning. This is further made clear by the application of abrogation to verses containing statements of facts (*akhbār*), whereas, properly speaking, abrogation could only take place in the case of verses containing a commandment or a prohibition (*amr* or *nahy*). In the ordinary sense of the word there could be no abrogation of a statement made in the Word of God, as that would suggest that God had made a wrong statement first and then recalled it. This use of the word "abrogation" by the earlier authorities

[29] Many instances of this may be quoted. In 2 : 284, it is said, "whether you manifest what is in your minds or hide it, Allāh will call you to account for it"; while according to 2 : 286, "Allāh does not impose on any soul a duty but to the extent of its ability". A report in *Bukhārī* says that one of the Companions of the Prophet, probably 'Abd Allāh ibn 'Umar held the opinion that the first verse was abrogated (*nusikhat*) by the second. What was meant by *naskh* (abrogation) in this case is made clear by another detailed report given in the *Musnad* (Ah. I, 332). According to this report when 2 : 284 was revealed, the Companions entertained an idea which they had never entertained before (or, according to another report, they were greatly grieved) and thought that they had not the power to bear it. The matter being brought to the notice of the Prophet, he said: "Rather say, We have heard and we obey and submit," and so God inspired faith in their hearts. As this report shows, what happened was this: that some Companion or Companions thought that 2 : 284 imposed a new burden on them, making every evil idea which entered the mind without taking root or ever being translated into action, punishable in the same manner as if it had been translated into action. 2 : 286 made it plain that this was not the meaning conveyed by 2 : 284, since, according to that verse, God did not impose on man a burden which he could not bear. This removal of a misconception was called abrogation (*naskh*) by Ibn 'Umar.

It may be added that there is nothing to show that 2 : 286 was revealed later than 2 : 284. On the other hand, the use of the words *we have heard and we obey* by the Prophet to remove the wrong notion which some Companions entertained — these very words occur in 2 : 285 — shows that the three verses, 284, 285, and 286 were all revealed together, and hence the abrogation, in the ordinary sense of the word, of one of them by another is meaningless. There are other instances in which a verse revealed later is thought to have been abrogated by a previous verse. But how could a later verse be abrogated by a previous one? Or what point can there be in giving an order which was cancelled before it was given? If, on the other hand, the *naskh* is taken to mean the placing of a limitation upon the meaning of a verse, or the removal of a wrong conception attached to it, no difficulty would arise, for even a previous verse may be spoken of as placing a limitation upon the meaning of a later verse or as removing a wrong conception arising therefrom.

[30] RM, I, p. 292.

[31] Ibid., p. 508.

regarding statements of facts[32] shows that they were using the word to signify the removal of a wrong conception regarding, or the placing of a limitation upon, the meaning of a certain verse. At the same time, it is true that the use of this word soon became indiscriminate, and when any one found himself unable to reconcile two verses, he would declare one of them to be abrogated by the other.

Basis of abrogation

The principle on which the theory of abrogation is based is unacceptable, being contrary to the clear teachings of the Qur'ān. A verse is considered to be abrogated by another when the two cannot be reconciled with each other; in other words, when they appear to contradict each other. But the Qur'ān destroys this foundation when it declares that no part of it is at variance with another: "Will they not then meditate on the Qur'ān? And if it were from any other than Allāh, they would have found in it many a discrepancy" (4 : 82). It was due to lack of meditation that one verse was thought to be at variance with another; and hence it is that in almost all cases where abrogation has been upheld by one person, there has been another who, being able to reconcile the two, has repudiated the alleged abrogation.

Sayūṭī on abrogation

It is only among the later commentators that we meet with the tendency to augment the number of verses thought to have been abrogated, and by some of these the figure has been placed as high as five hundred. In this

[32] One example of one statement being spoken of as abrogated by another is that of 2 : 284, 286 (for which see the previous footnote). Another is furnished by 8 : 65, 66, where the first verse states that in war the Muslims shall overcome ten times their numbers, and the second, after referring to their weakness at the time — which meant the paucity of trained men among them and their lack of the implements and necessaries of war — states that they shall overcome double their numbers. Now the two verses relate to two different conditions and they may be said to place a limitation upon the meaning of each other, but one of them cannot be spoken of as abrogating the other. In the time of the Prophet when the Muslims were weak, when every man, old or young, had to be called upon to take the field, and the Muslim army was but ill-equipped, the Muslims overcame double, even thrice their numbers; but in the wars with the Persian and Roman empires, they vanquished ten times their numbers. Both statements were true; they only related to different circumstances and the one placed a limitation upon the meaning of the other, but neither of them actually abrogated the other.

connection, Sayūṭī, one of the well-known commentators, says: "Those who multiply (the number of abrogated verses) have included many kinds — one kind being that in which there is neither abrogation, nor any particularization (of a general statement), nor has it any connection with any one of them, for various reasons. And this is as in the words of God: 'And spend out of what We have given them' (2 : 3); 'And spend out of what We have given you' (63 : 10); and the like. It is said that these are abrogated by the verse dealing with charity (*zakāt*), while it is not so, they being still in force".[33] Sayūṭī himself brings the number of verses which he thinks to be abrogated down to twenty-one,[34] in some of which he considers there is abrogation, while in others he finds that it is only the particularization of a general injunction that is effected by a later verse; but he admits that there is a difference of opinion even about these.

Shāh Walī Allāh's verdict on five verses

A later writer, however, the famous Shāh Walī Allāh of India, commenting on this in his *Fauz al-Kabīr*, says that abrogation cannot be proved in the case of sixteen out of Sayūṭī's twenty-one verses, but in the case of the remaining five he is of the opinion that the verdict of abrogation is final. These five verses are dealt with as follows:

(1) 2 : 180 "It is prescribed for you, when death approaches one of you, if he leaves behind wealth, for parents and near relations, to make a bequest in a kindly manner." As a matter of fact, both Baidzāwī and Ibn Jarīr[35] quote authorities who state that this verse was not abrogated; and it is surprising that it is considered as being abrogated by 4 : 11, 12, which speak of the shares to be given "after the payment of a bequest he may have bequeathed or a debt," showing clearly that the bequest spoken of in 2 : 180 was still in force. This verse in fact speaks of bequest for charitable objects which is even now recognized by Muslims to the extent of one-third of the property.[36]

(2) 2 : 240: "And those of you who die and leave wives behind, should make a bequest in favour of their wives of maintenance for a year without

33 It. II, p. 22.

34 *Ibid.*, p. 23.

35 Famous commentators of the Qur'ān.

36 This is discussed further in the chapter on *Inheritance*.

turning them out.'' But we have the word of no less an authority than Mujāhid that this verse is not abrogated: ''Allāh gave her (the widow) the whole of a year, seven months and twenty days being optional, under the bequest; if she desired she could stay according to the bequest (having maintenance and residence for a year), and if she desired she could leave the house (and remarry), as the Qur'ān says: 'Then if they leave of their own accord, there is no blame on you''' (Bu. 65, Surah ii : 41). This verse, therefore, does not contradict v.234. Moreover, there is proof that it was revealed after v.234, and hence it cannot be said to have been abrogated by the verse.

(3) 8 : 65: ''If there are twenty patient ones of you, they shall overcome two hundred'', etc. This is said to have been abrogated by the verse that follows it: ''Now Allāh has made light your burden and He knows that there is weakness in you. So if there be of you a hundred steadfast, they shall overcome two hundred.'' That the question of abrogation does not arise here at all is apparent from the words of the second verse which clearly refers to the early times when the Muslims were weak, having neither munitions of war nor experience of warfare, and when old and young had to go out and fight; while the first verse refers to a later period when the Muslim armies were fully organized and equipped.

(4) 33 : 52: ''It is not allowed to thee to take women after this.'' This is said to have been abrogated by a verse which was apparently revealed before it: ''O Prophet! We have made lawful to thee thy wives'' (33 : 50). The whole issue has been misunderstood. As stated before, a verse cannot be abrogated by one revealed before it. Apparently what happened was this. When 4 : 3 was revealed, limiting the number of wives to four, should exceptional circumstances require, the Prophet was told not to divorce the excess number, and this was effected by 33 : 50; but at the same time he was told not to take any woman in marriage after that, and this was done by 33 : 52.

(5) 58 : 12: ''O you who believe! when you consult the Messenger, offer something in charity before your consultation. That is better for you and purer. But if you have not the means then surely Allāh is Forgiving, Merciful.'' This is said to have been abrogated by the verse that follows: ''Do you fear that you will not be able to give in charity before your consultation? So when you do it not and Allāh has turned to you mercifully, keep up prayer and pay the poor-rate.'' It is not easy to see how one of these injunctions is abrogated by the other, since there is not the slightest difference in what they say. The second verse merely gives further explanation to show that the injunction is only in the nature of a recommendation, that

is to say, a man may give in charity whatever he can easily spare, the legal alms (*zakāt*) being the only obligatory charity.

Thus the theory of abrogation falls to the ground on all consideration.

Interpretation of the Qur'ān

The rule as to the interpretation of the Qur'ān is thus given in the Book itself: "He it is Who has revealed the Book to thee; some of its verses are decisive — they are the basis of the Book — and others are allegorical. Then those in whose hearts is perversity follow the part of it which is allegorical, seeking to mislead, and seeking to give it their own interpretation. And none knows its interpretation except Allāh, and those firmly rooted in knowledge. They say: We believe in it, it is all from our Lord. And none do mind except men of understanding" (3 : 6). In the first place,it is stated here that there are two kinds of verses in the Qur'ān, namely, the decisive and the allegorical — the latter being those which are capable of different interpretations. Next we are told that the decisive verses are the basis of the Book, that is, that they contain the fundamental principles of religion. Hence whatever may be the differences of interpretation, the fundamentals of religion are not affected by them, all such differences relating only to secondary matters. The third point is that some people seek to give their own interpretation to allegorical statements and are thus misled. In other words, serious errors arise only when a wrong interpretation is placed on words which are susceptible of two meanings. Lastly, in the concluding words, a clue is given as to the right mode of interpretation in the case of allegorical statements: "It is all from our Lord" — meaning that there is no disagreement between the various portions of the Book. This statement has in fact been made elsewhere also, as already quoted (see 4 : 82). The important principle to be borne in mind in the interpretation of the Qurān, therefore, is that the meaning should be sought from within the Qur'ān, and never should a passage be interpreted in such a manner that it may be at variance with any other passage, but more especially with the basic principles laid down in the decisive verses. This principle, in the revealed words, is followed by "those well-grounded in knowledge."[37] The following rules may, therefore, be laid down:

[37] The subject of the interpretation of the Quranic verses is very appropriately dealt with in the opening verses of the third chapter which begins with a discussion with the followers of Christianity, for, it must be borne in mind, that it is on a wrong interpretation of certain allegorical statements that the fundamental principles of Christianity are actually based. The basic doctrine of the religion of all the prophets in the Old Testament is

—The principles of Islām are enunciated in decisive words in the Qur'ān; and, therefore, no attempt should be made to establish a principle on the strength of an allegorical passage, or of words susceptible of different meanings.

—The explanation of the Book should in the first place be sought in the Qur'ān itself; for, whatever it has stated briefly, or merely hinted at, in one place, will be found expanded and fully explained elsewhere in it.

—It is very important to remember that the Qur'ān contains allegory and metaphor along with what is plain and decisive, and the only safeguard against beng misled by what is allegorical or metaphorical is that the interpretation of such passages must be strictly in consonance with what is laid down in clear and decisive words, and not at variance therewith.

—When a law or principle is laid down, any statement carrying a doubtful significance, or a statement apparently opposed to the law so laid down, must be interpreted subject to the principle enunicated. Similarly that which is particular must be read in connection with and subject to more general statements.

Value of Tradition and commentaries in interpreting the Qur'ān

In this connection, it may also be added that the Tradition also affords an explanation of the Qur'ān but a tradition can only be accepted when

the Unity of God, but there are a number of prophecies couched in allegorical language having reference to the advent of Christ. The Christians, instead of interpreting these in accordance with the clear words of the principle of Divine Unity, laid the foundations of Christianity on the metaphorical language of the prophecies, and thus by neglect of the true rule of interpretation were misled to such an extent as to ignore the very essentials of the religion of the prophets. Christ was believed to be God on the strength of metaphorical expressions, and the doctrine of the Trinity thus became the basis of a new religion. The epithet "son of God" was freely used in Israelite literature, and was always taken allegorically. The term occurs as early as Gen. 6 : 2 where the "sons of God" are spoken of as taking the daughters of men for wives. It occurs again in Job 1 : 6 and 38 : 7, and good men are no doubt meant in both places. In Ex. 4 : 22 and many other places, the Israelites are spoken of as the children of God: "Israel is my son, even my first born." The expression is used in the same metaphorical sense in the Gospels. Even in the fourth Gospel, where the Divinity of Christ is looked upon as finding a bolder expression than in the synoptics, Jesus Christ is reported as saying in answer to those who accused him of blasphemy for speaking of himself as the son of God: "Is it not written in your law, I said, Ye are gods? If He called them gods, unto whom the word of God came, and the scripture cannot be broken; say ye of him, whom the Father hath sanctified, and sent into the world. Thou blasphemest, because I said, I am the Son of God?" (Jn 10 : 34-36). It is thus clear that even in the mouth of Jesus the term "son of God" was a metaphorical expression, and by taking it literally the Church has destroyed the very foundations of religion. It is to this fundamental mistake of Christianity that the Qur'ān refers by giving the rule for the interpretation of allegorical verses in a discussion of the Christian religion.

it is reliable and not opposed to what is clearly stated in the Qur'ān.[38] As regards commentaries, a word of warning is necesary against the tendency to regard what is stated in them as being the final word on interpretation, since by so doing the great treasures of knowledge which an exposition of the Qur'ān in the new light of modern progress reveals are shut out, and the Qur'ān becomes a sealed book to the present generation. The learned men of yore all freely sought its meaning according to their understanding and circumstances, and the same right accrues to the present generation. It must also be added that though the commentaries are valuable stores of learning for a knowledge of the Qur'ān, the numerous anecdotes and legends with which many of them are filled can only be accepted with the greatest caution and after the most careful sifting.[39]

Divisions of the Qur'ān

The Qur'ān is divided into 114 chapters, each of which is called a *sūrah.*[40] The chapters are of varying length, the longest comprising one-twelfth of the entire Book. All the chapters, with the exception of the last thirty-five, are divided into sections (*rukū'*), each section dealing generally with one subject, and the different sections being interrelated to each other. Each section contains a number of verses (*āyah*).[41] The total number of verses is 6,240,[42] or including the 113 verses "in the name of Allāh" (*bismillāh*) with which the chapters open, 6,353.[43] For the purpose of recitation, the Qur'ān is divided into thirty equal parts (*juz*), each of these being again subdivided into four equal parts. Another division is into seven portions (*manzil*), which is designed for the completion of its recital in seven days. These divisions for the purpose of recitation have nothing to do with the subject-matter of the Qur'ān.

38 See also chapter on *Tradition (Sunnah or Ḥadith)*.

39 Such stories are mostly taken from the Jews and the Christians, and on this point I would refer the reader to my remarks under the heading "Reports in Biographies and Commentaries" in the next chapter, where I have shown that the best authorities have condemned most of this material as derived from Jewish and Christian sources.

40 Meaning literally *eminence* or *high degree* (R.), and also *any degree of a structure* (LL.).

41 Meaning originally a *sign* or a *communication from God.*

42 There existed a slight difference in the numbering of verses in the different centres of learning. Kūfah readers counting them 6,239, Baṣrah 6,204, Syria 6,225, Makkah 6,219, Madīnah 6,211. But this is a difference of computation only, some readers marking the end of a verse where others do not.

43 Every chapter of the Qur'ān begins with the *Bismillāh* verse, except the ninth.

Makkah and Madīnah sūrahs

An important division of the Qur'ān relates to the Makkah and Madīnah chapters. After the Call, the Prophet passed 13 years at Makkah, and was then forced to migrate with his Companions to Madīnah where he spent the last ten years of his life. Out of the total of 114 chapters of the Book, 92 were revealed during the Makkah period and 22 during the Madīnah period,[44] but the Madīnah chapters, being generally longer, contain about one-third of the Holy Book. In arrangement, the Makkah revelation is intermingled with that of Madīnah; the number of Makkah and Madīnah chapters following each other alternately, being 1, 4, 2, 2, 14, 1, 8, 1, 13, 3, 7, 10, 48. On referring to the subject-matter of the Makkah and Madīnah revelations, we find the following three broad features distinguishing the two groups of chapters. Firstly, the Makkah revelation deals chiefly with faith in God and is particularly devoted to grounding the Muslims in that faith, while the Madīnah revelation is mainly intended to translate that faith into action. It is true that exhortations to good and noble deeds are met with in the Makkah revelation, and in the Madīnah revelation faith is still shown to be the foundation on which the structure of deeds should be built, but, in the main, stress is laid in the former on faith in an Omnipotent and Omnipresent God Who requites every good and every evil deed, and the latter deals chiefly with what is good and what is evil, in other words, with the details of the law. The second feature distinguishing the two revelations is that while that of Makkah is generally prophetical, that of Madīnah deals with the fulfilment of prophecy. Thirdly, while the former shows how true happiness of mind may be sought in communion with God, the latter points out how man's dealing with man may also be a source of bliss and comfort to him. Hence a scientific arrangement of the Qur'ān must of necessity rest on the intermingling of the two revelations, blending of faith with deeds, of prophecy with fulfilment of prophecy, of Divine communion with man's relation to and treatment of man.

It may be added here that the idea that the proper arrangement of the Qur'ān should be in chronological order is a mistaken one. Most of the chapters were revealed piecemeal, and hence a chronological order of revelation would destroy the chapter arrangement altogether. Take, for example, the very first chapter chronologically, the 96th in the present order.

[44] Ch.110 was revealed at Makkah during the Farewell Pilgrimage and therefore belongs to the Madīnah period.

While its first five verses are undoubtedly the first revelation that came to the Prophet, the rest of the chapter was not revealed before the fourth year of his ministry. Similarly with the second chapter in the present arrangement; while the major portion of it was revealed in the first and the second years of the Hijrah, some verses were revealed as late as the closing days of the Prophet's life. Chronological order is, therefore, an impossibility.

The place of the Qur'ān in world literature

That the Qur'ān occupies a place of eminence in Arabic literature which has not fallen to the lot of any other book goes without saying; but we may say more and assert with confidence that the place so occupied has not been attained at any time by any book anywhere. For what book is there in the whole history of the human race that, through thirteen long centuries, has not only remained admittedly the standard of the language in which it is written but has also originated a world-wide literature? The feat accomplished by the Qur'ān is unique in the whole history of the written word. It transformed a dialect, spoken in a very limited area of a forgotten corner of the world, into a world-wide language which became the mother-tongue of vast countries and mighty empires, and produced a literature which is the basis of the culture of powerful nations from one end of the world to the other. There was no literature, properly speaking, in Arabic before the Qur'ān; the few pieces of poetry that did exist never soared beyond the praise of wine or woman, or horse or sword. It was with the Qur'ān that Arabic literature originated, and through it that Arabic became a powerful language spoken in many countries and casting its influence on the literary histories of many others. Without the Qur'ān, the Arabic language would have been nowhere in the world. As Dr. Steingass says:

"But we may well ask ourselves, what would in all probability have become of this language without Muḥammad and his Qur'ān? This is not at all an idle and desultory speculation. It is true the Arabic language had already produced numerous fine specimens of genuine and high-flown poetry, but such poetry was chiefly, if not exclusively, preserved in the memory of the people...Moreover, poetry is not tantamount to literature...Divided among themselves into numerous tribes, who were engaged in a perpetual warfare against each other, the Arabs, and with them their various dialects, would more and more have drifted asunder, poetry would have followed in the wake, and the population of Arabia would have broken up into a multitude of clans, with their particular bards, whose love-and-war songs enterprising travellers of our day might now collect... It seems, then, that it is only a work of the nature of the Qur'ān which could develop ancient Arabic into a literary language... But not only by raising a dialect, through its generalization, to the power of a language, and by rendering the adoption of writing indispensable, has the Qur'ān initiated the development of an Arabic literature; its composition itself has contributed two factors absolutely needful to this development: it has added to the existing poetry the origins of rhetoric and prose... But Muḥammad made a still greater and more decisive step towards creating a literature for his people. In those sūrahs, in which he regulated the private and public life of the Muslim, he originated a prose, which has remained the standard of classical purity ever since''.[45]

There are other considerations which entitle the Qur'ān to a place of eminence to which no other book can aspire. It throws light on all the fundamentals of religion,[46] the existence and unity of God, the reward of good and evil, the life after death, paradise and hell, revelation, etc. In addition to expounding to us the mysteries of the unseen, it offers a solution of the most difficult problems of this life, such as the distribution of wealth, the sex-problem, and all other questions on which depends in any degree the happiness and advancement of man. And the value of this copiousness of ideas is further enhanced when it is seen that it does not confront man with dogmas but gives reasons for every assertion made, whether relating to the spiritual or the physical life. There are hundreds of topics on which it has enriched the literature of the world, and whether it discusses questions relating to spiritual existence or to physical life here on earth, it adopts a rational approach and convinces by agrument and not by dogma.

More wonderful still is the effect which the Qur'ān has produced. The transformation it brought about is unparalleled in the history of the world. A complete change was wrought in the lives of a whole nation in an incredibly short time — a period of no more than twenty-three years. The Qur'ān found the Arabs worshippers of idols, unhewn stones, trees and heaps of sand, yet in less than a quarter of a century the worship of the One God ruled the whole land and idolatry had been wiped out from one end of the country to the other. It swept all superstitions before it and,

[45] Hughes' *Dictionary of Islam,* art. Qur'ān, pp. 528, 529.

[46] This subject has been fully dealt with in the second part of this book.

in their place, gave the most rational religion the world could dream of. The Arab who had been wont to pride himself on his ignorance transformed into the lover of knowledge, drinking deep at every fountain of learning to which he could gain access. And this was directly the effect of the teaching of the Qur'ān, which not only appealed to reason, ever and again, but declared man's thirst for knowledge to be insatiable. And along with superstition went the deepest vices of the Arab, and in their place the Holy Book put a burning desire for the best and noblest deeds in the service of humanity. Yet it was not the transformation of the individual alone that the Qur'ān had accomplished; equally was it a transformation of the family, of society, of the very nation itself. From the warring elements of the Arab race, it welded a nation, united and full of life and vigour, before whose onward march the greatest kingdoms of the world crumbled as if they had been but toys before the reality of the new faith. Thus the Qur'ān effected a transformation of humanity itself — a transformation material as well as moral, an awakening intellectual as well as spiritual. There is no other book which has brought about a change so miraculous in the lives of men.

European writers on the Qur'ān

To this position of the Qur'ān in world literature, testimony is borne by even the most biased European writers:

"The style of the Koran is generally beautiful and fluent ... and in many places, especially where the majesty and attributes of God are described, sublime and magnificent... He succeeded so well, and so strangely captivated the minds of his audience, that several of his opponents thought it the effect of witchcraft and enchantment".[47]

"That the best of Arab writers has never succeeded in producing anything equal in merit to the Qur'ān itself is not surprising".[48]

"The earliest Mekka revelations are those which contain what is highest in a great religion and what was purest in a great man".[49]

"However often we turn to it, at first disgusting us each time afresh, it soon attracts, astounds, and in the end enforces our reverence... Its style, in accordance with its contents and aim, is stern, grand, terrible — ever and

[47] Sale, *Preliminary Discourse*, p. 48.

[48] Palmer, *Intro.*, p.lv.

[49] Lane's *Selections*, Intro., p. cvi.

anon truly sublime... Thus this book will go on exercising through all ages a most potent influence''.[50]

''We may well say the Qur'ān is one of the grandest books ever written... Sublime and chaste, where the supreme truth of God's unity is to be proclaimed; appealing in high-pitched strains to the imagination of a poetically-gifted people where the eternal consequences of man's submission to God's holy will, or of rebellion against it, are pictured; touching in its simple, almost crude, earnestness, when it seeks again and again encouragement or consolation for God's Messenger, and a solemn warning for those to whom he has been sent, in the histories of the prophets of old: the language of the Qur'ān adapts itself to the exigencies of everyday life, when this everyday life, in its private and public bearings, is to be brought in harmony with the fundamental principles of the new dispensation.

''Here therefore its merits as a literary production should, perhaps, not be measured by some preconceived maxims of subjective and aesthetic taste, but by the effects which it produced in Muḥammad's contemporaries and fellow-countrymen. If it spoke so powerfully and convincingly to the hearts of his hearers as to weld hitherto centrifugal and antagonistic elements into one compact and well-organized body animated by ideas far beyond those which had until now ruled the Arabian mind, then its eloquence was perfect, simply because it created a civilized nation out of savage tribes, and shot a fresh woof into the old warp of history''.[51]

''From time beyond memory, Mecca and the whole Peninsula had been steeped in spiritual torpor. The slight and transient influences of Judaism, Christianity, or philosophical inquiry upon the Arab mind had been but as the ruffling here and there of the surface of a quiet lake; all remained still and motionless below. The people were sunk in superstition, cruelty, and vice... Their religion was a gross idolatry; and their faith the dark superstitious dread of unseen beings... Thirteen years before the Hegira, Mecca lay lifeless in this debased state. What a change had those thirteen years now produced... Jewish truth had long sounded in the ears of the men of Medina; but it was not until they heard the spirit-stirring strains of the Arabian Prophet that they too awoke from their slumber, and sprang suddenly into a new and earnest life''.[52]

50 Goethe — Hughes' *Dictionary of Islam*, p. 526.

51 Steingass — Hughes' *Dictionary of Islam*, pp. 527, 528.

52 Muir's *Life of Mahomet*, pp. 155, 156.

"A more disunited people it would be hard to find till suddenly the miracle took place! A man arose who, by his personality and by his claim to direct Divine guidance, actually brought about the impossible — namely, the union of all these warring factions".[53]

"It was the one miracle claimed by Mohammed — his 'standing miracle' he called it: and a miracle indeed it is".[54]

"Never has a people been led more rapidly to civilization, such as it was, than were the Arabs through Islam".[55]

"The Qur'ān is unapproachable as regards convincing power, eloquence, and even composition...And to it was also indirectly due the marvellous development of all branches of science in the Moslim world".[56]

Translation of the Qur'ān

Certain religious scholars (*Ulamā*) have held that the Qur'ān should not be translated into any language, but this position is clearly untenable. The Holy Book is plainly intended for all the nations; it is again and again called "a reminder for all the nations" (68 : 52; 81 : 27; etc.), and the Prophet is spoken of as "a warner for the nations" (25 : 1). No warning could be conveyed to a nation except in its own language, and the Qur'ān could not be spoken of as a reminder for the nations unless its message was meant to be given to them in their own language. Its translation into other languages was, therefore, contemplated by the Holy Book itself.[57]

53 *Ins and Outs of Mesopotamia.*

54 Bosworth Smith's *Mohammed*, p. 290

55 Hirschfeld's *New Researches*, p. 5.

56 *Ibid.*, pp. 8, 9.

57 Translations have actually been done into many languages by Muslims themselves. A Persian translation is attributed to Shaikh Sa'dī, while another rendering into Persian was the work of the famous Indian saint, Shāh Walī Allāh who died over 150 years ago. Translations were made into Urdu by other members of Shāh Walī Allāh's family, Shāh Rafi' al-Din and Shāh 'Abd al-Qādir, while many more have been added recently. Translations also exist in many other languages. The earliest translations in European languages have been listed as follows in Hughes' *Dictionary of Islam*:

"The first translation attempted by Europeans was a Latin version translated by an Englishman, Robert of Retina, and a German, Hermann of Dalmatia. This translation, which was done at the request of Peter, Abbot of the Monastery of Clugny, A.D. 1143, remained hidden nearly 400 years till it was published at Basle, 1543, by Theodore Bibliander, and was afterwards rendered into Italian, German and Dutch.... The oldest French translation was done by M. Du Ryer (Paris, 1647). A Russian version appeared at St. Petersberg in 1776... The first English Qur'ān was Alexander Ross's translation of Du Ryer's French version (1649-1688). Sale's well-known work first appeared in 1734 ... A translation by the Rev. J.M. Rodwell ... was printed in 1861... Professor Palmer, of Cambridge, translated the Qurān in 1880" (p. 523).

CHAPTER II

THE TRADITION (SUNNAH or ḤADĪTH)

Sunnah and Ḥadīth

Sunnah or *Ḥadīth* (the practice and the sayings of Prophet Muḥammad) is the second and, undoubtedly, secondary source from which the teachings of Islām are drawn.[1] In its original sense *Sunnah* indicates the doings and *Ḥadīth* the sayings of the Prophet; but in effect both cover the same ground and are applicable to his actions, practices, and sayings, *Ḥadīth* being the narration and record of the *Sunnah* but containing, in addition, various prophetical and historical elements. There are three kinds of *Sunnah*. It may be a saying of the Prophet (*qaul*) which has a bearing on a religious question, an action or a practice of his (*fi'l*), or his silent approval of the action or practice of another (*taqrīr*).

We have now to consider to what extent the teachings of Islām, its principles and its laws, can be drawn from this source. Any student of the Qur'ān will see that the Holy Book generally deals wih the broad principles or essentials of religion, going into details in rare cases. The details were supplied by the Prophet himself, either by showing in his practice how an injunction was to be carried out, or by giving an explanation in words.

The *Sunnah* or *Ḥadīth* of the Prophet was not, as is generally supposed, a thing whereof the need may have been felt only after his death, for it was as much needed in his lifetime. The two most important religious institutions of Islām, for instance, are prayer and the compulsory charity of *zakāt*; yet when the injunctions relating to these were delivered — and they are repeatedly met with both in Makkah and Madīnah revelations — no details were supplied. "Keep up prayer" (*aqīmu al-ṣalāta*) is the Quranic injunction and it was the Prophet himself who by his own actions gave the details of the service. "Pay the *zakāt*" (*ātū*

[1] *Sunnah* literally means *a way* or *rule* or *manner of acting* or *mode of life*, and *ḥadith* a saying conveyed to man either through hearing or *through revelation*. Hence the Holy Qur'ān is also spoken of as *ḥadith* (18 : 6; 39 : 23). The word *sunnah* is used in the Qur'ān in a general sense meaning *a way* or *rule*. Thus *sunnat al awwalīn* (8 : 38; 15 : 13; 18 : 55; 35 : 43) means *the way or example of the former people*, and is frequently used in the Qur'ān as signifying God's way of dealing with people, which is also spoken of as *sunnat Allāh* or God's way. Once, however, the plural *sunan* is used as indicating the ways in which men ought to walk: "Allāh desires to explain to you, and to guide you into the ways (*sunan*) of those before you" (4 : 26).

al-zakāh) is again an injunction frequently repeated in the Qur'ān, yet it was the Prophet who gave the rules and regulations for its payment and collection. These are but two examples; but since Islām covered the whole sphere of human activity, hundreds of points had to be explained by the Prophet by his example in action and word, while on the moral side, his was the pattern which every Muslim was required to follow (33 : 21). The man, therefore, who embraced Islām stood in immediate need of both the Qur'ān and the Sunnah.

Transmission of Tradition in Prophet's lifetime

The transmission of the practices and sayings of the Prophet from one person to another, thus became necessary during the Prophet's lifetime. In fact, the Prophet himself used to give instructions about the transmission of what he taught. Thus when a deputation of the tribe of Rabī'ah came to wait upon him in the early days of Madīnah, he concluded his instructions to them with the words: "Remember this and report it to those whom you have left behind."[2] Similar were his instructions in another case: "Go back to your people and teach them these things" (Bu. 3 : 25). There is another report according to which on the occasion of a pilgrimage, the Prophet, after enjoining on the Muslims the duty of holding sacred each other's life, property and honour, added: "He who is present here should carry this message to him who is absent" (Bu. 3 : 37). Again, there is ample historical evidence that whenever a people embraced Islām, the Prophet used to send them one or more of his missionaries who not only taught them the Qur'ān but also explained to them how its injunctions were to be carried out in practice. It is also on record that people came to the Prophet and demanded teachers who could teach them the Qur'ān and the *Sunnah*. And the Companions of the Prophet knew full well that his actions and practices were to be followed, should no express direction be met with in the Qur'ān. It is related that when Mu'ādh ibn Jabal, on being appointed Governor of Yaman by the Prophet, was asked how he would judge cases, his reply was, "by the Book of Allāh." Asked what he would do if he did not find a direction in the Book of Allāh, he replied "by the *Sunnah* of the Messenger of Allāh" (AD. 23 : 11). The *Sunnah* was, therefore, recognized in the very lifetime of the Prophet as affording guidance in religious matters.

[2] *Mishkāt al-Maṣābīḥ*, 1 : 1-i.

Writing of Tradition in Prophet's lifetime

The popular idea in the West that the need for *Sunnah* was felt, and the force of law given to Tradition, after the death of the Prophet,[3] is falsified by the above facts. Nor was the preservation of what the Prophet did or said an after-thought on the part of the Muslims, for the Companions while translating into practice most of his sayings, endeavoured also to preserve them in memory as well as on paper. The need of the *Sunnah*, its force as law, and its preservation are all traceable to the lifetime of the Prophet. A special importance was, from the first, attached to his sayings and deeds which were looked upon as a source of guidance by his followers. They were conscious of the fact that these things must be preserved for future generations; hence they not only kept them in their memory but even resorted to pen and ink for their preservation. Abū Hurairah tells us that when one of the *Anṣār* complained to the Prophet of his inability to remember what he heard from him, the Prophet's reply was that he should seek the help of his right hand (referring to the use of pen).[4] Another well-known report is from 'Abd Allāh ibn 'Amr: "I used to write everything that I heard from the Prophet, intending to commit it to memory. (On some people taking objection to this) I spoke about it to the Prophet who said: "Write down, for I only speak the truth".[5] Yet again there is another report from Abū Hurairah: "None of the Companions preserved more traditions than myself, but 'Abd Allāh ibn 'Amr is an exception, for he used to write and I did not".[6] Anas ibn

[3] Thus Muir writes in his introduction to the *Life of Mahomet:* "The Arabs, a simple and unsophisticated race, found in the Coran ample provisions for the regulation of their affairs — religious, social and political. But this aspect of Islam soon underwent a mighty change. Scarcely was the Prophet buried when his followers issued forth from their barren Peninsula resolved to impose the faith of Islam upon all the nations of the earth...Crowded cities, like Cufa, Cairo, and Damascus, required elaborate laws for the guidance of their courts of justice; widening political relations demanded a system of international equity... All called loudly for the enlargement of the scanty and naked dogmas of the Revelation... The difficulty was resolved by adopting the Custom (Sunnat) of Mahomet; that is, his sayings and his practice, as supplementary of the Coran...Tradition was thus invested with the force of law, and with something of the authority of inspiration" (p.xxix). And even a recent writer, Guillaume, writes in the *Traditions of Islam*: "While the Prophet was alive he was the sole guide in all matters whether spiritual or secular. Ḥadīth, or tradition in the technical sense, may be said to have begun at his death" (p.13).

[4] Tr. 39 : 12. Note that this saying exists in many forms.

[5] AD. 24 : 3. This saying is well-known and exists in thirty various forms with slight difference.

[6] Bukhārī, 3 : 39.

Mālik states that Abū Bakr wrote down for him the laws regarding alms.[7] 'Alī had also a saying of the Prophet with him in writing.[8] In the year of the conquest of Makkah, the Prophet delivered a sermon on the occasion of a man being killed by way of retaliation for some old grievance. When the sermon was over, one from among the people of Yaman came forward and requested him to have it written down for him, and the Prophet gave orders to that effect.[9] These reports show that while generally Tradition was committed to memory, it was occasionally, when there was need for it, written down. The last-mentioned incident affords the clearest testimony that, whatever the Companions heard from the Prophet, they tried to keep in their memory, for how else could an order be given for the writing of a sermon which had been delivered orally?

Why Traditions were not generally written

It is, however, a fact that the sayings of the Prophet were not generally written, and memory was the chief means of their preservation. The Prophet sometimes did object to the writing down of his sayings. Abū Hurairah is reported to have said: "The Prophet of God came to us while we were writing traditions and said: What is this that you are writing? We said: Sayings which we hear from thee. He said: What! a book other than the Book of God?" Now the disapproval in this case clearly shows fear lest his sayings be mixed up with the revealed word of the Qur'ān, though there was nothing essentially wrong in writing these down nor did the Prophet ever forbid this being done. On the other hand, as late as the conquest of Makkah, we find him giving orders himself for the writing down of a certain saying at the request of a hearer. He also wrote letters, and treaties were put down in writing too, which shows that he never meant that the writing of anything besides the Qur'ān was illegal. What he feared as the report shows, was that if his sayings were written down generally like the Qur'ān, the two might get mixed up, and the purity of the text of the Qur'ān might be affected.

Memory could be trusted for preservation of knowledge

Memory was by no means an unreliable mode for the preservation of Tradition, for the Qur'ān itself was safely preserved in the memory of

7 8 9 — see next page.

the Companions of the Prophet in addition to being committed to writing. In fact, had the Qur'ān been simply preserved in writing, it could not have been handed down intact to future generations. The aid of memory was invoked to make the purity of the Text doubly sure. The Arab had a wonderfully retentive memory in which he had to store up his knowledge of countless things. It was in this safe custody that all the poetry of the pre-Islamic days had been kept alive and intact. Indeed, before Islām, writing was but rarely resorted to, and memory was chiefly relied upon in all important matters. Hundreds and even thousands of verses could be recited from memory by one man, and the reciters would also remember the names of the persons through whom those verses had been transmitted to them. Aṣma'ī, a later transmitter of traditions, says that he learned twelve thousand verses by heart before he reached majority; of Abū Dzamdzam, Aṣma'ī says that he recited verses from a hundred poets in a single sitting; Sha'bī says that he knew so many verses by heart that he could continue repeating them for a month; and these verses were the basis of the Arabic vocabulary and even of Arabic grammar. Among the Companions of the Prophet were many who knew by heart thousands of the verses of pre-Islamic poetry, and of these one was 'Ā'ishah, the Prophet's wife. The famous Bukhārī trusted to memory alone for the retention of as many as six hundred thousand sayings and many students corrected their manuscripts by comparing them with what he had only retained in his memory.

Collection of Tradition: First stage

The first steps for the preservation of Tradition were thus taken in the lifetime of the Prophet,[10] but all his followers were not equally interested in the matter, nor had all equal chances of being so. Everyone had to work for his living, while on most of them the defence of the Muslim commu-

[7] Bukhhārī, 24 : 39.

[8] *Ibid.*, 3 : 39.

[9] *Ibid.*

[10] Thus Guillaume writes in the *Traditions of Islam:* "The ḥadīth last quoted do not invalidate the statements that traditions were written down from the mouth of the Prophet; the extraordinary importance attached to every utterance of his would naturally lead his followers who were able to write to record his words in order to repeat them to those who clamoured to know what he had said; and there is nothing at all in any demonstrably early writing to suggest that such a practice would be distasteful to Muḥammad" (p.17).

nity against overwhelming odds had placed an additional burden. There was, however, a party of students called the *Aṣḥāb al-Ṣuffah* who lived in the mosque itself, and who were specially equipped for the teaching of religion to the tribes outside Madīnah. Some of these would go to the market and do a little work to earn livelihood; others would not care to do even that. Of this little band, the most famous was Abū Hurairah, who would remain in the Prophet's company at all costs, and store up in his memory everything which the Prophet said or did. His efforts were, from the first, directed towards the preservation of Tradition. He himself is reported to have said once: "You say, Abū Hurairah is profuse in narrating traditions from the Prophet; and you say, How is it that the Refugees (*Muhājirīn*) and the Helpers (*Anṣār*) do not narrate traditions from the Prophet like Abū Hurairah? The truth is that our brethren from among the Refugees were occupied in transacting business in the market and I used to remain with the Prophet having filled my belly; so I was present when they were absent and I remembered what they forgot; and our brethren from among the Helpers were occupied with work on their lands, and I was a poor man from among the poor inmates of the Ṣuffa, so I retained what they forgot" (Bu. 34 : 1). Another Companion, Ṭalḥa, son of 'Ubaid Allāh, is reported to have said of Abū Hurairah: "There is no doubt that he heard from the Prophet what we did not hear. The reason was that he was a poor man who possessed nothing and was, therefore, a guest of the Prophet." Here is another report from Muḥammad ibn 'Amāra: "He sat in a company of the older Companions of the Prophet in which there were over ten men. Abū Hurairah began to relate a certain saying of the Prophet, which some of them did not know, so they questioned him over and over again until they were satisfied. Again, he related to them a saying in the same manner and he did this over and over again, and I was convinced that Abū Hurairah had the best memory."[11] According to another report, people used to say in the lifetime of the Prophet that Abū Hurairah narrated many sayings of the Prophet. So Abū Hurairah enquired of one of them as to which chapters the Prophet had recited in his night prayers the day before. The man being unable to answer the question, Abū Hurairah himself named the chapters[12] which shows not only that he had a wonderful memory but also that he tried his utmost to remember everything.

[11] Bq.— FB.I, p.191.

[12] Bukhārī, 21 : 18.

'Ā'ishah, the Prophet's wife, was also one of those who sought to preserve the practice of the Prophet. She too had a marvellous memory, and was, in addition, gifted with a clear intellect, by virtue of which she refused to accept anything which she did not understand. There is a report about her, according to which "she never heard anything she did not recognize but she questioned about it again and again".[13] In other words, she accepted nothing, even from the lips of the Prophet himself, until she was fully satisfied as to its meaning. 'Abd Allāh ibn 'Umar and 'Abd Allāh ibn 'Abbās are two other Companions who were specially engaged in the work of preserving and transmitting the knowledge of the Qur'ān and the Tradition as also was 'Abd Allāh ibn 'Amr who used to write down the sayings of the Prophet. And in addition to these, every Companion did his utmost to preserve such of his words and deeds as came to his knowledge. 'Umar who resided about three miles from Madīnah, had made arrangements with a neighbour so that each remained in the company of the Prophet on alternate days, in order to report to the other what happened in his absence.[14] And, most important of all, the Prophet had repeatedly laid an obligation on everyone of his followers to transmit his words to others: "Let him who is present deliver to him who is absent"[15] is the concluding sentence of many of his most important utterances all of which afford a clear proof that the work of preservation and transmission of the practice and sayings of the Prophet had begun in his lifetime. This was the first stage in the collection of the Tradition.

Collection of Tradition: Second Stage

With the Prophet's death, the work of the collection of Tradition entered on a second stage. Every case that came up for decision had now to be referred either to the Qur'ān or to some judgement or saying of the Prophet, which judgements or sayings, therefore, obtained a wide reputation. There are numerous cases on record in which a right was claimed on the basis of a judgment or saying of the Prophet, and evidence was demanded as to the authenticity of that saying.[16] Thus there was a double

[13] Bukhārī, 3 : 35.
[14] *Ibid.*, 3 : 27.
[15] *Ibid.*, 3 : 37.
[16] A Companion, Qabīṣa by name, reports that the grandmother of a deceased person came to Abū Bakr, the first Caliph, and claimed a right in inheritance. The latter said that he could find neither in the Book of God nor in the practice of the Prophet that she was entitled to any share, but that he would make enquiries about it from others. In this en-

process at work; not only was the trustworthiness of the particular tradition established beyond all doubt, it also obtained a wide circulation. Thus the multiple needs of a rapidly growing and widely-spreading community, whose necessities had increased tenfold on account of its onward march to civilization, brought into prominence a large number of traditions, knowledge of which had been limited to one or a few only, with the seal of confirmation on their truth, because at that time direct evidence of that truth was available.

This was not the only factor that gave an impetus to a dissemination of the knowledge of Tradition. The influx into Islām of large numbers of people who had never seen the Prophet himself, but who could behold for themselves the astounding transformation brought about by him, and to whom, therefore, his memory was sacred, in the highest degree, formed in itself an important factor in the general eagerness to discover everything which the great man had said or done. It was natural that each new convert should be anxious to know all there was to know about the great Teacher who had infused a new life into a dead world. Everyone who had seen him would thus become a source of knowledge for the later converts and since the incidents were fresh in the memories of the Companions they would be conveyed with fair accuracy to the new generation.

It must be remembered that the wonderful success which Islām achieved within so short a time, and the rapidity with which the reputation of its Prophet advanced, were the very reasons which led to the preservation of the actual facts concerning him. The personality of the Prophet and his religion assumed an unparalleled importance in Arabia within twenty years of the day on which he began the work of a reformer, and within ten years of his death Islām spread to many countries beyond the borders of Arabia. Everything relating to the Prophet, therefore, became a matter of discussion among Arabs and non-Arabs, friends and foes. Had he remained in oblivion for a century or so, and then risen to fame, probably

quiry, Mughīra gave evidence that the Prophet gave the grand-mother one-sixth of the property. Abū Bakr asked him to bring another witness in support of it, and Muḥammad ibn Maslama appeared before him corroborating the evidence of Mughīra. Judgment was accordingly given in favour of the grandmother (Tr. 28 : 9; AD. 18 : 5). Again, Fātimah, the Prophet's daughter, claimed that she was entitled to an inheritance from her father. As against this, Abū Bakr cited a saying of the Prophet: "We prophets do not leave an inheritance; whatever we leave is a charity." The truth of this tradition was not questioned by any one, and Fāṭimah's claim was rejected (Bu. 85 : 2). Such incidents happened daily and became the occasion of establishing or otherwise the truth of many sayings of the Prophet.

much of what he had said or done would have been lost to the world, and the exaggerations of a later generation, and not facts, would have been handed down to posterity. But with him the case was quite different. From the humblest position he had risen to the highest eminence to which man can rise, and that in less than a quarter of a century, and, therefore, there was not an incident of his life but had become public property before it could be forgotten.

There was another factor of the utmost importance which gave impetus to the knowledge of Tradition at this stage. To the Companions of the Prophet, the religion which he had brought was so priceless that they valued it above all else in the world. For its sake they had given up their business, their homes and their kinsfolk; to defend it they had laid down their lives. To carry this blessing, this greatest gift of God, to other people had become the supreme object of their lives; hence a dissemination of its knowledge was their first and foremost concern. In addition to this, the great Master had laid on those who were present, on those who saw him and listened to his words, the duty of carrying what they saw and heard, to those who were absent, to those who came after him. "*Let him who is present carry this to him who is absent,* was the phrase which on account of the frequency of its repetition rang continually in their ears. And they were faithful to the great charge which was laid on them. They travelled eastward and westward, northward and southward, and in whichever direction they went, and whichever country they reached, they carried with them the Qur'ān and the Tradition. Everyone of them who had but the knowledge of one incident relating to the Prophet's life deemed it his duty to deliver it to another. And individuals like 'Ā'ishah, Abū Hurairah, 'Abd Allāh ibn 'Abbas, 'Abd Allāh ibn 'Umar, 'Abd Allāh ibn 'Amr, Anas ibn Mālik and many others who had made the preservation of the Sayings and Practice of the Prophet first object of their lives, became, as it were, centres to whom people resorted from different quarters of the kingdom of Islām to gain knowledge of Islām and its Prophet. Their places of residence became in fact so many colleges for the dissemination of the knowledge of Tradition. Abū Hurairah alone had eight hundred disciples. 'Ā'ishah's house, too, was resorted to by hundreds of ardent pupils. The reputation of 'Abd Allāh ibn 'Abbās was equally great and, notwithstanding his youth, he was one of the foremost among the counsellors of 'Umar, on account of his knowledge of the Qur'ān and the Tradition. The zeal of the new generation for the acquisition of knowledge was so great that students were wont to travel from one place to another to complete their religious studies, and some would journey long distances to obtain first-hand information about one tradition only.[17]

Collection of Tradition: Third Stage

With the passing of the generation that had seen and heard the Prophet, the work of the collection of Tradition entered upon a third stage. There were no more reports to be investigated from different persons, and the whole Tradition was now the property of teachers who taught at various centres, and, therefore, in the third stage it could all be learnt by repairing to these centres instead of enquiring about it from individuals. At this stage, moreover, the writing of Tradition became more common. The large number of the students at different centres, having abundance of material to digest, to which was also added the further task of remembering the names of the transmitters, sought aid from the pen, so that the work might be easier. By this time the practice of writing had become general and writing material abundant. Moreover, there was now no fear of the Tradition being confused with the Qur'ān. It must, however, be remembered that at this stage the traditions were written merely as an aid to memory; the mere fact that a report was found among the manuscripts of a person was no evidence of its authenticity, which could be established only by tracing it to a reliable transmitter. 'Umar ibn 'Abd al-'Azīz, commonly known as 'Umar II, the Umayyad Caliph, who ruled towards the close of the first century of Hijrah, was the first man to issue definite orders to the effect that written collections should be made. He is reported to have written to Abū Bakr ibn Ḥazm: "See whatever saying of the Prophet can be found, and write it down, for I fear the loss of knowledge and the disapearance of the learned men; and do not accept

[17] It is reported that Jābir ibn 'Abd Allāh travelled from Madīnah to Syria for the sake of a single tradition (FB. I, p. 158). It was a month's journey as Jābir himself states (Bu. 3 : 19.) *Bukhārī's* famous commentary, *Fatḥ al-Bārī,* relates several incidents of the same type. Abū Ayyūb Anṣārī, for instance, is related to have undertaken a long journey to hear a saying of the Prophet from 'Aqabāh ibn 'Āmir. Sa'īd ibn Musayyab is reported to have said that he used to travel for days and nights in search of a single saying. Another Companion of the Prophet is said to have undertaken a journey to Egypt for the sake of one tradition. The zeal of the next generation was equally great. Abul 'Āliyāh is reported to have said: "We heard of a saying of the Prophet but we were not satisfied until we went to the Companion concerned in person and heard it from him direct" (FB. I, p. 159). AD. reports that Abū al-Dardā'was sitting in a mosque in Damascus when a man came to him and questioned him about a tradition, saying at the same time that he had come for no other object but the verification of a tradition which he (Abū al-Dardā') related (AD. 24 : 1).

anything but the Tradition of the Prophet; and people should make knowledge public and should sit in companies, so that he who does not know should come to know, for knowledge does not disappear until it is concealed from the public.[18] The importance of this incident lies in the fact that the Caliph himself took an interest in the collection of Tradition, the Umayyads generally having stood aloof from the great work up to this time. Abū Bakr ibn Ḥazm was the Caliph's Governor at Madīnah, and there is evidence that similar letters were written to other centres.[19] But 'Umar II died after a short reign of two and a half years, and his successor does not seem to have been interested in the matter. Even if a collection had been made in pursuance of these orders, which is very doubtful, no copy has reached us.[20] But the work was taken up independently of government patronage in the next century, which marks the commencement of the fourth stage in the collection of Tradition.

Collection of Tradition: Fourth Stage

Before the middle of the second century, Tradition started to assume a more permanent shape, and written collections began to see the light of day. Hundreds of the students were engaged in the work of learning Tradition in the various centres, but with every new teacher and student the work of preserving the name of the transmitter along with the text was becoming more difficult. Written collections had thus become indispensable. The first known work on the subject is that of Imām 'Abd al-Mālik ibn 'Abd al-'Azīz ibn Juraij, commonly known as Ibn Juraij. According to some, however, Sa'īd ibn Abī 'Arūba or Rabī' ibn Ṣuhaib has precedence in this matter. All these authors died about the middle of the

[18] Bu. 3 : 34.

[19] FB. I, p.174.

[20] Guillaume thinks that the issuing of orders by 'Umar II for the collection of Tradition is a later invention. The reason given by him is that no such collection has come down to us, nor is there any mention of it in any other work. But as I have pointed out, the reason for any such collection not being made, if really it has not disappeared, was the shortness of 'Umar's reign and the indifference of the other Umayyad Caliphs. Another reason given is that the name of Ibn Shahāb al-Zuhrī is, according to one report, connected with this order. But this rather confirms the authenticity of 'Umar's orders, because,as I have said before, the orders were circular. Muir is right when he says: "About a hundred years after Mahomet, the Caliph Omar II issued circular orders for the formal collection of all extant traditions. The task, thus begun, continued to be vigorously prosecuted" (*Life of Mahomet,* intr., p.xxx).

second century. Ibn Juraij lived at Makkah, while others who wrote books on Tradition in the second century are Imām Mālik ibn Anas and Sufyān ibn 'Uyaina in Madīnah, 'Abd Allāh ibn Wahb in Egypt, Ma'mar and 'Abd al-Razzāq in Yaman, Sufyān Thaurī and Muḥammad ibn Fudzail in Kūfa, Hammād ibn Salma and Rauḥ ibn 'Ubāda in Baṣra, Ḥushaim ibn Wāsiṭ and 'Abd Allāh ibn Mubārak in Khurāsān, by far the most important of the collections of these authors is the *Muwaṭṭā* of Imām Mālik. All these books, however, were far from being exhaustive. In the first place, the object of their compilation was simply the collection of such reports as touched on the daily life of the Muslims. Reports relating to a large number of topics, such as faith, knowledge, the life of the Prophet, wars, comments on the Qur'ān, were outside their scope. And secondly, every author collected only such reports as were taught at the centre where he worked. Even the *Muwaṭṭā* contains only the traditions which came through the people of Ḥijāz. All these works were, therefore, incomplete, but they were a great advance on oral transmission in the work of collecting Tradition.

Collection of Tradition: Fifth Stage

This great work was brought to completion in the third century of Hijrah. It was then that two kinds of collections were made, *Musnad* (the earlier type) and *Jāmi'* or *Muṣannaf. Musnad* is derived from *sanad* meaning *authority*, and the *isnād* of a tradition meant the tracing of it back through various transmitters to the Companion of the Prophet on whose authority it rested. The collections known as *Musnads* were arranged, not according to the subject-matter of the tradition, but under the name of the Companion on whose final authority the report rested. The most important of the works of this class is the *Musnad* of Imām Aḥmad ibn Ḥanbal,[21] which contains about thirty thousand reports. It is to the *Jāmi'*[22] or the *Muṣannaf*[23] that the honour is due of bringing the knowledge of Tradition to perfection. The *Jāmi'* not only arranges reports according to their subject-matter but is also of a more critical tone. Six books are recognized generally under the heading, being the collec-

[21] Born 164 A.H., died 241 A.H. He is one of the four recognized *Imāms* (jurists).

[22] Literally, *one that gathers together.*

[23] Literally, *compiled together.*

tions made by Muḥammad ibn Ismā'īl,[24] commonly known as Bukhārī (d.256 A.H.), Muslim (d.261 A.H.), Abū Dāwūd (d.275 A.H.), Tirmidzī (d.279 A.H.), Ibn Mājah (d.283 A.H.) and Nasā'ī (d.303 A.H.).[25] These books classified reports under various subjects and thus made Tradition easy for reference, not only for lawyers and judges but also for students and research scholars thus giving a further impetus to the study of Tradition.[26]

Bukhārī

Among the six[27] collections mentioned above, *Bukhārī* holds the first place in several respects while *Muslim* comes second.[28] In the first place, Bukhārī has the unquestioned distinction of being first, all the others modelling their writings on his. Secondly, he is the most critical of all.[29] He did not accept any report unless all its transmitters were reliable and until there was proof that the later transmitter had actually met the first; the mere fact that the two were contemporaries (which is the test adopted by Muslim) did not satisfy him. Thirdly, in his acumen (*Fiqāhah*) he surpasses all. Fourthly, he heads the more important of his chapter with text from the Qur'ān, and thus shows that Tradition is only an explanation of the Qur'ān, and as such a secondary source of the teaching of Islām.

24 Muḥammad ibn Ismā'īl Bukhārī was born at Bukhārā in 194 A.H. He began the study of Ḥadīth when only 11 years of age, and by the time that he was 16 had acquired a high reputation for his knowledge thereof. He had a wonderful memory, and the students of Ḥadīth used to correct their manuscripts by comparing them with what he recited from memory.

25 The works of Abū Dāwūd, Ibn Mājah and Nasā'ī are more generally known by the name of *Sunan* (pl.of *sunnah*).

26 The Shī'ās recognize the following five collections of Ḥadīth: 1.The *Kāfi* by Abū Ja'far Muḥammad ibn Ya'qūb (329 A.H.); 2. *Man lā yastiḥdziru-hu-l Faqīh* by Shaikh 'Alī (381 A.H.); 3. The *Tahdhīb* by Shaikh Abū Ja'far Muḥammad ibn 'Alī ibn Ḥusain (466 A.H.); 4. The *Istibṣār* by the same author; 5. The *Nahj al-Balaghah* by Sayyid al-Rāzī (406 A.H.). It will be seen that all these collections are of a much later date.

27 These are known as *Ṣiḥāḥ Sittah* or *the Six reliable collections.*

28 The two together are known as *Ṣaḥīḥain* or the *two reliable books.*

29 A modern writer, and one who has made a special study of Ḥadīth expresses the following opinion about Bukhārī: "So far as one is able to judge, Bukhārī published the result of his researches into the content of what he believed to be genuine tradition with all the painstaking accuracy of a modern editor. Thus he records even trifling variants in the ḥadīth, and wherever he feels that an explanatory gloss is necessary either in *isnād* or *matn* it is clearly marked as his own" (*Tr. Is.*, p. 29).

Method of counting the number of different reports

European critics are generally under the impression that when the authors of the *Muṣannafāt* set to work, there was such a vast mass of spurious traditions that the collectors did not credit more than one or two per cent of the prevailing mass as being genuine, and that these were taken to be genuine on the slender authority of the reliability of transmitters without any regard to the subject-matter.[30] The impression that the vast mass of reports taught at different centres in the third century was fabricated is based on a misconception. It is true that Bukhārī took cognizance of 600,000 reports and knew some 200,000 of these by heart. It is also a fact that his book contains no more than 9,000 traditions. But it is not true that he found the other 591,000 reports to be false or fabricated. It must be clearly understood that those who were engaged in the dissemination and study of Tradition looked upon every report as a different tradition when even a single transmitter was changed. Let us, for instance, take a tradition for which the original authority is Abū Hurairah. Now Abū Hurairah had about 800 disciples and the same tradition may have been reported by, say, ten of his disciples with or without any variation. Each of these reports would, according to the collectors, form a separate tradition. Again, suppose each of the transmitters of Abū Hurairah's tradition had two reporters, the same tradition would then be counted as twenty different reports. The number would thus go on increasing as the number of reporters increased. At the time when Bukhārī applied himself to Tradition in the first decade of the third century of Hijrah, there were schools of Tradition at different centres, and hundreds of students learned and transmitted reports to others. In a chain of ordinarily four or five

30 Writing of Bukhārī, Guillaume says: "Tradition reports that this remarkable man took cognizance of 600,000 aḥadīth, and himself memorized more than 200,000. Of these he has preserved to us 7,397, or according to other authorities, 7,295. If one adds to these the fragmentary traditions embodied in the *tarjamah*, the total is 9,082... When one reflects from these figures furnished by a Muslim historian that hardly more than one per cent of the Hadīth said to be openly circulating with the authority of the Prophet behind them were accounted geniune by the pious Bukhārī, one's confidence in the authenticity of the residue is sorely tried. Where such an enormous preponderance of material is judged false, nothing but the successful application of modern canons of evidence can restore faith in the credibility of the remainder" (*Tr. Is.*, pp. 28, 29). And Muir writes: "It is proved by the testimony of the Collectors themselves, that thousands and tens of thousands of traditions were current in their times which possessed not even the shadow of authority... Bokhary ... came to the conclusion, after many years' sifting, that out of 600,000 traditions ascertained by him to be then current, only 4,000 were authentic" (*Life of Mahomet*, intr., p. xxxvii).

transmitters, consider the number of reports that would arise from the same tradition on account of the variation of transmitters, and it is easy to understand that 600,000 did not mean so many reports relating to various subjects, but so many reports coming through different transmitters, many of them referring to the same incident or conveying the same subject-matter with or without variation of words. That this was the method of Bukhārī's counting of reports is clear from his book, the *Ṣaḥīḥ Bukhārī*, which, with the change of even one transmitter in a chain of, say, four or five, considers the report to be distinct.[31] What is called repetition in *Bukhārī* is due to this circumstance.

Reports in biographies and commentaries

European criticism has often mixed up Tradition with the reports met with in the biographies of the Prophet and in the commentaries on the Qur'ān. No Muslim scholar has ever attached the same value to the biographical reports as to traditions narrated in the above-mentioned collections. On the other hand, all Muslim critics recognize that the biographers never made much effort to sift truth from error. Imām Aḥmad ibn Ḥanbal sums up the Muslim point of view as regards the trustworthiness of the biographical reports when he declares that the biographies "are not based on any principle,"[32] and Ḥāfiz Zain al-Dīn 'Irāqī says that "they contain what is true and what is false." In fact, much of the adverse European criticism of Tradition would have been more suitably levelled at the biographical reports; and the same is true of the reports met with in the commentaries, which are still more unreliable. Many careless commentators confounded Tradition with Jewish and Christian stories, and made free use of the latter as if they were so many reports. Speaking of the commentaries, Ibn Khaldūn says: "Their books and their reports contain what is bad and what is good and what may be accepted and what should be rejected, and the reason is that the Arabs were an ignorant race without literature and without knowledge, and desert life and ignorance were their chief characteristics, and whenever they desired, as mortals do desire, to obtain knowledge of the cause of existence and the origin of creation and the mysteries of the universe, they turned

[31] "On the other hand, the same tradition is often repeated more than once under different chapters (*abwāb*), so that if repetitions are disregarded the number of distinct traditions is reduced to 2,762" (*Tr. Is.*, p.28).

[32] Mau., p.58.

for information to the followers of the Book, the Jews and such of the Christians as practised their faith. But these people of the Book were like themselves, and their knowledge of these things went no further than the knowledge of the ignorant masses... So when these people embraced Islām, they retained their stories which had no connection with the commandments of the Islamic law, such as the stories of the origin of creation, and things relating to the future and the wars, etc. These people were like Ka'b Aḥbār, Wahb ibn Munabbah, 'Abd Allāh ibn Salām and others. Commentaries on the Qur'ān were soon filled with these stories of theirs. And in such matters, the reports do not go beyond them, and as these do not deal with commandments, so their correctness is not sought after to the extent of acting upon them, and the commentators take them rather carelessly, and they have thus filled up their commentaries with them''.[33]

Shāh Walī Allāh writes in a similar strain: ''It is necessary to know that most of the Israelite stories that have found their way into the commentaries and histories are copied from the stories of the Jews and the Christians, and no commandment or belief can be based upon them''.[34]

In fact, in some of the commentaries, the reports cited do not make sense. Even the commentary of Ibn Jarīr, with all its value as a literary production, cannot be relied upon. Ibn Kathīr's commentary is, however, an exception, as it contains chiefly traditions taken from reliable collections.

Story-tellers

Yet another thing to beware of is the mixing up of Tradition with stories. As in every other nation, there had grown up among the Muslims a class of fable-mongers whose business it was to tickle the fancies of the masses by false stories. These were either drawn from the Jews, Christians and Persians, with whom the Muslims came in contact, or they were simply concocted. The professional story-tellers[35] seem to have sprung up early, for as Rāzī says, the Caliph 'Alī ordered that whosoever should relate the story of David as the story-tellers relate it (reference being to the story taken from the Bible as to David having committed adultery with Uriah's wife), should be given 160 stripes, that being

[33] Mq. I, p. 481, chapter *'Ulūm al-Qur'ān.*

[34] Hj. I, p. 171, chapter *I'tiṣām bi-l-kitāb.*

[35] They were called *quṣṣaṣ* (sing *qaṣṣ*), derived from *qaṣṣa* meaning *he related a story.*

double the punishment of the ordinary slanderer.[36] This shows that the story-teller had begun his work even at that early date, but then it must be remembered that he was never confounded with the reporter of Tradition, even by the ignorant masses. His vocation, being of a lower status, was necessarily quite distinct. Tradition was regularly taught in schools in different centres, as already known, and its teachers were in the first instance well-known Companions of the Prophet, such as Abū Hurairah, Ibn 'Umar, and 'Ā'ishah, whose place was later taken by equally well-known masters of Tradition from among the successors of the Companions (*Tābi'īn*). No story-teller, whose sphere of action was limited to some street corner, where he might attract the attention of passers-by, and perhaps gather round him a few loiterers, could aspire even to approach a school of Tradition. As a writer says: "They collect a great crowd of people round them: one *Qāṣṣ* stations himself at one end of the street and narrates traditions about the merits of 'Alī, while his fellow stands at the other end of the street exalting the virtues of Abū Bakr. Thus they secure the pence of the *Nāṣibī* as well as the *Shī'ī*, and divide their gains equally afterwards".[37] It is difficult to believe that such story-mongers could be mistaken for reporters of Tradition by any sensible person; yet scholars like Sir William Muir and other famous Orientalists often try to confound the two and speak of these stories as though they had some connection with Tradition. Even if it be true that some of them have found a place in certain commentaries, whose authors had a love for the curious and gave but scant heed to the sifting of truth from error, the collectors of Tradition (*Muḥaddithīn*) would never dream of accepting a story from such a source. They knew the story-tellers and their absurdities well enough, and indeed so scrupulous were they in making their selections that they would not accept a report if one of the reporters was known ever to have told a lie or fabricated a report[38] in a single instance. This much every European critic of Tradition must needs admit; how then could such people accept the puerile inventions of the street story-teller who followed his vocation merely for the few coins it might bring? That there are some incredible stories even in the collections of Tradition is true,

[36] Rz. VII, p.187, 38 : 21-25.

[37] Quoted by Guillaume, *Tr. Is.*, p.82.

[38] While speaking of *ta'n (i.e.*, accusation against a transmitter), Ibn Hajar in his *Sharḥ Nukhbāt al-Fikr,* says, that if a transmitter is shown to have told a lie in transmitting a ḥadīth, or even if he is accused of having told a lie, he is discredited (p.66).

but they are so rare that not the least discredit can justly be thrown on the collections themselves on that account, the reason for their existence being something quite different.

European criticism of Tradition

Among European critics, almost without exception, there is a prevalent idea that the Muslim critics of Tradition have never gone beyond the transmission line, and that the subject-matter has been left quite untouched. Suggestions have also been made that even the Companions of the Prophet were at times so unscrupulous as to fabricate traditions, while it should be common knowledge that the strictest Muslim critics of the transmitters are all agreed that when a report is traced back to a Companion, its authenticity is placed beyond all question. A European writer makes the suggestion that Abū Hurairah was in the habit of fabricating traditions: "A most significant recognition within ḥadīth itself of the untrustworthiness of guarantors is to be found in *Bukhārī*. Ibn 'Umar reports that Muḥammad ordered all dogs to be killed save sheep-dogs and hounds. Abū Hurairah added the word *au zar'in*; whereupon Ibn 'Umar makes the remark, Abū Hurairah owned cultivated land. A better illustration of the underlying motive of some ḥadīth can hardly be found".[39]

In the above quotation *zar'in* means *"cultivated land"*, and the suggestion is that Abū Hurairah added this word for personal motives. In the first place, Abū Hurairah is not alone in reporting that dogs may be kept for hunting as well as for keeping watch over sheep or tillage (*zar'*). Bukhārī reports a tradition from Sufyān ibn Abī Zubair in the following words: " I heard the Messenger of Allāh say: Whoever keeps a dog which does not serve him in keeping watch over cultivated land or goats, one *qīrāt* of his reward is diminished every day. The man who reported from him said, Hast thou heard this from the Messenger of Allāh? He said, Yea, by the Lord of this Mosque".[40] Now this report clearly mentions watch dogs kept for sheep as well as those kept for tillage, but not dogs kept for hunting, which the Qur'ān explicitly allows.[41] Abū Hurairah's report in the same chapter, preceding that cited above, expressly mentions all these kinds, watch dogs kept for sheep or tillage and dogs

[39] Guillaume, *Tr. Is.*, p.78.

[40] Bu. 41 : 3.

[41] Cf. The Qur'ān, 5 : 4.

for hunting, which only shows that he had the more retentive memory. And as for Ibn 'Umar's remark, there is not the least evidence that it contained any insinuation against Abū Hurairah's integrity. It may be just an explanatory remark, or a suggestion that the latter took care to preserve that part of the saying, because he himself had to keep watch dogs for his cultivated land. With all the mistakes that Abū Hurairah may have made in reporting so many traditions, no critic has ever yet questioned his integrity; in fact, critics are unanimous in maintaining that no Companion of the Prophet ever told a lie. Thus, Ibn Ḥajar says: "The *Ahl Sunnah* are unanimous that all (the Companions) are truthful (*'adūl*)".[42]

Further, the same European writer asserts that independent thinkers in the second and third century not only questioned the authority of Tradition altogether but derided the very system: "There was still a large circle outside the orthodox thinkers who rejected the whole system of ḥadīth. They were not concerned to adopt those which happened to fit in with the views and doctrines of the doctors, or even with those which might fairly be held to support their own view of life. So far from being impressed by the earnestness of the traditionists who scrupulously examined the *isnād*, or by the halo of sanctity which had gathered round the early guarantors of traditions, the independent thinkers of the second and third centuries openly mocked and derided the system as a whole and the persons and matters named therein".[43]

And, as evidence in support of these sweeping statements, he adds: "Some of the most flagrant examples of these lampoons will be found in the Book of Songs, where indecent stories are cast into the form in which Tradition was customarily handed down to posterity".[44]

Thus the "independent thinkers" who rejected the system of Tradition and "openly mocked and derided the system as a whole" are only the lampooners mentioned in the concluding portion of the paragraph. The *Aghānī*,[45] the Book of Songs, which is referred to as if it were a collection of lampoons directed against Tradition, is an important collection of ballads by the famous Arabian historian, Abū al-Faraj 'Alī ibn

[42] *Is. I,* pg. 6. The word *'adāla*, as used regarding transmitters of reports, means that there has been no intentional deviation from the truth, and this is not due merely to the respect in which the Companions are held, for the critics of the transmitters of Tradition never spared any one simply because he held a place of honour in their hearts.

[43] *Tr. Is.*, p.80

[44] Ibid.

[45] — see next page.

Ḥusain, commonly known as Isfahānī (born in 284 A.H.). One is at a loss to understand why the learned Western author should look upon it as an attempt to mock and deride the system of Tradition. There may be some indecent stories connected with these songs, but the presence of such stories does not alter the essential character of the work which is in the nature of an historical collection.[46] Neither in the book itself nor in any earlier writing is there a word to show that the collection was made in a spirit of mockery; and as to the fact that with the songs collected are given the names of those through whom the songs are handed down, that was the common method adopted in all historical writings and collections of the time, as may be readily seen by reference to the historical writings of Ibn Sa'd, or Ibn Jarīr; and it was chosen not to insult the method of transmission of Tradition but simply on account of its historical value. Guillaume, the European critic, has also mentioned the names of two great Muslim thinkers, Ibn Qutaibah and Ibn Khaldūn, in this connection, but they neither rejected the Tradition system as a whole nor ever mocked or derided that system or the persons and matters mentioned therein. Ibn Qutaibah rather defended the Qur'ān and Tradition against scepticism, and Guillaume has himself quoted with approval Dr. Nicholson's remarks that "every impartial student will admit the justice of Ibn Qutaybah's claim that no religion has such historical attestations as Islam."[47] The Arabic word *asnād* used in the original, and translated as *historical attestations*, is the plural of *sanad* which means *an authority*, and refers especially to the reporters on whose authority Tradition is accepted. Thus Ibn Qutaibah claims for Tradition a higher authority than that claimed in any other historical work of the time, and the claim is admitted by both Nicholson and Guillaime. In the *Encyclopaedia of Islām*, it is plainly

45 *The Encyclopaedia of Islam* speaks of the *Aghānī*, in the following words: " His chief work, which alone has been preserved, is the great *Kitāb al-Aghānī* in this he collected the songs which were popular in his time, adding the accounts of their authors and their origin which appeared of interest to him... With every song there is indicated, besides the text, the air according to the musical terminology ... to these are added very detailed accounts concerning the poet, often also concerning composers and singers of both sexes. In spite of its unsystematic order this book is our most important authority not only for literary history till into the third century of the Hidjra but also for the history of civilization" (Art. Abu'l Faradj).

46 There are indecent stories in some of the books of the Bible, but still the Bible does not cease to have a sacred character.

47 *Tr. Is.*, p.77.

stated that Ibn Qutaibah "defended the Qur'ān and Tradition against the attacks of philosophic scepticism." Ibn Khaldūn, too, never attacked Tradition itself, and his strictures are applicable only to stories which have generally been rejected by the collectors.

Canons of criticism of Tradition as accepted by Muslims

There is no doubt that the collectors of Tradition attached the utmost importance to the trustworthiness of the narrators. As Guillaume says: "Inquiries were made as to the character of the guarantors, whether they were morally and religiously satisfactory, whether they were tainted with heretical doctrines, whether they had a reputation for truthfulness, and had the ability to transmit what they had themselves heard. Finally, it was necessary that they should be competent witnesses whose testimony would be accepted in a court of civil law".[48] More than this, they tried their best to find out whether each report was actually traceable to the Prophet through the various necessary stages. Even the Companions did not accept any tradition which was brought to their notice until they were fully satisfied that it came from the Prophet. But the collectors went beyond the narrators, and they had rules of criticism which were applied to the subject-matter. In judging whether a certain report was spurious or genuine, the collectors not only made a thorough investigation of the trustworthiness of the transmitters but also applied other rules of criticism which are in no way inferior to modern methods. Shāh 'Abd al-'Azīz has summarized these rules in *Ujālah Nafi'ah*, and according to them a report was not accepted under any of the following circumstances:

—If it was opposed to recognized historical facts.

—If the reporter was a Shī'ah and the tradition was of the nature of an accusation against the Companions, or if the reporter was a Khārijī and the report was of the nature of an accusation against a member of the Prophet's family. If, however, such a report was corroborated by independent testimony, it was accepted.

—If it was of such a nature that to know it and act upon it was incumbent upon all, and it was reported by a single man.

[48] *Tr. Is.*, p. 83.

—If the time and the circumstances of its narration contained evidence of its forgery.[49]

—If it was against reason[50] or against the plain teachings of Islam.[51]

—If it mentioned an incident which, had it happened, would have been known to and reported by large numbers, while as a matter of fact that incident was not reported by any one except the particular reporter.

—If its subject-matter or words were unsound or incorrect; for instance, the words were not in accordance with Arabic idiom, or the subject-matter was unbecoming the Prophet's dignity.

—If it contained threatenings of heavy punishment for ordinary sins, or promises of mighty reward for slight good deeds.

—If it spoke of the reward of prophets and messengers to the doer of good.

—If the narrator confessed that he fabricated the report.[52]

The Qur'ān as the greatest test for judging Tradition

In addition to these rules of criticism, there is another very important test whereby the trustworthiness of Tradition may be judged, and it is a test the application whereof was commanded by the Prophet himself. "There will be narrators," he is reported to have said, " reporting Tradition from me, so judge by the Qur'ān; if a report agrees with the Qurān, accept it; otherwise, reject it." The genuineness of this saying is beyond

[49] An example of this is met with in the following incident related in *Ḥayāt al-Ḥayawān*. Hārūn al-Rashīd loved pigeons. A pigeon was sent to him as a present. Qādzī Abul Bakhtārī was sitting by him at the time, and to please the monarch he narrated a tradition to the effect that there should be no betting except in racing or archery or flying of birds. Now the concluding words were a forgery, and the Caliph knew this. So when the Qādzī was gone, he ordered the pigeon to be slaughtered, adding that the fabrication of this portion of the report was due to that pigeon. The collectors of Tradition on that account did not accept any report of Abul Bakhtārī.

[50] Ibn 'Abd al-Barr (d.463) and Al-Nawāwī (d.676) do not hesitate to assail traditions which seem to them to be contrary to reason or derogatory to the dignity of the Prophet (*Tr. Is., p.94*).

[51] Examples of this are the traditions relating to *Qadzā 'Umri, i.e.,* going through the performance of the *rak'ahs* of daily prayers on the last Friday in the month of Ramadzān as an atonement for not saying prayers regularly, or the report which says: Do not eat melon until you slaughter it.

[52] Similar rules of criticism are laid down by Mulla 'Alī Qārī in his *Maudzu'āt*, and by Ibn al-Jauzī in *Fatḥ al-Mughīth*, as well as by Ibn Hajar in *Nuzhat al-Naẓar*.

all question, as it stands on the soundest basis.[53] That Tradition was in vogue in the time of the Prophet is a fact admitted by even European critics, as already shown, and that the authority of the Qur'ān was higher than that of Tradition appears from numerous circumstances. "I am no more than a man," the Prophet is reported to have said according to a very reliable report. "When I order you anything respecting religion receive it, and when I order anything about the affairs of the world, I am no more than a man".[54] There is another saying of his: "My sayings do not abrogate the word of Allāh, but the word of Allāh can abrogate my sayings".[55] The ḥadīth relating to Mu'ādh which has been quoted elsewhere,[56] places the Qur'ān first, and the Tradition after that. 'Ā'ishah used to quote a verse of the Qur'ān on hearing words from the mouth of the Prophet when she thought that the purport of what the Prophet said did not agree with the Qurān. The great Imām Bukhārī quotes a verse of the Qur'ān whenever he finds one suiting his text, before citing a tradition, thus showing that the Qur'ān holds precedence over Tradition; and by common consent of the Muslim community, the *Bukhārī*, which is considered to be the most trustworthy of all collections of Tradition, is called the most reliable of books *after* the Book of God.[57] This verdict of the community as a whole is enough proof that even if the *Bukhārī* disagrees with the Qur'ān, it is the *Bukhārī* that must be rejected and not the Book of God. And, as has already been stated at the

[53] A tradition, however sound the statement it contains and however great the authority on which it is based, is readily condemned as a fabrication by European critics when it does not suit their canons of criticism. Thus Guillaume, after quoting the well-known tradition, which is reported by a very large number of Companions — so large that not the least doubt can be entertained as to its genuineness — "Whoever shall repeat of me that which I have not said, his resting-place shall be in hell," remarks: "A study of the theological systems of the world would hardly reveal more naive attempt to tread the *ṣirāṭ al-mustaqīm*" (*Tr. Is.*, p. 79). Referring to the same tradition, the same author remarks: "In order to combat false tradition they invented others equally destitute of prophetic authority" (*Tr. Is.*, p.78). Such irresponsible remarks ill befit a work of criticism. The genuineness of this report is beyond all doubt, and it has been accepted as such by collectors. It cannot be denied that there are theological systems whose basic principles are the concoctions of pious men, but in Islām the very details are matters of history, and "pious lies" could not find here any ground whereon to prosper.

[54] MM. I : 6 — *i*.

[55] *Ibid.*, I : 6 — *iii*.

[56] On being appointed Governor of Yaman, Mu'ādh was asked by the Prophet as to the rule by which he would abide. "By the law of the Qur'ān," he replied. "But if you do not find any direction therein," asked the Prophet. "Then I will act according to the Sunnah of the Prophet," was the reply. And the Prophet approved of it (AD. 23 : 11).

[57] Aṣah al-kutūbī ba'da kitāb-Allāh.

commencement of this chapter, Tradition is only an explanation of the Qur'ān, and hence also the latter must have precedence. And last of all, both Muslim and non-Muslm historians are agreed that the Qur'ān has been handed down intact, every word and every letter of it, while Tradition cannot claim that purity. All these considerations show that the saying that Tradition must be judged by Qur'ān is quite in accordance with the teachings of the Prophet, and there is really no ground for doubting its genuineness. Even if there were no such saying, the test therein suggested would still have been the right test, because the Qur'ān deals with the principles of the Islamic law while Tradition deals with its details, and it is just and reasonable that only such details should be accepted as are in consonance with the principles. Again, as the Prophet is plainly represented in the Qur'ān as not following "aught save that which is revealed" to him[58] and as not disobeying a word of that which was revealed to him,[59] it follows clearly that if there is anything in the Tradition which is not in consonance with the Qur'ān, it could not have proceeded from the Prophet, and must, therefore, be rejected.

How far did the Collectors apply these tests?

But the question arises as to whether all the collectors paid equal regard to the above canons of criticism. It is clear that they did not. The earliest of them, Bukhārī, is, by a happy coincidence, also the soundest. He was not only most careful in accepting the trustworthiness of the narrators but he also paid the utmost attention to the last of the critical tests enumerated above: the test of judging Tradition by the Qur'ān. Many of his books and chapters are headed by Qur'ānic verses, and occasionally he has contented himself with a verse of the Qur'ān in support of his text. This shows that his criticism of Tradition was not limited to a mere examination of the guarantors, as every European critic seems to think, but that he also applied other tests. The act of criticism was, of course, applied mentally and one should not expect a record of the processes of that criticism in the book itself. So with the other collectors. They followed the necessary rules of criticism but were not all equally careful, nor did they all possess equal critical acumen or experience. Indeed, they sometimes intentionally relaxed the rules of criticism, both as regards the examina-

[58] 6 : 50; 7 : 203; 46 : 9.

[59] 6: 15; 10 : 15.

tion of the narrators and the critical tests. They also made a distinction between traditions relating to matters of jurisprudence and others, such as those having to do with past history or with prophecies, or with other material which had no bearing on the practical life of man. We are told that they were stricter in matter of jurisprudence than in other traditions. Thus in his *Kitāb al-Madkhal* Baihaqi says: "When we narrate from the Prophet in what is allowed and what is prohibited, we are strict in the chain of transmission and in the criticism of the narrators, but when we relate reports on the merits of people, and about reward and punishment, we are lax in the line of transmission and overlook the defects of the narrators." And Aḥmad ibn Ḥanbal says: "Ibn Isḥāq is a man from whom such reports may be taken (*i.e.*, those which relate to the life of the Prophet), but when the question is about what is allowed and what is forbidden, we have recourse to a (strong) people like this, and he inserted the fingers of one hand amid those of the other," conjoining the hands, and thus pointing to the strength of character of the transmitters.

It must, however, be admitted that most of the collectors paid more attention to the investigation of the narrators than to the other critical tests; they were justified in this, for their object was to produce reliable collections and, therefore, their first concern was to see that the traditions could be authentically traced back to the Prophet through a trustworthy chain of narrators. This part of the criticism was more essential, as the longer the chain of narrators, the more difficult would it have been to test their reliability. Other tests could be applied to any tradition at any time, and the lapse of a thousand years could in no way affect the value of these tests, but the passing away of another century would have rendered the task of the examination of the chain of narrators so difficult as to be for all practical purposes impossible. Hence the collectors rightly focussed their attention on this test. Nor did the work of collecting the tradition close the door to further criticism. The collectors contented themselves with producing collections reliable in the main, leaving the rest of work of criticism to future generations. They never claimed faultlessness for their works; even Bukhārī did not do that. They exercised their judgments to the best of their ability, but they never claimed, nor does any Muslim claim on their behalf, infallibility of judgment. In fact,they had started a work which was to continue for generations. If possible, a hundred more canons of criticism might be laid down, but it would still be the judgment of one man as to whether a certain tradition should be accepted or rejected. Every collection is the work of one collector, and even if ninety-nine per cent of his judgments are correct, there is still room for the exercise of judgment by others. The Western critic errs in thinking that infallibility is claimed for any of the collectors of Tradition, and that the exercise of judgment by a certain collector precludes the exercise of judgment by others as to the reliability of a report.

We must also remember that, however much the collectors might have differed in their judgments as to the necessity for rigour in the rules of criticism, they set to work with minds absolutely free from bias or external influence. They would lay down their lives rather than swerve from what they deemed to be the truth. Many of the famous religious personalities preferred punishment or jail to uttering a word against their convictions. The fact is generally admitted as regards the Umayyad rule. As a European writer says: "They laboured to establish the *sunnah* of the community as it was, or as it was thought to have been, under the Prophet's rule, and so they found their bitterest enemies in the ruling house".[60] The independence of thought of the great Muslim divines under the Abbaside rule had not deteriorated in the least. They would not even accept office under a Muslim ruler: "It is well-known," says Th. W. Juynboll in the *Encyclopaedia of Islam*, "that many pious, independent men in those days deemed it wrong and refused to enter the servicc of the Government or to accept an office dependent on it" (p.91).

Different classes of Tradition

Ibn Ḥajar has dealt with different classes of Tradition in the *Sharḥ Nukhbat al-Fikr* at great length. The most important division of Tradition is into *mutawātir* (continuous) and *aḥād* (isolated). A tradition is said to be *mutawātir* (lit.*repeated successively* or *by one after another*) when it is reported by such a large number that it is impossible that they should have agreed upon falsehood, so that the very fact that it is commonly accepted makes its authority unquestionable. To this category belong traditions that have been accepted by every Muslim generation down from the time of the Prophet.[61] The *mutawātir* traditions are accepted without criticizing their narrators. All others are called *aḥād* (*pl.* of *aḥad* or *wāḥid* meaning *one, i.e.,* isolated).

[60] Guillaume, *Tr. Is.*, p.42.

[61] There is difference of opinion as to the number of reporters of the *mutawātir* traditions, some considering four to be the minimum required, others five or seven or ten, others still raising it further to forty or even seventy. But the commonly accepted opinion is that it is only the extensive acceptance of a tradition which raises it to the rank of *mutawātir*.

The *aḥād* traditions are divided into three classes, *mashhūr* (lit. *well-known*), technically traditions which are reported through more than two channels at every stage; *'azīz* (lit. *strong*), that is, traditions that are not reported through less than two channels; and *gharīb* (lit. *strange* or *unfamiliar*), namely traditions in whose link of narrators there is only a single person at any stage. It should be noted that in this classification the condition as to the traditions being narrated by more than two or two or less than two persons at any stage applies only to the three generations following the Companions of the Prophet.

Of the two chief classes of traditions, the *mutawātir* and the *aḥād*, the first are all accepted so far as the line of transmission is concerned, but the latter are further sub-divided into two classes, *maqbūl* or those which may be accepted, and *mardūd* or those which may be rejected. Those that are *maqbūl*, or acceptable, are again subdivided into two classes, *ṣaḥīḥ* (lit. *sound*), and *ḥasan* (lit. *fair*). The condition for a tradition being *ṣaḥīḥ* or sound is that its narrators are *'adl* (men whose sayings and decisions are approved or whom desire does not deviate from the right course), and *tāmm al-dzabṭ* (guarding or taking care of tradition effectually); that it is *muttaṣil al-sanad, i.e.*, that the authorities narrating it should be in contact with each other, so that there is no break in the transmission; that it is *ghair mu'allal i.e.*, that there is no *'illah* or defect in it; and that it is not *shādhdh* (lit. *a thing apart from the general mass*) *i.e.,* against the general trend of Tradition or at variance with the overwhelming evidence of others. A tradition that falls short of this high standard, and fulfils the other conditions but does not fulfil the condition of its narrators being *tāmm al-dzabṭ* (guarding or taking care of tradition effectually), is called *ḥasan (fair)*. Such a tradition is regarded sound (*ṣaḥīḥ*) when the deficiency of effectual guarding is made up for by the large number of its transmitters. A *sound* tradition is accepted unless there is stronger testimony to rebut what is stated therein. It has already been said that it is recognized by the collectors that a tradition may be unacceptable either because of some defect in its transmitters or because its subject-matter is unacceptable. Thus Ibn Ḥajar says that among the reasons for which a tradition may be rejected is its subject-matter. For example if a report contradicts a verse of the Qur'ān or a recognized tradition or the unanimous verdict of the Muslim community or common-sense, it is not accepted.

As regards defects in transmission, a tradition is said to be *marfū'* when it is traced back to the Prophet without any defect in transmission, *muttaṣal* when its *isnād* is uninterrupted, *mauqūf* when it does not go back to the Prophet, *mu'an'an* when it is linked by a word which does not show personal contact between two narrators, and *mu'allaq* when the name of one or more transmitters is missing (being *munqaṭa'* if the name is missing from the middle, and *mursal* if it is from the end).

Chapter III

IJTIHĀD OR EXERCISE OF JUDGMENT

Ijtihād is the third source from which the laws of Islām are drawn. The word itself is derived from the root *jahd* which means *exerting oneself to the utmost* or *to the best of one's ability,* and *Ijtihād,* which literally conveys the same significance, is technically applicable to a *lawyer's exerting the faculties of mind to the utmost for the purpose of forming an opinion in a case of law respecting a doubtful and difficult point* (LL.).

Value of reason recognized

Reasoning or the exercise of judgment, in theological as well as in legal matters, plays a very important part in the religion of Islām, and the value of reason is expressly recognized in the Qur'ān, which is full of exhortations like the following: "Do you not reflect?" "Do you not understand?" "Have you no sense?" "There are signs in this for a people who reflect;" "There are signs in this for a people who understand;" and so on. Those who do not use their reasoning faculty are compared to animals, and spoken of as being deaf, dumb and blind:

"And the parable of those who disbelieve is as the parable of one who calls out to that which hears no more than a call and a cry. Deaf, dumb, blind, so they have no sense" (2 : 171).

"They have hearts wherewith they understand not, and they have eyes wherewith they see not, and they have ears wherewith they hear not. They are as cattle; nay, they are more astray" (7 : 179).

"The vilest of beasts in Allāh's sight are the deaf, the dumb, who understand not" (8 : 22). "Or thinkest thou that most of them hear or understand? They are but as the cattle; nay, they are farther astray from the path" (25 : 44).

While those who do not exercise their reason or judgment are condemned, those who do it are praised:

"In the creation of the heavens and the earth and the alternation of the night and the day, there are surely signs for men of understanding. Those who remember Allāh standing and sitting and (lying) on their sides, and reflect on the creation of the heavens and the earth" (3 : 189, 190).

The Qur'ān does recognize revelation as a source of knowledge higher than reason, but at the same time admits that the truth of the principles established by revelation may be judged by reason, and hence it is that it repeatedly appeals to reason and denounces those who do not use their reasoning faculty. It also recognizes the necessity of the exercise of judgment in order to arrive at a decision: "But if any news of security or fear comes to them, they spread it abroad. And if they had referred it to the Messenger and to those in authority among them, those of them who can *search out the knowledge* of it would have known it" (4 : 83).[1]

The verse recognizes the principle of the exercise of judgment which is the same as *Ijtihād*, and though the occasion on which it is mentioned is a particular one, the principle recognized is general.

The Prophet allowed exercise of judgment in religious matters

The exercise of judgment *(ijtihād)* is recognized in Tradition as the means by which a decision may be arrived at when there is no direction in the Qur'ān or Tradition. The following tradition is regarded as the basis of *Ijtihād* in Islām: "On being appointed Governor of Yaman, Mu'ādh was asked by the Prophet as to the rule by which he would abide. He replied, 'By the law of the Qur'ān.' 'But if you do not find any direction therein,' asked the Prophet. 'Then I will act according to the practice *(Sunnah)* of the Prophet,' was the reply. 'But if you do not find any direction therein,' he was again asked. 'Then I will exercise my judgment (*ajtahidu*) and act on that,' came the reply. The Prophet raised his hands and said: 'Praise be to Allāh Who guides the messenger of His Apostle as He pleases' " (AD. 23 : 11). This tradition shows not only that the Prophet approved of the exercise of judgment, but also that his Companions were well aware of the principle, and that reasoning or exercise of judgment by others was freely resorted to when necessary, even in the Prophet's lifetime.

Exercise of Judgment by the Companions

It is a mistake to suppose that the exercise of judgment to meet the new circumstances only came into vogue with the four great jurists (*Imāms*) whose opinion is now generally accepted in the Islamic world. The work

[1] The original word for the italicized portion is *yastanbiṭūn* from *istinbāṭ* which is derived from *nabaṭ al-bi'ra*, meaning "he dug out a well and brought forth water." The *istinbaṭ* of the jurist is derived from this, and it signifies the searching out of the hidden meaning by his *ijtihād* and is the same as *istikhrāj, i.e.*, analogical deduction (TA.).

had begun, as already shown, in the Prophet's lifetime, since it was impossible to refer every case to him. After the Prophet's death, the principle of *Ijtihād* obtained a wider prevalence, and as new areas were added to the material and spiritual realm of Islām, the need of resorting to the exercise of the judgment became greater. Nor did the Caliphs arrogate all authority to themselves. They had a council to which every important case was referred, and its decision by a majority of votes was accepted by the Caliph as well as by the Muslim public. Thus Sayūṭi writes in his *History of the Caliphs* on the authority of Abū al-Qāsim Baghwi reporting from Maimūn son of Mihrān: "When a case came before Abū Bakr (the first Caliph), he used to consult the Book of God; if he found anything in it by which he could decide, he did so; if he did not find it in the Book, and he knew of a practice or saying of the Messenger of God, he decided according to it; and if he was unable to find anything there, he used to question the Muslims if they knew of any decision of the Prophet in a matter of that kind, and a company of people thus gathered round him, every one of whom stated what he knew from the Prophet, and Abū Bakr would say, Praise be to God Who had kept among us those who remember what the Prophet said; but if he was unable to find anything in the practice of the Prophet, he gathered the heads of the people, and the best of them, and consulted them, and if they agreed upon one opinion (by a majority) he decided accordingly".[2]

It is true that it was not exactly a legislative assembly in the modern sense, but the nucleus of a legislative assembly can clearly be seen in this council which decided all important affairs and, when necessary, promulgated laws. It was also supreme in both religious and temporal matters. The same rule was followed by 'Umar, the second Caliph, who resorted to *Ijtihād* very freely, but took care always to gather the most learned Companions for consultation. When there was a difference of opinion, the decision of the majority was acted upon. Besides this council, there were great individual teachers, such as 'Ā'ishah, Ibn 'Abbās, Ibn 'Umar and others, whose opinion was highly revered. Decisions were given and laws made and promulgated subject only to the one condition that they were neither contrary to the Qur'ān nor to the practice of the Prophet.

Great Jurists: Imām Abū Hanifah

In the second century of the Hijrah era arose the great jurists who codi-

[2] *T.Kh.*, p.40.

fied the Islamic law according to the need of their time. The first of these, and the one who claims the allegiance of the greater part of the Muslim world, was Abū Ḥanīfah Nu'mān ibn Thābit, born in Baṣrah in 80 A.H. (699 A.D.), a Persian by descent. His centre of activity, however, was Kūfah, and he passed away in 150 A.H. (767 A.D.). The basis of his analogical reasoning *(qiyās)* was the Qur'ān, and he accepted Tradition only when he was fully satisfied as to its authenticity; and, as the collectors had not yet commenced the work of collection, and Kūfah itself was not a great centre of that branch of learning, naturally Abū Ḥanīfah accepted very few traditions, and always resorted to the Qur'ān for his juristic views. Later on when Tradition was collected, and was more in vogue, the followers of the Ḥanafī system — as Abū Ḥanīfah's school of thought was called — introduced into it more traditions. Abū Ḥanīfah had two famous disciples, Muḥammad and Abū Yūsuf, and it is mostly their views of the great master's teaching that now form the basis of the Ḥanafī system. Abū Ḥanīfah was a man of highly independent character, and when, towards the close of his life, the then Muslim Government wanted to win him over to its side, he preferred imprisonment to an office which would have interfered with his independence of thought. His system is not only the first in point of time but is also that which claims allegiance from the great majority of Muslims, and a development of which on the right lines would have resulted in immense benefit to the Muslim world. It was he who first directed attention to the great value of analogical reasoning (*qiyās*) in legislation. He also laid down the principle of equity, whereby not only could new laws be made, but even logical conclusions could be controverted when proved inequitable. He recognized the authority of customs and usages, but exercised and inculcated independence of judgment to such an extent that he and his followers were called "upholders of private judgment" *(ahl al-ra'y)* by the followers of other schools.

Imām Mālik

The second famous jurist, Mālik ibn Anas, was born in Madīnah in 93 A.H. (713 A.D.); he worked and died there at the age of eighty-two. He limited himself almost entirely to the traditions which he found in Madīnah, relating more especially to the practice which prevailed there, and his system of jurisprudence is based entirely on the traditions and practices of the people of Madīnah. He was scrupulously careful in giving judgment, and whenever he had the least doubt as to the correctness of his decision, he would say: "I do not know." His book, *Muwaṭṭā*, though a comparatively small collection of Tradition, and limited only to the traditions and practices of the people of Madīnah, is the first work of its kind, and one of the most authoritative.

Imām Shāfi'ī

The third jurist, Abū 'Abd Allāh Muḥammad ibn Idrīs al-Shāfi'ī, was born in Palestine in the year 150 A.H. (767 A.D.). He passed his youth at Makkah, but he worked for the most part in Egypt, where he died in 204 A.H. In his day he was unrivalled for his knowledge of the Qur'ān, and took immense pains in studying the Traditions, travelling from place to place in search of information. He was intimately acquainted with the Ḥanafī and the Mālikī schools of thought, but that which he himself founded was based largely on Tradition, as distinguished from the Ḥanafī system which was founded on the Qur'ān and made very little use of Tradition. Over the Mālikī system, which is also based on Traditions, it had this advantage that the Tradition made use of by Shafi'ī was more extensive, and was collected from different centres, while Mālik contented himself only with what he found at Madīnah.

Imām Aḥmad

The last of the four great jurists was Aḥmad ibn Ḥanbal, who was born in Baghdād in 164 A.H. and died there in 241. He too made a very extensive study of Tradition, his famous work on the subject — the *Musnad* of Aḥmad ibn Hanbal — containing nearly thirty thousand traditions. This monumental compilation, prepared by his son 'Abd Allāh, was based on the material collected by the Imām himself. In the *Musnad,* however, as already remarked, traditions are not arranged according to subject-matter but according to names of the Companions to whom they are ultimately traced. Though the *Musnad* of Aḥmad contains a large number of traditions, it does not apply those strict rules of criticism favoured by men like Bukhārī and Muslim. It was indeed only an arrangement according to subject-matter that made a criticism of Tradition possible, and the *Musnads,* in which reports relating to the same matter were scattered throughout the book, could not devote much attention to the subject matter, and were not even sufficiently strict in scrutinizing the line of transmission. Accordingly, the *Musnad* of Aḥmad cannot claim the same reliability as regards its material as can the collections of the other famous collectors. From the very nature of his exertions, it is evident that Aḥmad ibn Ḥanbal made very little use of reasoning, and as he depended almost entirely on Tradition, the result was that he admitted even the weakest report. It would thus appear that from the system of Abū Ḥanīfah, who applied reasoning very freely and sought to deduce all questions from the Qur'ān by the help of reason, the system of Aḥmad ibn Ḥanbal is distinguished by the fact that it makes the least possible use of reason, and thus there was a marked falling off in the last of the four great jurists from the high ideals of the first, so far as the application of reason to matters of religion is concerned. Even the system of Abū Ḥanīfah himself deteriorated on account of the later jurists of that school not developing the master's high ideal, with the consequence that the world of Islām gradually gave up reasoning or exercise of judgment (*Ijtihād*) and stagnation reigned in the place of healthy development.

Different methods of formulating new laws

The four Jurists (*Imāms*) who are accepted by the entire *Sunnī* world of Islām, are thus agreed in giving an important place in legistation to *Ijtihād*, and the Shī'as attached to it an even greater importance.[3] In fact, the sphere of *Ijtihād* is a very wide one, since it seeks to fulfil all the requirements of the Muslim community which are not met with expressly in the Qur'ān and the Tradition. The great jurists of Islām have endeavoured to meet these demands by various methods, technically known as *qiyās* (analogical reasoning), *istiḥsān* (equity), *istiṣlāh* (public good), and *istidlāl* (inference). Before proceeding further, a brief description of these methods may be given to show how new laws are evolved by adopting them.[4]

[3] *Ijmā'*, of which I shall speak later, and which means really the *Ijtihād* of many, and *Ijtihād*, are thus looked upon as two more sources of the Islamic law along with the Qur'ān and the Sunnah, though only the latter two regarded *as al-adillat al-qaṭ'iyya* or absolute arguments or authorities, the former two being called *al-adillat al-ijtihādiyya* or arguments obtained by exertion.

[4] Sir 'Abd al-Raḥīm has very ably dealt with this subject in his *Muhammadan Jurisprudence* where he has referred to original authorities. I am indebted to him for the material used here.

Qiyās *or reasoning based on analogy*

The most important of these methods, and the one which has almost a universal sanction, is *qiyās*[5] which may be described as 'reasoning based on analogy'. A case comes up for decision, which is not expressly provided for either in the Qur'ān or in the Tradition. The jurist looks for a case resembling it in the Qur'ān or in Tradition, and, by reasoning on the basis of analogy, arrives at a decision. Thus it is an extension of the law as met with in the Qur'ān and Tradition, but it is not of equal authority with them, for no jurist has ever claimed infallibility for analogical deductions, or for decisions and laws which are based on *qiyās*; and it is a recognized principle of *Ijtihād* that the jurist may err in his judgment. Hence it is that so many differences of juristic deductions exist even among the highest authorities. From its very nature the *qiyās* of one generation may be rejected by a following generation.

Istiḥsān *or Exercise of Private Judgment and* Istiṣlāh *or Deduction based on Public Good*

Istiḥṣān,[6] in the terminology of the jurists, means the *exercise of private judgment, not on the basis of analogy but on that of public good or the interest of justice*. According to the Ḥanafī school,when a deduction based on analogy is not acceptable either because it is against the broader rules of justice or because it is not in the interest of the public good, and is likely to cause undue inconvenience to those to whom it is applied, the jurist is at liberty to reject the same, and to adopt instead a rule which is conducive to public good, or is in consonance with the broader rules of justice. This method is peculiar to the Ḥanafī system, but owing to strong opposition from the other schools of thought, it has not, even in that system, been developed to its full extent. The principle underlying it is, however, a very sound one and is quite in accordance with the spirit of the Qur'ān. There is, moreover, less liability to error in this method than in far-fetched analogy, which often leads to narrow results opposed

[5] Literally, *measuring by* or *comparing with,* or *judging by comparing with, a thing*, while the jurists apply it to "a process of deduction by which the law of a text is applied to cases which, though not covered by the language, are governed by the reason of the text" (MJ.).

[6] Literally, *considering a thing to be good* or *preferring a thing.*

to the broad spirit of the Holy Book. In the school of Imām Mālik, a similar rule is adopted under the name of *istiṣlāh* which means "*a deduction of law based on considerations of public good*".

Istidlāl *or inference*

Istidlāl literally signifies *the inferring of one thing from another*, and the two chief sources recognized for such inferences are customs and usages, and the laws of religions revealed before Islām. It is admitted that customs and usages which prevailed in Arabia at the advent of Islām, and which were not abrogated by Islām, have the force of law. On the same principle, customs and usages prevailing anywhere, when not opposed to the spirit of the teachings of the Qur'ān or not forbidden by it, would be admissible, because, according to a well-known maxim of the jurists, "permissibility is the original principle,"and therefore what has not been declared unlawful is permissible. In fact, as a custom is recognized by a vast majority of the people, it is looked upon as having the force of *Ijmā'*, and, hence, it has precedence over a rule of law derived from analogy. The only condition required is that it must not be opposed to a clear text of the Qur'ān or a reliable tradition of the Prophet. The Ḥanafī law lays special stress on the value of customs and usages.[7] As regards laws revealed previous to Islām, opinion is divided. Some jurists hold that all such laws as have not been expressly abrogated have the force of law even now, while others argue that they have not. According to the Ḥanafī school, those laws of the previous religions are binding which have been mentioned in the Qur'ān without being abrogated.

Ijmā' *or consensus of opinion*

In the terminology of the Muslim jurists, *Ijmā'*[8] means a consensus of opinion of the Muslim jurists of a particular age on a question of law. This agreement is inferred in three ways: firstly, by word (*qaul*), *i.e.*, by recognized jurists expressing an opinion on the point in question;

[7] It is thus laid down in *Al-Ashbāh wal-Naẓā'ir*: "Many decisions of law are based on usage and customs, so much so that it has been taken as a principle of laws" (MJ.).

[8] The word *ijmā'* is derived from *jam'* which means *collecting* or *gathering together*, and *ijmā'* carries the double significance of composing and settling a thing which has been unsettled and hence *determining and resolving upon an affair*, and also agreeing or *uniting in opinion* (LL).

secondly, by deed (*fi'l*), *i.e.*, when there is unanimity in practice; and thirdly, by silence (*sukūt*) — when the recognized jurists do not controvert an opinion expressed by one or more of them. It is generally held that *Ijmā'* means the consensus of opinion of such authorities only (*mujtahids*), and those who are not learned in law do not participate in it, but some are of opinion that it means the agreement of all Muslims. There is a difference of opinion as to whether *Ijmā'* is confined to a particular place or to one or more particular generations. Imām Mālik based his *Ijtihād* on the consensus of opinion of the people of Madīnah. Theoretically, such a limitation is untenable, as learned men were not confined to Madīnah, and were sent out to outlying parts of the country even in the Prophet's lifetime. The more generally received opinion is that men of all places must be included. Again, the Sunnī schools of thought exclude the Shī'a jurists (*mujtahids*) from the purview of *Ijmā'*, and *vice versa*. The Shī'as further hold that only the descendants of 'Alī and the Prophet's daughter Fāṭimah are the proper persons to exercise *Ijtihād*. Among the Sunnīs, some jurists are of opinion that *Ijmā'* is restricted only to the Companions of the Prophet, others extending it to the next generation, but the general opinion is that it is not confined to any one generation, nor to any one country, and therefore only the consensus of opinion of all the Jurists of all countries in any one age is an effective *Ijmā'*, and this is almost an impossibility.

There is considerable difference of opinion as to whether an effective *Ijmā'* is formed by a majority of the jurists or by the agreement of the entire body of them. Most authorities require the unanimity of opinion of all the jurists of a particular age, but others have held the opposite view. However, it is generally agreed that if there is an overwhelming preponderance of jurists holding a certain view, that view is valid and binding, though not absolute.[9] *Ijmā'* is said to be complete when all the jurists of a particular age have come to an agreement on a certain question, though according to some it is necessary that all of them should have passed away without changing their opinion on that question. Some go still further and assert that no *Ijmā'* is effective unless it is shown that no jurist born in that age has expressed a contrary opinion.

When *Ijmā'* is established on a point, its effect is that no single jurist is permitted to reopen it, unless some jurist of the age in which the *Ijmā'* came about had expressed a different view. One *Ijmā'* may, however, be repealed by another in the same age or in a subsequent age,

9 Mkh. II, p. 35; JJ. III, p. 291.

with this reservation that the *Ijmā'* of the Companions of the Prophet cannot be reversed by any later generation.[10] Views differ as to whether or not, when there is disagreement on a question among the Companions, an *Ijmā'* upholding one view or the other is debarred. The fact that even a Companion may have made an error in forming a judgment is admitted on all hands, and therefore technically, there can be no objection to an *Ijmā'* which goes against the opinion of a Companion.

Two more points have to be elucidated in order to realize the full force of *Ijmā'*. From what has been stated above, it would seem that a very large number of jurists would be needed for a valid *Ijmā'*. It is, however, held that if three or even two of them take part in deliberating on a question, the *Ijmā'* is valid, while one jurist is of opinion that, if in any particular age there is only one jurist his solitary opinion would have the authority of *Ijmā'*. And now we come to the most important question: What is the authority on which *Ijmā'* is to be based? According to the four great *Imāms*, it may be based on the Qur'ān or on Tradition or on analogy. The Mu'tazilas, however, hold that it cannot be based on isolated traditions or on analogy.[11] They, and some others, hold that as *Ijmā'* is absolute, the authority on which it is based must also be absolute.

Ijmā' *is only* **Ijtihād** *on a wider basis*

It would thus be seen that it is a mistake to call *Ijmā'* an independent source of the laws of Islām. It is essentially reasoning or exercise of judgment (*Ijtihād*), with this distinction that it is *Ijtihād* on which all or the majority of the jurists of a certain generation are agreed. It is even admitted that, barring the *Ijmā'* of the Companions, the *Ijmā'* of one generation of Muslims may be set aside by that of another. The fact, however, is that if *Ijmā'* is taken to mean the consensus of opinion of all the jurists of a certain generation of Muslims, it has never been practicable after perhaps the early days of the Companions. The Muslims having spread far and wide and living, as they did, in distant places, could not all be occupied with the discussion of a certain question at one and the same time. Even in one country the same question need not occupy the attention of all the jurists simultaneously. There is, however, no denying

[10] KA. III, p. 262

[11] JJ. III, p. 396.

the fact that, if many of them are agreed on a certain question, their opinion would carry greater weight than that of a single one, but even the opinion of many, or of all, is not infallible. *Ijmā'*, after all, is only *Ijtihād* on a wider basis, and like the latter it is always open to correction.

To differ with majority is no sin

It may be added here that the sense in which the word *Ijmā'* is commonly used nowadays is quite erroneous, for it is taken to mean the opinion of the majority, and it is generally thought that it is a sin on the part of a Muslim to differ with the views of the majority. But honest difference of opinion, instead of being a sin, is called a mercy by the Prophet, who is reported to have said: "The differences of my people are a mercy".[12] Difference of opinion is called a mercy because it is only through encouraging it that the reasoning faculty is developed, and the truth ultimately discovered. There were many differences of opinion among the Companions, and there were also matters on which a single man used to express boldly his dissent from all the rest. For example, Abū Dharr was alone in holding that to have wealth in one's possession was a sin. His opinion was that no one should amass wealth, and that immediately one came into possession of it, he must distribute it to the poor. All the other Companions were opposed to this view, yet the authority of the majority was never quoted against him, nor did anyone dare say that he deserved to be punished for this difference of opinion with the whole body of Companions.[13] *Ijtihād*, on the other hand, is encouraged by a saying of the Prophet, which promises reward even to the man who makes an error in it: "When the judge gives a judgment and he exercises his reasoning faculty and is right, he has a double reward, and when he gives a judgment and exercises his reasoning faculty and makes a mistake, there is a reward for him.[14]

Three degrees of **Ijtihād**

Later jurists speak of three degrees of *Ijtihād*, though there is no authority for this in either the Qur'ān or the Tradition or in the writings

[12] [13] [14] — see next page.

of the great Imāms. These three are: exercise of judgment in legislation (*Ijtihād filshar'*) in a juristic system, (*Ijtihād fil-madhhab*), and in particular cases (*Ijtihād fil-masā'il*). The first kind of *Ijtihād* (exercise of judgment) in the making of new laws, is supposed to have been limited to the first three centuries and, practically, it centres in the four Imāms who, it is thought, codified all law and included in their systems whatever was reported from the Companions and the generation next to them (*Tābi'in*). Of course, it is not laid down in so many clear words that the door of *Ijtihād* for making laws is closed after the second century of Hijrah, but it is said that the conditions necessary for a jurist of the first degree have not been met with in any person after the first four Imāms, and it is further supposed that they will not be met with in any person till the Day of Judgment. These conditions are three: a comprehensive knowledge of the Qur'ān in its different aspects, a knowledge of the Tradition with its lines of transmission, text and varieties of significance, and a knowledge of the different aspects of *qiyās* (reasoning).[15] No reason is given why these conditions were met with only in four men in the second century of Hijrah, and why they were not met with in any person among the Companions or in the first century. It is an assertion without a basis. The second degree of *Ijtihād* — exercise of judgment in a juristic system — is said to have been granted to the immediate disciples of the first four Imāms. Muḥammad and Abū Yūsuf, the two famous disciples of Abū Ḥanīfah, belong to this class, and their unanimous opinion on any point must be accepted, even if it goes against that of their master. The third degee of *Ijtihād* — pertaining to particular cases — was attainable by later jurists who could solve special cases that came before them which had not been decided by the jurists of the first two degrees, but such decisions must be in absolute accordance with the opinion of the latter. The door of such *Ijtihād* is also supposed to have been closed after the sixth century of Hijrah. And at present, it is said, there can be only *muqallidīn*, literally "those who follow another in what he says or does, firmly believing him to be right therein, regardless of proof or evidence." They may only quote a decision (*fatwā*) from any of the earlier authorities, or when there are differing opinions of the earlier jurisconsults they can choose one of them, but they cannot question the cor-

[12] JS. p. 11

[13] IS. T. IV. I, p. 166.

[14] MM. 17 : 3-i.

[15] KA. IV, p. 15.

rectness of what has been said. Thus *Ijtihād* which was never considered to be an absolute authority by the great Imāms or their immediate disciples is now practically placed on the same level with the Qur'ān and the Tradition and hence no one now is considered to be fit for *Ijtihād*.

The door of **Ijtihād** *is still open*

But it is a mistake to suppose that the door of *Ijtihād* was closed after the four Imāms mentioned above. It is quite clear that the free exercise of judgment was allowed by the Qur'ān, while both the Qur'ān and the Tradition explicitly allowed analogical deduction (*istinbāṭ*), and it was on the basis of these directions that the Muslim world continued to exercise its judgment in making laws for itself. The Companions made use of it even in the Prophet's lifetime, when it was not convenient to refer a matter to him personally; and after his death, as new circumstances arose, new laws were made by the majority of the Caliph's council and new decisions given by the learned among the Companions; the next generation (*Tābi'ūṇ*) added up to the knowledge of the Companions; and each succeeding generation, not satisfied with what the previous one had achieved, freely applied its judgment. The second century saw the four great luminaries appear on the horizon of *Ijtihād*, and the appearance of these great jurists one after another, each evidently dissatisfied with what his predecessor had achieved, is another conclusive argument that Islām permitted human judgment to be exercised freely to meet new circumstances. Mālik was not content with what his great predecessor Abū Ḥanīfah had accomplished, nor Shāfi'ī with what his two predecessors had done; and in spite of the three having practically exhausted the well of jurisprudence, Aḥmad ibn Ḥanbal gave to a world, whose thirst for knowledge was ever on the increase, the result of the application of his own judgment. The great jurists not only applied their judgment to new circumstances but they also differed in their principle of jurisprudence, which shows that no one of them considered the others infallible. If they were not infallible then, how did they become such after so many centuries when the mere lapse of time necessitated new legislation to meet new requirements? That the Prophet opened the door of *Ijtihād* is only too clear, that he never ordered it to be closed after a certain time is admitted on all hands; and even the great Imāms never closed that door. Neither Abū Ḥanīfah, nor Mālik, nor Shafi'ī, nor yet Aḥmad ibn Ḥanbal ever said that no one after him shall be permitted to exercise his own judgment, nor did any one of them claim to be infallible; neither does any book on the principles of jurisprudence (*uṣūl*) lay down that the exercise of a man's own judgment for the making of new laws was forbidden to the Muslims after the four Imāms, not yet that their *Ijtihād* has the same absolute authority as the Qur'ān and the Tradition. *Ijtihād* was a great blessing to the Muslim people; it was the only way through which the needs of succeeding generations and the requirements of different races merging into Islām could be met. Neither the Prophet, nor any of his Companions, nor any of the great jurists ever said that Muslims were forbidden to apply their own judgment to new circumstances and the ever changing needs of a growing community after a certain time; nor has any one of them said, what in fact no one could say, that no new circumstances would arise after the second century. What happened was that the attention of the great intellects of the third century was directed towards the collection and criticism of the Tradition. On the other hand, the four Imāms rose so high above the ordinary jurists that the latter were dwarfed into insignificance, and the impression gained ground gradually that no one could exercise his judgment independently of the former. This impression in its turn led to limitations upon *Ijtihād* and the independence of thought to which Islām had given an impetus. Being thus restrained by a false impression, the intellect of Islām suffered a heavy loss and the increasing demand of knowledge being brought to a standstill, stagnation and ignorance took its place.

Independence of thought recognized

The Qur'ān recognizes independence of opinion for one and all, and requires that absolute obedience be given only to God and His Messenger: "O you who believe, obey Allāh and obey the Messenger and those in authority from among you; then if you quarrel about anything, refer it to Allāh and the Messenger"(4 : 59). This verse speaks first of obedience to those in authority (*ulu-l-amr*), along with the obedience to the Messenger, and then mentions disputes which, it says, must be settled by referring them to God and His Messenger. The omission of *ulu-l-amr* from the latter portion of the verse shows clearly that the *quarrel* here spoken of relates to differences with *ulu-l-amr*, and in the case of such a difference the only authority is that of God and the Messenger, or the Qur'ān and the Tradition. Every authority in Islām, whether temporal or spiritual, is included in *ulu-l-amr*, and independence of thought for every Muslim is thus recognized by allowing him to differ with all except the Qur'ān and the Tradition. The Companions, the Collectors of Tradition, the four Imāms and the other jurists being thus included in *ulu-l-amr*, must be obeyed ordinarily, but to differ with any one or all of them, when one has the authority of the Qur'ān and the Tradition is expressly permitted. And since the ultimate test of the correctness of Tradition is the Qur'ān itself, the conclusion is evident that Islām allows independence of thought subject only to one thing, that the principles laid down in the Qur'ān are not contravened.

It will thus be seen that any Muslim community has the right to make any law for itself, the only condition being that such law shall not contravene any principle laid down by the Qur'ān. The impression prevailing in the Muslim world at present that no one has the right, even in the light of the new circumstances which a thousand years of the world's progress have brought about, to differ with the four Imāms, is entirely a mistaken one. The right to differ with the highest of men below the Prophet is a Muslims' birthright, and to take away that right is to stifle the very existence of Islām. Under the present circumstances, when conditions have quite changed and the world has been moving on for a thousand years, while the Muslims have more or less stagnated, it is the duty of Muslim states and Muslim peoples to apply their own judgment to the changed conditions, and find out the ways and means for their temporal salvation. In fact, the closing of the door on the free exercise of judgment, and the tendency to stifle independence of thought which took hold of the Muslim world after the third century of Hijrah, was condemned by the Prophet himself who said: "The best of the generations is my generation, then the second and then the third; then will come a people in which there is no good".[16] And again he said: "The best of this community (*ummah*) are the first of them and the last of them; among the first of them is the Messenger of Allāh, and among the last of them is Jesus, son of Mary,[17] and between these is a crooked way, they are not of me nor am I of them".[18]

The three generations in the first tradition refer to three centuries, the first century being the century of the Companions, since the last of them died at the end of the first century after the Prophet and the second and third being those of the next two generations known as *Tābi'īn* and *taba' Tābi'īn*. As a matter of fact, we find that while independence of

16 17 18 — see next page.

thought was freely exercised in the first three centuries, and even Muḥammad and Abū Yūsuf, the immediate followers of Abū Ḥanīfah, did not hesitate to differ with their great leader, rigidity became the rule thereafter with only rare exceptions. The time when independence of thought was not exercised is, therefore, denounced by the Prophet himself, as the time of a crooked company.

16 KU. VI, 2068.

17 By Jesus, son of Mary, is meant the Messiah who was promised to the Muslims, as he is plainly called *imāmukum min-kum i.e.*, "your Imām from among yourselves" (Bu. 60 : 49).

18 KU.VI, 2073.

PART TWO

THE PRINCIPLES OF ISLĀM

Chapter I

IMĀN OR FAITH

Faith and action

The religion of Islām may be broadly divided into two parts — the theoretical, or, what may be called, its articles of faith or its doctrines, and the practical, which includes all that a Muslim is required to do, that is to say, the practical course to which he must conform his life. The former are called *uṣūl* (plural of *aṣl*, meaning *a root* or *a principle*), and the latter *furū'* (plural of *far'*, which means *a branch*). The former are also called *'aqā'id* (pl.of *'aqīdah*, lit., *what one is bound to*) or beliefs, and the latter *aḥkām* (pl. of *ḥukm*, lit., *an order*) or the ordinances and regulations of Islām. According to Shahrastāni, the former is *ma'rifah* or knowledge, and the latter *tā'ah* or obedience. Thus knowledge is the root; and obedience or practice, the branch. In the Qur'ān the two broad divisions are repeatedly referred to as *īmān*[1] (faith or belief) and *'amal* (deed or action) and the two words are often used together to describe a believer; *those who believe and do good* is the oft recurring description of true believers. The relation of faith with deeds must be constantly borne in mind in order to understand the true meaning of Islām.

Use of the word Īmān in the Qur'ān

The word *īmān*, generally translated as *faith* or *belief*, is used in two different senses in the Qur'ān. According to Rāghib, the famous lexicologist of the Qur'ān, *īmān* is sometimes nothing more than a confession with the tongue that one believes in Muḥammad, as for example in these verses: "Those who believe (*āmanū*) and those who are Jews, and the Christians, and the Sabians, whoever believes in Allāh and the Last Day and does good, they have their reward with their Lord..." (2 : 62);

[1] The word *īmān*, generally translated as faith or belief, is derived from *āmana* (ordinarily rendered as *he believed*) which means, when used intransitively, *he came into peace* or *security*; and, when used transitively, *he granted (him) peace or security*. Hence the believer is called *al-mu'min*, meaning *one who has come into peace* or *security* because he has accepted the principles which bring about peace of mind or security from fear; and God is called *al-Mu'min* meaning *the Granter of security* (59 : 23).

"O you who believe (*āmanū*)! Believe in Allāh and His Messenger and the Book which He has revealed to His Messenger" (4 : 136). But, as Rāghib has further explained, *īmān* also implies the condition in which a confession with the tongue is accompanied by an assent of the heart[2] and the carrying into practice of what is believed,[3] as in this verse: "And for those who believe in Allāh and His Messengers, they are the truthful and the faithful ones with their Lord" (57 : 19).

The word *īmān* is, however, also used in either of the two latter senses, meaning simply the assent of the heart or the doing of good deeds. Examples of this are: "The dwellers of the desert say: We believe (*āmanna*). Say: You believe not, but say, We submit; and faith has not yet entered into your hearts" (49 : 14). Here belief clearly stands for the assent of the heart as explained in the verse itself. Or, "What reason have you that you believe not in Allāh, and the Messenger invites you that you may believe in your Lord and He has indeed made a covenant with you if you are believers" (57 : 8), where "believe in Allāh" means *make sacrifices in the cause of truth*, as the context shows. Thus the word *īmān*, as used in the Qur'ān, signifies either simply a confession of the truth with the tongue, or simply an assent of the heart and a firm conviction of the truth brought by the Prophet, or the doing of good deeds and carrying into practice of the principle accepted, or it may signify a combination of the three. Generally, however, it is employed to indicate an assent of the heart, combined, of course, with a confession with the tongue, to what the prophets bring from God, as distinguished from the doing of good deeds, and hence it is that the righteous, as already remarked, are spoken of as those *who believe and do good*.

Īmān *in Ḥadīth*

In Tradition, the word *īmān* is frequently used in its wider sense, that is to say, as including good deeds, and sometimes simply as standing for good deeds. Thus the Prophet is reported to have said: "*Īmān* (faith) has over sixty branches, and modesty (*ḥayā'*) is a branch of faith" (Bu. 2 : 3). In another tradition the words are: "*Īmān* has over seventy branches, the highest of which is (the belief) that nothing deserves to be worshipped except Allāh (*Lā ilāha ill-Allāh*), and the lowest of which is

[2] *Taṣdīq-un bi-l-qalb.*

[3] *'Amal-un bi-l-jawāriḥ.*

the removal from the way of that which might cause injury to any one'' (M. 1 : 10). According to one report: ''Love of the Anṣār[4] is a sign of faith'' (Bu. 2 : 10); according to another: ''One of you has no faith unless he loves for his brother what he loves for himself'' (Bu. 2 : 7). And a third says: ''One of you has no faith unless he has greater love for me than he has for his father and his son and all the people'' (Bu.2 : 8). The word *īmān* is thus applied to all good deeds and the Bukhārī has as the heading of one of his chapters in the *Kitāb al-Īmān* (Book 2): ''He who says, *Īmān* is nothing but the doing of good;'' in support of which he quotes verses of the Qur'ān. He argues from verses which speak of faith being increased,[5] that good deeds are a part of faith, because otherwise faith could not be thus spoken of.

Kufr *or unbelief*

Just as faith (*īmān*) is the acceptance of the truth brought by the Prophet, so unbelief (*kufr*) is its rejection, and as the practical acceptance of the truth or the doing of a good deed is called *īmān* or part of *īmān*, so the practical rejection of the truth or the doing of an evil deed is called *kufr* or part of *kufr*. The heading of a chapter in the *Bukhārī* is as follows: ''Acts of disobedience (*ma'āṣī*) are of the affairs of *jāhiliyyah*'' (Bu. 2 : 22). Now *jāhiliyyah* (lit. *ignorance*), in the terminology of Islām, means the ''time of ignorance'' before the advent of the Prophet, and is thus synonymous with *kufr* or unbelief. In support of this is quoted a report relating to Abū Dharr who said that he abused a man, addressing him as the son of a Negress, upon which the Prophet remarked: ''Abū Dharr! Thou findest fault with him on account of his mother; surely thou art a man in whom is *jāhiliyyah*'' (Bu. 2 : 22). Thus the mere act of finding fault with a man on account of his negro origin is called *jāhiliyyah* or *kufr*. According to another tradition, the Prophet is reported to have warned his Companions in the following words: ''Beware, do not become unbelievers (*kuffār*, pl. of *kāfir*) after me, so that some of you should strike off the necks of others'' (Bu. 25 : 132). Here the slaying of Muslims by Muslims is condemned as an act of unbelief.

[4] The residents of Madīnah who helped the Prophet on the occasion of his flight to that city are called *Anṣār*, plural of *nāṣir* meaning *a helper*.

[5] ''He it is Who sent down tranquillity into the hearts of the believers that they may have more of faith added to their faith'' (48 : 4). ''And those who believe may increase in faith'' (74 : 31). ''But this increased their faith'' (3 : 172).

In another tradition, it is said: "Abusing a Muslim is transgression and fighting with him is unbelief (*kufr*)" (Bu. 2 : 36). Yet in spite of the fact that the fighting of Muslims with one another is called *kufr* — and those who fight among themselves are even termed *unbelievers* (*kāfirs*) — in these traditions, the Qur'ān speaks of two parties of Muslims at war with one another as believers (*mu'minīn*) (49 : 9).[6] It is, therefore, clear that such conduct is called an act of unbelief (*kufr*) simply as being an act of disobedience. This point has been explained by Ibn Athīr in his well-known dictionary of tradition, the *Nihāyah*. Writing under the word *kufr*, he says: "*Kufr* (unbelief) is of two kinds: one is denial of the faith itself, and that is the opposite of faith; and the other is denial of a *far'* (branch) of the *furū'* (branches) of Islām, and on account of it a man does not get out of the faith itself." As already shown, the *furū'* of Islām are its ordinances, and thus the practical rejection of an ordinance of Islām, while it is called *kufr*, is not *kufr* in the technical sense, *i.e.* a denial of Islām itself. He also tells of an incident which throws light on this question. Azhari was asked whether a man (*i.e.*, a Muslim) became a *kāfir* (unbeliever) simply because he held a certain opinion, and he replied that such an opinion was *kufr* (unbelief): and, when pressed further, added: "The Muslim is sometimes guilty of *kufr* (unbelief)". Thus it is clear that a Muslim remains a Muslim though he may be guilty of an act of unbelief (*kufr*).

A Muslim cannot be called a Kāfir

The concluding portion of the above paragraph makes it clear that a Muslim cannot properly be called a *kāfir* (unbeliever). Every evil deed or act of disobedience being part of *kufr*, even a Muslim may commit an act of unbelief. And the opposite is equally true, namely, that since every good deed is a part of faith, even an unbeliever may perform an act of faith. There is nothing paradoxical in these statements. The dividing line between a Muslim and a *kāfir*, or between a believer and an unbeliever, is confession of the Unity of God and the prophethood of Muḥammad — *Lā ilāha ill-Allāh Muḥammad-un Rasūlu-llāh*. A man becomes a Muslim or a believer by making this confession and as long as

[6] "And if two parties of believers fight, make peace between them, but if one of them acts wrongfully towards the other, fight that which acts wrongfully until it returns to Allāh's command" (49 : 9).

he does not renounce his faith in it, he remains a Muslim or a believer technically, in spite of any opinion he may hold on any religious question, or any evil which he may commit; and a man who does not make this confession is a non-Muslim or unbeliever technically, in spite of any good that he may do. It does not mean that the evil deeds of the Muslim are not punished, or that the good deeds of the non-Muslim are not rewarded. The law of the requital of good and evil is a law apart which goes on working irrespective of creeds, and the Qur'ān puts it in very clear words: "So he who has done an atom's weight of good will see it; and he who has done an atom's weight of evil will see it" (99 : 7,8). A believer is capable of doing evil and an unbeliever is capable of doing good, and each shall be requited for what he does. But no one has the right to expel any one from the brotherhood of Islām so long as he confesses the Unity of God and the prophethood of Muḥammad. The Qur'ān and the Tradition are quite clear on this point. Thus in the Qur'ān we have: "And say not to anyone who offers you salutation, Thou art not a believer" (4 : 94). The Muslim form of salutation—*al-sālamu 'alaikum*, or *peace be to you*—is thus considered a sufficient indication that the man who offers it is a Muslim, and no one has the right to say to him that he is not a believer, even though he may be insincere. The Qur'ān speaks of two parties of Muslims fighting with each other, and yet of both as believers (*mu'min*): "And if two parties of the believers (*mu'minīn*) fight with each other, make peace between them" (49 : 9). It then goes on to say: "The believers are but brethren; so, make peace between your brethren" (49 : 10).

Even those who were known to be hypocrites were treated as Muslims by the Prophet and his Companions, though they refused to join the Muslims in the struggle in which the latter had to engage in self-defence, and when the reputed chief of these hypocrites, the notorious 'Abd Allāh ibn Ubayy, died, the Prophet offered funeral prayers on his grave and treated him as a Muslim. Tradition is equally clear on this point. According to one tradition the Prophet is reported to have said: "Whoever offers prayers as we do and turns his face to our Qiblah and eats the animal slaughtered by us, he is a Muslim for whom is the covenant of Allāh and His Messenger, so do not violate Allāh's covenant" (Bu. 8 : 28). In another report we are told: "Three things are the basis of faith: to withhold from one who confesses faith in *lā ilāha ill-Allāh*,[7] you should not

[7] The *kalimah*, or the declaration of the unity of God and the prophethood of Muḥammad.

call him *kāfir* for any sin, nor expel him from Islām for any deed...'' (AD. 15 : 33). And according to a third, reported by Ibn 'Umar, he said: ''Whoever calls the people of *lā ilāha ill-Allāh* unbeliever (*kāfir*) is himself nearer to unbelief (*kufr*)'' (Tb.). By the 'people of *lā ilāha ill-Allāh*', or the upholders of the Unity, are clearly meant the Muslims, and it is made quite evident that any one who makes a confession of the *Kalimah*, that there is no god but Allāh and Muḥammad is His Messenger, becomes a Muslim, and to call him a *kāfir* is the greatest of sins. Thus it will be seen that membership of the brotherhood of Islām is a thing not to be tested by some great theologian, well-versed in logical quibbling, but rather by the man in the street, by the man of commonsense, or even by the illiterate man who can judge of another by his very appearance, who is satisfied with even a greeting in the Muslim style who requires no further argument when he sees a man turn his face to Qiblah, and to whom Islām means the confession of the Unity of God and the prophethood of Muḥammad.

A doctrine so plainly and so forcefully taught in the Qur'ān and the Tradition stands in need of no support from the great and learned men among the Muslims. But, notwithstanding the schisms and differences that arose afterwards, and the numerous intricacies that were introduced into the simple faith of Islām by the logical niceties of later theologians, the principle stated above is upheld by all authorities on Islām. Thus the author of *Mawāqif* sums up the views of Muslim theologians in the following words: ''The generality of the theologians and the jurists are agreed that none of the *Ahl Qiblah* (the people who recognize the Ka'bah as *qiblah*) can be called a *kāfir*'' (Mf. p. 600). And the famous Abu'l-Ḥasan Ash'arī writes in the very beginning of his book *Maqālāt al-Islāmiyyīn wa Ikhtilāfāt al-Muṣallīn*: ''After the death of their Prophet, the Muslims became divided on many points, some of them called others *dzāll* (straying from the right path), and some shunned others, so that they became sects entirely separated from each other, and scattered parties, but Islām gathers them all and includes them all in its sphere'' (MI. pp. 1, 2).[8] Ṭahāwī, too, is reported as saying that ''nothing can drive a man

[8] Ash'arī states this principle by way of a preliminary to a discussion on the different sects of Islām, and then he goes on to speak of the Muslims as being divided into the Shī'a, the Khwārij, the Murji'ah, the Mu'tazilah, etc. Next he proceeds to discuss the main subdivisions of these heads, those of the Shī'a being the *Ghāliyah* (Extremists) who are again subdivided into fifteen sects, the *Rāfidzah* who are subdivided into twenty-four different sects, and the *Zaidiyah* who have six branches. Fifteen subdivisions of the Khwārij are spoken of, and so on with regard to the other main sects. All these different sects

out of *Īmān* except the denial of what makes him enter it'' (Rd. III, p. 310). Similarly Aḥmad ibn al-Muṣṭafā says that it is only bigoted people who call each other *kāfirs*, for, he adds: ''Trustworthy Imāms from among the Ḥanafīs and the Shāfi'īs and the Mālikīs and the Ḥanbalīs and the Ash'arīs hold that none of the *Ahl Qiblah* can be called a *kāfir*'' (MD. I, p. 46). In fact, it is the Khwārij who first introduced divisions or sectarianism into Islām by calling their Muslim brethren *kāfirs*, simply because they disagreed with their views.

Īmān *and* Islām

The lexicology of *īmān* and *Islām* has already been explained. Originally the word *īmān* signifies *conviction of the heart*, while the word *Islām* signifies *submission* and hence relates primarily to action. This difference in the original meaning finds expression both in the Qur'ān and the Tradition, though in ordinary use they both convey the same significance, and *mu'min* and Muslim are generally used interchangeably. An example of the distinction in their use in the Qur'ān is afforded in 49 : 14: ''The dwellers of the desert say, we believe (*āmannā* from *īmān*); say, you believe not but say, We submit (*aslamnā* from *islām*); and faith has not yet entered into your hearts. And if you obey Allāh and His Messenger, He will not diminish aught of your deeds; for Allāh is Forgiving, Merciful.''[9] This does not mean, of course, that they did

and sub-sects are spoken of by Ash'arī as being Muslims, and not even the *Ghūliyah* are excluded from Islām, though almost all of them believed in one of their leaders as a prophet, and legalized certain things expressly forbidden in the Qur'ān. For instance, the *Bayāniyah* believed in the prophethood of Bayān, their founder; the followers of 'Abd Allāh ibn Mu'āwiyah believed in their founder as Lord and as a prophet; and so it was with many others of them. Even these people are called Muslims because they still believed in the prophethood of Muḥammad and in the Divine origin of the Qur'ān and followed the law of Islām. The modern followers of Ash'arī who call their Muslim brethren *kāfirs* for the slightest differences should take a lesson from this.

[9] The use of *īmān* and Islām in Tradition points occasionally to a similar distinction in use, though ordinarily they are used interchangeably. Thus in the *Kitāb al-Īmān*, Bukhārī relates the following from Abū Hurairah: ''The Prophet; may peace and the blessings of Allāh be upon him, was one day sitting outside among the people when a man came to him and asked: What is *īmān*? He replied: *Īmān* is this that thou believe in Allāh and His angels and in the meeting with Him and His messengers, and that thou believe in life after death. He asked, What is Islām? He replied: Islām is this that thou worship Allāh and do not associate with Him aught, and keep up prayer and pay the obligatory alms (*zakāt*) and keep fast in Ramaḍān''. (Bu. 2 : 37). In another report narrated in the same book, it is stated how when a Companion of the Prophet speaking of another repeat-

not believe in the prophethood of Muḥammad. The significance of faith entering into the heart is made clear in the very next verse: "The believers are those only who believe in Allāh and His Messenger, then they doubt not and struggle hard with their wealth and their lives in the way of Allāh. Such are the truthful ones" (49 : 15). In fact, both the words, *īmān* and Islām, are used to signify two different stages in the spiritual growth of man. A man is said to have believed (*āmana*) when he simply declares his faith in the Unity of God and the prophethood of Muḥammad, which in fact is the first stage of belief, because it is only by declaration of the acceptance of a principle that one makes a start; and a man is also said to have believed (*āmana*) when he carries into practice to their utmost extent the principles in which he has declared his faith. Examples of both these uses have already been given: examples of the first are 2 : 62, 4 : 136; an example of the latter (49 : 15) has just been quoted above. The only difference is that in the first use, belief or *īmān* is in its first stage a confession of the tongue—a declaration of the principle; and in the second, *īmān* has been perfected and indicates the last stage of faith which has then entered into the depths of the heart, and brought about the change required. The same is the case with the use of the word *Islām*; in its first stage it is simply a willingness to submit, as in the verse quoted above (49 : 14); in its last it is entire submission, as in 2 : 112: "Nay, whoever submits himself (*aslama*) entirely to Allāh, and he is the doer of good (to others), he has his reward from his Lord, and there is no fear for such nor shall they grieve." Thus both *īmān* and Islām are the same in their first and last stage—from a simple declaration they have developed into perfection—and cover all the intermediate stages. They have both a starting point and a goal; and the man who is at the starting point, the mere novice, and the man who has attained the goal, in spite of all the differences between them, are both called *mu'min* or Muslim, as are also those who are on their way at different stages of the journey.

edly said that he thought him to be a believer (*mu'min*), the Prophet every time said, Rather a Muslim (Bu. 2 : 19); thus, indicating that men could judge of each other only from outward acts. In the beginning of that book, however, a tradition is narrated from Ibn 'Umar showing that Islām also includes belief: "Islām is based on five fundamentals, the bearing of witness (*shahādah*) that there is no god but Allāh and that Muḥammad is the Messenger of Allāh, and the keeping up of prayer, and the giving of *zakāt*, and the pilgrimage, and fasting in the month of Ramaḍān"(Bu.2 : 1). The word used here is, however, *shahādah* (or, *the bearing of witness*), not *īmān* or *believing*, and *shahādah* in this case, though requiring belief in the truth of what is stated, is still an outward act.

No dogmas in Islām

The above discussion leads us also to the conclusion that there are no dogmas in Islām, no mere beliefs forced upon a man for his alleged salvation. Belief, according to Islām, is not only a conviction of the truth of a given proposition, but it is essentially the acceptance of a proposition as a basis for action. The Qur'ān definitely upholds this view, for, according to it, while the proposition of the existence of devils is as true as that of the existence of angels, a belief in angels is again and again mentioned as part of a Muslim's faith, whereas a disbelief in devils is as clearly mentioned as necessary: "So whoever disbelieves (*yakfur*) in the devil and believes (*yu'min*) in Allāh, he indeed has laid hold on the firmest handle" (2 : 256). The words used here for believing in God and disbelieving in devils are, respectively, *īmān* and *kufr*. If *īmān* meant simply a belief in the existence of a thing, and *kufr* the denial of its existence, a disbelief in devils could not have been spoken of as necessary along with a belief in God. God exists, the angels exist, the devil exists; but while we must believe in God and His angels, we must disbelieve in the devil. This is because the angel, according to the Qur'ān, is the being that prompts the doing of good, and the devil is the being that prompts the doing of evil, so that a belief in angels means really acting upon the promptings to do good, and a disbelief in the devil means refusing to entertain evil promptings. Thus *īmān* (belief) really signifies the acceptance of a principle as a basis for action, and every doctrine of Islām answers to this description. There are no dogmas, no mysteries, no faith which does not require action; for every article of faith means a principle to be carried into practice for the higher development of man.

Principles of faith

The whole of the religion of Islām is briefly summed up in the two short sentences, *Lā ilāha ill-Allāh, i.e.*, there is no god but Allāh, or, nothing deserves to be made an object of love and worship except Allāh, and *Muḥammad-un Rasūlullāh*, Muḥammad is the Messenger of Allāh. It is simply by bearing witness to the truth of these two simple propositions that a man enters the fold of Islām. The first part of the creed is the constant theme of the Qur'ān, and a faith in the Unity of God, in the fact that there is no god except Allāh, is repeatedly mentioned as the basic principle, not only of Islām but of every religion revealed by God. It takes several forms: "Have they a god with Allāh?" "Have they a god besides Allāh?" "There is no god except Allāh;" "There is no god but He;" "There is no god but Thou;" "There is no god but I". The second part of the creed concerning the apostleship of Prophet Muḥammad is also a constant theme of the Qur'ān, and the very words *Muḥammad-un Rasūlullāh* occcur in 48 : 29. From Tradition, too, it appears that the essential condition of the acceptance of Islām was the acceptance of these two component parts of the creed (Bu. 2 : 40).

The above, in the terminology of the later theologians, is called "a brief expression of faith" (*īmān mujmal*), while the detailed expression of faith, which the later theologians call *mufaṣṣal*, is set forth in the very beginning of the Qur'ān as follows: a belief in the Unseen (*i.e.* God), a belief in that which was revealed to the Prophet Muḥammad and in that which was revealed to the Prophets before him, and a belief in the Hereafter (2 : 2-4). Further on in the same chapter, five principles of faith are clearly mentioned: "That one should believe in Allāh and the Last Day and the Angels and the Book and the Prophets." (2 : 177). Again and again, the Qur'ān makes it clear that it is only in relation to these five that belief is required. In the Tradition there is a slight variation. *Bukhārī* has it as follows: "That thou believe in Allāh and His Angels and in the meeting with Him and His Messengers and that thou believe in the Life after death" (Bu. 2 : 37). It will be seen that a belief in the meeting with God is mentioned distinctly here, and while this is included in the belief in God in the Qur'ān in the verse quoted above, it is also mentioned distinctly on many occasions, as in verse 13 : 2. Again, in the Tradition, the Books are not mentioned distinctly and are included in the word "Messengers." Thus the basis of belief rests on five principles, according to the Qur'ān and Tradition: God, His Angels, His Prophets, His Books, and a Life after death.[10]

[10] In some traditions the words are added: "That thou believe in *qadar*"(lit. *the measure*). *Qadar* is, no doubt, spoken of in the Qur'ān as a law of God, but never as an article of faith, and all the Divine laws are accepted as true by every Muslim. See chapter on *Qadar or Taqdeer*.

Significance of faith

As already stated, all articles of faith are in reality principles of action. Allāh is the Being Who possesses all the perfect attributes and when a man is required to believe in Allāh, he is really required to make himself possessor of the highest moral qualities, his goal being the attainment of the Divine Attributes. He must set before himself the highest and purest ideal which the heart of man can conceive, and make his conduct conform to that ideal. Belief in the angels means that the believer should follow the good impulses which are inherent in him, for the angel is the being who prompts the doing of good. Belief in the books of God signifies that we should follow the directions contained in them for the development of our inner faculties. Belief in apostles means that we are to model ourselves on their noble example and sacrifice our lives for humanity even as they did. Belief in the Hereafter or the Last Day tells us that physical or material advancement is not the end or goal of life; but that its real purpose is an infinitely higher one, of which the Resurrection, or the Last Day, is but the beginning.

Chapter II

THE DIVINE BEING

SEC I. — THE EXISTENCE OF GOD

Material, inner and spiritual experience of humanity

In all religious books the existence of God is taken almost as an axiomatic truth. The Qur'ān, however, advances numerous arguments to prove the existence of a Supreme Being Who is the Creator and Controller of this universe. These are, broadly speaking, of three kinds. Firstly, there are the arguments drawn from the creation, which relate to the lower or material experience of humanity; secondly, the evidence of human nature, which concerns the inner experience of humanity; and thirdly, there are arguments based on Divine revelation to man, which may be called the higher or spiritual experience of humanity. It will be seen, from what is said further on, that, as the scope of experience is narrowed down, so the arguments gain in effectiveness. The argument from creation simply shows that there *must be* a Creator of this universe, Who is also its Controller, but it does not go so far as to show that there *is* a God. The testimony of human nature proceeds a step further, since there is in it a consciousness of Divine existence, though that consciousness may differ in different natures according as the inner light is bright or dim. It is only revelation that discloses God in the full splendour of His light, and shows the sublime attributes which man must emulate if he is to attain perfection, together with the means whereby he can hold communion with the Divine Being.

The law of evolution as an evidence of purpose and wisdom

The first argument, drawn from the creation, centres round the word *Rabb*. In the very first revelation that came to the Prophet, he was told to "read in the name of the *Rabb* Who created" (96 : 1). The word *Rabb*, which is generally translated as 'Lord', carries really quite a different significance. According to the best authorities on Arabic lexicology, it combines two senses, that of *fostering, bringing up* or *nourishing*, and that of *regulating, completing* and *accomplishing* (LL., TA.). Thus its underlying idea is that of fostering things from the crudest state to that of highest perfection, in other words, the idea of evolution. Rāghib[1] is even more explicit on this point. According to him, *Rabb* signifies *the fostering of a thing in such a manner as to make it attain one condition after another until it reaches its goal of perfection.* There is thus, in the use of the word *Rabb*, an indication that everything created by God bears the impress of Divine creation, in the characteristic of moving on from lower to higher stages until it reaches perfection. This argument is expanded and made clearer in another very early revelation which runs thus: "Glorify the name of thy *Rabb*, the Most High! Who creates, then makes complete, and Who measures, then guides" (87 : 1-3). The full meaning of *Rabb* is explained here: He creates things and brings them to perfection; He makes things according to a measure and shows them the ways whereby they may attain to perfection. The idea of evolution is fully developed in the first two actions, the creation and the completion, so that everything created by God must attain to its destined completion. The last two actions show how the completion or evolution is brought about. Everything is made according to a measure, that is to say, certain laws of development are inherent in it; and it is also shown a way, that is to say, it knows the line along which it must proceed, so that it may reach its goal of completion. It thus appears that the creative force is not a blind force but one possessing wisdom and acting with a purpose. Even to the ordinary eye, wisdom and purpose are observable in the whole of the Divine creation, from the tiniest particle of dust or blade of grass to the mighty spheres moving in the universe on their appointed courses, because everyone of them is travelling along a certain line to its appointed goal of completion.

In this connection attention may be drawn to another characteristic of God's creation. Everything, we are told, is created in pairs: "And the heaven, We raised it high with power, and We are the maker of the vast extent. And the earth, We have spread it out; how well have We prepared it! And of everything We have created pairs that you may be mindful" (51 : 47-49), "Glory be to Him Who created pairs of all things, of what the earth grows and of their kind and of what they know not!" (36 : 36). "And Who created pairs of all things" (43 : 12). This shows that there are pairs not only in the animal creation but also in "what the earth grows," that is, in the vegetable kingdom, and further in "what they know not". In fact, the idea of pairing is carried to its furthest extent, so that even the heavens and the earth are described as if they were a pair, because of the quality of activity in the one and of passivity in the

[1] A famous lexicologist of the Qur'ān.

other. This deep interrelationship of things is also an evidence of Divine purpose in the whole of creation.

One law prevails in the whole universe

A further point upon which the Qur'ān lays especial stress is the fact that, notwithstanding its immensity and variety, there is but one law for the whole universe: "Who created the seven heavens alike; thou seest no incongruity in the creation of the Beneficent God. Then look again: can thou see any disorder? Then turn the eye again and again — thy look shall come back to thee confused, while it is fatigued" (67 : 3, 4). Here we are told that there is in creation neither incongruity, whereby things belonging to the same class are subject to different laws, nor disorder, whereby the law cannot work uniformly; so that the miraculous regularity and uniformity of law in the midst of the unimaginable variety of conflicting conditions existing in the universe is also evidence of a Divine purpose and wisdom in the creation of things. From the smallest particle to the largest heavenly body, everything is held under control and is subject to a law; no one thing interferes with the course of another or hampers it; while, on the other hand, all things are helping each other on to attain perfection. The Qur'ān stresses this fact frequently: "The sun and the moon follow a reckoning. And the herbs and the trees adore (Him)" (55 : 5, 6). "And the sun moves on to its destination. That is the ordinance of the Mighty, the Knower. And for the moon, We have ordained for it stages till it becomes again as an old dry palm branch. Neither is it for the sun to overtake the moon, nor can the night outstrip the day. And all float on in an orbit" (36 : 38-40). "Then He directed Himself to the heaven and it was a vapour, so He said to it and to the earth: Come both, willingly or unwillingly. They both said: We come willingly" (41 : 11). "Allāh is He Who made subservient to you the sea that the ships may glide therein by His command, and that you may seek of His grace, and that you may give thanks. And He has made subservient to you whatsoever is in the heavens and whatsosever is in the earth, all from Himself. Surely there are signs in this for a people who reflect" (45: 12, 13). "And He created the sun and the moon and the stars, made subservient by His command; surely His is the creation and the command" (7 : 54). All these verses show that, inasmuch as everything is subject to command and control for the fulfilment of a certain purpose, there must be an All-Wise Controller of the whole.

Guidance afforded by human nature

The second kind of argument for the existence of God relates to the human soul. In the first place, there is the consciousness of the existence of God. There is an inner light within each man telling him that there is a Higher Being, a God, a Creator. This inner evidence is often brought out in the form of a question. It is like an appeal to man's inner self. The question is sometimes left unanswered, as if man were called upon to give it a deeper thought: "Or were they created without a (creative) agency? Or are they the creators (of their own souls)? Or did they create the heavens and the earth?" (52 : 35, 36). Sometimes the answer is given: "And if thou ask them, Who created the heavens and the earth? They would say: The Mighty, the Knowing One has created them" (43 : 9). On one occasion, the question is put direct to the human soul by God Himself: "And when thy Lord brought forth from the children of Adam, from their loins, their descendants and made them bear witness about themselves: Am I not your Lord (*Rabb*)? They said: Yes, we bear witness" (7 : 172). This is clearly the evidence of human nature which is elsewhere spoken of as being "the nature made by Allāh in which He has created all men" (30 : 30). Sometimes this consciousness on the part of the human soul is mentioned in terms of its unimaginable nearness to the Divine Spirit: "We are nearer to him than his life-vein" (50 : 16). And again, "We are nearer to it (the soul) than you" (56 : 85). The idea that God is nearer to man than his own self only shows that the consciousness of the existence of God in the human soul is even clearer than the consciousness of its own existence.

If then, the human soul has such a clear consciousness of the existence of God, how is it, the question may be asked, that there are men who deny the existence of God? Here, two things must be borne in mind. In the first place the inner light within each man, which makes him conscious of the existence of God, is not equally clear in all cases. With some, as with the great divines of every age and country, that light shines forth in its full glory, and their consciousness of the Divine presence is very strong. In the case of ordinary men, consciousness is generally weaker and the inner light more dim; there may even be cases in which that consciousness is only in a state of inertia, and the inner light has almost gone out. Secondly, even the atheist or the agnostic recognizes a First Cause, or a Higher Power, though he may deny the existence of a God with particular attributes; and occasionally that consciousness is awakened in him, and the inner light asserts itself, especially in times of distress or affliction. It looks very much as though ease and comfort, like evil, cast a veil over the inner light of man, and the veil is removed by distress — a fact to which the Qur'ān has repeatedly called attention: "And when We show favour to man, he turns away and withdraws himself; but when evil touches him, he is full of lengthy supplications" (41 : 51). "And when harm afflicts men, they call upon their Lord turning to Him" (30 : 33). "And when a wave like awnings covers them they call upon Allāh, being sincere to Him in obedience. But when He brings them safe to the land, some of them follow the middle course" (31 : 32). "And whatever good you have, it is from Allāh; then when evil afflicts you, to Him do you cry for aid" (16 : 53).

There is in man's soul something more than mere consciousness of the existence of God; there is in it a yearning after its Maker — the instinct to turn to God for help; there is implanted in it the love of God for Whose sake it is ready to make every sacrifice. Finally, it cannot find complete contentment without God.

Guidance afforded by Divine revelation

The third group of arguments found in the Qur'ān, to prove the existence of God, relates to Divine revelation — the clearest and surest evidence — which not only establishes the truth of the existence of God but also casts a flood of light on the Divine attributes without which the existence of the Divine Being would remain mere dogma. It is through this disclosure of the Divine attributes that belief in God becomes the most important factor in the evolution of man, since a knowledge of those attributes enables him to set before himself the high ideal of imitating Divine morals; and it is only thus that man can rise to the highest moral eminence. God is the Nourisher of everything in the creation, so His worshipper will do his utmost to serve the cause not only of humanity but also of all creatures. God is Loving and Affectionate to His creatures, so one who believes in Him will be moved by the impulse of love and affection towards His creation. God is Merciful and Forgiving, so His servant must be merciful and forgiving to his fellow-beings. A belief in a God possessing the perfect attributes made known by Divine revelation is the highest ideal which a man can place before himself; and without this ideal there is a void in man's life, a lack of all earnestness and every noble aspiration.

In another way, Divine revelation brings man closer to God and makes

His existence felt as a reality in his life, and that is through the example of the perfect man who holds communion with the Divine Being. That God is a Reality, a Truth — in fact, the greatest reality in this world — that man can feel His presence and realize Him in each hour of his everyday life, and have the closest relations with Him; that such a realization of the Divine Being works a change in the life of man, making him an irresistible spiritual force in the world, is not the solitary experience of one individual or of one nation, but the universal experience of all men in all nations, all countries and all ages. Abraham, Moses, Christ, Confucius, Zoroaster, Rama, Krishna, Buddha and Muḥammad, each and every one of these luminaries brought about a moral, and in some cases also a material, revolution in the world, which the combined resources of whole nations were powerless to resist, and lifted up humanity from the depths of degradation to the greatest heights of moral, and even material, prosperity; which only shows what heights man's soul may rise if only it works in true relationship with the Divine Being.

One example may be considered in greater detail — that of the Holy Prophet Muḥammad. A solitary man arose in the midst of a whole nation which was sunk deep in all kinds of vice and degradation. He had no power at his back, not even a man to second him, and without any preliminaries at all, he set his hand to the unimaginable and apparently impossible task of the reformation, not merely of that one nation but, through it, of the whole of humanity. He started with that one Force, the Force Divine, which makes possible the impossible — "Read in the name of thy Lord!" "Arise and warn and thy Lord do magnify." The cause was Divine, and it was on Divine help that its success depended. With every new dawn the task grew harder, and the opposition waxed stronger, until, to an onlooker, there was nothing but disappointment everywhere. Nonetheless, his determination grew stronger with the strength of the opposition and, while in the earlier revelation there were only general statements of the triumph of his cause and the failure of the enemy, those statements became clearer and more definite as the prospects, to all outward appearance, grew more hopeless. Some of these verses in the order of their revelation are: "By the grace of thy Lord thou art not mad. And thine is surely a reward never to be cut off" (68 : 2, 3). "Surely We have given thee abundance of good" (108 : 1). "Surely with difficulty is ease" (94 : 5). "And surely the latter state is better for thee than the former, and soon will thy Lord give thee so that thou wilt be well pleased" (93 : 4, 5). "Surely it is the word of an honoured Messenger, the possessor of strength, having an honourable place with the Lord of the Throne"

(81 : 19, 20). "And during a part of the night, keep awake by it (*i.e.*, the Qur'ān) ... maybe, thy Lord will raise thee to a position of great glory" (17 : 79). "O man! We have not revealed the Qur'ān to thee that thou mayest be unsuccessful" (20 : 1, 2). "And on that day the believers will rejoice in Allāh's help" (30 : 4, 5). "We certainly help Our Messenger, and those who believe, in this world's life and on the day when the witnesses arise" (40 : 51). "Blessed is He Who, if He please, will give thee better gardens than these: Gardens in which flow rivers. And He will give thee palaces" (25 : 10). 'Allāh has promised those of you who believe and do good that He will surely make them rulers in the earth as He made those before them rulers, and that He will surely establish for them their religion, which He has chosen for them, and that He will surely give them security in exchange after their fear" (24 : 55). "He it is Who sent His Messenger with the guidance and the religion of Truth, that He may make it prevail over all religions" (48 : 28).

In like manner, the end of opposition is described more clearly in the later revelations than in the earlier, although that opposition grew more and more powerful as days went on. The following three verses belong to three different periods: "Till when they see that which they are promised, they will know who is weaker in helpers and less in number" (72 : 24). "Or say they, We are a host allied together to help each other"? Soon shall the hosts be routed and they will show (their) backs" (54 : 44, 45). "Say to those who disbelieve: You shall soon be vanquished" (3 : 11). And all this did happen a few years after these things had been foretold, though at that time there was nothing to justify such prophecies and all the circumstances were against them. No man could possibly have foreseen what was so clearly stated as certain to come about, and no human power could have brought to utter failure the whole nation with all its resources ranged against a solitary man and determined to destroy him. Divine revelation thus affords the clearest and surest testimony of the existence of God, in Whose knowledge, past, present and future are alike and Who controls both the forces of nature and the destiny of man.

SEC. 2 — THE UNITY OF GOD

The Unity of God

All the basic principles of Islām are fully dealt with in the Qur'ān, and so is the doctrine of faith in God, of which the corner-stone is belief in the Unity of God (*tauḥīd*). The best-known expression of Divine Unity is that contained in the declaration of *lā ilāha ill-Allāh*. It is made up of four words, *lā* (no), *ilāh* (that which is worshipped), *illā* (except) and Allāh (the proper name of the Divine Being). Thus these words, which are commonly rendered into English as meaning "there is no god but Allāh," convey the significance that there is nothing which deserves to be worshipped except Allāh. It is this confession which when combined with the confession of the prophethood of Muhammad — *Muḥammad-un Rasūlullāh* —, admits a man into the fold of Islam. The Unity of God, according to the Qur'an, implies that God is One in His person (*dhāt*), One in His attributes (*ṣifāt*) and One in His works (*af'āl*). His Oneness in His person means that there is neither plurality of gods nor plurality of persons in the Godhead; His Oneness in attributes implies that no other being possesses one or more of the Divine attributes in perfection; His Oneness in works implies that none can do that which God has done, or which God may do.[2] The doctrine of Unity is beautifully summed up in one of the shortest and earliest chapters of the Qur'ān: "Say: He, Allāh, is One; Allāh is He on Whom all depend; He begets not; nor is He begotten; and none is like Him" (ch. 112).

The Gravity of **shirk**

The opposite of Unity (*Tauḥīd*) is *shirk*, implying *partnership*.[3] In the Qur'ān, *shirk* is used to signify the associating of gods with God, whether such association be with respect to the person of God or His attributes or His works, or with respect to the obedience which is due to Him alone. *Shirk* is said to be the gravest of all sins: "Surely, ascribing partners to Him (*shirk*) is a grievous iniquity" (31 : 13); "Allāh forgives not that a partner should be set up with Him and forgives all besides that to whom He pleases" (4 : 48). This is not due to a feeling of jealousy on the part of God — in fact jealousy, according to the Qur'ān, is quite unthinkable as an attribute of the Divine Being; it is due to the fact that *shirk* demoralizes man, while Divine Unity brings about his moral elevation. According to the Qur'ān, man is God's vicegerent (*khalīfa*) on earth (2 : 30), and this shows that he is gifted with the power of con-

[2] Some have explained Oneness in attributes as meaning that He does not possess two powers, two knowledges, etc., and Oneness in works as meaning that no other being has influence over Him.

[3] *Sharīk* (pl. *shurakā'*) means a partner.

trolling the rest of the earthly creation. We are told expressly that he has been made to rule the world: "Allāh is He Who made subservient to you the sea that the ships may glide therein by His command, and that you may seek His grace, and that you may give thanks. And He has made subservient to you whatsoever is in the heavens and whatsoever is in the earth, all from Himself; surely there are signs in this for a people who reflect" (45 : 12, 13). Man is thus placed above the whole of creation. He is placed even above the angels who are spoken of as making obeisance to him (2 : 34). If, then, man has been created to rule the universe and is gifted with the power to subdue everything and to turn it to his use, does he not degrade himself by taking other things for gods, by bowing before the very things which he has been created to conquer and rule? This is an argument which the Qur'ān has itself advanced against *shirk*. Thus the words, "Shall I seek a lord other than Allāh, while He is the Lord of all things" (6 : 165), are followed in the next verse by "And He it is Who has made you successors in the land." And again: "Shall I seek for you a god other than Allāh, while He has made you excel all created things?" (7 : 140). *Shirk* is, therefore, of all sins the most serious because it degrades man and renders him unfit for attaining the high position destined for him in the Divine scheme.

Various forms of **shirk**

The various forms of *shirk* mentioned in the Qur'ān are an indication of the ennobling message underlying the teaching of Divine Unity. These are summed up in the verse: "That we shall worship[4] (or serve) none but Allāh and that we shall not associate aught with Him and that some of us shall not take others for lords besides Allāh" (3 : 63). These are really three forms of *shirk*— a fourth is mentioned separately. The most palpable form of *shirk* is that in which anything besides God is worshipped, such as stones, idols, trees, animals, tombs, heavenly bodies, forces of nature, or human beings who are supposed to be demi-gods or gods or incarnations of God or sons or daughters of God. The second

[4] The Arabic word for worship is *ibādah*, which carries originally a wide significance, *the showing of submission to the utmost extent*, or *obedience which is combined with the utmost humility*, but in ordinary usage means the adopting of a reverential attitude of the body towards a thing, while the mind is engrossed with ideas of greatness and mightiness, and the making of supplications to it. It is in this sense that the word *ibādah* is used here.

kind of *shirk*, which is less palpable, is the associating of other things with God, that is, to suppose that other things and beings possess the same attributes as the Divine Being. The beliefs that there are three persons in the Godhead, and that the Son and the Holy Ghost are eternal, Omnipotent and Omniscient like God Himself, as in the Christian creed, or that there is a Creator of Evil along with a Creator of Good, as in Zoroastrianism, or that matter and soul are co-eternal with God and self-existing like Himself, as in Hinduism — all come under this head. The last kind of *shirk* is that in which some men take others for their lords. The meaning of this was explained by the Prophet himself, in answer to a question put to him. When verse 9 : 31 was revealed — "they have taken their doctors of law and their monks for lords besides Allāh" — 'Adiyy ibn Hātim, a convert from Christianity, said to the Prophet that the Jews and the Christians did not worship the doctors of law and the monks. The Prophet asked him if it was not true that they blindly obeyed them in what they enjoined and what they forbade, and 'Adiyy answered in the affirmative. This report shows that to follow the behests of great men blindly was also considered *shirk*. The fourth kind of *shirk* is referred to in the verse: "Hast thou seen him who takes his low desires for his god?" (25 : 43). Here the blind submission to one's own desires is described in words used for *shirk*. Thus belief in the Unity of God means that true obedience is due to God alone, and whosoever obeys either any one else, or his own low desires, in preference to the Divine commandments, is really guilty of *shirk*.

Idolatry

Of the different forms of *shirk*, idolatry is cited more frequently than all the others, and is denounced in the most scathing terms in the Qur'ān. This is because idolatry is the most heinous form of *shirk* and also was the most rampant throughout the world at the advent of Islām. Not only is idolatry condemned in its gross form, which takes it for granted that an idol can cause benefit or do harm, but the idea is also controverted that there is any meaning underlying this gross form of worship: "And those who choose protectors besides Him, (say): We serve them only that they may bring us nearer to Allāh. Surely Allāh will judge between them in that in which they differ" (39 : 3). A similar excuse is put forward today by some of the idolators. It is said that an idol is used only to enable a worshipper to concentrate his attention, and become more deeply engrossed in Divine contemplation. This idea is controverted in the verse quoted above — "that they may bring us nearer to Allāh." But even in this case the worshipper must believe that the idol on which he centres his attention is a symbol of the Divine Being, which is a grossly false notion; and, moreover, it is the idol on which the worshipper's attention is centred, not the Divine Being. It is also wrong to suppose that a material symbol is necessary for concentration, for attention can be every whit as easily concentrated on a spiritual object, and it is only when the object of attention is spiritual that concentration helps the development of will-power. Along with idol-worship, the Qur'ān also prohibits dedication to idols (6 : 137).

Nature worship

Another form of prevailing *shirk* denounced in the Qur'ān is the worship of the sun, the moon, the stars, in fact everything which might appear to control the destinies of man. This is expressly forbidden: "And of His signs are the night and the day and the sun and the moon. Adore not the sun nor the moon, but adore Allāh Who created them" (41 : 37)[5]. The argument advanced against the worship of the sun and the moon not only applies to all heavenly bodies[6] but also, and equally well, to all the forces of nature, which are in fact again and again mentioned as being made subservient to man.

Trinity

The Trinity is also denounced as a form of *shirk*: "So believe in Allāh and His messengers and say not, Three. Desist, it is better for you; Allāh is only One God" (4 : 171). It is sometimes alleged that the Quranic conception of the Trinity is a mistaken one, because it speaks

[5] The argument is also clearly put forth in Abraham's controversy with his people that these things are themselves under the control of a Higher Power: "And thus did We show Abraham the kingdom of the heavens and the earth and that he might be of those who are sure. So when night overshadowed him, he saw a star. Said he, Is this my Lord? And when it set, he said, I love not the setting ones. Then when he saw the moon rising, he said, Is this my Lord? When it set, he said, If my Lord had not guided me, I should be of the erring people. Then when he saw the sun rising, he said, Is this my Lord? Is this the greatest? And when it set, he said, O my people! I am clear of what you set up with Allāh. I have turned myself, being upright, wholly to Him Who originated the heavens and the earth and I am not of the polytheists" (6 : 76 - 80).

[6] The worship of Sirius is alluded to in 53 : 49, where God is called the Lord of Sirius.

of Jesus and Mary as having been taken for two gods: ''O Jesus, son of Mary! Didst thou say to men, Take me and my mother for two gods, besides Allāh?'' (5 : 116). The reference here is to Mariolatry. That Mary was worshipped is a fact, and the Qur'ān's reference to it is significant,[7] but it should be noted that neither the Qur'ān nor the Prophet has anywhere said that Mary was the third person of the Trinity. Where the Qur'ān denounces the Trinity, it speaks of the doctrine of sonship but does not speak of the worship of Mary at all; and where it speaks of the worship of Mary, it does not refer to the Trinity.

Doctrine of sonship

Another form of *shirk*, refuted in the Qur'ān, is the doctrine that God has sons or daughters. The pagan Arabs ascribed daughters to God while the Christians hold that God has a son. Though the doctrine of ascribing daughters to god is mentioned in the Qur'ān several times,[8] yet it is against the Christian doctrine that the Holy Book speaks with gravest emphasis: ''And they say: The Beneficent God has taken to Himself a son. Certainly you have made an abominable assertion! The heavens may almost be rent thereat, and the earth cleave asunder, and the mountains fall down in pieces, that they ascribe a son to the Beneficent God!'' (19 : 88 - 91). The doctrine is denounced repeatedly,[9] even in the earliest revelations,

[7] The doctrine and practice of Mariolatry, as it is called by the Protestant controversialists, is too well-known. In the catechism of the Roman Church the following doctrines are to be found: ''That she is truly the mother of God ...; That she is the mother of Pity and very specially our advocate; that her images are of the utmost utility.'' It is also stated that her intercessions are directly appealed to in the Litany. And further that there were women in Thrace, Scythia and Arabia who were in the habit of worshipping the Virgin as a goddess, the offer of a cake being one of the features of their worship. ''From the time of the Council of Ephesus, to exhibit figures of the Virgin and Child became the approved expression of orthodoxy... Of the growth of the Marian cultus, alike in the East and the West, after the decision at Ephesus, it would be impossible to trace the history... Justinian in one of his laws bespeaks her advocacy for the empire... Narses looks to her for directions on the field of battle. The emperor Heraclius bears her image on his banner. John of Damascus speaks of her as the sovereign lady to whom the whole creation has been made subject by her son. Peter Damian recognizes her as the most exalted of all creatures, and apostrophizes her as deified and endowed with all power in heaven and in earth'' (En. Br., 11th ed. XVII, p. 813).

[8] See 16 : 57; 17 : 40; 37 : 149.

[9] For instance in 2 : 116; 6 : 102-104; 10 : 68; 17 : 111; 18 : 4, 5; 19 : 35, 91, 92; 23: 91; 37 : 151, 152,; 112 :3. Of these, ch. 112 is undoubtedly one of the earliest revelations, while the 17th, 18th and 19th chapters also belong to the early Makkah period.

which shows that from the very first the Qur'ān set before itself the correction of this great error. It will be observed that a mention of the doctrine of sonship is often followed by the word *subḥāna-hū*, which word is used to indicate the purity of God from all defects. The reason for this is that the doctrine of sonship is due to the supposition that God cannot forgive sins unless He receives some satisfaction therefor, and this satisfaction is supposed to have been afforded by the crucifixion of the Son of God, who alone is said to be sinless. The doctrine of sonship is thus practically a denial of the quality of forgiveness in God, and this amounts to attributing a defect to Him. It is for this reason also that a most forcible denunciation of the doctrine of sonship is followed by the words: "It is not worthy of the Beneficent God (*Raḥmān*) that He should take to Himself a son" (19 : 92). the word *Raḥmān* signifies originally the Lord of immeasurable mercy Who requires no satisfaction or compensation for a display of the quality of mercy which is inherent in Him, and the attribute of being *Raḥmān* negatives the doctrine of sonship.

Significance underlying the doctrine of Unity

That various kinds of *shirk* mentioned in the Qur'ān show that, in the doctrine of Unity, it gives to the world an ennobling message of advancement all round, physical as well as moral and spiritual. Man is freed not only from slavery to animate and inanimate objects, but also from subservience to the great and wondrous forces of nature which, he is told, he can subdue for his benefit. It goes further and delivers man from that greatest of slaveries, slavery to man. It does not allow to any mortal the dignity of Godhead, or of being more than a mortal; for the greatest of mortals is commanded to say: "I am only a mortal like you; it is revealed to me that your God is One God" (18 : 110). Thus all the bonds which fettered the mind of man were broken, and he was set on the road to progress. A slave mind, as the Qur'ān plainly says, is incapable of doing anything good and great,[10] and hence the first condition for the advancement of man was that his mind should be set free from the trammels of all kinds of slavery, which was accomplished in the message of Divine Unity.

[10] — see next page.

Unity of human race underlies Unity of God

The doctrine of the Unity of God, besides casting off the bonds of slavery which had enthralled the human mind, and thus opening the way for its advancement, carries another significance equally great, if not greater, to wit, the idea of the unity of the human race. He is the *Rabb* of all the nations (*Rabb al-'ālamīn*). *Rabb* in Arabic signifies the *Fosterer of a thing in such a manner as to make it attain one condition after another until it reaches its goal of completion* (R.). The words *Rabb al-'ālamīn* thus signify that all the nations of the world are, as it were, the children of one Father, and that He takes equal care of all, bringing all to their goal of completion by degrees. Hence God is spoken of in the Qur'ān as granting not only His physical but also His spiritual sustenance, His revelation, to all the nations of the world: "And for every nation there is a messenger" (10 : 47); "There is not a people but a warner has gone among them" (35 : 24). We further find that the Qur'ān upholds the idea that God, being the God of all nations, deals with all of them alike. He hearkens to the prayers of all, whatever their religion or nationality. He is equally merciful to all and forgives the sins of all. He rewards the good deeds of the Muslim and the non-Muslim alike; and not only does He deal with all nations alike, but we are further told that He created them all alike, in the Divine nature: "The nature made by Allāh in which He has created men" (30 : 30). And this unity of the human race, which is thus a natural corollary of the doctrine of the Unity of God, is further stressed in the plain words that "Mankind is a single nation" (2 : 213) and that, "all are but a single nation" (10 : 19).

SEC. 3 — THE ATTRIBUTES OF GOD

Nature of the Divine attributes

Before speaking of the Divine attributes it will be necessary to warn the reader against a certain misconception as to the nature of the Divine

10 "Allāh sets forth a parable: there is a slave, the property of another, controlling naught, and there is one whom We have granted from Ourselves goodly provisions, so he spends from it secretly and openly. Are the two alike?... And Allāh sets forth a parable of two men: one of them dumb, controlling naught and he is a burden to his master; wherever he sends him, he brings no good. Is he equal with him who enjoins justice?" (16 : 75, 76). "He has made subservient to you the sun and the moon pursuing their courses, and He has made subservient to you the night and the day" (14 : 33); "And the stars are

Being. God is spoken of in the Qur'ān as seeing, hearing, speaking, being displeased, loving, being affectionate, grasping, controlling, etc; but the use of these words must not be taken in any sense as indicating an anthropomorphic conception of the Divine Being.[11] For, He is plainly stated to be above all material conceptions: "Vision comprehends Him not and He comprehends all vision" (6 : 104). And He is not only above all material limitations but even above the limitation of metaphor: "Nothing is like Him" (42 : 11). To indicate His love, power, knowledge and other attributes, the same words had to be used as are in ordinary use for human beings, but the conception is not quite the same. Even the "hands" of God are spoken of in the Qur'ān (5 : 64), but it is simply to give expression to His unlimited power in bestowing His favours on whom He will. The word *yad* which means *hand* is also used metaphorically to indicate favour (*ni'ma*) or *protection* (*ḥifāẓa*) (R.). Thus in 2 : 237 occur the words "in whose hand (*yad*) is the marriage tie," where the word *yad* is used in a metaphorical sense. In the *Nihāya*, the word *yad* is explained as meaning *ḥifẓ* (protection) and *difā'* (defence), and in support of this is

made subservient by His command... And He it is Who has made the sea subservient...and thou seest the ships cleaving through it" (16 : 12 - 14); "See you not that Allāh has made subservient to you whatever is in the heavens and whatever is in the earth?" (31 : 20); and so on.

[11] The anthropomorphic view which likens God to man has never found favour among the Muslims. A very insignificant sect known as the Karrāmiyah (after the founder, Muḥammad Karrām) or the Mujassimah (from *jism* meaning body, after the doctrine advocated by them) held the view that God was corporeal, but this has always been rejected by the learned among the Muslims. In one tradition it is no doubt stated that the Prophet, in a vision, felt a touch of the Divine hand between his shoulders, but it is unreasonable to take for reality what was seen in a vision. Ash'arī says: "The Ahl Sunnah and the followers of Ḥadīth hold that God is not a *jism* (corporeal) and He is not like anything else and that He is on the 'Arsh... and that the nature of His *istiwā* is not known (*bi-lā kaif*), and that He is Light" (MI. p. 211). He also says that He has hands the nature of which is not known (*bi-lā kaif*) and eyes the nature of which is not known (*bi-lā kaif*) and so on. It is also laid down as a basic principle regarding the Divine attributes that "He does not resemble His creatures in anything, nor does any of His creatures resemble Him" (FA. p. 14). And further that the attributes of the Divine Being are to be taken as referring to the ultimate end (Bai.). Shāh Walī Allāh is more express and says in clear words that the *basṭ al-yad* in His case means only *being bountiful* (Hj. I p. 63); while regarding Divine attributes in general, he writes in the same strain as Baidzāwī, saying that "their use is only in the sense of the ultimate end of those words," adding that His *raḥmah* for instance only means the bestowal of good things, not an actual inclining of the heart (Hj.).

quoted the hadīth which speaks of Gog and Magog in the words *la-yadāni li-ahad-in bi-qitālihim*, which signify that no one shall have the power (*yadān*, lit., *two hands*) to fight with them. Hence *the hands of God* in 5 : 64 stand for *His favours* according to the Arabic idiom.

Another, and a greater, misunderstanding exists as to the meaning of the expression commonly translated as "uncovering of the leg" (*kashf-'ani-l-sāq*). Here it is nothing but gross ignorance of Arabic idiom that has led some to translate it as such. The expression is used twice in the Qur'ān, once with regard to the queen of Sheba (27 : 44) and once passively without indicating the subject (68 : 42). It has never been used in relation to God. The word *sāq*, which means *shank*, is used in the expression *kashf'ani-l-sāq* in quite a different sense, for *sāq* also means *difficulty* or *distress*, and the expression under discussion means either to *prepare oneself to meet a difficulty* or *the disclosure of distress* (TA., LL.).

'Arsh ***or Throne***

God's *Arsh* or Throne is spoken of, yet does not signify any place, rather representing His control of things as a monarch's throne is a symbol of his power to rule: "The *'Arsh* of Allāh is one of the things which mankind knows not in reality but only in name, and it is not as the imaginations of the vulgar hold it to be ... And it is taken as indicating *might* or *power* and *authority* and *dominion*" (R.). *Istawā 'ala-l-'Arsh* is the form which occurs more often in connection with the mention of *'Arsh*, and a reference to it is invariably made after mentioning the creation of the heavens and the earth, and in relation to the Divine control of creation, and the law and order to which the universe is made to submit by its great Author. *Istawā* followed by *'alā* means *he had mastery* or *control of a thing* or *ascendency over it* (R.). It is nowhere said in the Qur'ān that God sits on *'Arsh*; it is always His controlling power that is mentioned in connection therewith. A similar misunderstanding exists with regard to *kursī* (lit., *throne* or *chair*) which is also supposed by some to be a material thing, whereas no less an authority than Ibn 'Abbās explains the word *kursī* as meaning *'ilm* or *knowledge* (Bai. 2 : 255), and even according to lexicologists *kursī* here may mean *knowledge* or *kingdom* (R.). *Kursī* and *'Arsh*, therefore, stand only for the knowledge and control of God.

Proper name of the Divine Being

Allāh is the proper or personal name — *ism dhāt* — of the Divine Being, as distinguished from all other names which are called *asmā' al-ṣifāt* or names denoting attributes. It is also known as the greatest name of God (*ism a'ẓam*). Being a proper name it does not carry any significance, but being the proper name of the Divine Being it comprises all the attributes which are contained separately in the attributive names. Hence the name Allāh is said to gather together in itself all the perfect attributes of God. The word Allāh being a proper name is *jāmid*, that is to say, it is not derived from any other word. Nor has it any connection with the word *ilāh*[12] (god or object of worship). It is sometimes said that Allāh is a contracted form of *al-ilāh*, but that is a mistake, for if *al* in Allāh were an additional prefix, the form *yā Allāh*, which is correct, would not have been permitted, since *yā al-ilāh* or *yā al-Raḥmān* are not permissible. Moreover, this supposition would mean that there were different gods (*āliha*, pl. of *ilāh*), one of which became gradually known as *al-ilāh* and was then contracted into Allāh. This is against facts, since Allāh "has ever been the name of the Eternal Being" (DI.). Nor has the word Allāh ever been applied to any but the Divine Being, according to all authorities on Arabic lexicology. The Arabs had numerous *ilāhs* or gods but none of them was ever called Allāh, while a Supreme Being called Allāh was recognized above them all as the Creator of the universe (29 : 61), and no other deity, however great, was so regarded.

Four chief attributes

Among the attributive names of the Divine Being occurring in the Qur'ān, four stand out prominently, and these four are exactly the names mentioned in the Opening chapter (*Fātiḥah*), which by a consensus of opinion, and according to a saying of the Prophet, is the quintessence of the Book. The chapter opens with the proper name Allāh, and then follows the greatest of all attributive names *Rabb* which, for want of a proper equivalent, is translated "Lord". Its real significance, according to the best authority on Quranic lexicology, is the *Fosterer of*

[12] Which is either derived from the root *āliha* meaning *taḥayyara* or *he became astonished*, or it is a changed form of *wilāh* from the root *waliha*, which means *he became infatuated*.

a thing in such a manner as to make it attain one condition after another until it reaches its goal of completion (R.). *Rabb*, therefore, means the Lord Who brings all that is in this universe to a state of perfection through various stages of growth,[13] and as these stages include the lowest and the remotest, which, as we go back farther and farther, dwindle into nothingness, the word *Rabb* carries with it the idea of the Author of all existence. *Rabb*, is thus the chief attribute of the Divine Being, and hence it is that prayers are generally addressed to *Rabb*, and begin with the words *Rabba-nā*, that is, our Lord.[14] Indeed after the proper name Allāh, the Qur'ān has given the greatest prominence to the name *Rabb*.

The order adopted by the Qur'ān in speaking of the Divine attributes is a highly scientific one. Allāh, the proper name, comes first of all in the Opening chapter, and this is followed by *Rabb*, the most important of the attributive names. Their relative importance is further shown by the fact that while the name Allāh is found in the Qur'ān some 2,800 times, the name *Rabb* occurs about 960 times, no other name being so frequently mentioned. Next in importance to *Rabb* are the names *Raḥmān, Raḥīm*[15] and *Mālik* which follow *Rabb* in the Opening chapter. These three names in fact show how the attribute of *rabūbiyya*, or bringing to perfection by fostering, is brought into play. *Raḥmān* signifies that love is so predominant in the Divine nature that He bestows His favours and shows His mercy even though man has done nothing to deserve

[13] The theory of evolution, to which a reference is undoubtedly contained in the word *Rabb*, is expressly referred to on several occasions in the Qur'ān. Thus, speaking of the first state of the heavens and the earth, it says: "The heavens and the earth were closed up so We rent them" (21 : 30). This, no doubt, refers to an early stage in evolution when there was a state of chaos, out of which the present highly complicated but completely regulated system has grown up. And speaking of the creation of man, it says: "And indeed He has created you by various stages" (71 : 14), showing that man has been brought to the present stage of physical perfection after passing through various conditions. In another place it is said that man "shall certainly ascend to one state after another" (84 : 19), which is in all likelihood a reference to the spiritual evolution of man.

[14] It should be noted here that Jesus Christ addressed the Divine Being as *Ab* or Father, instead of which the Qur'ān adopts *Rabb*. Now while *Ab* or Father carries with it the idea of paternal affection combined with fostering, the word *Rabb* carries a far grander idea, the idea of the unbounded love and affection of the Author of all existence, Who has not only given to the whole creation its means of nourishment but has also ordained beforehand for all a sphere of capacity and within that sphere provided the means by which they may continue to attain gradually to their goal of perfection. It shows how highly the Quranic revelation has developed the simpler ideas of previous revelations.

[15] — see next page.

them. The granting of the means of subsistence for the development of physical life, and of Divine revelation for man's spiritual growth, are due to this attribute of unbounded love in the Divine Being. Then follows the stage in which man takes advantage of these various means which help the development of his physical and spiritual life, and turns them to his use. It is at this stage that the third attribute of the Divine Being, *Raḥīm,* comes into play, whereby He rewards every effort made by man in the right direction; and since man is making constant and continual efforts, the attribute of mercy conveyed in the name *Raḥīm* is also displayed continually. This is true both as regards the physical and spiritual development of man. The Prophet himself is reported to have said: "*Al-Raḥmān* is the Beneficent God Whose love and mercy are manifested in the creation of this world, and *al-Raḥīm* is the Merciful God Whose love and mercy are manifested in the state that comes after" (BM. I, p. 17).

To bring creation to perfection, however, the manifestation of yet another attribute is needed. As submission to the law results in the advancement of man which brings reward, disobedience to the law must result in retarding his progress or bringing down punishment upon him. In fact, the punishment of wrong is as necessary in the Divine scheme as is the reward of good, and punishment is really only a different phase of the exercise of the attribute of *rabūbiyyah* (fostering); for ultimate good is still the object. Therefore, just as *Raḥīm* is needed to bring his reward to one who does good or submits to the law, there must be another attribute to bring about the requital of evil. Hence in the Opening chapter of the Qur'ān, *Raḥīm* is followed by *Māliki yaum al-dīn* or "Master of the Day of Requital." The adoption of the word *Mālik*, or Master, in connection with the requital of evil is significant, as, ordinarily, it would be expected that there should be a judge to mete out the requital of evil. The essential difference between a judge and a master is that the former is bound to do justice and must punish the evil-doer for every evil, while the latter, the master, can exercise his discretion, and may either punish the evil-doer or forgive him and pass over even the greatest of his iniquities.[16] This idea is fully developed in the Qur'ān, where we are

[15] *Raḥmān* and *Raḥīm* are derived from the one root *raḥma*, which means *tenderness requiring the exercise of beneficence*, and thus comprise the ideas of love and mercy. *Raḥmān* is of the measure of *fa'lān* and gives expression to the preponderance of *raḥma* in Divine nature, and *Raḥīm* is of the measure of *fa'īl* and gives expression to the repetition of the quality of *raḥma*.

[16] See next page.

repeatedly told that while good is rewarded ten times over or even more, evil is either forgiven or requited with its equivalent. In one place, indeed, the unbounded mercy of the Divine Being is said to be so great that "He forgives the sins altogether" (39 : 53). Hence the attributive name *Mālik* is introduced to link the idea of requital with that of forgiveness, and that is why, while the Opening chapter mentions the name *Mālik* as the next in importance to *Raḥīm*, in the body of the Qur'ān it is the name *Ghafūr* (Forgiving) which occupies that place of importance, the first two, *Raḥmān* and *Raḥīm*, along with the cognate verb forms, occurring some 560 times, and *Ghafūr*, the next in point of frequency, occurring in its noun and verb forms about 230 times. Hence it will be seen that the Qur'an gives prominence to the attributes of love and mercy in God to an extent whereof the parallel is not to be met with in any other revealed book.

Ninety-nine names

From the explanations thus given of the four names *Rabb, Raḥmān, Raḥīm* and *Mālik*, from the frequency of their mention in the Qur'ān, to which no approach is made by any other name, and from their mention in the Opening chapter of the Qur'ān, it is clear that these four names are the chief attributive names of the Divine Being, and all His other attributes are but offshoots of these four essential attributes. On the basis of a report from Abū Hurairah, which, however, is regarded as weak (*gharīb)* by Tirmidhī, ninety-nine names of God are generally mentioned, the hundredth being Allāh; but while some of them occur in the Qur'ān, others are only inferred from some act of the Divine Being, as finding expression in the Holy Book. There is, however, no authority whatsoever for the practice of repeating these names on a rosary or otherwise. Neither the Prophet, nor any of his Companions ever used a rosary. In the Qur'ān, it is said: "And Allāh's are the best names, so call on Him thereby, and leave alone those who violate the sanctity of His names"

[16] It is here that the makers of the Christian creed have made their greatest error. They think that the Son of God is needed to atone or make compensation for the evil deeds of humanity, since God, being a judge, cannot forgive sins unless somebody can be found to provide a compensation. In the Qur'ān we are told that God is a Master and He can, therefore, forgive. In fact, the Lord's Prayer belies the Christian creed, because there we are told to pray that God may forgive us our sins as we forgive our debtors. How do we forgive a debtor? Not by pocketing the money but by relinquishing the debt. And if man can forgive, why not God?

(7 : 180). The context shows that calling on God by His excellent names only means that nothing derogatory to His dignity should be attributed to Him; for, in the second part of the verse, those who violate the sanctity of the Divine names are rebuked,[17] and the violation of the sanctity of the Divine names has been clearly explained to mean either ascribing to God attributes which do not befit His high dignity, or ascribing Divine attributes to that which is not Divine. Hence calling on God by His excellent names merely means that only those high attributes should be ascribed to Him which befit His dignity. The particular names of God mentioned in the Qur'ān are:

1. As relating to His person, *al-Wāḥid* or *Aḥad* (the One), *al-Ḥaqq* (the True), *al-Quddūs* (the Holy), *al-Ṣamad* (on Whom all depend while He does not depend on any), *al-Ghanī* (the Self-sufficient), *al-Awwal* (the First), *al-Ākhir* (the Last), *al-Ḥayy* (the Ever-living), *al-Qayyūm* (the Self-subsisting).

2. As relating to the act of creation, *al-Khāliq* (the Creator), *al-Bāri'* (the Creator of the soul), *al-Muṣawwir* (the Fashioner of shapes), *al-Badī'* (the Originator).

3. As relating to the attributes of love and mercy, (besides *Rabb, al-Raḥmān*, and *al-Raḥīm), al-Ra'ūf* (the Affectionate), *al-Wadūd* (the Loving), *al-Laṭīf* (the Benignant), *al-Tawwāb* (the Oft-returning to mercy), *al-Ḥalīm* (the Forbearing), *al-'Afuww* (the Pardoner), *al-Shakūr* (the Multiplier of rewards), *al-Salām* (the Author of peace), *al-Mu'min* (the Granter of security), *al-Barr* (the Benign), *Rāfi' al-darajāt* (the Exalter of ranks), *al-Razzāq* (the Bestower of sustenance), *al-Wahhāb* (the Great Giver), *al-Wāsi'* (the Ample-giving).

4. As relating to His greatness and glory, *al-'Azīm* (the Grand), *al-'Azīz* (the Mighty), *al-'Aliyy* or *Muta'āl* (the Exalted or the High), *al-Qawiyy* (the Strong), *al-Qahhār* (the Supreme), *al-Jabbār* (one Who sets things aright by supreme power),[18] *al-Mutakabbir* (the Possessor of greatness), *al-Kabīr* (the Great), *al-Karīm* (the Honoured), *al-Ḥamīd*

[17] Sanctity of the Divine names may be violated in three ways: (1) By giving the holy names of God to other beings; (2) by giving God names which do not befit him; and (3) by calling God by names of which the meaning is unknown (Rz.). According to Rāghib, violation of the sanctity of the Divine names is of two kinds: (1) giving Him an improper or inaccurate attribute, and (2) interpreting His attributes in a manner which does not befit Him (R.).

[18] See next page.

(the Praiseworthy), *al-Majīd* (the Glorious), *al-Matīn* (the Strong), *al-Ẓāhir* (Ascendant over all), *Dhu-l-jalāli wa-l-ikrām* (the Lord of glory and honour).

5. As relating to His knowledge, *al-'Alīm* (the Knowing), *al-Ḥakīm* (the Wise), *al-Samī'* (the Hearing), *al-Khabīr* (the Aware), *al-Baṣīr* (the Seeing), *al-Shahīd* (the Witness), *al-Raqīb* (the Watcher), *al-Bāṭin* (the Knower of hidden things), *al-Muhaimin* (the Guardian over all).

6. As relating to His power and control of things, *al-Qādir* or *Qadir* or *Muqtadir* (the Powerful), *al-Wakīl* (the One having all things in His charge), *al-Waliyy* (the Guardian), *al-Ḥafīz* (the Keeper), *al-Malik* (the King), *al-Mālik* (the Master), *al-Fattāḥ* (the Greatest Judge), *al-Ḥāsib* or *Ḥasīb* (the One Who takes account), *al-Muntaqim* or *Dhuntiqām* (the Inflictor of retribution), *al-Muqīt* (the Controller of all things).

The other names which are taken from some act or attribute of God mentioned in the Holy Qur'ān are *al-Qābidz* (the One Who straitens),

[18] Considerable misconception prevails as to the true significance of the name *al-Jabbār*, a recent writer in the *Encyclopaedia of Islam* going so far as to translate it by the word *Tyrant*, while the next name *al-Mutakabbir* is rendered, by the same writer, *Haughty*. This rendering is no doubt due to an obsession on the part of Christian writers that the God of Islām is an embodiment of cruelty, tyranny and frightfulness, and that a Loving and Merciful God is peculiar to the Christian religion. If the writer had consulted even Hughes' *Dictionary of Islam*, he would not have made such a blunder. Hughes renders *al-Jabbār* as meaning *Repairer*, and *al-Mutakabbir* as meaning *the Great*. The rendering in the *Encylopaedia* is distortion of the worst type. Becuase, he says, the word *jabbār* has been used for men in a bad sense, the same sense is conveyed when it is spoken of God. There are hundreds of words in every language which are used in a good as well as in a bad sense, and no reasonable person would contend that because a word has been used in a bad sense, it cannot be used in a good one. The Qur'ān lays it down plainly that God's are the most excellent names; would the rendering *haughty* or *tyrant* be in consonance with that statement? Again the Qur'ān declares on more occasions than one that God is "not in the least unjust" to men (41 : 46; 50 : 29), and that He does not do injustice to the weight of an atom (4 : 40). Can we in the face of this description of God call Him a tyrant? If we go to Arabic lexicology, we find that the word *jabr,* from which *al-jabbār* is derived, means originally *repairing* or *setting a thing aright by supreme power (islāk al-shai'i bi-dzarb-in min-al-qahri).* (R.). The same authority goes on to say that it is used to indicate simply *repairing* or *setting aright*, and sometimes simply *dominance* or *supreme power.* When man makes a wrong use of dominance, he becomes a *jabbār* in a bad sense. But in the Qur'ān itself, this word *jabbār* is used of men simply in the sense of *mighty*. When Moses asked his people to enter the Holy Land, they said: "O Moses! There are *mighty men (jabbārīn)* in it, and we will on no account enter it until they go out from it (5 : 22). All authorities are agreed that *al-Jabbār*, spoken of God, means either *One Who sets aright by supreme power* or *the Supreme One Who is above His creation*.

al-Bāsit (the One Who amplifies), *al-Rāfi'* (the One Who exalts), *al-Mu'izz* (the One Who gives honour), *al-Mudhill* (the One Who brings disgrace), *al-Mujīb* (the One Who accepts prayers), *al-Bāi'th* (the One Who raises the dead to life), *al-Muḥṣī* (the One Who records or numbers things), *al-Mubdi'* (the One Who begins), *al-Mu'īd* (the One Who reproduces), *al-Muḥyī* (the One Who gives life), *al-Mumīt* (the One Who causes death), *Mālik al-mulk* (the Master of the kingdom), *al-Jāmi'* (the One Who gathers), *al-Mughnī* (the One Who enriches), *al-Mu'ṭi* (the One Who grants), *al-Māni'* (the One Who withholds), *al-Hādī* (the One Who guides), *al-Bāqī* (the One Who endures for ever), *al-Wārith* (the One Who inherits everything).

Of the rest of the ninety-nine names, *al-Nūr* (the Light) is not really a name of the Divine Being — God is called *Nūr* in the sense of being the Giver of light (24 : 35); *al-Sabūr* (the Patient), *al-Rashīd* (the One Who directs), *al-Muqsiṭ* (the Equitable), *al-Wālī* (the One Who governs), *al-Jalīl* (the Majestic), *al-'Adl* (the Just), *al-Khāfidz* (the One Who abases), *al-Wājid* (the Existing), *al-Muqaddim* (the One Who brings forward), *al-Mu'akhkhir* (the One Who puts off), *al-Dzarr* (the One Who brings distress), *al-Nāfi'* (the One Who confers benefits), may be taken from the sense. Two more attributes falling under this head will be referred to later on because they require a detailed treatment; these are the attributes of *speech* and *will*, which are dealt with in the chapters *Revealed Books* and *Predestination (Qadar)*, respectively.

Predominance of love and mercy in Divine nature

It will be seen that the attributes of God given above have nothing to do with the autocracy, inexorability, vengeance and cruelty which European writers have generally associated with the picture of Him as drawn in the Qur'ān. On the contrary, the qualities of love and mercy in God are emphasized in the Qur'ān more than in any other sacred book. Not only does every chapter open with the two names *Rahmān* and *Rahīm*, thus showing that the qualities of love and mercy are predominant in Divine nature, but the Holy Book goes further and lays the greatest stress in explicit words on the immeasurable vastness of the Divine mercy. The following may be taken as examples:

"He has ordained mercy on Himself" (6 : 12, 54). "Your Lord is the Lord of all encompassing mercy" (6 : 148). "And My mercy encompasses all things" (7 : 156). "Except those on whom thy Lord has mercy, and for this did He create them" (11 : 119). "O My servants who have been prodigal regarding their own souls, despair not of the mercy of Allāh, surely Allāh forgives sins altogether" (39 : 53). "Our Lord! Thou embracest all things in mercy and knowledge" (40 : 7).

So great is the Divine mercy that it encompasses believers and unbelievers alike as the above verses show. Even the enemies of the Prophet are spoken of as having mercy shown to them: "And when We make people taste of mercy after an affliction touches them, lo! they devise plans against Our messages" (10 : 21). The polytheists are repeatedly spoken of as calling upon God in distress, and God as removing their distress. The picture of the Divine attributes portrayed in the Qur'ān is, first and last, a picture of love and mercy, and while these are mentioned under many different names and repeated hundreds of times, His attribute of punishment — Exactor of retribution — occurs but four times in the whole of the Qur'ān.[19] It is true that the punishment of evil is a subject on which the Qur'ān is most emphatic, but its purpose in this case is simply to impress upon man that evil is a most hateful thing which ought to be shunned; and, by way of set-off, not only does it lay great stress on the reward of good deeds, but goes further and declares over and over again that evil is either forgiven or punished only with the like of it, but that good is rewarded tenfold, and hundredfold, or even without measure. But at the same time it must be borne in mind that punishment itself, as described in the Qur'ān, is of a remedial nature, and has in it nothing of vengeance — it is the treatment of a disease which man has brought upon himself. It is still love, for its object is still to set a man on the road to spiritual progress by healing the disease. One of the names of God, included in the ninety-nine names by the later theologians, though not mentioned in the Qur'ān, is *al-Dzārr* or One Who causes distress, but this bringing about of distress is only in the limited sense that it is a punishment for wrong-doing with the underlying object of reformation: "We seized them with distress and affliction in order that they might humble themselves" (6 : 42, 7: 94).

[19] 3 : 3; 5 : 95; 14 : 47; 39 : 37.

Divine attributes as the great ideal to be attained

Just a belief in the Unity of God is a source of man's uplift, making him conscious of the dignity of human nature, and inspiring him with the grand ideas of the conquest of nature and of the equality of man with man, so the numerous attributes of the Divine Being, as revealed in the Qur'ān, are really meant for the perfection of human character. The Divine attributes really serve as an ideal to which man must strive to attain. God is *Rabb al-'ālamīn,* the Fosterer and Nourisher of the worlds; keeping that as an ideal before himself, man must endeavour to make the service of humanity, even that of dumb creation, the object of his life. God is *Raḥmān,* conferring benefits on man and showing him love without his having done anything to deserve it; the man who seeks to attain to perfection must do good even to those of his fellow-men from whom he has not himself received, and does not expect to receive, any benefit. God is *Raḥīm,* making every good deed bear fruit; man must also do good for any good that he receives from another. God is *Mālik,* requiting evil, not in a spirit of vengeance or even of unbending justice, but in a spirit of forgiveness, in the spirit of a master dealing with his servant; so must man be forgiving in his dealings with others, if he will attain to perfection.

The above are the four chief attributes of the Divine Being, and it is easily seen how they serve as ideals for man. So it is with all His other attributes. Take, for example, those of love and mercy. God is Affectionate, Loving-kind, Benignant, Oft-returning to mercy, Forbearing, Pardoner, Multiplier of rewards, Author of peace, Granter of security, Restorer of loss, Benign, Exalter of ranks, Ample-giving, Bestower of sustenance and so on; all this man must also try to be. Again let us take His attributes of knowledge. God is Knowing, Wise, Aware, Seeing, Watcher, Knower of hidden things; man must also try to perfect his knowledge of things and acquire wisdom. In fact, where man is spoken of as having been made a vicegerent of God, his chief characteristic, that which marks him out as the ruler of creation, is stated to be a knowledge of things.[20] And as regards wisdom, the Qur'ān says that the Prophet was raised to teach wisdom.[21] Then there are His attributes of power and

[20] See 2 : 30 and 2 : 31.

[21] 2 : 151; 3 : 163; 62 : 2.

greatness and control of all things; even the angels are commanded to make obeisance to man, showing that man is destined to exercise control over them too. Man is told again and again that everything in the heavens and in the earth has been made subservient to him. It is true that man's love, mercy, knowledge, wisdom, and control of things are all insignificant as compared with their Divine models, but however imperfectly he may achieve it, the fact remains that he has before him the ideal of Divine morals, which he must try to imitate.

CHAPTER III

ANGELS

Angels are immaterial beings

The Arabic word for angel is *malak*, of which the plural form is *malā'ika*.[1] The Qur'ān speaks of the creation of man from dust and of the creation of *jinn* from fire, but it does not speak of the origin of *angels*. There is, however, a report from 'Ā'ishah, according to which the Prophet said that the *jinn* are created from fire (*nār*), and that the angels are created from light (*nūr*) (M. 52 : 22). This shows that the angels are immaterial beings, and further, that the *jinn* and the angels are two different classes of beings, and that it is a mistake to consider them as belonging to one class. In the Qur'ān angels are spoken of as "messengers (*rusul*) flying on wings"[2] (35 : 1). Their description as *rusul*[3] has reference to their spiritual function of bearing Divine messages. Sacred history, indeed, represents angels as possessing wings, but so far as the Qur'ān is concerned, it would be a grievous mistake to confuse the (*janāḥ*) wing of an angel with the fore-limb of a bird which fits it for flight. The wing is a symbol of the *power* which enables those immaterial beings to execute their functions with all speed; and in Arabic, the word *janāḥ* is used in a variety of senses. In birds it is the wing; the two sides of a thing are called its *janāḥain* (two *janāḥs*); and in man, his hand is spoken of as his *janāḥ* (R.). The word has further been used metaphorically in the Qur'ān in several places, as in 15 : 88 and 26 : 215, where the "lowering of the *janāḥ*" stands for "being kind." The Arabic proverb, *huwa maqṣūṣ al-janāḥ* (lit., he has his *janāḥ* — wing — clipped), really means, *he lacks the power to do a thing* (LL.), which also shows that *janāh* is used for *power* in Arabic. In the immaterial beings called

1 The root from which the word is derived is *'alk* or *'alūka* meaning *risāla* or *the bearing of messages*. The *hamza*(') was dropped from the singular form which was originally *ma'lak* and afterwards changed into *mal'ak* (hence the plural *malā'ika*), such changes being very common in the Arabic language. Some authorities, however, consider the form *malak* to be the original form and trace it to the root *malk* or *milk* meaning *power*, and this difference of opinion has been turned by D.B. Macdonald into an *argument* that the word is borrowed from the Hebrew, though he admits that "there is no trace of a verb in Hebrew (nor in Phoenician, where the noun occurs in later inscriptions)" (En. Is., art. *Malā'ika*).

2 *Ajniha* pl. of *janāḥ*.

3 Pl. of *rasūl*, meaning *a messenger*.

angels who are created from light (*nūr*), and in whom therefore a material *janāḥ* cannot be thought of, it is simply the symbol of a *power* which is speedily brought into action.

Can angels be seen?

It is commonly thought that the immaterial beings, whom we call angels, can assume any shape they like, but the Qur'ān gives no countenance to this idea. On the contrary, it is repeatedly stated in answer to the demands of the Prophet's opponents, who desired to see an angel or to have an angel as a messenger, that angels could not be seen and that an angel would have been sent as a messenger had angels, and not human beings, lived on earth: "And nothing prevents people from believing when the guidance comes to them except that they say, Has Allāh raised up a mortal to be a messenger? Say, Had there been in the earth angels walking about secure, We would have sent down to them from the heaven an angel as a messenger" (17 : 94, 95). Twice it is related in the Qur'ān that the angelic hosts sent to help the Muslims were not seen by human eye: "Then Allāh sent down His calm upon His Apostle and upon the believers, and sent hosts which you saw not" (9 : 26); "Call to mind the favour of Allāh to you when there came against you hosts, so We sent against them a strong wind and hosts that you saw not" (33 : 9). The Qur'ān further states that the devils or *jinn* cannot be seen by human eye: "He sees you, he as well as his host, from whence you see them not" (7 : 27).

Abraham's guests

Two cases have, however, to be considered. In the first place, there is a story related about Abraham's guests[4] who first came to him and gave him the good news of a son, Isaac, and then went to Lot and bade him leave the city along with his followers, since punishment was about to overtake his people. It is generally supposed that these were angels, as angels alone are deputed to deliver messages to prophets, and the Bible says that they were angels. But the Qur'ān speaks of them only as the guests of Abraham and as "Our messengers," and nowhere says that they were angels. Had they been angels, they would have delivered the

[4] 11 : 69, 70; 15 : 51, 52; 51 : 24, 25

Divine message to Abraham and Lot in the manner in which the angels deliver such messages, which is by revealing the Divine message to the heart of the prophet: "He revealed it to thy heart by Allāh's command" (2 : 97); and the angel, though he may come in the shape of a man, is not seen by the physical eye of the prophet but by his spiritual eye. Therefore, if the guests spoken of were angels, their appearance to both Abraham and Lot must have been in vision, in which state it is that revelation comes to the prophets of God; but if it was with the physical eye that Abraham and Lot beheld them, then they were men and not angels. The fact that they did not take any food when it was offered by Abraham merely shows that they did not need it, or that they were fasting at the time. Abraham had received the news of a son independently of them and Lot had also been informed of the impending fate of his people without their agency.[5]

Hārūt and Mārūt

The other case is that of Hārūt and Mārūt. Special stress has been laid on this point by Western writers generally, and by the Christian missionaries in particular, and the inference is drawn, from what is related of them in the Qur'ān, that angels are not immaterial creatures and that they have desires like human beings; and thus it is sought to contradict the whole teaching of the Qur'ān on angels by a story which is based neither on the Qur'ān nor on any authentic tradition. In fact, the Qur'ān rejects the story which was current among the Magi and the Jews about these two angels. According to Sale, the Persian Magi "mention two rebellious angels of the same names, now hung up by the feet, with their heads downwards, in the territory of Babel." And he adds: "The Jews have something like this, of the angel Shamhozai, who, having debauched himself with women, repented, and by way of penance hung himself up between heaven and earth." These stories, and others ascribing evil practices to Solomon, were rejected by the Qur'ān in the following words: "And Solomon disbelieved not, but the devils disbelieved, teaching men enchantment. And it was not revealed to the two angels in Babel, Hārūt and Mārūt. Nor did they teach it to any one, so that they should have said, We are only a trial, so disbelieve not" (2 : 102). The statement made

[5] "And We made known to him (*i.e.*, to Lot) this decree that the roots of these should be cut off in the morning" (15 : 66).

here amounts to this. The Jews instead of following the word of God went after certain evil crafts which they attributed to Solomon and to two angels at Babel. Solomon is declared to be innocent of evil practices, and the story of the two angels a fabrication. All reliable commentators have taken the same view of the Quranic statement. The tradition which is quoted in support of the other view is not to be met with in the six reliable collections, but only in the *Musnad* of Aḥmad, and the *Musnad* contains many untrustworthy reports. Moreover, nothing which contradicts the very principles laid down in the Qur'ān can be accepted on the basis of such weak authority. The commentators have actually condemned the alleged report as untrue (*fāsid*) and repudiated (*mardūd*) (Rz.). Another authority says that nothing in this story can be traced to the Prophet and calls it puerile and worthless (*Khurāfāt*) (RM.). Hence the alleged story of Hārūt and Mārūt which is rejected by the Qur'ān, and is not based on any authentic tradition, cannot be made a basis for rejecting the principles laid down in the Qur'ān that angels cannot be seen.

Nature of angels

Though angels are spoken of as *beings*, they are not endowed with powers of discrimination like those of human beings; in this respect, indeed, they may be said to partake more of the attributes of the powers of nature than of man. Their function is to obey and they cannot disobey. The Qur'ān says plainly: "They do not disobey Allāh in that which He commands them, but (they) do as they are commanded" (66 : 6); which also shows that the story of Hārūt and Mārūt, which ascribes disobedience to angels, is without foundation. And inasmuch as man is endowed with a will while the angel is not, man is superior to the angel; which superiority is also evident from the fact that angels were commanded to make obeisance to him (2 : 34).

The angel's coming to the Prophet

It is true that the angel Gabriel is spoken of as coming to the Prophet with the Divine revelation, but as has been already shown, it was with the spiritual senses that the Holy Prophet received the revelation, and therefore it was not with the physical eye that he beheld Gabriel. The angel came to him sometimes in the shape of a man; the Prophet heard the words of revelation, on occasions, with the force of the ringing of a bell; yet those who were sitting next to him, while fully conscious of the change coming over him, neither saw the angel, nor heard the words of the revelation. Numerous incidents are related in which the Prophet received the revelation while he was sitting among his Companions, yet not one of the Companions ever saw the angel, or even heard his voice. And even when Gabriel came to him at other times, it was always with the spiritual eye that the Prophet saw him. 'Ā'ishah is very explicit on this point. It is related that on a certain occasion the Prophet said to her: "O 'Ā'ishah! Here is Gabriel offering salutation to thee." She said: "And on him be peace and the mercy and blessings of Allāh; thou seest what I do not see" (Bu. 59 : 6). This shows that even 'Ā'ishah never saw Gabriel, whether he came with revelation or on other occasions.

There are, however, a few stray incidents, related in certain traditions, from which inference is drawn that others besides the Prophet saw Gabriel, but, from what has been stated above, it is clear that either it was in a vision (a state of *kashf*), and therefore with the spiritual senses, that they saw him or that there had been some misunderstanding in the relation of the incident. For instance, it is stated that a stranger came to the Prophet while he was sitting with his Companions, and asked him questions about faith and religion; and when he went away, the Prophet said that it was Gabriel who had come to teach them their religion (Bu.2 : 37). But it is doubtful whether the Prophet meant that the man who put the questions was Gabriel, or that the answers which he gave to the stranger were at the prompting of Gabriel. The latter interpretation of his words is more in consonance with the principle laid down that the angel cannot be seen with the physical eye, and with the vast majority of other incidents in which Gabriel came to the Prophet and was seen by him but not by others present at the same time. It is also possible that the few people who were present with the Prophet shared his vision and saw Gabriel with the spiritual eye.

There are two other cases in which there seems to be a misunderstanding. The first is the case of Umm Salama, the Prophet's wife. Some one was talking with the Prophet, and Umm Salama thought it was Diḥya. Afterwards she heard the Prophet delivering a sermon which gave her to understand that it was Gabriel (Bu.66 : 1). Here, clearly there seems to be a misunderstanding. The Prophet never told Umm Salama or anybody else that it was Gabriel who talked to him in the presence of Umm Salama. Her first impression was that it was Diḥya, and when she expressed that opinion to the Prophet, he did not contradict her, which shows that she was right. Afterwards certain words of the sermon gave her the impression that it was Gabriel, but she never expressed that opinion to the Prophet, and therefore her second impression cannot be accepted in face of the fact that whenever Gabriel appeared to the Prophet, whether with or without a revelation, he was never seen by any one except the Prophet, and that too with the inner light. The second is an incident recorded by Ibn Sa'd about 'Ā'ishah having seen Gabriel.[6] It cannot be accepted when, according to the report earlier quoted from *Bukhārī*, 'Ā'ishah had herself told the Prophet that she could not see the angel whom he saw.

Angelic function

In the Qur'ān, angels are generally described as having a connection with the spiritual state of man. It was an angel, Gabriel by name, who brought revelation to the Prophet (2 : 97; 26 : 193, 194) and the prophets before him (4 : 163). The same angel is mentioned as strengthening the prophets (2 : 87) and the believers (58 : 22). While angels generally are spoken of as descending on believers and comforting them (41 : 30), they are also intermediaries in bringing revelation to those who are not prophets, as in the case of Zacharias (3 ; 38) and Mary (3 : 41, 44). Angels were sent to help the believers against their enemies (3 : 123, 124; 8 : 12); they pray for blessings on the Holy Prophet (33 : 56) and on the believers (33 : 43); they ask forgiveness for all men, believers as well as non-believers (42 : 5); they cause believers to die (16 : 32) and also non-believers (4 : 97; 16 : 28); they write down the deeds of men (82 : 10, 12); they will intercede for men on the Day of Judgment (53 : 26). There is no clear reference to their function in the physical world unless the causing of death may be treated as such, but I have classed it as a spiritual function because death makes both the believers and unbelievers enter a new life. It may be added here that the Tradition mentions an angel of birth, that is an angel appointed for every man when he quickens in the mother's womb (Bu. 59 : 6). There are, however, verses in the Qur'ān which show that the angelic hosts have some sort of connection with the physical world. The most important of these verses are those which speak of the creation of man (Adam). When God wished to create man, He communicated His wish to the angels (2 : 30; 15 : 28; 38 : 71). This shows that the angels were there before man was created, and, there-

[6] Is. VIII, p.140.

fore, must have had some sort of connection with the physical world and with the forces which brought about the creation of man. Unless they are treated as intermediaries carrying out the Divine will, the communication to them of the Divine will to create man is meaningless. These verses, therefore, lead us to the conclusion that the laws of nature find expression through angels. It is due to this function of theirs that they are called messengers (*rusul*) (22 : 75; 35 : 1). Expression of the Divine will is a Divine message, and the angels as bearers of that message carry it into execution. Their description as bearers of the Throne (*'Arsh*) of the Lord (40 : 7; 69 : 17) leads to the same conclusion for, as already stated, the *'Arsh* stands for the Divine control of the universe, and the angels, the bearers of that control, are in fact the intermediaries through whom that control is exercised.

Vastly greater importance is, however, attached to the angelic function in the spiritual world, because it is primarily with the spiritual development of man that the Qur'ān is concerned. To put it briefly, the function of the angel in the spiritual world is the same as his function in the physical world — to serve as an intermediary in carrying out the Divine will which, in the latter case, is to bring about the evolution of creation, and in the former, the evolution of man. According to the teachings of Islām, the angel has a close connection with the life of man from his birth, even from the time he is in the mother's womb till his death, and even after death, in his spiritual progress in Paradise and his spiritual treatment in Hell. The different functions of the angel in connection with the spiritual life of man may be broadly divided into seven classes which are detailed below.

Angels as intermediaries in bringing revelation

The most important and, at the same time, the most prominent function of the angel, in the spiritual realm, is the bringing down of Divine revelation or the communication of Divine messages to the prophets. The prophet not only sees the angel but also hears his voice, and the angel is to him, therefore, a reality. This has been the universal experience of humanity in all ages. As the angel is an immaterial being, the prophet sees him sometimes in the shape of a human being and sometimes in other forms. Thus the angel Gabriel often appeared to the Prophet in the shape of a man, but sometimes he saw him "in his shape" (*fī ṣūrati-hī*) "filling the whole horizon" (Bu. 59 : 7). It is not stated what that shape was, and probably it could not be described; only the spiritual eye could recognize it. Once, also, he saw his six hundred wings (*ajniḥah*) (Bu. 59 : 7) which no doubt stand for his immense power. On another occasion he saw him in a cloud (Bu. 59 : 6), the cloud itself being probably a part of the vision.

According to the Qur'ān, the angel who brought revelation to the Prophet is known by the name of Gabriel (2 : 98). The Arabic form is *Jibrīl* which according to 'Ikrimah[7] is composed of *jibr* meaning *servant* (*'abd*) and *'īl* meaning *God* (2 : 97, Bu. 65). Gabriel is also mentioned in the Qur'ān as *Ruḥ al-Amīn* or the Faithful Spirit (26 : 193, 194), and *Rūḥ al-Qudus* or the Holy Spirit (16 : 102). In all these places, Gabriel or the Faithful Spirit or the Holy Spirit is said to have revealed the Qur'ān to the Prophet. The revelation to the prophets that appeared before him is said to have been granted in a similar manner (4 : 163). In Tradition, Gabriel is spoken of *as the great angel who is entrusted with secret messages (al-Nāmūs al-akbar)*, and the same *Nāmūs* is said to have appeared to Moses (Bu. 1 : 1). Gabriel is also called the messenger (*rasūl*) through whom God speaks to His prophets (42 : 51).

While Gabriel is thus spoken of as bringing revelation to the prophets, angels generally are said to bring revelation to other righteous servants of God: "He sends down the angels with revelation (*al-rūḥ*) by His command on whom He pleases of His servants" (16 : 2). And again: "Exalter of degrees, Lord of the Throne; He makes the spirit (*al-rūḥ*) to light by His command on whom He pleases of His servants" (40 : 15). These are general statements; and in the case of Mary who was undoubtedly not a prophet, the angels are also spoken of as bearing Divine messages: "And when the angels said, O Mary, surely Allāh has chosen thee and purified thee" (3 : 41); and again: "When the angels said, O Mary, surely Allāh gives thee good news with a word from Him of one whose name is the Messiah" (3 : 44). And so in the case of Zacharias, the father of John the Baptist: "The angels called to him as he stood praying in the sanctuary: Allāh gives thee good news of John" (3 : 38). And the believers generally are thus spoken of: "As for those who say, Our Lord is Allāh, then continue in the right way, the angels descend upon them, saying: Fear not, nor be grieved, and receive good news of the Garden which you were promised" (41 : 30).

[7] The same authority says that Michael (*Mīkāīl*) also has the same meaning, being *Mīkā-'īl, Mīk* bearing the significance of *'abd*.

Angels as intermediaries in strengthening believers

The second function of the angels, as revealed in the Qur'ān, is to strengthen the righteous servants of God, prophets as well as others, and to give them comfort in trials and affliction. Jesus Christ is specially mentioned in this connection because of the serious allegations of the Jews against him. Thrice[8] it is stated in the Qur'ān that Jesus Christ was strengthened with the Holy Spirit which, as shown earlier, is another name of Gabriel, according to the Qur'ān.[9] And the believers generally are said to be strengthened with the Spirit: "These are they into whose hearts He has impressed faith, and strengthened them with a Spirit from Him" (58 : 22), where instead of the *Rūḥ al-Qudus* we have *Rūḥ-in min-hu* (Spirit from Him), the meaning being the same. In one tradition, the Prophet is reported as asking Ḥassān, the poet, to defend him against the abuse of the unbelievers and adding: "O Allāh! Strengthen him with the Holy Spirit" (Bu.8 : 68). Elsewhere the words are: "And Gabriel is with thee"(Bu. 59 : 6). And again we find in the Qur'ān that the angels are spoken of as friends (*awliyā*) or guardians of the faithful in this life and in the Hereafter (41 : 31). It was in this sense, *i.e.*, to strengthen the believers, that the angels were sent to help them in their struggle against the unbelievers, as in these verses: "When you sought the aid of your Lord, so He answered you: I will assist you with a thousand[10] of the angels" (8 : 9); "Does it not suffice you that your Lord should help you with three thousand[11] angels sent down" (3 : 123); while yet on a third field of battle the Muslims were promised the help of five thousand angels (3 : 124). The Qur'ān itself explains why the angels were sent: "And Allāh made it only a good news for you and that your hearts might be at ease thereby" (3 : 125; 8 : 10). It was through the strengthening of the believers' hearts that the angels worked (8 : 12).[12] These angelic hosts were sent when the Muslims had to fight in defence against heavy odds, 300 against a thousand, 700 against three thousand, and 1,500 against 15,000. And on all three fields the Muslims were victorious and the

[8] 2 : 87, 253; 5 : 110.

[9] See 16 : 102 and 2 : 97.

[10 & 11] The enemy numbered one thousand in the battle of Badr and three thousand in the battle of Uḥud.

[12] "When thy Lord revealed to the angels: I am with you, so make firm those who believe. I will cast terror into the hearts of those who disbelieve" (8 : 12).

unbelievers had to go back without attaining their objective.[13] The strengthening of heart through the angels is, therefore, a solid fact of history.

Angels as intermediaries in carrying out Divine punishment

Closely allied with this strengthening of the believers is the third function of the angels—that of executing Divine punishment against the wicked, because in the contest between the righteous and the wicked the punishment of the latter and the help of the former are identical. Often would those who sought to extirpate the truth by physical force say that if there were a God Whose messenger the Prophet was, and if there were angels who could help his cause, why did they not come? "Why have not angels been sent down to us, or why do we not see our Lord?" (25 : 21). "They wait for naught but that Allāh should come to them in the shadows of the clouds with angels, and the matter has already been decided" (2 : 210). "Await they ought — but that the angels should come to them or that thy Lord's command should come to pass" (16 : 33). "They wait not aught but that the angels should come to them or that thy Lord should come, or that some of the signs of thy Lord should come" (6 : 159).

To these demands, the Qur'ān replies in the following words: "And on the day when the heaven bursts asunder with clouds, and the angels are sent down, as they are sent. The Kingdom on that day rightly belongs to the Beneficent, and it will be a hard day for the disbelievers" (25 : 25, 26). This shows that it was the promised punishment of the unjust which was hinted at in the coming of the angels. Elsewhere it is said: "And if thou couldst see when the angels cause to die those who disbelieve, smiting their faces and their backs?" (8 : 50). "But how will it be when the angels cause them to die, smiting their faces and their backs?" (47 : 27). And on one occasion, the demand and the answer are thus put together: "Why bringest thou not the angels to us if thou art of the truthful? We send not the angels but with truth, and then they would not be respited" (15 : 7, 8).

Angels' intercession and prayers for men

Another very important function of the angels is that of intercession—an intercession which includes both the believer and the unbeliever. As

[13] "...So that they should return in failure" (3 : 126).

God "has ordained mercy on Himself" (6 : 12), and His "mercy encompasses all things" (7 : 156) — in fact, it was to show mercy that "He created them" (11 : 119) — it was necessary that His angels, who are intermediaries carrying out His will, should include all in their intercession. The intercession of the angels is mentioned in the Qur'ān on one occasion in particular: "And how many angels are there in the heavens whose intercession avails not except after Allāh gives permission to whom He pleases and chooses" (53 : 26). The Tradition also speaks of the intercession of angels (Bu. 98 : 24). Now intercession is really a prayer to God on behalf of the sinners on the Day of Judgment, but we are told that the angels pray for men even in this life: "The angels celebrate the praise of their Lord and ask forgiveness for those on earth" (42 : 5), "those on earth" including both the believer and the unbeliever. And while this prayer is all-comprehensive, it grows stronger in the case of believers: "Those who bear the Throne of Power and those around it celebrate the praise of their Lord and believe in Him and ask protection for those who believe: Our Lord, Thou embracest all things in mercy and knowledge, so protect those who turn to Thee and follow Thy way... (and) make them enter the Gardens of perpetuity which Thou hast promised them and such of their fathers and their wives and their offspring as are good...and guard them from evil" (40 : 7-9). As a result of the prayers of the angels, the faithful are actually guided forth from every kind of darkness into light: "He it is Who sends His blessings on you and (so do) His angels, that He may bring you forth out of darkness into the light" (33 : 43). And as regards the Prophet, the angels bless him: "Surely Allāh and His angels bless the Prophet. O you who believe, call for blessings on him" (33 : 56). Thus the angels' connection with man grows stronger as he advances in righteousness. As regards men generally, the angels pray for their forgiveness so that punishment in respect of their evil deeds may be averted; as regards the faithful, they lead them forth from darkness into light, and thus enable them to make progress spiritually; and as regards the Prophet, they bless him and are thus helpful in advancing his cause in the world.

Angels help in the spiritual progress of man

It will be seen that in his spiritual function the angel is meant to render help in the spiritual advancement of man. The angel brings Divine revelation, and it is only with the help of such revelation that man is able to realize what the spiritual life is, and to make advancement spiritually by a development of his inner faculties. The angel strengthens the Prophet, through whom the law of spiritual progress is revealed, and also the believers who are instrumental in carrying the ennobling message to humanity, and thus renders help in establishing the law of spiritual advancement; and the same end is achieved by the punishment of those who try to exterminate that law and its upholders. The angels' intercession and prayer even for the unbeliever are undoubtedly meant to set him on the road to spiritual progress, while his bringing of the believers from darkness into light, and his blessings on the Prophet, are the advancement of the cause of spiritual progress. Thus, if analyzed, each one of the functions of the angel is aimed at helping the spiritual advancement of man and bringing about his spiritual perfection. This is further borne out by the fact that there are angels even in Paradise and Hell[14] which are really two different places or conditions, wherein man is enabled to carry on his spiritual progress after death, the former opening the way to immeasurable heights of spiritual progress,[15] and the latter cleansing man of the spiritual diseases[16] which he has himself contracted by leading an evil life in this world.

Angels' promptings to noble deeds

Every good and noble deed is the result of the promptings of the angel. The Qur'ān speaks of the angel and the devil as leading man to two different courses of life: the former, as shown above, to a good and noble life aiming at the development of the human faculties, and the latter, as will be shown later, to a base and wicked life tending to the deadening of those faculties. Every man is said to have two associates, an associate angel and an associate devil. The first is called a 'witness' (*shahīd*), and the second a 'driver' (*sā'iq*): "And every soul comes, with it a driver and a witness. Thou wert indeed heedless of this, but now We have

14 Speaking of those in Paradise, the Qur'ān says: "And the angels will enter in upon them from every gate" (13 : 23). And of Hell it says: "And We have made none but angels the guardians of the fire" (74 : 31).

15 A single day of that progress is said to extend over fifty thousand years: "To Him ascend the angels and the spirit (of man) in a day, the measure of which is fifty thousand years" (70 : 4).

16 See the discussion on Hell.

removed from thee thy veil, so that thy sight is sharp this day'' (50 : 21, 22). The *driver* is the devil who makes evil suggestions and leads man to a state of degradation, and the *witness* is the angel who helps man on to a good and noble end. Man is said to be heedless of it here, there being a veil over his eyes, so that he cannot see to what condition he is being led, but he will see the result clearly on the Day of Judgment. In Tradition we are told that every man has an associate angel and an associate devil. Thus Muslim reports from Ibn Mas'ūd: ''The Prophet said, There is not one among you but there is appointed over him his associate from among the jinn and his associate from among the angels. The Companions said, And what about thee, Prophet of Allāh? He said, The same is the case with me, but Allāh has helped me over him (*i.e.*, the associate jinn) so he has submitted and does not command me aught but good''.[17] According to another tradition, the Prophet is reported to have said: ''There are suggestions which the devil makes to the son of man, and suggestions which the angel makes. The devil's suggestion is for evil and giving the lie to the truth, and the angel's suggestion is for good and the acceptance of truth''.[18]

Angels recording deeds of men

Another spiritual function of the angels, on which special stress is laid in the Qur'ān, is the recording of the good and evil deeds of man. These angels are called 'honourable recorders' (*kirām-an Kātibīn*), the words being taken from the verse of the Qur'ān: ''And surely there are keepers over you, honourable recorders, they know what you do'' (82 : 10-12). and elsewhere we have:''When the two receivers receive, sitting on the right and on the left. He utters not a word but there is by him a watcher at hand'' (50 : 17,18). ''Alike (to Him) among you is he who conceals the word and he who speaks openly, and he who hides himself by night and who goes forth by day. For him are (angels) guarding the consequences (of his deeds), before him and behind him, who guard him by Allāh's command'' (13 : 10, 11).

The guarding in the last verse refers to the guarding of man's deeds. The angels are immaterial beings, and hence also their recording is

[17] MM. 1 : 3—i; Ah. I, pp. 385, 397, 401.

[18] MM. 1 : 3—ii.

effected in a different manner from that in which a man would prepare a record. In fact, their record exists, as elsewhere stated, in the form of the effect which an action produces: "And We have made every man's actions cling to his neck, and We shall bring forth to him on the Day of Resurrection a book which he will find wide open" (17 : 13). The clinging of a man's actions to his neck is clearly the effect which his actions produce and which he is powerless to obliterate, and we are told that this effect will be met with in the form of an open book on the Resurrection Day, thus showing that the angel's recording of a deed is actually the producing of an effect.

Faith in angels

The different functions of angels in the spiritual world are thus connected, in one way or another, either with the awakening of the spiritual life in man or its advancement and progress. Herein lies the reason why faith in angels is required along with a faith in God: "Righteous is the one who believes in Allāh, and the Last Day, and the angels, and the Book and the prophets" (2 : 177). "The Messenger believes in what has been revealed to him from his Lord, and so do the believers. They all believe in Allāh and His angels and His books and His messengers" (2 : 285).

Faith or belief in any doctrine, according to the Qur'ān, is essentially the acceptance of a proposition as a basis for action. Faith in angels, therefore, means that there is a spiritual life for man, and that he must develop that life by working in accordance with the promptings of the angel and by bringing into play the faculties which God has given him; and that is why—though the existence of the devil, who makes the evil suggestions, is as much a fact as the existence of the angel who makes the good suggestions — the Qur'ān requires a belief in angels and a disbelief in devils.[19] This, of course, is not to say that one must deny the existence of the devil. The significance is clear enough: one must obey the commandments of God and refuse to follow the suggestions of the devil. Faith in the angels, therefore, only means that every good suggestion—and such is the suggestion of the angel--must be accepted, because it leads to the spiritual development of man.

[19] "So whoever disbelieves in the devil and believes in Allāh, he indeed lays hold on the firmest handle" (2 : 256).

Iblīs *is not an angel but one of the jinn*

There is a popular misconception, into which many writers of repute have fallen, that *Iblīs* or the Devil is one of the angels. The misconception has arisen from the fact that where the angels are commanded to make obeisance to Adam, there is also mention of *Iblīs* and his refusal to make obeisance: "And when We said to the angels, Be submissive to Adam, they submitted, but[20] *Iblīs* (did not). He refused and was proud, and he was one of the disbelievers" (2 : 34). From these words it is clear enough that *Iblīs* or the Devil was one of the unbelievers and refused to obey, and, therefore, he could not be an angel, because, of the angels, it is plainly said that "they do not disobey Allāh in that which He commands them, but do as they are commanded" (66 : 6). And elsewhere it is stated in so many words that *Iblīs* was not from among the angels but from among the jinn: "And when We said to the angels, Make submission to Adam, they submitted except *Iblīs*. He was of the jinn, so he transgressed the commandment of his Lord" (18 : 50). Now jinn and angels are two different classes of beings; their origin and their functions have nothing in common. The jinn, as we have seen, are mentioned as being created from fire, while the angels are created from light; and the function of the jinn has also been shown to be quite different from the function of the angel. It is, therefore, an obvious error to look upon the jinn as being a branch of the angelic creation.

The Jinn

The word *jinn* is derived from *janna* meaning *he covered* or *concealed* or *hid* or *protected*.[21] The word *jinn* has been used in the Qur'ān

[20] The word *illā*, which ordinarily means *except* and is used as indicating *istithnā'* (exception), is sometimes used to indicate *istithnā' munqaṭi'* (lit. *an exception which is cut off*), the thing excepted being disunited in kind from that from which the exception is made, so that the two belong to two classes. Thus they say, *jā' al-qaumu illā ḥimār-an*, the meaning of which is that the people came but an ass did not come, the people and the ass belonging to two quite different classes. It is exactly in this sense that the word *illā* is used here, the angels and *Iblīs* belonging to two quite different classes. Hence the rendering adopted. It is sometimes argued that if the devil were not an angel, he would not have been spoken of at all in connection with the commandment to the angels to make obeisance to man. The fact is that the commandment to the angels was in fact a commandment to all creation, and the lower beings jinn, were, therefore, included in it. The words *idh amartu-ka* (when I commanded thee), occurring in 7 : 12 regarding the devil, show that the lower beings called jinn were included by implication in the commandment to the higher beings.

[21] See next page.

distinctly in two senses. It is applied in the first place to the spirits of evil or the beings that invite man to evil, as opposed to the angels who invite him to good, both being imperceptible with the senses.[22] The origin of these beings is said to be fire, and their function is described as that of exciting evil passions or low desires. The Qur'ān is explicit on both these points. As regards the creation of jinn, it says: "And the jinn We created before of intensely hot fire" (15 : 27); and again: "And He created the jinn of a flame of fire" (55 : 15). And to show that the jinn and the devils are one, the devil is spoken of as saying: "I am better than he (*i.e.*, man); Thou hast created me of fire while him Thou didst create of dust" (7 : 12). As regards the function of jinn, the Qur'ān is equally clear: "The slinking devil who whispers into the hearts of men, from among the jinn and the men" (114 : 4-6). Traditions have already been quoted showing that every man has with him an associate from among the angels who inspires him with good and noble ideas and an associate from among the jinn who excites his baser passions.

The devil

The question is often asked why has God created beings which lead man astray? There is a misunderstanding in this question. God has created man with two kinds of passions, the higher which awaken in him a higher or spiritual life, and the lower which relate to his physical existence; and corresponding to these two passions there are two kinds of beings, the angels and the devils. The lower passions are necessary for man's physical life, but they become a hindrance to him in his advancement to a higher life when they run riot and are out of control. Man is required to keep these passions in control. If he can do so, they become a help to him in

[21] All Arabic lexicologists are agreed on its Arabic origin and, moreover, there are numerous words in use in Arabic which are derived from the same root, such as the verb *janna* meaning *it covered* or *overshadowed* (6 : 77), or the noun *janna* meaning *garden* because its trees cover the ground, or *janān* meaning *the heart* because it is concealed from the senses, and *majann* or *junna* meaning *shield* because it protects a man, and *janīn* or the *foetus*, so long as it is in the mother's womb. In spite of this the writer in the *Encyclopaedia of Islam* calls it a loan-word.

[22] In the second place, this word is applied in the Qur'ān to great potentates or powerful leaders who, through their importance and detachment from the masses, do not mix freely with them, and remain distant or 'hidden from their eyes." This use of the word is discussed later.

his advancement instead of a hindrance. This is the meaning underlying the Prophet's reply in the tradition already quoted, when he was asked if he too had an associate jinn. "Yes," he said, "but Allāh has helped me to overcome him, so he has submitted and does not command me aught but good." His devil is said to have submitted to him (*aslama*), and instead of making evil suggestions commanded him naught but good, that is to say, became a help to him in the development of his higher life.

Such is the true significance underlying the story of Adam. The devil at first refuses to make obeisance to man, *i.e.*, to become helpful in his spiritual advancement, and is determined, by hook or by crook, to set him on the wrong course and excite his baser passions: "Certainly I will take of Thy servants an appointed portion; and certainly I will lead them astray and excite in them vain desires" (4 : 118,119). But he is subdued by the help of the Divine revelation, and those who follow the revelation have no fear of the devil's misleading: "Then Adam received (revealed) words from his Lord, and He turned to him mercifully... Surely there will come to you guidance from Me, then whoever follows My guidance, no fear shall come upon them, nor shall they grieve" (2 : 37, 38). The presence of the devil thus indicates that, in the earlier stages of spiritual development, man has to contend with him by refusing to obey his evil promptings, and any one who makes this struggle is sure to subdue the evil one; while in the higher stages, the lower passions having been brought into subjection, the devil actually becomes helpful, "commanding naught but good," so that even physical desires become a help in the spiritual life of man. Without struggle there is no advancement in life, and thus even in the earlier stages, the devil is the ultimate means of man's good, unless, of course, man chooses to follow instead of stubbornly resisting him.

The word **jinn** *as applied to men*

The other use of the word *jinn* is with regard to men of a certain class.[23] Even the word *devil* (*shaiṭān*), or *devils* (*shayāṭīn*), has been applied to

[23] Some authorities have held that the word *jinn* is also applicable to the angels, but it should be borne in mind that it is in a strictly literal sense that the word has been so used. The literal significance of the word *jinn* is *a being hidden from the human eye*, and as the angels are also invisible beings, they may be called *jinn* in a literal sense. Otherwise they have nothing in common with jinn.

men in the Qur'ān, and the leaders of evil are again and again called devils.[24] But the use of the word *jinn* when speaking of men was recognized in Arabic literature before Islām. The verse of Mūsā ibn Jābir *fa-mā nafarat jinn*, which would literally mean, *and my jinn did not flee*, has been explained as meaning, "and my companions who were like the jinn, did not flee"(LL.). Here the word *jinn* is clearly explained as meaning human beings. And Tabrezi says, further, that the *Arabs liken a man who is sharp and clever in affairs to a jinni and a shaiṭān.*[25] There are other examples in pre-Islamic poetry in which the word *jinn* has been used to denote great or brave men.[26] In addition to this, the word *jinn* is explained by Arabic lexicologists as meaning *mu'aẓẓam al-nās* (Q., TA.), *i.e, the main body of men* or *the bulk of mankind* (LL.). In the mouth of an Arab, the main body of men would mean the non-Arab world. They called all foreigners *jinn* because they were concealed from their eyes. It is in this sense that the word *jinn* is used in the Qur'ān in the story of Solomon: "And of the *jinn* there were those who worked before him by the command of his Lord... They made for him what he pleased of synagogues and images" (34 : 12, 13). The description of the *jinn* here as builders shows them to have been men. And they are also spoken of as devils (*shayāṭīn*) in 38 : 37, where they are called builders and divers, and it is further added that some of them were "fettered in chains." Surely those who built buildings and dived into the sea were not invisible spirits, nor do invisible spirits require to be fettered in chains. These were in fact the strangers whom Solomon had subjected to his rule and forced into service.[27]

In one place in the Qur'ān jinn and men are addressed as one class or community (*ma'shar*).[28] In this verse both jinn and men are asked the question: "Did there not come to you messengers from among you?" Now the messengers who are mentioned in the Qur'ān or Tradition all belong to mankind, and the Holy Book does not speak of a single messenger from among the jinn. The jinn in this case, therefore, are either non-Arabs

[24] 2 : 14; 3 : 174; 8 : 48; 15 : 17; 21 : 82, etc.

[25] TH. I, p.193.

[26] I have quoted these verses in my Urdu commentary, the *Bayān al-Qur'ān* under 6 : 128.

[27] A comparison with II Chron. 2 : 18 would further clear the point: "And he set threescore and ten thousand of them to be bearers of burdens, and fourscore thousand to be hewers in the mountain."

[28] "O community (*ma'shar*) of jinn and men, did there not come to you messengers from among you, relating to you My messages and warning you of the meeting of this day of yours?" (6 : 131). *Ma'shar* is *a class* or *community whose affair is one* (LA).

or the iniquitous leaders who mislead others. In one verse, it is stated that "if jinn and men should combine together to bring the like of this Qur'ān, they could not bring the like of it" (17 : 88), while in another, in an exactly similar challenge the expression "your helpers" or "leaders" have been used instead of jinn (2: 23). The jinn mentioned in the first section of ch. 72 are evidently foreign Christians, since they are spoken of as holding the doctrine of sonship (72 : 3,4). In 72 : 6, they are called *rijāl* (pl. of *rajul*), which word is applicable to the males of human beings only (LA.). Again, in the 46th chapter the word *jinn* has been used in the sense of foreigners when a party of the jinn is stated to have come to the Prophet and listened to the Holy Book and believed in it,[29] because all the injunctions contained in the Qur'ān are for men, and there is not one for the jinn. This was evidently a party of the Jews of Nisibus as reports show, and the Qur'ān speaks of them as believers in Moses.[30] Commenting on this incident, Ibn Kat͟hīr has quoted several reports from the *Musnad* of Aḥmad, which establish the following facts. The Prophet met a party of jinn at Nak͟hla when returning from Ṭā'if in the tenth year of the Call. These are said to have come from Nineveh. On the other hand, there is a well-stablished story that the Prophet on his way back from Ṭā'if took rest in a garden where he met a Christian who was a resident of Nineveh; and the man listened to his message and believed in him. It may be that he had other companions to whom he spoke of the Prophet, and that these came to him later on. Another party of jinn is said to have waited on him when he was at Makkah, and he is reported to have gone out of the city to a lonely place at night time, and to have spent the whole night with them. And we are told that their traces and the traces of the fire which they had burned during the night were visible in the morning. When prayer-time came and the Prophet said his prayers in the company of Ibn Mas'ūd, the narrator, two of them are said to have come and joined the service. They are supposed to have been Jews of Nisibus and were seven in number (IK. 46 : 29). The Prophet went to see them outside Makkah, evidently because the Quraish would have interfered with the meeting and ill-treated any who came to see him. At any rate the Qur'ān and the Tradition do not speak of the jinn as they

[29] "And when We turned towards thee a party of the jinn, who listened to the Qur'ān...Then when it was finished they turned back to their people warning them" (46 : 29).

[30] "They said: O our people, we have heard a book revealed after Moses, verifying that which is before it, guiding to the truth and to the right path" (46 : 30).

exist in the popular imagination, interfering in human affairs or controlling the forces of nature or assuming human or any other shape or taking possession of men or women and affecting them with certain diseases.[31]

The jinn have no access to Divine secrets

There is another misundersanding in connection with the devils or the jinn which should be removed. It is thought that according to the teachings of the Qur'ān, the devils have access to the Divine secrets, and stealthily overhear the Divine revelation which is communicated to the angels. This was an Arab superstition borrowed either from the Jews[32] or the Persians, and the Qur'ān has rejected it in emphatic words. Thus, speaking of the revelation of the Holy Book, it says: "And surely this is a revelation from the Lord of the worlds. The Faithful Spirit has brought it on thy heart...And the devils have not brought it. And it behoves them not, nor have they the power to do it. Surely they are far removed even from hearing it" (26 : 192-212). In the face of these words, it is impossible to maintain that the Qur'ān upholds the doctrine of the devils' access to Divine secrets. The Divine message is entrusted to Gabriel, who is here called the Faithful Spirit to show that it is quite safe with him; and this message he brings direct to the heart of the Prophet. The idea that the devils can overhear it by eavesdropping is strongly condemned; they do not ascend to heaven as is popularly supposed, nor do they come down to earth with the Divine secrets; nor does it behove them, nor have

31 Such ideas are unfortunately associated with the existence of jinn in the Gospels. The stories of Jesus casting out devils are more wondrous than fairy tales: "And devils also came out of many, crying out, and saying, Thou art Christ the Son of God" (Lk. 4 : 41). A devil was cast out of a dumb man and he began to speak (Mt. 9 : 33); a woman from Canaan had a daughter possessed with the devil and Jesus at first refused to cast out the devil because she was not an Israelite (Mt. 15 : 22-24); as many as seven devils went out of Mary Megdalene (Lk. 8 : 2); the devils cast out of another two men were sufficient for a whole herd of swine: "They went into the herd of swine: and, behold, the whole herd of swine ran violently down a steep place into the sea, and perished in the waters" (Mt. 8 : 32). And this power of casting out devils was given to all those who believed in Jesus (Mk. 16 : 17).

32 "The Talmud teaches that angels were created of fire and that they have various offices...that the jinn are an intermediate order between angels and men...that they know what is to happen in the future, because they listen to what is going on behind the curtain to steal God's secrets" (RI. p. 68). The Quranic teaching is opposed to this; it is not the angels that are created of fire but the jinn. The jinn are not an intermediate order between angels and men; man is placed highest of all, even above the angels; the jinn are invisible beings of a very low order, their only function is the insinuation of evil into the hearts of men, and they have no access to Divine secrets.

they the power to ascend to heaven and come down with the revelation; they are far removed even from the hearing of it, so their stealthy listening to the Divine secrets is only a myth. Another verse states: "Or have they the means by which they listen (to Divine secrets)? Then let their listener bring a clear authority" (52 : 38). Here too the claim made by superstition on behalf of the devils, that they can ascend into heaven and listen to the Divine secrets, is plainly rejected. And yet in a third verse it is reported that Divine secrets are safely entrusted to the apostles, and that no one else has access to them: "He makes known to none His secrets except a messenger whom He chooses. For surely He makes a guard to go before him and after him" (72 : 26,27).

The entire idea of the devils'eavesdropping on Divine secrets appears to have arisen from a misunderstanding of certain words, particularly the words *shaiṭān* and *rajm*. *Shaiṭān* (devils), as already shown, has admittedly been used for the iniquitous leaders of opposition to the Prophet, as in the case of hypocrites: "And when they are alone with their devils (*shayāṭīn*), they say we are with you" (2 : 14). All commentators are agreed that here by *their devils* are meant their leaders in unbelief.[33] The opposition to the Prophet came chiefly from two sources, *viz.*, the worldly leaders and the diviners or soothsayers (*kāhin*). As the simple faith of Islām was the death-knell of all superstitions, and the office of *kāhin* represented one of the greatest superstitions that ever enthralled the Arab mind, at all times prone to superstition, the diviners fought the Prophet tooth and nail. They deceived the people by their oracular utterances, and by presuming to foretell that the Prophet would soon perish. Like the worldly leaders of the verse quoted above, these diviners are also spoken of in the Qur'ān as *shayāṭīn* (devils), because they led people to evil courses of life.

The other word of which the meaning has been misunderstood, is *rajm* (used in connection with these devils or diviners). *Rajm*, no doubt, does mean *the throwing of stone*, but it is also used to indicate *conjecture (zann), superstition (tawahhum), abusing (shaṭm)* or driving away (*ṭard*) (R.). It occurs in the sense of conjecture in 18 : 22 —"Making conjectures (*rajm-an*) at "what is unknown"—, and in the sense of *abuse* in 19 : 46 in which the word *la-arjumanna-ka* is explained as meaning, "I will speak to thee in words which thou dost not like" (R.). And it is added that

[33] IJ-C. I, p. 99; *Bdz.*; Rz., etc.

shaiṭān or the devil is called *rajīm*, because "he is driven away from all good and from the high places of the exalted assembly" (*mala' al-a'lā*) (R.).

The two words explained above occur in the following verse: "And We have adorned this lower heaven with lights and We have made them *rujūm-an li-l-shayāṭīn*," which words are wrongly translated as *missiles for the devils*.[34] In the light of what has been stated above, the meaning clearly is *means of conjecture for the devils* or *kāhins, i.e.*, the diviners and the astrologers. The following significance is accepted by the best authorities: "We have made them to be means of conjectures to the devils of mankind, *i.e.*, to the astrologers"(LL., Bdz., TA.). Another commentator says: "It is said that the meaning is that We made them so that the devils of mankind who are the astrologers make conjectures by them" (RM.). Ibn Athīr gives the following explanation: "It has been said that by *rujūm* are meant the conjectures which were made,...and what the astrologers state by guesses and surmises and by their coming to certain conclusions on account of the combination of the stars and their separation, and it is they that are meant by *shayāṭīn*, for they are the devils of mankind. And it has been stated in some tradition that whoever learns anything from astrology...learns the same from sorcery, and the astrologer is a *kāhin* (diviner or soothsayer) and the *kāhin* is a sorcerer and the sorcerer is an unbeliever, and thus the astrologer who claims to acquire a knowledge of the stars to decide the happenings (of the future) thereby, and ascribes to them the sources of good and evil, is called a *kāfir*" (N. art. *rajm*). Thus a plain verse of the Qur'ān which really condemns the practices of diviners and soothsayers has been misinterpreted to mean that the stars were used as missiles for the devils who went up to heaven. Reference to this subject is contained in two other places in the Qur'ān: "Surely We have adorned the lower heaven with an adornment, the stars. And (there is) a safeguard against every rebellious devil. They cannot listen to the exalted assembly and they are reproached from every side, (being) driven off, and for them is a perpetual chastisement; except him who snatches away but once, then there follows him a brightly shining flame" (37 : 6-10). "And certainly We have made strongholds in the

[34] This is even Mr. Pickthall's translation, though he adds a footnote which shows this translation to be incorrect: "On the authority of a tradition going back to Ibn 'Abbās, the allusion is to the soothsayers and astrologers who saw the source of good and evil in the stars."

heaven and We have made it fair-seeming to the beholders, and We guard it against every accursed devil, but he who steals a hearing; so there follows him a brightly shining flame''(15 : 16-18).[35] On both these occasions, the principle is again stated in forcible words that the soothsayers and diviners have no access to heaven or the stars on which they base their conjectures; it is they again who are here called the rebellious or accursed devils — ''They cannot listen to the exalted assembly.'' But we are also told that ''they are reproached from every side, being driven off,'' *i.e.*, their own votaries do not honour them, and they are reproached because what they assert proves untrue and therefore they live in perpetual torture. And then there is an exception: ''Except him who snatches off but once''. Now this snatching away of the soothsayers, after we are told that they are reproached from every side and driven off, clearly means nothing but that occasionally their conjecture turns out to be true. The same idea is expressed in the second verse by the words ''he who steals a hearing.'' It is of course not meant that the Divine secrets are being discussed aloud somewhere in heaven and that the devil is hiding and overhears them. Divine revelation, as already shown on the authority of the Qur'ān, is entrusted to the Faithful Spirit, that is Gabriel, who, in turn, discloses it to the heart of the Prophet — there is no question of overhearing in this process.[36] It has also been established on the authority of the Qur'ān that the devils cannot ascend to heaven, that they have no access to Divine secrets. It would, therefore, be a travesty of all these clearly established principles to say that the devils can overhear the Divine secrets. Obviously, in both verses, it is the *kāhins* of Arabia, the diviners and soothsayers, that are spoken of. The soothsayer's occasional snatching and his stealthy hearing refer only to his conjecture sometimes coming true, the visible flame which follows meaning the subsequent failure and disappointment due to the advent of Islām, which destroyed the whole effect of the soothsayer's pretensions. The description of spiritual truths in terms of physical laws which are prevalent in the world is of common occurrence in the Qur'ān; and it is a fact that the darkness of

[35] The Arabic words translated as ''brightly shining flame'' are *shihāb* and *thāqib*. The former means only a flame (LL. also compare 27 : 7 where Moses goes to bring a *shihāb*); and the latter means *that piercing through the darkness* or *brightly shining* (LL.) — the meaning being that a soothsayer gets but one opportunity but there soon follows a flame that dispels the darkness to which he leads men.

[36] — see next page.

superstition — and the office of the *kāhin* or the soothsayer was undoubtedly a superstition — was completely dispelled by the light of Islām, so that Islām may be said literally to have proved a flame of fire for the chaff of soothsaying and divination.

[36] The following tradition cannot be taken literally, inasmuch as certain portions thereof are opposed to the Qur'ān. The Prophet is reported to have said that when God intends to send a revelation, the heavens are shaken and the heavenly hosts swoon and fall down in prostration. Gabriel is the first to raise his head and to him God reveals His pleasure. The angels then enquire of Gabriel what God has said, and he replies: The Truth, and He is the High, the Great. The secret listeners hear a part of this. Some are destroyed by the flame of fire but some are successful in imparting the news to others before they themselves are destoyed, and these latter take the message to the *kāhin* (diviner) on earth (34 : I; Bu. 65). Different versions of this report are met with, but I have taken the most salient points of all. Now whereas a large number of reports state, and the Qur'ān also is explicit on this point, that revelation is communicated directly to the Prophet by Gabriel, without any intervention, this report says that it is communicated by Gabriel to other angels, and this is done in such a way that even the devils can hear it, while according to the Qur'ān the devils are ''far removed from the hearing of it'' (26 : 212). Hence the report being opposed to the Qur'ān and other traditions, cannot be accepted in its entirety. There has undoubtedly been some misunderstanding somewhere in the course of transmission, and the wrong view of some narrator has crept in.

CHAPTER IV
REVEALED BOOKS

Revealed books mentioned under three names

Revealed books are mentioned in the Qur'ān under three names. The first name is *kitāb* (pl. *kutub*), meaning a Book.[1] The word *al-Kitāb* has been used for the Qur'ān itself, for its chapters, for any previous revelation, (13 : 43), for all previous revelations taken together (98 : 3) and for all revealed books including the Qur'ān (3 : 118). Revealed books are also spoken of as *ṣuḥuf* (pl. of *ṣaḥīfa*)[2] as in 87 : 18, 19, where all previous books, particularly the books of Moses and Abraham are so called, or as in 80 : 13 and 98 : 2 where the Qur'ān itself is spoken of as *ṣuḥuf.* The third name under which revealed books are mentioned is *zubur* (pl. of *zabūr*),[3] as in 26 : 196, 4 : 163, etc. The singular form, *zabūr*, occurs only three times in the Qur'ān, twice in connection with the book of David: "And We gave to David a scripture (*zabūr*)" (4 : 163, 17 : 55); and on one occasion a quotation is given from *al-Zabūr*: "And truly We wrote in the Book (*al-Zabūr*) after the reminder that My righteous servants will inherit the land" (21 : 105).

Revelation to objects and beings other than man

The Arabic word for revelation, *waḥy*, has, in its highest form, come to signify the Divine word which is communicated to prophets (*anbiyā'*) and saints, or righteous servants of God (*auliyā'*) who have not been

[1] In 2 : 285 and in other places, the Prophet and the believers are spoken of as believing in *kutubī-hī* or His books. The word *kutub* is pl. of *kitāb*, which is derived from the root *kataba*, meaning *he wrote* or *he brought together*, and *kitāb (book)* is *a writing* which *is complete in itself.* Thus a letter may be called *kitāb*, in which sense the word occurs in 27 : 28, 29, regarding Solomon's letter to the queen of Sheba. The word *kitāb* has, however, been used to speak of the revelation of God to prophets whether written or not (R.), while it is also freely used regarding the Divine decrees or ordinances (see 8 : 68; 9 : 36; 13 : 38, etc.).

[2] The word *ṣaḥīfa* is derived from *ṣaḥf*, and *ṣaḥīfa* means *anything spread out* (R.). *Muṣḥaf* means *a collection of written pages*, and the Qur'ān is also called *muṣḥaf.*

[3] The word *zabūr* is derived from *zabara* which means *he wrote* or *he wrote it firmly* or *skilfully* or *engraved* or *inscribed on a stone* (TA.); and *zabūr* means *any writing* or *book*, and particularly *the Book of the Psalms* of David is called *al-Zabūr* (LL.).

raised to the dignity of prophethood[4]. (R.). According to the Qur'ān, revelation is a universal fact, so much so that it is even spoken of as being granted to inanimate objects: "Then He directed Himself to the heaven and it was a vapour, so He said to it and to the earth: Come both willingly or unwillingly. They both said: We come willingly. So He ordained them seven heavens in two periods, and revealed in every heaven its affair" (41 : 11, 12). On another occasion there is mention of revelation to the earth: "When the earth is shaken with her shaking, and the earth brings forth her burdens, and man says, What has befallen her? On that day she shall tell her news, as if thy Lord had revealed to her" (99 : 1 - 5). In the first instance, God's speaking to the earth and the heavens and His revelation to the heavens shows that there is a kind of revelation through which the Divine laws are made to operate in the universe; in the second, a great revolution that is brought about upon earth — its "bringing forth its burdens", explained as the laying open of its treasures (R.) in the form of minerals and other products — is spoken of as a kind of revelation. There is also a revelation to the lower animals: "And thy Lord revealed to the bee: Make hives in the mountains and in the trees and in what they build, then eat of all the fruits and walk in the ways of thy Lord submissively" (16 : 68, 69). This is really an example of the Divine revelation being granted also to the lower creation, so that what they do by instinct is really a revelation. These two examples show that Divine revelation is intended for the development and perfection of everything within its ordained sphere. Here may also be mentioned the revelation to angels: "When thy Lord revealed to the angels: I am with you, so make firm those who believe" (8 : 12). As revelation itself is communicated through angels, it appears that there are various orders of angels; and it is for this reason that Gabriel, the angel who brings revelation to the prophets of God, is regarded as the greatest of them all.

Revelation to **auliyā'**

Much misconception prevails as to the sphere of revelation to man. It is generally thought that revelation is limited to the prophets of God. This is not true, for the Qur'ān regards it, in one form or another, as the universal experience of all humanity. Rāghib, already quoted, defines revelation, in a strictly technical sense, as meaning the word of God as

[4] *Al-kalimatu-llatī tulqā ilā anbiyā'i-hī wa auliyā'i-hī waḥy-un.*

conveyed to the prophets (*anbiyā'*) and to other righteous servants (*auliyā*) of God. And on several occasions the Qur'ān speaks of revelation (*waḥy*) having been granted to such righteous servants of God as were not prophets, men as well as women. The mother of Moses is said to have received a revelation though she was undoubtedly not a prophet, and so are the disciples of Jesus who were not prophets: "And We revealed (*auḥainā*) to Moses' mother, saying: Give him suck; then when thou fearest for him, cast him into the river, and fear not, nor grieve; surely We shall bring him back to thee and make him one of the messengers" (28 : 7); "And when I revealed (*auḥaitu*) to the disciples (of Jesus), saying, Believe in Me and My messenger" (5 : 111). These verses leave not the least doubt that *waḥy* or revelation is granted to those who are not prophets as well as to prophets, and therefore the door to revelation is not closed, even though no prophet at all would come after Prophet Muḥammad. It is only authoritative revelation, the form of revelation peculiar to prophets, the revelation through Gabriel as explained in next paragraph, that has ceased after him.

Revelation to man granted in three ways

Revelation to inanimate objects, to the lower animals and to the angels is of a different nature from revelation to man, and it is the latter with which we are chiefly concerned. Divine revelation to man is stated to be of three kinds: "And it is not vouchsafed to a mortal that Allāh should speak to him except by revelation or from behind a veil, or by sending a messenger and revealing by His permission what He pleases;" (42 : 51). The first of these, which is called *waḥy* in the original, is the inspiring of an idea into the heart, for the word *waḥy* is used here in its primary significance of a *hasty suggestion* or *infusing into the heart*, as distinguished from a revelation in words.[5] In spite of the fact that this kind of revelation is the "infusing of an idea into the heart," it is called a form of God's speaking to man. This is technically called "inner revelation" (*waḥy khafī*) and the sayings of the Prophet touching religious matters are in this class. The Prophet himself is reported to have said on such an occasion: "The Holy Spirit has inspired (this) into my heart" (N.). It is an

[5] Since different kinds of revelation are spoken of here, the use of *waḥy* must be intended in its original significance, *viz.*, *a hasty suggestion* made directly to the heart of the inspired one. It is in this sense that revelation is spoken of as being granted to the mother of Moses (28 : 7) and to the disciples of Jesus who were not prophets (5 : 111).

idea put into the mind, as distinguished from revelation proper, which is a message conveyed in words. Revelation in this form is common to both prophets and those who are not prophets.[6]

The second mode of God's speaking to man is said to be "from behind a veil" (*min warāi' ḥijāb*), and this includes dream (*ru'yā*), vision (*kashf*) and *ilhām* (when voices are heard or uttered in a state of trance, the recipient being neither quite asleep, nor fully awake). This form of revelation is also common both to prophets and those who are not prophets, and in its simplest form, the *ru'yā* or the dream, is a universal experience of the whole of humanity. The Qur'ān tells us of the vision of a king, who was apparently not a believer in God (12 : 43) — a vision which had a deep underlying significance. This shows that, according to the Qur'ān, revelation in its lower forms is the common experience of all mankind, of the unbeliever as well as the believer, of the sinner as well as of the saint.

The third kind, which is peculiar to the prophets of God, is that in which the angel (Gabriel) brings the Divine message in words. This is the surest and clearest form of revelation, and such was the revelation of the Qur'ān to the Prophet. This is called *revelation that is recited in words (waḥy matluww)*. It is the highest and most developed form; and it was in this manner that revelation was granted to all the prophets of God in every nation.[7] The revealed books are a record of this highest revelation,

[6] It is more or less in this sense, the sense of putting a suggestion into the mind, or what is called a *limma* or *waswasa* of the devil, that the devils are spoken of as bringing *waḥy* to their friends: "And certainly the devils inspire (*yūḥūn* from *waḥy*) their friends" (6 : 122).

[7] Some Muslims have been misled, by the Christian conception of revelation, into the belief that revelation means only an illumination of the mind, and that to say that God *speaks* is merely a metaphor, because it is only the recipient of the revelation who speaks under a certain Divine influence. Unfortunately, the original Gospel, the revelation of Jesus Christ, having been lost, there arose four men who at different periods wrote four gospels containing the life-story of Jesus together with remnants of his teachings. These were believed to have been written under Divine influence and therefore the Christian conception of revelation could go no further. According to the Qur'ān, the illumination of the mind, or the inspiration of the mind of man with a certain idea, or, as it is called in the Qur'ān, the putting of a hasty suggestion into the mind, is only the lowest form of revelation, common both to the prophet and to him who is not a prophet, the only difference being that, in the case of the prophet, it is a very clear idea while in the case of others it may be clear or vague, according to the capacity of the recipient. Revelation, in which words are communicated to the Prophet through the angel Gabriel, is the highest and most developed form of revelation, while next to it in force and clarity come the words communicated to the righteous among the Muslims, or the visions shown to them.

and technically the word revelation (*waḥy*) is applied to this form as distinguished from the lower forms.

Object of God's revelation to man

Speaking of Adam, the Qur'ān has stated the reason why revelation from God was needed, and the purpose which it fulfilled. Man had two objects before him, to conquer nature and to conquer self, to bring under his control the powers of nature and his own desire. In the story of Adam as the prototype of man, as related in the Qur'ān[8], we are told that Adam was given the knowledge of things, that is to say that man was endowed with the capacity to obtain knowledge of all things; he was also gifted with the power to conquer nature, for the angels (beings controlling powers of nature) were made to submit to him; but Iblīs (the inciter of lower desires in man) did not make obeisance, and man fell a prey to his evil suggestions. Man was powerful against all, but weak against himself. He could attain perfection in one direction by his own exertions; he could conquer nature by his knowledge of things and the power granted

[8] See (2 : 30 - 38). I quote here the more important passages of this section: "And when thy Lord said to the angels, I am going to place a ruler in the earth, they said: Wilt Thou place in it such (beings) as make mischief in it and shed blood? And we celebrate Thy praise and extol Thy holiness. He said, Surely I know what you know not. And he taught Adam all the names (*i.e.*, gave Adam knowledge of all things)... And when We said to the angels, Be submissive to Adam, they submitted but Iblīs did not. He refused and he was proud, and he was one of the disbelievers. And We said, O Adam! dwell thou and thy wife in the garden, and eat from it a plenteous (food) wherever you wish, and approach not this tree, lest you be of the unjust. But the devil made them slip from it, and caused them to depart from the state in which they were.. And Adam received (revealed) words from his Lord, and He turned to him mercifully. Surely He is Oft-returning to mercy, the Merciful. We said, Go forth from this state all, so surely there will come to you a guidance from Me, then whoever follows My guidance, no fear shall come upon them, nor shall they grieve." Light is thrown on this subject by what is stated elsewhere in the same connection: "And We indeed created you, then We fashioned you, then We said to the angels, Make submission to Adam. So they submitted except Iblīs; he was not of those who submitted... And We said: O Adam! dwell thou and thy wife in the garden... But the devil made an evil suggestion to them that he might make manifest to them that which has been hidden from them of their shame (7 : 11 - 20). The latter passage shows that in the story of Adam, the story is related of every son of man, that it was by his evil suggestion that the devil misled man and that this suggestion was in connection with man's own evil inclination. This is made yet more clear by a warning to all sons of man: "O children of Adam! let not the devil seduce you as he expelled your parents from the garden, pulling off from them their clothing that he might show them their shame. He surely sees you, he as well as his host, from whence you see them not" (7 : 27).

to him; but the greater conquest and the greater perfection lay in the conquest of his inner self, and this conquest could only be brought about by a closer connection with the Divine Being. It was to make this perfection possible for him that revelation was needed. Thus, we are told, when man proved weak against his own desires and passions, Divine help came to him in the form of certain "words from his Lord", that is to say, in the form of Divine revelation which was granted to Adam. And as for his posterity, the Divine law was given: "Surely there will come to you a guidance from Me, then whoever follows My guidance, no fear shall come upon them, nor shall they grieve" (2 : 38). In these words man is told that, with the help of Divine revelation, he shall have no fear of the Devil's temptings, and so the hindrance of his progress and the obstacle to the development of his faculties being removed, he will go on advancing on the road to perfection.

Revelation is a universal fact

It has already been pointed out that revelation in its lower forms, in the form of inspiration or that of dreams or visions, is the universal experience of humanity, but even in its highest form, it is not, according to the Qur'ān, limited to one particular man or to one particular nation. It is, on the other hand, most emphatically stated that just as God has given His physical sustenance to each and every nation, even so He has endowed it with His spiritual sustenance for its moral and spiritual advancement. Two quotations from the Qur'ān will suffice to show that revelation in its highest form has been granted to every nation: "There is not a people but a warner has gone among them" (35 : 24). "And for every nation there is a messenger" (10 : 47). And thus the idea of revelation in Islām is as broad as humanity itself.

Belief in all sacred scriptures is an article of Muslim faith

The religion of Islām, therefore, requires a belief, not in the Qur'ān alone but in all the books of God, granted to all the nations of the world. At its very commencement it lays down in clear words: "And who believe in that which has been revealed to thee and that which was revealed before thee" (2 : 4). And again: "The Messenger believes in what has been revealed to him from his Lord, and so do the believers; they all believe in Allāh and His angels and His Books and His messengers" (2 : 285).

A book was granted to every prophet of God: "Mankind is a single nation. So Allāh raised prophets as bearers of good news and as warners, and He revealed with them the book with truth" (2 : 213); "But if they reject thee, so indeed were rejected before thee messengers who came with clear arguments and scriptures and the illuminating Book" (3 : 183). Only two books are mentioned by their special names, the *Taurāt* (Torah, or book of Moses) and the *Injīl* (Gospel, or book of Jesus). The giving of a scripture (*zabūr*) to David is also mentioned (17 : 55), and the scriptures (*ṣuḥuf*) of Abraham and Moses are mentioned together in 53 : 36, 37 and 87 : 19. But, as stated above, a Muslim is required to believe, not only in the particular books named but in all the books of all the prophets of God, in other words, in the sacred scriptures of every nation, because every nation had a prophet and every prophet had a book.

Revelation brought to perfection

According to the Qur'ān, revelation is not only universal but also progressive, attaining perfection in the last of the prophets, the Prophet Muḥummad. A revelation was granted to each nation according to its requirements, and in each age in accordance with the capacity of the people of that age. And as the human brain became more and more developed, more and yet more light was cast by revelation on matters relating to the unseen, on the existence and attributes of the Divine Being, on the nature of revelation from Him, on the requital of good and evil, on life after death, on Paradise and Hell. The Qur'ān is called a book "that makes manifest," because it shed complete light on the essentials of religion, and made manifest what had hitherto remained, of necessity, obscure. It is on account of this full resplendence of light which it casts on all religious problems that the Qur'ān claims to have brought religion to perfection: "This day have I perfected for you your religion and completed My favour to you and chosen for you Islām as a religion" (5 : 3). Six hundred years before this revelation, Jesus Christ said: 'I have yet many things to say unto you, but ye cannot bear them now. Howbeit when he, the Spirit of truth, is come, he will guide you into all truth" (Jn. 16 : 12, 13). This is clearly a reference to the coming of a revelation with which religion will come to perfection, and, among the sacred books of the world, the Qur'ān alone advances the claim that it has brought religion to perfection; and, in keeping with that claim, has cast the fullest light on all religious questions.

The Qur'ān as guardian and judge of previous revelation

Besides bringing revelation to perfection and making plain what was obscure in the previous scriptures, the Qur'ān claims to be a guardian over those scriptures, guarding the original teachings of the prophets of God, and a judge deciding the differences between them. Thus after speaking of the Torah and the Gospel (5 : 44, 47), it says: "And We have revealed to thee the Book with the truth, verifying that which is before it of the book and a guardian over it" (5 : 48). It is elsewhere pointed out in the Qur'ān that the teachings of the earlier scriptures had undergone alterations, and therefore only a revelation from God could separate the pure Divine teaching from the mass of error which had grown around it. This the Qur'ān did, and hence it is called a guardian over the earlier scriptures. As for its authority as a judge, we are told: "We certainly sent messengers to nations before thee... And We have not revealed to thee the Book except that thou mayest make clear to them that wherein they differ" (16 : 63, 64). Religious differences had grown to a large extent. All religions were from God, yet they all denounced one another as leading man to perdition; and their basic doctrines had come to differ from one another to such an extent that it had become simply unthinkable that they could have proceeded from the same Divine source; till the Qur'ān pointed out the common ground, namely, the Unity of God, and the universality of revelation.

Defects of earlier scriptures removed

There is much that is common to the Qur'ān and the previous scriptures, especially the Bible. The Qur'ān has repeatedly declared that the basic principles of all religions were the same, only the details differing according to the time and the stage of a people's development. All these principles in a more developed form are taught by the Qur'ān, and occasionally lessons have been drawn from previous history. But the remarkable thing is that, both in its discussion or religious principles and in its references to history, the Qur'ān has done away with the defects of the earlier books. Take, for example, the Bible. It mentions many incidents which, so far from conveying any ennobling lesson, are derogatory to the dignity of prophethood and, sometimes, even of an obscene nature. An educated Jew or Christian would prefer that his sacred book did not contain such statements as that Abraham, that great and revered patriarch of all nations, was a liar, that Lot committed incest with his own daughters, that Aaron made the image of a calf and led the Israelites to its worship; that David, whose beautiful Psalms are the texts of sermons in churches and synagogues, committed adultery with Uria's wife, and that Solomon with all his wisdom worshipped idols to please his wives! The Qur'ān speaks of all these great men but it accepts none of these statements and rejects most of them in unmistakable words. Again, it speaks of the Devil tempting Adam, but in a language which makes it clear that it is the story of man's everyday experience; there is no image of dust into whose nostrils the breath of life is breathed; no rib of Adam is taken out to make the woman; there is no Divine interdiction against the tree of the knowledge of good and evil; there is no serpent to beguile the woman, nor does the woman tempt the man; the Lord God does not walk in the garden in the cool of the day; no punishment is meted out to the serpent that he shall go on his belly and eat dust; the bringing forth of children is not a punishment for the woman, nor is labouring in the fields a punishment for the man. Similarly the Qur'ān relates the history of Noah several times, but not once does it state that there was a deluge which covered the whole earth and destroyed all living creatures on the face of the earth. It only speaks of a flood that destroyed Noah's people. There are many other examples[9] which show that, though the Qur'ān relates the histories of some of the prophets of yore in order to draw lessons therefrom, yet it does not borrow from the Bible. It is from the Divine source that its knowledge is drawn, and hence it is that when referring to those histories, it removes all their defects.

Alterations of the text of previous scriptures

The examples given above show that the old scriptures, though revealed by God, have undergone considerable changes; and this is not only true of the Bible but applies with equal truth to all the ancient revealed books. Modern criticism of the Bible, together with the accessibility of ancient manuscripts, has now established the fact that many alterations were made in it; it is over thirteen hundred years since the Qur'ān

[9] I have noted these and other differences between the Qur'ān and the Bible in the notes to my Translation of the Qur'ān to which I may refer the reader who seeks further information on this point.

charged the followers of the Bible with altering its text, and that at a time when nobody knew that such alterations had been made in its text. Only one quotation may be given in this connection: "Do you then hope that they would believe in you, and a party from among them indeed used to hear the word of Allāh, then altered it after they had understood it, and they know (this)... Woe, then, to those who write the book with their hands and then say, This is from Allāh; so that they may take for it a small price!" (2 : 75 - 79).[10] Hence it should be borne in mind that though the Qur'ān speaks again and again of "verifying" what is before it, yet

[10] The following examples of alterations in some of the Old and New Testament books are taken from a Christian commentator on the Bible. Regarding the authorship of the Pentateuch which has generally been ascribed to Moses, he says: "On close examination, however, it must be admitted that the Pentateuch reveals many features inconsistent with the tradional view that in its present form it is the work of Moses. For instance, it may be safely granted that Moses did not write the account of his own death in Dt. 34... In Gn. 14 : 14 and Dt. 34 mention is made of Dan; but the territory did not receive that name till it was conquered by the Danites, long after the death of Moses (Josh 19 : 47; Jg. 18 : 29). Again, in Nu. 21 : 14, 15 there is quoted as an ancient authority 'the book of the Wars of the Lord', which plainly could not have been earlier than the days of Moses. Other passages which can with difficulty be ascribed to him are Ex. 6 : 26, 27; 11 : 3; 16 : 35, 36; Lv. 18 : 24 - 28; Nu. 12 : 3; Dt. 2 : 12" (Dm. p. xxv). And again: "A careful examination has led many scholars to the conviction that the writings of Moses formed only the rough material or part of the material, and that in its present form it is not the work of one man, but a compilation made from previously existing documents" (*ibid.*, p. xxvi).

How true are the words of the Qur'ān, uttered 1300 years ago: "Who write the book with their hands, then say, This is from Allāh".

The case of other books of the Bible is no better. Even the Gospels are admitted to have been altered. The original Gospel of Jesus Christ is nowhere to be found. But even the authenticity of the authorship of St. Matthew and the others is doubtful. As Dummelow says, "Direct authorship of this Gospel by the apostle Matthew is improbable" (Dm. p. 620). As regards Mark, he says: "Internal evidence points definitely to the conclusion that the last twelve verses (*i.e.*, 16 : 9 - 20) are not by St. Mark" (*ibid.*, p. 732). The explanation as to how these verses found a place here is very interesting. It is stated that the Gospel of Mark, being the first authoritative account of the life of Jesus, gained a good circulation at first; but, later on, Matthew and Luke became more popular, and Mark was, so to say, put in the shade. "When at the close of the apostolic age an attempt was made (probably in Rome) to collect the authentic memorials of the Apostles and their companions, a copy of the neglected Second Gospel was not easily found. The one that was actually discovered, and was used to multiply copies, had lost its last leaf, and so a fitting termination (the present appendix) was added by another hand" (Dm. p. 733). Many other examples of changes made in the text can be quoted, but one more would suffice. Commenting on the well-known confession of Christ, "Why callest thou me good," (Mk. 10 : 18) Dummelow says that in the Revised Version of Matthew, Christ's reply is: "Why askest thou me concerning that which is good"; and adds: "The author of Matthew... altered the text slightly, to prevent the reader from supposing that Christ denied that He was good" (*ibid.*, p. 730).

it does not and cannot mean that there have been no alterations in them. On the other hand, it condemns many of the doctrines taught by the followers of the earlier scriptures, and this shows that while their origin is admitted to be Divine, it is at the same time pointed out that these books have not come down to us in their original purity, and that the truth revealed in them has been mixed up with errors due to alterations effected by human hands.

Door to revelation is not closed

In almost every great religion, Divine revelation is considered to be the particular experience of a particular race or nation, and even in that nation the door to revelation is looked upon as having been closed after some great personage or after a certain time. But Islām, while making revelation the universal experience of humanity, also considers its doors as standing open for all time. There is an erroneous idea in some minds that, in Islām, the door to revelation was closed with Prophet Muḥammad, because it is stated in the Qur'ān that he is the last of the prophets. Why there shall be no prophet after him will be discussed in the next chapter, but it is an error to confuse the discontinuance of prophethood with the discontinuation of revelation. It has been shown that of the three kinds of revelation, two are common to both prophets and those who are not prophets, while only one form of revelation, the highest, in which the angel Gabriel is sent with a message in words, is peculiar to the prophets; and therefore when it is said that no prophet shall appear after Prophet Muḥammad, the only conclusion that can be drawn from it is that door has been closed on that highest form of revelation; but by no stretch of words can revelation itself be said to have come to an end. The granting of revelation to those who are not prophets being an admitted fact, as shown before on the basis of clear Quranic verses, revelation remains, and humanity will always have access to this great Divine blessing, though prophethood, having reached its perfection, has naturally come to an end. The doctrine of the continuance of revelation is clearly upheld in the Qur'ān and the Tradition. The former says: "Those who believe and guard against evil, for them is good news (*bushrā*) in this world's life and in the hereafter" (10 : 63, 64). The *bushrā* granted in this world's life are "good visions which the Muslim sees or which are shown to him," according to a saying of the Prophet (Rz). And according to one of the most reliable traditions, *bushrā* or *mubashshirāt* — both words having the same significance — are a part of prophethood. Thus the Prophet is reported to have said: "Nothing remains of prophethood but *mubashshirāt*," (Bu. 92 : 5). Being asked what was meant by *mubashshirāt*, he replied, "good (or true) visions" (Bu. 92 : 5). According to another tradition he is reported to have said: "The vision of the believer is one of the forty-six parts of prophethood" (Bu. 92 : 4). In another version of the same report, instead of the *vision of the believer*, the words are *good* (or *true*) *visions (ru'yā ṣāliḥah)*. The word *vision* is used here in a wide sense, and includes the inspiration which is granted to the righteous. For we are told in yet another tradition: "There used to be among those who were before you persons who were spoken to (by God) though they were not prophets; if there is such a one among my people, it is 'Umar" (Bu. 62 : 6). All these traditions and the Quranic verses quoted above afford enough proof that revelation in some of its lower forms is continued after the Prophet, and it is only the highest form of revelation — that brought by Gabriel — which has been discontinued with the termination of prophethood.

Kalām ***(speaking) is an attribute of the Divine Being***

It is thus one of the basic principles of Islām that God speaks as He hears and sees. It has been said that God is never spoken of in the Qur'ān as *Mutakallim* or *Kalīm*, that is, as One Who speaks.[11] It has already been shown that there are many names of the Divine Being that are taken from some attribute or act ascribed to Him in the Qur'ān, as for instance, *al-Rāfi', al-Qābidz, al-Bā'siṭ, al-Mujīb, al-Muḥyī*, etc. There are even names that are taken not from an express attribute or act but from the sense simply, as *al-Wājid, al-Muqaddim, al-Mu'akhkhir*, etc. Now the attribute *kalām* of the Divine Being is mentioned frequently in the Qur'ān. God spoke to (*kallama*) Moses (4 : 164; 7 : 143); He spoke to (*kallama*) other prophets (2 : 253); He speaks to those who are not prophets (42 : 51). This leaves no doubt that speaking is an attribute of God according to the Qur'ān, just as seeing and hearing are His attributes. The list of the ninety-nine names that has been prepared may not include it, but the Qur'ān definitely and decidedly states again and again that God has been speaking to His servants. Hence, though no prophet

[11] En. Is., art. Kalām.

will come after Prophet Muḥammad, yet God still speaks to His righteous servants, because it is one of His attributes, and because His attributes cannot cease to function.

The useless controversy which once occupied the attention of the Muslim world as to whether the Qur'ān was created or uncreated, and whether it was eternal or came into existence afterwards (*muḥdath*), on account of which many men of note had to suffer great hardships, seems to have been due to some misunderstanding. It is recognized by all that speech (*kalām*) is an attribute of God, and all attributes of the Divine Being are inseparable from Him; indeed the Divine Being could not be conceived of as existing without these. Hence none of His attributes could be said either to have been created or to be *muḥdath*, that is, coming into existence afterwards. But there is equally no doubt that Divine attributes find expression at different times. God sees and hears from eternity, He sees and hears now and He will see and hear in the future. Similarly He speaks from eternity; He speaks even now and He will speak in the future. When Adam came into this world, He granted Him a revelation; afterwards He granted a revelation to Noah, then to Abraham, then to Moses. He granted revelations to all nations of the world, each at a particular time and in the language of that particular people. That revelation, and in fact all events of the future, existed in His unlimited knowledge from all eternity, but so far as human experience is concerned, it was new (*muḥdath*), and we have to speak in terms of human experience. Nothing is new in the sight of God, whenever done, but according to our conception of things, the revelations given to Adam and to Noah and to all other prophets were new when they were granted. The Qur'ān itself is explicit on this point: "There comes not to them a new (*muḥdath*) Reminder from their Lord but they hear it while they sport" (21 : 2). In this sense, the Qur'ān was also a new reminder, though it was there in the knowledge of God from all eternity. But things cannot be said to be eternal and uncreated, simply because they are in the knowledge of God from eternity.

CHAPTER V

PROPHETS

Nabī *and* **Rasūl**

The next article of faith in the Muslim catechism is belief in the prophets. The Arabic word for prophet is *nabī*, which is derived from *naba'*, meaning *an announcement of great utility*: *imparting knowledge of a thing* (R.). It is added by the same authority that the word *naba'* is applied only to such information as is free from any liability to untruth.[1] One lexicologist explains the word *nabī* as meaning *an ambassador between God and rational beings from among His creatures* (R.). According to another, a *nabī* is *the man who gives information about God* (Q.)[2] A *nabī* is also called a *rasūl*, which means *an apostle* or *messenger*.[3] The two words *nabī* and *rasūl* are used interchangeably in the Qur'ān, the same person being sometimes called *nabī* and sometimes *rasūl*; while occasionally both names are combined. The reason seems to be that the prophet has two capacities, *viz.*, he receives information from God, and he imparts the message to mankind. He is called a *nabī* in his first, and a *rasūl* in his second capacity, but there is one difference. The word *rasūl* has a wider significance, being applicable to every messenger in a literal sense; and the angels are called Divine "messengers",[4] because they are also bearers of Divine messages when complying with His Will.

Faith in Divine messengers

It has already been stated that a faith in Divine revelation is one of the essentials of Islām, and since revelation must be communicated through a man, faith in the messenger is a natural sequence, and is mentioned

[1] It should be noted that the *hamza (')* in the root-word *naba'* is dropped in the word *nabī*. It is for this reason that some authorities are of opinion that *nabī* is derived from *nubuwwa* meaning *the state of being exalted.*

[2] This is further explained as *the man to whom God gives information concerning His Unity and to whom He reveals secrets of the future and imparts the knowledge that he is His prophet* (TA.).

[3] Lit., *one sent*.

[4] *Rusul*, pl. of *rasūl*, see 351 : 1.

in the Qur'ān along with faith in the revealed books.[5] In fact there is a deeper significance underlying faith in the prophets, and hence the greater stress is laid upon this article of faith. The prophet is not only the bearer of the Divine message but he also shows how that message is to be interpreted in practical life; and therefore he is the model to be followed. It is the prophet's example that inspires a living faith in the hearts of his followers and brings about a real transformation in their lives. That is why the Qur'ān lays special stress on the fact that the prophet must be a human being: "Had there been in the earth angels walking about secure, We would have sent down to them an angel from the heaven as a messenger" (17 : 95); "And We sent not before thee any but men to whom We sent revelation...Nor did We give them bodies not eating food" (21 : 7, 8).

Universality of the institution of prophethood

Prophethood is a free Divine gift to man, *a mauhiba*,[6] according to the Qur'ān. Just as He has granted His gifts of physical sustenance to all men alike, so His spiritual gift of prophethood, through which a spiritual life is awakened in man, is also a free gift to all the nations of the world. It is not among the Israelites alone that prophets were raised as would appear from the Bible. According to the Qur'ān, there is not one nation in the world in which a prophet has not appeared: "There is not a people but a warner has gone among them" (35 : 24). And again: "For every nation there is a messenger" (10 : 47). We are further told that there have been prophets besides those mentioned in the Qur'ān: "And We sent messengers We have mentioned to thee before, and messengers We have not mentioned to thee" (4 : 164). It is, in fact, stated in a tradition that there have been 124,000 prophets, while the Qur'ān contains only about twenty-five names, among them being several non-Biblical prophets, Hūd and Ṣāliḥ in Arabia, Luqmān in Ethiopia, a contemporary of Moses (generally known as *Khidzr*) in Sūdān, and Dhu-l-Qarnain

[5] See 2 : 177, 285.

[6] The Qur'ān itself is called a gift of God: "The Beneficent God (*al-Raḥmān*) taught the Qur'ān" (55 ; 1, 2). That is to say, it is a free gift of God, not the result of anything done on the part of man, because *al-Raḥmān* means the bestower of free gifts. We are also told that no man can rise to the dignity of prophethood by his own efforts; it is God Who raises someone to that dignity when He intends to reform men. Thus the unbelievers' question, as to why revelation is not sent to them is met with the reply: "God knows best where He places His message" (6 : 125).

(Darius I, who was also a king) in Persia; all of which is quite in accordance with the theory of the universality of prophethood. And as the Holy Book has plainly said that prophets have appeared in all nations and that it has not named all of them, which in fact was unnecessary, a Muslim may accept the great luminaries who are accepted by other nations as having brought light to them, as the prophets of those nations.

A Muslim must believe in all the prophets

The Qur'ān, however, not only establishes the theory that prophets have appeared in all nations; it goes further and renders it necessary that a Muslim should believe in all those prophets. In the very beginning we are told that a Muslim must "believe in that which has been revealed to thee and that which was revealed before thee" (2 : 4); and a little further on: "We believe in Allāh and in that which has been revealed to us and in that which was revealed to Abraham and Ishmael and Isaac and Jacob and the tribes, and in that which was given to Moses and Jesus, and in that which was given to the prophets from their Lord; we do not make any distinction between any of them" (2 : 136), where the word *prophets* clearly refers to the prophets of other nations. And again, the Qur'ān speaks of Muslims as believing in all the prophets of God and not in Prophet Muḥammad alone : "Righteous is the one who believes in Allāh and the Last Day and the angels and the Book[7] and the prophets" (2 : 177); "The Messenger believes in what has been revealed to him from his Lord, and so do the believers; they all believe in Allāh and His angels and His Books and His messengers; we make no distinction between any of His messengers" (2 : 285). In fact, to believe in some prophets and reject others is condemned as unbelief (*kufr*): "Those who disbelieve in Allāh and His messengers,and desire to make a distinction between Allāh and His messengers and say: We believe in some and disbelieve in others, and desire to take a course in between — these are truly disbelievers" (4 : 150, 151). A belief in all the prophets of the world is thus an essential principle of the religion of Islām, and though the faith of Islām is summed up in two brief sentences, there is no god but Allāh and Muḥammad is His apostle, yet the man who confesses belief in Prophet

[7] While a belief in all the prophets is stated to be necessary, *the Book* is spoken of in singular in this verse. *The Book* therefore stands for Divine Revelation in general or the scriptures of all the prophets; or because the Qur'ān is a book "wherein are all the right books" (98 : 3), it might mean the Qur'ān.

Muḥammad, in so doing, accepts all the prophets of the world, whether their names are mentioned in the Qur'ān or not. Islām claims a universality to which no other religion can aspire, and lays the foundation of a brotherhood as vast as humanity itself.

National Prophets

The Divine scheme whereby prophets were raised for the regeneration of the world, as disclosed in the Qur'ān, may be briefly summed up as follows. Prophets appeared in every nation, but their message was limited to that particular nation and in some cases to one or a few generations. All these prophets were, so to say, national prophets, and their work was limited to the moral upliftment and spiritual regeneration of one nation only. But while national growth was of necessity the first step, when each nation lived almost an exclusive life and the means of communication were wanting, the grand aim which the Divine scheme had in view was the upliftment and unification of the whole human race. Humanity could not remain for ever divided into water-tight compartments of nationality, formed on the basis of blood or geographical limitations. In fact these divisions had, through jealousy, become the means of discord and hatred among different nations, each looking upon itself as the only chosen nation, and despising the rest. Such views tended to extinguish any faint glimmerings of aspirations for the unity of the human race. The final step, therefore, in the institution of prophethood was the coming of one prophet for all the nations, so that the consciousness of being one whole might be brought to the human race. The day of the national prophet was ended; it had served the purpose for which it was meant, and the day of the world-prophet dawned upon humanity in the person of Prophet Muḥammad.

The world-prophet

The idea of the world-prophet is not based on a solitary passage occurring in the Qur'ān, as to the extent of the mission of this or that prophet; but is a fully developed Divine scheme. When mentioning the earlier prophets the Qur'ān says that Noah was sent "to his people",[8]

[8] 7 : 59; 71 : 1.

and so Hūd[9] and Ṣāliḥ[10] and Shu'aib[11] — everyone of them was sent to *his* people. It speaks of Moses as being commanded to "bring forth *thy* people from darkness into light",[12] it speaks of Jesus as "a messenger to the children of Israel"[13] but in speaking of Prophet Muḥammad it says in unequivocal words that "We have not sent thee but as a bearer of good news and as a warner *to all mankind*[14]. On another occasion also, the universality of the Prophet's mission is thus stressed: "Say, O mankind, surely I am the Messenger of Allāh to you all, of Him Whose is the kingdom of the heavens and the earth" (7 : 158). One thing is sure that no other prophet is spoken of either in the Qur'ān or in any other scripture[15] as having been sent to the whole of humanity or to all people or all nations; nor is Prophet Muḥammad ever spoken of in the Qur'ān as having been sent to *his people* only.[16] The Qur'ān itself is repeatedly termed "a Reminder for the nations".[17] And the Prophet is not only a warner to all the nations but a mercy to all of them as well: "And We have not sent thee but as a mercy to the nations" (21 : 107).

The idea that a world-prophet must follow the national prophets is further developed in the Qur'ān. It is in a Madīnah revelation[18] that the whole

[9] 7 : 65.

[10] 7 : 73.

[11] 7 : 85.

[12] 14 : 5.

[13] 3 : 48.

[14] The Arabic words for *all mankind* are *kāffat-an li-l-nās,* where even *al-nās* carries the idea of *all people,* and the addition of *kāffah* is meant to emphasize further that not a single nation was excluded from the heavenly ministration of the Prophet Muḥammad.

[15] Jesus Christ was the last of these national prophets; and though the message of Christianity has now been conveyed to all the nations of the world, yet that was never Christ's own idea. He was perfectly sure that he was "not sent but unto the lost sheep of the house of Israel" (Mt. 15 : 24); so sure indeed that he did not hesitate to call those who were not Israelites "dogs" in comparison with the "the children" who were the Israelites (Mt.15 : 26), and the bread of the children could not be cast to the dogs. Nevertheless, the idea of casting the heavenly bread of Jesus to the same non-Israelite "dogs" entered the head of one of his disciples, after "the children" had shown no desire to accept that bread.

[16] It is, no doubt, true that he is commanded to warn "a people whose fathers were not warned" (36 : 6), but that does not mean that he was not to warn others than Arabs, for in 25 : 1 he is expressly described as being "a warner to all the nations."

[17] 68 : 52; 81 : 27; 38 : 87; 12 : 104.

[18] — see next page.

proposition, the appearance of a world-prophet, the distinguishing feature of his religion and the necessity for believing in him is laid down in clear words. The complete passage is as follows: "And when Allāh made a covenant through the prophets: Certainly what I have given you of Book and wisdom — then a messenger comes to you verifying that which is with you, you shall believe in him, and you shall aid him. He said, Do you affirm and accept My compact in this matter? They said, We do affirm. He said, Then bear witness, and I too am of the bearers of witness with you. Whoever then turns back after this, these are the transgressors. Seek they then other than Allāh's religion? And to Him submits whoever is in the heavens and the earth, willingly or unwillingly, and to Him they will be returned. Say: We believe in Allāh and that which is revealed to us, and that which was revealed to Abraham, and Ishmael and Isaac and Jacob and the tribes, and that which was given to Moses and Jesus and to the prophets from their Lord; we do not make any distinction between any of them, and to Him we submit. And whoever seeks a religion other than Islām, it will not be accepted from him, and in the Hereafter he will be one of the losers" (3 : 80-84).

That a world-prophet is spoken of here is evident from the fact that his acceptance — "you must believe in him and you must aid him" — is made obligatory on the followers of all the prophets that had passed away before him. As prophets had been sent, according to the teachings of the Qur'ān, to every nation, the conclusion is obvious that the followers of every prophet are required to believe in this, the final Prophet. The distinguishing feature of the world-prophet as mentioned here is that he will "verify that which is with you," in other words, that he will bear testimony to the truth of all the prophets of the world. One may turn the pages of all the sacred books and search the sacred history of every nation, and it would be found that there was but One Prophet who verified the scriptures of *all* religions and bore testimony to the truth of the prophets of every nation. In fact, no one could aspire to the dignity of world-prophet

[18] A. J. Wensinck advances a new theory in his book, *The Creed of Islam,* to the effect that though there are passages in the Qur'ān which speak of a universal mission of Prophet Muḥammad, but it was an earlier idea given up later: "It is true that there are in the Kuran expressions that seem to cover a wider field. We have already seen an example of this in the verse, 'Say to them, O men! verily I am unto you all the Apostle of God.' None of these passages, however, seem to have been revealed after the Hidjra"(p.7). One fails to understand the force of the agrument, if there be one, conveyed in these words. When a proposition is so clearly stated, what difference does it make whether it was uttered in Makkah or Madīnah. As a matter of fact, Madīnah and Makkah revelations are equally clear as to the universality of the Prophet's mission.

who did not treat the whole humanity as one; and Muḥammad is the only man who did so by declaring that prophets of God had appeared in every nation and that every one who believed in him must also believe in *all* the prophets of the world. Hence it is that the verse requiring a belief in all the prophets of God — a belief in Abraham, in Ishmael, in Isaac, in Jacob, in Moses, in Jesus, and finally and comprehensively in *the prophets*, — which occurs several times in the Qur'ān, is repeated here again, and followed by the clear statement that Islām, or *belief in all the prophets of God,* is the only religion with God, and whosoever desires a religion *other than Islām* — a belief only in one prophet while rejecting all others — it shall not be accepted from him, because belief in *one* prophet is, after all, only acceptance of partial truth, and tantamount to the rejection of the whole truth, to wit, that there have been prophets in every nation.

Muḥammad (peace be on him), therefore, does not only claim to have been sent to the whole world, to be a warner to all peoples and a mercy to all nations but lays the foundations of a world-religion, by making a belief in the prophet of every nation the basic principle of his faith. It is the only principle on which the whole of humanity can agree, the only basis of equal treatment for all nations. The idea of a world-prophet is not a stray idea met with in the Qur'ān; it is not based simply on one or two passages, stating that he had been raised for the regeneration of all nations; but the idea is here developed at length, and all the principles which can form the basis of a world-religion are fully enunciated. The whole of humanity is declared to be one nation (2 : 213); God is said to be the *Rabb* (lit. *the Nourisher unto perfection*) of all nations (1 : 1); prophets are declared to have been raised in all the nations for their uplift (35 : 24); all prejudices of colour, race and language are demolished (30 : 22; 49 : 13); and a vast brotherhood, extending over all the world, has been established, every member of which is bound to accept the prophets of all nations, and to treat all nations equally. Thus not only is the Prophet Muḥammad a world-prophet who takes the place of the national prophets but he had also established a world-religion wherein the idea of nationality is superseded by the consciousness of the unity of the human race.

All prophets are one community

All prophets, being from God, are as it were brethren. This doctrine of the brotherhood of all prophets is not only taught in the interdiction against making distinctions between the prophets of God, as stated above, but is laid down in the plainest words in both the Qur'ān and Tradition. Thus, after speaking of various prophets in the chapter *Prophets*, we are told: "Surely this your community is a single community" (21 : 92). And again: "O ye messengers, eat of the good things and do good. Surely I am Knower of what you do. And surely this your community is one community and I am your Lord" (23 : 51, 52). Tradition also tells us that all prophets are as brothers: "The prophets are, as it were, brothers on the mothers' side, their affair is one and their followers are different" (Bu. 60 : 48). Every prophet may have some special characteristic of his own, but, generally, what is said of one in the Qur'ān, of his high morals or sublime character or noble teachings or trust in God, is true of all. Thus of Abraham we are told that he was "a truthful man" (19 : 41); of Moses that he was "one purified" (19 : 51), or that he was "brought up before My eyes" (20 : 39); of Ishmael that he was "truthful in promise" or "one in whom his Lord was well pleased" (19 : 54, 55); of Noah, Hūd, Sāliḥ, and Lot that they were "faithful" (26 : 107, 125, 143, 162); of Jesus that he was "worthy of regard in this world and the hereafter, and one of those who are drawn nigh to Allāh" (3 : 44); of John the Baptist that "We granted him wisdom ... and kind-heartedness from Us and purity, and he was dutiful and kindly to his parents and he was not insolent, disobedient (19 : 12-14), or that he was "honourable and chaste" (3 : 38). It is the gravest mistake to think that the high qualities attributed to one prophet may be wanting in others. The prophets are all one community; they were all raised for one purpose; the teachings of all were essentially the same; they were all truthful, all faithful, all worthy of regard; all were made near to God, all were pure, all of them guarded against evil, all were honourable and chaste, and none of them was insolent or disobedient to God.[19]

[19] As the Christian religion is based on the supposition that Jesus Christ was the son of God and that he alone, being sinless, could be an atonement for the sins of humanity, every Christian writer has taken pains to call in the help of the Qur'ān for the exclusive sinlessness of Jesus Christ, while the Gospels deal a death-blow to that sinlessness by the plain answer he is said to have given to one who called him "good master": "Why callest thou me good? There is none good but one, that is God" (Mt. 19 : 17; Mk. 10 : 18). In the Qur'ān, all prophets are treated as one community. The Christian argument that Jesus is spoken of as "worthy of regard" and as "one drawn nigh to Allāh"and that therefore other prophets were not such would, if applied against Jesus, mean that, since of John it is said that he was "chaste" and "one who guarded against evil," therefore Jesus Christ was not chaste, nor did he guard against evil; or since of Abraham it is said that he was "truthful" but not so of Jesus, therefore Jesus was not truthful. It

Why prophets are raised

The prophets are raised for the uplift of humanity and for freeing men from the bondage of sin. It has been shown in the last chapter that Divine revelation was needed to enable man to subdue the devil, who would, otherwise, be a great hindrance in his moral and spiritual progress. Man was commanded to live in a spiritual paradise, but since he was unable to withstand the temptations of the devil, the Divine revelation came to his aid; and a rule for all time was laid down for the guidance of all men: "There will come to you a guidance from Me, then whoever follows My guidance, no fear shall come upon them, nor shall they grieve" (2 : 38). The negation of fear refers to the fear of the devil's temptation, as a remedy against which Divine revelation was first granted to man. Again, every prophet brings the message of the Unity of God, and the significance underlying this message has already been shown (in ch.2) to be the all-round advancement of man, physical as well as spiritual and moral. And every

should be noted that the Qurān speaks of Jesus as "one drawn nigh to Allāh" and, on another occasion, of the Companions of the Prophet as being *muqarrabūn* or *those made nigh to God* (56 : 11). The exclusive sinlessness of Jesus Christ is quite unknown to the Qur'ān; neither does the fact that Jesus Christ is called *kalimatu-hū* (His word) and *rūḥ-un min-hu* (a spirit from Him) in any way establish that he is looked upon as more than mortal, since his mortality is repeatedly established in the clearest words: "The likeness of Jesus with Allāh is truly as the likeness of Adam" (3 : 58); "The Messiah, son of Mary, was only a messenger; messengers before him had indeed passed away. And his mother was a truthful woman; they both used to eat food" (5 : 75). And if Jesus Christ is called God's word, it only shows that he is looked upon as a created being like other mortals, for all created things are called *words of God*: "If the sea were ink for the words of my Lord, the sea would surely be consumed before the words of my Lord are exhausted, though We brought the like of it to add thereto" (18 : 109). Jesus Christ is thus one of these numberless words. Similarly, he is called *a* spirit from God, not *the* spirit of God, as Christian writers have generally supposed: "O people of the Book, exceed not the limits in your religion, nor speak anything about Allāh but the truth. The Messiah, Jesus son of Mary, is only a messenger of Allāh, and His word which He communicated to Mary and a mercy from Him" (4 : 171). The Arabic word *rūḥ* has been translated as *mercy*. *Rauḥ* and *Rūḥ* both mean *mercy* of Allāh according to Az. (See LL. under *rauḥ*). *Rūḥ* also signifies *inspiration* or *Divine revelation* (T., LL.). The verse would then mean that the advent of Jesus was in accordance with a prophecy and an inspiration from the Divine Being. Even if we take *spirit* to be the meaning of *rūḥ*, it does not carry Jesus a step beyond the limits of mortality, for of Adam also it has been said, I *breathed My spirit into him* (15 : 29).

In fact, every man is spoken of as having the spirit of God breathed into him: "Then He made his progeny of an extract of worthless water. Then He made him complete and breathed into him of His spirit" (32 : 8, 9). Thus every man is a spirit from God; nay, he is more than this, inasmuch as every man is called a vicegerent of God (*khalīfah*) (2 : 30). Sometimes a tradition is quoted in support of the theory of the exclusive sinlessness

prophet is called *giver of good news* (*mubashshir*) and *warner* (*mundhir*) (2 : 213); the good news relating to his advancement and elevation, the warning to the retarding of or interference with his progress. The four works entrusted to the Prophet, as mentioned several times in the Qur'ān, are stated thus: "We have sent a Messenger to you from among you who recites to you Our messages and purifies you and teaches you the Book and the Wisdom" (2 : 151, etc.). The Arabic word for purifying is *yuzakkī* which is derived from *zakā*, originally meaning, according to Rāghib, the *progress attained by Divine blessing (i.e.* by the development of the faculties placed by God within man), and relates to the affairs of this world as well as the Hereafter, that is to say, to man's physical as well as spiritual advancement. The Prophet's message of *purification*, therefore, signifies not only purification from sin but also man's

of Jesus: "No child is born but the devil touches him when he is born, so he raises a cry for help on account of his touching him, except Mary and her son" (Bu. 60 : 44). A similar report is related about John the Baptist: "There is no man (*'abd*) but he will meet Allāh in a state of being sinful except John (Yaḥyā)" (IK.). Now these traditions contradict each other; for, according to the first, even John was born with a touch of the devil, while, according to the latter, even Mary and Jesus are sinful. It is therefore out of the question to take them literally. In fact, Mary and her son, in the first report and John, in the second, are mentioned as prototypes of the righteous man. The Qurān itself tells us that Mary stands for a believer: "And Allāh sets forth to those who believe the example of the wife of Pharaoh...and of Mary, the daughter of 'Imrān, who guarded her chastity, so We breathed into him of Our inspiration, and she accepted the truth of the words of her Lord and His books, and she was of the obedient ones" (66 : 11,12). The believer not yet emancipated from the bondage of sin is compared to Pharaoh's wife; Pharaoh being, as it were, the embodiment of evil; and the believer so emancipated is likened to Mary who guarded her chastity and accepted the truth of the words of her Lord. Mary, therefore, according to the Qurān, typifies the man whom the devil cannot mislead, or, in the words of the tradition, whom the devil does not touch; while her son is described in the same verse, as one into whom "We breathed of Our inspiration." The tradition therefore tells us that two kinds of men are not tempted by Satan or touched by him; of such as are not prophets, those, like Mary, who guard themselves and are perfectly obedient, and the prophets, like Jesus, who are the recipients of Divine revelation. In the second tradition, both these are called *Yaḥyā* which literally means *he is alive, i.e.*, people in whom the life spiritual is awakened. All others are said to be touched by the devil, *i.e.*, the devil misleads them at times, but being believers in God they *cry aloud for help*, such being the significance of the word *ṣārikh* used in the tradition. The time of birth mentioned indicates the spiritual birth, the first beginnings of which are marked by the struggle against evil, or the temptations of the devil, which struggle is spoken of as the crying for help to God against those temptations. Both these reports, therefore, must be accepted only metaphorically; for if they are taken in a literal sense, they contradict each other, and, not only each other but all principles of religion also, and are therefore clearly unacceptable.

setting forth on the road to physical and moral advancement.[20] All these references to the Holy Book show that the object of sending prophets was no other than the uplift of man, to enable him to subjugate his animal passions, to inspire him with nobler and higher sentiments, and to imbue him with Divine morals.

Sinlessness of prophets

The men who are commissioned for the high office of prophethood must themselves be free from the bondage of sin, and more than that be the possessors of high morals if they are to fulfil the mission entrusted to them. The doctrine of the sinlessness of prophets has therefore always been an admitted principle among Muslims. Christian writers on Islām, however, have laboured to show that this doctrine is opposed to the Qur'ān,[21] but nothing could be further from the truth. The Qur'ān not

[20] Christian theologians have greatly misunderstood the object with which prophets are raised. They think that to be delivered from the bondage of sin is the be-all and end-all of man's earthly life, the highest spiritual stage to which man can rise; and therefore they believe that prophets were sent solely for this purpose. The Qur'ān, on the other hand, looks upon sinlessness as the starting point of man's spiritual advancement. It teaches, of course, that man must resist the temptation of the devil, but that is only the first step for the proper development of the great faculties which God has granted to man and man's advancement is so limitless that it continues even after death, in a new life.

[21] Sell in *The Faith of Islam* admits that "the orthodox belief is that prophets are free from sin" (p.299), and then goes on to say that this "does not agree with actual facts." Klein in *The Religion of Islam*, while conceding the point that according to the teachings of Islām, a prophet must possess faithfulness, truthfulness and the like, and that it is impossible to ascribe to prophets attributes opposed to these, such as unfaithfulness, falseness, mendaciousness, want of intelligence, dullness, or concealing the message (pp.73,74), says that there is a "contradiction between the teaching of the Qur'ān and that of the theologians." The fact is that the Christian doctrine of Atonement is responsible for all these quibblings of the Christian controversialists. Because the "Son of God" was needed to make atonement for the sins of men, therefore all the prophets sent for the regeneration of man must be sinful. If others, besides Jesus Christ, were sinless, the world would have no need for a "Son of God". The Bible itself, notwithstanding the many alterations in it, contains clear evidence of the sinlessness of the prophets. Of Noah it is said that he "was a just man and perfect in his generations" (Gen. 6 : 9). To Abraham, the Lord said: "Walk before Me and be thou perfect" (Gen.17 : 1). To Moses, He said: "Thou shalt be perfect with the Lord thy God" (Deut.18 : 13). Now *perfect* is more than *sinless*. The Bible itself says: "Blessed are the perfect in the way, who walk in the law of the Lord...They also do no iniquity: they walk in His ways" (Ps. 119 : 1, 3). And again: "The law of his God is in his heart; none of his steps shall slide" (Ps. 37 : 31). Zacharias, according to the writers of the Gospels, was not a prophet, and yet both he and his wife

only speaks of individual prophets in terms of the highest praise, but also lays down clearly in general terms that the prophets cannot go, either in word or in deed, against any commandment of God: "And We sent no messenger before thee but We revealed to him that there is no God but Me, so serve Me. And they say, The Beneficent God has taken to Himself a son. Glory be to Him! Nay, they are honoured servants; they speak not before He speaks and according to His command they act" (21 : 25-27).[22] And elsewhere it is said: "It is not for a prophet to act dishonestly" (3 : 160). These two verses set out in general words the principle of the sinlessness of prophets, while it has already been shown how each individual prophet has been spoken of in terms of the highest praise; one is called a *Ṣiddīq* (*i.e.*, one who has never told a lie); another is said to have been purified by God's hand and to have been brought up in the Divine presence; a third is described as being one in whom God was well pleased; a fourth is mentioned as having been granted purity and as one who guarded against evil and never disobeyed; a fifth is said to be worthy of regard and one of those who are near to God; and many of them, including Prophet Muḥammad, are described as being *amīn*, which means *one who is completely faithful to God.* The Qurān, therefore leaves not the least doubt as to the sinlessness of the prophets.

are declared to be sinless: "And they were both righteous before God, walking in all the commandments and ordinances of the Lord, blameless" (Lk. 1 : 6). And of John, their son, it is said that he was "filled with the Holy Ghost, even from his mother's womb" (Lk. 1 : 15). In the face of such clear words upholding the sinlessness of prophets, and of even the righteous persons who were not prophets, it is sheer defiance of sacred authority to call the prophets sinful, for the sake of one who rebuked others for calling him "good" (Mk. 10 : 17, 18). The doctrine of the sinlessness of the prophets is therefore based on both the Qur'ān and the Bible.

[22] Commentators who have taken the last words as applying to angels, have done so only because they have paid no attention to the context. There is no doubt that, elsewhere, similar words are used about angels: "Who do not disobey Allāh in what He commands them, and do as they are commanded" (66 : 6). But the context here is too clear to need any comment. It speaks of the prophets, and then it speaks of the Christian doctrine that God has taken a son to Himself, which is based on the theory of the sinfulness of all prophets, as already shown, and hence it goes on to state in clear words that all prophets are sinless.

It may be added that while referring to the doctrine that Jesus Christ is the son of God, it is added that *they are honoured servants.* These words draw attention to the fact that others beside Jesus were spoken of as the Sons of God, but the title signified nothing more than that they were honoured servants.

Istighfār

There are, however, certain words which have been misunderstood by some critics, who have straightaway rushed to the erroneous conclusion that the Qur'ān gives no support to the doctrine of the sinlessness of prophets. The most important of these words is *istighfār* which is generally taken as meaning *asking for forgiveness of sins*. It, however, carries a wide significance. *Seeking of protection from sin*[23] is as much a meaning of *istighfār* as the *seeking of protection from the punishment of sin*. When it is established that, according to the teachings of the Qur'ān, the prophets are sinless, *istighfār* can, in their case, only be taken as meaning the *seeking of protection from the sins to which man is liable*, for it is through Divine protection alone that they can remain sinless. Hence the Prophet is spoken of in a tradition as saying *istighfār* a hundred times a day; that is to say, he was every moment seeking the protection of God, and praying to Him, that he may not go against His will. *Istighfār* or the prayer for protection (*ghafr*) is in fact a prayer for Divine help in the advancement to higher and higher stages of spiritual perfection. Thus, even those who have been admitted into Paradise are described as praying to God for His *ghafr*: "Our Lord! make perfect for us our light and grant us protection (*ghaffir*); surely, Thou art possessor of power over all things" (66 : 8). The ordinary rendering is "forgive us", but forgiveness, in the narrow sense of pardoning of sins, is meaningless here, because none can be admitted into Paradise unless his sins are pardoned. *Ghafr* or forgiveness, therefore, stands here for Divine help in the spiritual advancement of man, which will continue even after death. On another occasion, *maghfirah*, which is the same as *ghafr*, is described as a blessing of Paradise: "For them therein are all fruits and protection (*maghfirat*) from their Lord" (47 : 15). *Maghfirat* is therefore one of the blessings which the righteous shall enjoy in Paradise, and therefore a Divine help in the onward progress of man therein.

Dhanb

Another misunderstood word is *dhanb* which is generally translated as meaning sin; but *dhanb* also is a word with a very wide significance.[24] It is as much applicable to sins due to perversity as to shortcomings resulting

23 24 — see next page.

from inadvertence. In respect of the latter, there is a vast difference between the righteous man and the sinner. A righteous man, without in the least departing from the course of righteousness, would always feel that he had fallen short in doing some good to humanity or in doing his duty to God; and thus, even though he is engaged in doing good, he feels that there is something lacking in him. Between the shortcoming of such a one and that of the sinner is a world of difference. The sinner's shortcoming or *dhanb* is that he has set himself against the will of God deliberately and done evil, while the righteous man's shortcoming lies in the fact that he is not satisfied that he has done all the good that it was in his power to do.

Khaṭā'

Another word which requires to be explained in this connection is *khaṭ'a* or *khaṭā'*. This word too has a wide significance and covers all unintended actions and mistakes and errors of judgment.[25] Its mention, therefore, in connection with a prophet, does not imply sinfulness.

Individual cases: Noah and Abraham

Christian criticism of Islām has been particularly directed against the doctrine of the sinlessness of the prophets, and this, as already pointed

[23] *Istighfār* is derived from the root *ghafr* which means *the covering of a thing with that which will protect it from dirt* (R.). Hence *istighfār* means only *the seeking of a covering* or *protection*. Qaṣtalānī, in his commentary on *Bukhārī*, makes this quite clear, and adds that *ghafr* means *sitr* or *covering, which is either betwen man and his sin* or *between sin and its punishment* (Qs. I, p. 85.)

[24] According to one authority, *dhanb* is originally *taking the tail of a thing*, and it is applied to *every act the consequence of which is disagreeable* or *unwholesome* (R.). According to another, it means either *a sin*, or *a crime* or *a fault*, and it is said to differ from *ithm* in being either intentional or committed through inadvertence, whereas *ithm* is definitely intentional (LL.).

[25] According to Rāghib, *when a man intends the doing of a good thing but he happens to do instead something which he never intended*, that is also *khaṭī'a* (mistake). According to another authority, the difference between *khaṭī'a* (mistake) and *ithm* (sin) is that in the latter there is intention, which is not necessary in the former (IJ-C. V, p.162). When the *mujtahid* (one who exercises his reasoning faculty) does not arrive at a right conclusion and makes a *khaṭā'* (mistake) in his judgment, he is still said to merit a reward, since his intention was good. Hence the word *khaṭī'a* or *khaṭā'* does not necessarily imply sin.

out, is due to the Christian doctrine of Atonement which falls *ipso facto* the moment any one else is regarded as sharing with Jesus Christ the honour of sinlessness. This criticism is, however, based, not on any principle enunciated in the Qur'ān, for it is there stated in clear words that all prophets of God are faithful, both in word and deed, to the Divine commandments, but on certain cases of individual prophets. Most of this misdirected criticism is due to a wrong conception of the four words explained above, *viz.*, *ghafr, istighfār, dhanb* and *khaṭā'*. For example, it is said that Noah was a sinner because he prayed to God, saying: "My Lord! I seek refuge in Thee from asking Thee that of which I have no knowledge. And unless Thou forgive (*taghfir*) me and have mercy on me, I shall be of the losers" (11 : 47). The word used for forgiving is from *ghafr*, which, as shown above, also means the granting of protection and the prayer has not the remotest reference to any confession of sin on the part of Noah. Similarly, Abraham is looked upon as a sinner because he is spoken of as expressing the hope that God "will forgive me my mistake (*khaṭī'atī*) on the Day of Judgment" (26 : 82). It is one thing to commit a mistake and quite a different thing to go against the Divine commandments, and no sensible critic could twist such words into a confession of sin.

Prophet Muḥammad

Prophet Muḥammad is said by these critics of Islām to be a sinner because he is commended to seek Divine protection (*istaghfir*) for his *dhanb* (40 : 55). Now to seek protection against sin does not mean that sin has been commited — he who seeks Divine protection rather guards himself against the commission of sin; and, moreover, the word used here is *dhanb* which means any human shortcoming. The following verses may, however, be discussed at greater length: "Surely We have granted thee a clear victory, that Allāh may cover for thee thy (alleged) shortcomings in the past and those to come" (48 : 1, 2). The Arabic words used are *dhanbi-ka*. Even if the meaning *thy dhanb* or *thy fault* is adopted, there is no imputation of sin, but only of human shortcomings, for, as has been already shown, *dhanb* carries that wider significance. But as a matter of fact *dhanbi-ka* here means the *dhanb attributed to thee*[26] not *thy dhanb*. The

[26] This significance of the *idzāfa* is a commonplace of the Arabic language. Again and again the Qur'ān speaks of *shurakā'* (associates) of God, though the meaning is that they are the associates *attributed* to the Divine Being by polytheists. Similarly in 5 : 29, the word *ithmī* does not mean *my sin*, but *the sin committed against me*: "I would rather that thou shouldst bear the sin against me (*ithmī*) and thy own sin."

victory spoken of in the first sentence is, on the best authority,[27] the Ḥudaibiyah truce. During a prolonged state of hostilities, between the Muslims and their opponents, the latter had had no opportunity for reflecting on the beauties of Islām, but had, in fact, contracted a certain hatred towards it. They did not come into contact with the Prophet except as enemies on the field of battle, and hence they drew a dark picture of him as an enemy. The truce drawn up at Ḥudaibiyah was a victory for Islām, or, at any rate, a gain to the cause of Islām, since it put a stop to hostilities; and peace being established in the country, the non-Muslims freely mixed with the Muslims, and the good points of Islām together with the high morality of the Prophet made their impression. Misunderstandings were removed, and people began to be attracted by the bright picture of Islām. It was in this sense that the Ḥudaibiyah truce, which is called a clear victory of Islām, became the means of protection (*ghafr*) to the Prophet against the evil things which had been said concerning him. It was a victory over the hearts of men, and it changed their mental attitude towards Islām, while the number of Muslims increased by leaps and bounds. The reference in "those to come" is to the later carpings of the critics of Islām, and means that evil things will be said about the Prophet at a later date as well, and that all such misrepresentations and misunderstandings will, in their turn, be swept away.

Moses

Moses is also said to have committed a sin by killing a Copt, but the Qur'ān makes it clear that he simply used his fist to ward off an attack against an Israelite who was being illtreated (28 : 15), and thus death was only accidental. No law would hold a man to be guilty under such circumstances. It is true that the word *dzāll* is used of Moses in connection with this incident on another occasion (26:20), but *dzalla* means *he was perplexed* or *confused* (LL.), and it is in this sense that the word is used there. *Dzāll* is also employed with reference to Prophet Muḥammad in 93 : 7 in almost the same sense, *i.e.*, one unable, by himself, to find the way to prophethood (R.).[28] This is not only made clear by the context but also by the history of the Prophet's life, which shows that from his very childhood he shunned not only idolatry but all the evil

[27] 48 : 1; Bu. 64 : 37.

[28] *Ghaira muhtad-in li-mā sīqa ilaihi min al-nubuwwatī.*

practices of Arab society. Living in the midst of such a society, he was not only free from its evils but was further anxious to find a way for its delivery from those evils. He saw around him the degraded condition of a fallen humanity but could not see the way to raise it up; it was God Who showed him that way, as the verse runs: "(Did He not) find thee groping, so He showed the way" (93 : 7)

Adam

Concerning Adam, it is undoubtedly said that "Adam disobeyed his Lord" (20 : 121), but even here there is no commission of sin, for as a preliminary to that incident, it is clearly stated: "And certainly We gave a commandment to Adam before, but he forgot; and We found in him no resolve (to disobey)" (20 : 115). There was no intention on the part of Adam to disobey the Divine commandment; it was simply forgetfulness that brought about the disobedience. In 2 : 36, where the same incident is related, the word used instead of *disobedience* is a derivation of *zallat* which means a *slip* or *a mistake*. Thus, individually, none of the prophets is spoken of in the Qur'ān as having committed a sin, and therefore the doctrine of the sinlessness of the prophets is unassailable.

Conception of miracles in Islām

The word employed in the Qur'ān for miracle is *āyat*, the primary meaning of which is *an apparent sign or mark by which a thing is known* (R.). As there used, it generally carries one of two significations, *an indication, evidence* or *proof*, and a *Divine message* or *communication*. In the first sense, it includes the miracle in its meaning, and in the second, a verse of the Qurān. The adoption of the same word to indicate a Divine message and its proof is noteworthy. It shows that the Divine message itself is first and foremost proof of its own truth, and hence it is that the Qur'ān has always been looked upon by all Muslims as the greatest miracle of the Prophet. And it is indeed the greatest miracle ever vouchsafed to a prophet because it stands in need of no other evidence whatever, but is itself a living proof of its own truth for all time.

Christian writers on Islām are generally of opinion that though the Qur'ān records certain miracles of other prophets, it denies that any signs at all were vouchsafed to Prophet Muḥammad save and except the Holy Book itself. It is true that the Quranic conception of miracles is quite different from that of the Christian. In Christianity, miracles are all in all. Not only do they take the place of argument, but the central doctrine of the Christian religion is itself based on an alleged miracle. For what is the rising of Jesus from the dead but a miracle? And a miracle, too, without a shred of evidence. Yet if Jesus did not rise from the dead, the pillar on which the whole structure of Christianity rests crashes to the ground. The basic doctrine of Christianity thus being a miracle, it is not surprising that, in the Gospels, miracles take the place, not only of argument, but also of religious duties, moral teachings and spiritual awakening. The dead are made to rise from the graves, multitudes of the sick are healed, sight is restored to the blind, the lame are made to walk, the deaf to hear, water is turned into wine, devils are cast out and many other wonderful deeds are done.[29] That these are only exaggerations or misunderstandings or even pure inventions is quite another matter; the impression one gains is that the great object before the reformer is not to bring

[29] Though the Gospels lay so much stress on miracles, the whole force out of the argument of miracles, if there be any argument, is taken away by two outstanding facts. In the first place, similar miracles were, according to the Gospels, worked even by the opponents of Jesus Christ, for he is himself made to say: "And if I by Beelzebub cast out devils, by whom do your children cast them out?" (M.12 : 27; Lk.11 : 19). The disciples of the Pharisees could therefore work the miracles which Jesus did. And again, he is reported as saying: "Many will say to me in that day, Lord, Lord, have we not prophesied in thy name? And in thy name have cast out devils? And in thy name done many wonderful works?" (Mt.7 : 22). Even false Christs could work the miracles which Jesus showed: "For there shall arise false Christs and false prophets, and shall show great signs and wonders" (Mt. 24 : 24). And last of all there was the healing pool of those days: "Now there is at Jerusalem by the sheep market a pool, which is called in the Hebrew tongue Bethesda, having five porches. In these lay a great multitude of impotent folk, of blind, halt, withered, waiting for the moving of the water. For an angel went down at a certain season into the pool, and troubled the water: whosoever then first after the troubling of the water stepped in was made whole of whatsoever disease he had" (Jn. 5 : 2-4). If miracles were so cheap in those days, if even the disciples of the Pharisees and iniquitous and false Messiahs could perform the self-same miracles which the "Son of God" was performing, if there was such a miraculous pool, what evidence can these miracles possibly afford?

Yet another consideration makes the evidence of the Gospel miracles worthless. The miraculous in a prophet's life is needed to assure the people to whom he is sent of the truth of his message, and to convince the ordinary mind that some supernatural power is at his back. The question, therefore, is, supposing Jesus wrought the miracles which are recorded of him in the Gospels, what was the effect produced by those miracles? Certainly if such wonderful deeds were done, the masses ought to have followed him without hesitation. But the Gospels tell us that though multitudes of the sick followed him and were healed, and though faith was a condition precedent to healing, yet Jesus never had multitudes of followers. His following was very poor, perhaps no more than five hundred

about a transformation by implanting faith in God in the mind of man; and that conviction of the truth is sought, not by argument or appeal to the heart, but by overawing the mind by the miraculous. The conception of the miracle, as given by the Qur'ān, is quite different. Here the supreme object before the Prophet is to effect a moral and spiritual transformation; the means adopted are an appeal to the reasoning faculty, an appeal to the heart of man to convince him that the Divine message is meant for his own uplift, and lessons drawn from previous history showing how the acceptance of truth has always benefited man, and its rejection has worked to his own undoing. The miracle has its own place in the Divine scheme; something great and beyond human power and comprehension is wrought now and again to show that the source of the great Message of Truth is supernatural, Divine. Thus the Qur'ān makes it clear that the bringing about of a transformation is the real object for which prophets are raised that this object is attained by several means, each of which, therefore, has but a secondary value, and that among these evidences of the truth of the Prophet, the miracle occupies not the highest place.

Thus it is that, while the Qur'ān is full of arguments, makes frequent appeals to human nature, and repeatedly refers to the histories of previous peoples, the mention of miracles in it is very rare. But still they are not denied: "And they swear their strongest oaths by Allāh that if a sign came to them they would most certainly believe in it. Say, Signs are with Allāh. And what should make you know that when they come they believe not" (6 : 110). The words "signs are only with Allāh" clearly imply, as do those that follow, that extraordinary signs will be shown as an evidence of the Divine mission of the Prophet. Strange it is that there are critics who see in this verse a denial of signs, only because it is said that signs are with God. It is true that the Qur'ān does not represent Prophet Muḥammad as a wonder-worker, as the Gospels represent Jesus Christ. Signs were shown, not when the Prophet so desired, or when his opponents demanded, but when it was the will of God; hence, whenever an extraordinary sign of the Prophet's truth was demanded, the reply was that such a sign would come when God willed it.

men. His own disciples also did not show in any marked degree the effect of the miraculous upon their lives. Of the twelve specially chosen, one turned traitor, another cursed and the rest all fled, leaving the master in a sad plight. Therefore even if Jesus worked miracles, they would seem never to have fulfilled the object for which miraculous power is vouchsafed.

Another much misunderstood verse of the Qurān relating to the showing of signs is: "And nothing hindered Us from sending signs but the ancients rejected them ... and We send not signs, but to warn." (17 : 59) These words do not signify that because the former people had rejected the signs, therefore God would send no more. Had this been their meaning, God would have ceased to send even Divine messages, because the ancients had already rejected such messages. But, since the word *ā yat* means both a *sign* and a *communication*, the argument of rejection applies to both equally well. The meaning of the words is quite clear. If anything could have been considered as hindering God from sending a new communication or a sign, it would surely have been the rejection of such by previous generations, but it never did. The Divine Being has been equally merciful to all generations, and rejection by former was no ground for depriving later generations of signs and Divine guidance.

The miracles of Islām

As already stated, the greatest miracle of Islām is the Qur'ān. Nor is this an after-thought on the part of the Muslims, for the Holy Book itself claims to be a miracle and has challenged the world to produce its like: "If men and jinn should combine together to bring the like of this Qur'ā n, they could not bring the like of it, though some of them were aiders of others" (17 : 88). "Or, say they, He has forged it. Say: Then bring ten forged chapters like it, and call upon whom you can besides Allāh, if you are truthful" (11 : 13). "Or, say they: He has forged it? Say: Then bring a chapter like it and invite whom you can besides Allāh, if you are truthful" (10 : 38). "And if you are in doubt as to that which We have revealed to Our servant, then produce a chapter like it, and call on your helpers besides Allāh, if you are truthful" (2 : 23).

The proof of this claim lies in the result achieved — a miraculous transformation — which has been acknowledged alike by friends and critics of Islām. Some of the recent writers say: "It was the one miracle claimed by Mohammed — his 'standing miracle' he called it; and a miracle indeed it is".[30] "The Qoran is unapproachable as regards convincing power, eloquence and even composition ... Never has a people been led more rapidly to civilization, such as it was, than were the Arabs through Islām".[31] "A more disunited people it would be hard to find, till

[30] Bosworth Smith, *Life of Mohammed,* p. 290.

[31] Hirschfeld, *New Researches,* p. 85.

suddenly, the miracle took place! A man arose who, by his personality and by his claim to direct Divine guidance, actually brought about the impossible — namely the union of all these warring factions.''[32] ''That the best of Arab writers has never succeeded in producing anything equal in merit to the Qur'ān itself is not surprising''.[33]

In short, the Qur'ān is a miracle because it brought about the greatest transformation that the world has ever witnessed — a transformation of the individual, of the family, of society, of the nation, of the country, an awakening material as well as moral, intellectual as well as spiritual. It produced an effect far greater than that of any other miracle recorded of any prophet; hence its claim to be the greatest of all miracles is incontestable and uncontested.

Prophecy

Of all miracles, the Qur'ān gives the first place to prophecy, and, in fact, prophecy does, in some respects, enjoy a distinction beyond that attributed to other miracles. Miracles generally are manifestations of the powers of God, and prophecy gives prominence to God's infinite knowledge which comprehends the future as well as the past and present. But there is one great disadvantage attaching to all miracles which are merely manifestations of power. It is very difficult to secure reliable evidence for them under all circumstances. Certain men may have witnessed the performance of such a miracle and their evidence may satisfy their contemporaries, but, with the lapse of time, their testimony loses much of its value. Therefore a miracle stands in need of being proved up to the hilt before it may be used as evidence of a prophet's claim, and in most cases it is very hard, if not impossible, to adduce any proof that the miracle ever actually took place. Another difficulty in the matter of miracles generally is to be found in the fact that, however wonderful a performance, it may be explained scientifically, and thus lose all value as a sign of the Divine mission of its worker. Take for instance the great miracles of Jesus Christ. The greatest of these is his raising the dead to life, and in one case, that of the ruler's daughter, Jesus is reported as saying: ''The maid is not dead, but sleepeth'' (Mt.9 : 24). There was no doctor's certificate at hand to show that the maid actually was dead,

[32] *The Ins and Outs of Mesopotamia,* p. 99.

[33] Palmer, Introduction to *Translation of Qur'ān*, p.1v

and, notwithstanding the impression of the relatives that such was the case, Jesus Christ himself knew that she was only sleeping or, perhaps, in a state of stupor. If then the disciples did not misunderstand his symbolical words — and Jesus used to talk much in figurative language[34] — there is still the possibility that a person who was taken for dead was not actually dead. And this is exactly what happened in the case of Jesus himself who was taken for dead but was not actually dead, as is shown by facts recorded about him in the Gospels. Jesus' miracles of healing are still more doubtful in view of the fact that similar miracles were also performed by his opponents, and that there was, as we have seen, a Pool of Healing in those days, which restored sight to the blind and cured all kinds of ailments. Such doubts, however, do not exist in the case of prophecy, which can stand the test of scientific investigation. Moreover, the evidence in such case rests on a firmer basis altogther, and its fulfilment generally comes to pass after a long time. A prophecy which proceeds from a Divine source must, of course, disclose some event which is beyond the scope of human knowledge and which cannot possibly be discovered by human foresight. It must also be connected with some deep Divine purpose in relation to the elevation of humanity, for prophecies are not meant merely to satisfy human curiosity. Lastly, it must have behind it the force of conviction, so that it is not only uttered with the utmost certainty but even in circumstances which apparently conflict with what is disclosed in the prophecy. A prophecy that fulfils these three conditions is one of the greatest miracles, a miracle which by an appeal to reason shows that there is a God Who reveals deep secrets to man and with Whom man can hold communion.

[34] There is not the least doubt that Jesus often spoke in parables and used symbolic language freely: "Let the dead bury their dead" (Mt. 8 : 22); "The hour is coming, and now is, when the dead shall hear the voice of the Son of God...for the hour is coming, in which all that are in the graves shall hear his voice and shall come forth" (Jn. 5 : 25-29) There seems to be no doubt that words like these were the source from which sprang marvels like the following: "And, behold, the veil of the temple was rent in twain from the top to the bottom; and the earth did quake, and the rocks rent; And the graves were opened; and many bodies of the saints which slept arose, And came out of the graves after his resurrection and went into the holy city, and appeared unto many" (Mt. 27 : 51-53). A recent commentator says of this incident that it "seems to be a pictorial setting forth of the truth that in the Resurrection of Christ is involved the resurrection of all His saints, so that on Easter Day all Christians may be said in a certain sense to have risen with Him" (Dummelow's *Bible Commentary*).

Prophecy of the triumph of Islām

The prophecies mentioned in the Qur'ān and those uttered by the Prophet, of which Tradition literature is full, cover so vast a ground and relate to a future so distant that they require separate treatment. But one example may be given in illustration of what has been said above. The Qur'ān gives prominence to the great prophecy of the triumph of Islām, and its earlier chapters are full of such prophecies uttered in various forms. Now these chapters were revealed, and these prophecies announced, at a time when the Prophet was quite alone and helpless, beset on all sides by enemies plotting to put an end to his life. The few adherents to his cause had been forced by cruel persecution to leave their homes and to take shelter in a foreign land. There was not the remotest prospect of Islām ever making any headway against the mighty forces of polytheism and idolatry, the mass of superstition and evil of every kind ranged against it. All previous attempts at the regeneration of Arabia, those of the Jewish nation which had settled down in various parts of Arabia, of the Christian missionaries who had the backing of the powerful Roman empire on the north and of Abyssinia in the south and west, the indigenous Arab attempt known as Hanīfism, had all proved utter failures, and thus the fate of each previous attempt was only a symbol of despair for any fresh reform movement. Yet under these adverse circumstances, amidst nothing but despair on every side, we find prophecy after prophecy announced in the surest and most certain terms to the effect that the great forces of opposition would be brought to naught, that the enemies of Islām would be put to shame and perish, that Islām would become the religion of the whole of Arabia, that the empire of Islām would be established and battles be fought in which the Muslims would be victorious and the enemy brought low, that Islām would spread to the farthest corners of the earth and that it would ultimately be triumphant over the religions of the world.[35]

[35] I give a few quotations from the Holy Book: "Are your unbelievers better than these (Pharaoh and others), or have you an immunity in the scriptures? Or say they: We are a host allied together to help each other? Soon shall the hosts be routed, and they will show (their) backs" (54 : 43-45).

"And you dwell in the abodes of those who were wronged themselves, and it is clear to you how We dealt with them and We made them examples for you. And they have indeed planned their plan, and their plan is with Allāh, though their plan is such that the mountains should be moved thereby. So think not that Allāh will fail in His promise to His Messengers; for Allāh is Mighty, the Lord of retribution" (14 : 45-47).

All this has been stated in the Qur'ān in plain words, and at a time when there was not the least prospect of Islām gaining ground, and all this was brought to fulfilment, against all expectations, in the lifetime of the Prophet. No one who has the slightest acquaintance with the Qur'ān and the history of Islām can have any doubts on this score.

The value of prophecy, as a miracle of Islām, is, however, much more extensive. There are great and wonderful prophecies in the Book, and more still in Tradition, extending into the far future, many of which have been fulfilled in our own age, and almost every generation of Muslims sees with its own eyes the fulfilment of one or more of these great prophecies, and needs not to turn the pages of history to find out what miracles were performed by the Prophet in a previous age. Another feature of this miracle is that it has been vouchsafed even to the righteous followers of the Prophet in every age. Thus it is not only the Prophet's own prophecies that are witnessed in every age, for prophecy is also a heritage to his devout and faithful followers.[36]

"Those who disbelieve, neither their wealth nor their children shall avail them aught against Allāh... As was the case of the people of Pharaoh, and those before them. They rejected Our messages, so Allāh destroyed them on account of their sins and Allāh is Severe in requiting (evil). Say to those who disbelieve: You shall be vanquished and driven together to hell" (3 : 9-11).

"We will soon show them Our signs in farthest regions and among their own people, until it is quite clear to them that it is the truth" (41 : 53).

"And those who disbelieved said to their messengers: We will certainly drive you out of our land, unless you come back into our religion. So their Lord revealed to them, We shall certainly destroy the wrongdoers and We shall certainly settle you in the land after them" (14 : 13, 14).

"And certainly We wrote in the Book after the reminder that My righteous servants will inherit the land. Surely in this is a message to a people who serve Us" (21 : 105-106).

"Allāh has promised to those of you who believe and do good that He will surely make them rulers in the earth as He made those before them rulers, and that He will surely establish for them their religion which He has chosen for them, and that He will surely give them security in exchange after their fear" (24 : 55).

"He it is Who sent His Messenger with the guidance and the true religion, that He may make it overcome the religions, all of them" (61 : 9; 48 : 28; 9 : 33).

[36] Speaking of the faithful, the Qur'ān says: "They will have good news (*bushrā*) in this world's life" (10 : 64); and elsewhere: "The angels descend upon them, saying, Fear not, nor be grieved, and receive good news of the garden which you were promised" (41 : 30). And according to Tradition, "nothing remains of prophethood except *mubashshirāt*" (Bu. 92 : 5), and these are explained to be true visions and are called a part of the prophethood (Bu. 92 : 4).

Intercession : God is the real Intercessor

There is one more point on which light should be thrown in connection with the place of prophets in Islām, and that is the doctrine of intercession. The Arabic word for intercession is shafa'[37] which signifies *the joining of a man to another assisting him*, especially when a man who enjoys a high rank and honour joins himself to a man of a lower position (R.). In the Qur'ān, God is spoken of as the real Intercessor (*Shāfi'*): "There is no protector (*waliyy*) for them, nor any intercessor (*shāfi'*) besides Him" (6 : 51, 70). And on another accasion: "Allāh's is the intercession altogether" (39 : 44). It is sometimes spoken of in connection with the Divine control of things: "Allāh is He Who created the heavens and the earth and what is between them in six periods, and He is established on the Throne of Power. You have not besides Him a guardian or an intercessor. Will you not then mind?" (32 : 4). Thus intercession, according to the Qur'ān, is really in the hands of God, just as the control of things is really in His hands, and hence the oft-repeated expression that none can intercede with God except with His permission (10 : 3; 2 : 255).[38]

Intercession is denied in the case of those that are set up as gods: "And they will have no intercessors from among their associate gods" (30 : 13); "And they serve besides Allāh what can neither harm them nor profit them, and they say, These are our intercessors with Allāh" (10 : 18).

Who can intercede?

Among those who can intercede with God with His permission, angels are mentioned. "And how many angels are there in the heavens whose intercession avails not except after Allāh gives permission to whom He pleases and chooses" (53 : 26). Prophets are also spoken of as intercessors: "And We sent no messenger before thee but We revealed to him that there is no God but Me, therefore serve Me. And they say, The Beneficent (God) has taken to Himself a son. Glory be to Him! Nay, they are

[37] It is derived from *shafa' meaning the making a thing to be one of a pair* (TA.), or *the adjoining a thing to its like* (R.).

[38] The writer of the article on *shafā'a* in the *Encyclopaedia of Islam* is evidently wrong when he translates the *shafā'a* passage as meaning "Who should intervene with Him, *even* with His permission." The Arabic words are *illā bi-idhni-hī*, and any one having even a superficial knowledge of Arabic knows that *illā* means *except*, not *even*. The erroneous rendering has entirely changed the sense of the passage.

honoured servants.[39] They speak not before He speaks and according to His command they act. He knows what is before them and what is behind them, and they intercede not except for him whom He approves'' (21 : 25-28). Believers are also spoken of as interceding: ''And those whom they call upon besides Him control not intercession, but he who bears witness to the Truth and they know (him)'' (43 : 86). Since every believer bears witness to the Truth, this verse may fairly be taken as referring to the intercession of believers. Another verse is as follows: ''They have no power of intercession, save him who has made a covenant with the Beneficent (God)'' (19 : 87), since every true believer may be said to have made a covenant with God, the verse apparently also speaks of the intercession of true believers. Tradition also speaks of the intercession of God, of angels, of prophets and of believers. Thus a report relating to *shafā'ah*, accepted by both Bukhārī and Muslim, concludes with the words: ''Then Allāh will say, The angels have interceded and the prophets have interceded and the believers have interceded, and there remains the most Merciful of all merciful ones; then He will take a handful out of fire and bring forth from it a people who have never done any good'' (M. 1 : 72). It may be noted that the handful of God cannot leave anything behind.

God's intercession

As already shown, with reference to Arabic lexicons, the true meaning of *shafā'a* is the rendering of assistance by one who holds a high position to one in a low position and standing in need of such help. The word has been used in exactly the same sense in the Qur'ān. The idea of mediation, which depicts a wrathful Being, on the one hand, determined to execute the sentence of punishment, and, on the other, a suppliant on behalf of a sinner, is not the Quranic sense of intercession or *shafā'a*. For here the real intercessor or *Shāfi* is God Himself, not the wrathful God Who is bound to punish the sinners for what they have or even for what they have not done,[40] but the most Merciful of all merciful ones, Who is moved for humanity's sake to such an extent that He takes out from the fire even those who have never done any good. The intercession (*shafā'a*) of God is, therefore, the merciful Divine help which enables

39 See also footnote 22 on page 176.

40 According to the Christian Church, man must suffer for what is called Original Sin, *i.e.*, the sin not committed by man but by some distant forefather of his in the remote past.

the sinners to escape from the evil consequences of what they have done, when all other means have failed.

Intercession of the angels

The intercession of angels is thus spoken of in the Qur'ān: "Those who bear the Throne of power and those around it celebrate the praise of their Lord and believe in Him and ask protection for those who believe: Our Lord, Thou embracest all things in mercy and knowledge, so protect those who turn (to Thee) and follow Thy way, and save them from the chastisement of hell: Our Lord, make them enter the Gardens of perpetuity which Thou hast promised them and such of their fathers and their wives and their offspring as are good. Surely Thou art the Mighty, the Wise. And guard them from evil, and whom Thou guardest from evil this day, Thou hast indeed mercy on him, and that is the mighty achievement" (40 : 7-9). "The heavens may almost be rent asunder above them, while the angels celebrate the praise of their Lord and ask forgiveness for those on earth. Now surely Allāh is the Forgiving, the Merciful" (42 : 5).

In the first of these passages, the angels are spoken of as asking for Divine protection and Divine mercy for the believers specially, though their fathers, wives and offspring are afterwards included; and in the second passage, the angels are spoken of as asking forgiveness for believers as well as unbelievers. The intercession of the angels is, therefore, common to both believers and unbelievers. The spiritual relation of the angel with man[41] is one of prompting to noble and virtuous deeds, and hence the angels' intercession is in connection with those who have done some sort of good, whether they be believers in a prophet or not. And this intercession takes the form of a prayer that mercy and forgiveness be shown by God to His creatures.

Intercession of prophets and believers

Divine mercy is also manifested through the prophets, and this is the intercession (*shafā'ah*) of the prophets. It is a mistake to suppose that it will be exercised only on the Day of Judgment; nor is it limited to the

41 See chapter on Angels.

prayers of forgiveness for the dead.[42] The Prophet's intercession is witnessed in the change he brings about in the life of a people, in delivering them from the bondage of evil, and setting them on the road to advancement. Thus it is stated that the Prophet Muḥammad was raised so that he might purify the people,[43] and the miraculous purification of Arabia and its advancement, physical, intellectual, moral and spiritual, is the clearest evidence of the success of his intercession (*shafā'a*). He prayed incessantly for the well-being of his followers, and his prayer is said to be "a relief" to those for whom he prayed.[44] He is also commanded to seek God's protection for them,[45] and this was clearly, as in the case of angels, intercession on their behalf.

The intercession of the believers is of a similar nature. The believers who are on a higher spiritual plane help those who are on a lower level, by their example and by their prayers. Intercession by example is clearly spoken of in the Qur'ān: Whoever intercedes (*yashfa'*) in a good cause (*shafa'at-an hasanat-an*) has a share of it" (4 : 85). The original word used here is *shafā'a*, and the meaning is that when a man sets a good example which others follow and benefit thereby, he is rewarded for it.

Intercession on the Judgment Day

It is clear from the above that the the doctrine of intercession (*shafā'a*) in Islām is really meant to give expression to the boundless mercy of the Divine Being. This *shafā'a* is exercised, in the first instance, in this life. There are the angels of God who prompt men to do good and pray to God that men may be saved from falling into evil, and that Divine blessings and mercy may be extended to them; there are the prophets of God who are commissioned with the express object of delivering men from the bondage of sin and setting them on the right course

[42] In the article on *Shafā'a* in the *Encyclopaedia of Islam* we have: "But it should be noted that the Prophet even in his lifetime is said to have made intercession. 'Ā'ishah relates that he often slipped quietly from her side at night to go to the cemetery of Baqī' al-Gharqad to beseech forgiveness of Allāh for the dead... Similarly his *istighfār* is mentioned in the *ṣalāt al-janā'iz* ... and its efficacy explained... The prayer for the forgiveness of sins then became or remained an integral part of this *ṣalāt*... to which a high degree of importance was attributed."

[43] See 2 : 151. The Arabic word for purification is *yuzakkī*, derived from *zakā* whereof the original meaning is *the progress attained by Divine blessing* (R.).

[44] 9 : 103.

[45] 3 : 158; 4 : 64; 24 : 62; 47 : 19; 60 : 12.

to advancement and who, by their example and by their prayers, lead men out of the darkness of evil into the light of the Divine mercy and blessings; and there are believers who have attained to perfection, and who, following in the footsteps of the great prophets of God, intercede for those who are left behind. But, according to the Qur'ān, the progress of man is not limited to this life. Far more extensive fields of activity are awaiting him in the life after death, and the Day of Resurrection is the great day when the consequences of all good and evil deeds shall be made fully manifest. The intercession (*shafā'a*) of Prophet Muḥammad on that day is given precedence and the greatest prominence, according to a tradition.[46] This is so because even in this life, the *shafā'a* exercised by him transcends that of every other prophet. The material, moral and spiritual revolution brought about by Prophet Muḥammad has been so tremendous that by a consensus of opinion he is admitted to be the "most successful of all prophets and religious personalities".[47] God had been showering His blessings on mankind through angels and through prophets and their righteous followers, and the help which they have rendered to mankind is itself evidence that in the higher life they will render similar help; but, inasmuch as God's mercy knows no bounds, even those who responded neither to the call of the angel in this life, nor to the call of the prophets of God, nor yet to the call of other righteous servants of God, those who, in the words of the tradition already referred to, have never done any good, shall be lifted up by Divine mercy, by the most Merciful of all merciful ones, and being delivered from the evil consequences of what they have wrought, shall be set up on the road to unlimited progress which the Resurrection shall open up for mankind.

Finality of prophethood

In the Qur'ān, Prophet Muḥammad is spoken of as the last of the prophets: "Muḥammad is not the father of any of your men, but he is the Messenger of Allāh and the last of the prophets (*khātam al-nabiyyīn*), and Allāh is ever Knower of all things" (33 : 40.) The words *khātam al-nabiyyīn* and *khātim al-nabiyyīn* mean *the last of the prophets*, for both the words *khātam* and *khātim* mean *the last portion of anything* (LL.). The best Arabic lexicologists are agreed that *khātam al-qaum* means *the last of a people* (TA.). The doctrine of the finality

46 Bu. 81 : 51.

47 *En. Br.*, art. Koran, 11th Ed.

of prophethood in Muḥammad, therefore, rests on the clear words of the Qur'ān.

Tradition is even clearer on this point. The meaning of khātam *al-nabiyyīn* was thus explained by the Prophet himself: "My example and the example of the prophets before me is the example of a man who built a house and he made it very good and very beautiful with the exception of a stone in the corner, so people began to go round it and to wonder at it and to say, Why has not this stone been placed? The Prophet said, I am this stone and I am the last of the prophets" (Bu. 61 : 18). This tradition, in which the Prophet speaks of himself as the corner-stone of prophethood and the last of the prophets, is related by Muslim and Tirmidhī as well, and also by Aḥmad in more than ten places. Another report in which the Prophet speaks of himself as the last of the prophets is contained in the following words: "The Israelites were led by prophets; whenever a prophet died, another came after him; surely after me there is no prophet, but there will be successors" (Bu. 60 : 50). This is also narrated by Muslim and Aḥmad in several places. According to another tradition, the Prophet is reported to have said to 'Alī, when on the occasion of the Tabūk expedition he left him in Madīnah in his place: "Art thou not pleased that thou shouldst stand to me in the same relation as Aaron stood to Moses except that there is no prophet after me" (Bu. 62 : 9). Similar reports in which the Prophet made it clear that no prophet would appear after him abound in other books of Tradition.

A Prophet for all peoples and all ages

The idea that prophethood came to a close in the person of Prophet Muḥammad is not a stray idea. On the other hand, it is the natural conclusion of the universalization of the theory of revelation which is the basic principle of the religion of Islām. Revelation, according to the Qur'ān, is not the solitary experience of this or that nation but the spiritual experience of the whole of the human race. Allāh is spoken of in the very opening verse as the *Rabb* of all the nations of the world, the *Nourisher unto perfection,* physically as well as spiritually, of the whole human race. Starting from that broad basis, the Qur'ān develops the theory that prophets were sent to every nation: "There is not a people but a warner has gone among them" (35 : 24); "And for every nation there is a messenger" (10 : 47). At the same time it is stated that every prophet was sent to a single nation and, therefore, though prophethood was in one sense a universal fact, it was more or less a national institution, the scope of the preaching of every prophet being limited to his own nation. The advent of Prophet Muḥammad universalized the institution of prophethood in a real sense. The day of the national prophet was over, and one prophet was raised for the whole world, for all nations and for all ages: "Blessed is He Who sent down the *Furqān*[48] upon His servant that he may be a warner to all the nations" (25 : 1). "Say, O mankind, surely I am the Messenger of Allāh to you all, of Him Whose is the kingdom of the heavens and the earth" (7 : 158). "And We have not sent thee but as a bearer of good news and as a warner to all mankind, but most men know not" (34 : 28).

Unification of human race based on finality of prophethood

The world-prophet therefore took the place of the national prophets, and the grand idea of unifying the whole human race, and gathering it together under one banner, was thus brought to perfection. All geographical limitations were swept away as were all bars of colour and race, and the basis of the unity of the human race was laid upon the grand principle that the whole human race was one, and that all men, wherever they may be found, were a single nation (2 : 213). Such unity could not be accomplished unless the finality of prophethood was established, for if prophets continued to appear after the world-prophet, they would undoubtedly demand the allegiance of this or that section, and shatter the very foundations of the unity at which Islām aimed by giving a single prophet to the whole world.

Significance underlying finality

It may, however, be further added that by bringing prophethood to a close, Islām has not deprived the world of a blessing which was available to previous generations. The object of sending a prophet to a people was to make known the Divine will, and point out the ways by walking in which men could hold communion with God. That object was also brought to perfection through the great World-Prophet, whose message was so perfect that it met the requirements not only of all contemporary

[48] *Furqān* (lit., *discrimination*) is one of the names of the Qur'ān, because of the clear distinction it brought about between truth and falsehood.

nations but of all future generations as well. This is plainly claimed by the Qur'ān, a claim not put forward by any other heavenly book or any other religion: "This day have I perfected for you your religion and completed My favour to you and chosen for you Islām as a religion" (5 : 3). The perfection of religion and the completion of the blessing of prophethood thus go hand in hand, and the blessing of prophethood being made complete in the person of the Prophet, it is a distortion of facts to say that, if no more prophets appeared, the Muslims would be without the blessing of prophethood, since they possess that blessing in its most complete form. Religion being made perfect, and prophethood being made complete, there remained no need for another religion after Islām or for another prophet after Prophet Muḥammad.

Appearance of the Messiah

There is a prophecy in books of tradition which states that the Messiah would appear among the Muslims. The words in *Bukhārī* are: "How would you feel when the son of Mary makes his appearance among you, and he will be your Imām from among yourselves (*imāmu-kum minkum*)" (Bu. 60 : 49). In *Muslim* instead of *imāmu-kum min-kum*, the words are *amma-kum min-kum* (M. 1 : 67), the significance being exactly the same as that of *Bukhārī's* words. This prophecy has given rise to a more or less general misconception that the Israelite prophet Jesus Christ would appear among the Muslims, a misconception due to not giving proper attention to the doctrine of finality of prophethood, for if there is *no need* for a prophet, as clearly set forth in the Qur'ān, neither a new nor an old prophet can appear. In fact, the appearance of an old prophet would be as much subversive of the doctrine of the finality of prophethood, and as derogatory to the dignity of the *last* prophet of the world, as would the appearance of a new prophet. The words of the prophecy are so clear that, if due attention had been paid to them, there could never have been a misconception. The son of Mary spoken of in the prophecy is clearly called "your Imām *from among yourselves*," and therefore the Israelite prophet Jesus Christ, who was from among the Israelites, could *not* be meant.

The prophecy relating to the appearance of the Messiah among the Muslims is on all fours with the prophecy relating to the second advent of Elias (Elijah) among the Israelites. In fact, there is a strange coincidence between the cases of Elijah and Jesus Christ. Of Elijah it is said in the

Bible: "Elijah went up by a whirlwind into heaven" (II Kings 2 : 11). On the strength of this inspired evidence, the Jews believed that Elijah was alive in heaven. Then there was the prophecy : "Behold, I will send you Elijah the prophet before the coming of the great and dreadful day of the Lord" (Mal. 4 : 5), which showed that he would return to this earth before the Messiah appeared. Yet these hopes based on such strong evidence were not fulfilled. Jesus Christ was confronted with this difficulty: "And his disciples asked him saying, Why then say the scribes that Elias must first come? (Mt. 17 : 10). Jesus' reply is recorded in the following words: "Elias truly shall first come ... But I say unto you, That Elias is come already, and they knew him not, but have done unto him whatsoever they listed... Then the disciples understood that he spake unto them of John the Baptist" (Mt. 17 : 11-13). And John the Baptist was called Elias in prophecy because it had been said of him: "And he shall go before him in the spirit and power of Elias" (Lk. 1 : 17).

Now of Jesus Christ it is nowhere said in the Qur'ān that he went up into heaven. On the other hand, it is plainly stated that he died a natural death.[49] Therefore there is not the least ground for supposing that Jesus

[49] "O Jesus! *I will cause thee to die* and exalt thee in My presence and clear thee of those who disbelieve and make those who follow thee above those who disbelieve to the Day of Resurrection" (3 : 54).

"And when Allāh will say: O Jesus, son of Mary! Didst thou say to men, Take me and my mother for two gods besides Allāh, he will say ... I said to them naught save as Thou didst command me: Serve Allāh, my Lord and your Lord; and I was a witness of them *so long as I was among them, but when Thou didst cause me to die*, Thou wast the watcher over them, and Thou art witness of all things" (5 : 116, 117).

The words *mutawaffi-ka* and *tawaffaita-ni*, which have been translated as *I will cause thee to die* and *Thou didst cause me to die* carry exactly this significance and nothing else. I'Ab says the significance of the former is *mumītu-ka* (*i.e.*, I will cause you to die). According to LA "you say *tawaffā-hu-llāhu* when you mean Allāh took his soul or caused him to die". And according to LL it signifies, "God took his soul (S.Q.) ... or cause him to die" (Msb). Thus no other significance can be attached to these words when thus used.

Pickthall translates the first verse as 'I am gathering thee' and this is the Biblical idiom for causing to die. 'Abdullāh Yūsuf 'Alī, in the first edition of English Translation of the Qur'ān, translated the words as *I will cause thee to die*, but in the second edition he changed it to *I will take thee*.

In the first verse the *raf'* of Jesus Christ to Allāh is spoken of. *Raf'* means *raising* or *elevating* and also *exalting* and *making honourable* (T., LL.). But wherever the *raf'* of a man to God is spoken of in the Qur'ān or in the religious literature of Islām, it is always in the latter sense, for raising a man in his body to Himself would mean that the Divine Being is limited to a place. This is also evident by the prayer every Muslim repeats several times daily in his prayers in the sitting position between the two prostrations; *wa-raf'-nī*, meaning *and exalt me*. Commenting on this verse Rz. says: *this shows that* raf' *here is the exalting in degree and in praise, not in place and direction.*

Christ is alive in heavens. Again, the Bible states that Elijah will be sent, but the Tradition prophecy about the advent of the Messiah adds the clear words that "he will be your Imām from among yourselves." Even if Jesus had been alive and the words quoted above had not made clear the true significance of the prophecy, the analogy of the prophecy of Elijah's advent would have been sufficient to eradicate all misconceptions regarding the re-appearance of Jesus Christ. But in addition to all this, there is the clearly defined and strongly established fact of the finality of prophethood which bars the advent of any prophet, old or new, after Prophet Muḥammad.

Appearance of reformers

It must however be borne in mind that, as shown in the last chapter, Divine revelation is granted to prophets as well as to those who are not prophets, and that, therefore, though prophethood, being no more needed, has been brought to a close, the gift of Divine revelation to the righteous servants of God is still granted as heretofore.Men do not stand in need of a new prophet because they have a perfect law in the Qur'ān, but they do stand in need of Divine blessings, and Divine revelation is the highest of all blessings. Moreover, speaking is an attribute of the Divine Being, just as hearing and seeing are His attributes also, and Divine attributes never cease to function. It has also been shown in the last chapter that, according to a most reliable tradition, a part of prophethood called *mubashshirāt* (lit., *good visions*) remains after prophethood has ceased (Bu. 92 : 5), and according to another, God speaks to the righteous in this community (*ummah*) though they are not prophets (Bu. 62 : 6). There is another report showing that *mujaddids* (reformers) will appear among the Muslims: "Surely Allāh will raise for this community (of Muslims), at the commencement of every century, one who will reform their religion" (AD. 36 : 1). A *mujaddid* is a reformer commissioned to remove errors that have crept in among the Muslims, and to shed new light on the great religious truths of Islām in the new circumstances which the Muslim community will be called upon to face.

Chapter VI

LIFE AFTER DEATH

Al-ākhirah

A faith in a life after death is the last of the basic principles of Islām. The word generally used in the Qur'ān to indicate this life is *al-ākhirah.*[1] Death, according to the Qur'ān, is not the end of man's life; it only opens the door to another, a higher, form of life: "We have ordained death among you and We are not to be overcome, that We may change your state and make you grow into what you know not" (56 : 60 - 61). Just as from the small life-germ grows the man, and he does not lose his individuality for all the changes which he undergoes, so from this man is made the higher man, his state being changed, and he himself being made to grow into what he cannot conceive at present. That this new life is a higher form of life is also made plain: "See how We have made some of them to excel others. And certainly the Hereafter is greater in degrees and greater in excellence" (17 : 21).

Importance of faith in Future Life

The Qur'ān accords to faith in the Future Life an importance which is next only to faith in God. Very often all the doctrines of faith are summed up as amounting to belief in God and the Future Life: "And there are some people who say, We believe in Allāh and the Last Day, and they are not believers" (2 : 8); "Whoever believes in Allāh and the Last Day and does good, they have their reward with their Lord" (2 : 62).

The Opening chapter of the Qur'ān, entitled the *Fātiḥah*, is not only looked upon as the quintessence of the Book but it is actually the chapter

[1] *Ākhir* is the opposite of *awwal* (which means *the first*), and thus signifies *that which comes after*, or *the future* or *the last. Al-yaum al-ākhir* or *the last day* is used instead of *al-ākhirah* (2 : 8, 62, etc.); sometimes *al-dār al-ākhirah, the next* or *the future* or *the last abode*, is used (28 : 77; 29 : 64; 33 : 29), and once *al-nash'at al-ākhirah* or *the future* or *the next life*, which is the real meaning conveyed by all these terms.

Occasionally, the word *al-ākhirah* is used to indicate the future condition in this very life as compared with the previous state, as in 93 : 4: "And that which comes after (*al-ākhirat*) is certainly better for thee than that which has gone before", where the meaning is that the future had great eventualities in store for the Prophet, and his cause would continue to gain as time went on.

which plays the greatest part in creating a true Muslim mentality; for the Muslim must recite it in the five prayers, over thirty times daily. In this chapter God is spoken of as the "Master of the Day of Requital", and thus the idea that every deed must be requited is brought before the mind of the Muslim continually. This constant repetition of the idea of a requital of deeds, undoubtedly impresses on the mind the reality of a future life, when every deed shall find its full reward. The reason for attaching so much importance to a life after death is clear. The greater the faith in the good or bad consequences of a deed, the greater is the incentive which urges a man to or withholds him from that deed. Therefore this belief is both the greatest impetus towards good and noble, and the greatest restraint upon evil or irresponsible deeds. But more than this, such a belief purifies the motives with which a deed is done. It makes a man work with the most selfless of motives, for he seeks no reward for what he does; his work is for higher and nobler ends relating to the life beyond the grave.

Connection between the two lives

The Qur'ān not only speaks of a life after death which opens out for man a new world of advancement, before which the progress of this life sinks into insignificance; it also shows that the basis of that life is laid in this our life on earth. The Hereafter is not a mystery beyond the grave; it begins in this life. For the good, the heavenly life, and for the wicked, a life in hell, begin even here, though the limitations of this life do not allow most people to realize this. "Thou wast indeed heedless of this, but now We have removed from thee thy veil, so thy sight is sharp this day" (50 : 22). This shows that the spiritual life which is hidden from the human eye by reason of material limitations, will become manifest in the Resurrection; because human perception will then be clearer, the veil of material limitations having been removed. The Qur'ān speaks of two paradises for the righteous and two chastisements for the wicked, as also of a heavenly and hellish life each beginning here: "And for him who fears to stand before his Lord are two Gardens" (55 : 46). "O soul that art at rest! Return to thy Lord well pleased, well pleasing. So enter among My servants and enter My Garden" (89 : 27 - 30). "Nay, would that you knew with a certain knowledge, you would certainly see Hell" (102 : 5, 6). "It is the fire kindled by Allāh *which rises over the hearts*" (104 : 6, 7). "And whoever is blind in this life, shall also be blind in the Hereafter'' (17 : 72). ''Such is the chastisement, and certainly the chastisement of the hereafter is greater, did they but know'' (68 : 33).

Barzakh

The state between death and Resurrection is called *barzakh* which literally means *a thing that intervenes between two things*, or *an obstacle* or *a hindrance* (LL.). The word *barzakh* has been used in this latter sense of an obstacle in two places in the Qur'ān (25 : 53 and 55 : 20), where a barrier between two seas is spoken of as *barzakh*. As signifying the state between death and Resurrection, it occurs in the following verses: ''Until when death overtakes one of them, he says, My Lord, send me back, that I may do good in that which I have left. By no means! it is but a word that he speaks. And before them is *barzakh* until the day when they are raised'' (23 : 99, 100). This intervening state is also known by the name of *qabr*, which means *grave*, but has also been used in the wider sense of the state which follows death. Thus the three states, death, the grave and Resurrection, are spoken of, where the *grave* undoubtedly stands for *barzakh*: ''Then He causes him to die, then assigns to him a grave (*aqbara-hū*); then when He will, He raises him to life again'' (80 : 21, 22). And the raising to life on the Day of Resurrection is spoken of as the raising of those who are in their graves, as in 100 : 9 and 22 : 7, where all people are meant, whether actually buried or not. The state of *qabr* is therefore the same state as that of *Barzakh*, the state in which every man is placed after death, and before the Resurrection.

Second stage of the higher life

Since the Qur'ān speaks of the growth of a higher life even in the life of this world, the spiritual experience of man is the first stage of the higher life. Yet, ordinarily, man is neglectful of this higher experience, and it is only persons of a very high spiritual development that are in any way conscious of that higher life. *Barzakh* is really the second stage in the development of this higher life, and it appears that all men have a certain consciousness of the higher life at this stage, though full development has not yet taken place. In the Qur'ān, even the development of the physical life is mentioned as passing through three stages. The first stage of that life is the state of being in the earth; the second, that of being in the mother's womb; and the third, that in which the child is born. Thus we have: "He knows you best when He brings you forth from the earth and when you are embryos in the wombs of your mothers" (53 : 32); "And He began the creation of man from dust. Then He made his progeny of an extract of worthless water. Then He made him complete and breathed into him of His spirit" (32 : 7 - 9); "And certainly We create man of an extract of clay; then We make him a small life-germ in a firm resting-place..., then We cause it to grow into another creation, so blessed be Allāh, the Best of creators!" (23 : 12 - 14). Corresponding to these three stages in the physical development of man, the stage of dust, the stage of embryo and the stage of birth into life, the Qur'ān speaks of three stages in his spiritual development. The first is the growth of a spiritual life which begins in this very life, but it is a stage at which ordinarily there is no consciousness of this life, like the dust stage in the physical development of man. Then there comes death, and with it is entered the second stage of a higher or spiritual life, the *barzakh* or the *qabr* stage, corresponding to the embryo stage in the physical development of man. At this stage, life has taken a definite form, and a certain consciousness of that life has grown up, but it is not yet the full consciousness of the final development which takes place with the Resurrection, and which may therefore be compared to the actual birth of man, to his setting forth on the road to real advancement, to a full awakening of the great truth. The develpment of the higher life in *barzakh* is as necessary a stage in the spiritual world as is the development of physical life in the embryonic state. The two thus stand on a par.

Spiritual experience in the **barzakh** *stage*

That there is some kind of awakening to a new spiritual experience immediately after death is abundantly evident from various Quaranic statements. For example, the verses in which *barzakh* is spoken of[2] set forth the spiritual experience of the evil-doer, who immediately becomes conscious of the fact that, in his first life, he has been doing something which is now detrimental to the growth of the higher life in him, and hence desires to go back, so that he may do good deeds which may help the development of the higher life. It shows that the consciousness of a higher life

[2] 23 : 99, 100.

has sprung up in him immediately after death. On another occasion, we are told that evil-doers are made to taste of the evil consequences of their deeds in this state of *barzakh*, the consciousness of the chastisement becoming clear on the Resurrection Day: "And the evil chastisement overtook Pharaoh's people — the Fire; they are brought before it every morning and evening and on the day when the Hour comes to pass: Make Pharaoh's people enter the severest chastisement" (40 : 45, 46).

It should be noted that while, in the Qur'ān, the guilty are spoken of as receiving chastisement in the state of *barzakh*, in Traditions this punishment is spoken of as *'adhāb al-qabr*, or the punishment meted out in the grave. In *Bukhạrī* the chapter on *'adhāb al-qabr*[3] begins with quotations from the Qur'ān, one of which is the verse relating to the punishment of Pharaoh's people in *barzakh* quoted at the conclusion of the previous paragraph. This shows that *Bukhārī* regards these two punishments as one, and thus he establishes the identity of *qabr* and *barzakh*. Again, the 90th chapter of the same book has the following heading: "The dead man is shown his abode morning and evening" (Bu. 23 : 90). Under this heading, a tradition is narrated from 'Abd Allāh ibn 'Umar reporting the Prophet as saying that "when a man dies, his abode (in the next life) is brought before him morning and evening, in Paradise if he is one of the inmates of Paradise, and in fire if he is one of the inmates of fire" (Bu. 23 : 90). This report also shows that the punishment meted out in the grave (*'adhāb al-qabr*) means only the spiritual condition of the guilty people in the state of *barzakh*.

Similarly, the righteous are spoken of as tasting the fruits of good deeds immediately after death: "And think not of those who are killed in Allāh's way as dead. Nay, they are alive, being provided sustenance from their Lord; rejoicing in what Allāh has given them out of His grace; and they rejoice for the sake of those who, being left behind, have not yet joined them, that they have no fear nor shall they grieve" (3 : 168, 169). These verses show that the departed ones are even conscious of what they have left behind, and this establishes some sort of connection between this world and the next.

Duration of barzakh

All questions connected with the life of the other world are of an intricate nature, inasmuch as they are not things that can be perceived by human

[3] Bu. 23 : 87.

senses; they are "secrets" that shall be made known only after death, according to the Qur'ān[4] and, according to a saying of the Prophet, "things which no eye has seen, nor has ear heard, nor have they entered into the heart of man" (Bu. 59 : 8). As will be shown later on, the very ideas of time and space as relating to the next world are different from those here, and therefore we cannot conceive of the duration of *barzakh* in terms of this world's time. Moreover, the full awakening to the higher life will take place in the Resurrection, and the state of *barzakh* is therefore a state, as it were, of semi-consciousness. Hence it is that it is sometimes likened to a state of sleep as compared with the great awakening of the Resurrection, for the unbelievers are made to say: "O woe to us! who has raised us up from our sleeping-place?" (36 : 52). The state of *barzakh*, as regards those who have wasted their opportunities in this life, lasts according to the Qur'ān, till the Day of Resurrection: "And before them is *barzakh* until the day when they are raised" (23 : 100). The question of a longer duration of *barzakh* for some, and a shorter one for others, does not arise, as they do not seem to have consciousness of the length of time: "And the day when the Hour comes, the guilty will swear that they did not tarry but an hour. Thus are they ever turned away. And those who are given knowledge and faith will say: Certainly you tarried according to the ordinance of Allāh till the Day of Resurrection — so this is the Day of Resurrection — but you did not know" (30 : 55, 56). As regards those in whom the life spiritual has been awakened during the life on earth, consciousness in the *barzakh* state will undoubtedly be more vivid, and there is a tradition which speaks of the righteous being exalted to a higher state (*raf'*) after forty days, and thus making progress even in that state.

Various names of Resurrection

The Resurrection is spoken of under various names, the most frequent of which is *yaum al-qiyāmah* or *the Day of the Great Rising*, which occurs seventy times in the Qur'ān. Next to it is *al-sā'ah* which means *the Hour*, and occurs forty times; *yaum al-ākhir* or *the Last Day* occurs twenty-six times, while *al-ākhirah* as meaning *the Future Life* occurs over a hundred times. Next in importance is *yaum al-dīn* which means *the Day of Requital. Yaum al-faṣl* or *the Day of Decision* occurs six times,

[4] 32 : 17.

and *yaum al-ḥisāb* or *the Day of Reckoning* five times. Other names occur only once or twice, such as *yaum al-fatḥ* (*the Day of Judgment*), *yaum al-talāq* (*the Day of Meeting*), *yaum al-jam'* (*the Day of Gathering*), *yaum al-khulūd* (*the Day of Abiding*), *yaum al-khurūj* (*the Day of Coming Forth*), *yaum al-ba'th* (*the Day of being Raised to Life*), *yaum al-ḥasrat* (*the Day of Regret*), *yaum al-tanād* (*the Day of Calling Forth*), *yaum al-āzifah* (*the Day that draws near*), *yaum al-taghābun* (*the Day of Manifestation of Losses*). Other names which occur once or twice without the word *yaum* (day) are *al-qāri'ah* (*the striking Calamity*), *al-ghāshiyah* (*the Overwhelming Calamity*), *al-sākhkhah* (*the Deafening Calamity*), *al-tāmmah* (*the Predominating Calamity*), *al-ḥāqqah* (*the Great Truth*), and *al-wāqi'ah* (*the Great Event*).

A general destruction and a general awakening

It will be seen that most of these names refer either to a destruction or an awakening and rising to a new life; they relate to the sweeping off of an old order and the establishment of a new one. A few quotations descriptive of the Resurrection will make the point clearer. "He asks: When is the Day of Resurrection? So when the sight is confused, and the moon becomes dark, and the sun and the moon are brought together. Man shall say on that day, whither to flee? No! There is no refuge! With thy Lord on that day is the place of rest. Man will that day be informed of what he sent before and what he put off... Nay, but you love the present life; and neglect the Hereafter. (Some) faces that day will be bright, looking to their Lord. And (other) faces that day will be gloomy, knowing that a great disaster will be made to befall them" (75 : 6 - 25). "When the stars are made to disappear, and when the heaven is rent asunder, and when the mountains are carried away as dust, and when the messengers are made to reach their appointed time" (77 : 8 - 11). "Surely the Day of Decision is appointed — the day when the trumpet is blown, so you come forth in hosts; and the heaven is opened so it becomes as doors; and the mountains are moved off so that they remain a semblance" (78 : 17 - 20). "The day when the quaking one shall quake — The consequence will follow it. Hearts that day will palpitate, their eyes cast down... It is only a single cry, when lo! they will be awakened" (79 : 6 - 14). "They ask thee about the Hour: When will that take place about which thou remindest... To thy Lord is the goal of it" (79 : 42 - 44). "When the earth is shaken with her shaking, and the earth brings forth her burdens... On that day men will come forth in sundry bodies that they may be shown their works'' (99 : 1 - 6). ''The day on which they shall come forth from their graves in haste, as if they were hastening on to a goal'' (70 : 43). ''And when the trumpet is blown with a single blast, and the earth and the mountains are borne away and crushed with one crash; on that day will the Event come to pass... On that day you shall be exposed to view — no secret of yours will remain hidden'' (69 : 13 - 18). ''When the Event comes to pass — there is no belying its coming to pass — abasing (some), exalting (others)'' (56 : 1 - 3). ''On the day when the earth shall be changed into a different earth and the heavens as well'' (14 : 48).

Three Resurrections

The two words used most frequently regarding the Resurrection are *al-qiyāmah* and *al-sā'ah.* The first of these refers, apparently, to the *rising*, which is its literal significance, the second to destruction, being *the hour of doom.* As regards this latter word, Rāghib says that there are three *sā'ahs* in the sense of resurrection: *viz., the greater resurrection (kubrā)* which is the rising up of the people for reckoning, *the middle resurrection (wusṭā)* which is the passing away of one generation, and *the minor resurrection (sughrā)* which coincides with the death of the individual. An example of the last use of the word *sā'ah* from the Qur'ān is: ''They are losers indeed who reject the meeting with Allāh, until when the hour comes upon them suddenly'' (6 : 31). Here the *hour (al-sā'ah)* clearly stands for the death of the person. As regards the use of *al-sā'ah* in the sense of the end of a generation, a tradition of the Prophet is quoted according to which he is reported to have said about 'Abd Allāh ibn Unais, who was then only a boy: ''If the life of this boy is lengthened, he will not die till the hour (*al-sā'ah*) comes to pass'' (R.); and it is related that he was the last to die from among the Companions of the Prophet; in other words, *al-sā'ah* in this case signifies the passing away of the generation of the Companions. There are examples of this use in the Qur'ān also: ''The hour (*al-sā'ah*) drew nigh and the moon was rent asunder'' (54 : 1). ''The hour,'' in this case, stands for the doom of the opponents of the Prophet. And again: ''Or say they, We are a host allied together to help each other. Soon shall the hosts be routed and they will show their backs. Nay, the Hour (*al-sā'ah*) is their promised time and the hour is most grievous and bitter'' (54 : 44 - 46). Bukhārī tells us, in his comment on these verses, that, when the Prophet was faced with a most serious situation on the day of the battle of Badr, the Muslims being in danger of utter annihilation at the hands of their powerful opponents, and was praying for their safety, he was reminded of this prophecy, and comforted his Companions by reciting these verses aloud,[5] showing that *the hour (al-sā'ah)* here meant the hour of the enemy's defeat.

Spiritual resurrection and the greater resurrection

Just as the word *al-sā'ah* is used in a wider sense, and indicates, besides the Doomsday, sometimes the death of an individual and sometimes the passing of a generation, so do the words *qiyāma* (rising) and *ba'th* (raising the dead to life) sometimes occur, each in a wider sense. Thus there is a saying of the Prophet: "Whoever dies, his resurrection had indeed come to pass."[6] Here the state of *barzakh* is called a resurrection, and this shows that no sooner does a man die than he is raised to a new life. It should be further borne in mind that on many occasions when the Qur'ān speaks of the dead, it means those who are spiritually dead, and by giving life to them it means the bringing about of a spiritual awakening in them, as for example: "Is he who was dead, then We raised him to life and made for him a light by which he walks among the people, like him whose likeness is that of one in darkness whence he cannot come forth?" (6: 123). Here, clearly, the dead one is he who is spiritually dead, and God's raising him to life is giving him the life spiritual. On one occasion even, by "those in the graves" are meant those who are dead spiritually: "Neither are the living and the dead alike. Surely Allāh makes him whom He pleases hear, and thou canst not make those hear who are in the graves. Thou art naught but a warner" (35 : 22, 23). The context shows that by "those in the graves" are meant those whom death has overtaken spiritually, whom the Prophet would warn but they would not listen. On another occasion, where those in the graves are mentioned, the words convey a double significance, referring to the spiritual awakening brought about by the Prophet as well as to the new life in the Resurrection: "And thou seest the earth barren, but when We send down thereon water it stirs and swells and brings forth a beautiful growth of every kind.

[5] Bu. 64 : 4.

[6] MM. 26 : 7.

This is because Allāh, He is the Truth, and He gives life to the dead and He is possessor of power over all things, and the Hour is coming, there is no doubt about it; and Allāh will raise up those who are in the graves'' (22 : 5 - 7). The first part of this passage, describing the giving of life to dead soil by means of rain, shows that the second part refers to the giving of spiritual life by means of Divine revelation, a comparison between rain and revelation being of frequent occurrence in the Qur'ān. ''The Hour'' here, as in so many other places, refers to the doom of the opponents of the Prophet, and ''the dead'' and ''those in the graves'' are evidently the spiritually dead. But, though speaking primarily of the spiritual resurrection, there is also a reference to the great Resurrection of the dead. In fact, not only here but in many other places in the Qur'ān, the spiritual resurrection, to be brought about by the Prophet, and the greater Resurrection of the dead are mentioned together, the one being as it were an evidence of the other,[7] because an awakening to spiritual life shows the existence of a higher life, the development of which is the real aim of the greater resurrection. This is the first great argument running throughout the pages of the Qur'ān as to the truth of the greater resurrection. The spiritual resurrection brought about by the Prophet, the awakening to a spiritual life, makes the higher life an experience of humanity, and thus clears the way for a development of that life in a higher sphere, above the limitations of this material world.

[7] This is specially the case when the giving of life to the dead earth, by means of rain, is spoken of as an evidence of the Resurrection. In such cases, both the spiritual resurrection and the greater resurrection are meant, the one in fact being evidence of the other. That the spiritual resurrection serves as an argument for the greater resurrection is clearly pointed out in the following verses: ''Nay! I swear by the Day of Resurrection. Nay! I swear by the self-accusing spirit'' (75 : 1, 2). Now here the resurrection is spoken of as an evidence of the Resurrection, and what is really meant is that the spiritual resurrection to be brought about by the Prophet (such being the significance of *qiyāma* here) shall serve as an evidence of the greater resurrection which is implied. And the fact that it is the spiritual resurrection that is produced as an evidence is made clear by mentioning along with it the self-accusing spirit which is the first stage of the growth of spiritual life in man, because it is when the inner self of man accuses him of wrong-doing that his struggle against evil is begun in earnest, which struggle is the first indication of the growth of spiritual life; but when evil is done without the inner voice asserting itself, it is a sign that the man is spiritually dead. The self-accusing spirit is the lower stage of the growth of a spiritual life, the higher stage being called ''the spirit at rest'' or *al-nafs al-muṭma'inna*, which enters into paradise even in this life (89 : 27 - 30).

Life has an aim

That the whole of creation on this earth is for the service of man, and that human life has some great aim and purpose to fulfil, is yet another argument for Resurrection advanced by the Qur'ān: "Does man think that he will be left aimless?" (75 : 36); "Do you then think that We have created you in vain and that you will not be returned to Us?" (23 : 115). Just as the God-idea ennobles man's life, and endows it with the purest and highest impulses, so does the resurrection-idea introduce a seriousness into man's life which cannot be otherwise attained. It will be taking too low a view of human nature to imagine that with all those vast capacities for ruling nature and its wonderful forces, human life itself has no aim. If everything in nature is intended for the service of man, human life itself could not be without purpose. The Qur'ān refers to this argument in the following verses: "Certainly We have created man in the best make, then We render him the lowest of the low, except those who believe and do good, so their's is a reward never to be cut off" (95 : 4 - 6). The last words clearly refer to the higher life which is never to be cut off. It cannot be that the whole of creation should serve a purpose and that man alone who is lord of it and endowed with capabilities for ruling the universe, should have a purposeless existence. It is the Resurrection alone that solves this difficulty. Man has a higher object to fulfill, he has a higher life to live beyond this world; which is the aim of human life in this world.

Good and evil must have their reward

Another argument adduced by the Qur'ān in support of the resurrection is that good and evil must have their reward. Of the whole living creation, man alone has the power to discriminate between good and evil. And so acute is his perception of good and evil that he strives with all his might to promote good and to eradicate evil. He makes laws for this purpose, and uses the whole machinery of power at his disposal to enforce them. Yet what do we see in practical life? Good is often neglected and starves, while evil prospers. That is not as it should be. "Allāh wastes not the reward of the doers of good" (11 : 115; 12 : 90, etc.); "We waste not the reward of him who does a good work" (18 : 30); "I will not suffer the work of any worker among you to be lost, whether male or female, the one of you being from the other" (3 : 194); "So he who does an atom's weight of good will see it. And he who does an atom's weight of evil will see it'' (99 : 7, 8) — such are some of the plain declarations made by the Qur'ān. And when we look at nature around us, we find the same law at work. Every cause has its effect, and everything done must bear a fruit. Even that which man does in the physical world must bear a fruit. Why should man's good or evil deeds be an exception to this general rule working in the whole universe? And if they are not an exception, as they should not be, the conclusion is evident that good and evil must bear their full fruit in another life, which indicates the continuity of the life of man in another world, when death has put an end to it in this.

Resurrection as a workable principle of life

It will be seen from the above that the Resurrection is not a dogma in which a man is required to believe for his salvation in another life; rather it is a principle of human life, a principle which makes that life more serious and more useful, while at the same time awakening in him the consciousness of a life that is higher. The man who sincerely believes in the Resurrection will try his utmost to take advantage of every opportunity that is offered him to live his life to the best purpose; he will try hard to do any good that he possibly can to the creatures of God, and he will shun every evil deed as far as he can. Thus a belief in the Resurrection is needed in the first place to make this lower life worth living. Without such a belief, life loses not only its meaning, leaving man without any real or abiding aim, but also all incentive to do good and eschew evil.

Resurrection is quite consistent with present scientific knowledge

The idea of a life after death is so strange to the average mind that the Qur'ān has, again and again, to answer the question, how will it be? And the answer given in all cases is that the great Author of all existence Who made this vast universe out of nothing, could also bring about a new creation. ``Were We then fatigued, with the first creation? Yet they are in doubt about a new creation'' (50 : 15). ``But they say, Who will return us (to a new creation)? Say, He Who created you at first'' (17 : 51). ``And they say: When we are bones and decayed particles, shall we then be raised up into a new creation? See they not that Allāh, Who created the heavens and the earth, is able to create the like of them?'' (17 : 98 - 99). ``Seest thou not that Allāh created the heavens and the earth with truth? If He please, He will take you away and bring a new creation. And that is not difficult for Allāh. And they will all come forth to Allāh'' (14 : 19 - 21).

The subject is reverted too often to enable all the verses bearing on it to be reproduced, but the one underlying idea running through them all is that this old creation, the earth and its heaven, and the rest of the universe, would give place to a new creation. The old order would be changed into an entirely new one. It shall be a day ''when the earth shall be changed into a different earth and the heavens as well'' (14 : 48). Just as this universe has grown out of chaos and a nebulous mass into its present state of systems of galaxies and stars and their families, it will, in its turn, give place to a higher order which will be evolved from it. The idea is quite consistent with the scientific knowledge of the universe to which man has attained at the present-day — the idea of evolution, order out of chaos, a higher order out of a lower order, and with this order of the universe, a higher order of human life of which our present senses cannot conceive.

Will the Resurrection be corporeal?

Another question connected with the Resurrection is whether it would be a corporeal resurrection. So far as our present experience goes, it is through the body that the spirit receives all its impressions of pleasure and pain, that it gets knowledge and perception of things, that its impulses and sentiments are developed. In fact, according to the present state of our knowledge, we cannot conceive of the soul without a body. But whether the soul in Resurrection will receive back the same body which it left in this world is quite another question. There is nothing in the Qur'ān to show that the body which the soul left at death will be restored to it. On the other hand, there are statements to show that it will be a new creation altogether. The verses quoted in the last paragraph give a clear indication that it is not the old creation that will be restored at the Day of Resurrection. Even the old heaven and the old earth will pass away and there will be a new heaven and a new earth (14 : 48). If the very earth and heaven have changed at the Resurrection, how can the human body remain the same? And in fact the Qur'ān has stated clearly that it shall be a new body altogether. In one place, the human beings at the Resurrection are called the likes of the present race: ''Do they not consider that Allāh Who created the heavens and the earth is able to create their likes?'' (17 : 99), where the Arabic words for *their likes* are *mithlahum*, the personal pronoun *hum* referring to men, not to heaven and earth. In another place, the statement that the bodies would be changed is even clearer. There, the question of the unbelievers is first mentioned: "When we die and have become dust and bones, shall we then indeed be raised?" (56 : 47). And the reply is given: "Have you considered the life-germ? Is it you that create it or are We the Creators? We have ordained death among you and We are not to be overcome, that We may change your state and make you grow into what you know not. And certainly you know the first growth, why do you not then mind?" (56 : 58 - 62). After men have become dust and bones, they shall be raised up again but their "state" will be entirely "changed," and the new growth will be one which "you know not", while "you know the first growth." The human body at the Resurrection is, therefore, a new growth with our present senses, which we cannot even know. And this is as true of the human body as of all things of the next life, of the blessings of Paradise as well as of the chastisement of Hell, that they are things which according to a saying of the Prophet, "the eye has not seen, nor has the ear heard, nor has it entered into the heart of man to conceive of them" (Bu. 59 : 8). The resurrection-body has therefore nothing in common with the body of this world except the name or the form which preserves the individuality.

A body prepared from the good and evil deeds of man

To understand how, what may be called the spiritual body of the life after death, is prepared, one must turn again to the Qur'ān. There it is stated that angels have been appointed to record the good and evil deeds of man. Thus in the opening sections of the 13th chapter, a denial of the Resurrection — "When we are dust, shall we then be in a new creation?" (13 : 5) — is followed by the answer: "Alike (to Him) among you is he who conceals his words and he who speaks them openly, and he who hides himself by night and who goes forth by day. For him are angels guarding the consequences of his deeds, before him and behind him who guard him by Allāh's command" (13 : 10, 11). It is first stated that to God all are alike, those who conceal their words and those who speak them openly, and those that do a good or evil deed in the darkness of the night and those who do it in the light of the day: and it is then added that there are angels before and behind man that guard him. The guarding of the man and the guarding of his deeds are thus one and the same thing. In fact, this has been made clear in an earlier chapter — earlier in point of revelation: "Nay, but you give the lie to the Judgment, and surely there are keepers over you, honourable recorders, they know what you do'' (82 : 9 - 12). Here the angels that are called ''keepers over you'', being undoubtedly the guarding angels (13 : 11), are plainly described as the recording angels who know what man does. Thus both these verses show that an inner self of man is being developed, all along, through his deeds, and that is what is meant by guarding man in one case and guarding *his deeds* in the other. It is the inner self that assumes a shape after death and forms first the body in *barzakh* and is then developed into the body in Resurrection.

Elsewhere, a similar denial of the Resurrection is rebutted by saying[8] that God knows that the body becomes dust, and is followed by the words: ''And with Us is a book that preserves'' (50 : 4), *i.e.*, there is with God a writing that preserves what is essential to growth in the next life. That 'preserving writing' is the record of good and evil deeds kept by the guardian angels, so that, here again, we are told that while the outer garb of the soul, the body, becomes dust and goes back to the earth, the inner self is preserved and forms the basis of the higher life — life in the Resurrection.

Spiritualities materialized

This materialization of spiritualities — not a materialization in the sense in which it is accepted in this life, but a materialization of the new world to be evolved from the present world — is spoken of frequently in the Qur'ān as well as in Tradition. For instance, those who are guided by the light of faith in this life shall have a light running before them and behind them on the Day of Resurrection: ''Is he who was dead, then We raised him to life and made for him a light by which he walks among the people, like him whose likeness is that of one in darkness whence he cannot come forth?'' (6 : 123); ''On that day thou wilt see the faithful men and the faithful women, their light gleaming before them and on their right hand'' (57 : 12). And the fruits of good deeds are spoken of as fruits of Paradise: ''And give good news to those who believe and do good deeds, that for them are gardens in which rivers flow. Whenever they are given

[8] The actual words used are literally translated as ''We know indeed what the earth diminishes of them'', *i.e.*, the body becomes dust.

a portion of the fruit thereof, they will say: This is what was given to us before; and they are given the like of it'' (2 : 25). Similarly the fire which burns within the heart of man in this life, by reason of inordinate love of wealth, becomes the fire of Hell in the next life: ''It is the Fire kindled by Allāh, which rises above the hearts'' (104 : 6, 7). And the spiritual blindness of this life turns into blindness in the next life: ''And whoever is blind in this (world), he will be blind in the Hereafter'' (17 : 72). The seventy years of evil-doing — seventy being the average span of human life — are turned into a chain of seventy cubits (69 : 32). The man who acts according to the Book of God, or takes it in his right hand here, shall be given his book in the right hand on the Resurrection Day, and the man who will have none of it, and throws it behind his back, shall be given his book behind his back or in his left hand (69 : 19, 25; 84 : 7, 10). Tradition also is full of examples of this. The spiritualities of this life take an actual shape in the Hereafter. This is the truth underlying all the blessings of Paradise and the torments of Hell.

The book of deeds

It will have been noticed that the guarding of the good and evil deeds of man, which form the basis of the higher life, is spoken of as writing them down; and a book of good and evil deeds is repeatedly mentioned. To quote further: ''Or do they think that We hear not their secrets and their private counsels? Aye! and Our messengers with them write down'' (43 : 80). ''This is Our record that speaks against you with truth. Surely We wrote what you did'' (45 : 29). ''And the book is placed, then thou seest the guilty fearing for what is in it, and they say: O woe to us! what a book is this! It leaves out neither a small thing nor a great one, but numbers them all'' (18 : 49). ''So whoever does good deeds and he is a believer, there is no rejection of his effort, and We write it down for him'' (21 : 94).

Not only has every individual his book of deeds, but even nations are spoken of as having their books of deeds: ''And thou wilt see every nation kneeling down; every nation will be called to its record.[9] This day you are requited for what you did'' (45 : 28).

A nation's record or book of deeds explains what is meant by the individual's book of deeds. The expression means nothing but the effect

[9] The Arabic word used is *kitāb*.

of the deeds done by the individual or the nation. It is a mistake to take the word *kitāb* in the sense of a collection of pages written down with pen and ink in connection with the writing of good and evil deeds. *Kitāb* does not always mean *a collection of written leaves*; it sometimes signifies the *knowledge of Allāh*, or His *command*, or *what He has made obligatory* (R.). And *kataba* does not always mean that *he wrote certain words on paper with ink and pen*; it also means *he made a thing obligatory* or *decreed* or *ordained* or *prescribed a thing (Ibid.)*. According to the same authority, the significance of *kitāb (writing)* in 21 : 49, where the writing of good deeds is spoken of, is that God will preserve those deeds for the doer, and requite him for them.

A study of the verses in which the recording of actions, or the books of deeds, is referred to, leads to the conclusion that it is the effect produced by those actions that is meant. For instance: "And We have made every man's actions to cling to his neck, and We shall bring forth to him on the Day of Resurrection a book which he will find wide open" (17 : 13). Making the actions cling to the doer's neck is clearly causing the effect of the actions to appear on the person concerned; in other words, all actions, good or bad, have their impress on the man.[10] This is in accordance with what has been already stated, namely that an inner self of man is being prepared in this life. That inner self is really his book of deeds, a book in which is noted down the effect of every deed done. It is to this that the concluding words of the verse allude where it is said that this book of deeds, the inner self, which here is hidden from the human eye, will become an open book on the Day of Resurrection. And, quite in consonance with this, the next verse goes on to say: "Read thy book; thine own soul is sufficient as a reckoner against thee this day" (17 : 14). In other words, the effect of a man's deeds becomes so manifest on the Resurrection Day that no outside reckoning is needed. It is man himself who reads his own book, that is to say, sees all his actions in the impress left on him, and judges himself because the reckoning has already appeared in his own self.

In agreement with this are two other verses of an earlier chapter: "Nay, surely the record (*kitāb*) of the wicked is in the prison" (83 : 7); 'Nay, surely the record (*kitāb*) of the righteous is in the highest places"

[10] The deed done is, in this verse, called a *ṭā'ir*, which means originally *a bird* or *a thing that flies off*, and also means *a deed*. A man's deed is called a *ṭā'ir* to show that it flies off as soon as it is done, so that it is not in a man's power to bring it back, as the verse clearly states, a permanent impress of it is left on the doer.

(83 : 18). As opposed to the righteous who are in the highest places, the wicked should have been spoken of as being in the lowest places, but instead of that they are stated to be in prison, which means that a bar is placed against their advancement; hence they are mentioned further on as being "debarred from their Lord" (83 : 15), while the righteous go on advancing to higher and higher places. The word 'record' or book (*kitā b*), here plainly stands for the inner self of the man; in any other sense, the placing of the book in a prison is meaningless. Thus it is clear from the various descriptions of the "book of deeds" or "the record of deeds" that it is the effect of good or evil deeds accelerating or retarding a man's spiritual progress, as the case may be, that is meant, and that the writing is nothing but the impress that is left on man when he does a good or bad deed — an impress which no human eye can see, but whose reality cannot be doubted by any conscientious thinker.

Balance or mīzān

A 'balance' is also spoken of in connection with the good and evil deeds of man. The *mīzān* or balance is again a misunderstood word. *Wazn* is simply *the knowing of the measure of a thing* (R.). It is true that the measure of material things is judged by a pair of scales or by some other implement, but the deeds of man need no scales for their measurement. Rā ghib is very clear on this point when he says that by *wazn* or *mīzān*, in connection with the deeds of men, is meant "the doing of justice in the reckoning of men." He quotes the following examples: "And the judging (*wazn*) on that day will be just" (7 : 8); "And We will set up a just balance (*mawāzin*, pl. of *mīzān*) on the Day of Resurrection" (21 : 47), where in fact the meaning is made clear in the Qur'ān itself by the addition of the words "no soul will be wronged in the least." So too elsewhere, a *mīzān* is referred to as working in nature itself: "And the heaven, He raised it high, and He set up the measure (*mīzān*) that you may not exceed the measure. And keep up the balance with equity nor fall short in the measure" (55 : 7 -9). Here the words used for *measure* or *balance* are the same words *mīzān* and *wazn*. A *mīzān* or balance is first spoken of as existing in connection with the creation of the heavens, and this is followed by an injunction that men should also preserve the balance with equity. Now the balance that is seen working in nature is the law to which everything is subject so that, while opposing forces do exist, yet each force is subject to a law. Everything works out its destiny according to a measure, and so should man also work out his destiny according to a measure. Hence the injunction not to get inordinate in respect of the measure.

The *mīzān* or 'measure' of men is clearly spoken of elsewhere as having been sent down by God: "Certainly We sent Our messengers with clear arguments, and sent down with them the Book and the measure (*mīzān*) that men may conduct themselves with equity" (57 : 25). Revelation, or the Book, is sent down by God to awaken the spiritual life in man, and therefore the measure, which is spoken of as having been sent down along with revelation, must also relate to the spiritual life of man. In his physical growth man is undoubtedly subject to the same balance as is the rest of nature, yet apart from that he has a higher life, the life spiritual, which is evolved out of the present life, and the book that is sent with the prophets and the measure both relate to the growth of their spiritual life. The book contains the directions in principle, to do good and shun evil, so that the spiritual life awakened in man takes a good or bad turn, a higher or lower form, according to the preponderance of good or evil. Thus not only do good and evil deeds leave their effect behind but also there is a balance which gives shape to that effect and makes the spiritual growth possible, or has a retarding effect on that growth if evil preponderates.

The 'balance' of the Hereafter, therefore, differs not at all from the 'balance' of this life, except that there it takes a more palpable form. The general principle is laid down in the following verses: "And We will set up a just balance on the Day of Resurrection, so no soul will be wronged in the least. And if there be the weight of a grain of mustard seed, We will bring it, and sufficient are We to take account" (21 : 47). "And the judging (*wazn*) on that day will be just, so as for those whose good deeds are heavy, they are the successful. And as for those whose good deeds are light, those are they who ruined their souls" (7 : 8, 9).

A certain class of persons is indicated in whose case no balance shall be set up at all. These are the people who waste away the whole of their energy in this world's doings: "Shall We inform you who are the greatest losers in respect of deeds? Those whose efforts go astray in this world's life... Nor shall We set up a balance for them on the Day of Resurrection" (18 : 103 - 105).

Jannah *or Paradise*

The life after death takes two forms: a life in Paradise for those in whom the good preponderates over the evil, and a life in Hell for those in whom the evil preponderates over the good. The word *Paradise (Firdaus)* occurs only twice in the Qur'ān; on one occasion in conjunction with *Gardens*[11] *(jannāt)* and on the other alone.[12] It is the word *garden (jannah* or its plural *jannāt)* that is generally used to indicate the abiding place of the righteous.[13] The use of this name for the abode of bliss has a deeper significance, since of Paradise it is plainly stated that its blessings are such as cannot be perceived by the physical senses. The description of Paradise usually given is *gardens in which rivers flow*, corresponding to which the description of the righteous generally is, *those who believe and do good.* These two descriptions, read in the light of what has gone before as to the materialization in the next world of the spiritualities of this life, are an indication of the fact that faith, which is the water of spiritual life, is converted into rivers, and good deeds, which spring from faith, are the seeds whence grow the trees of the next life.

Blessings of Paradise

The description of Paradise as a garden with rivers flowing in it, is clearly stated to be a parable or a likeness, not an actuality, in terms of this life: "A parable of the garden which is promised to those who keep their duty: therein flow rivers; its fruits are perpetual and its plenty" (13 : 35); "A parable of the garden which the dutiful are promised: therein are rivers of water not altering for the worse..." (47 : 15). And quite in keeping with this description is the statement made elsewhere, that the blessings of Paradise cannot be conceived of in this life, not being things of this world: "No soul knows what refreshment of the eyes is hidden for them: a reward for what they did" (32 : 17). An explanation of these words was given by the Prophet himself when he said: "Allāh says I have prepared for My righteous servants what no eye has seen and no ear has heard,

[11] 18 : 107.

[12] 23 : 11.

[13] *Jannat* is derived from *janna* which signifies *the concealing of a thing so that it is not perceived by the senses*, and *jannat*, in the ordinary usage, means *a garden*, because its ground is covered by trees.

and what the mind of man has not conceived'' (Bu. 59 : 8). And Ibn 'Abbās, the famous companion and commentator, is reported to have said: "In Paradise there are no foods of this life except the names".[14]

A few examples may be added. *Ẓill* which means *a shadow*, is spoken of as one of the blessings of Paradise: "They and their wives are in shades" (36 : 56); "The dutiful are amid shades and fountains" (77 : 41); "Its fruits are perpetual and its *ẓill*" (13 : 35). *Ẓill*[15] actually does not in all these cases bear the significance of *shade*; the name is there but its import is quite different. In fact we are plainly told in the Qur'ān that there is no sun in Paradise: "They will see therein neither sun nor intense cold" (76 : 13). Hence in the case of Paradise, *ẓill* signifies *protection* or *plenty*, as being the idea underlying the word *shade* (R.).

Those in Paradise are spoken of as being given *sustenance (rizq)*. But it cannot mean what sustains the body here. It is the sustenance that is needed for the inner self of man, and it is for this reason that prayer is also called sustenance.[16] The fruits of Paradise, whether mentioned under a particular name or generally, are not the fruits of this life, but of deeds done. The name is the same, but the significance is quite different. Thus we are told: "Whenever they are given a portion of the fruit thereof, they will say: This is what was given to us before" (2 : 25). Evidently the fruits of good deeds are meant here, and not the fruits that the earth grows, because the latter are not given to all the true believers here while the former are. Similar is the case with the rivers of water, milk and honey all of which are plainly spoken of as a parable;[17] the thrones, the cushions and carpets;[18] the ornaments, the bracelets, the silk robes[19] — all these are not things of this life, but are mentioned simply to show that whatever may serve to perfect the picture of the happiness of man, will be there. As for the exact form they will take, that cannot be made known to man, because his senses are incapable of perceiving it. All descriptions of the

[14] RM. 1, p. 172.

[15] The same word has also been used in connection with the rigours of Hell. "And the shade of black smoke, neither cool nor honourable" (56 : 43, 44). "Walk on to the shade having three branches" (77 : 30). Rāghib adds that *ẓill* is *every covering whether good or bad*; and hence *ẓill* is also spoken of as one of the severities of Hell.

[16] 20 : 131.

[17] 47 : 15.

[18] 88 : 13 - 16.

[19] 18 : 31.

blessing of the next life are only *a likeness* or *a parable* (*mat͟hal*) as is explained in the Qur'ān.[20]

As already stated, the Resurrection means quite a new life and a new order of things, a new heaven and a new earth. A little consideration will show that our ideas of space and time are inapplicable to the next life. Paradise extends over the whole of the heavens and the earth, that is to say, the whole of this universe: "And hasten to forgiveness from your Lord and a Garden as wide as the heavens and the earth" (3 : 132; 57 : 21). And when the Prophet was asked where was Hell, if Paradise extended over the whole of the heavens and the earth, he replied "Where is the night when the day comes?"[21] This shows that Paradise and Hell are more like two conditions than two places. Again, notwithstanding the fact that the two are poles asunder, the one being the highest of the high and the other the lowest of the low, they are separated only by a thin partition: "Then a wall, with a door in it, will be raised between them; within it shall be mercy and outside of it chastisement" (57 : 13). And elsewhere, speaking of the inmates of Paradise and the inmates of Hell, it is said: "And between them is a veil" (7 : 46). It is impossible, with our present ideas of space, to conceive of these two things at one and the same time. Again, a "vehement raging and roaring" of hell-fire is repeatedly mentioned,[22] but those in Paradise shall "not hear its faintest sound"[23] while they will hear the call of the inmates of that fire: And the companions of the fire shall call out to the owners of the Garden: "Pour on us some water or some of that which Allāh has provided for you. They say: Surely Allāh has prohibited them both to the disbelievers, who take their religion for an idle sport and a play, and this world's life deceives them" (7 : 50, 51). Thus those in Paradise shall hear the talk of those in Hell, but they shall not hear the roaring of the fire of Hell. This shows that the change, that will come over man in the Resurrection, will be so thorough that even his present senses will be changed into others of which it is impossible for him to conceive in this life, senses which would hear the lowest tones of one kind, but not the most terrible sounds of another.

[20] 13 : 35; 47 : 15.

[21] RM. 1, p. 670.

[22] 25 : 12; 67 : 7

[23] 21 : 102.

Women in Paradise

The things mentioned among the blessings of Paradise are, therefore, not the things of this world but things which we have neither seen nor heard of in this life; nor, with our present senses, can we even conceive of them. All descriptions given are simply to show that the life of the righteous will be perfect in the Resurrection. It is with the same end in view that mention is made of the company of men and women in that state, to which sensually minded people have attached a sensual significance. Writing under the word *zauj*, used in the Qur'ān in connection with the companionship of men and women, Rāghib[24] says that "the meaning of *zawwajnā-hum bi-ḥūr-in 'īn* is that we have given them *ḥūr* as companions *(qarannāhum bi-hinna)*, and the Qur'ān does not say *zawwajnā-ḥūm ḥūr-an*, as you say in the case of the marriage of a man with a woman, *zawwajtu-hū imra'at-an*, hinting that the relations there will not be as they are known to us here in this life".[25] It is also stated that in the "relations with women in Paradise there is no suggestion of procreation";[26] and as sexual relationship, as understood in this life, is a requirement of nature to help the act of procreation, it is clear that the relationship of sexes or the company of men and women in the Resurrection has quite a different significance.

The mention of women in the Qur'ān is, in the first place, to show that men and women are both equal in the sight of God, and that both will enjoy the higher life in the Resurrection. That women, in general, shall have access to Paradise like men, is made clear in many places: "And whoever does good, whether male or female, and is a believer, these shall enter the Garden" (40 : 40; 4 : 124). "Whoever does good deeds, whether male or female, and is a believer, We shall certainly make him live a good life" (16 : 97). "I will not suffer the work of any worker among you to be lost whether male or female, the one of you being from the other" (3 : 194).

[24] The famous lexicologist of the Qur'ān.

[25] See also LL., which confirms that the use of the word *zauj* as a double transitive verb without being followed by a particle means marrying and when made doubly transitive with particle *bi* to join and unite a thing to its fellow or like. Along with it is quoted 81 : 7 which is translated as meaning *and when the souls shall be paired* or *united with their fellows.*

[26] RM. 1, p. 172.

The wives of the righteous are mentioned particularly as accompanying their husbands in Paradise: "They and their wives are in shades, reclining on raised couches" (36 : 56). "Our Lord! make them enter the Gardens of perpetuity, which Thou hast promised them and such of their fathers and their wives and their offspring as are good" (40 : 8). "Enter the garden, you and your wives; being made happy" (43 : 70).

Ḥūr

Among the various descriptions of women in Paradise is the word *ḥūr*, which occurs four times in the Qur'ān. It is a plural of *aḥwar* (applied to a man) and of *ḥaurā'* (applied to a woman), signifying *one having eyes characterized by* the quality termed *ḥawar* (LL.)[27] Purity is the prevailing idea in the meaning of *ḥawar*, and therefore *hawārī*,[28] which is derived from the same root, means *a pure and sincere friend*. Hence "pure ones" is the nearest rendering of the word *ḥūr*, in English. The four occasions on which the women of Paradise are spoken of as *ḥūr* are: "Those who keep their duty are indeed in a secure place, in gardens and springs... and We shall join them to pure (*ḥūr*), beautiful ones" (44: 51- 54). "The dutiful will be surely in Gardens and bliss... Reclining on thrones set in lines, and We will join them to pure (*ḥūr*), beautiful ones" (52 : 17 - 20). "Therein (*i.e.*, in the gardens) are goodly beautiful ones... Pure ones (*ḥūr*) confined to the pavilions" (55 : 70 - 72). "And the foremost are the foremost, these are drawn nigh (to God). In Gardens of bliss... On thrones inwrought... And pure (*ḥūr*), beautiful ones, the likes of hidden pearls: a reward for what they did" (56 : 10 - 24).

Are *ḥūr* the women that go to Paradise, the wives of the righteous? A hint to this effect is given in a tradition. The last of the occasions on which the *ḥūr* are spoken of is 56 : 10 - 24, and in continuation of the subject there occur the words: "Surely We have created them a new creation, so We have made them virgins, loving, equals in age, for those

[27] *Ḥawar* means originally *whiteness* (which is a symbol of purity), and the word *ḥaurā*, is applied to *a woman who is of a white colour and whose white of the eye is intensely white and the black thereof intensely black* (LA). *Aḥwar*, besides being applied to a man of a similar description, also signifies *pure* or *clear intellect* (LL.).

[28] In the Qur'ān this word has been particularly applied to the chosen disciples of Jesus, but in Tradition it is used in a general sense in connection with the chosen friends of any prophet.

on the right hand'' (56 : 35 - 38). In connection with their being a new creation, the Prophet is reported to have said that, by this are meant women who have grown old here.[29] The meaning, therefore is that all good women will be in a new creation in the life of the Resurrection so that they shall all be virgins, equals in age. The Prophet's explanation shows that the word *ḥūr* is used to describe the new growth into which women of the world will grow. An anecdote is also related that an old woman came to the Prophet when he was sitting with his Companions, and asked him if she would go to Paradise. In a spirit of mirth, the Prophet remarked that there would be no old women in Paradise. She was about to turn away rather sorrowfully, when the Prophet comforted her with the words that all women shall be made to grow into a new growth, so that there shall be no old women in Paradise, and recited the verses quoted above.[30]

Ḥūr as a blessing of Paradise

The conclusion to which this tradition leads is further supported by what is stated in the Qur'ān. The description of *ḥūr*, as given in the Qur'ān, contains the best qualities of a good woman, purity of character, beauty, youthful appearance, restrained eyes and love for her husband. But even if the *ḥūr* are taken to be a blessing of Paradise, and not the women of this world, it is a blessing as well for men as for women. Just as the gardens, rivers, milk, honey, fruits, and numerous other things of Paradise are both for men and women, even so are *ḥūr*. What these blessings actually are, no one knows, but the whole picture of Paradise drawn in the Qur'ān strongly condemns the association of any sensual idea therewith. It may, however, be asked, why are these blessings described in words which apply to women? The fact is that the reward spoken of here has special reference to the purity and beauty of character, and if there is an emblem of purity and beauty, it is womanhood, not manhood.

Children in Paradise

What is true of women is also true of *ghilmān* (children). The Qur'ān speaks, on one occasion, of the presence in Paradise of *ghilmān* (pl. of *ghulām* meaning *a boy*), and on two occasions of *wildān* (pl. of *walad*

[29] Tr. 44 : Surah 56.
[30] RM. VIII, p. 320.

meaning *a son* or *a child*): ''And round them go boys (*ghilmān*) of theirs as if they were hidden pearls'' (52 : 24); ''And round about them shall go youths (*wildān*) never altering in age'' (56 : 17; 76 : 19). In the first case, there is a double indication showing that these boys, called the *ghilmān*, are the offspring of the faithful; they are called *ghilmān-un la-ḥum* or their boys, and it is clearly stated that God will ''unite with them (*i.e.*, the righteous) their offspring'' (52 : 21). To the same effect, it is elsewhere said that the ''offspring'' of the faithful will be made to enter Paradise with them (40 : 8). Hence the *ghilmān* and the *wildān* are the young children who have died in childhood. There is, however, a possibility that these boys are only a blessing of Paradise, as boyhood is, like womanhood, an emblem of purity and beauty.

Abode of peace

No reader of the Qur'ān can fail to see that the real picture of Paradise, therein portrayed, has no implication whatsoever, of any sensual pleasure. Some of the verses which reveal the true nature of Paradise may be quoted: ''Allāh has promised to the believing men and the believing women gardens in which rivers flow, to abide in them, and goodly dwellings in gardens of perpetual abode; and greatest of all is Allāh's goodly pleasure, that is the grand achievement'' (9 : 72). ''Those who believe and do good, their Lord guides them by their faith; rivers will flow beneath them in Gardens of bliss. Their cry in it will be, Glory to Thee, O Allāh! and their greeting, Peace! And the last of their cry will be: Praise be to Allāh, the Lord of the worlds'' (10 : 9, 10). ''Their greeting therein is, Peace!'' (14 : 23). ''Surely those who keep their duty are in Gardens and fountains: Enter them in peace, secure. And We shall root out whatever of rancour is in their breasts — as brethren, on raised couches, face to face. Toil afflicts them not in it, nor will they be ejected therefrom'' (15 : 45 - 48). ''And they say: Praise be to Allāh, Who has removed grief from us! Surely our Lord is Forgiving, Multiplier of rewards, Who out of His grace has made us alight in a house abiding for ever therein; toil touches us not, nor does fatigue afflict us therein'' (35 : 34 - 35). ''They have fruits therein, and they have whatever they desire. Peace! a word from the Merciful Lord'' (36 : 57 - 58). ''Enter it in peace. That is the day of abiding. For them therein is all they wish and with Us is yet more'' (50 : 34 - 35). ''They hear therein no vain or sinful talk but only the saying, Peace! Peace!'' (57 : 25 - 26).

Quite in accordance with this description of Paradise, one of the names by which Paradise is mentioned in the Qur'ān is *abode of peace*[31] (*dār al-salām*).

Liqā Allāh *or the meeting with God*

The ultimate object of the life of man is described as *liqā' Allāh* which means *the meeting with God.* In one of the earliest chapters we are told: "O man! Thou must strive a hard striving (to attain) to thy Lord until thou meet Him" (84 : 6). But this object cannot be fully attained in this life; it is only in the life after death, the higher life, that man is able to reach this stage. Hence it is that those who deny the life after death are said to be deniers of the meeting with God: "And they say: When we are lost in the earth, shall we then be in a new creation? Nay, they are disbelievers in the meeting with their Lord" (32 : 10). To be content with this life, and not to look forward to a higher goal and a higher life, is repeatedly condemned: "Those who expect not the meeting with Us, and are pleased with this world's life and are satisfied with it, and those who are heedless of Our communications — these, their abode is the Fire" (10 : 7, 8); 'We leave those alone who have no hope of meeting with Us, in their inordinacy, blindly wandering on" (10 : 11); "And those who disbelieve in the messages of Allāh and the meeting with Him, they despair of My mercy, and for them is a painful chastisement" (29 : 23); "They know the outward of this world's life, but of the Hereafter they are heedless. Do they not reflect within themselves? Allāh did not create the heavens and the earth and what is between them but with truth and for an appointed term. And surely most of the people are deniers of the meeting with their Lord" (30 : 7, 8). Only those who are sure that they will meet their Lord work on patiently for this great object: "And seek assistance through patience and prayer, and this is hard except for the humble ones, who know that they will meet their Lord and that to Him they will return" (2 : 45, 46). The meeting with the Lord is the great goal to attain for which all good deeds are done: "So whoever hopes to meet his Lord, he should do good deeds, and join no one in the service of his Lord" (18 : 110). And what is Hell itself but being debarred from the Divine presence: "Nay, rather, what they earned is rust upon their hearts. Nay, surely they are that day debarred from their Lord. Then they

[31] 6 : 128; 10 : 25.

will surely enter the burning Fire'' (83 : 14 - 16). Paradise is therefore the place of meeting with God, and life in Paradise is above all corporeal conceptions.

Advancement in the higher life

That, however, is only the beginning of the higher life. The goal has been attained, but it only opens out wide fields for further advancement. If man has been granted such vast capabilities even in this physical life that his advancement knows no bounds, that advancement could not cease with the attainment of the higher life. In accordance with the idea of the Resurrection as the birth into a higher life, the Qur'ān speaks of an unending progress in that life, of the righteous ever rising to higher and higher stages. Rest and enjoyment are not the goal of human existence. Just as there is a desire implanted in the human soul to advance further and further in this life, even so there will be such a desire in Paradise: ''O you who believe, turn to Allāh with sincere repentance. It may be your Lord will remove from you your evil and cause you to enter Gardens wherein flow rivers, on the day on which Allāh will not abase the Prophet and those who believe with him. Their light will gleam before them and on their right hands — they will say: Our Lord, make perfect for us our light and grant us protection; surely Thou art possessor of power over all things'' (66 :8). It is clear from the first part of this verse that all evil is removed from those who enter into Paradise, and as clear from the concluding portion that the soul of the righteous shall still be animated by a desire for more and more light, which evidently indicates a desire to attain to higher and ever higher stages of spiritual life. And there shall be means of fulfilment of every desire in Paradise: ''They have fruits therein and they have whatever they desire'' (36 : 57). So the desire to attain to higher and higher stages cannot remain unfulfilled: ''But those who keep their duty to their Lord, for them are high places, above them higher places (still), built for them'' (39 : 20). The new life granted to the righteous in Paradise is thus the starting-point for a new advancement, in which man shall continue to rise to higher and higher places. Nor shall man ever grow weary in the attainment of these high stages of which even a conception cannot be now formed, for ''therein toil touches us not nor does fatigue afflict us therein'' (35 : 35); ''Nor shall they be ever ejected from it'' (15 : 48). The joys of Paradise are thus really the true joys of advancement.

Different names of Hell

Hell is described by seven different names in the Qur'ān, and these are supposed by some to be the seven divisions of Hell. The most frequently occurring is *Jahannam*, which is, as it were, a proper name for Hell.[32] Its meaning signifies a great depth. Another name for Hell which bears a similar significance, but which occurs only once in the Qur'ān,[33] is *hā wiya*, meaning *an abyss* or *a deep place of which the bottom cannot be reached* (LA.).[34] Four names of Hell are taken from the analogy of fire, *viz., jaḥīm*, derived from *jaḥum*, signifying the *burning* or *blazing of fire*, but this word is applied to the fury of war as well as of fire, while *tajaḥḥama*, another measure from the same root, means *he burned with vehemence of desire* or *covetousness and niggardliness*, also *he became strained in disposition* (LL.); *sa'ir* from *sa'r* which means the *kindling of fire* and is metaphorically applied to *the raging of war* (R.);[35] *saqar* from *saqara* which means *the heat of the sun scorched a man* (R.); *lazā* which means *the flame* of the fire, and in one form (*talazza*) is metaphorically used for *"burning with anger"* (LA). The seventh name *ḥuṭamah*, which occurs only twice in the same context, (104 : 4, 5), is derived from *ḥaṭam* which means *the breaking of a thing*, also *breaking* or *rendering infirm* or *weak with age*, while *ḥuṭamah* means *a vehement fire*, and *ḥuṭmah* sterility (LL.).[36]

Hell, a manifestation of spiritualities

It will be seen from the above that the different names of Hell convey three different ideas, the idea of falling down to a great depth, the idea of burning and the idea of being broken down. Thus as the idea of rising higher and higher is connected with Paradise, that of falling down to abysmal depth is essentially connected with Hell; and as the ideas of contentment and happiness are associated with Paradise, the idea of burning is

[32] *Jahannam* signifies *great depth*, and *bi'r-un jahannam-un* means *a well whose depth is very great* (LA.).

[33] 101 : 9.

[34] The root being *hawā* which means *falling down to a depth from a height*, and hence indicating low desires (R.).

[35] The word *su'ur* has been used in the sense of *distress* in the Holy Qur'ān (54 : 24).

[36] The word *ḥuṭām*, derived from the same root, is used in 57 : 20 and elsewhere for "dried up and broken down" vegetation.

associated with Hell which is itself but the result of burning with passion in this life; and lastly, as the idea of a fruitful life is associated with Paradise, life in Hell is represented as an unfruitful life. All this is the result of man's own deeds. Because he follows his low desires and baser passions, he makes himself fall into the depths; the burning caused by worldly desires and passions changes into a flaming fire after death; and since the only end in view is some sort of gain in this life, such deeds can bear no fruit after death. Just as the blessings of Paradise are a manifestation of the hidden realities of this life, so are the depths, the fire and unfruitfulness of the next, the Day of Resurrection being the day of the manifestation of hidden realities[37] when the veil shall be removed from the eyes of man so that he shall see clearly the consequences of the deeds of which he took no heed in this life.[38] In other words, the spiritual torments and mental pangs, that are generally felt almost imperceptibly in this life, assume a palpable shape in the life after death. The answer to the question, what is Hell? is unequivocally given as "Fire kindled by Allāh which rises over the hearts" (104 : 6, 7). Now the fire which consumes the hearts is that caused by inordinate passions. Regret for the evil done is also spoken of as fire: "Thus will Allāh show them their deeds to be intense regret to them, and they will not escapc from the fire" (2 : 167). The low desires of this life (*ahwā*), that are so often a hindrance in man's awakening to a higher life and nobler aims, become the abysmal depth (*hāwiyah* or *jahannam*), to which the evil-doer makes himself fall. Even so, in the Qur'ān we are told: "So shun the filth of the idols and shun false words, being upright for Allāh, not associating aught with Him; and whoever associates aught with Allāh, it is as though he had fallen from on high" (22 : 30 - 31). And of the people whose exertions are all limited in this world's life, it is said: "They whose efforts go astray in this world's life and they think that they are making good manufactures: those are they who disbelieve in the messages of their Lord and meeting with Him, so their works are in vain. Nor shall We set up a balance for them on the Day of Resurrection. That is their reward — Hell" (18 : 104 - 106).

Though fire is so frequently mentioned as the consequence of evil, reasons for which will be given later on, yet there are a number of other aspects of the evil consequences of evil deeds. For example, it is said: "For those who do good is good (reward) and more (than this). Neither blackness or ignominy will cover their faces. These are the owners of

[37] 86 : 9.

[38] 50 : 22.

the Garden; therein they will abide. And those who earned evil, the punishment of an evil is the like thereof, and abasement will cover them — they will have none to protect them from Allāh — as if their faces had been covered with slices of the dense darkness of night. These are the companions of the fire; therein they will abide;; (10 : 26, 27). Blackness of the face is again mentioned as the chastisement of Hell: "On the Day when some faces turn white and some faces turn black. Then as to those whose faces are black: Did you disbelieve after your belief? So taste the chastisement because you disbelieved" (3 : 105). So, too in the earlier revelation: "And faces on that day will have dust on them, darkness covering them. Those are the disbelievers, the wicked" (80 : 40 - 42).

Disgrace is mentioned as the chastisement of evil-doers in many other places: "Then on the Resurrection Day, He will bring them to disgrace... Surely disgrace this day and evil are upon the unbelievers" (16 : 27); "... that We may make them taste the chastisement of abasement in this world's life. And the chastisement of the Hereafter is truly more abasing, and they will not be helped" (41 : 16). Again, those in Hell are sometimes spoken of as asking for water and sustenance from those in Paradise: "And the companions of the fire call out to the owners of the Garden: Pour on us some water or some of that which Allāh has provided for you" (7 : 50). The water they have is "boiling and intensely cold" (78 : 25). On other occasions, however, it is light that they cry for: "On the day when the hypocrites, men and women, will say to those who believe: Wait for us that we may borrow from your light. It will be said: Turn back and seek a light" (57 : 13).

Remedial nature of Hell

Hell, therefore, only represents the evil consequences of evil deeds, but still it is not a place merely for undergoing the consequences of what has been done; it is also a remedial plan. In other words, its chastisement is not for the purpose of torture but for purification; so that man, rid of the evil consequences which he has brought about with his own hands, may be made fit for spiritual advancement. The Qur'ān has clearly laid down the same law even for those punishments which are inflicted on man here on earth: "And We did not send a prophet to a town, but We seized its people with distress and affliction that they might humble themselves" (7 : 94). It is clear from this that God brings down His punishment upon a sinning people in order that they may turn to Him, in other words, that they may be awakened to a higher life. The same must therefore be the object of punishment in Hell.

In fact, a little consideration would show that good is enjoined because it helps the progress of man, and evil is prohibited because it retards that progress. If a man does good, he himself gets the advantage of it; if he does evil, it is to his own detriment. It is a subject to which the Qur'ān returns over and over again: "He is indeed successful who causes it[39] to grow, and he indeed fails who buries it" (91 : 9, 10). "Your striving is surely for diverse ends. Then as for him who gives (in charity) and keeps his duty, and accepts what is good — We facilitate for him (the way to) ease. And for him who is niggardly and considers himself self-sufficient, and rejects what is good, We facilitate for him (the way to) distress" (92 : 4 - 10). "If you do good, you do good for your own souls, and if you do evil, it is for them" (17 : 7). "Whoever does good, it is for his own soul; and whoever does evil, it is against it. And thy Lord is not in the least unjust to the servants" (41 : 46). "Whoever does good, it is for himself, and whoever does evil, it is against himself; then to your Lord you will be brought back" (45 : 15).

Purification being the great object, the man who has wasted his opportunity here must undergo the ordeal of Hell in order to obtain it. Various other considerations lead to the same conclusion. In the first place, such great prominence is given to the attribute of mercy in God that He is spoken of as having "ordained mercy on Himself";[40] the Divine mercy is described as encompassing all things,[41] so that even those who have acted extravagantly, against their own souls, should not despair of the mercy of God;[42] and finally it is laid down that for mercy did He create all men.[43] Such a merciful Being could not chastise man unless for some great purpose, which is to set him again on the road to the higher life, after purifying him from evil.

The ultimate object of the life of man is that he shall live in the service of God: "And I have not created the jinn and the men except that they

[39] Refers to the soul and the faculties given to man.

[40] 6: 12, 54

[41] 6: 148; 7 : 156; 40 : 7.

[42] 39 : 53.

[43] 11 : 119.

should serve Me'' (51 : 56). The man who lives in sin is debarred from the Divine presence,[44] but, being purified by fire, is again made fit for Divine service. Hence Hell is called, in one place, the *friend (maulā)* of the sinners,[45] and their *mother (umm)* in another.[46] Both descriptions are a clear indication that Hell is intended to raise up man by purifying him from the dross of evil, just as fire purifies gold of dross. It is to point to this truth that the Qur'ān uses the word *fitnah (the assaying of gold,* or *casting it into the fire to purify it)*, both of the persecutions which the faithful undergo in this life[47] and of the punishment which the evil-doers shall suffer in Hell.[48] Thus the faithful are purified through their suffering, in the way of God, in this life; and the evil-doers shall be purified by hell-fire. Hell is called a ''friend'' of sinners, because through suffering it will fit them for spiritual progress, and it is called their ''mother'', because in its bosom they will be brought up, so that they may be able to tread the path of a new life.

Another consideration, which shows that this chastisement is of a remedial nature, is that, according to the teachings of the Qur'ān and the Sayings of the Prophet, all those who are in Hell, shall ultimately, when they are fit for a new life, be released from it. This is a point on which great misunderstanding prevails even among Muslim theologians. They make a distinction between the Muslim sinners and the non-Muslim sinners, holding that all Muslim sinners shall be ultimately taken out of Hell, but not the non-Muslim sinners. Neither the Qur'ān nor the Tradition upholds this view. There are two words *khulūd* and *abad* used in connection with the abiding in Hell or Paradise, and both these words, while, no doubt, indicating *eternity*, also bear significace of *a long time*. Not only do all authorities on Arabic lexicology agree on this, but the use of these words in the Qur'ān also makes it quite clear. The word *khulū d* has been freely used regarding the chastisement in Hell of Muslim as well as of non-Muslim sinners. One example of its use for Muslim sinners is that after stating the law of inheritance, it is said: ''These are Allā h's limits; and... whoever disobeys Allāh and His Messenger and goes

[44] 83 : 15.

[45] 57 : 15.

[46] 101 : 9.

[47] 2 : 191; 29 : 2, 10.

[48] 37 : 63.

beyond His limits, He causes him to enter fire, to abide in it (*khālidīn*), and for him is an abasing chastisement'' (4 : 13, 14). Here clearly Muslim sinners are spoken of, and yet their abiding in Hell is expressed by the word *khulūd*.

Take the other word *abad*. This word occurs thrice in the Qur'ān, in connection with the abiding of sinners in Hell. Ordinarily, it is taken as meaning *for ever* or *eternally*, but that it sometimes signifies only *a long time*, is abundantly clear from the fact that both its dual and plural forms are in use. Rāghib says that this is owing to the fact that the word is, in that case, used to express *a part of time*. And explaining its verb form *ta'abbada*, he says it signifies the thing *existed for abad*, and is taken to mean *what remains for a long time*. Thus *a long time*, as the significance of *abad*, is fully recognized in Arabic lexicology. That in the case of those in Hell, it signifies *a long time* and not *for ever*, is clear from the fact that the abiding in Hell of even the unbelievers is elsewhere stated to be for *aḥqāb*, which is the plural of *ḥuqbah*, meaning *a year* or *many years* (LA.)., or *eighty years* (R.). At all events it indicates a definite period of time, and hence serves as a clear indication that even *abad*, in the case of abiding in Hell, means *a long time*.

The two words *khulūd* and *abad*, which are generally construed as leading to an eternity of Hell, being thus disposed of, the verses which are generally adduced in support of the idea that those in Hell shall for ever and ever suffer its endless tortures may be considered: ''Thus will Allāh show them their deeds to be intense regret to them, and they will not escape from the fire'' (2 : 167). ''Those who disbelieve, even if they had all that is in the earth, and the like of it with it, to ransom themselves with it from the chastisement of the Day of Resurrection, it would not be accepted from them and theirs is a painful chastisement. They would desire to come forth from the fire, and they will not come forth from it, and theirs is a lasting chastisement'' (5 : 36, 37). ''Whenever they desire to go forth from it, from grief, they are turned back into it'' (22 : 22). ''And as for those who transgress, their refuge is the Fire. Whenever they desire to go forth from it they are brought back into it, and it is said to them, Taste the chastisement of the Fire, which you called a lie'' (32 : 20).

These verses are self-explanatory. Those in Hell shall desire to escape from it but shall not be able to do so; even if they could offer the whole earth as a ransom, they would not be able to get out. The evil consequences of sin cannot be avoided, howsoever one may desire, and even so is the fire of Hell. None can escape from it. But not a word is there in any of these verses to show that God will not take them out of it, or that the tortures of Hell are endless. They only show that every sinner must suffer the consequences of what he has done, and that he cannot escape them; but that he may be set free when he has undergone the necessary chastisement, or that God may, of His boundless mercy, deliver the sinners when He pleases, is not denied here.

Even if *abad* is taken to mean eternity, the abiding in Hell, according to the Qur'ān, must cease at some time, because a limit is placed on it by the addition of the words *except as Allāh pleases (illā mā shā'a Allāh)* which clearly indicate the ultimate deliverance of those in Hell. The following two verses may be noted in this connection: "He will say, The fire is your abode — you shall abide therein, except as Allāh pleases. Surely thy Lord is Wise, Knowing" (6 : 129). "Then as to those who are unhappy, they will be in the fire; for them will be sighing and groaning — abiding therein so long as the heavens and the earth endure, except as thy Lord pleases. Surely thy Lord is the mighty Doer of what He intends" (11 : 106, 107).

Both these verses show that the abiding in Hell must come to an end. To make this connection clearer still, the Qur'ān has used a similar expression for those in Paradise but with quite a different ending: "And as for those who are made happy, they will be in the Garden, abiding therein so long as the heavens and the earth endure, except as thy Lord pleases — a gift never to be cut off" (11 : 108). The two expressions are similar; those in Hell and those in Paradise abide, each in his place, as long as the heavens and the earth endure, with an exception added in each case — except as thy Lord pleases — showing that they may be taken out of that condition. But the concluding statements are different. In the case of Paradise, the idea that those in it may be taken out of it, if God pleases, is immediately followed by the statement that it is a gift that shall never be cut off, showing that they shall not be taken out of Paradise; while in the case of Hell, the idea that those in it will be taken out is confirmed by the concluding statement, that God does as He intends.

This conclusion is corroborated by Tradition. The Prophet is reported to have said: "Then Allāh will say, The angels have interceded and the prophets have interceded and the faithful have interceded and none remains but the most Merciful of all merciful ones. So He will take out a handful from the fire and bring out a people who have never done any good" (M. 1 : 72). Three kinds of intercession are spoken of in this tradition — of the faithful, of prophets and of the angels — and the intercession of each class is undoubtedly meant for people who have some sort of close relation with that class. The faithful will intercede for people who have come into contact with them personally; the prophets will intercede for their followers; the angels, who move men to do good, will intercede for people who are not followers of a prophet, but who have done some good. And the report adds that the most Merciful of all still remains, so He will bring out from the fire even people who have never done any good. It follows that, thereafter, none can remain in Hell, and in fact the handful of God cannot leave anything behind.

Other traditions state even more explicitly that all men shall be taken out of Hell. "Surely a day will come over Hell when it will be like a field of corn that has dried up after flourishing for a while" (KU.). "Surely a day will come over Hell when there shall not be a single human being in it" (FBn. IV, p. 372). And a saying of 'Umar, the second Caliph, is recorded as follows: "Even if the dwellers in Hell may be numberless as the sands of the desert, a day will come when they will be taken out of it"(FBn. IV, p. 372). A similar saying is recorded from Ibn Mas'ūd: "Surely a time will come over Hell when its gates shall be blown by wind, there shall be none in it, and this shall be after they have remained therein for many years."[49] Similar sayings are reported from many other Companions such as Ibn 'Umar, Jābir, Abū Sa'īd, Abū Hurairah, etc., and also from the learned men of the next generation (*Tābi'īn*) (FBn.). And later Imāms, such as Ibn 'Arabī, Ibn Taimiyah, Ibn Qayyim, and many others, have held similar views (*ibid.*). Thus there can be but little doubt left that Hell is a temporary place for the sinner, whether Muslim or non-Muslim, and this also supports the view that the chastisement of Hell is not for torture but as a remedy, to heal the spiritual diseases which a man has incurred by his own negligence, and to enable him to start again on the road to the higher life. The truth of this has already been established from the Qur'ān, but a tradition also may be quoted here which expressly speaks of inmates of the fire as being set on the road to the higher life: "Then will Allāh say, Bring out (of the fire) every one in whose heart there is faith or goodness to the extent of a mustard seed, so they will be taken out having become quite black; then they will be thrown into the river of life and they will grow as grows a seed by the side of the river" (Bu. 2 : 15). This report is conclusive as to the remedial nature of Hell and establishes beyond a doubt that all men will ultimately be set on the way to the higher life.

[49] IJ — C. XII, p. 66.

Chapter VII

TAQDĪR OR PREDESTINATION

A great deal of misunderstanding prevails about the doctrine of predestination and the absolute decree of good and evil by God. It is necessary first to understand the correct meaning of the Arabic words *qadar* and *taqdīr* — the ideas commonly associated with their meaning being unknown both to the Qur'ān and to Arabic lexicology. *Qadar* and *taqdīr,* according to Rāghib, mean *the making manifest of the measure (kamiyya) of a thing*, or simply *measure.*[1] In the words of the same authority, God's *taqdīr* of things is in two ways, by granting *qudra, i.e., power* or by making them in a particular measure and in a particular manner, as wisdom requires. An example of this is given in the *taqdīr* of the date-stone, out of which it it is the palm only that grows, not an apple or olive tree, or in the *taqdīr* of the sperm of man, out of which grows man only, not any other animal. *Taqdīr* is therefore the law or the ordinance or the measure which is working throughout the creation; and this is exactly the sense in which the word is used in the Qur'ān. For

[1] The word *qadzā* is generally associated with *qadar*, and in common parlance, *qadzā wa qadar* of God are spoken of together. But while *qadar* means the Divine measure of things, *qadzā*, according to Rāghib, means the *deciding of an affair whether it be by word or by deed.* It is further stated to be of two kinds, either as relating to man or as relating to God. An example of the *qadzā* of God in word is 17 : 4 where *qadzainā*(present plural preterite form of *qadzā*) means, according to Rāghib, *we made known to them and revealed to them a decisive revelation*: "And We made known (*qadzainā*) to the children of Israel in the Book. Certainly you will make mischief in the land twice". So also in 15 : 66 which runs thus: "And We revealed (*qadzainā*) to him this affair that the roots of these shall be cut off in the morning." In both these places *qadzā* means the making known of a Divine order by way of prophecy. An example of the deciding of an affair by deed is 40 : 20, where God's judgment is called His *qadzā*: "And Allāh judges with the truth." or 41 : 12, etc. where the creation of heavens is spoken of : "So He ordained them (*qadzā-hunna*) seven heavens." Referring to the distinction between *qadzā* and *qadar*, Rāghib says that *qadar* is the measure, while *qadzā* is the decision or the bringing of it into action. Thus when the Caliph 'Umar ordered Abū 'Ubaida to give up a plague-stricken place to which 'Umar refused to go, and to remove his troops to a healthier spot, he was met with the objection: "Dost thou fly from the *qadzā of Allāh?" i.e.*, from what God has ordered. 'Umar's reply was: "I fly from the *qadzā* of Allāh to the *qadar* of Allāh." What he meant evidently was that if God had brought about plague by His *qadzā* in one place, another place was free from it, and it was His *qadar, i.e.*, a Divine law, that they should betake themselves to a place of safety (R.) *Qadzā* is, therefore, only the ordering of a thing to come to pass, while *qadar* signifies the creating of things subject to certain laws.

example, it speaks of a *taqdīr* for each and everything that has been created: "Glorify the name of thy Lord, the Most High, Who creates, then makes complete, and Who measures (*qaddara* from *taqdīr*), then guides" (87 : 1-3). "Who created everything, then ordained for it a measure (*taqdīr*) (25 : 2). "Surely We have created everything according to a measure (*qadar*)" (54 : 49). "And the sun moves on to its destination. That is the ordinance (*taqdīr*) of the Mighty, the Knowing. And the moon, We have ordained (*qaddarnā* from *taqdīr*) for it stages" (36 : 38, 39).

The law according to which foods, provisions and other things are provided in the earth is also called a *taqdīr* of God, and so, also, the law according to which rain falls on the earth, and that according to which night and day follow each other: "And He made in it mountains above its surface, and He blessed therein and ordained (*qaddara*) therein its foods" (41 : 10). "And there is not a thing but with Us are the treasures of it, and We send it not down but in a known measure (*qadar*)" (15 : 21). "And We send down water from the cloud according to a measure (*qadar*)" (23 : 18; 43 : 11). "And Allāh measures (*yuqaddiru* from *taqdīr*) the night and the day" (73 : 20).

Though man is included in the creation, and his *taqdīr* is therefore the same as that of the whole creation, he is also separately spoken of as having a *taqdīr* similar to the law of growth and development in other things: "Of what thing did He create him? Of a small life-germ. He creates him, then *proportions him*[2] (*qaddara-hū*)" (80 : 18, 19).

All these verses go to show that, as according to lexicologists, *taqdīr*, in the language of the Qur'ān, is the universal law of God, operating as much in the case of man as in the rest of nature: a law extending to the sun, the moon, the stars, the earth and the heavens and all that exists in them. This universal law is fully explained in two short verses already quoted: "Who creates, then makes complete, and Who measures, then guides". Four things are mentioned regarding every object of creation, including man: its creation (*khalq*), its completion (*taswīya*), its measure (*taqdīr*), and its guidance to its goal (*ḥidāya*). The law of life, as witnessed in nature, is exactly the law described here. Everything is created so as finally to attain to its completion, this completion being brought about according to a law or a measure within which everything works by Divine guidance. Thus the *taqdīr* of a thing is the law or the measure of its

[2] Or *makes him according to a measure.*

growth and development and the *taqdīr* of man is not different in nature from the *taqdīr* of other things.

Creation of good and evil

Taqdīr, meaning the *absolute decree of good and evil by God*, an idea with which the word is now indissolubly connected by the popular mind as well as by thinking writers, is neither known to the Qur'ān,[3] nor even to Arabic lexicology. The doctrine of predestination is of later growth, and seems to have been the result of the clash of Islām with Persian religious thought. The doctrine that there are two creators, a creator of good and a creator of evil, had become the central doctrine of the Magian religion, just as the Trinity had become that of the Christian faith. The religion of Islām taught the purest monotheism, and it was probably in controverting the dualistic doctrine of the Magian religion, that the discussion arose as to whether or not God was the Creator of evil and many side-issues sprang up. All this was due only to a misunderstanding of the nature of good and evil. God created man with certain powers which he could exercise under certain limitations, and it is the exercise of these powers in one way or another that produces good or evil. For instance, God has gifted man with the power of speech, which he can use either to do good or evil to humanity, either to tell a truth and say a good word, or to utter falsehood and slander. Similarly, man has been endowed with numerous other powers which may be used either for good or for evil. Hence the controversy, as to whether God was the Creator of good and evil, arose simply out of a misconception of the nature of good and evil. The same act may be a virtue on one occasion and evil on another. A blow struck in self-defence or in defence of a helpless man is right, and a blow struck aggressively is wrong. Hence evil is also called *ẓulm*, which, according to lexicologists, means *the placing of a thing in a place other than that which is meant for it, either by falling short or by excess or by deviation from its time or its place* (R.). Thus the use of a power in

[3] There is only one occasion in the Qur'ān on which a derivative of *taqdīr* is used to indicate the fate of a person. Speaking of the wife of Lot, the Qur'ān says: "We ordained (*qaddarnā*) that she shall surely be of those who remain behind" (15 : 60; 27 : 57). But even here it does not mean that God had ordained that she should be a doer of evil. There is mention here of an ordinance which holds good in the case of all evil-doers that they should suffer the evil consequences of what they have done; she was not one of the faithful, but a disbeliever, so that when Divine punishment overtook the evil-doers, she was ordained to be with them.

the right manner, or at the right moment, or in the right place is a virtue, and its use in a wrong manner or at a wrong moment, or at the wrong place is a vice. The Qur'ān, therefore, has not dealt with the question of the creation of good and evil at all. It speaks of the creation of heavens and earth and all that is in them; it speaks of the creation of man; it speaks of endowing him with certain faculties and granting him certain powers; it tells us that he can use these powers and faculties within certain limitations, just as all other created things are placed within certain limitations — and the limitations of each kind are its *taqdīr*. But in the Qur'ān, there is no mention of a *taqdīr* to mean either the creation of good and evil deeds, or an absolute decree of good and evil by God.

The following verse is sometimes quoted as showing that God is the Creator of the actions of man: "And Allāh has created you and what you make" (37 : 96). The Arabic word for "you make" is *ta'malūn,* from *'aml* which means both *doing* and *making*. So the words are sometimes taken as meaning "what you do" instead of "what you make," and from this it is concluded that God is the Creator of the actions of man, and as these actions are good as well as bad, therefore God is the Creator of the evil deeds of man. The context, however, shows that *mā ta'malūn* here means "what you make," and not "what you do," and the verse in question does not speak of the good and evil deeds of man, but of the idols and stones which were worshipped. The preceding verses 91-93 speak of Abraham's breaking the idols; v. 94 says that when the people saw their idols broken, they advanced towards him; vv. 95, 96 contain Abraham's arguments against idol-worship: "Do you worship that which you hew out? And Allāh has created you and what you make." Now the concluding words "what you make" clearly refer to the idols which they made, and the argument is clear that what was hewed out by man's own hands could not be God, God being the Creator of man as well as of the stones which were made into idols. This interpretation has been accepted by the best commentators.[4]

It may, however, be added that God is recognized by the Qur'ān as the first and ultimate cause of all things; but this does not mean that He is the Creator of the deeds of man. He has, of course, created man; He has also created the circumstances under which he lives and acts; but still He has endowed man with a discretion to choose how to act, which he can exercise under certain limitations, just as all his other powers and

[4] R.M. VII, p. 300. According to some commentators, the concluding words are interrogatory: "And Allāh has created you — and what is it that you do?"

faculties are exercised under limitations and only in accordance with certain laws. Thus it is said in the Qur'ān: "The truth is from your Lord; so let him who please believe and let him who please disbelieve" (18 : 29). And as he can exercise his discretion or his will in doing a thing or not doing it, he is responsible for his own deeds and is made to suffer the consequences.[5]

The will of God and the will of man

A great deal of misunderstanding exists as to the relation of the Divine will to the will of man. All the faculties with which man has been endowed have emanated from the great Divine attributes. Yet all human attributes are imperfect, and can be exercised only under certain limitations and to a certain extent. God is All-Seeing and All-Hearing; man also sees and hears, but these attributes in him bear no comparison to the Divine attributes of seeing and hearing, being only imperfect and miniature images of the perfect and infinite attributes of the Divine Being, even as the reflecting mirror of human nature is itself imperfect and finite. For the very same reason, man's exercise of these attributes is also subject to certain limitations and laws. Man's knowledge of things, his exercise of power over things and his exercise of his will in relation to things stand on a par. All these are subject to limitations and laws. Man's will stands

5 The useless controversy as to whether God was or was not the Creator of man's deeds divided the Muslim world at one time into three camps. The Jabarīyah held that God was the Creator of man's deeds, whether good or evil, and man was entirely powerless in the matter. He moved as the Divine hand moved him, having neither the choice, nor the power, nor the will to swerve a hair's breadth from what God had decreed. Another party went to the other extreme holding that man, being the creator of his own actions, had full control over them. This was the view adopted later on by the Mu'tazila whose founder was Wāṣil ibn 'Aṭā. Their argument was that it was impossible that God should first compel a man to do a thing and then punish him for it. The general body of the Muslims held that both these were extreme views. But in marking out an intermediate course, they adopted a position which was not very clear. They held that faith was the *via media* between *jabr* and *qadar*, but to effect a reconciliation between these two extreme views they introduced the theory of *kasb* which means *acquisition*. The gist of this theory was "that man is neither absolutely compelled, nor an absolutely free agent" (RI., p. 104) So far the position was logical, but further discussions led the holders of this view to the absurd position that man was only outwardly free, being inwardly forced. It is true that man's will works under certain limitations, *qadar* or *taqdīr* of God, but it is not true that the Divine will compels him to take a certain course. There may be a hundred and one causes of his decision in a particular case, and his responsibility may vary according to those circumstances; but still the choice is his and so is the responsibility.

in the same relation to the Divine will as his other attributes to the attributes of the Divine Being. He can exercise it under limitations and laws, and there is a very large variety of circumstances which may determine his choice in each case. Yet it is not true that the choice to exercise it has been taken away from him; and the fact is that, notwithstanding all the limitations, he is free to exercise his will, and, therefore, though he may not be responsible to the same extent for everything and in all cases — and a variety of circumstances must determine the extent of his responsibility, which may be very small, almost negligible, in some cases, and very great in others — yet he is a free agent and responsible for what he does.

The Quranic verses bearing on this subject may be considered. The argument that man does an evil deed because God wills it so, is put into the mouth of the opponents of the Prophet on several occasions. For instance: "The polytheists says: If Allāh had pleased, we would not have set up aught with Him, nor our fathers, nor would we have made anything unlawful. Thus did those before them reject (the truth) until they tasted Our punishment. Say, Have you any knowledge so you would bring it forth to Us? You only follow a conjecture and you only tell lies. Say, Then Allāh's is the conclusive argument; so if He had pleased, He would have guided you all" (6 : 149, 150). The polytheists' contention here is that what they do is in accordance with the will of God, and this is condemned as a mere conjecture and a lie. And against it, two arguments are adduced. The first is that previous people were punished when they persisted in their evil courses; if what they did was because God had so willed it, He would not have punished them for it. The second is that God had never said so through any of His prophets: "Have you any knowledge with you so you should bring it forth to Us?" And in the verse that follows, the argument is carried further: "If He had willed, He would have guided you all." The conclusion is clear. If it were the Divine will that people should be compelled to one course that would have been the course of guidance. But men are not compelled to accept even the right way: much less could they be compelled to follow the wrong course. This is clearly laid down: "We have truly shown the way, he may be thankful or un-thankful" (76 : 3). And again: "The truth is from your Lord, so let him who please believe, and let him who please disbelieve" (18 : 29). The Divine will is therefore exercised in the raising up of prophets, and in the pointing out of the courses of good and evil, and human will is exercised in the choice of one course or the other.

It is this very law that is expressed at the end of ch. 76: "Surely this is a Reminder, so whoever will, let him take a way to his Lord. And you will not, unless Allāh please'' (76 : 29, 30). And again to the same effect: ''It is naught but a Reminder for the nations, for him among you who will go straight. And you will not, except Allāh please, the Lord of the worlds'' (81 : 27-29). In both these places, the Qur'ān is spoken of as having been revealed for the upliftment of man, yet, it is added, only he will derive benefit from it who chooses to go straight or takes a way to his Lord, that is, exercises his will in the right direction. Thus man is left to make his choice after God has sent down a revelation, and the will of man to make a choice is thus exercised only after the will of God has been exercised in the sending down of a revelation. If God had not pleased to reveal the reminder, man would have had no choice. Thus the words ''you will not, unless Allāh please,'' mean only this that if God had not pleased to send a revelation, man would not have been able to make his choice of good or evil.[6]

[6] The Western critics of Islām have hastily formed the opinion that the Prophet was an opportunist, and that the Qur'ān makes contradictory statements, preaching free will at one time and laying stress on predestination at another. Thus Macdonald writes in the *Encyclopaedia of Islam* under *Kadar*: ''The contradictory statements of the Qur'ān on free will and predestination show that Muḥammad was an opportunist preacher and politician, and not a systematic theologian.'' The same view has been expressed by Sell: ''The quotations made from the Qur'ān in the last few pages will have shown that whilst some passages seem to attribute freedom to man, and speak of his consequent responsibility, others teach a clear and distinct fatalism'' (*Faith of Islam,* p.338). Both these writers have not taken the trouble to study the Qur'ān for themselves, and have based the above opinion simply on the fact that the contending Muslim sections have, all of them quoted the Qur'ān in their support, as if the numerous sects of Christianity had never quoted the Bible text in support of their contradictory assertions! The verse which I have discussed here is looked upon by Sell as the ''famous text''in support of predestination. Yet if a little consideration had been given to the words, the meaning could have been easily discovered. There is rather a tendency to force the conclusion of fatalism even upon plain words.

I may here note some of the verses which Hughes has quoted in his *Dictionary of Islam* in support of the doctrine of predestination: ''All sovereignty is in the Hands of God'' (13 : 30); ''God slew them and those shafts were God's, not thine'' (8 : 17). Now these two verses have apparently not the least bearing on predestination; the first speaks of God's sovereignty and the second says that the defeat and slaughter of the overwhelming Quraish forces could not be brought about by the Prophet, and that it was brought about by God. Two other verses quoted by Hughes have been wrongly translated, but in spite of that they do not lend any colour to the decree of good and evil: ''All things have been created after fixed decree'' (54 : 49); ''The Lord hath created and balanced all things and hath fixed their destinies and guided them'' (87: 2, 3).

Now the translation of *qadar* by *fixed decree* and that of *qaddara* by *He has fixed their destinies* is opposed to all Arabic lexicons. The wish of the writer has here taken the place of rules of interpretation. The other verses quoted by him have been fully discussed by me, and none of them speaks of predestination.

Foreknowledge of God

The doctrine of predestination, or the decreeing of a good course for one man and an evil course for another, thus finds no support from the Qur'ān which gives to man the choice to follow one way or the other. But, it is said, the doctrine of the decreeing of good and evil follows from the doctrine of the foreknowledge of God. If God knows what will happen in the future, whether a particular man will take a good or an evil course, it follows that that man must take that particular course, for the knowledge of God cannot be untrue. Now in the first place, it must be clearly understood what God's knowledge of the future means. The fact is that the future is an open book to God. The limitations of time and space, which are everything to man, are nothing to God. Man's knowledge of things is limited both by time and space but to the Infinite Being, unlimited space is as it were a single point and the past and the future are like the present. God sees or knows the future as a man would know what is passing before his eyes. God's knowledge of the future therefore, though far above and far superior to man's knowledge, is like his knowledge of the present, and mere knowledge of a thing does not interfere with the choice of the agent or the doer. Hence God's foreknowledge has nothing to do with predestination.

God's writing of adversities

Statements are frequently met with in the Qur'ān in which God is spoken of as having written down the doom of a nation, or a man's term of life, or an affliction. Such verses have also been misconstrued as upholding the doctrine of predestination. The misconception is due to a wrong interpretation of the word *kitāb*, which ordinarily carries the significance of *writing,* but has been freely used in Arabic literature and in the Qur'ān itself in a variety of senses.[7] Examples of these uses are: "Allāh has *written down* (*kataba*), I shall certainly prevail, I and My messengers" (58 : 21). "Nothing will afflict us save what Allāh has *ordained (kataba)* for us" (9 : 51). "Say, Had you remained in your houses, those for

[7] Rāghib says: "The word *kitāba* carries the significance of *ithbāt i.e., establishing* or *confirming*, and *taqdīr, i.e., measuring out* and *ijāb, i.e., making obligatory*, and *fardz, i.e, making incumbent*, and *'azm bi'l-kitāba, i.e., determination to write down.*" And further on, it is stated that *kitābat* also signifies *qadzā, i.e., what has been brought to pass*, and *ḥukm, i.e., order*, and *'ilm, i.e., knowledge.*

whom slaughter was *ordained (kutiba)* would have gone forth to the places where they would be slain (3 : 153). In all these instances there is no mention of predestination or the fixing before-hand of an evil course for the evil-doer. In the first example the meaning is clearly this, that the order or command has gone forth from God, that the Prophet will triumph, and God's orders must come to pass. "God has written down" only means that it is God's order that such a thing should happen. It is not necessary to seek a reference to any previous writing or previous order, because the order or writing is there in these words themselves, but, if necessary, the reference may be to the numerous prophecies that are met with in the Qur'ān regarding the ultimate triumph of the Prophet, and which were in fact written down in a literal sense.

In the other two examples, there is mention of distress or death having been ordained or written down. In the first place, it must be borne in mind that even if by the writing down of death or distress it is meant that such was preordained for them, it does not lend any support to the doctrine of predestination, which means that the evil course of an evil-doer has been fixed for him beforehand, and that no choice is left to him to adopt either a good or an evil course. Death or distress is due to circumstances over which man has no control, while the doing of good or evil is a matter entirely of man's own choice, according to the Qur'ān. But, as a matter of fact, there is no mention of preordaining here, for *kitāba* is used in the sense of *ordering* or *ordaining* and not preordaining.[8] The following two verses may be compared: "No disaster befalls in the earth or in yourselves, but it is in a book before We bring it into existence" (57 : 22); "No calamity befalls but by Allāh's permission (*idhn*)" (64 : 11). The word *idhn* used here means, according to Rāghib, knowledge of a thing, where there is with it also *mashīa i.e.*, permission or order. It is clear, from a comparison of these two verses, that what is called *kitāba* in one place is called *idhn* in another. Thus the writing of Allāh is only His knowledge or permission or order.

The Holy Book throws further light on this subject where it makes mention of the Divine intention to bring the faithful to perfection through adversities. Thus, speaking of the believers in particular, it says: "And We shall certainly try you with something of fear and hunger and loss

[8] In fact, the word sometimes means simply *intending* a thing: "The reason is that a thing is first intended, then spoken and then written. So intention is the beginning and writing the end, and therefore the word *kitāba* is used to signify mere *intention,* which is the beginning, when it is meant to emphasize it by writing" (R.).

of property and lives and fruits; and give good news to the patient, who, when a misfortune befalls them, say: 'Surely we are Allāh's and to Him we shall return'. Those are they on whom are blessings and mercy from their Lord and those are the followers of the right course'' (2 : 155-157). The principle is laid down here that the faithful are brought to perfection through adversities and trials, because we are told that Allāh intends to try the believers by means of various kinds of affliction, and through patience in suffering, they make themselves deserving of Divine blessings and mercy. Therefore when the faithful are made to say, ''Nothing will afflict us save what Allāh has ordained for us'' (9 : 51), it is in reference to the Divine will, as expressed above, and they are made to suffer afflictions for their own perfection. God's writing down afflictions for them means, therefore, only that the Divine law is that they will be brought to perfection through afflictions. Of like significance is 3 : 153.

Both the verses quoted above and other similar verses, which speak of the writing down of afflictions for the believers, only teach that greatest lesson of life, resignation in adversities. Muslims are taught to remain absolutely contented when they have to meet adversity or death in fulfilment of their duties. If a Muslim meets adversity or even death, he must believe that it is by God's order, that being the real meaning of *kitābat* in such cases. That faith upholds a Muslim in adversity because he knows that, out of an adversity which is by the order of the good God, will undoubtedly come good. There is a message in these verses that Muslims must face all adversities manfully and never despair of the mercy of God.

Lauḥ maḥfūẓ

A few words may be added in this connection on the *lauḥ maḥfūẓ*, which is generally supposed to contain all the decrees of God in writing. The word *lauḥ* means *a plank*,[9] and also *a tablet for writing*, and *maḥfūẓ*, means *that which is guarded*. The expression *lauḥ maḥfūẓ* occurs but once in the Qur'ān, and there it is mentioned in connection with the guarding of the Qur'ān itself: ''Nay, it is a glorious Qur'ān, in a guarded tablet'' (85 : 21, 22). The word *lauḥ* in its plural form *alwāḥ* is used in connection with the books of Moses: ''And We ordained for him in the tablets (*alwāḥ*) admonition of every kind and clear explanation of all things'' (7 : 145). The *alwāḥ* of Moses and the *lauḥ* of the

[9] As in 54 : 13.

Qur'ān are the same; only in the case of the Qur'ān the *lauḥ* is stated to be *guarded* or *maḥfūẓ*, for which the explanation is given "that the Qur'ān is protected against change and alteration" (R.). The meaning conveyed is therefore exactly the same as is elsewhere stated about the Qur'ān: "Surely We have revealed the Reminder, and surely We are its guardian" (15 : 9). The significance in both cases is that no alteration shall find a way into the text of the Qur'ān, and that it shall be preserved in full purity. So far as the Qur'ān is concerned, there is no mention in it of a *lauḥ maḥfūẓ* in which the decrees of God are written. God's writing is not of the same nature as man's writing; for man stands in need of pen, ink and writing material. This has elsewhere been explained in connection with the Divine attributes, where it has been shown that though speaking, seeing, hearing and other deeds are ascribed to God, yet the nature of these deeds is quite different from that of man's deeds, for God does not stand in need of means for the doing of an act, while man does. The writing of God therefore does not stand in need of a tablet or ink or pen, and if a *guarded tablet* (*lauḥ maḥfūẓ*) is spoken of in certain traditions, it stands only for the great and all-comprehensive knowledge of God, before which everything is as clear as written words on a tablet are before man.

God does not lead astray

A great misconception regarding the teachings of the Qur'ān is that it ascribes to God the attribute of leading astray. Nothing could be farther from the truth. While *al-Hādī*, or the *One Who guides*, is one of the ninety-nine names of Allāh, as accepted by all Muslims, *al-Mudzill*, or *the One Who leads astray*, has never been recognized as such. If *leading astray* were an attribute of God, as *guiding* certainly is, the name *al-Mudzill* should have been included in the list of His names, as *al-Hādī* is. But the Qur'ān, which repeatedly says that God's are all the excellent names, could not ascribe to Him what it has plainly ascribed to the Devil, *viz.*, the leading astray of men. This act is conclusive so far as the leading astray of men is concerned, but there are several other considerations which confirm it. The sinners' own confession, as repeatedly mentioned in the Qur'ān, is that their great leaders misled them, or that the Devil misled them. Not once do they put forward the excuse that it was God Himself Who misled them: "Until when they all follow one another into it (the fire), the last of them will say with regard to the first of them: Our Lord! these led us astray, so give them a double chastisement of the Fire'' (7 : 38). ''O woe is me! Would that I had not taken such a one for a friend! Certainly he led me astray from the Reminder after it had come to me (25 : 28, 29). ''And none but the guilty led us astray'' (26 : 99). ''And they say, Our Lord, surely we obeyed our leaders and our great men, so they led us astray from the path. Our Lord! Give them a double chastisement and curse them with a great curse'' (33 : 67, 68). ''And those who disbelieve will say: Our Lord, show us those who led us astray from among the jinn and the men that we may trample them under our feet, so that they may be of the lowest'' (41 : 29).

If God had really led men astray, their best excuse on the Day of Judgment would have been that they did not deserve to be punished, because it was God Himself Who led them astray. But not once is that excuse advanced, and it is always the guilty leaders, both from among men and jinn, who are denounced by the followers as having misled them. This is another conclusive argument that it is not God Who leads men astray.

In the third place, the Qur'ān is full of statements to the effect that God sends His prophets and grants revelation for the guidance of the people. The general rule laid down with regard to Divine dealing with humanity is thus made clear in the very beginning: ''Surely there will come to you a guidance from Me, then whoever follows My guidance, no fear *shall come upon them,* nor shall they grieve'' (2 : 38). It is impossible that God, Who is so solicitous for the guidance of man, should Himself lead him astray. Guiding and leading astray are two contradictions which could not be gathered together in one being. The Qur'ān itself draws attention to this point: ''And it is not attributable to Allāh that He should lead a people astray after He has guided them, so far so that He makes clear to them what they should guard against'' (9 : 115). The argument is evident. The Being Who sends guidance to a people could not lead them astray; how, then, could it be ascribed to God that He makes men fall into evil when He sends His messengers to explain to people that they should guard against evil?

Idzlāl as ascribed to God

The mistaken idea that God leads people astray arises out of a misconception of the meaning of the word *idzlāl* when it is ascribed to God. The word *idzlāl* carries a variety of meanings besides *leading astray*. It should be noted that wherever *idzlāl* is attributed to God, it is only in connection with the transgressors,[10] the unjust,[11] and the extravagant,[12] never for people generally. *Idzlāl* is the causative form of *dzlāl*, which means *swerving from the straight path,* and the word is applied to every swerving from the right path whether it is intentional or unintentional, and whether it is very small or very great; ... wherefore it may be used of him who commits any mistake whatever (R.). According to the same authority, *idzlāl* is of two kinds. The first kind is that in which *dzlāl* (or going astray) is the cause of *idzlāl*. This again may be in two ways: (1) when a thing has itself gone astray from you, as you say, *adzlaltu-l-ba'īra*, the meaning of which is, *I lost the camel* not *I led the camel astray*, which is not true in this case; and (2) when you judge a person to be in error or going astray; and in both these cases going astray on the part of the object of *idzlāl* is the cause of *idzlāl* or leading astray. The second kind is that in which *idzlāl* or *leading astray* is the cause of the going astray of the object of *idzlāl* and it is in this way that you embellish evil to a man so that he may fall into it'' (R.). The word, as used in the Qur'ān with reference to God means *judging or finding one to be in error.* This was a recognized use of the words among the Arabs. Thus in a verse of Tarfah, the words *adzallanī ṣadīqī* mean *my friend judged me to be in error* (LA.). And in a tradition it is said that the Prophet came to a people *fa-adzalla-hum, i.e., he found them adopting a wrong course, not following the true path* (N). Ibn Athīr gives further examples showing that *adzalla-hū* means *he found him in error* just as *aḥmadtu-hū* means *I found him in a praiseworthy condition*, and *abkhaltu-hū* means *I found him a niggard* (N.). In fact, this sense of the word is recognized by all lexicologists. Explaining *adzalla-hū,* Lane says: ''And *he found him to be erring, straying*...like as one says *aḥmada-hū* and *abkhala-hū*'' (LL.), and this explanation is quoted from the *Tāj al-'Arūs*.

Hence, since *idzlāl* cannot be applied to God in the sense of *leading astray*, and since it is always the transgressors and the extravagant whose *idzlāl* by God is spoken of, the only significance that can be attached to that word, in this case, is God's judging them to be in error or finding them in error, or in some cases, God's bringing them to destruction which is also an approved significance.

[10] 2 : 26.

[11] 14 : 27.

[12] 40 : 34.

God's sealing of hearts

Another misconception which must be removed in this connection is that relating to God setting seals on hearts. The misconception in this case is that it is thought that God has created some men with seals on their hearts, while others have been created with free and open hearts. No trace of any such distinction is met with anywhere either in the Qur'ān or in Tradition. All men are created sinless, all men are created pure, that is the express teaching of Islām. The Qur'ān says: "So set thy face for religion being upright, the nature (*fiṭra*) made by Allāh in which He has created men. There is no altering Allāh's creation. That is the right religion" (30 : 30). According to this verse all men have been created in pure nature, and a tradition of the Prophet, which is really an explanation of this verse, says: "Every child that is born conforms to *fiṭra* (human nature), and it is his parents who make him a Jew or a Christian or a Magian" (Bu.23 : 80). The idea that some men are born with a seal on their hearts is directly opposed to this teaching. The Qur'ān does speak of God setting seals on some hearts, but it says expressly that seals are set on the hearts of the reprobate, the hardened sinners who pay no heed to the call of the Prophet. In the very beginning of the Qur'ān, it is stated: "Those who disbelieve — it being alike to them whether thou warn them or warn them not — they will not believe. Allāh has sealed their hearts and their hearing, and there is a covering over their eyes" (2 : 6, 7). It should be noted that though sealing is spoken of here, yet it is in connection with those who have so hardened their hearts that they do not pay any heed to the Prophet's warning. They refuse to open their hearts to receive the truth, and do not lend their ears to listen to it, nor use their eyes to discern the truth from falsehood. As is elsewhere stated: "They have hearts wherewith they understand not, and they have eyes wherewith they see not, and they have ears wherewith they hear not. They are as cattle" (7 : 179). And again, they are made to say: "Our hearts are under coverings from that to which thou callest us, and there is a deafness in our ears, and there is a veil between us and thee" (41 : 5). It is always the reprobate whose heart is said to be sealed. "Thus does Allāh seal every heart of a proud, haughty one" (40 : 35). The fact that the cause of the seal is the sinner's own act of not heeding the warning, is made clear on another occasion also: "And there are those of them who seek to listen to thee, till, when they go forth from thee, they say to those who have been given knowledge: What was it that he said just now? These are they whose hearts Allāh has sealed and they follow their low desires'' (47 : 16).

All these verses show that God sets a seal upon the hearts of certain people as a result of their own actions. They do not listen to the Prophet's call, they give no heed to his warning, they do not try to understand what he says, and the result is that God seals their hearts. If a person closes upon himself the doors of his house, he will naturally be in darkness. Just in the same manner, those who themselves close the doors of their hearts are visited with the natural consequence of this, the setting of a seal. The seal, therefore, being the consequence of a man's own deeds, has nothing to do with the doctrine of predestination.

Tradition and predestination

Some of the traditions from which predestination is concluded may now be considered, but it has to be borne in mind clearly that tradition must be read subject to the broad principles established in the Qur'ān, and must be so interpreted as not to clash with the Book of God, and that in case of a clash it is the tradition that must be rejected; for its words are often the words of narrators, and in such metaphysical subjects there has been a good deal of mixing up of the ideas of the narrators through a long chain of transmitters. There is a great deal of difference between tradition relating to the rules and regulations of daily life, which every man could easily understand and retain in memory, and those relating to metaphysical subjects where the ideas of the transmitters would, sometimes quite unintentionally, and sometimes on account of not clearly understanding the real concept of the words, affect the narration of the report, and where the change of a single word may sometimes change the underlying idea entirely.

Bearing this in mind we may consider the reports narrated in the Book of Qadar in *Bukhārī*, but first a tradition may be considered which, though not accredited by the best authorities, is the stock argument of Western writers regarding predestination in Islām. This tradition occurs in several different forms in *Abū Dāwūd, Tirmidhī* and *Aḥmad*, and the gist of it is that when God created Adam, He also brought forth the souls of his children. The particular form of this tradition, which appeals to the Western writers, is that occurring in one report of *Aḥmad*: ''He said to the souls on His right hand, To Paradise and I do not care; and He said to those on His left hand, To the fire and I do not care'' (MM.1 :

4—*iii*). This tradition discloses such a distorted picture of Divine dealing with man that there should not be the least hesitation in rejecting it. The Qur'ān says in plain words that it is for mercy that He created all men;[13] it speaks of the Divine mercy as encompassing all things, like His knowledge;[14] it tells the most obdurate sinner not to despair of His mercy, for "Allāh forgives the sins altogether";[15] it describes God again and again as the most Merciful of all merciful ones.[16] Tradition draws a similar picture of the indescribable mercy of God. It tells us that God wrote down, when He ordered creation, that "His mercy shall take precedence of His displeasure";[17] it describes God as having divided His mercy into a hundred parts and as having sent into the world only one part, the whole of love finding expression in the created beings, including the love of a mother for her offspring, being a manifestation of that hundredth part, and the other ninety-nine parts finding their expression on the Day of Resurrecion, so that if the unbeliever knew of the whole of Divine mercy, he would not despair of going to Paradise;[18] it draws a picture of the unbounded mercy of God when it speaks of how the Prophet, on seeing mother pressing her child to her bosom, remarked to his Companions: "Do you think that she can throw this child into the fire?" And on their replying in the negative, added: "Allāh is much more merciful to His creatures than this woman to her child".[19] Could God with all this mercy, which is beyond human conception, be in the same breath described as saying: "These to fire and I do not care?" Certainly these cannot be the words of the Prophet. It is the error of some narrator in the long chain of the transmission of the report.

In another form the same tradition occurs as an explanation of a verse of the Qur'ān, and runs as follows: "Allāh created Adam and then He touched his back with His right hand and brought forth from it children, and said, These I have created for Paradise and they will do the works of the inmates of Paradise: again He touched his back and brought forth children and said, These I have created for the fire and they will do the works of the inmates of the fire" (MM.1 : 4—*ii*). This does not mean

[13] 11 : 119.

[14] 40 : 7.

[15] 39 : 53.

[16] 7 : 151; 12 : 64, 92; 21 : 83; 23 : 109, 118.

[17] Bu. 59 : 1.

[18] Bu. 81 : 19; 78 : 19; M. 49 : 4.

[19] Bu. 78 : 18.

that, in creating men, God had decreed one portion for Paradise and another for the fire. It denotes only the all-comprehending knowledge of God. However, if we read the verse of which this tradition is said to be an explanation, we shall find that the two have nothing in common except the idea of bringing forth offspring. The verse in question is: "And when thy Lord brought forth from the children of Adam, from their loins, their descendants, and made them bear witness about themselves: Am I not your Lord? They said: Yes; we bear witness" (7 : 172). It will be seen that the tradition contains no explanation of the verse at all, which speaks of something quite different.

The real explanation of the verse occurs in another tradition, and undoubtedly there was some misunderstanding on the part of some narrator, which misled him into giving an explanation having nothing in common with the original and, indeed, quite opposed to the Quranic text of which it is alleged to be an explanation. Quoting the verse, Ubayy ibn Ka'b explains it thus: "He gathered them and made them pairs, gave them forms and made them speak so that they talked. Then He took a promise and agreement from them and made them bear witness about themselves, saying, Am I not your Lord? They said, Yes. He said, I call to witness against you the seven heavens and the seven earths, and I call to witness against you your father Adam, lest you say on the Day of Resurrection, We did not know this. Know that there is no God but I, and there is no Lord but I, and do not associate anything with Me; I will surely send to you My messengers who will remind you of this My promise and this My covenant, and I will reveal to you My books. They said, We bear witness that Thou art our Lord and our God; we have no Lord besides Thee and we have no God besides Thee" (MM. 1 : 4—*iii*).

If we take the verse itself, we find it so clear that not only does it need no explanation but it even removes the obscurity of the so-called explanations; for it speaks plainly of the bringing forth of the children, not from the loins of Adam but from the loins of the "children of Adam". The verse, therefore, clearly refers to every human being as he comes into existence, and the evidence referred to is that which is afforded by human nature itself, that God is its Creator. This is said elsewhere too: "So set thy face for religion being upright, the nature made by Allāh in which He has created men. There is no altering of Allāh's creation. That is the right religion, but most people do not know" (30 : 30). Both these verses announce in clear words that every human child is born into the world in a pure state; none comes into life with the impress of hell on it. Human nature is so made that it is not compelled to follow the evil course. It is free from every taint. Even Tradition states that "every child is born in the *fiṭra*" (the right state or the condition of Islām), and that it is his parents who later on "make him a Jew or a Christian or a Magian" (Bu. 23 : 80, 93). Thus both the Qur'ān and the Tradition cut at the root of the doctrine of predestination.

It is quite in consonance with this principle that Islām recognizes that all children, whether born of believing or unbelieving parents, go to Paradise if they die before attaining the age of discretion. Even if this had not been expressly stated, it would have been a foregone conclusion of the principle laid down above on the basis of the Qur'ān and the Tradition that evey child is born with a pure nature, a Muslim. But there is a clear Tradition to that effect. It is related that the Holy Prophet saw in a vision an old man at the foot of a large tree and around him were children, and in the vision he was told that the old man was Abraham and the children that were around him were the children who died before *attaining the age of discretion* (*'ala-l-fiṭra*). "At this some of the Muslims asked him: And the children of polytheists, too, O Messenger of Allāh!" The Prophet replied: "The children of polytheists as well" (Bu. 92 : 48). Being with Abraham clearly meant being in Paradise. According to another report, when the Prophet was questioned about the children of the polytheists, he is reported to have said: "When Allāh created them, He knew what they would do" (Bu. 23 : 93). These words have been variously interpreted, but it would be wrong to give them a significance contradicting the plain words of the first report. At any rate, it does not mean that God knew what they would do after attaining majority, since they were to die before that. It, therefore, means that God knew that they would die in the condition in which they were born, *i.e.*, the condition of Islām, because He knew that they would not attain to the age of discretion, when they would be able to judge between right and wrong and adopt the one course or the other.

It would be difficult to consider here all the Traditions relating to *qadar*. Only *Bukhārī*, the most reliable collection of Traditions, may be considered. In the first place, Bukhārī does not relate a single report speaking of faith in *qadar*, and thus the question that such a faith is one of the fundamentals of Islām is disposed of, for faith in *qadar* is unknown both to the Qur'ān and to the most reliable collection of Tradition. Coming to the actual traditions which Bukhārī has related in his Jāmi' in book 82, called *Qadar*, one finds that not a single report in this chapter lends any support to the theory that a good or an evil course has been chalked out beforehand and is forced upon man. The Traditions related here, as well as in other collections, generally speak either of the Divine knowledge of things or of the Divine command prevailing over all. The most well-known report from which predestination is concluded is that speaking of an angel being in charge of the embryo — "an angel is sent to the embryo, and he is commanded with four things; his sustenance and his term of life and whether he is unhappy or happy (Bu. 82 : 1). The same tradition occurring elsewhere is in the following words: "Then an angel is sent and he is commanded with four words. It is said to him, Write down his actions and his sustenance and his term of life and whether he is unhappy or happy" (Bu. 59 : 6). The writing down of actions in the state of embryo seems to be a case of a clear mistake; for the Qur'ān plainly speaks of angels writing down the deeds when they are done, and in this connection not one, but two angels are spoken of.[20] But even if the words are accepted as correct they can be interpreted in consonance with the teachings of the Qur'ān to mean that the Divine knowledge of things is all-comprehensive, so much so that He knows all about a man even in the embryonic state. The angel's record, as already shown does not mean actually writing down in a book; it is only expressive of Divine knowledge. As the properties of the seed are all in the seed, so even the embryo shows what the man will develop into. No human eye can see these hidden potentialities; but nothing is hidden from God.

Another tradition bearing on the subject is that which speaks of Adam's argument with Moses. Moses is reported to have said to Adam that it was his own fault that caused him to get out of the garden, to which Adam replied: "Dost thou blame me for a matter which had been ordained for me before I was created" (Bu. 60 : 31). It is added in the report that Adam prevailed over Moses in argument. A reference to the Qur'ān will show that Adam's fault was not really the cause of his children living in a particular state, for it is after forgiveness of Adam's fault that mankind are told to live in that particular state, the state of *hubūṭ* as it is called, which is the state of struggle with the devil. It is not actually a *fall*, though there is in it the liability to fall, but there is also along with it the chance to conquer, and to subjugate the devil and thus rise to perfection. Man could be placed in one of the two conditions. He could be made to live either in a state in which there would be no struggle, but then there would be also no chance to conquer, no hope of rising to great spiritual heights; or he could be placed in a state of struggle in which there is the liability

[20] 50 : 17; 82 : 10-12. See also chapter *Angels*.

to fall and the chance to conquer and rise to greatness. This latter condition is called the state of *hubūṭ*[21] in the Qur'ān. Adam was no doubt placed in a garden and he could be spoken of as going forth from it, but his posterity was never placed in that garden and therefore they could not be spoken of as going forth from it. No one can be spoken of as going forth from a condition or a place in which he has never been. Therefore the *hubūṭ* is quite different from getting out of the garden, and it is after forgiveness even of Adam's fault that the *hubūṭ* of mankind is spoken of. Thus 2 : 36 speaks of Adam's fault, 2 : 37 speaks of the fault being forgiven, and 2 : 38 speaks of the *hubūṭ* of Adam's children, the last two verses being: "Then Adam received revealed words from his Lord, and He turned to him mercifully. Surely He is oft-returning to mercy, the Merciful. We said, Go forth (*ihbiṭū*) from this state all. Surely there will come to you a guidance from Me, then whoever follows My guidance, no fear shall come upon them nor shall they grieve" (2 : 37, 38). Elsewhere also: "Then his Lord chose him, so He turned to him (mercifully) and guided (him). He said, Go forth herefrom both — all (of you) — one of you (is) enemy to another. So there will surely come to you guidance from Me; then whoever follows My guidance, he shall not go astray, nor be unhappy" (20 : 122, 123). Thus Adam's reply to Moses was that it was not due to his fault that men had to live in a state of struggle with the devil, for such was the Divine scheme even before he was born.

The details of the rest of the traditions of Bukhārī need not be gone into. Many of them are wrongly interpreted. For example, one report mentions the death of a grandson of the Prophet, and of the Prophet comforting the child's mother with the words: "Allāh's is what He takes away and Allāh's is what He gives; every one has a term of life, so let her be patient" (Bu. 82 : 3). This report makes no mention at all of any decree of good and evil deeds. It speaks of a term of life, for every person has a term of life in God's knowledge. Many other traditions of a similar nature

[21] The word *hubūṭ* has the same meaning as *nazūl* (T.A.) which means *alighting* in a particular place or a particular condition, there being this difference that in *nazūl* there is the idea of an honourable entry into a state (R.). In the Qur'ān, *hubūṭ* is used always in connection with Adam and his progeny living in a particular state, except on one occasion where it is used for the Israelites in the simple sense of alighting in a city or living in a settled state and resorting to agriculture. The Israelites asked Moses to pray to God that they may have "what the earth grows," "its herbs and its cucumbers" etc., and the reply is: "Enter (*ihbiṭū* from *habṭ*) a ctiy, so you will have what you ask for" (2 : 61). It will be seen that the word *habṭ* or *hubūṭ* is used here simply in the sense of entering or alighting in a place or a condition, without any idea of fall or disgrace being attached to it.

are wrongly supposed to lend support to the doctrine of predestination. In one, the Prophet is reported to have remarked in a certain company that there was not a man but his place in fire or in Paradise was written down. Thereupon a man said: "Shall we not rely then (and give up the doing of deeds), O Messenger of Allāh?" The Prophet said: "No: do work, for to every one it is made easy" (Bu. 82 : 3); and then he recited the following verse: "Then for him who gives (charity) and keeps his duty and accepts what is good — We facilitate for him the (way to) ease. And as for him who is niggardly and considers himself self-sufficient and rejects what is good — We facilitate for him the (way to) distress" (92 : 5-10). If any conclusion of predestination could be drawn from the words of tradition, the verses quoted by the Prophet, in support of what he said, negative such a conclusion, for they speak of two different ends for two different kinds of workers. The words of the Prophet himself lead to the same conclusion, for he laid stress on works. Nor do his concluding words "to every one it is made easy" lead to any other conclusion, for the meaning is that to the worker of good, the good end, and to the worker of evil, the evil end, is made easy, as stated in the Quranic verses quoted in support of his assertion.

Faith in qadar *finds no place in the Qur'ān and Bukhārī*

The real issue may now be dealt with. It has been shown, firstly, that though the Qur'ān speaks of *qadar* or *taqdīr*, these words by no means carry the significance of predestination or of a decree of good and evil for man; secondly, that the *qadar* or *taqdīr* of which the Holy Book speaks is of a general nature, a law prevailing in the whole of the universe, a limitation under which the whole of creation is moving onward, and that therefore *qadar* or *taqdīr* has nothing to do with the good and evil deeds which are special to man; thirdly, that there is, in the Qur'ān or in the most reliable traditions, no mention at all of the necessity of faith (*īmān*) in *qadar* or *taqdīr*; and fourthly, that it is never mentioned as one of the fundamentals of religion like faith in God and His angels and His books and His apostles and a life after death. *Qadar* or *taqdīr* is spoken of simply as a Divine law prevailing in the universe, like many other laws, and no question concerning faith in them arises. It must also be clearly understood that the fundamentals of religion are all fully explained in the Qur'ān itself; and a thing cannot be accepted as a fundamental of Islām of which there is no mention in the

Holy Book. Tradition is only a secondary source of the religion of Islām and, as a matter of fact, it deals only with secondary matters of religion or its details. The great principles, the basic doctrines, must all be sought from the Qur'ān, which neither mentions *qadar* among the fundamentals of Islām, nor even speaks of a faith in it. It is only in Tradition that we find mention of *qadar*, and even here the most reliable of all collections, the *Bukhārī*, does not contain any report mentioning faith in *qadar* as an article of Islām. Thus to both the Qur'ān and the *Bukhārī*, faith in *qadar* is unknown, and therefore to speak of it as a fundamental of Islām is a mistake.

Faith in qadar *is a doctrine of later growth*

There is indeed one tradition which shows that faith in *qadar* is of later growth. In his second book, the book of *Faith*, Bukhārī relates the following report from Abū Hurairah: "The Holy Prophet was one day sitting outside among a number of people when there came to him a man and said, What is faith? The Prophet replied, Faith is this that thou believe in Allāh and His angels and the meeting with Him, and His messengers, and that thou believe in life after death" (Bu. 2 : 37). The report is a lengthy one and only the first portion relating to the subject of discussion has been quoted. This same report is also related in *Muslim* through three different channels. In the first channel, the four narrators are the same as in *Bukhārī*, and the words are also almost the same: "The Holy Prophet was one day sitting outside among a number of people when there came to him a man and said, What is faith, O Messenger of Allāh? The Holy Prophet replied, That thou believe in Allāh and His angels and His Book and the meeting with Him, and His messengers, and that thou believe in the life after death" (M.1 : 1). In his second channel, the first three narrators are again the same as in *Bukhārī* and the report is narrated in the words quoted above. In his third channel, only the first two narrators are the same, the rest being different, and a change is introduced into the words, the portion relating to the Prophet's reply now assuming the following form: "That thou believe in Allāh and His angels and His Book and the meeting with Him, and His messengers, and that thou believe in the life after death and that thou believe in *qadar*, in the whole of it" (M.1 : 1). It will be noticed that when the narrators are the same as in *Bukhārī* (with the exception of the last narrator from whom *Muslim* took his words), the words of the tradition are almost the same, there being only an addition of the words "and His Book." These words have either been added by one of Muslim's narrators, as the natural result of faith in messengers of God, or they have been left out by one of Bukhārī's narrators, as being included in faith in the Divine messengers. Otherwise, the fundamentals of faith are exactly the same and so even the words in both narrations. Even when Muslim has only Bukhārī's three top narrators, the words of the report are still the same. But in the third channel, where only two top narrators of Bukhārī, Abū Hurairah and Abū Zar'a, are retained, the words are changed, and quite a new element is introduced into it by the addition of *faith in qadar,* which the original does not contain. This shows beyond the shadow of a doubt that the words "faith in *qadar*" were added by the third narrator, and that these words were not spoken either by Abū Hurairah or even by the next narrator, Abū Zar'a, and thus there remains not the least doubt that the inclusion of faith in *qadar* among the fundamentals of faith, is an addition of about the end of the first century of Hijrah. There is no doubt that discussion about *qadar* arose later, and it was during these discussions that, through inadvertence or otherwise, some narrator put these words into the mouth of Abū Hurairah.

The same tradition has again been narrated by *Muslim* through quite a different channel, with an introductory note from the last narrator, Yaḥyā ibn Ya'mar, as follows: "the first man who held the view of *qadar* in Baṣra was Ma'bad al-Juhānī, so I and Ḥumaid ibn 'Abd al-Raḥmān went out on a pilgrimage, and we said that if we meet any Companion of the Prophet, we will question him about what these persons say regarding *qadar,* and it was granted to us to meet 'Abd Allāh ibn 'Umar entering the mosque" (M. 1 : 1). The note then goes on to say that the narrator asked 'Abd Allāh " about people who say there is no *qadar*[22] and that the affair begins just now." Then the same tradition is

[22] These people are here spoken of as denying *qadar*, but the name given to them by later theologians is Qādarīya which would mean "upholders of *qadar.*" Hence it was the Mu'tazila, who later on became the upholders of this theory, argued that the name Qādarīya could not be applied to them but to the upholders of the doctrine of *qadar*. The orthodox argument, on the other hand, was that the Mu'tazila, or their predecessors, who questioned the *qadar* of God, set up a rival *qadar* of man, inasmuch as they believed that man was the creator of his own deeds. But perhaps the word *qadar* was used by these disputants in the sense of *qudrat, i.e., power,* and the two contending parties had gone to two extremes, those who upheld the absolute power of God, refusing that man had any free choice, and those who upheld the theory of the absolute power of man over his deeds. The truth lies midway between these two extreme views.

related in different words, and the part of it under discussion runs thus: "That thou believe in Allāh and His angels and His Books and His messengers and the last day and that thou believe in the *qadar*, the good of it and the evil of it." It will be noticed that the words "meeting with Him (*liqāi-hī*)" are omitted in this report, while to the belief in the *qadar* of Abū Hurairah's report are added the words *the good of it and the evil of it* (*khairi-hī wa sharri-hī*). The introductory note is too clear. Discussions were being carried on relating to *qadar*, and a party had arisen which entirely denied it. 'Abd Allāh ibn 'Umar lived till the 73rd year of the Hijrah, and on being questioned about the matter, he is alleged not only to have upheld *qadar* but also to have related a tradition which mentioned belief in it, as one of the fundamentals of Islām. Bukhārī has not accepted this tradition, while Muslim, granting the correctness of Bukhārī's tradition which does not make any mention of *qadar*, has shown that Ibn 'Umar's report cannot be relied upon, and probably the anxiety to silence opponents had led to indiscretion on the part of some controversialist.

Significance of faith in qadar

It is difficult to say what meaning *faith* in *qadar* carried. The words occuring in one report are "that thou believe in *qadar* in the whole of it," and in a second, "that thou believe in *qadar*, in the good of it and the evil of it". A third version, "that thou believe in *qadar*, in the good of it and the evil of it, being from Allāh," which is ordinarily met with in the books on beliefs (*'aqā'īd*) cannot be traced to any tradition. It is very probable that the latter two additions were even later than the first formulation of belief in *qadar*. If we take the word *qadar* in the original sense in which it is used in the Qur'ān, a belief "in *qadar*, in the whole of it" would only mean that one must believe that everything in this universe is subject to a law and under a limitation, God alone being the Controller of all. If we take the next form, "that thou believe in *qadar*, in the good of it and the evil of it," "the good and the evil" does not refer to the good or evil deeds of man, but to the good or bad *circumstances* under which man is placed to work out his destiny. The original words *khair* and *sharr* have been freely used in the Qur'ān in this sense.[23] *Khair* is anything which brings good, and its opposite is *sharr*

[23] — see next page.

(R.); and *khair* or *sharr* means *doing good* or *doing evil* only when a word meaning *doing* is added to it, the equivalent for which is *'amal*. The good of *qadar* and the evil of *qadar*, therefore, mean only whatever of good fortune or evil fortune comes to man. The meaning would therefore be that whatever of good or evil fortune comes to man, it must be accepted as coming from God; in other words a man must completely surrender himself to the Divine will under all circumstances. This, as already shown, is one of the great lessons of life which has been taught to the Muslim.

Ash'arī's view

The first man who formulated the orthodox views which are accepted by the general body of Muslims was Imām Abū-l-Ḥasan Ash'arī, after whom his followers are known as Asha'riah, and he plainly states this to be the significance of a faith in *qadar*; for, speaking of the beliefs of Ahl Sunnah and the followers of *Ḥadīth*, he says: "And that good (*khair*) and evil (*sharr*) are by the *qadzā* of Allāh and by His *qadar*, and they believe in the *qadzā* of Allāh and His *qadar*, in the good of it and the evil of it, the sweet of it and the bitter of it, and that they do not control for themselves any profit or any loss" (MI. p. 292). Evidently the words "sweet" and "bitter" (*huluwei-hī wa murri-hī*) and the words "profit" and "loss" are added to explain that by good and evil, *khair* and *sharr*, are meant good fortune and evil fortune, ease and hardship, not good and evil deeds done by man. This contentment under all conditions, is, as already shown, one of the great lessons of life taught to a Muslim, but it is neither a doctrine nor a principle of faith.

This much is certain that belief in *qadar* does not mean belief in predestination; for predestination, for which the Arabic word is *jabr*, has never been the belief of the Muslim community. The Jabariyah, or believers in predestination, have, on the other hand, been recognized as a heretical sect. A strict predestinarian, who believes that man has no control at all over his actions, would deny the very basic principle of religion, that is,

[23] For example: "Surely man is created impatient—fretful when evil (*sharr*) afflicts him, and niggardly when good (*khair*) befalls him" (70 : 19-21); "And man prays for evil (*sharr*) as he ought to pray for good (*khair*) and man is ever hasty" (17 : 11); "And if Allāh were to hasten for men the (consequences of) evil (*sharr*) as they would hasten on the good (*khair*), their doom would certainly have been decreed for them" (10 : 11); "Every soul must taste of death, and We test you by evil (*sharr*) and good (*khair*) by way of trial" (21 : 35).

the responsibility of man for his actions. The orthodox position has always been the middle one. Man has a free will, but that will is exercised under certain limitations. It is only the Divine will that can be called an absolutely free will, a will under no limitations; but eveything created, and therefore everything human, is subject to *qadar*, to a Divine measure of things, to limitations imposed upon it by a Higher controlling Power. Man is the possessor neither of absolute knowledge, nor of absolute power, nor yet of absolute will. All these atributes belong properly to God. Human knowledge, human power and human will are all subject to limitations, and these limitations are placed upon man by the Divine measure which is called *qadar*. It is only in this sense that a Muslim can be said to have faith in *qadar*.

PART THREE

LAWS AND REGULATIONS OF ISLĀM

CHAPTER I

PRAYER

SEC. 1. — VALUE OF PRAYER

Importance of prayer in Islām

Five fundamental religious duties are recognizedby Islām, *viz.*, prayer, zakāt or poor-rate, fasting, pilgrimage and jihād, but while jihād is a national duty, the first four are, more or less, individual duties, though having an important national significance. Among these four, prayer undoubtedly occupies the most important position, and is given the greatest prominence in the Qur'ān, poor-rate coming next to it.

The importance of prayer may be judged from the following facts: that it was the first duty enjoined on the Prophet; that, though prayer and zakāt are often mentioned together in the Qur'ān, prayer always takes precedence; and that the keeping up of prayer is the frequently repeated injunction of the Qur'ān. It has also been generally recognized as the first and foremost duty of a Muslim. There are several reasons why prayer has been given this importance. It is really the first step in the onward progress of man, and yet it is also his highest spiritual ascent (*mi'rāj*). Prayer keeps man away from evil; it helps him to realize the Divine in him, and that realization not only urges him to do disinterested service for humanity but also makes him attain the highest degree of moral and spiritual perfection. Prayer is also the means of levelling all differences of rank, colour and nationality, and the means of bringing about a cohesion and unity among men which is the necessary basis of a living civilization.

Self-development though prayer

What prayer really aims at is stated in the very beginning of the Qur'ān. There we are told that a Muslim, who would tread the road to self-development, must accept certain principles and carry out certain duties: "This Book, there is no doubt in it, is a guide to those who keep their duty, who believe in the Unseen and keep up prayer and spend out of what We have given them, and who believe in that which has been revealed to thee and that which was revealed before thee; and of the Hereafter they are sure. These are on a right course from their Lord, and these it is that are successful[1] (*mufliḥūn*)'' (2 : 2 - 5). *Falāḥ,* the infinitive form of *mufliḥūn*, whether relating to this life or to the next, carries with it the idea of the complete development of the inner faculties of man, and the achievement of both material and moral greatness; what, in other words, may be called the full self-development of man. This self-development is reached, according to the Qur'ān, by the acceptance of three principles, the existence of God, His revealing Himself to man, and the Hereafter; and by the exercise of two duties, the keeping up of prayer, or seeking communion with God, and the spending of one's wealth for others or the service of humanity. The place of prayer in the self-development of man is given such a prominence in Islām that in the call to prayer the words ''come to prayer'' are immediately followed by the words ''come to *falāḥ,*'' thus showing that self-development is attained through prayer. And on another occasion, the Qur'ān says: ''Successful indeed are the believers, who are humble in their prayers'' (23 : 1, 2); where the word used for *being successful* is *aflaḥa*, carrying the significance of achieving full self-development.

Prayer as the means of realizing the Divine in man

Belief in God is the fundamental principle of every religion; nevertheless the object of religion is not simply to preach the doctrine of the existence of God as a theory; it goes far beyond that. Religion seeks to instil the conviction that God is a living force in the life of man; and prayer is the means by which it is sought to achieve this great end. The real conviction that *God is* comes to man, not by the belief that there is a God in the outer world, but by the realization of the Divine within himself; and that this realization is attained through prayer is made clear by what

[1] *Mufliḥūn* is the plural of *mufliḥ*, which is derived from the root *falḥ*, meaning *cleaving asunder a thing*. *Falāh*, the infinitive form of *mufliḥ*, means *success and complete attainment of what is desired* (R.). The same authority says that *falāḥ* is of two kinds, one relating to this life and the other relating to the next. The former stands for the attainment of those good things whereby the life of this world is made good; and these are *baqā (existence), ghinā (freedom from want,* i.e., *wealth)* and *'izz (honour)*. The *falāh* relating to the next life includes, according to Rāghib, four things that is to say, life with which there is no death, wealth with which there is no want, honour with which there is no disgrace, and knowledge with which there is no ignorance.

is stated in the beginning of the Qur'ān, as quoted above. The three requisites of a true Muslim are there given in their natural order. The first is a belief in the Unseen, which means a belief in God, the great *Unseen* Who cannot be perceived by the physical eye of man. The second, which follows immediately the belief in the Unseen, is the keeping up of prayer, thus showing that belief in the Unseen is turned into a certainty of the Divine existence, a realization of the Divine within man, by means of prayer; and it is with reference to this realization that we are told, a little further on: "And seek assistance through patience and prayer, and this is hard except for the humble, who know that they will meet their Lord and that to Him they will return" (2 : 45, 46). The third requisite, spending out of what God has given, is the natural sequel of the second, and shows that the realization of the Divine in man leads to the service of humanity. In one of the earliest revealed chapters of the Qur'ān, it is stated that prayer is useless unless it leads to the service of humanity: "So woe to the praying ones, who are unmindful of their prayer, who do good to be seen, and refrain from acts of kindness" (107 : 4 - 7).

The experience of humanity

The universal experience of humanity bears out the truth of what the Qur'ān has said. Though to most people now-a-days the existence of God amounts to little more than a theory, yet in every age and in every nation there have been men who, through prayer, have realized the great truth of the Divine existence within their hearts, and have laid down their lives for the good of humanity. In their case belief in the existence of God was a moral force which not only brought about a complete change in their own lives but also enabled them to transform the lives of entire nations for centuries and change the histories of peoples and of countries. Their selflessness and truthfulness were beyond reproach, and their testimony, which is really the testimony of all nations in all ages, establishes one fact, that belief in the existence of God becomes a moral force of the first magnitude when once it is realized in the heart of man through prayer to the Divine Being; so great a moral force is it, indeed, that even the most powerful material forces give way before it. Is not the experience of those great personalities a beacon-light for others showing them that they also can make God a moral force in their lives? The powers and faculties that are given to one man are also given to another, and through their proper use one man can do what another, before him, has done.

Prayer, a means of attaining to moral greatness

Again if, apart from the experience of humanity, we consider the question rationally, prayer to God is the natural sequel of the acceptance, in theory, of the existence of God. The aspiration to rise to moral greatness is implanted in human nature more deeply than even the aspiration to rise to material greatness; but the only way in which the former can be realized is to be in touch with the All-Pervading Spirit, the fountain-head of purity and the source of the highest morality. "All the perfect attributes are Allāh's" says the Qur'ān (7 : 180). But man stands in need of perfect attributes as well for there is implanted in him the unquenchable desire to rise higher and higher. How can he do so except by being in touch with the Being that possesses the perfect attributes, the Being that is free from all defects? And prayer is but an attempt to be in touch with Him. And the only way to become imbued with Divine morals is to get in touch with the Divine Spirit, to be drawn away from all worldly trammels for a while, and to drink deep at that source, which is prayer to God. In many traditions, prayer is spoken of as *munājāt* or *confidential intercourse* with the Lord (Bu. 8 : 38; 9 : 8; 21 : 12). In one it is related that man should pray to God as if he were seeing Him (Bu. 2 : 37). Such descriptions of prayer show its real nature to be that of being in actual intercourse with the Divine Being and intercourse means nothing but becoming imbued with Divine morals.

Prayer as the means of purification of heart

The right development of human faculties depends upon the purification of man's inner self and the suppression of evil tendencies: "He is indeed successful who purifies it" (91 : 9), says the Qur'ān, referring to the soul. Prayer is spoken of as a means of purification for the heart. "Recite that which has been revealed to thee of the Book and keep up prayer; surely prayer keeps one away from indecency and evil" (29 : 45). Elsewhere too: "And keep up prayer at the two ends of the day and in the first hours of the night; surely good deeds take away evil deeds" (11 : 114). In a tradition, the saying of prayers is compared to washing oneself in a river: "Abū Hurairah says that he heard the Prophet say, If one of you has a river at his door in which he washes himself five times a day, what do you think? Would it leave any dirt on him? The Companions said, It would not leave any dirt on him (and he would be perfectly clean). The Prophet said, This is an example of the five prayers, with which Allāh blots off all the evils of a man'' (Bu. 9 : 6). There are many other traditions in which it is stated that prayer is a means of suppressing the evil tendencies of man (*kaffārah*). The reason is plain. In 20 : 14, ''the remembrance of Allāh'' is stated to be the object of keeping up prayer, while in 29 : 45, it is stated that ''the remembrance of Allāh is the greatest restraint'' upon sin. A little consideration will show that a law generally requires a sanction behind it, and behind all Divine laws which relate to the development of man and to his moral betterment, the only sanction is a belief in the great Author of those laws. The oftener, therefore, a man reverts to prayer, to that state in which, disengaging himself from all wordly attractions, he feels the Divine presence as an actual fact, the greater is his certainty about the existence of God; and the greater the restraint upon the tendency to break that law. Prayer, thus, by checking the evil tendencies of man, purifies his heart of all evil, and sets him on the right road to the development of his inner faculties.

Unification of the human race through Divine service

The service of prayer is divided into two parts, one to be said in private and the other to be performed in congregation, preferably in a mosque. While the private prayer is meant simply for the development of the inner self of man, the public one has other ends as well in view, ends, indeed, that make the Islamic prayer a mighty force in the unification of the human race. In the first place, this gathering of all people living in the same vicinity five times daily in the mosque is a help to the establishment of healthy social relations. In the daily prayer services these relations are limited to a narrow circle, *i.e.*, only to members of the same neighbourhood, but the circle becomes wider in the weekly Friday service which gathers together all Muslim members of a particular locality, and still wider in the two great 'Id gatherings. Far more important than this, however, is the levelling of social differences brought about by means of congregational prayer. Once within the doors of the mosque, every Muslim finds himself in an atmosphere of equality and love. Before their Maker they all stand shoulder to shoulder, the king along with his poorest subject, the rich arrayed in gorgeous robes with the beggar child clad in rags, the white man with the black. Nay, the king or rich man standing in a back row will have to lay his head, prostrate himself before God, at the feet of a slave or a beggar standing in the front. There could be no more levelling influence in the world. Differences of rank, wealth and colour vanish within the mosque, and quite a new atmosphere, an atmosphere of brotherhood, equality and love, totally differing from the outside world, prevails within the holy precincts. To be able to breathe, five times daily in an atmosphere of perfect peace within a world of strife and struggle, of equality where inequality is the order of the day, and of love amid the petty jealousies and enmities of daily life, is indeed a blessing. But it is more than a blessing; for it is the great lesson of life. Man has to work amidst inequalities, amidst strife and struggle, amidst scenes of hatred and enmity, and yet he is drawn out of these five times a day, and made to realize that equality, fraternity and love are the real sources of human happiness. The time spent on prayer is not, therefore, wasted even from the point of view of active humanitarianism; on the contrary, the best use of it is made in learning those great lessons which make life worth living. And these lessons of fraternity, equality and love, when put into practice in daily life, serve as foundations for the unification of the human race and of the lasting civilization of mankind. In fact, the five daily congregational prayers are meant, among other things, to carry into practice the theoretical lessons of equality and fraternity for which Islām stands; and however much Islām may have preached in words the equality of man and the fraternity of the community of Islām, all this would have remained a dead-letter, had it not been translated into the everyday life of man through the institution of five daily congregational prayers.

Regulation of prayer

Prayer, in Islām, thus not only enables man to realize the Divine in him, not only makes him drink deep at the fountain of Divine morals, purifies his heart and sets him on the right road to the development of human faculties; but it goes a step further and, levelling all differences, brings about love, concord and a true union of humanity. This last object, it can be easily seen, cannot be achieved without a regularly instituted form of prayer, so that all men should gather together in mosques at the stated times and should stand up reverently, bow down and prostrate themselves before their great Maker as one. But even apart from that consideration, it was necessary that permanence should be given to the institution of prayer by requiring its observance at stated times and in a particular manner. The truth is that the grand idea of holding communion with God or realizing the Divine within man, which is so essential to the moral elevation of man, could not have been kept alive unless there was an outward form to which all people should try to conform. In the first place, no idea can live unless there is an institution to keep it alive. Secondly, the masses in any community, even though it may be educated, can be awakened to the recognition of a truth only through some outward form, which reminds them of the underlying idea. And thirdly, there can be no uniformity without a form, and without uniformity the community or nation, as a whole, cannot make any progress, the end in view being the moral elevation of the community as a whole and not the elevation of particular individuals. It is a fact that Muslims as a nation have a more vital faith in God than the followers of any other religion. It is this faith in God that accounts for the early Muslim conquests, before which the mightiest empires were swept away like a straw; it is this same faith in God that enabled the Muslims to hold their own against the onslaughts of Christian Europe during the Crusades; and it is this faith in God again that enables Muslims today to carry on the spiritual contest with Christianity, in spite of the fact that all the material forces in this contest, such as wealth, power and organization, are on the side of Christianity. The Islamic institution of prayer which keeps the spirit of the Muslim in touch with the Divine Spirit is without doubt the basis on which this strong faith in God rests, and the value of prayer in the formation of this noble trait in the Muslim national character is incalculable.

It must, however, be added that prayer in Islām is not so rigid as it is generally thought to be. It is true that all Musims are required to assemble at particular times in the mosques, and to follow the lead of the *Imām*, as an army would obey the orders of its general; and such uniformity is essential to enable prayer to serve the double purpose of bringing about the communion of man with God and the union of man with man; but every prayer is divided into two parts, one to be performed in congregation, the other alone. Even in the congregational part there is ample scope for the individual to give expression to the soul's sincerest desire before its Maker, and for an outpouring of the true sentiments of the heart. But in the private part of the prayer, it is not only left to the individual to select the portions of the Qur'ān which he likes, but he can also give vent to his own feelings by making any supplications that he likes and in any language that he chooses, in any of the four postures, the posture of standing, bowing, prostration and sitting.

Times of prayer

In Islām there is no Sabbath. A day is not set apart for worship, as in Judaism and Christianity. One day of prayer with no business and six days of business with no prayer, is not the Muslim's rule of life. Prayer is made a part of the everyday affairs of man. There is a prayer in the morning before sunrise when a man rises from his bed; another just after midday, a third in the afternoon; a fourth at sunset; and a fifth before going to bed. Prayer is thus the first daily act of a Muslim and it is also his last act of the day, and between these two there are other prayers during hours of business or recreation. Thus Islām requires that, in all the varying conditions through which man has to pass, his spirit should be in touch with the Divine Spirit. Even when busiest, he should still be able to disengage himself from all wordly occupations for a short while and resort to prayer. The object in view in this arrangement is clearly that man should feel the Divine presence under all conditions, so that while he is doing his work, God should still be nearest to his heart. It would readily be seen how immensely such arrangement must enhance the value of prayer as a moral force in the transaction of everyday affairs.

Mode of worship

The Islamic mode of worship is calculated to concentrate attention on one object, the realization of the Divine presence. The ablution preceding prayer, the reverential attitude in standing, the bowing down, the kneeling with the forehead placed on the ground, and the reverent sitting posture — all help the mind to realize the Divine presence as a fact; and the worshipper, as it were, finds his heart's joy in doing honour to the Great Master, not only with his tongue but with his whole body, adopting a reverent attitude. There is not the least doubt that the spirit of humility in man finds particular expression in the reverential postures which must be adopted in prayer. The whole prayer is a most solemn and serious affair during which the worshipper does not turn his attention to anything else, nor does he indulge in any movement which should distract his attention or disturb his prayerful attitude. The prayer is thus an undisturbed meditation on the Divine, and it is for this reason that in Islām it is not accompanied with music but by recitations from the Qur'ān speaking of Divine love, mercy, power and knowledge. In fact, what is considered ritualism in the Islamic institution of prayer is only a way to feel the Divine presence and ponder over His greatness, glory and love by adopting certain reverential postures, and it would be seen that the Islamic mode of worship combines in it all the reverential postures that can possibly be adopted, the posture of standing, sitting, bowing down and prostration.[2]

It cannot be denied that a particular posture of the body will generate in man feelings of pride and haughtiness while another is suggestive of true humility, and it is only the latter frame of mind that can bring man closer to God. If, therefore, humility is the essence of prayer, the particular postures of standing, sitting, bowing down and prostration are also essential for creating that spirit in man, and any change would be a change for the worse, a change that might well bring about failure to achieve the very end for which prayer is intended.[3]

[2] The movement among some Muslims, however small their number, that the different postures in prayer should be revised so as to suit the ways of life in the cities of the West, is based on a miscalculation as to the value of prayer. It is, for example, suggested that, instead of standing or sitting on the floor, the worshippers should have the option of sitting on chairs and, instead of bowing down and the prostration, there should be the option of simply bowing the head a little. This departure from postures prescribed by the Prophet would not only cause a divergence which would know no end but also reduce the usefulness of prayer by destroying its uniformity. If there were mosques in which some people sit on chairs and others stand on the ground, some who bow down or prostrate themselves before God while others simply bend their heads, prayer would have failed altogether in attaining its great object, that of levelling down differences of rank and bringing about a unification of humanity. If it be urged that mosques in the West may be modelled on the fashion of the churches, then the unity of the worldwide brotherhood of Islām would have gone altogether. And when these Westerners will come to the East, they will not be able to join the congregational prayer of their Eastern brethren, and Islām will have failed to bring about the great object of joining the West with the East, and establishing a common brotherhood for all mankind. Apart from the consideration of uniformity, however, there is the fact that the form in which prayer has been inculcated by the Founder himself is calculated to produce in the mind of man a spirit of true humility which is essential if he is to receive the Divine spirit. If prayer is intended to realize the Divine in man and bring him in touch with the great Spirit of the universe, that object can best be attained only by adopting the reverent method which the Prophet has taught.

[3] It is true that, in cases of sickness, or when a man is on a journey, the worshipper is permitted to say his prayers in any posture which he finds convenient, but that is under compulsion. In such a case he is willing to humble himself in any position, but since his bodily condition does not allow him to assume the prescribed posture, and the object of all is the creation of a true spirit of humility, a departure from regular procedure in that case does not affect the sincerity of him who prays or the efficacy of his prayer.

Language of prayer

Naturally a man would like to unfold his heart before his Maker by praying in the language in which he can most readily express his feelings, and this is fully recognized in Islām. Not only in private prayer but in the course of the public service as well, the worshipper is at liberty to pray to God in his own tongue, after or during the recitation of portions of the Qur'ān in a standing posture, or after utterance of words of Divine glory in that of bowing down or prostration. In the public service such prayers would undoubtedly be limited, since the worshipper must follow the *Imām*, but in the private portion they may be of any length.

The question, however, assumes a different aspect when the public service itself is considered, for, unless the public service is conducted in a language which is common to all Muslims, there must again be a failure in achieving the great end for which prayer is instituted. As already stated, the unification of Muslims through prayer is as much an end and object of prayer as to bring man into communion with God. It is prayer that daily gathers together persons of different callings and different ranks and positions in society, under one roof, and on a perfect status of equality, and these homogeneous units are again united by the more extensive gathering for the Friday prayers, or the still larger assemblies at 'Id prayers, culminating in that mighty assemblage at Makkah of all nations and all races on the most perfect status of equality — European, Asian and African, king and beggar, all clad in one dress — the annual concourse of the pilgrims from the farthest corners of the earth. Now all these various gatherings, from the great gathering of all nations at Makkah down to the smallest gathering in a village mosque, are expressly for Divine worship, and if there were a babel of languages prevailing in these gatherings, the object of unification of the human race through Divine service — an idea unique to Islām — would fail altogether. The bond of a common language is one of the greatest factors towards unification, and this bond Islām has established by the use of a common language at the Divine service. This language, it is evident, could be none other than Arabic, the language of the Qur'ān. Any one who realizes the grand object which Islām has set before itself of unifying the human race through Divine service, will at once appreciate the necessity of having that service in Arabic.

It is only short-sightedness, intensified by ignorance of the wider issues of unification, that makes some men think that the Divine service must be held in the language proper to each nation, and that a service held in any other language will not fulfil the purpose of worship. In the first place, the Islamic prayer does not consist of mere words of praise of the Divine glory and majesty, or the mere expression, in words, of the inner feelings of the heart. That no doubt is an important part of prayer but even more important than this is the attitude of mind, the inner feeling itself, of which the words are meant to be an expression. Now this attitude of mind is produced, in the first place, by the atmosphere about the worshipper and by the particular postures of reverence which he adopts. The mood, more than words, generates a true spirit of humility, and the first condition of a prayerful mind is humility, as the Qur'ān itself lays down: "Successful indeed are the believers, who are humble in their prayers" (23 : 1, 2). Suppose there is a man who takes part in a public service without understanding a word of Arabic. It would be entirely wrong to say that prayer does not benefit him, for there are the movements of his body, the raising of the hands to the ears, the standing up with folded hands, the bowing down, the placing of the forehead on the ground, the sitting down in a particular attitude of reverence, which all go a long way towards producing in him humility and consciousness of the Divine presence. He may not understand the language used, but here he is himself giving expression to his inner feelings in the language of his bodily movements. In fact, his whole self is expressive of what the words convey. It will indeed be highly more beneficial if he understands the spoken language also, but it is absurd to say that the language of movements has no meaning for him.

Now let us come to the language of words. The oftest repeated expressions in the Islamic service are *Allāhu Akbar, Subḥāna Rabbiy-al-'Aẓīm, Subḥāna Rabbiy-al-A'lā*, and the opening chapter of the Qur'ān, called *al-Fātiḥah*. As regards the first expression there is hardly a Muslim in the world, whatever language he may speak, and whether educated or uneducated, young or old, male or female, who does not understand the meaning of *Allāhu Akbar*. It is with this expression that a man enters into the Divine service and it is with it that he changes one posture of the body to another, so that with the very entrance in prayer, the mind receives an impression of the glory and majesty of God and assumes an attitude of prayerfulness to God and of humbleness before Him, and this impression on the mind is renewed at every change of movement, and thus the contemplation of Divine glory and greatness is the one occupation of mind during the service. Take the next two expressions, *Subḥāna Rabbiy-al-'Aẓīm*, repeated when the worshipper is bowing down, and *Subḥāna Rabbiy-al-A'lā*, repeated in the state of prostration. Even if a man does not understand their meaning, he does realize, when bowing that he is bowing before the great God, and does realize when lying down prostrate that he has laid his forehead on the ground before Him Who is the Highest. Yet, even a child would not take more than half an hour to learn these phrases and their meaning. And similar is the case with the opening chapter of the Qur'ān which is so often repeated in prayer. The seven short sentences of this chapter can be learnt, along with their meanings, in a short time and with very little effort. Even if one were to conduct Divine service in one's own language, still he would have to spend some time in learning it, and the learning of the significance of the Arabic words would only require a little additional time. Keeping in view the grand object of unifying the human race through Divine service, the time thus spent would represent the most usefully spent period of one's life.

Other advantages of maintaining Arabic in Divine service

There are two other considerations which make it necessary to maintain the Arabic language in Divine service. The Qur'ān, parts of which are recited in the service, was revealed in the Arabic language, and it is a generally admitted fact that a translation can never fully express the ideas of the original. And when the original is the word of God, and the ideas expressed are those relating to God's majesty and glory, it is still more difficult to convey the full significance in a translation.[4] Again there is a music in the original which no translation can possibly render. The music of the Qur'ān is not only in its rhythm but also in its diction. Now music plays an important part in producing an effect on the mind, and the recitation of the Qur'ān thus serves the purpose of communicating grand and beautiful ideas to the accompaniment of music. Hence it is that the Islamic service has never stood in need of the artificial music of the organ, having within itself the true music of the human soul. Even if a translation could convey something of the grand and rich ideas of the Qur'an, it could not convey the music which, along with the idea,

[4] Thus Sale in the Preliminary Discourse to his Translation of the Qur'ān, speaking of the style of the Holy Book, says: "and in many places, especially where the majesty and the attributes of God are described, sublime and magnificent; of which the reader cannot but observe several instances, though he must not imagine the translation comes up to the original, notwithstanding my endeavours to do it justice" (p. 48).

exercises such a potent influence on the mind of man. A Western orientalist remarks in the introduction of his translation of the Qur'ān: "The Arabs made use of a rhymed and rhythmical prose, the origin of which it is not difficult to imagine. The Arabic language consists for the most part of triliteral roots, *i.e.*, the single words expressing individual ideas consist generally of three consonants each, and the derivative forms expressing modifications of the original idea are not made by affixes and terminations alone but also by the insertion of letters in the root... A sentence, therefore, consists of a series of words which would each require to be expressed in clauses of several words in other languages, and it is easy to see how a next following sentence, explanatory of or completing the first, would be much more clear and forcible if it consisted of words of a similar shape and implying similar modifications of other ideas. It follows then that the two sentences would be necessarily symmetrical, and the presence of rhythm would not only please the ear but contribute to the better understanding of the sense, while the rhyme would mark the pause in the sense and emphasize the proportion".[5]

Another orientalist pays a tribute to the language of the Qur'ān as follows: "The language has the ring of poetry, though no part of the Qur'ān complies with the demands of Arab metre. The sentences are short and full of half-restrained energy, yet with a musical cadence. The thought is often only half expressed; one feels the speaker has essayed a thing beyond words, and has suddenly discovered the importance of language, and broken off with the sentence unfinished. There is the fascination of true poetry about these earliest sūrahs; as we read them we understand the enthusiasm of the Prophet's followers, though we cannot fully realise the beauty and the power."[6]

The Fātiḥah

It will be seen from these two quotations that even Western writers who have read the Qur'ān in the original recognize that its translation can convey neither the elements of music in its recitation, nor yet the full significance of the original. The opening chapter of the Qur'ān can be taken as an example. This chapter, the *Fātiḥah*, is the most essential

[5] Palmer, pp. liv, lv.

[6] Stanley Lane-Poole, *Selections from the Kur'ān*, p. civ.

part of the Islamic prayer. The seven verses of this chapter must be recited in every *rak'ah* of every prayer, whether private or public. Take the recitation first. A reference to the transliteration and translation, given further on, will show that the translation has in it nothing of the musical cadence of the original, and the effect upon the ear of the mere recitation of words is quite lost in the translation. But even more important than this is the inability of any language to convey the exact significance of the short words of the original, even in long sentences. Take, for instance, the word *Rabb* which occurs here first of all as an attribute of the Divine Being, and is the most frequently repeated of attributes in the whole of the Qur'ān. In English it is generally translated as *Lord*, but that word does not at all convey the real significance of the Arabic word *Rabb*, which, as already pointed out, carries with it the idea of *the fostering of a thing in such a manner as to make it attain one condition after another until it reaches its goal of completion*. It is a word composed of but two letters, *ra* and *ba*, yet the significance which it carries is so vast that a whole sentence would be required in other languages to convey its meaning fully. The word *Lord* or *Father* does not express that idea at all. The same is the case with the next following attributes, *Raḥmān* and *Raḥīm*, which are both derived from the same root *raḥmah* signifying *tenderness requiring the exercise of beneficence*, and are closely related in meaning; the former indicating that quality of love and mercy which comes into operation, even before the creation of man, by providing for him things which are necessary for his life; and the latter that which comes into operation when man makes use of these things and has thus done something to deserve it. No words in any other language can fully express these great ideas and this fine distinction. Similar is the case with *ibādah*, used in the middle verse, which is rendered in English by *worshipping*, but which really carried the meaning of *obedience coupled with the utmost submissiveness*.[7] The word *ihdi*, occuring in the fourth verse, is rendered *guide*, but *hidāyah*, the root from which it is derived, means *guiding and leading on the right way with kindness until one reaches the goal.*[8] How could these ideas be expressed in small and simple words, suitable for prayer, in any other language? Indeed, this petition, which is the essence of the

7 *Al-'ibādah al-ṭā'ah ma'-al-khudz'ūi* (TA.).

8 *Al-hidāyah al-rashād wa-l-dalālah bi-luṭf-in ilā mā yūṣilu-ila-l-maṭlūb*. (TA.).

whole institution of Islamic prayer, would lose its real significance by being translated into any other language.

Prayer as index of Muslim mentality

Thus the *Fātiḥah*, being the only essential portion of the Qur'ān which must be repeated in every *rak'ah* of a prayer, may rightly claim to be the guiding principle of a Muslim's life and a true index of his mentality. The main principles underlying the *Fātiḥah* may be considered briefly here. These are, firstly, the desire to give praise to the Divine Being under all circumstances, for the chapter opens with the words "All praise is due to Allāh". The Muslim has to come to prayer five times a day whatever the circumstances may be. There may be occasions when he is in distress, has suffered a reverse or a defeat, has a friend or near relative in distress, when some one very dear to him has just passed away and he is under the burden of a great bereavement, yet in all these conditions he is required to give praise to God Who brings about all these conditions, just as he would do had he received a blessing or some great benefit from God. The attitude of mind thus produced is to live in perfect peace with one's environment, neither to be carried away by joy, nor give way to dejection or depression. It is an attitude of mind which keeps a man steadfast in pleasure as well as pain, in joy as well as sorrow.

The second and third main ideas which determine a Muslim's mental attitude towards things are contained in the words *Rabbi-l-'ālamīn*, the Nourisher unto perfection of all the worlds or all the nations. This attribute of God brings to the man the comfort of knowing that whatever may happen to him, whether he receives a blessing or faces disaster, he must still be sure that he is being led on to perfection through these different stages. The addition of the words *al-'ālamīn*, all worlds or all nations, opens up his mind and widens the sphere of his love and sympathy not only towards all men, to whatever nation or creed they may belong, but also to the whole of God's creation. The man who recognizes that God is the Nourisher unto perfection of all men cannot bear hatred towards them. He must recognize, in fact, that God is much more to all men than is a father to his sons.

The fourth main idea is carried in the words *Raḥmān* and *Raḥīm*. God is Loving and Beneficient; He has provided man with everything necessary for his development, physical as well as moral and spiritual; but still that development depends on the right use of outward things as well as of the inner faculties which are meant for this object. The choice is man's whether he takes advantage of those means and reaches the goal, or rejects or ignores them and suffers the evil consequences thereof.

The fifth and sixth great ideas contained in the *Fātiḥah* are those conveyed in the words *Mālik yaum al-dīn* or Master of the Day of Requital. God is here called the *Mālik* or the Master, and not *Malik* or King. The two words are almost alike, but there is this vast difference between a *Mālik* and a *Malik* that the latter is bound to give to each what he deserves, but the former may, if he likes, forgive an offender altogether. There are some religions that lay so much stress on Divine justice that they refuse to recognize a God who can forgive offenders without having some compensation. Such a narrow view of Divine justice has a corresponding effect on the morals of a man. The word *Mālik* rejects this idea, and shows God to be a Master, Who can forgive if He likes, however great the offence may be. The addition of the words *yaum al-dīn*, the Day of Requital, is by way of reminder that man must face the consequence of his own deeds. There is no deed, good or bad, that is without a consequence, and if these consequences are not seen by man in this life, there is still a Day of Requital, even after death.

The seventh idea is contained in the words *iyyāka na'budu*, the idea of rendering obedience to God with entire submission. This is meant to create in man the mentality of obedience to the Divine commandments, even when these are opposed to the commandments of some temporal authority or to his own wishes. This attitude also gives man the strength to carry out the Divine commandments.

The eighth idea is contained in the words *iyyāka nasta'īn* (Thee do we beseech for help). The mental attitude which it is sought to create by these words is that of entire dependence on God and never despairing of the attainment of an object, for even if outward means have failed, there is God, the Controller of all means, Whose help will not fail the man who depends on Him.

The ninth idea is contained in the words *ihdi-nā*. This signifies the soul's inner desire — prayer being nothing but the expression of the soul's inmost desire — of being led on and on to the goal, such being the significance of *hidāyah*. These words also show that the mentality of being content to live in perfect peace with one's environment is not a negation of action. The Muslim attitude towards the world is not one of inaction or listlessness; on the contrary, it comprises both the desire to remain in peace with his environment, and the desire to move on and on so as to reach the great goal. He gives praise to God at every step, yet his is not a stationary condition; he is not the slave of his environment, but for ever struggling and striving to master it; he does not stand for peace without progress, nor yet for progress without peace, but for peace and progress combined.

The tenth idea ruling the Muslim mentality, as disclosed in the *Fātiḥah*, is the longing to walk in the footsteps of those who have received Divine blessings of any kind, temporal or spiritual, and the desire to be able to avoid the errors of those who have been the objects of Divine displeasure or those who have gone astray. The latter are the followers of the two extremes, while those who have received the Divine favours are those who keep to the middle path — which is the straight path.

With these ten ideas ruling man's mind (and this is what is aimed at by the frequent repetition of the Opening Chapter in prayer), a man is armed with the best weapons both for happiness and success.

It is sometimes said that prayer leads to idleness and indolence, because it causes a man to depend on his supplications for what he wants instead of working for it. The objection is, of course, due to a complete misconception as to the nature of prayer. Prayer to God does not mean that a man has simply to entreat the Divine Being to grant him this or that favour and do nothing himself towards attaining it. Prayer is, in fact, a search for means and is thus an incentive to action. The *Fātiḥah* is the most important Muslim prayer, yet as already shown, its central idea is one of action or being led on to action, for here the supplicator does not ask for certain favours but only to be guided on the right path. The actual prayer is contained in the words *ihdi-naṣ-ṣirāṭ al-mustaqīm, i.e., guide us on the right path,* or, as shown with reference to the meaning of *hidāyah, lead on to the goal by keeping us on the right path.* Prayer is thus only the means of leading a man onwards and discovering the path by walking whereon he may attain the goal. It is a search for means to attain to a goal and a yearning to walk on a certain path. In face of this clear teaching, it is a mistake to suppose that prayer for any object negatives the adoption of human means to gain it. Elsewhere the acceptance of prayer is spoken of as rewarding a man for the hard work he has done: "So their Lord accepted their prayer, saying, I will not suffer the work of any worker among you to be lost, whether male or female, the one of you being from the other" (3: 194).

The rule has been laid down in the Qur'ān in several places that no end can be gained without making a hard struggle for it: "We have certainly created man to face difficulties" (90 : 4); "And that man can have nothing but what he strives for; and that his striving will soon be seen;

then he will be rewarded for it with the fullest reward'' (53 : 39 - 41); ''Say: O my people! work in your place. Surely I am a worker'' (39 : 39). The question may however be asked, what is the need for prayer if man must work for an end and avail himself of the means to gain it? Here, again, is a misconception as to the capabilities of man. It often happens that, notwithstanding the hardest struggle, a man is unable to gain an end, and finds himself quite helpless. In such a case prayer is a help, a source of strength, to the worker. He does not lose heart nor does he despair, because he believes that, though the means at his disposal have failed, though all around there are difficulties and darkness, though his own strength is failing, yet there is a Higher Power with Whom nothing is impossible, Who can still bring a ray of light to dispel the darkness and Who remains a perpetual source of strength for him in his helplessness, and that by praying to Him he can still achieve what seems otherwise quite unattainable. That is the function of prayer, and it is thus one of the means to gain an end when all other means have failed, and a source of strength to man at all times, but especially in moments of utter weakness and despair.

That such is the true function of prayer, and that it is only a source of greater energy and greater strength to enable man to face difficulties and achieve an end, is shown by the early history of Islām. Prophet Muḥammad and his Companions were undoubtedly the greatest believers in prayer — they are spoken of in the Qur'ān as spending two-thirds of the night, half the night or one-third of the night in prayer (73 : 20) —, and yet this was the very band of men whose love for work knew no bounds, whose energy was inexhaustible and who faced extreme difficulties with an iron determination. Surely the men who in ten years conquered two of the most powerful empires of the world, who with but the scantiest of resources faced armies double and treble and, on occasions, ten times the size of their own, whatever other charges may be brought against them, cannot be said to have been idle and inefficient. And it is a fact of history that, whenever the great Muslim conquerors were faced with the most critical situation, they fell down in prostration before God, seeking strength from the Source of real strength. Prayer, in fact, transformed the neglected race of the Arabs into the most distinguished nation which history can show, turned an idle and inefficient people into the most zealous and untiring workers for the progress of humanity, in all phases of its advancement. Truly, prayer is meant to awaken, and does awaken, the latent energies of the human soul.

SEC. 2 — THE MOSQUE

No consecration is necessary

In a discussion on prayer, it is necessary to speak of the mosque. The Arabic word for mosque is *masjid*, which means *a place where one prostrates oneself*, or *a place of worship*. It should be borne in mind, in the first place, that prayer can be performed anywhere. No particularly consecrated place is necessary for the holding of the Divine service. To this effect there is an express saying of the Prophet, who, speaking of some of his peculiarities, is reported to have said: "The whole of the earth has been made a mosque for me" (Bu. 8 : 56). A Muslim may, therefore, say his prayers anywhere he likes. The mere fact that he does so elsewhere than in a mosque detracts in no way from the efficacy of the prayer; nor does a building when constructed for the express purpose of prayer stand in need of consecration. All that is required is that the builder should declare his intention to have that building used as a place of prayer.

The mosque as a religious centre

But, in spite of what has been stated above, the mosque plays a more important part in Islām than does any other house of worship in any other religion. Where the Qur'ān speaks of the Muslim's duty to defend and protect all houses of worship, to whatever religion they may belong, it speaks, of the mosque last of all, but it mentions its distinctive characteristic, namely that the name of God is remembered there most of all: "And if Allāh did not repel some people by others, cloisters and churches and synagogues and mosques in which Allāh's name is much remembered, would have been pulled down" (22 : 40). The concluding words of the verse — *mosque in which Allāh's name is much remembered* — are significant. All religious buildings are resorted to generally once a week, but the mosque is visited five times a day for the remembrance of God's name. In fact, if any house on earth can be called God's house, on account of its association with the Divine name, that house is the mosque which pre-eminently deserves the name, all other religious houses seem neglected in comparision with it. The whole atmosphere of the mosque is charged with the electricity of the Divine name; there is the call to prayer five times a day, which render the air with cries of the greatness and unity of God — *Allāhu Akbar, Allāhu Akbar* and *lā ilāha ill-Allāh*; there is the individual service, carried on in silence, but with God's name on the lips of every individual worshipper; there is the public service in which the *Imām* recites aloud portions of the Qur'ān, that tell of Divine grandeur and glory, with the refrain of *Allāhu Akbar* repeated at every change of movement; and when the prayer is finished, there is again a chorus of voices speaking of Divine greatness, making the mosque echo and re-echo with the remembrance of God. It is true that God does not dwell in the mosque, but surely one feels His presence there. It will thus be seen that the mosque is the centre of Muslim religious life. It is not a place to which a man may resort once a week to be inspired with a spiritual idea, which he will in all likelihood forget during the six days to follow; it is a place which sends forth, as it were, the blood of spiritual life, hour after hour, into the veins of the Muslim, and thus keeps his mind imbued with higher thoughts, and his heart alive in a real sense.

A training ground of equality

Being a meeting-place of Muslims five times daily, the mosque serves as a training ground where the doctrine of thc equality and fraternity of mankind is put into practical working. It is undoubtedly true that every religion is based on the two fundamental principles of the Fatherhood of God and the brotherhood of man, but it is equally true that no religion has been so successful in establishing a living brotherhood of man as has Islām, and the secret of this unparalleled success lies in the mosque. The mosque enables Muslims to meet five times a day, on terms of perfect equality and in a spirit of true brotherhood, all standing in a row before their great Maker, knowing no difference of colour or rank, all following the lead of one man. All differences and distinctions are, for the time being, obliterated. Without the mosque, the mere teaching of the brotherhood of man would have remained a dead letter as it is in so many other religions.

The mosque as a cultural centre

Besides being its religious centre, the mosque is also the cultural centre of the Muslim community. Here the Muslim community is educated on all questions of its welfare. The Friday sermon is a regular weekly lecture on all such questions, but, besides that, whenever in the time of the Prophet and his early successors it became necessary to inform the Muslim community on any matter of importance, a sermon or a lecture was delivered in the mosque. Even during his last illness the Prophet came out into the mosque and delivered a sermon to the people.

In additon to this mass education in the Prophet's Mosque, there were also arrangements for the education of those who wanted to acquire learning. Men who had to be trained as missionaries for the spread of light and learning in distant parts of the country not only received their education in the mosque but also lodged in a place, called the *Ṣuffa*, attached to the mosque. The *Ṣuffa* was situated in the northern part of the mosque, covered with a roof but with open sides, from which those students received the name of *ahl al-Ṣuffa* or *aṣḥāb al-Ṣuffa, i.e.*, the dwellers of the *Ṣuffa*. It is a mistake to think that homeless people were lodged in it, for among those mentioned as having lived there are men like Sa'd ibn Abī Waqqāṣ,[9] while there were many poor immigrants who never lived there. The fact is that those who wanted to acquire knowledge of the Qur'ān and the religion of Islām were lodged there, and their numbers is said to have reached four hundred at times. It was out of these that missionaries were sent sometimes in batches of ten or twelve, and once, even in a batch of seventy, to educate the people in the country. Almost every mosque to this day has to some extent, arrangements for the education of students, the *maktab* or the *madrasah* (the school), being a necessary adjunct to the mosque. Many important mosques have also some trust property attached to them, their income going towards the upkeep of the students and their teachers. In later times, libraries, some of them very large, were also kept in parts of the mosque.

The mosque as a general centre

But this is not all. In the time of the Prophet and his early successors, the mosque was the centre of all kinds of Muslim activities. Here all important national questions were settled. When the Muslim community was forced to take up arms in self-defence, it was in the mosque that measures of defence and expeditions were concerted. It was, again, to the

[9] One of the prominent Companions of the Prophet, who belonged to a comparatively well-to-do family.

mosque that the people were asked to repair when there was news of importance to be communicated, and the mosque also served as the council-hall of the Muslims. In the time of ‘Umar, when two councils were appointed to advise the Caliph, it was in the mosque that these councils met. Deputations from Muslim as well as non-Muslim tribes were received in the mosque, and some of the more important deputations were also lodged there, as in the case of the famous Christian deputation from Najrān, and the deputation of Thaqīf, a polytheist tribe; and for this purpose tents were set up in the yard of the mosque.[10] Indeed, once on the occasion of a festival, the Prophet even allowed certain Abyssinians to give a display with shield and lance in the mosque (Bu. 8 : 69). Ḥassān ibn Thābit used to recite in the mosque his verses in defence of the Prophet against the abuse of his enemies (Bu. 8 : 68). Juridical affairs were also settled in the mosque (Bu. 8 : 44; 93 : 18), and it was used in a number of other ways. For example, a tent was set up for Sa‘d ibn Mu‘ādh in the yard of the mosque when he received fatal wounds in the battle of the Ditch (Bu. 8 : 77), and it was in this tent that he died. A freed handmaid had also a tent in the mosque where she resided (Bu. 8 : 57). The mosque was thus not only the spiritual centre of the Muslims but also their political, educational and social centre. It was, indeed, their national centre in the truest and most comprehensive sense of the word.

Respect for mosques

The fact, however, that the mosque may be used for other objects than the saying of prayer, does not in any way detract from its sacred character. It is primarily a place for Divine worship and must be treated as such. Nor are any proceedings allowed in the mosque, except such as related to the welfare of the Muslim community or have a national importance. The carrying on of any business or trade in the mosque is expressly forbidden (AD. 2 : 216). Due respect must be shown to the house of God;

[10] In the Qur’ān it is said: “The idolators have no right to frequent the mosques of Allāh while bearing witness to unbelief against themselves” (9 : 17). This verse does not mean that a non-Muslim cannot be allowed to pay a visit to a mosque. By “the mosques of Allāh”, here in fact is meant the *Masjid al-Ḥarām*, the Sacred Mosque of the Ka‘bah, which is really a centre of all the mosques of the world; and as the words of the verse show, the polytheists who had long been in possession of the Ka‘bah were told that they had now no right to frequent that mosque, as it had been cleared of all traces of polytheism. Moreoever, for the non-Muslims to have a *right* to pay visits to mosques is quite different from the Muslims allowing them to come into the mosques.

thus even the raising of loud voices is denounced (Bu. 8 : 83), and spitting is expressly prohibited (Bu. 8 : 37). Saying prayers, with the shoes on, is permitted (Bu. 8 : 24), but the shoes must be clean and not dirty. The practice has, however, grown of removing the shoes at the door of the mosque as a mark of respect to the mosque and to ensure cleanliness. Keeping the mosque clean and neat is an act of great merit. (Bu. 8 : 72).

Mosques should face the Ka'bah

The Ka'bah, or the Sacred Mosque of Makkah, is, according to the Qur'ān, the first house for the worship of God that was ever built on this earth: "Certainly the first house appointed for men is the one at Bakkah,[11] blessed, and a guidance for nations" (3 : 95). An account of its building by Abraham and Ishmael is given in the Qur'ān in 2 : 127, but that it was only a reconstruction of a fallen building is shown by 2 : 125, where the purification of the house of idols that had been placed in it is mentioned before its construction in 2 : 127. Even Muir ascribes "an extremely remote age" to the Ka'bah. The Ka'bah, being thus the first mosque on earth, all mosques are built to face it. This practice is based on an express injunction contained in the Qur'ān. The first injunction relating thereto appears in connection with Abraham: "And when We made the House (the Ka'bah), a resort for men and a place of security; and take ye the place of Abraham (the Ka'bah) for a place of prayer"[12] (2 : 125). And, further on, more expressly: "And from whatsoever place thou comest forth, turn thy Face towards the Sacred Mosque; and wherever you are, turn your faces towards it" (2 : 150). This order that all places of worship should converge towards the Ka'bah had an underlying purpose which is hinted at in the Qur'ān in connection with the subject of the *Qiblah*,[13]

[11] Bakkah is the same as Makkah.

[12] Ḥasan is reported to have said that by *muṣallā* (lit., a place of prayer) is meant *qiblah* (Rz.), or the direction facing which prayer is to be said. This verse was revealed about sixteen months after the Hijrah. Up to that time prayers were said facing Jerusalem, the *qiblah* of the Israelite prophets. It is noteworthy that so long as the Prophet was in Makkah, where there were no Jews or Christians, he said his prayers facing Jerusalem, for he had not received any revelation on the point and naturally followed the *qiblah* of the Israelite prophets. But when he came to Madīnah, where the Jewish element of the population was very strong, he was ordered not to face Jerusalem any more, as the Ka'bah was to be the future *qiblah* of the Muslims.

[13] *Qiblah* literally means *the direction* or *point towards which one turns his face* (LL.). In its religious usage it means the direction towards which one turns his face when saying his prayers, and the *qiblah* is thus the Spiritual Centre of a people.

"And every one has a goal to which he turns himself, therefore vie with one another in good works; wherever you are, Allāh will bring you all together" (2 : 148). The *bringing of all together* clearly means *the making of all as one people*, so that beneath the ostensible unity of direction lies the real unity of purpose. Just as they have all one centre to turn to, they must set one goal before themselves. Thus the unity of the *Qiblah* among Muslims stands for their unity of purpose, and forms the basis on which rests the brotherhood of Islām. Hence the Prophet's saying: "Do not call those who follow your *Qiblah (ahl Qiblah)* disbelievers (*kāfir*)" (N. art. *Kufr).*

Building of the mosque

The only requirement of the law of Islām regarding the building of a mosque is that it should face the Ka'bah. Tradition, however, further recommends that the building should be as simple as possible. All adornments are generally avoided, in accordance with a saying of the Prophet: "I have not been commanded to raise the mosques high" (AD. 2 : 11). To this Ibn 'Abbās adds: "You will surely adorn them as the Jews and the Christians adorn (their places of worship)." According to another tradition, the Prophet is reported to have said: "The hour of doom (*al-sā'ah*)[14] will not come till people vie with one another in (the building of) mosques" (AD. 2 : 11). The mosque built by the Prophet himself at Madīnah, called the Prophet's Mosque, was a simple structure in a vast courtyard in which tents could be pitched in time of need. The building was made of bricks baked in the sun, and the roofed portion, resting on columns consisting of the stems of palm-trees was covered with palm-leaves and clay. Both Abū Bakr and 'Umar, the first and second Caliphs, rebuilt it with the same material, though the latter extended it considerably (AD. 2 : 11). The great mosques of Islām erected in the time of 'Umar in Baṣrah, Kūfah and Fusṭāt, the new towns built by the Muslims, or in old towns such as Madā'in, Damascus and Jerusalem, were all simple structures like the Prophet's Mosque at Madīnah built either of reeds or bricks baked in the sun, with vast courtyards, large enough to accommodate congregations of even 40,000 men, the floors being generally strewn with pebbles. These mosques were built by the Government and had the Government House attached to them, the

[14] As shown elsewhere, *al-sā'ah* or *the hour* in this case means *the doom* or *the time of the fall of a nation.*

Governors themselves leading the prayers. Quite in accordance with the simplicity of their structure, the mosques were unfurnished except for mats or carpets and a pulpit from which the sermon was delivered on Fridays. 'Uthmān, the third Caliph, rebuilt the Prophet's Mosque at Madīnah with hewn stone and mortar (AD. 2 : 11). The custom of building mosques with domes and having one or more minarets grew up later, but even these are, notwithstanding their grandeur, monuments of simplicity, their chief adornment being the writing on theirs walls, in mosaic, of verses from the Qur'ān.

Tribal and sectarian mosques

Every Muslim is free to build a mosque, and so people living in different quarters of a town may build mosques for themselves. Abū Bakr had erected a mosque in the courtyard of his house while still at Makkah at a very early period (Bu. 46 : 22). Another Companion, 'Itbān ibn Mālik, once invited the Prophet to say prayers in a particular part of his house which he might use as a mosque, since he was unable to reach the mosque of his people in the rainy season (Bu. 8 : 46). A mosque was built at Qubā, in the suburbs of Madīnah, for the people of that locality, the tribe of 'Amr ibn 'Auf, and the Prophet used to visit it once a week (Bu. 20 : 2). Another mosque at Madīnah is spoken of as the mosque of Banī Zuraiq (Bu. 8 : 41). And *Bukhārī* has the following heading for this chapter: "Can a mosque be called the 'mosque of so and so?' " Thus a name may be given to any mosque, either that of the founder or of the people who resort to it, or any other name. In later times, Muslims belonging to different sects had their own mosques, the Ka'bah, the Central Mosque, gathering all together at the time of Pilgrimage. But when a mosque has once been built it is open to Muslims of all persuasions and no one has the right to prohibit Muslims of a certain persuasion or sect from entering it. This is a point on which the Qur'ān contains a clear injunction: "And who is more unjust than he who prevents men from the mosques of Allāh, from His name being remembered in them, and strives to ruin them?" (2 : 114).

Admission of women to mosques

The custom of *pardah* in certain countries of the Muslim world raises the question as to whether women may go to the mosques. There was no such question in the Prophet's time, when women freely took part in religious services. There is indeed a tradition which tells us that on a certain night the Prophet was very late in coming out to lead the night prayers, when the people had assembled in the mosque; and he came only on hearing 'Umar call out, "The women and the children are going to sleep" (Bu. 9 : 22). This shows that women were in the mosque even at such a late hour. According to another tradition narrated by 'Āishah, women used to be present at the morning prayer, which was said at an hour so early that they returned to their houses while it was still dark (Bu. 8 : 13). Yet another tradition shows that even women who had children to suckle would come to the mosque, and that when the Prophet heard a baby crying, he would shorten his prayer lest the mother should feel inconvenience (Bu. 10 : 65); while in one tradition it is stated that when the Prophet had finished his prayers, he used to stay a little and did not rise until the women had left the mosque (Bu. 10 : 152). All these traditions afford overwhelming evidence of the fact that women, just in the same way as men, used to frequent the mosques and that there was not the least restriction in this matter. "There are other traditions which show that the Prophet had given orders not to prohibit women from going to the mosque. For instance, there is onc which quotes the Prophet as saying: "Do not prohibit the handmaids of Allāh from going to the mosques of Allāh" (Bu. 11 :12). According to another, the Prophet is reported to have said that, if a woman wanted to go to the mosque at night, she should not be prohibited from doing so (Bu. 10 : 162). The words of a third tradition are more general: "When the wife of one of you asks permission to go out, she should not be prohibited from doing so" (Bu. 10 : 166). There was an express injunction that on the occasion of the 'Īd festival women should go out to the place where prayers were said; even women in a state of menstruation were to be present, though they would not join the prayers (Bu. 13 : 15, 20). The practice for women to be present in the mosques at the time of prayer seems to have continued long enough after the Prophet's time. Within the mosque they were not separated from men by any screen or curtain; only they formed into a line behind the men (Bu. 10 : 164); and though they were covered decently with an over-garment, they did not wear a veil. On the occasion of the great gathering of the Pilgrimage a woman is expressly forbidden to wear a veil (Bu. 25 : 23). Many other traditions show that women formed themselves into a back row and that the men retained their seats until they had gone out of the mosque (Bu. 10 : 164). This practice seems to have existed for a very long time. Thus we read of women calling out *Allāhu Akbar* along with men in the mosque during the three days following *'Īd al-Adzhā* as late as the time of 'Umar ibn 'Abd al-'Azīz, the Umayyad Caliph, who ruled about the end of the first century A.H. (Bu. 13 : 12). In the year 256 A.H., the Governor of Makkah is said to have tied ropes between the columns to make a separate place for women (*En. Is.*, art. *Masjid*). Later on, the practice grew up of erecting a wooden barrier in the mosque to form a separate enclosure for women, but by and by the *pardah* conception grew so strong that women were altogether shut out from the mosques.

Another question connected with this subject relates to the entrance of women into mosques during their menstruation. It must be borne in mind, in the first place that in Islām a state of menstruation or confinement is not looked upon as a state of impurity, as in many other religions. All that the Qur'ān says about menstruation is that conjugal relations should be discontinued during the state of menstruation: "And they ask thee about menstruation. Say, It is harmful; so keep aloof from women during the menstrual discharge" (2 : 222).[15] According to tradition, a woman is exempted from saying her prayers, or keeping the fast, as long as menstruation lasts. As regards pilgrimage, she may perform all obligations except *ṭawāf* (making the circuits of the Ka'bah), but there is no idea of impurity attaching to her in this condition. There is a very large number of traditions showing that all kinds of social relations with women in this condition were permitted, that the husband and wife could occupy the same bed, that the Prophet used to recite the Qur'ān when sitting in close contact with his wife who had her courses on, and that a woman in this condition was allowed to handle the Qur'ān (Bu. 6 : 2, 3, 5, 6, 7). There is, however, a tradition from which the conclusion is drawn that a woman should not enter the mosque during the menstrual discharge, but evidently there is some misunderstanding here, for if she could handle the Qur'ān why could she not enter the mosque? The tradition runs thus: " 'Ā'ishah says that the Prophet said to her, Hand me over the mat from the mosque. I said I am in a state of menstruation. The Prophet said, Thy menstruation is not in thy hands" (AD. 1 : 104). Apparently the Prophet wanted a mat which was in the mosque and he asked 'Ā'ishah to hand

[15] Keeping aloof in this condition relates only to conjugal relations, not to social relations, as the words, that follow, show: "Then when they have cleansed themselves, go into them as Allāh has commanded you" (2 : 222). The cleansing spoken of here signifies having a bath when the menstrual discharge is over.

it over to him. Now the general opinion concerning a menstruating woman, before Islām, was that she was defiled, and 'Ā'ishah's reply seems to have been given under that impression. The Prophet's reply, on the other hand, clearly shows this conception to have been a mistaken one, and that menstruation did not defile a woman; it was quite a different thing that she was required to abstain from saying her prayers when in that state. There is, however, another tradition which represents the Prophet as saying: "I do not make the mosque lawful for a menstruating woman or for a person who is under an obligation to perform a total ablution" (AD. 1 : 93). But this tradition has been called weak and cannot therefore be relied on. Or, the mosque here simply represents the prayer service from which such persons are exempted. As the traditions quoted earlier show, there is not the least idea of defilement in a menstruating woman. Similarly there are traditions showing that what a menstruating woman touches with her mouth is not defiled (AD. 1 : 103). Even the very clothes which she wears need not be washed if they are not actually defiled (Bu. 6 : 11). The tradition mentioned above is therefore no bar against a woman's entrance into the mosque when she is menstruating, but as she is to abstain from prayer, she has no need to go there.

Office-bearers of the mosque

Every mosque will ordinarily have a *Mutawallī* (lit., *guardian*), who is charged with its management by those who have built it. The *mutawallī* has the right to appoint the *Imām*, or the man who leads the prayers, but he has no right to prohibit Muslims, on account of sectarian differences, from entering the mosque. Every mosque has also generally a *mu'adhdhin* who gives the call for prayers. The *mu'adhdhin* may also look after the mosque. But the most important man in the mosque is the *Imām*, the man who leads the prayers and delivers the sermon (*khuṭbah*) on Friday. The honour of leading the prayers was, in the time of the Prophet, and also for a long time after that, given to the best man in the community. *Bukhārī* has the following heading for one of his chapters: "Those who are well-grounded in knowledge and possess the greatest excellence are most entitled to lead prayer" (Bu. 10 : 46). Under this heading, he quotes a tradition in which it is narrated that when the Prophet was on his death-bed, he appointed Abū Bakr to lead the prayers in his place, and when he was requested to appoint 'Umar instead, as Abū Bakr was too tender-hearted, he refused to do so. Abū Dāwūd narrates sayings of the Prophet requiring the honour of leading the prayer to be conferred on the man who was most learned in the Qur'ān, or in a case where two men were equal in that respect, other considerations were to be applied. The Prophet himself was the Imām in the central mosque at Madīnah and, after him, his successors, the respective caliphs, Abū Bakr, 'Umar and 'Uthmān. When a governor was appointed to a province, he was also appointed as Imām to lead the prayers, and this practice continued for a long time. In fact, the honour of leading the prayers (*imāmat*) in Islām was as great as the honour of kingship, and the two offices, the office of the spiritual leader and that of the temporal leader, were combined in one person for a long time. As the ruler himself was the Imām at the centre, so were his governors the Imāms in the different provincial headquarters. The priest and the present-day *mulla* had no place in early Islām. Nor does the Imām, like the mosque, stand in need of consecration, because every one is consecrated by entering into the fold of Islām. Any one can lead the prayers in the absence of the Imām, and any one may act as Imām when several people are gathered together. The present practice of having paid Imāms, whose only duty is to lead the prayers, is to a very large extent responsible for the degeneration of the Muslims. These people have generally no sense of the dignity of Islām and its institutions, nor have they the light, learning and general experience which should entitle them to claim to lead the Muslims spiritually. A woman is also spoken of as acting as an Imām, while men followed her, though it was in her own house (AD. 2 : 60).

SEC. 3 — PURIFICATION

Outward purification as a prelude to prayer

Prayer, according to the Qur'ān and Tradition, is the means for the purification of soul, and of the body and the garments a man wears, which is declared to be necessary as a preparation for prayer. By a consensus of opinion, the 74th chapter of the Qur'ān is the second revelation which the Prophet received after the first five verses of the 96th chapter, and the first five verses of the former may here be quoted to show the importance of outward cleanliness in the religion of Islām: "O thou who wrappest thyself up! Arise and warn, and thy Lord do magnify, and thy garments do purify, and uncleanliness do shun" (74 : 1 - 5). Thus warning the people, magnifying the Lord which is done through prayer, and purifying the garments and the body, are laid down here as three fundamental duties. The two ideas, the purification of the body and of the soul, are very often mentioned together in the Qur'ān. To quote one more example: "Surely Allāh loves those who turn much to Him, and He loves those who purify themselves" (2 : 222). Tradition also lays special stress on outward purification. According to one, "purification is the key to prayer" (Tr. 1 : 3); according to another, "religion is built on cleanliness"; and in a third tradition it is stated that "purification is one-half of faith" (IM. 1 : 5). The implication is clear. Inward purity is the real aim, but outward purity is a necessary preparation. A pure mind in a pure body is the watchword of Islām.

The making of outward purification as a necessary preparation for prayer is intended not only to direct attention to the real aim which is the purity of the soul but also to ensure constant purification of the body which is in itself a great necessity of life, for the man who purifies himself five times a day would undoubtedly be in a constant state of physical purity. The Qur'ān recommends good clothing generally: "Say, Who has prohibited the adornment of Allāh which He has brought forth for His servants and the good provisions?" (7 : 32). Here clothing is called an adornment, to show that good clothes add to beauty; and elsewhere it is stated they they are meant as a covering and also as a beauty" (7 : 26). And in the case of prayer, it is further stated: "O children of Adam! attend to your adornment at every time of prayer" (7 : 31). This shows that when assembling in mosques for prayer, attention must be paid to outward appearance and purity as well. One reason for this direction is that an assemblage of people in prayer, dirty in clothing or person, would undoubtedly be offensive to others. Hence it is specially laid down that, in the larger gatherings on Fridays, every one should preferably take a bath before coming to prayer, and use scent if possible.

Wudzū'

The first condition of bodily purification is *wudzū'*[16] which, in the terminology of Islamic law, means the washing of certain parts of the body before prayers, and may be described as partial ablution. The necessary details of *wudzū'* are given in the Qur'ān in one of the latest surahs,[17]

[16] The word *wudzū'* is derived from *wadzā'* which means *ḥusn* or beauty (N.).

[17] — see next page.

though in practice it is traceable to the very time when prayer was made obligatory. To this practice which the Prophet undoubtedly instituted by Divine light, or inner revelation (*waḥy khafiyy*), sanction is given in the following words: "O you who believe ! when you rise up for prayer, wash your faces and your hands up to the elbows, and wipe your heads, and (wash)[18] your feet up to the ankles" (5 : 6).

The practice of the Prophet, as recorded in Tradition contains substantially the same details. Briefly these may be described as follows:

1. The hands are first washed up to the wrists.

2. The mouth is then cleaned with water, or by rinsing with a toothbrush and by gargling if necessary.

3. The nostrils are then cleaned by snuffing a little water into them and blowing the nose if necessary.[19]

4. The face is then washed from the forehead to the chin and from one ear to the other.

5. Then the right arm and after that the left, is washed from the wrist to the elbow.

[17] In Tradition certain precautions are recommended in the case of natural evacuations, so that no part of the excrement or filth should remain on the body or defile the clothes. These consist in the use of pebbles — whose place may be taken by toilet paper — and water, after the passing of urine or stools, or simply water. These are apparently very minor details of life but they play an important part in the preservation of cleanliness and health. Similarly removal of superfluous hair, *i.e.*, hair under the arm-pit or that of *regis pubis*, is enjoined for the same purpose, that is to say, for the sake of cleanliness and health. The practice of circumcision, or the removal of superfluous flesh, which, according to the Bible, dates back to Abraham, has its origin in the same idea. That circumcision is also a remedy for many kinds of diseases is now generally recognized by medical opinion.

[18] The Shī'ahs hold that the feet are simply to be wiped like the head, but in the received text of the Qur'ān, the words used are *arjula-kum*, where *arjula* (feet) having a *naṣab* over it, is the objective case and is governed by the verb *aghsilū* which means *wash*, the meaning thus being "wash your feet." If *arjul* had been governed by *imsaḥū-bi* meaning "wipe your feet", the words would have read *arjuli-kum*, not *arjula-kum.*

[19] It will be seen that the Qur'ān, in speaking of *wudzū'*, begins with the washing of the face, without speaking of the first three stages. The reason is that the washing of the face includes these three things, the washing of the hands to wrists as a preliminary to, and cleansing the mouth and the nose as part of the washing of the face. The Tradition only gives greater details.

6. The head is then wiped over with wet hands, three fingers of both hands, between the little finger and the thumb, being joined together, and the inner side of the ears wiped with forefingers and its outer side with thumbs.

7. The feet are then washed up to ankles, the right foot being washed first.

If socks or stockings are being worn, and they have been put on after performing an ablution, it is not necessary to take them off; the three fingers of the wet hand may be passed over them. The same practice may be resorted to in the case of shoes. If the socks or the shoes are then taken off, the *wudzū'* remains. It is, however, necessary that the feet should be wahsed once in every twenty-four hours.[20]

Wudzū' may be performed before every prayer, but the necessity for it arises only when there has been a natural evacuation[21], or when a man has been fast asleep.

The tooth-brush

It will be seen that, besides the religious object which is to remind man of the necessity for inner purification, the great aim in *wudzū'* is to foster habits of cleanliness. Such parts of the body as are generally exposed are washed time after time, so that dust or uncleanness of any kind may be removed and they may be clean at all times. That health and cleanliness are two of the great purposes which *wudzū'* serves, in addition to its spiritual meaning, is shown by the stress which is laid on rinsing the mouth with the aid of a tooth-brush (*miswāk*).

[20] *Wudzū'*, as described here, is taken from the most authentic traditions, and is a very simple process, the object of which is to cleanse the parts which are generally exposed. Later theologians have added a large number of unnecesary details. Everybody knows best how to clean a particular part of the body and whether to wash it once or twice or thrice. As regards the particular *adhkār* (recitations) to be repeated at the washing of particular parts, authoritative opinion is that all these *adhkār* are fabrications, with the exception of saying *bismillāh* at the beginning and repeating the *kalimah* at the end, adding the words *Allāh-ummaj'al-nī min al-tawwābīn waj'al-nī min al-mutaṭahhirīn.* "O Allāh! make me of those who turn to Thee again and again and make me of those who purify themselves" (ZM. I, p. 50).

[21] Natural evacuation includes the passing of urine, stools and wind. The Qur'ān speaks of natural evacuation as *coming from ghā'it* (4 : 43), the last word meaning *low land* to which people generally resorted for a privy. The use of this word indicates that anything which offends others should be done in a lonely place, and the mosque, where other people are assembled, is not such a place.

Clean mouth and teeth not only improve the general cleanliness of the body but also exclude a large number of diseases. The Prophet thought so highly of the tooth-brush that he never neglected it under any condition; even on his death-bed he asked for a tooth-brush, and expired only a few minutes afterwards (Bu. 64 : 85). It was his custom to arise for the *Tahajjud* prayer soon after midnight, and even at that hour he used first to clean his mouth and teeth with a tooth-brush (Bu. 4 : 73; M. 2 : 13). He attached such importance to the cleansing of the mouth that he used repeatedly to say that the only thing which prevented him from declaring the use of the tooth-brush obligatory at every prayer (*i.e.*, at least five times daily) was the fear that it might be a burden on his community (Bu. 11 : 8; 30 : 27). On another occasion he is reported to have said that the tooth-brush cleans the mouth and brings about the pleasure of God (*mardzāt-un li-l-Rabb*) (Bu. 30 : 27). Similarly gargling is recommended to keep the throat clean, which is also beneficial to health.

Taking a bath

The taking of a bath is rendered necessary in certain cases.[22] It should be noted in this connection that it is a mistake to call the state in which a man is under an obligation to perform a *wudzū'* or take a bath, a state of defilement. It is simply a first step towards going to prayer, and undoubtedly promotes habits of cleanliness and is conducive to health. The direction is contained in the Qur'ān itself: "And if you are under an obligation to perform a total ablution (*Junub*), then wash yourselves" (5 : 6). Bathing is also enjoined in Tradition on occasions of large gatherings, such as the Friday prayers and the 'Id prayers, when clean clothes must also be put on and scent used if available. These directions have

[22] These cases are: (1) *pallutio nocturna* or *iḥtilām*, (2) *coitus* or sexual intercourse; and in the case of women especially, (3) menses or *ḥaidz* and (4) *puerperium* or *nifās*. During the period of menses and *puerperium* a woman is exempted from prayer. Menstruation generally lasts from three to ten days, and a bath should be taken, when the flow stops, after a minimum period of three days, the maximum limit being ten days, after which bath should be necessarily taken. In the first two conditions a man is called *junub*, from *janb* meaning *a side*. To call this a state of pollution or defilement is not correct, and no lexicologist supports it. On a certain occasion when one such person, a *junub*, described himself as *najs (polluted* or *defiled)* in the presence of the Prophet, he corrected him by saying that a Muslim does not become defiled (Bu. 5 : 23). It is a technical term and means *one who is under an obligation to perform a total ablution or bathing* (LL.). The connection with the root-meaning is that such a person is *on a side* or *remote* from prayer (R.).

thus both a religious and a hygienic value. They serve as a kind of preparation for going before a higher Presence, and help to wrest the attention of man from lower objects and divert it to the higher, and they also make the atmosphere in which gatherings of men take place, purer and healthier.

Tayammum

That there is in *wudzū'* and the bath a religious purpose besides the hygienic one is shown by the fact that when water is not available, still it is necessary to perform an act which diverts attention from bodily purification to the purity of the soul, which is the aim of prayer. The direction is thus laid down in the Qur'ān: "And if you are sick or on a journey or one of you comes from the privy, or you have had contact with women, and you cannot find water, betake yourselves (*tayammamū*) to pure earth and wipe your faces and your hands therewith. Allāh desires not to place a burden on you but He wishes to purify you and that He may complete His favour on you, so that you may give thanks" (5 : 6). Thus when a man is unable to find water, or when the use of water or the taking of a bath is harmful, he is enjoined to avail himself of pure earth, and this use of earth, instead of water, is stated to be a means of purification. Now, though earth may, under certain conditions, be a purifier, it is clear that the wiping of the face and the hands with it does not serve the purpose of bodily purification; yet it is plainly called a means of purification, and therefore it is the purification of the soul which is intended here. By the order of *tayammum*,[23] attention is thus drawn to the inner purpose underlying *wudzū'* and the bath. As stated in the Qur'ān, and amplified in Tradition, *tayammum* consists in striking both hands on pure earth or anything containing pure dust, then blowing off the excess of dust from the hands, and passing the hands over the face and the backs of the two hands, the left over the right and the right over the left[24] (Bu. 7 : 4, 5).

[23] The word *tayammum* is derived from *amma* meaning *he repaired to a thing*, and *tayammum* therefore means, originally, simply *betaking oneself to a thing*, and since the word is used here in connection with betaking oneself to pure earth, *tayammum* has come technically to mean this particular practice.

[24] There are certain traditions which speak of passing the hands over the parts of the body which are washed in *wudzū'*, but Bukhārī gives no credit to these reports, and heads the fifth chapter of his book of *Tayammum* with the express words: "*Tayammum* is only for *wajh* (the face) and *kaffain* (the two hands)."

SEC. 4 — THE CALL TO PRAYER (ADH̲ĀN)

The origin of **adh̲ān**

The word *adh̲ān* is derived from *idh̲n* which means originally *anything that is heard* (*udh̲un* meaning *the ear*), and hence it comes to mean *knowledge* or *giving knowledge* that a thing is permitted (R.), and *adh̲ān* or *ta'dh̲īn* means an *announcement*, or an *announcement of prayer* and *of the time thereof* — the *call to prayer* (LL.).[25] Regarding the origin of *adh̲ān*, Buk̲h̲ārī tells us that when the Muslims came to Madīnah, they used, at first, to have a time appointed for prayer, at which they all gathered together, but this arrangement being unsatisfactory, a consultation was held at which suggestions for ringing a bell or blowing a horn having been rejected, 'Umar proposed that a man should be appointed who should call out for prayer, at which the Prophet ordered Bilāl to call out for prayers in the words of *adh̲ān* as we now have it (Bu. 10 : 1, 2).[26] The need for the call to prayer was felt after the emigration of the Muslims to Madīnah, because at Makkah the unbelievers did not allow the Muslims to say their prayers openly.

The delivery of **adh̲ān**

The *adh̲ān* is delivered in every mosque, or wherever there is a gathering for congregational prayer,[27] five times a day. The call is given out from a minaret or some raised platform, in as loud a voice as possible, so that it may reach the ears of the greatest possible number of men. The man giving the call stands with his face to the *Qiblah*, *i.e.*, towards Makkah, with both hands raised to the ears, chanting the following sentences in the order given:

[25] The words *adh̲ān* (9 : 3) and *adh̲dh̲ana*, the perfect form of *ta'dh̲īn* and *mu'adh̲dh̲in*, the nominative form (7 : 44; 12 : 70), have been used in the Qur'ān in the general sense of *making an announcement*, while the call to prayer is expressed by the word *nidā* (5 : 58; 62 : 9), which means *calling out*, with the addition of the words *li-l-ṣalāh*, or *for prayer*.

[26] There are other traditions which speak of the visions of 'Abd Allāh ibn Zaid and 'Umar who saw a man calling out for prayer in the words ordered by the Prophet, but it appears also from traditions that the Prophet gave orders before these visions were related to him, and that it was Divine inspiration which guided him to the *adh̲ān*.

[27] Bu. 10 : 18.

اللهُ أَكْبَرُ اللهُ أَكْبَرُ اللهُ أَكْبَرُ اللهُ أَكْبَرُ	Allāhu Akbar, Allāhu Akbar, Allāhu Akbar, Allāhu Akbar.	Allāh is the Greatest (repeated four times).
أَشْهَدُ أَنْ لَّا إِلٰهَ إِلَّا اللهُ أَشْهَدُ أَنْ لَّا إِلٰهَ إِلَّا اللهُ	Ashhadu an lā ilāha ill-Allāh, Ashhadu an lā ilāha ill-Allāh.	I bear witness that nothing deserves to be worshiped except Allāh (repeated twice).
أَشْهَدُ أَنَّ مُحَمَّدًا رَّسُوْلُ اللهِ أَشْهَدُ أَنَّ مُحَمَّدًا رَّسُوْلُ اللهِ	Ashhadu anna Muḥammad-an Rasūlu-llāh, Ashhadu anna Muḥammad-an Rasūlu-llāh.	I bear witness that Muḥammad is the Apostle of Allāh (repeated twice).
حَيَّ عَلَى الصَّلٰوةِ حَيَّ عَلَى الصَّلٰوةِ	Ḥayya 'ala-ṣ-ṣalāḥ, Ḥayya 'ala-ṣ-ṣalāḥ.	Come to prayer (repeated twice, turning the face to the right).
حَيَّ عَلَى الْفَلَاحِ حَيَّ عَلَى الْفَلَاحِ	Ḥayya 'ala-l-falāḥ, Ḥayya 'ala-l-falāḥ.	Come to success (repeated twice, turning the face to the left).
اللهُ أَكْبَرُ اللهُ أَكْبَرُ	Allāhu Akbar, Allāhu Akbar.	Allāh is the Greatest (repeated twice).
لَا إِلٰهَ إِلَّا اللهُ	Lā ilāha ill-Allāh.	Nothing deserves to be worshipped except Allāh.

The following sentence is added in the call to morning prayer after *Ḥayya 'ala-l-falāḥ*:

اَلصَّلٰوةُ خَيْرٌ مِّنَ النَّوْمِ اَلصَّلٰوةُ خَيْرٌ مِّنَ النَّوْمِ	Aṣ-ṣalātu khair-un minan-naum, Aṣ-ṣalātu khair-un minan-naum.	Prayer is better than sleep (repeated twice).

When the call to prayer is finished, the crier as well as the hearers may pray briefly in the following words:

اَللّٰهُمَّ رَبَّ هٰذِهِ الدَّعْوَةِ التَّامَّةِ وَالصَّلٰوةِ الْقَآئِمَةِ اٰتِ مُحَمَّدَنِ الْوَسِيْلَةَ وَالْفَضِيْلَةَ وَابْعَثْهُ مَقَامًا مَّحْمُوْدَانِ الَّذِيْ وَعَدْتَّهٗ	Allāh-umma Rabba hādhihi-da 'wati-t-tāmmati wa-ṣ-ṣalāti-l-qā'imati āti Muḥamada-ni-l-wasīlata wa-l-fadzīlata wa-b'ath-hu maqām-an maḥmūda-nilladhī wa'adta-hū.	O Allāh! the Lord of this perfect call and ever-living prayer, grant to Muḥammad nearness and excellence and raise him to the position of glory which Thou hast promised him.

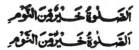

Significance of adhān

The *adhān* is not only an announcement of the time of prayer, but also of the great principles of the faith of Islām and of the significance underlying them. It is an announcement, made five times daily, from hundreds of thousands of minarets, of the unity of God and of the prophethood of Muḥammad, which are the two fundamental principles of Islām. But this announcement goes further and carries also the real significance of the Unity of God which is contained in the words *Allāhu Akbar* or Allāh is the Greatest, so that man must bow only before Him, and before none else. And the real message of religion, the realization of the Divine in man, is declared with equal force — "Come to prayer," and, immediately thereafter — "Come to success"; coming to prayer is the attainment of success in life, because it is only through the realization of the Divine in man that complete self-development (*falāḥ*) is attained. What a noble idea! The meaningless ringing of the bell or the blowing of the trumpet is replaced by an announcement of the principles of Islām and their significance, by a declaration made five times daily, that any one may attain to success in life through the door of the mosque. No more effective propaganda can be thought of. No one need remain in doubt as to what Islām is and what its message is. No one need read books to get at the principles of Islam; no one need listen to a philosophical dissertation as to the significance of those principles; no one need have a doubt as to the end in view in accepting these principles. To every one's door, nay, to his very ears, is carried the message every morning, noon, afternoon, evening and at the time of going to bed, that the Unity of God and the apostleship of Muḥammad are the fundamental principles of Islām, that man must not bow before anything but God, that any one can attain to complete self-development, which is success in life, through the realization of the Divine in him, which is brought about by prayer to God.

SEC. 5 — TIMES OF PRAYER

Regularization of prayer

The institution of prayer in Islām is a perfectly regularized institution, and it is the first lesson which a Muslim learns in the organization of things. Without divesting the individual of his liberty to pray to God at whatsoever place and time and in whatsoever manner he likes, Islām has thoroughly organized the institution of prayer. As stated earlier, prayer brings about not only the development of the individual but also a perfect development of society, being a means for the unification of humanity. This latter object cannot be obtained without a properly organized institution of prayer with a fixed place and fixed times and a uniform method, so that through it individuals may be brought together. Hence it is that the Qur'ān requires prayer to be said at appointed times: "Prayer indeed has been enjoined on the believers at fixed times" (4 : 103).

Times of prayer

The Qur'ān does not explicity state that prayer should be said at such and such times, but it does give indications of the times of prayer. For example, it is stated in a very early revelation: "Keep up prayer from the declining of the sun till the darkness of the night, and the recital of the Qur'ān[28] at dawn; surely the recital of the Qur'ān at dawn is witnessed" (17 : 78). There are four prayers which follow one another successively, the two afternoon prayers and the two evening prayers; and the time of each of these extends till the time of the next following prayer, with the exception of a very short interval, when the sun is actually setting, between the late afternoon and the sunset prayer. These four prayers are, therefore, spoken of together in the words "from the declining of the sun till the darkness of the night", and the morning prayer is mentioned separately. In another verse it is stated: "And celebrate the praise of thy Lord before the rising of the sun and before its setting, and glorify Him during hours of the night and parts of the day, that thou mayest be well-pleased" (20 : 130). That the glorification here referred to is prayer, is shown by the context, since 20 : 132 says: "And enjoin prayer on thy people and steadily adhere to it." Here the morning prayer and the late afternoon prayer are indicated, while the two evening prayers are spoken of together. A third verse of the later Makkan period throws further light on the times of the prayers: "And keep up prayer in the two parts of the day and in the first hour of the night" (11 : 114). The addition of the words "first hours" of the night here makes it clear that, apart from a prayer in the darkness of the night, which is spoken of in

[28] The name given to the early morning prayer is an indication that there is usually a comparatively longer recitation of the Qur'ān in it.

17 : 78, there is also a prayer in the "first hours," that is to say, immediately after sunset. Thus the morning prayer, the early afternoon and the night prayer are referred to in 17 : 78, the late afternoon prayer in 20 : 130, and the sunset prayer in 11 : 114.

Five obligatory prayers

The five times of prayer are thus mentioned in the Qur'ān, not in one place but in many, as if by way of reference to something which already existed. As a matter of fact, the Qur'ān only enjoins the *iqāmah*, or organization, of prayer and the details of that organization were given by the Prophet guided by the Holy Spirit (Bu. 9 : 1) or by inner revelation (*waḥy kh̲afiyy*). The following are the times of the five obligatory prayers, and their names according to the practice (*Sunnah*) of the Prophet:

1. *Fajr*, or the early morning prayer, is said after dawn and before sunrise. It is mentioned by this name in the Qur'ān in 17 : 78 and 24 : 58. This prayer is to be said when a man rises from his sleep in the morning. A Muslim must therefore habituate himelf to rising before sunrise, but if he gets up late sometimes, then the prayer may still be said even though the sun may have risen (Bu. 9 : 35).

2. *Ẓuhr*, or the early afternoon prayer, is said when the sun begins to decline, and its time extends until the next prayer. In the hot season it is better to delay it till the severity of the sun is mitigated a little (Bu. 9 : 9).

3. *Aṣr*, or the late afternoon prayer, is said when the sun is about midway on its course to setting, and its time extends till the sun begins to set. But it is better to say it when the sun is yet high (Bu. 9 : 11).

4. *Mag̲h̲rib*, or the sunset prayer, is said immediately after the sun sets, and its time extends till the red glow in the west disappears.

5. *'Is̲h̲ā'* or the night prayer, is said when the red glow in the west disappears, and its time extends till midnight. It is mentioned by name in the Qur'ān in 24 : 58. This prayer must be said at the time of going to bed, so that it is the last act of the day, just as the morning prayer is the first act of the day.

Combining prayers

The two afternoons prayers, *Ẓuhr* and *'Aṣr*, may be combined when one is on a journey, and so may the two night prayers, *Mag̲h̲rib* and

'Ishā' (Bu. 18 : 13, 14, 15). Such a combination is also allowed in inclement weather, and according to one tradition this combination may be effected even when there is neither journey nor rain. Thus Ibn 'Abbās says: "The Prophet (may peace and the blessings of Allāh be upon him) combined the *Ẓuhr* and *'Aṣr* prayers, eight *rak'ahs*, and the *Maghrib* and *'Isha'* prayers, seven *rak'ahs* , and this was in Madīnah. Ayyub said, "It may have been on a rainy night." He replied "May be" (Bu. 9 : 12). The Prophet was in this case in Madīnah, and therefore not journeying, and as to rain, the narrator was not sure. The same tradition appearing in *Muslim* is clearer on this point. Ibn 'Abbās' report, there, is in the following words: "The Prophet combined the *Ẓuhr* and *'Aṣr* prayers and the *Magṛib* and *'Ishā'* prayers when there was neither journey nor fear," and being asked why he did it, the reply was, "so that his followers may not be in difficulty" (M. 6 : 8). According to another report, the words are that combination was effected in Madīnah when there was neither fear nor rain (M. 6 : 5). This combination is called *jam' bain al-ṣalātain* or the combination of two prayers, and both prayers may be said at the time of the earlier prayer, which is called *jam' taqdīm*, or an early combination, or at the time of the later prayer, which is called *jam' tạkhir*, or a late combination.

Voluntary prayers

The only voluntary prayer spoken of in the Qurān is *Tahajjud*[29] (17 : 79). This night prayer finds frequent mention in the Qur'ān and, while it is voluntary for the Muslims generally, the Prophet, in one of the earliest revelations, was commanded to observe it: "O thou who hast wrapped up thyself! Rise to pray by night except a little, half of it, or lessen it a little, or add to it, and recite the Qur'ān in a leisurely manner" (73 : 1 - 4). And in the same chapter, we are told further on, that this prayer was regularly observed by the Prophet and even by his Companions: "Thy Lord knows indeed that thou passest in prayer nearly two-thirds of the night and sometimes half of it, and sometimes a third of it, and also a party of those with thee" (73 : 20). Still, as 17 : 79 shows, it is called a voluntary prayer (*nāfilah*). It is said after midnight, after one has had some sleep.[30]

[29] *Tahajjud* is derived from *hajada* meaning *he was wakeful in the night* (LL.).

[30] In some traditions another voluntary prayer, the *Ḍuḥā*, is mentioned. *Dzuḥā* is the time before noon, when the sun is high on the horizon, and the prayer said at this time is called *Ḍuḥā*.

SEC. 6 — THE SERVICE

The form of the prayer

The Arabic word for prayer is *ṣalāt*, which originally means *praying* or *the making of a supplication*, and was employed in this sense before Islām. In the Qur'ān, the word is used both in the technical sense of Divine service as established by Islām, and in a general sense. In the latter, it means simply *praying* or *making a supplication.*[31] In the technical sense it is almost always used with one of the derivatives of the word *iqāmah*. *Aqāmah* means *he kept a thing* or *an affair in a right state* (LL.). Hence the *iqāma* of *ṣalāh* would mean the *keeping of the prayer in a right state*, which includes both the proper observance of the outward form and maintaining its true spirit. The purification before prayer, the mosque, the fixing of times and finally the settling of the form, are all parts of the outward organization, without which the spirit could not have been kept alive. To keep alive the spirit, an outward form is essential, for the spirit cannot live without a body. This is as true of institutions as of life. To maintain the spirit of law and order is the object of every good government, yet this spirit cannot be maintained without an external form. If therefore the object of religion is to enable man to seek and maintain a relationship with the Divine Spirit, that object cannot be attained without a form. In fact, as already stated, the great end in view, *viz.*, to bring about the unity of the human race through Divine service, could not have been attained without a regularity in form and without a uniformity prevailing throughout the whole of the Muslim world. Hence a form has been fixed for the institution of the Islamic prayer, the individual having, in addition, liberty to pray to God in accordance with the desire of his own soul, when and where and as he likes. Like the times of prayer, the form was revealed to the Prophet by the Holy Spirit or Gabriel.

The maintenance of the spirit of prayer

The outward form is not, however, the end; it is only a help, a means to gain the end which is the maintaining of a true relationship with the

[31] As in the verse: "Take alms out of their property — thou wouldst cleanse them and purify them thereby — and pray for them; surely thy prayer (*salāh*) is a relief to them" (9 : 103).

Divine Spirit and purification of all evil inclinations. Thus in the Qur'ān, the observance of the form of the prayer is spoken of as being meant to free a man from evil: "And keep up prayer at the two ends of the day and in the first hours of the night. Surely good deeds take away evil deeds. This is a reminder for the mindful" (11 : 114). And only they are said to attain self-development or success, who are true to the spirit of the prayer: "Successful indeed are the believers, who are humble in their prayers" (23 : 1, 2). And the mere form without the spirit is condemned in one of the earliest revelations: "So woe to the praying ones, who are unmindful of (the spirit of) their prayers" (107 : 4, 5). It is a mistake to think that Islām only requires the form to be observed; it no doubt enjoins a form, but only a form with a spirit in it.

Parts of Divine service

The Divine service, as already shown, is held five times a day, and each service has two parts, the congregational, which is called *fardz* (obligatory), and individual, which is called *sunnah* (the Prophet's practice). Each is made up of a number of *rak'ahs*[32] varying from two to four. Technically *rak'ah* means one complete act of devotion which includes standing, bowing down, prostration and sitting reverentially, and is thus a kind of a unit in the Divine service. The order in which these different postures are adopted is a natural order. The worshipper first stands reverentially, and offers certain prayers; then he bows down and glorifies God; then he stands up again praising God; then falls prostrate placing his forehead on the ground and glorifying God; then he sits down in a reverential position and makes a petition; then again falls down in prostration. Each change of posture[33] is performed with the utterance of the words *Allāhu Akbar* meaning "Allāh is the Greatest". This is called *takbīr* which means *magnifying* or *extolling the greatness (of God).*

The obligatory part of the prayer (*fardz*), which, in a congregation, is performed after the *Imām*, contains the following number of *rak'ahs*:

1. *Fajr,* or morning prayer...	2 *rak'ahs.*
2. *Ẓuhr,* or early afternoon prayer...	4 *rak'ahs.*
3. *'Aṣr,* or late afternoon prayer...	4 *rak'ahs.*

[32] The word *rak'ah* is derived from *raka'a* meaning *he bowed down,* and literally the *rak'ah* is an act of bowing down before God.

[33] With two exceptions mentioned later.

4. *Maghrib,* or sunset prayer... 3 *rak'ahs.*
5. *'Ishā'* or night prayer... 4 *rak'ahs.*

The individual parts which are called *sunnah* (Prophet's practice) contain the following number of *rak'ahs:*

1. *Fajr,* 2 *rak'ahs* before the congregational prayer.
2. *Ẓuhr,* 4 *rak'ahs* before the congregational prayer and 2 after it.
3. *Maghrib,* 2 *rak'ahs* after the congregational prayer.
4. *'Ishā',* 2 *rak'ahs* after the congregational prayer, followed by three *rak'ahs* called *witr* (lit., *odd number*). The latter are really a part of the voluntary prayer (*Tahajjud*) which consists of two *rak'ahs* said successively four times, followed by three *rak'ahs.*

Posture of qiyām

Every *rak'ah* consists of four parts. The first of these is the standing position (*qiyām*), with which the prayer is started. The worshipper, turning his face towards the Ka'bah, the Central Mosque of the world, raises both hands to his ears and utters the *takbīr.*[34] As a sign of reverence for the Holy Presence, before Whom the worshipper stands, the hands are thereafter folded on the breast, the wrist of the right hand being just over the wrist of the left. That is the preferable position, but they may as well be folded lower below the navel, the palm of the right hand being over the left. Or they may be left quite free in the natural position.[35] These are small matters in which people may differ according to their tastes. The essential factor is that the worshipper should stand in a reverential position, having the feeling that he is standing before the Holy and Majestic Presence. In this standing position (*qiyām*), the Divine Being is praised and prayers are addressed to Him and certain portions of the Qur'ān are recited, as will be explained later on.

[34] The utterance of the same words at the opening of prayers is called *takbīr taḥrīma* or *takbīrat al-iḥrām*, the words *tahrīm* and *iḥrām* meaning *prohibition.* This particular name is given to this *tabkīr* because with its utterance, attention to everything but prayer is prohibited.

[35] According to Imām Abū Hanīfah the hands are folded below the navel, and according to Shāfi'ī over the breast, while Imām Mālik is reported as leaving the hands free (H. *Kitāb al-ṣalāt*), the Shi'ahs doing the same. But there is a report from Imām Mālik that the hands must be folded (Ma. 8 : 3).

Posture of **rukū‘**

The *qiyām* is followed by the *rukū‘* which means *bowing down*. In this posture the worshipper, while standing, bows forward and places both his hands on his knees and utters words declaring Divine glory.

Posture of **sajdah**

Next comes the *sajdah*, or prostration, but before falling down in *sajdah* the worshipper rises up from the *rukū‘*, so that he again assumes the standing position with both hands hanging down freely, and along with the assumption of this position the following words, and not *takbīr*, are uttered: *Sami‘ Allāhu li-man ḥamidah*, meaning, Allāh listens to him who praises Him. And, with this, words of Divine praise are uttered, *Rabba-nā wa la-k-al-ḥamd*, that is, "Our Lord! all praise is due to Thee".[36] After thus standing up, the worshipper prostrates himself with "Allāhu Akbar" on his lips. In this state, the toes of both feet, both knees, both hands and the forehead touch the ground, and thus a posture of the utmost humility is assumed, while words declaring the Divine glory and Divine greatness are on the lips of the worshipper. This posture is assumed twice, the worshipper in between raising his head with the *takbīr* on his lips, and briefly assumes the sitting position, as described in the next paragraph.

Posture of **qa‘dah**

The *qa‘dah*, meaning *sitting*, follows every two *rak‘ahs*.[37] If it is the first *rak‘ah*, then after performing the second *sajdah*, the worshipper stands up and performs the second *rak‘ah* in exactly the same manner as the first, after which the sitting position (*qa‘dah*) is assumed. In this posture, the right foot remains in a standing position, as in the *sajdah*, the tips of the toes touching the ground, while the left foot is spread with its back in contact with the ground, and the open hands placed on the knees.[38] This

[36] This is one of the exceptions to the utterance of *takbīr* on the change of posture, the other being the final act of finishing the prayer which is by means of a salutation instead of *takbīr*.

[37] The short sitting between two sajdahs being called *Jalsah* which also means *sitting*.

[38] If a man by reason of any difficulty cannot assume this position with ease, he may adopt any reverential sitting posture which he finds easy.

position is kept so long as the necessary recitals are made. If the prayer consists of two *rak'ahs*, it ends in this position. In the case of three or four *rak'ahs* the standing position is again assumed and the required number of *rak'ahs* performed in the same manner. The last position, with which the prayer comes to an end, is in all cases the sitting position (*qa'dah*), and the prayer concludes with *taslīm i.e.*, the utterance of the words *al-salāmu 'alai-kum wa raḥmatu-llah*, or "Peace be on you and the mercy of Allāh!"

Is a departure from these postures allowable?

It may be added here that the four positions, *qiyām, rukū', sajdah* and *qa'dah*, are all the possible positions which a man can assume to show reverence, and, so far as the physical position of the worshipper is concerned, the form adopted is the most perfect possible and leaves nothing to be desired. The different postures, even if unaccompanied by any prayers to or praise of the Divine Being, with silent contemplation of the Divine Presence, are sufficient to inspire the heart of the worshipper with true awe of the Divine Being, and to bring before his mind a picture of the great majesty and glory of God, as he stands up, then bows down, then places his forehead on the ground. The law allows certain modifications in certain cases; as, for instance, when a person is sick, he may say his prayers in a sitting position, or if unable to sit down, he may say them while lying down, dispensing with even the *rukū'* and the *sajdah* if necessary. So, on a journey, a man is allowed to say his prayers while riding a horse or a camel (Bu. 18 : 7, 19), and though this is expressly allowed only in the case of voluntary prayers, the obligatory (*fardz*) prayer, in a railway carriage, on a boat or in an aeroplane seat would follow the same rule, and the postures adopted in all such cases must be subject to the exigencies of the situation. Even the direction may not be towards *Qiblah*. But when there is no exigency, a departure from the form prescribed by the Prophet may not be made.

The question is sometimes asked if these positions are essential, and if an alteration in them would, in any way, affect the value of the prayer. Suppose a man simply kneels down and bows his head a little; another man on a chair bows his forehead on to a table placed before him; would it not answer the purpose? Another suggestion is that there should be arrangements in mosques similar to those in churches. These are undoubtedly the suggestions of persons who do not want to mix with their humbler brethen, and the next step would be to have separate seats for distinguished men, so that they may be able to hold their heads above others proudly even in the House of God. The result would be a death-blow to the very object at which Islām aims through the institution of prayer — *i.e.*, the creating of a spirit of humility and the levelling of differences between man and man. The spiritual experience of the man who lays his forehead on the ground, as a sign of the utmost humility, must be altogether different from that of him who sits in a chair; for it cannot be denied that the different postures of the body have a corresponding effect on the mind, and Islām seeks to make the spiritual experience of the Muslim perfect by making him assume one position of reverential humility after another, so that he may pass from one experience to another. And what, after all, is the idea at the bottom of all these suggestions? Only that such a man thinks himself too important to place his forehead on the ground before his Maker. Surely such a man will fail to acquire any spiritual experience of true humility, and prayer for him will have no value.

Dhikr

Corresponding to the different postures of humility which the worshipper assumes in saying his prayers, he is enjoined to give expression to the praise and glory of God, to His great attributes of love, mercy, forgiveness, etc., to confess his own weakness, to pray for Divine help to support him in his weakness and for Divine guidance to lead him aright and make him achieve the goal of his existence. All such expressions are known in Arabic by the one name *dhikr*, which is generally translated as *remembrance*. The whole of prayer is called in the Qur'ān *dhikr-Allāh*, or the remembrance of Allāh.[39] The Qur'ān itself is also frequently referred to as *dhikr*. Hence, whether a portion of the Qur'ān is recited in prayer, or words giving expression to Divine glory and greatness are uttered, as taught by the Prophet, all goes by the name of *dhikr*.

[39] 29 : 45; 62 : 9; 63 : 9 etc.

Dhikr *in* qiyām

The *qiyām* (standing posture) starts with the *takbīr*[40] or the utterance of "Allāhu Akbar". Nothing besides the *takbīr* must be said to open the prayers. To announce that the worshipper intends to say so many *rak'ahs, fardz* or *sunnah*, having his face towards the *Qiblah*, and so on, is simply absurd, as no trace of it is met with in the practice of the Prophet (*Sunnah*) or in the practice of sayings of the Companions or the followers of the four *Imāms* (ZM. I, p. 51).

Between the first *takbīr* and the recital of the Opening chapter of the Qur'ān, which is the most essential part of the prayer, several kinds of *dhikr*[41] are reported from the Prophet. The best known, which the Caliph 'Umar used to recite,[42] is as follows:

سُبْحَانَكَ اللّٰهُمَّ وَبِحَمْدِكَ وَتَبَارَكَ
اسْمُكَ وَتَعَالٰى جَدُّكَ وَلَآ
اِلٰهَ غَيْرُكَ

Subḥāna-k-Allāh-umma wa bi-ḥamdi-ka wa tabā-raka-smu-ka wa ta-'alā jaddu-ka wa lā ilāha ghairu-ka (Ad. 2 : 120).

Glory to Thee, O Allāh, and Thine is the praise, and blessed is Thy name, and exalted is Thy majesty, and there is none to be served besides Thee.

This *dhikr* is uttered in a low voice not heard by others. Bukhārī however relates a tradition from Abū Hurairah, according to which the Prophet addressed the following prayer after the first *takbīr*:

اللّٰهُمَّ بَاعِدْ بَيْنِيْ وَبَيْنَ خَطَايَايَ
كَمَا بَاعَدْتَ بَيْنَ الْمَشْرِقِ
وَالْمَغْرِبِ اللّٰهُمَّ نَقِّنِيْ مِنَ الْخَطَايَا
كَمَا يُنَقَّى الثَّوْبُ الْاَبْيَضُ مِنَ
الدَّنَسِ اللّٰهُمَّ اغْسِلْ خَطَايَايَ
بِالْمَاءِ وَالثَّلْجِ وَالْبَرَدِ

Allāh-umma bā'id bainī wa baina khaṭāyā-ya kamā bā'adta bain-al-mashriqi wa-l-maghribi; Allāh-umma naqqinī min-al-khaṭāyā kamā yunaqqa-th-thaub-ul-abyadzu min-ad-danasi; Allaḥ-umma aghsil khaṭāyā-ya bi-l-mā'i wa-th-thalji wa-l-baradi (Bu. 10 : 80).

O Allāh! keep faults as distant from me as the east is distant from the west; O Allāh! cleanse me of all faults as a white cloth is cleansed of dirt; O Allāh! wash away my faults with water and snow and hail.

40 Called *takbīr al-iḥrām.*

41 This *dhikr* is called *istiftāh.*

42 This is met with in a tradition of the *Sunan* (ZM. I, p. 52).

Still another form, mentioned in other traditions, is as follows:

إني وجهت وجهي للذي فطر
السموات والأرض حنيفا وما أنا
من المشركين ۝ إن صلاتي
ونسكي ومحياي ومماتي لله رب
العلمين ۝ لا شريك له وبذلك
أمرت وأنا من المسلمين ۝ اللهم
أنت الملك لا إله إلا أنت أنت
ربي وأنا عبدك ظلمت نفسي
واعترفت بذنبي فاغفر لي
ذنوبي جميعا لا يغفر الذنوب
إلا أنت واهدني لأحسن الأخلاق
لا يهدي لأحسنها إلا أنت واصرف
عني سيئها لا يصرف سيئها
إلا أنت

Innī wajjahtu wajhiya li-lladhi faṭar-al-samāwāti wa-l-ardza ḥanīf-an wa mā anā min-al-mushrikīn. Inna ṣalāṭī wa nusukī wa maḥyā-ya wa mamātī li-llāhi Rabbi-l-‘ālamin. lā sharīka la-hū wa bi-dhā-lika umirtu wa anā min-al-Muslimīn. Allāh-umma anta-l Maliku lā ilāha illā anta. anta Rabbī wa anā ‘abdu-ka, ẓalamtu nafsī wa‘-taraftu bi-dhanbī fa-ghfir-lī dhunūbī jamī‘-an lā yaghfiru-l-dhunūba illā anta, wah-di-nī li-aḥsani-l-akhlāqi lā yahdī li-aḥsani-hā illā anta wa-ṣrif ‘anni sayyi’a-hā lā yaṣrifu sayyi’a-hā illā anta. (AD. 2 : 119).

Surely I have turned myself, being upright, wholly to Him Who originated the heavens and the earth and I am not of the polytheists. Surely my prayer and my sacrifice and my life and my death are for Allāh, the Lord of the worlds, no associate has He; and this I am commanded and I am one of those who submit. O Allāh! Thou art the King, none is to be served but Thee; Thou art my Lord and I am Thy servant; I have been unjust to myself and I confess my shortcomings, so forgive Thou all my shortcomings, for none forgives the shortcomings but Thou. O Allāh! Guide me to the best of morals, none guides to the best of them but Thou, and turn away from me bad morals, none can turn away bad morals but Thou.

Some other forms are also given in Tradition, which shows that if the worshipper offers any other prayer or utters any other words glorifying the Divine Being it is quite permissible to do so.

The above *dhikr* is followed by the words:

أعوذ بالله من الشيطن الرجيم ۝

A’ūdhū bi-llāhi mina l-shaiṭani-l-rajīm.

I seek the refuge of Allāh from the accursed devil.

The *dhikr* mentioned above is peculiar, to the opening *rak‘ah* of a prayer. It is actually with the Opening chapter of the Qur’ān (*Fātiḥah*) that the prayer opens, for it is this short chapter (*sūrah*) that is recited in every *rak‘ah*. The *Fātiḥah*, the salient points of which have already been given, runs thus:

بِسْمِ اللّٰهِ الرَّحْمٰنِ الرَّحِيْمِ ○
اَلْحَمْدُ لِلّٰهِ رَبِّ الْعٰلَمِيْنَ ○
الرَّحْمٰنِ الرَّحِيْمِ ○ مٰلِكِ يَوْمِ
الدِّيْنِ ○ اِيَّاكَ نَعْبُدُ وَاِيَّاكَ
نَسْتَعِيْنُ ○ اِهْدِنَا الصِّرَاطَ
الْمُسْتَقِيْمَ ○ صِرَاطَ الَّذِيْنَ
اَنْعَمْتَ عَلَيْهِمْ ۙ غَيْرِ الْمَغْضُوْبِ
عَلَيْهِمْ وَلَا الضَّآلِّيْنَ ○

Bi-smi-llāhi-r-Raḥmāni-r-Raḥim.	In the name of Allāh, the Beneficent, the Merciful.
1. Al-ḥamdu li-llāhi Rabbi-l-'ālamīn.	1. Praise be to Allāh, the Lord of the worlds.
2. Ar-Raḥmāni-r-Raḥīm.	2. The Beneficent, the Merciful.
3. Māliki yaumi-d-dīn.	3. Master of the Day of Requital.
4. Iyyā-ka na'budu wa iyyā-ka nasta'īn.	4. Thee do we serve and Thee do we beseech for help.
5. Ihdi-na-ṣ-ṣirāṭ-al-mustaqīm:	5. Guide us on the right path:
6. Ṣirāṭ-alladhīna an'amta 'alai-him.	6. The path of those upon whom Thou hast bestowed favours.
7. Ghairi-l-maghdzūbi 'alai-him wa la-dz dzāllīn.	7. Not those upon whom wrath is brought down, nor those who go astray.

At the close of the above is said "Āmin!" which means "Be it so!"[43]

The recital of the *Fātiḥah* is followed by any other portion of the Qur'ān,[44] it may be a short or a long chapter or it may be one or more verses selected from anywhere. A short chapter, *al-Ikhlās* or Unity[45] which in its four very short verses contains the doctrine of the Unity of the Divine Being in its perfection, is given below:

بِسْمِ اللّٰهِ الرَّحْمٰنِ الرَّحِيْمِ ○
قُلْ هُوَ اللّٰهُ اَحَدٌ ○ اَللّٰهُ الصَّمَدُ ○
لَمْ يَلِدْ وَلَمْ يُوْلَدْ ○ وَلَمْ يَكُنْ
لَّهٗ كُفُوًا اَحَدٌ ○

Bi-smi-llāhi-r-Raḥmāni-r-Raḥim.	In the name of Allāh, the Beneficent, the Merciful.
1. Qul huw-Allāhu Aḥad.	1. Say, He, Allāh, is One.
2. Allāhu-l-Ṣamad.	2. Allāh is He on Whom all depend.
3. Lam yalid wa lam yūlad.	3. He begets not nor is He begotten.
4. Wa lam yakun la-hū kufuwan aḥad.[46]	4. And none is like Him.

[43] The Prophet used to pause a little after the recital of the *Fātiḥah* (Bu. 10 : 39; ZM. I, p. 53); perhaps he used this pause to offer some prayer to the Divine Being on his own behalf or on behalf of his community.

[44] Called *qirā'ah*.

[45] The 112th chapter of the Qur'ān.

[46] The first verse declares the Oneness of God and thus denies any sort of plurality in the Divine Being, such as the Christian doctrine of the Trinity or the Magian doctrine of duality or the Hindu doctrine of polytheism. The second verse declares that nothing

It may be noted here that while the Opening chapter *Fātiḥah* is essential to prayer and must be recited in every *rak'ah* in the standing position, the addition thereto of any other portion of the Qur'an is dispensed with in certain cases, as in the third or fourth *rak'ah* in case of a congregational prayer. A little pause was also generally observed by the Prophet after *qira'āh* before assuming the next posture (*rukū'*).

Dhikr *in* rukū' *and* sajdah

The *dhikr* in the state of *sajdah* differs but slightly from that in *rukū'*. Of the following, the first is the best-known *dhikr* for *rukū'*, the second for *sajdah*, while the third is an alternative form for either:

(١) سُبْحَانَ رَبِّيَ الْعَظِيْمِ	1. Subḥāna Rabbiy-al-'Aẓim (AD. 2 : 149).	Glory to my Lord, the Great.
(٢) سُبْحَانَ رَبِّيَ الْأَعْلٰى	2. Subḥān Rabbiy-al-'A'la (*Ibid.*)	Glory to my Lord, the most High.
(٣) سُبْحَانَكَ اللّٰهُمَّ رَبَّنَا وَبِحَمْدِكَ اللّٰهُمَّ اغْفِرْ لِيْ	3. Subḥāna-k-Allāh-umma Rabba-nā wa bi-ḥamdi-ka Allāh-ummagh-fir-lī (*Ibid.*).	Glory to Thee, O Allāh our Lord! and Thine is the praise; O Allāh, grant me protection!

This *dhikr* is repeated thrice, while to it may be added any other prayer. The *sajdah*, in particular, is the most fitting position for addressing any prayer in any language to the Almighty. There are reports showing that the Prophet used to pray in the *sajdah* in both forms: in the form of glorifying and praising the Divine Being and in the form of petition or asking the Divine Being for His favours (ZM. I, p. 60). Numerous forms of these prayers are given in Tradition, and all of them show an outpouring of the soul in a state of true submission, which is what, in fact, every worshipper needs, and therefore he is free to express the yearning of his soul before his great Maker in any way that he likes.

is independent of God, and thus denies the independent existence of matter and soul, a doctrine held by a Hindū sect of recent growth, the Ārya Samāj. The third verse is plain enough: God cannot be described either as a Father or as a Son as the Christians hold, nor has He any daughters as some idolators said. The fourth verse declares that none is like God, and thus deals a death-blow to such doctrines as those of Incarnation and Manifestation, the latter being the basic doctrine of the Bahā'ī religion.

Dhikr *in the sitting posture*

There are two sitting postures, the first being the *jalsa*, the short sitting between the two *sajdahs*. The prayer addressed in this position is as follows:

اَللّٰهُمَّ اغْفِرْ لِيْ وَارْحَمْنِيْ وَاهْدِنِيْ
وَعَافِنِيْ وَارْزُقْنِيْ (ابو داؤد)
وَاجْبُرْنِيْ وَارْفَعْنِيْ (ابن ماجہ)

Allāh-umma-ghfir-lī wa rḥam-nī wa-hdi-nī wa 'āfi-nī wa-rzuq-nī (AD. 2 : 143).
wa-jbur-nī wa-rfa'nī (IM. 5 : 23).

O Allāh! grant me protection and have mercy on me and grant me security and guide me and grant me sustenance and set right my affairs and exalt me!

The second sitting position, the *qa'dah*, is assumed after two *rak'ahs* have been offered. And then the following prayer, called *al-tashshahud*, is offered.

اَلتَّحِيَّاتُ لِلّٰهِ وَالصَّلَوٰتُ وَالطَّيِّبَاتُ
اَلسَّلَامُ عَلَيْكَ اَيُّهَا النَّبِيُّ وَرَحْمَةُ
اللّٰهِ وَبَرَكَاتُهٗ اَلسَّلَامُ عَلَيْنَا
وَعَلٰى عِبَادِ اللّٰهِ الصّٰلِحِيْنَ اَشْهَدُ
اَنْ لَّآ اِلٰهَ اِلَّا اللّٰهُ وَاَشْهَدُ اَنَّ
مُحَمَّدًا عَبْدُهٗ وَرَسُوْلُهٗ

At-taḥyyātu li-llāhi wa-ṣ-ṣalawātu wa-ṭayyi bātu; as-salāmu 'alai-ka ayyuha-n-nabiyyu wa raḥmatu-llāhi wa bara-kātuhū, as-salāmu 'alai-nā wa 'alā 'ibādi-llāhi-ṣ-ṣāliḥ īn. Ashadu an lā ilāha ill-Allāhu wa ashhadu anna Muḥammad-an 'abdu-hū wa rasūluh. (Tr. 2 : 100).

All services rendered by words and bodily actions and sacrifice of wealth are due to Allāh. Peace be on thee, O Prophet! and the mercy of Allāh and His blessings. Peace be on us and on the righteous servants of Allāh. I bear witness that none deserves to be worshipped but Allāh, and I bear witness that Muḥammad is His servant and His Apostle.

If this is only the intermediate sitting in a prayer of three or four *rak'ahs*, the worshipper stands up after the above-mentioned *dhikr*, but if it is the final sitting, whether in a prayer of two or three or four *rak'ahs*, the following *dhikr*, called *al-ṣalā 'ala-l-Nabiyy*, is added:

اَللّٰهُمَّ صَلِّ عَلٰى مُحَمَّدٍ وَّعَلٰى
اٰلِ مُحَمَّدٍ كَمَا صَلَّيْتَ عَلٰى اِبْرٰهِيْمَ
وَعَلٰى اٰلِ اِبْرٰهِيْمَ اِنَّكَ حَمِيْدٌ
مَّجِيْدٌ اَللّٰهُمَّ بَارِكْ عَلٰى مُحَمَّدٍ
وَّعَلٰى اٰلِ مُحَمَّدٍ كَمَا بَارَكْتَ عَلٰى
اِبْرٰهِيْمَ وَعَلٰى اٰلِ اِبْرٰهِيْمَ اِنَّكَ
حَمِيْدٌ مَّجِيْدٌ

Allāh-umma ṣalli 'alā Muḥammad-in wa 'alā āli Muḥummad-in kamā ṣallai-ta 'alā Ibrāhīma wa 'alā ā li Ibrāhima inna-ka Ham-īd-un Majīd. Allāhu-umma bārik 'alā Muḥammad-in wa alā āli Muḥammad-in kamā bā rakta 'alā Ibrāhīma wa 'alā āli Ibrāhīma inna-ka Hamī d-un Majīd. (AD. 2 : 181).

O Allāh! Exalt Muḥammad and the true followers of Muḥammad as Thou didst exalt, Abraham and the true followers of Abraham; surely Thou art Praised, Magnified. O Allāh! Bless Muḥammad and the true followers of Muḥammad as Thou didst bless Abraham and the true followers of Abraham; surely Thou art Praised, Magnified.

The following prayer is then added:

رَبِّ اجْعَلْنِي مُقِيمَ الصَّلٰوةِ وَمِنْ ذُرِّيَّتِي ۖ رَبَّنَا وَتَقَبَّلْ دُعَاءِ رَبَّنَا اغْفِرْ لِي وَلِوَالِدَيَّ وَلِلْمُؤْمِنِينَ يَوْمَ يَقُومُ الْحِسَابُ	Rabbi-j'al-nī muqīma-l-ṣalāti wa min dhurriyyatī Rabba-nā wa taqabbal du'ā'i; Rabba-na-ghfir-lī wa li-wālidayya wa li-l-mu'minīna yauma yaqū mu-l-ḥisāb.	My Lord! make me and my offspring keep up prayer; our Lord! and accept my prayer; our Lord! grant protection to me and my parents and to the believers on the day when the reckoning will take place.

This may be followed by any other prayer which the worshipper may wish to offer. One such prayer, comprehensive in its content, which is given in a tradition, is reproduced below:

اللّٰهُمَّ إِنِّي أَعُوذُ بِكَ مِنَ الْهَمِّ وَالْحُزْنِ وَأَعُوذُ بِكَ مِنَ الْعَجْزِ وَالْكَسَلِ وَأَعُوذُ بِكَ مِنَ الْجُبْنِ وَالْبُخْلِ وَأَعُوذُ بِكَ مِنْ غَلَبَةِ الدَّيْنِ وَقَهْرِ الرِّجَالِ اللّٰهُمَّ اكْفِنِي بِحَلَالِكَ عَنْ حَرَامِكَ وَأَغْنِنِي بِفَضْلِكَ عَمَّنْ سِوَاكَ	Allāh-umma innī a'ūdhu-bi-ka min-al-hammi wa-l-ḥuzni wa a'ụdhu-bi-ka min'al''ijzi wa-l-kasali wa a'ūdhu-bi-ka min-al-'jubni wa-l-bukhli wa a'ụdhu-bi-kamin ghalabati-d-daini wa qahri-r-rijāl; Allāh-umma k-fi-nī bi-ḥalāli-ka 'an ḥarāmi-ka wa-ghni-nī bī-fadzli-ka 'an man siwā-ka.	O Allāh! I seek Thy refuge from anxiety and grief, and I seek Thy refuge from lack of strength and laziness, and I seek Thy refuge from cowardice and niggardliness, and I seek Thy refuge from being overpowered by debt and the oppression of men; O Allāh! suffice Thou me with what is lawful, to keep me away from what is prohibited, and with thy grace make me free from want of what is besides Thee!

The concluding *dhikr* in the sitting position is *taslīm,* or the utterance of the following words:

السَّلَامُ عَلَيْكُمْ وَرَحْمَةُ اللّٰهِ	As-salāmu 'alai-kum wa raḥmatu-llāh.	Peace be on you and the mercy of Allāh.

These words are uttered twice, first turning the face to the right and then turning to the left.

The qunūt

Qunūt comes from *qanata* which means *he was humble in obedience* to God, and *qunūt* is really *a prayer of humility*, but it also means *standing long in prayer*. There are two kinds of *qunūt* spoken of in traditions.

One of these was the prayer which was specially addressed to the Divine Being on the occasion of some great tribulation, as happened when seventy Muslim missionaries were treacherously murdered by the tribes of Ra'l, Dhakwān, etc. (Bu. 14 : 7; 56 : 19). It was a prayer calling for Divine punishment on the tyrants who butchered absolutely innocent people, and this prayer was offered after rising from *rukū'* in the morning and evening congregational prayers. It was on this occasion that the prophet received a revelation (3 : 127), not to pray for the punishment of a people, but still his practice of offering *qunūt* at the time of great disaster or imminent danger was acted upon by his Companions, as by Abū Bakr before the battle with Musailimah (ZM. I, p. 75). The *qunūt* in this case was a prayer to God to avert a calamity.

The more well-known *qunūt* is, however, that offered in the *witr* prayer in the third *rak'ah*. It is based on a tradition related in the *Sunan* and the *Musnad* of Aḥmad, and the words of this prayer, as reported by Ḥasan, son of 'Alī, are as follows:

اَللّٰهُمَّ اهْدِنِيْ فِيْمَنْ هَدَيْتَ
وَعَافِنِيْ فِيْمَنْ عَافَيْتَ وَتَوَلَّنِيْ
فِيْمَنْ تَوَلَّيْتَ وَبَارِكْ لِيْ فِيْمَآ
اَعْطَيْتَ وَقِنِيْ شَرَّ مَا قَضَيْتَ
اِنَّكَ تَقْضِيْ وَلَا يُقْضٰى عَلَيْكَ
اِنَّهٗ لَا يَذِلُّ مَنْ وَّالَيْتَ تَبَارَكْتَ
رَبَّنَا وَتَعَالَيْتَ

Allāh-umma-hdi-nī fī-man hadaita wa 'āfi-nī fī-man 'āfaita wa tawalla-nī fī man tawallaita wa bārik lī fī-ma a'ṭaita wa-qi-nī sharra mā qadzaita inna-ka taqdzī wa lā yuqdzā 'alai-ka, inna-hū lā yadhillu man wālaita tabārakta Rabba-nā wa ta'ālaita (ZM . I, p. 70).

O Allāh! Guide me among those whom Thou hast guided, and preserve me among those whom Thou hast preserved, and befriend me among those whom Thou hast befriended, and bless me in what Thou hast granted, and save me from the evil of what Thou hast ordained, for Thou dost order and no order is given against Thy order; surely he is not disgraced whom Thou befriendest; blessed art Thou, our Lord! and highly exalted.

Another form of *qunūt* is the following:

اللّٰهُمَّ إِنَّا نَسْتَعِينُكَ وَنَسْتَغْفِرُكَ وَنُؤْمِنُ بِكَ وَنَتَوَكَّلُ عَلَيْكَ وَنُثْنِي عَلَيْكَ الْخَيْرَ وَنَشْكُرُكَ وَلَا نَكْفُرُكَ وَنَخْلَعُ وَنَتْرُكُ مَنْ يَفْجُرُكَ اللّٰهُمَّ إِيَّاكَ نَعْبُدُ وَلَكَ نُصَلِّي وَنَسْجُدُ وَإِلَيْكَ نَسْعَى وَنَحْفِدُ وَنَرْجُوا رَحْمَتَكَ وَنَخْشَى عَذَابَكَ إِنَّ عَذَابَكَ بِالْكُفَّارِ مُلْحِقٌ

Allāh-umma innā nasta'īnu-ka wa nastaghfiru-ka wa nu'minu bi-ka wa natawakkalu 'alaika wa nuthnī 'alaik-al-khaira wa nashkuru-ka wa lā nakfuru-ka wa nakhla'u wa natruku man yafjuru-ka Allāh-umma iyyā-ka na'budu wa la-ka nuṣallī wa nasjudu wa-ilai-ka nas'ā wa naḥfidu wa narjū raḥmata-ka wa nakhshā 'adhāba-ka inna 'adhāba-ka bi l-kuffāri mulḥiq.

O Allāh! We beseech Thee for help, and seek Thy protection and believe in Thee and rely on Thee and extol Thee and are thankful to Thee and are not ungrateful to Thee and we declare ourselves clear of, and forsake, him who disobeys Thee. O Allāh! Thee do we serve and for Thee do we pray and prostrate ourselves and to Thee do we betake ourselves and to obey Thee we are quick, and Thy mercy do we hope for, and Thy punishment do we fear, for Thy punishment overtakes the unbelievers.

Dhikr *after finishing prayer*

There is no reference in any tradition to the Prophet raising up the hands for supplication after offering prayers, as is the general practice, but some kinds of *dhikr* are recommended:

أَسْتَغْفِرُ اللّٰهَ رَبِّي مِنْ كُلِّ ذَنْبٍ وَّأَتُوبُ إِلَيْهِ

Astaghfiru-llāh Rabbī min kulli dhanb-in wa atūbu ilai-hi.

I seek the protection of Allāh, my Lord, from every fault and turn to Him.

اللّٰهُمَّ أَنْتَ السَّلَامُ وَمِنْكَ السَّلَامُ تَبَارَكْتَ يَا ذَا الْجَلَالِ وَالْإِكْرَامِ

Allāh-umma anta-s-salāmu wa min-ka-s-salāmu, tabārakta yā dha-l-jalāli wa-l-ikrām.

O Allāh! Thou art the Author of peace, and from Thee comes peace, blessed art Thou, O Lord of Glory and Honour.

لَا إِلٰهَ إِلَّا اللّٰهُ وَحْدَهُ لَا شَرِيكَ لَهُ لَهُ الْمُلْكُ وَالْحَمْدُ وَهُوَ عَلَى كُلِّ شَيْءٍ قَدِيرٌ

Lā ilāha ill-Allāhu waḥda-hū lā sharkīa la-hū, la hu-l-mulku wa-l-ḥamdu wa huwa 'alā kulli shai'-in qadir;

Nothing deserves to be worshipped except Allāh, He is One and has no associate; His is the kingdom and for Him is praise, and He has power over all things.

اللّٰهُمَّ لَا مَانِعَ لِمَا أَعْطَيْتَ وَلَا مُعْطِيَ لِمَا مَنَعْتَ وَلَا يَنْفَعُ ذَا الْجَدِّ مِنْكَ الْجَدُّ

Allāh-umma lā māni'a li-mā a'ṭaita wa lā mu'ṭiya li-mā mana'ta wa lā yanfa'u dha-l-jaddi min-ka-l-jaddu.

O Allāh! there is none who can withhold what Thou grantest, and there is none who can give what Thou withholdest, and greatness does not benefit any possessor of greatness as against Thee.

In addition to these prayers, the recital of verse 2 : 255 of the Qur'ān (*āyat al-kursiyy*) is also recommended, as well as that of the words *subḥān-Allāh* (glory be to Allāh), *al-ḥamduli-ilāh* (praise be to Allāh), and *Allāhu Akbar* (Allāh is the Greatest), several times each.

The congregation

As already noted, the essential part of the obligatory prayers called *fardz* is said in congregation. The very form of the different prayers to be recited shows that Islām has laid special stress on prayer in congregation. The whole Muslim body that can assemble in one place, both men and women, must gather at the appointed time, praise and glorify God, and address their petitions to Him in a body. All people stand shoulder to shoulder in a row, or in several rows, as the case may be, their feet being in one line, and one person, chosen from among them and called the Imām, which means *leader*, leads the prayer and stands in front of all. If, however, there are women in the congregation, they form a row by themselves at the back, and after the congregational prayer is over the men are not allowed to leave their places until the women have gone out. The distance between the Imām and the first row, or between the different rows, is such that the persons in each row may be able to prostrate themselves, so that their heads may be almost at the feet of the front row. This distance would generally be four feet. The smallest number of people that can form a congregation is two, one leading the prayer and the other following, and these two stand together, the Imām a little ahead, say about six inches, and standing to the left while the follower stands on the right. If a third person joins while the prayer is thus being led, either the Imām moves forward or the person following moves backward, so that the two who follow form a row. The people who stand behind are called *muqtadūn* or *followers*, and the discipline is so perfect that the followers are bound to obey the Imām, even though he may make a mistake, though they have the right to point out the mistake, by pronouncing the words *subḥan-Allāh* (glory be to Allāh). This amounts to a hint that God alone is free from all defects, such being the meaning of the word *subḥāna*. It is however the judgment of the Imām which is the decisive factor, and the followers, after giving the hint, must still obey him.

Iqāmah

To announce that the congregational prayer is ready, the *iqāmah* (which means *causing to stand*) is pronounced in a loud voice, though not so loud as the call to prayer (*adhān*). The sentences of the *adhān* are also the sentences which form the *iqāmah*, but with the difference that they may be uttered only once and not repeated, and the following sentence is uttered twice after *ḥayya 'ala-l-falāḥ*:

قد قامت الصلوة Qad qāmati-ṣ-ṣalāh Prayer is ready.

The additional words of the morning *adhān* also do not find a place in the *iqāmah*, which is generally recited by the person who calls out the *adhān*, though in his absence any one else standing behind the Imām may do so.

Congregational prayer

When the *iqāmah* has been called out, the followers do not begin the prayer until the Imām starts it by saying: "Allāhu Akbar" in a loud voice. With the utterance of these words by the Imām, the whole congregation, like the Imām, raises hands to ears while uttering the same words in a low voice. Both the Imām and the followers then recite, still in a low voice, some introductory *dhikr*, as stated above, after which the Imām recites the Opening Chapter of the Qur'ān (*Fātiḥah*) in a loud voice, pausing slightly after every verse, so that during the interval the followers may slowly repeat each sentence. The Ḥanafis,[47] however, hold that the Imām's recitation is sufficient, and that the followers need not recite the sentences of the *Fātiḥah*.

After the Imām has recited *Fātiḥah*, the whole congregation says *Amīn*, either in a loud or a low voice, the former, no doubt, having the greater effect. After this, the Imām recites in a loud voice any portion of the Qur'ān, the followers listening in silence, occasionally glorifying God or praising Him or addressing some petition to Him in accordance with the subject-matter of the verses that are being recited. This procedure is followed in the case of the morning prayer, which consists of only two *rak'ahs* of *fardz*, and of the first two *rak'ahs* of the evening and early night prayers. In the case of the first two *rak'ahs* of the early after-

[47] Belonging to the school of thought of Imām Abū Ḥanīfh.

noon and the late afternoon, prayer is more in the nature of a meditation than a recital, like the private prayer, and the Imām and the followers individually recite the *Fātiḥah* and a portion of the Qur'ān inaudibly. In the last two *rak'ahs* of both the afternoon prayers and the early night prayer, as well as in the last *rak'ah* of the sunset prayer, the *Fātiḥah* is recited in a similar manner, individually and inaudibly. All the *takbīrs* uttered at the changes of posture, and the final *taslīm* ending the prayer, are, however, uttered by the Imām in a loud voice in all congregational prayers, and so is the *dhikr Sami' Allāhu li-man ḥamida-hū* recited on rising from *rukū'*, while the followers in this last case say in a low voice, *Rabba-nā wa la-kal ḥamd*. The *dkikr* in *rukū'* and *sajdah* and the sitting posture is repeated in a low voice by the Imām, as well as those who follow him.

Sajdah sahw

If a mistake is made in prayer, or the worshipper is doubtful about the number of *rak'ahs*, he adds, what is called, *sajdah sahw*, (*sahw* meaning *mistake*) at the close of prayer, just before the *taslīm*. The *sajdah sahw* consists in performing a double prostration like the ordinary prostration in prayer. If the Imām has made a similar mistake, he, along with the whole congregation, performs *sajdah sahw*.

Late-comers

A person who comes in late and joins the congregational service when it has already started, must, if he has missed one or more *rak'ahs*, complete the number after the Imām has finished. A *rak'ah* is deemed to have been completed when a person joins the *rukū'*, though he may have missed the *qiyām*.

Prayer in the case of one who is on a journey

If one is on a journey,[48] the prayers are shortened. The *sunnahs* are all dropped with the exception of the two of the morning prayer, and the number of obligatory *rak'ahs* in the *Ẓuhr, 'Aṣr* and *'Ishā'* prayers,

[48] There is some difference of opinion as to whether it is necesary that the journey should extend over a certain specified distance or a certain specified time. But the best judge on this matter is the person concerned. A time-limit of a day and a night as the minimum is favoured.

which is four ordinarily, is reduced to two. In addition to this, the man who is journeying is allowed to combine the *Ẓuhr* and *'Aṣr* prayers and also the *Maghrib* and *'Ishā* prayers. The *witr* of the *'Ishā'* prayer are also retained. If a man who is on a journey is chosen to lead the prayers, he shortens the prayers, while such of the followers who are not on a journey complete the number of *rak'ahs*; but if the Imām is not on a journey, while some or all of the followers are, the latter do not shorten the prayer.

Prayer service in battles

So much importance is given by the Qur'ān to the holding of Divine service that, even when facing the enemy, it must be held just the same. But this service is much shortened, and its holding is expressly mentioned in the Qur'ān thus: "And when you journey in the earth, there is no blame on you if you shorten the prayer, if you fear that those who disbelieve will give you trouble. Surely the disbelievers are your open enemies. And when thou art among them and leadest the prayer for them, let a party of them stand up with thee and let them take their arms; then when they have performed their prostration, let them go to your rear,and let another party who have not prayed come forward and pray with thee" (4 : 101, 102).

It appears from this that in case when there is fear of enemy's attack, the congregation is divided into two parties, each saying only one *rak'ah* of prayer with the Imām, while the Imām says only two *rak'ahs*. This is called *ṣalāt al-khauf* (or *prayer when there is fear*) (Bu. 12 : 1). In case of still greater fear, it is permitted to say prayers whether on foot or riding (Bu. 12 : 2), as the Qur'ān says: "But if you are in danger, then say your prayers on foot or on horseback" (2 : 239). This, it is explained, is the saying of prayer by *īmā*, *i.e.*, simply by nodding of the head (Bu. 12 : 5).

SEC. 7 — THE FRIDAY SERVICE

Friday service specially ordained

There is no sabbath in Islām, and the number of prayers on Friday is the same as on any other day, with this difference, that the specially ordained Friday service takes the place of the early afternoon prayer. It is the greater congregation of the Muslims at which the people of a place must all gather together, as the very name of the day[49] indicates. Though all prayers are equally obligatory, yet the Qurān has specially ordained the Friday service, and thereat it enjoins all Muslims to gather together: "O you who believe! when the call is sounded for prayer on Friday, hasten to the remembrance of Allāh and leave off traffic; that is better for you if you know" (62 : 9). Any other prayer may be said singly under special circumstances, but not so the Friday service which is essentially a congregational service. For the holding of the Friday service, later jurists have laid down certain conditions which are not met with either in the Qur'ān or in Tradition. The call to prayer, which is mentioned in the Qur'ān, may be made from any mosque whether it be situated in a village or a town or in a certain quarter of a town, or it may even be given, when necessary, from a place where there is no mosque. Bukhārī has a special chapter devoted to this subject headed "Friday service in villages and towns", and he cites the case of Ruzaiq who was manager of a farm and whom Ibn Shahāb enjoined to hold the Friday service on his land (Bu. 11 : 11). It is, however, true that the practice has been for all Muslims, who can do so, to gather together at a central mosque, because the underlying idea is, undoubtedly, to enable the Muslims to meet together once a week in as large a number as possible.

Preparations for the Friday service

The importance of the occasion and the greater number of the persons assembled have made it necessary to issue further instructions regarding cleanliness in preparation for the Friday service. For example, it is recommended that a bath be taken before attending (Bu. 11 : 2); that scent be used (Bu. 11 : 3), and the best clothes available be worn (Bu. 11 : 7); also that the mouth be well-cleaned with a tooth-brush (Bu. 11 : 8). These instructions are intended to foster habits of cleanliness and to make the great concourse of people in Divine service on Friday as little offensive as possible.

[49] *Yaum al-jumu'ah,* literally *the day of gathering.*

The Sermon

A special feature of the Friday service is the sermon (*khuṭbah*)[50] by the Imām, before the prayer Service is held. After the people have assembled in the mosque, the *mu'-adhdhin* makes a call for prayer while the Imām is sitting. When the *adhān* is finished, the Imām stands up facing the audience and delivers the *khuṭbah*. He begins with the *kalimah shahādah*,[51] or words speaking of the praise and glory of God, and then goes on to recite a Qur'ānic text[52] which he expounds to the audience, who are specially enjoined to remain sitting and silent during the sermon (Bu. 11 : 29). This is delivered in two parts, the Imām taking a little rest by assuming the sitting position in the middle of the sermon, and then continuing. Any subject relating to the welfare of the community may be dealt with in the sermon. The Prophet is reported to have once prayed for rain during the sermon,after somebody had directed his attention to the fact that the cattle and the people were in severe hardship on account of drought (Bu. 11 : 35). According to another report, a certain person came to the Prophet when he was delivering a sermon and questioned him about faith, and the Prophet explained to him what faith was and then resumed the sermon (M. 7 : 13). As regards the 'Īd sermons, it is expressly stated that the Prophet used to order the raising of an army, if necessary, in the sermon, to give any other orders which he deemed necessary, in addition to admonitions of a general nature (ZM. I, p. 125). All these facts show that the sermon is for the education of the masses, to awaken them to a general sense of duty, to lead them to the ways of their welfare and prosperity and warn them against that which is a source of loss or ruin to them. Therefore it must be delivered in a language which the people understand, and there is no sense in delivering it in Arabic to an audience which does not know the language. Divine service is quite a different thing from the sermon. The sermon is meant to exhort the people, to give them information as what to do under certain circumstances and what not to do; it is meant, in fact, to throw light on all questions of life; and to understand a sermon in a foreign language requires an extensive, almost an exhaustive, knowledge of that language. Not so in

[50] Lit. an *address*.

[51] *Ashihadu an la ilāha ill-Allāhu wa ashhadū anna Muḥammad-an 'abdu-hū wa rasūlu-hu*. Between the *kalimah shahādah* and recital of a Quranic text occur the words *ammā ba'du,* which mean *after this*.

[52] There is a tradition in *Muslim*, according to which a certain woman learnt the chapter entitled *Qāf* (ch. 50) from the Prophet's recital of it on the pulpit (M. 7 : 13).

the case of Divine service, which consists of a number of stated sentences and the meaning of which can be fully learnt, even by a child, in a short period. Moreover, in Divine service the different postures of the body are in themselves expressive of Divine praise and glory, even if the worshipper does not understand the significance of the words. It is, therefore, of the utmost importance that the masses should know what the preacher is saying in the Friday service which is the best means of education for the masses and for maintaining the vitality of the Muslim community as a whole.

The Friday service

After the sermon is over, the *iqāmah* is pronounced and a congregational service of two *rak'ahs* is held, in which the Imām recites the Opening chapter and a portion of the Qur'ān in a loud voice, as he does in the morning and evening prayers. This is the only obligatory service, but two *rak'ahs sunnah* are said as soon as a man enters the mosque; even if he comes late and the Imām has already started the sermon, the latecomer must still perform these two *rak'ahs* (Bu. 11 : 33). Two *rak'ahs sunnah* are also said after the service has ended (Bu. 11 : 39). There is not the least authority for saying *Ẓuhr* prayers[53] after the Friday service, which in fact takes the place of *Ẓuhr* prayers.

As already stated, there is in Islām no sabbath, or seventh day for Divine worship. Hence the Qur'ān plainly speaks of daily business being done before the Friday service, leaving it only for the sake of the service, and again it speaks of business being done after the service has been held: "But when the prayer is ended, disperse abroad in the land and seek of Allāh's grace" (62 : 10). But as a seventh day is necessary for rest from work, Friday may be chosen, if the choice lies with the Muslims. At any rate, Muslims have a religious right to attend the Friday service even when they are under non-Muslim rule.

[53] The origin of this practice is in the wrong impression that Friday service can only be held in a city or under the Muslim rule. As a matter of fact, as already shown, it may be held in a city or in a village, or anywhere else. So also the condition that it can only be held under Muslim rule is simply absurd. The Qur'ān and the Ḥadīth place no such limitation on the Friday service or any other service.

SEC. 8 — THE 'ĪD PRAYERS

Festivals of Islām

There are, in Islām, two great festivals having a religious sanction, and in connection with both of them a congregational service of two *rak'ahs* is held, followed by a sermon. Both these festivals go under the name of *'Īd*[54] which means *a recurring happiness*. The first of these is called the *'Īd al-fiṭr*,[55] and takes place immediately after the month of fasting. The other is called *'Īd al-Adẕḥā*.[56] Both these festivals are connected with the performance of some duty, in the first case the duty of fasting, and in the second the duty of sacrifice. A day of happiness following the performance of duty is intended to show that true happiness lies in the performance of duty. One characteristic of the Islamic festivals, therefore, is that they have, underlying them, a deep spiritual meaning. But they have another characteristic as well. In the moment of their greatest joy, the Muslims gather in as vast a congregation as possible and fall prostrate before their great Maker, giving thanks to Him that He has enabled them to perform their duty or to make a sacrifice. The spiritual significance of both festivals is thus brought out in the Divine service which is the chief feature of the day of festival.

Gathering for the 'Īd

The preparation for 'Īd is similar to the preparation for the Friday service. One must take a bath, put on one's best clothes, use scent, and do everything possible to appear neat and tidy. The gathering in the 'Īd should preferably be in an open place, but if necessary, a mosque may also be used for holding the Divine service. An open space is preferable on account of the size of the congregation, which a mosque might not be able to hold. No *a͟dhān* is called out for the 'Īd prayers, nor an

[54] Derived from *'aud*, meaning *to return*.

[55] The word *fiṭr* meaning *to begin*, from which is also derived *fiṭrah* meaning *nature*. *Ifṭār* means *the breaking of the fast*, as if the faster had returned to a natural course or fulfilled the demand of nature, and it is from this that the name *'Īd al-Fiṭr* seems to have been taken, because it follows the month of fasts and takes place on the first of S͟hawwāl.

[56] *Adẕḥā* being the plural of *adẕḥāṭ*, meaning *a sacrifice*.

iqāmah for the arranging of the lines (Bu. 13: 7).[57] Though women take part in all the prayers and in the Friday service, they are specially enjoined to be present at the ʻĪd gatherings, for the Prophet is reported to have said that "the young girls and those that have taken to seclusion and those that have their menses on, should all go out (for the ʻĪd) and be present at the prayers of the Muslims" (Bu. 13 : 15; 6 : 23). The time of ʻĪd prayers is any time after sunrise and before noon.

The ʻĪd service

The ʻĪd service consists only of two *rakʻahs* in congregation. The Imām recites the *Fātiḥah* and a portion of the Qur'ān in a loud voice, as in the Friday service. As already noted, there is neither *a<u>dh</u>ān* nor *iqāmah* for the ʻĪd prayer, but there is a number of *takbīrs* in addition to those that are meant to indicate the changes of position. On the best authority, the number of these additional *takbīrs* is seven in the first *rakʻah* and five in the second before the recital of the *Fātiḥah* in both *rakʻahs* (Tr. 5 : 5).[58] The *takbīrs* are uttered aloud by the Imām, one after another, as he raises both hands to the ears and then leaves them free in the natural position. Those who stand behind him raise and lower their hands similarly.

The ʻĪd Sermon

The ʻĪd sermon is delivered after Divine service is over. As regards the manner and the subjects dealt with, it is similar to the Friday sermon, except that it is not necessary to break it up into two parts by assuming the sitting posture in the middle of it. It was the Prophet's practice to address the women separately, who were all required to be present whether they joined in the service or not.

57 Some think that the sentence *al-ṣalātu jāmiʻat-un* should be called aloud but such a practice is not traceable to the Prophet (ZM. I, p. 124).

58 As stated above, the number of additional *takbīrs* given here is on the best authority available. A difference of opinion does, however, exist on this point. But much importance should not be attached to these matters. Some people say four additional *takbīrs*, in the first *rakʻah* and three in the second, in the latter case before going to *rukūʻ*. The tradition, however, on which this is based, is not reliable (ZM. I, p. 124).

The 'Īd charity

While celebrating the great 'Īd festivals, a Muslim not only remembers God (by attending Divine service) but he is also enjoined to remember his poorer brethren. The institution of a charitable fund is associated with both 'Īds. On the occasion of the *'Īd al-Fiṭr*, every Muslim is required to give *ṣadaqa al-Fiṭr* (lit., the *Fiṭr charity*) which amounts to three or four seers[59] of wheat, barley, rice or any other staple food of the country, or its equivalent in money, per head of the family, including the old as well as the youngest members, males as well as females (Bu. 24 : 70). The payment is to be made before the service is held, and it is obligatory (*fardz*). Like zakāt, the *Fiṭr* charity was an organized institution, as expressly mentioned in a tradition: "They gave this charity to be gathered together, and it was not given away to beggars" (Bu. 24 : 77). According to another tradition, Abū Hurairah said that "the Holy Prophet gave me charge of the zakāt of Ramadzān" (Bu. 40 : 10). The principle of gathering the *Fiṭr* charity, so clearly laid down in these traditions, has now been abandoned by the Muslims, and the result is that a most beneficial institution of Islām for the uplift of the poor and needy has been thrown into neglect, and considerable amounts which could strengthen national funds thrown away.

'Īd al-Adzḥā also furnishes an occasion for the exercise of charity. The sacrifice of an animal on that day (for which see the next paragraph), not only makes the poorest members of the community enjoy the festival with a good feast of meat but national funds for the amelioration of the poor or the welfare of the community can be considerably strengthened if the skins of the sacrificed animals are devoted to this purpose. In addition to this, in places where the number of sacrificed animals is in excess of the needs of the population, the surplus meat may be preserved and sold, and the proceeds thereof used for some charitable object.[60] Islām does not allow the wastage of natural resources, and it has organized all its charities in such a manner that they can be turned to the best use.

Besides these obligatory charities at the two 'Īds, the Prophet used to exhort people in his 'Īd sermons to contribute whatever they could, voluntarily, for the national cause; and there is mention of women giving away their jewelry at such times (Bu. 13 : 8). The two 'Īd festivals of

[59] One seer is equal to approximately one kilogram.

[60] It is to be regretted that the surplus meat in Makkah is buried away instead of being turned to any useful purpose.

Islām could thus be made occasions for strengthening national funds and for the relief of the poor, if the directions of the Prophet were followed faithfully.

The Sacrifice

At the *'Īd al-Adzḥā*, every Muslim who can afford to do sacrifices an animal. In the case of a goat or a sheep, one animal suffices for one household (Tr. 18 : 8). In the case of a cow or a camel, seven men may be partners (Tr. 18 : 7). The animal is sacrificed after the 'Īd prayers are over. It may be sacrificed on the day of 'Īd or during the two or three days that follow, called the *tashrīq* days, the time during which pilgrims stop in Minā (MM. 4 : 49-iii). The two days' limit is preferable, because the pilgrims are allowed to leave after two days.[61] The animal sacrificed must be free from apparent physical defects, and full-grown (*musinna*). The goat or sheep should be at least a year old, the cow two years and the camel five (H. ch. *al-Adzḥiya*). As regards the meat of the slaughtered animals, the Qur'ān says: " Eat of them and feed the contented one and the beggar" (22 : 36). There is no harm if it is dried and sold and the proceeds used for the feeding of the poor. The idea that the meat of the sacrifices should not be stored or eaten for more than three days is contradicted by a saying of the Prophet: "Jābir ibn 'Abd Allāh says, We did not use to eat the flesh of our sacrifices for more than the three days of Minā; so the Prophet gave us permission and said, Eat and take it as a provision for the way; so we ate and made it provision for the way" (Bu. 25 : 124). The giving of one-third, or more, or less, to the poor is simply optional. No hard and fast rules have been laid down. The skin of the animal must, however, be disposed of in charity (Bu. 25 : 121).

Can sacrifice be replaced by charity?

To the ordinary mind, the idea underlying sacrifice seems no more than charity, and the question has often been asked, May not a Muslim instead of sacrificing an animal, give away its price in charity? The answer to this question, in the light of the Islamic law, is in the negative. The

61 "Then whoever hastens off in two days, it is no sin for him, and whoever stays behind it is no sin for him" (2 : 203).

sacrifice by the Muslims throughout the world on the 'Īd day is intended to make Muslim hearts, throughout the world, beat in unison with the hearts of the unparalleled assemblage at Makkah, the centre of Islām. Millions of people assemble there from all quarters of the world, people who have sacrificed all comforts of life for no object except to develop the idea of sacrifice, a sacrifice selfless beyond all measure, because it has no personal or even national end in view, a sacrifice for the sake of God alone. However grand that idea, it receives a greater grandeur from the fact that the people who have been unable to make that sacrifice actually, are made to share the same desire and show their willingness to make the same sacrifice by the ostensible act of the sacrifice of an animal, which is the final act of the pilgrimage. One desire moves the hearts of the whole Muslim world from one end to the other at one moment, and this is made possible only by the institution of sacrifice, the red letters of which can be read by the ignorant and the learned alike. That this institution should also serve the purpose of charity is quite a different thing. Islām does not allow its rich members to forget their poorer brethren in the hour of their joy at a time of festival, but charity is not the idea underlying the sacrifice on the occasion of the 'Īd or the pilgrimage, and therefore no mere charity can take the place of sacrifice.

The idea underlying sacrifice

The sacrifice does not consist in the act of shedding the blood of an animal or feeding on its meat is made plain by the Qur'ān: "Not their flesh, nor their blood, reaches Allāh, but to Him is acceptable observance of duty on your part" (22 : 37). The underlying significance is made clearer still in the another verse: "And for every nation We appointed acts of devotion that they might mention the name of Allāh on what He has given them of the cattle quadrupeds. So your God is One God, therefore to Him should you submit; and give good news to the humble, whose hearts tremble when Allāh is mentioned, and who are patient in their afflictions" (22 : 34, 35). The act of the sacrifice of an animal is thus in some way connected with righteousness, with submission to One God, with humbleness of heart, with patience under sufferings: and the sacrifice of the animal is plainly regarded as affecting the heart, as making it tremble at the mention of Allāh's name. Here we are told that it is not any empty mention of a word that they make, but the underlying meaning is that their hearts should thrill at the mention of that name. Taking away the life of an animal and shedding its blood, does not make them ferocious but creates humbleness in their hearts, because they realize that if they have sacrificed an animal over which they hold control, it is their duty to lay down their own lives in the way of Allāh, Who is not only their Master but also their Creator and Sustainer, and Who therefore exercises a far greater authority over them than they do over the animals. Hence, in the midst of verses speaking of sacrifice, is introduced a verse which requires the faithful to be patient under trials and hardships, in the way of Allāh. In the sacrifice of animals, the Qur'ān thus gives to its followers the lesson of laying down their own lives in the cause of truth; and the lesson is made clearer still when this section on sacrifice, verses of which have been quoted above, is straightaway followed by a section which requires believers to lay down their lives in the defence of truth, the very first verse of that section running thus: "Permission to fight is given to those on whom war is made because they are oppressed" (22 : 39).

It will thus be seen that Islām has invested the principle of sacrifice with a new meaning. The institution of sacrifice has been accepted in one form or another by all the nations of the world. Like all other religious principles which are universally recognized, the principle of sacrifice finds a deeper meaning in Islām. The outward act is still there as of old, but it no longer conveys the meaning attached to it in some ancient religions, namely that of appeasing an offended deity or serving as an atonement for sin. In Islām it signifies the sacrifice of the sacrificer himself, and thus becomes an outward symbol of his readiness to lay down his life, and to sacrifice all his interests and desires in the cause of truth. The animal that is sacrificed really stands for the animal within him. And one day, and one particular moment on that day, is chosen so that all Muslim hearts from one end of the world to the other may pulsate with one idea at a particular moment, and thus lead to the development of the idea of self-sacrifice in the community as a whole.

SEC. 9 — SERVICE ON THE DEAD

Preparatory to service

A Divine service is held over the dead body of every Muslim, young or old, even of infants who have lived only for a few minutes or seconds. It is called *ṣalāt al-janā'iz*.[62] When a person dies, the body is washed with soap or some other disinfectant and cleansed of all impurities which may be due to disease. In washing the dead body, the parts which are washed in *wudzū* are taken first, and then the whole body is washed (Bu. 23 : 8, 9, 11). It is then wrapped in one or more white sheets (Bu. 23 : 19, 20, 27) and scent is also added (Bu. 23 : 21). In the case of martyrs, or persons slain in battle, the washing and wrapping in white cloth is dispensed with (Bu. 23 : 73). The dead body is then placed on a bier, or, if necessary, in a coffin, and carried on the shoulders, as a mark of respect, to its last resting-place, though the carrying of the body by any other means is not prohibited.[63] The Prophet stood up when he saw the bier of a Jew pass by. He did this to show respect to the dead, and then enjoined his followers to stand up as a mark of respect when a bier passed by, whether it is a Muslim or a non-Muslim (Bu. 23 : 50).

The service

Following the dead body to the grave and taking part in the Divine service held over it is regarded as a duty which a Muslim owes to a Muslim, and so is also the visiting of the sick (Bu. 23 : 2). Technically, taking part in Divine service is called *fardz kifāyah*, which means that it is sufficient that some Muslims should take part in it. Women are not prohibited from going with the bier, thought their presence is not considered desirable, because being more emotional and tender-hearted than men they may break down. The service may be held anywhere, in a mosque or in an open space or even in the graveyard if sufficient ground is available there. All those who take part in the service must perform *wudzū'*. The bier is placed in front; the Imām stands facing the middle of the bier whether the body be of a male or a female (Bu. 23 : 64),[64] and the people form themselves into lines according to the number of those who take

62 *Janā'iz* is the plural of *jināzah* or *janāzah* meaning *the dead body lying on a bier* or *the bier*, from *janaza* meaning *he concealed* or *hid* (a thing). According to some *jināzah* means *the bier*, and *janāzah* the *dead body*, or *vice versa* (LL.).

63 There is a difference of opinion as to the legality of driving or riding when following a bier (AD. 20 : 45, 46). But if the dead body itself is being borne on a carriage, there is no harm in driving when following it, nor so when there is a valid reason.

64 According to one ḥadīth, Anas ibn Mālik, when leading the *janāzah* prayer, took up a position in the middle of the bier in the case of a woman and a position nearer the head in the case of a man, and on being questioned said that such was the practice of the Prophet (AD. 20 : 54).

part, facing the Qiblah. The general practice is to have three rows at least, but Bukhārī is expressly of opinion that there may be two rows or three or more (Bu. 23 : 54). If the number of people is very small, there is no harm if they form only a single line. The service starts with the *takbīr*, with the pronouncement of which hands are raised to the ears and placed in the same position as in prayer. Four *takbīrs* in all are pronounced loudly by the Imām (Bu. 23 : 65). After the first *takbīr*, the same *dhikr* relating to the praise and glory of God is repeated in a low voice by the Imām as well as those who follow, as in the first *rak'ah* of the daily service, followed by the Opening chapter of the Qur'ān (*Fātiḥah*), but without adding any portion of the Qur'ān (Bu. 23 : 66). The second *takbīr* is then pronounced without raising the hands to the ears, and the *dhikr* known as *al-ṣalā 'ala-l'Nabiyy* is recited in a low voice as in the *qa'dah* (see p. 313). After the third *takbīr*, a prayer for the forgiveness of the deceased is addressed to God. Different forms of this prayer are reported as having been offered by the Prophet, and it seems that prayer in any form is permissible. The following are the most well-known:

اللّٰهُمَّ اغْفِرْ لِحَيِّنَا وَمَيِّتِنَا وَشَاهِدِنَا وَغَائِبِنَا وَصَغِيْرِنَا وَكَبِيْرِنَا وَذَكَرِنَا وَأُنْثَانَا	Allāh-umma-ghfir li-ḥayyi nā wa mayyiti-nā wa shāhidi-nā wa ghā'ibi-nā wa ṣaghīri-nā wa kabīri-na wa zakari-na wa unthā-nā;	O Allāh! Grant protection to our living and to our dead and to those of us who are present and those who are absent, and to our young and our old folk and to our males and our females;
اللّٰهُمَّ مَنْ أَحْيَيْتَهُ مِنَّا فَأَحْيِهِ عَلَى الْإِسْلَامِ وَمَنْ تَوَفَّيْتَهُ مِنَّا فَتَوَفَّهُ عَلَى الْإِيْمَانِ	Allāh-umma man aḥyaita-hū minnā fa-aḥyi-hi 'ala-l-Islāmi wa man tawaffai-ta-hū minnā fatawaffa-hū 'ala-l-īmani;	O Allāh! Whomsoever Thou grantest to live from among us, cause him to live in Islām (submission) and whomsoever of us Thou causest to die, make him die in faith;
اللّٰهُمَّ لَا تَحْرِمْنَا أَجْرَهُ وَلَا تَفْتِنَّا بَعْدَهُ	Allāh-umma lā taḥrim-nā ajra-hū wa la taftinnā ba'da-hū (MM 5 : 5-ii).	O Allāh! Do not deprive us of his reward and do not make us fall into a trial after him.

Another prayer runs thus:

اللّٰهُمَّ اغْفِرْ لَهُ وَارْحَمْهُ وَعَافِهِ وَاعْفُ عَنْهُ وَأَكْرِمْ نُزُلَهُ وَوَسِّعْ مَدْخَلَهُ وَاغْسِلْهُ بِالْمَاءِ وَالثَّلْجِ وَالْبَرَدِ وَنَقِّهِ مِنَ الْخَطَايَا كَمَا نَقَّيْتَ الثَّوْبَ الْأَبْيَضَ مِنَ الدَّنَسِ

Allāh-umma-ghfir la-hū wa-rḥam-hu wa ‘āfi-hī wa‘-fu ‘an-hu wa akrim nuzula-hū wa wassi‘ madkhala-hū wa-ghsil-hu bi-l-mā’i wa-th-thalji wa-l-baradi wa naqqi-hī min al-khaṭāyā kamā naqqaita-th-thaub al-abyadz min-ad-danasi (M. 11 : 27).

O Allāh! Grant him protection, and have mercy on him, and keep him in good condition, and pardon him, and make his entertainment honourable, and expand his place of entering, and wash him with water and snow and hail and clean him of faults as the white cloth is cleaned of dross.

After the fourth *takbīr*, the *taslīm* is pronounced loudly by the Imām, as at the close of prayer (see p. 314). A similar Divine service may be held in the case of a dead man when the dead body is not present. A funeral service was held by the Prophet himself in Madīnah when news of the death of the Negus of Abyssinia reached him (Bu. 23 : 4). When the service is over, the bier is taken to the grave and buried. The grave is dug in such a manner that the dead body may be laid in it facing Makkah. It is generally between four and six feet deep, and an oblong excavation is made on one side, wherein the dead body is to be placed. This is called the *laḥd*. The dead body is made to rest in the *laḥd* facing the Qiblah. If the dead body is contained in a coffin, the *laḥd* may be dispensed with. The following words are reported in a tradition as having been uttered by the Prophet when placing a dead body in the grave:

بِسْمِ اللّٰهِ وَبِاللّٰهِ وَعَلٰى سُنَّةِ رَسُوْلِ اللّٰهِ

Bi-smi-llāhi wa billāhi wa ‘alā sunnati Rasūli-llāh (Tr. 10 : 53).

In the name of Allāh and with Allāh and according to the sunnah of the Messenger of Allāh.

The grave is then filled in and a prayer is again offered for the dead one and the people then depart (AD. 20 : 70). The funeral service of a child[65] is similar to that of one who has reached the age of discretion, except that the prayer after the third *takbīr* is different:

اللّٰهُمَّ اجْعَلْهُ لَنَا فَرَطًا وَسَلَفًا وَذُخْرًا وَأَجْرًا

Allāh-umma-j‘al-hu la-nā faraṭ-an wa salaf-an wa dhukhr-an wa ajr-an (Bu. 23 : 66).[66]

O Allāh! Make him for us a cause of recompense in the life to come and as one going before and a treasure and a reward.

[65] Funeral service is held over a child that is born alive and then dies; according to one tradition, however, funeral service may be held also over the *siqṭ*, *i.e.*, a child that is born dead but has the form developed (AD. 20 : 46).

[66] The words *wa dhukhr-an, i.e.* "and a treasure" are not in *Bukhārī*.

It will be seen that the funeral service for children is not a prayer for their forgiveness but a prayer that the young ones who have gone before may be a means of recompense and reward for the parents. There are other traditions which speak of one afflicted with the death of young children as being made to enter Paradise: "A person, three of whose children die before reaching the age of discretion,is saved from the fire, or goes to Paradise" (Bu. 23 : 92). In the heading of his chapter, Bukhārī limits this to the offspring of Muslims (though there are no such words in the tradition itself) and then adds a long tradition in which the Prophet saw in a vision "the children of all people", *i.e.*, Muslims as well as non-Muslims, around Abraham (Bu. 23 : 93). The word of this latter report are thus explained in another version of it: "As regards the children around Abraham, they are the children who die *'ala-l-fiṭrah* (lit., *in the state in which they are born*, that being called expressly the state of Islām), or before attaining the age of discretion. Some of the Muslims said: O Messenger of Allāh! are the children of the polytheists also there? He said: Yes, the children of polytheists also" (Bu. 92 : 48). Thus all children go to Paradise; more than this, the death of young children is an affliction which becomes the means of taking one to Paradise, perhaps because it brings about a change in the hearts of the parents.

Patience enjoined under afflictions

It may also be added in this connection that Islām forbids indulgence in intemperate grief for the dead. It requires that all affliction be borne patiently, as the Qur'ān says: "And We shall certainly try you with something of fear and hunger and loss of property and lives and fruits; and give good news to the patient, who, when a misfortune befalls them, say, Surely we are Allāh's and to Him we shall return" (2 : 155, 156). On hearing of the death of a relative or a friend or of any other affliction, a Muslim is enjoined to say *Innā li-llāhi wa innā ilai-hi rāji'ūn:* "We are Allāh's and to Him we shall return." These words are a source of unlimited solace and comfort in bereavement. Allāh has taken away His own; all of us come from God and must return to Him. Hence it is forbidden that one should indulge in regular mourning or ostentatious grief. When visiting a cemetary, the following words are recommended:

السَّلَامُ عَلَيْكُمْ أَهْلَ الدِّيَارِ مِنَ الْمُؤْمِنِينَ وَالْمُسْلِمِينَ وَإِنَّا إِنْ شَاءَ اللّٰهُ بِكُمْ لَلَاحِقُونَ نَسْأَلُ اللّٰهَ لَنَا وَلَكُمُ الْعَافِيَةَ	As-salāmu ‘alai-kum ahl-ad-diyāri min al-mu’minīna wa-l-Muslimīna wa innā inshā Allāhu bi-kum la-lāḥiqūn; nas’alu-llāha la-nā wa la-kum-ul-āfiyah (M. 12: 36).	Peace be on you, O residents of this world from among the faithful and the Muslims, and we will surely join you, if it please Allāh. We pray to Allāh for security for you and for ourselves.

With small variations this prayer is repeated in several traditions.

A very large number of innovations has grown up about what may be done for the benefit of the dead. There is no mention of any tradition of distributing charity at the grave, or having the Qur’ān recited at the grave or elsewhere for the benefit of the dead. There are traditions speaking of the Qur’ān being read to the dying person (AD. 20: 21); but there is no mention at all of its being read over the dead body or over the grave. Neither is there any mention of saying the *Fātiḥah*, or a prayer for the dead, when people come to console the relatives of the departed. The Prophet is, however, reported as having prayed for the dead when visiting their graves, and the simple act of asking forgiveness for the deceased is not forbidden. The preparing of food on the third or tenth or fortieth day after death is also an innovation. There is no mention of it in any tradition. Instead of the family of the deceased preparing food for others, it is recommended that food should be prepared and sent to the family of the deceased by others (Bu. 70 : 24; AD. 20 : 27). Alms may, however, be given on behalf of the deceased, and doing deeds of charity is the only thing allowed. It is stated in a tradition that “a man came to the Prophet and said that his mother had died suddenly, and he was sure that if she could speak, she would give something in charity, and enquired whether she would get any reward if he gave charity on her behalf.” The Prophet is reported to have replied in the affirmative (Bu. 23 : 95). In another tradition it is related that Sa‘d ibn ‘Ubāda asked the Prophet if it would benefit his deceased mother, who had died while he was away, if he gave something in charity on her behalf, and the Prophet, in this case also, replied in the affirmative (Bu. 55 : 15).

SEC. 10 — TAHAJJUD AND TARĀWĪḤ

Tahajjud *prayer is voluntary*

The word *tahajjud* is derived from *hujūd* which means *sleep*, and *tahajjud* literally signifies the *giving up of sleep* (R.). The *Tahajjud* prayer is so called because it is said after one has had some sleep, and sleep is then given up for the sake of prayer. It is specially mentioned, even enjoined, in the Qur'ān itself in the very earliest revelations, but it is expressly stated to be voluntary. The following verses may be noted in this connection:

"O thou covering thyself up! Rise to pray by night except a little, half of it, or lessen it a little or add to it, and recite the Qur'ān in a leisurely manner... The rising by night is surely the firmest way to tread and most effective in speech" (73 : 1 - 6).

"Thy Lord knows indeed that thou passest in prayer nearly two-thirds of the night, and (sometimes) half of it, and (sometimes) a third of it, as do a party of those with thee" (73 : 20).

"And during a part of the night, keep awake by it, beyond what is incumbent on thee; maybe thy Lord will raise thee to a position of great glory" (17 : 79).

The Prophet's **Tahajjud**

As the above quotation from the 73rd chapter shows, the Prophet used to pass half or even two-thirds of the night in prayer. His practice was to go to sleep immediately after the *'Iṣhā'* prayers, and then he generally woke up after midnight and passed almost all this latter half of the night in *Tahajjud* prayers, sometimes taking a short nap, which would give him a little rest, just before the morning prayer. This practice he kept up to the last. While in the congregational prayers the recitation of the Qur'ān was generally short, in consideration of the children, women and aged people among the audience, the recitation in the *Tahajjud* prayers was generally long, and it is related in traditions that he used to stand so long reciting the Qur'ān that his feet would get swollen[67] (Bu. 19 : 6).

The **Tahajjud** *prayer*

The *Tahajjud* prayer consists of eight *rak'ahs*, divided into a service of two at a time, followed by three *rak'ahs* of *witr*. To make it easier for the common people the *witr* prayer, which is really a part of *Tahajjud*, has been made a part of the voluntary portion of *'Ishā'* or night prayer, and therefore, if the *witr* prayer has been said with *'Ishā'*, *Tahajjud* would consist of only eight *rak'ahs*. But if there is not sufficient time, one may stop after any two *rak'ahs* (Bu. 19 : 10). The Prophet laid special stress on *Tahajjud* in the month of Ramadzān, and it was the *Tahajjud* prayer that ultimately took the form of *Tārawīḥ* in that month. He is reported to have said that whoever keeps awake at night to offer prayer in the month of Ramadzān, having faith and seeking only the Divine pleasure, his faults are covered (Bu. 2 : 27); and there are traditions showing that he used to awaken his wives to say prayers (Bu. 14 : 3). He is also said to have gone to the house of his daughter Fāṭima at night to awaken her and her husband 'Alī for *Tahajjud* prayers (Bu. 19 : 5). Owing to the emphasis laid by the Prophet on this prayer and the injunctions of the Qur'ān quoted above, the Companions of the Prophet were very particular about *Tahajjud* prayer, though they knew that it was not obligatory, and some of them used to come to the mosque during the latter part of the night to say their *Tahajjud* prayers. It is reported that the Prophet had a small closet made for himself in the mosque and furnished with a mat as a place of seclusion wherein to say his *Tahajjud* prayers during the month of Ramadzān, and on a certain night, when he rose up to say his *Tahajjud* prayers, some people who were in the mosque

[67] It is nothing but a distortion of facts to call such a person a voluptuary, simply because he took certain widows under the shelter of his roof and made them share the honour of partnership with him in matrimonial life. The man who passed half and even two-thirds of the night in prayer and who strenuously worked during the day-time for the all-round welfare of a whole nation, could not possibly have time for the indulgence of his passions. It is also a noteworthy fact that the only thing which kept him awake was a recitation of the Qur'ān, or the glorification of the Divine Being, and it is impossible to fathom the depth of his love for God and his love for the word of God, when it is borne in mind that only the greatest attraction could keep a man awake during the night and enable him to conquer sleep.

saw him and followed him in prayer, thus making a congregation. On the following night, this congregation increased, and swelled to still larger numbers on the third. On the fourth night, the Prophet did not come out, saying he feared lest it be made obligatory, and that it was preferable to say the *Tahajjud* prayers in one's own house (Bu. 10 : 80, 81). *Tahajjud*, except for these three days, thus remained an individual prayer during the lifetime of the Prophet, the caliphate of Abū Bakr, and the early part of the caliphate of 'Umar (Bu. 31 : 1). But later on, 'Umar introduced a change whereby this prayer became a congregational prayer during the early part of the night, and was said after the *'Ishā'* prayer. He himself is reported to have said that it was an innovation, though the latter part of night during which people kept on sleeping was preferable to the early part in which they said this prayer (Bu. 31 : 1). Doubtless he had had this suggestion from the example of the Prophet himself, who had said the *Tahajjud* prayer in congregation for three nights, and allowed the *witr*, which was also a part of *Tahajjud*, to be adjoined to the *'Iṣhā'* prayer. And though for the average man the change introduced by 'Umar is welcome, nevertheless in the month of fasting (Ramadzān) *Tahajjud* in the latter part of the night and as an individual prayer is preferable.

Tarāwīḥ

Tarāwīḥ is the plural of *Tarwīḥah* which is derived from *rāḥah* and means *the act of taking rest.* The name *Tarāwīḥ* seems to have been given to this prayer because the worshippers take a brief rest after every two *rak'ahs*. It is now the practice that the whole of the Qur'ān is recited in the *Tarāwīḥ* prayers in the month of Ramadzān. But to recite it in a single night is against the express injunctions of the Prophet (Bu. 30 : 58). The number of *rak'ahs* in the *Tarāwīḥ* prayers seems, at first, to have been eleven, being exactly the number of *rak'ahs* in the *Tahajjud* prayers (including of course three *witr rak'ahs*). It is stated that 'Umar at first ordered eleven *rak'ahs*, but later on, the number seems to have been increased to twenty *rak'ahs* of *Tarāwīḥ* and three *rak'ahs* of *witr*, now making a total of twenty-three.[68] And this practice is now generally maintained throughout the Muslim world, the Ahl Ḥadīth and the Aḥmadīs being almost the only exception. It is customary for the Imām to recite the whole of the Qur'ān in *Tarāwīḥ* during the month of fasting, whether the number of *rak'ahs* be eight or twenty.

[68] Ma. — *Targhīb fi-l-ṣalā fi Ramadzān.*

SEC. 11 — MISCELLANEOUS SERVICES

Service for rain

It is reported that on a certain occasion when there had been a prolonged drought, someone requested the Prophet, while he was delivering the Friday sermon in the mosque, to pray for rain, as both men and cattle were suffering severely, and in response, the Prophet raised his hands and prayed to God for rain (Bu. 11 : 35). Similarly he is reported to have prayed to God when there was excess of rain (Bu. 11 : 35). On another occasion, however, he is said to have gone out into the open with the congregation, and to have prayed for rain and then performed two *rak'ahs* of prayer in congregation, reading the *Fātiḥah* in a loud voice, as in the Friday service (Bu. 15 : 1, 16).[69]

Service during eclipse

A prayer service of two *rak'ahs* was held by the Prophet during an eclipse of the sun. This eclipse occurred on the day of the death of Ibrāhīm, the Prophet's eighteen months old son. The service differed from the ordinary prayer service in that there were two *qiyāms* and two *rukū's* in each *rak'ah*.[70] There is also mention of a sermon having been delivered after the service (Bu. 16 : 4). In this sermon, the Prophet, while enjoining charity and seeking of forgiveness from God (*istighfār*), referred particularly to Ibrāhīm's death. When the people saw that the sun had darkened, they began to say among themselves that this was due to Ibrāhīm's death. The Prophet rebutted this idea in his sermon, saying that "the sun and the moon do not suffer eclipse for any one's death or life" (Bu. 16 : 13). This was the only occasion of an eclipse on which a service was held by the Prophet (ZM. I, p. 129).

[69] In some traditions it is stated that before prayer, the Prophet turned over his *riḍā* (a loose wrapper worn over the shoulders). It seems, however, to have been only accidental, or it may have been simply a precautionary measure lest the *riḍā* should fall down in the raising up of the hands (FB. II, pp. 144, 415).

[70] After the first *qiyām* there was a rukū' as in the ordinary service, though of longer duration, and then a *qiyām* followed again in which a portion of the Qur'ān was recited; this was followed by a second *rukū'*, after rising from which the *sajdah* was performed as in the ordinary service; the recitation being in a loud voice, as in Friday and 'Id prayers (Bu. 18 : 2, 19).

Chapter II

ZAKĀT OR CHARITY

Charity as one of the two principal duties

Charity towards man, in its widest sense, is laid down in the Qur'ān as the second great pillar on which the structure of Islam stands. This is made plain in the very beginning of the Holy Book: "(Those) who believe in the Unseen and keep up prayer and spend out of what We have given them; and who believe in that which has been revealed to thee and that which was revealed before thee, and of the Hereafter they are sure. These are on a right course from their Lord, and these it is that are successful" (2 : 3-5). The main principles of Islām, as laid down here, are five: three theoretical and two practical. The three theoretical essentials are belief in God, in Divine revelation and in the Hereafter; and the two practical are keeping up prayer and spending out of what God has given to man. The first of these, which has already been discussed in the last chapter, *i.e.*, prayer, is the means of the realization of the Divine in man, while the second, or spending out of whatever has been given to man, stands for charity in a broad sense, *i.e.*, for all acts of benevolence and doing good to humanity in general. For what God has given to man is not only the wealth which he possesses but all the faculties and powers with which he has been gifted.

That benevolence, or the doing of good to man, is one of the two mainstays of religion, is a constant theme of the Qur'ān, and one more verse may be quoted. Speaking of the Jewish and Christian claims to salvation, on the basis of certain dogmas, the Holy Book says: "And they say, None shall enter the Garden except he who is a Jew, or the Christians. These are their vain desires. Say, Bring your proof if you are truthful. Nay, whoever submits himself entirely to Allāh and he is the doer of good to others, he has his reward from his Lord, and there is no fear for such nor shall they grieve" (2 : 111, 112). In this verse submission to Allāh takes the place of keeping up prayer, and the doing of good to humanity, that of spending out of what has been given to man. Thus, theoretically, Islām means a belief in God, in Divine revelation and in the Hereafter, and practically it means the realization of the Divine in man by prayer, or entire submission to God, and the service of humanity. The numerous ordinances relating to various aspects of life, whether contained in the

Qur'ān or in the practice and sayings (*Sunnah*) of the Prophet, are only offshoots of these two practical essentials of religion.

Prayer is useless if it does not lead to charity

The relation in which prayer stands to charity is made clear by the order in which the two are mentioned. When prayer and charity are spoken of together, and this combination is of frequent occurrence in the Qur'ān, prayer always takes precedence over charity, because prayer prepares a man for the service of humanity. In the verse which speaks of the five basic principles of Islām, mention of belief in the Unseen is immediately followed by an injunction to keep up prayer, and this again by another to do acts of benevolence. This is to show the natural order. Belief in the Unseen is the starting point of man's spiritual progress. But this would lead to no good if the next step, the seeking of communion with the Unseen through prayer, does not follow. And this again is meaningless if it does not lead to acts of benevolence. Prayer, therefore, is the first step because it leads to the second, that is, charity. This is elsewhere made plain: "Woe to the praying ones, who are unmindful of their prayers! who do (good) to be seen and refrain from acts of kindness" (107 : 4-7)

Conception of charity in Islām

The most frequently recurring words for charity are *infāq*[1] which means *spending benevolently, iḥsān* which means *the doing of good, zakāt* which means *growth* or *purification*, and *ṣadaqah* which is derived from the root *sidq*, meaning *truth*, and comes to signify a *charitable deed*. The very words used to denote charitable deeds are an indication of the broadness of its conception. The Qur'ān not only lays stress on such great deeds of charity as the emancipation of slaves,[2] the feeding of the poor,[3] taking care of orphans[4] and doing good to humanity in general,

[1] The words *fī sabīl Allāh* (meaning, *in the way of Allāh*) are sometimes added to the derivatives of *infāq* in the Qur'ān, but the significance is the same, even when the word is used without this addition.

[2] 90 : 13; 2 : 177.

[3] 69 : 34; 90 : 11-16; 107 : 1-3.

[4] 17 : 34; 76 : 8; 89 : 17; 90 : 15; 93 : 9; 107 : 2.

but gives equal emphasis to smaller acts of benevolence. It is for this reason that the withholding of *mā'ūn,*[5] which specially indicates *small acts of kindness and charity,* is stated to be against the spirit of prayer. And in a similar strain, the speaking of a kind word to parents is referred to as *iḥsān,*[6] and generally the use of kind words is recommended as in itself a charitable deed in many places.[7]

Tradition is much more explicit. To remove from the road anything which may cause hurt is called a *ṣadaqah* or a charitable deed (Bu. 46 : 24). According to another tradition "there is a *ṣadaqah* (charity) on every limb with every new sun, and to do justice among people is also a charity" (Bu. 53 : 11). Another report gives yet more detail: "On every limb there is a *ṣadaqah* (charity) every day; a man helps another to ride his animal, it is a charity; or he helps him to load his animal, this is also a charity; and so is a good word; and every step, which a man takes in going to pray, is a charity; and to show the way is a charity."[8] Examples of other charitable deeds are "your salutation to people," "your enjoining what is right and forbidding what is wrong,"[9] "refraining from doing evil to any one"[10] and so on. The circle of those towards whom an act of charity may be done is equally wide. To give food to one's wife or one's children is called a charitable deed, while to maintain even one's self is not excluded from the category of charitable deeds: "The Prophet said, Whatever you feed yourself with is a charity, and whatever you feed your children with is a charity, and whatever you feed your wife with is a charity, and whatever you feed your servant with is a charity".[11] The doing of good to the dumb creation is also called a charity: "Whoever tills a field and birds and beasts eat of it, it is a charity".[12] The Qur'ān also speaks of extending charity not only to all men including believers and unbelievers (2 : 272) but also to the dumb creation (51 : 19).

[5] 107 : 7.

[6] 17 : 23.

[7] 2 : 83; 4 : 8 etc.

[8] Bukhārī 56 : 72, 128.

[9] Ah. II, p. 329.

[10] Ah. IV, p. 395.

[11] Ah. IV, p. 131.

[12] Ah. IV, p. 55.

Voluntary charity

Charity, in the sense of giving away one's wealth, is of two kinds, voluntary and obligatory. Voluntary charity is generally mentioned in the Qur'ān as *infāq* or *iḥsan* or *ṣadaqah*, and though the Holy Book is full of injunctions on this subject, and hardly a leaf is turned which does not bring to the mind the grand object of the service of humanity as the goal of man's life, the subject is specially dealt with in the 36th and 37th sections of the second chapter. The reward of charity is first spoken of:

"The parable of those who spend their wealth in the way of Allāh is as the parable of a grain growing seven ears, in every ear a hundred grains; and Allāh multiplies further for whom He pleases" (2 : 261).

A charitable deed must be done as a duty which man owes to man, so that it conveys no idea of the superiority of the giver or the inferiority of the receiver:

"Those who spend their wealth in the way of Allāh, then follow not up what they have spent with reproach or injury, their reward is with their Lord... A kind word with forgiveness is better than charity followed by injury... O you who believe! make not your charity worthless by reproach and injury" (2 : 262-264).

Love of God should be the motive in all charitable deeds, so that the very doing of them fosters the feeling that all mankind is but a single family:

"And they give food out of love for Him to the poor and the orphan and the captive" (76 : 8).

"And give away wealth out of love for Him to the near of kin and the orphans and the needy and the wayfarer and to those who ask and to set slaves free" (2 :177).

"And the parable of those who spend their wealth to seek Allāh's pleasure and for the strengthening of their souls, is as the parable of a garden on elevated ground" (2 : 265).

Only good things and well-earned wealth should be given in charity:

"O you who believe! spend of the good things that you earned and of that which We bring forth for you out of the earth, and aim not at the bad to spend thereof" (2 : 267).

Charitable deeds may be done openly or secretly:

"If you manifest charity, how excellent it is! and if you hide it and give it to the poor, it is good for you" (2 : 271).

Those who do not beg should be the first to receive charity:

"For the poor who are confined in the way of Allāh, they cannot go about in the land, the ignorant man thinks them to be rich on account of their abstaining from begging. (2 : 273).

Significance of zakāt

Obligatory charity is generally mentioned under the name *zakāt*, but it is sometimes called a *ṣadaqah*, specially in traditions. The word *zakāt* is derived from *zakā*, which means *it* (a plant) *grew*. The other derivatives of this word, as used in the Qur'ān, carry the sense of *purification from sins*. The Prophet is again and again spoken of as *purifying* those who would follow him (*yuzakkī-him* or *yuzakkī-kum*)[13] and the purification of the soul is repeatedly mentioned as being real success in life.[14] The word *zakāt* is also used in the sense of purity from sin. Thus of John it is said: "And We granted him wisdom when a child, and kindheartedness from Us and purity (*zakāt*)" (19 : 12, 13). And on another occasion, one child is spoken of as being " better in purity (*zakāt*)" than another (18 : 81). The idea of purity, and that of the growth of human faculties and success in life, are thus connected together. According to Rāghib, *zakāt* is wealth which is taken from the rich and given to the poor, being so called because it makes wealth grow, or because the giving away of wealth is a source of purification. In fact both these reasons hold true. The giving away of wealth to the poorer members of the community, while, no doubt, a source of blessing to the individual, also increases the wealth of the community as a whole, and at the same time it purifies the giver's heart of the inordinate love of wealth which brings numerous sins in its train. The Prophet himself has described *zakāt* as wealth "which is taken from the rich and returned to the poor" (Bu.24 : 1).

Importance of zakāt *in Islām*

The two commandments, to keep up prayer and to give *zakāt*, often go together, and this combination of the two is met with in the earliest chapters of the Qur'ān, as well as in those which were revealed towards the end of the Prophet's life. Thus in ch.73, which is undoubtedly one of

[13] 2 : 129, 151; 3 : 163; 9 : 103; 62 : 2.

[14] 91 : 9; 92 : 18.

the very earliest revelations, we have: "And keep up prayer and pay the *zakāt* and offer to Allāh a goodly gift" (73 : 20). And in the ninth chapter, which is the latest in revelation, we have: "Only he can maintain the mosques of Allāh who believes in Allāh and the Last Day and keeps up prayer and pays the *zakāt* and fears none but Allāh" (9 : 18). Not only are prayer (*ṣalāt*) and *zakāt* mentioned together in a large number of passages[15] but also these two are treated as being the basic ordinances of the religion of Islām, and their carrying into practice is often mentioned as being sufficient indication that one is a believer in the religion of Islam. The two verses quoted above point to the same conclusion. A few more are:

"And they are enjoined naught but to serve Allāh, being sincere to Him in obedience, upright, and to keep up prayer and pay the *zakāt*, and that is the right religion" (98 : 5). "These are verses of the Book of wisdom, a guidance and a mercy for the doers of good, who keep up prayer and pay the *zakāt* and who are certain of the Hereafter" (31 : 2-4). "But if they repent and keep up prayer and pay the *zakāt*, they are your brethren-in-faith" (9 : 11).

Zakāt as the basic principle of every religion

Ṣalāt and *zakāt* are also spoken of together as the basic ordinances of the religion of every prophet. Thus of Abraham and his posterity, it is said: "And We made them leaders who guided people by Our command, and We revealed to them the doing of good and the keeping up of prayer and the giving of *zakāt*" (21 : 73). The Israelite law is also said to have contained a similar commandment: "And Allāh said: Surely I am with you. If you keep up prayer and pay the *zakāt* and believe in My messengers and assist them and offer to Allāh a goodly gift, I will certainly cover your evil deeds, and cause you to enter gardens in which rivers flow" (5 : 12). Ishmael is also spoken of as giving the same commandment to his followers: "And he enjoined on his people prayer and *zakāt*, and he was one in whom his Lord was well-pleased" (19 : 55). Even Jesus

[15] Klein says: "It is mentioned in eighty-two passages of the Qur'ān in close connection with prayer" (RI. p. 156, f.n.). I have not been able to trace the combination of *ṣalāt* and *zakāt* in more than 27 passages. But there are a few more passages in which prayer to God and the idea of charity in general are mentioned together.

is said to have received a similar Divine commandment: "And He has enjoined on me prayer and *zakāt* so long as I live" (19 : 31).[16]

This view of religion shows that, according to the Qur'ān, the service of humanity and the amelioration of the condition of the poor has always been among the principal aims and objects of religion. It is, however, true that the same stress has not been laid on this principle in the previous religions, and, moreover, the institution of *zakāt*, like every other principle of religion, has been brought to perfection, along with the perfection of religion, in Islām.

Problem of the distribution of wealth

One of the greatest problems facing humanity is undoubtedly the problem of the distribution of wealth, with which is also bound up the question of political power. The system of capitalism which is the foundation-stone, so to say, of the materialistic civilization of modern Europe, has led to the concentration of wealth in fewer and fewer hands. Political power has followed in the wake of wealth. The insatiable thirst for wealth on the part of the capitalists, who are the real controllers of political power, has reduced many nations of the world to a state of slavery, and regular plunder has been legalized under different high-sounding phrases such as colonization, occupation, mandate, sphere of influence, and so on.

The reaction against capitalism set in towards the middle of the nineteenth century. It came under the name of Socialism and gradually developed into what is now known as Bolshevism. It holds Russia in its grip, perhaps as severely as Capitalism still holds other European countries. Whether, in Russia, it has come to stay is a question which only the future can decide. But there is one thing that strikes one as very strange. Bolshevism, which had come in to liberate the people, is as much of a bondage as Capitalism. The autocracy of Czardom has only given place to the autocracy of the Soviet.

The question before us, however, is, has Bolshevism, by state-ownership of all means of production, finally solved the great problem of the distribution of wealth? A few years are but as one moment or even less in world

[16] The words, *so long as I live*, establish conclusively that Jesus is dead, because *zakāt* can only be given by one who is in possession of worldly wealth and of Jesus it could not be said that he was in possession of wealth in heaven, and even if it were so there would be none there to receive the *zakāt*.

history. To say that because the five-year plan has accelerated production to an extent which could hardly be imagined, and that therefore the state-ownership of means of production is the solution of the problem, is to show overhastiness in drawing a conclusion. Who knows that the people entrusted with the carrying out of the scheme, the state-agents, may not tomorrow degenerate into an oligarchy similar to the oligarchy of Capitalism? Human nature is too prone to these tendencies, and the Bloshevism offers hardly any remedy to check such tendencies. But there is more than this. Bolshevism which came as the friend of labour defeats its own end by denying to labour its fruits. The rigid system of doling out the necessaries of life to all alike, to the indolent and diligent, the stupid and the intelligent, will undoubtedly foster conditions which must soon become unbearable for humanity; for it is going directly against nature and nature's recognized laws. But its evil results cannot be seen in a day.

Islām's solution of wealth problem

To Islām is due the credit of not only solving the wealth problem but, at the same time, developing the higher sentiments and building up character, on which alone can be laid the foundations of a lasting civilization for the human race. The rigid laws of Bolshevism, which gave the body sufficient to live on, are killing the higher sentiments of human sympathy and love—qualities which not only make life worth living but lacking which humanity must degenerate into the worst barbarism. Islām accomplishes both objects by its state institution of charity, which goes under the name of *zakāt* or poor-rate. Every possessor of wealth in the Islamic commonwealth is required to contribute annually one-fortieth of his wealth to a common fund, which is managed by the state, or by the Muslim community where there is no Muslim state, and this fund is utilized by the state or community for the amelioration of the condition of the poor. *Zakāt*, therefore, acts not only as a levelling influence but, also a means of developing higher sentiments of man, the sentiments of love and sympathy towards his fellow-man; while the rigid system of state ownership and equality of distribution helps to kill man's higher instincts. By this means, too, wealth is made to circulate in the body-politic of Islām, just as blood circulates in a living organism, a fixed portion of the wealth of the richer members being drawn to the centre, whence it is sent forth to those parts of the body-politic which need it most. The institution of *zakāt* thus becomes not only a levelling influence but also one of the means for the uplift of the nation as a whole.

Zakāt *is a state institution*

It should be borne in mind that *zakāt* is not simply obligatory charity. It is a state institution or, where there is no Muslim state, a national institution. The individual is not at liberty to calculate and spend his *zakāt* as he likes. It must be collected by the state on a national basis, and spent by the state or community. Where the Qur'ān describes the main heads of the expenditure of *zakāt*, it mentions an item of expenditure on officals appointed to collect and distribute the same, which shows clearly that, by the institution of *zakāt*, it contemplated either a department of the state or at least a public fund managed entirely by a public body. The donor is not required to give a certain portion of his *zakāt* to deserving persons, but to contribute all of it to a fund which must be used for the uplift of the community. It was in this sense that the Prophet understood it, and when he assumed control of the government, he made *zakāt* a state institution, appointing officials to collect it and directing his governors to do the same in distant provinces.[17] Abū Bakr, the first caliph, followed in the footsteps of the Prophet when he declared war against some of the tribes which had refused to send their *zakāt* to the state treasury, adding: "*Zakāt* is the right (of the state or community) in the wealth (acquired by an individual), and by Allāh, if they refuse to make over even one lamb which they used to make over to the Prophet, I will fight against them" (Bu. 14 : 1).

Property on which zakāt *is payable*

Though injunctions relating to *zakāt* are met with in very early revelations, the details were given only after Islām was established at Madīnah. Silver and gold are the two commodities which man has always loved to hoard, and beside this these are the two precious metals which are the basis of the currencies of the world. These two, therefore find special mention as being articles on which *zakāt* must be paid. Ornaments made

[17] As in the case of Mu'ādh who was appointed Governor of Yaman (Bu. 24 : 1).

of silver or gold were treated as silver or gold. And cash, whether in the form of coins or notes or bank deposits, would follow the same rule. Precious stones were excepted from *zakāt*, because in taking a part, in this case, the whole would have to be broken up or damaged. Articles of merchandise were also considered as being subject to *zakāt* to whatever class they may belong.[18] Animals used for trade purposes were subject to *zakāt* only if they were kept on pastures belonging to the state. There is no mention of immovable property, such as agricultural lands and house property, among the things on which *zakāt* was levied, but the produce of land, whether cereals or fruits, was subject to a tax called *'ushr*, literally, the tenth part. It has been treated as *zakāt*; actually, however, it falls within the category of land revenue. Vegetables are excepted from *zakāt* (Tr. 7 : 13). Since *zakāt* is a tax on property, therefore it is realizable though the property may belong to a minor. According to a tradition, the Prophet is reported to have said: "Whoever is the guardian of an orphan, he should do trading by his property, and should not allow it to lie idle so that it may come to an end by the payment of *zakāt*" (Tr. 7 : 15).

Niṣāb

Zakāt was an annual charge on property which remained in the possession of a person for a whole year, when its value reached a certain limit, called *niṣāb*. *Niṣāb* differed with different kinds of property, the

[18] There is almost a consensus of opinion on this matter. Bukhārī mentions no tradition on this point, but the heading of one of his chapters, the 29th, in the book of *zakāt* is as follows: "The *ṣadaqah (zakāt)* of *kasb* (what is earned) and *tijārah* (merchandise)" (Bu. 24 : 29). He is unable, however, to find a tradition supporting it, and contents himself with quoting the following verse of the Qur'ān: "O you who believe! give in charity of the good things that you earn and of what We have brought forth for you out of the earth"(2 : 267). It may, however, be noted that this verse refers to voluntary gifts. Abū Dāwūd mentions a tradition from Sumra ibn Jundub: "The Prophet used to command us that we should pay *zakāt* out of what we had for sale" (AD. 9 : 31). Some have questioned the authenticity of this tradition, but it is supported by another tradition. For instance, there is a tradition reported by Dār Quṭnī and Ḥākam, according to which the Prophet mentioned *bazz* (cloth for sale) as being one of the things on which *zakāt* was payable. According to another, also reported by Dār Quṭnī, the Caliph 'Umar ordered a certain man who was carrying on trade in skins, to pay the *zakāt* by having the price estimated. There is also a tradition in *Baihaqī*, according to which Ibn 'Umar said that in *'urūdz* (commodities other than gold and silver), there was no *zakāt* unless they were meant for trade (AM-AD. II, p. 4). The last-mentioned tradition is also reported by Abū Dhar (Ah.V, p. 199).

most important being 200 dirhams or 52½ tolas (nearly 21 oz.) in the case of silver, and twenty *mithāls* or 7½ tolas (nearly 3 oz.) in the case of gold. The *niṣāb* of cash was the same as that of silver or gold, according as the cash was held in silver or gold. In the case of merchandise of all kinds, the value was calculated on the basis of, and the *niṣāb* was judged by, the silver standard. In the case of ornaments, the *niṣāb* was that of silver, if the ornaments were made of silver, and that of gold, if they were made of gold. But jewels and the like would be excepted, and only the weight of silver or gold would be considered in determining the *niṣāb*. In the case of animals, the *niṣāb* was five for camels, thirty for bulls or cows and forty for goats. In the case of horses, no particular *niṣāb* is mentioned, but as *zakāt* in this case was judged by the price, the *niṣāb* must also be judged by the same standard. In the case of cereals, the *niṣāb* was five *wasaq*, according to two different calculations; it comes to twenty-six maunds and ten seers, or eighteen maunds and thirty-five and a half seers, or nearly a ton in the first case, and about two-thirds of a ton in the second.[19]

Rate at which zakāt *must be paid*

With the exception of animals, *zakāt* was levied at almost a uniform rate, being 2½ per cent of the accumulated wealth. In the case of animals, camels and sheep, detailed rules were laid down, and animals of a particular age were taken as *zakāt* when the herd reached a specified number.[20] A perusal of the rates given in the footnote would show that,

[19] The difference arises from the measure of *ṣā'* which, according to the people of 'Irāq, is eight *raṭl* in weight, and according to the people of Ḥijāz, five and one-third *raṭl*.

[20] In the case of camels, the rule laid down was as follows: "One goat for five camels, and after that, one for each additional five or part of five, up to 24. When the number reached 25, a young she-camel, one year old, sufficed up to 34. For 35 to 45, the age was raised to two years; for 46 to 60, to three years; for 61 to 75, to four years. For 76 to 90, two young she-camels of the age of two years were given as *zakāt*; for 91 to 124, two of the age of three years, and after that one she-camel of the age of two years for every forty camels, or one of the age of three years for every fifty camels, was to be added. In the case of goats and sheep, the *zakāt* was one goat or sheep for 40 to 120, two for 121 to 200, three for 201 to 300, and after that one for each hundred or part of hundred (Bu. 24: 38). In the case of cows, a one-year old calf for every thirty cows, and a two-year old one for every forty, is the rule laid down in a ḥadīth (Tr. 7 : 5). According to Bukhārī (Bu. 24 : 45), horses are exempt from *zakāt*. The reason appears to be that they were needed in time of war. Later jurists, however, consider horses to be taxable according to their value at the rate of 2½ p.c. (H.I, p. 173).

though there is a slight variation, yet in the main, the rate of 2½ per cent seems to have been kept in view. The case of one full-grown cow out of every forty cows, one she camel, two years old, out of every forty camels, and one goat out of forty goats, makes this clear.

The case of treasure-trove, out of which one-fifth was taken, is quite a different matter, and can hardly fall within the category of *zakāt*, since it cannot be said to be a thing which has remained in the full possession of the owner for one year. In such circumstances, where other governments would take the whole treasure, the Muslim state takes only a fifth. In case of *'ushr*, as already stated, it is not technically *zakāt*; it is really land revenue. The state takes only one-tenth of the produce of agricultural land when it is grown with the aid of rain-water or natural springs, and one-twentieth when irrigated by wells or other artificial means in which labour is engaged by the owner of the land (IM.8 : 17).

Zakāt *under modern conditions*

It will thus be seen that *zakāt* proper is only a charge on accumulated wealth, and is intended to do away with the inequalities of Capitalism. Wealth has a tendency to accumulate, and *zakāt* aims at its partial redistribution in such a manner that the community, as a whole, may derive advantage from it. A part of the amassed wealth or capital of every individual is taken away annually and distributed among the poor and the needy. *Zakāt* would therefore be payable on all cash hoardings, or hoardings in gold or silver, as well as on any form of capital, whether in the shape of cash or kind. Precious stones, as already stated, are excepted, because the payment of *zakāt* on them would necessitate their sale. Machinery employed in industry must follow the same rule. It should, in fact, be regarded in the same light as the implements of an artisan, and its earnings become taxable when the necessary conditions as to the assessment of *zakāt* are fulfilled. Stock-in-trade should be treated in a similar manner; that is to say, only the yearly profit should be taxable, not the stock itself. In the case of all things on which *zakāt* is payable, whether cereals, live-stock or other articles of merchandise, their value should be determined, and *zakāt* levied at the universal rate of 2½ per cent. Where the Muslims live under non-Muslim governments, and the collection and disbursement of *zakāt* cannot be undertaken by these governments, the duty devolves on the Muslim community as a whole, and the institution of *zakāt* must take the shape of a national Muslim institution in every country where there is a Muslim population.

How **zakāt** *should be spent*

The items of the expenditure of *zakāt* are thus expressly stated in the Qur'ān: "Alms (*ṣadaqāt*) are only for the poor (*fuqarā'*), and the needy (*masākīn*), and the officials appointed over them, and those whose hearts are made to incline to truth (*al-mu'allafati qulūbu-hum*), and captives, and those in debt, and in the way of Allāh, and the wayfarer: an ordinance (*farīdzah*) from Allāh, and Allāh is Knowing, Wise" (9 : 60). As already noted, *zakāt* is sometimes mentioned under the name of *ṣadaqah*. That this is the significance of *ṣadaqāt* here is made clear by the concluding words of the verse, where it is called a *farīdzah*, or an obligatory duty, which word is applicable to *zakāt* only. The eight heads of expenditure spoken of here may be divided into three classes. The first relates to those who stand in need of help, including the poor, the needy, those whose hearts are made to incline to truth, captives, debtors and wayfarers. Secondly, there are the officials appointed for collection and disbursement of the fund. And, thirdly, a part of the *zakāt* is required to be spent in the way of Allāh. A few words of explanation may be added as regards each class.

It will be seen that six kinds of people fall under the first head. The first are *fuqarā'* (pl. of *faqīr*), derived from *faqr* which means *the breaking of the vertebrae of the back*, and faqīr therefore means literally *a man who has the vertebrae of his back broken* or *one afflicted by a calamity* (LL.). Apparently it refers to disabled people, who, on account of some defect, are unable to earn their living. The second are *masākīn* (pl. of *miskīn*), which is derived from *sakana* meaning *it became still* or *motionless. Miskīn* therefore signifies *one caused by poverty to have little power of motion* (LL.). There exists a good deal of difference as to the real distinction between the two words *faqīr* and *miskīn*; but, keeping the literal significance in view, the real distinction appears to be that *faqīr* is one who is disabled from earning on account of some physical disability, while *miskīn* is one who, though fit to earn sufficient, is unable to do so on account of poverty or lack of resources. The *miskīn* is the needy man who if given a little help can earn livelihood for himself. The unemployed would fall in this category.

These are the two chief classes for whose benefit the institution of *zakāt* is maintained, and hence they are separated from others by a mention of the establishment. The other groups falling in this class are also of persons who stand in need of help for some sufficient reason. There are *al-mu'allafāti qulābu-hum*, those whose hearts are made to incline to truth, that is, people who are in search of truth but unable to find means to have access to it on account of poverty. In this category would also fall new converts to Islām who are deprived of the means of their subsistence because of their conversion. Then there are the captives, or those who have been deprived of their liberty, and are unable to regain it by their own exertion. The freeing of slaves falls in this category. Then there are the debtors who are unable to pay off their own debts, and, lastly, there are the travellers who are stranded in a foreign country or in a distant place, and are unable to reach their homes.

There are two other heads of expenditure of *zakāt*, the first of which is the maintenance of an establishment and office for the collection of *zakāt*. This shows that *zakāt* was meant to be collected at some central place, and then distributed, and the maintenance of people who did this work was a charge under this head. The Qur'ān, therefore, does not allow the giving away or spending of *zakāt* according to the individual's choice.[21] The collection of *zakāt*, in spite of the remuneration paid for it, is regarded as an act of merit and according to one tradition, the collector of *zakāt* is equal in merit to one who takes part in *jihād* or in a war to defend religion.[22]

Zakāt ***may be spent in defence and propagation of Islām***

The establishment charge being a corollary of the nationalization of the institution of *zakāt*, the only item of expenditure besides the help of those in need, for one reason or another, is, what is called *fī sabīli-llāh*, or *in the way of Allāh*, which is accepted generally as meaning *warriors defending the faith*.[23] While such warriors are undoubtedly the most

[21] There is a tradition which states that the Prophet allowed one-third of the *zakāt* to be spent by an individual for those whom he thought fit to receive the *zakāt*. He is reported to have said: "When you estimate, leave one-third; if you do not leave one-third, then leave one-fourth"(AD. 9 : 14). Explaining this tradition, Imām Shāfi'i says that the one-third or one-fourth was to be left, so that the person from whom the *zakāt* was taken should spend the portion left on his relatives or neighbours as he desired (AM-AD. 9 : 15).

[22] AD. 19 : 6; Tr. 7 : 18.

[23] IJ-C. X, p.100

important national need of a community, it is equally true that they are an exception and not the rule, and hence the significance of the words *fī sabīli-llāh* cannot be limited to them. But there is another paramount need of the Muslim community which is called *jihād kabīr*, or the *great jihād*, in the Qur'ān: "And if We had pleased, We would have raised a warner in every town. So do not follow the unbelievers, and strive against them a mighty striving (*jihād-an kabīr-an*) with it" (25 : 51-52). The personal pronoun *it*, as the context clearly shows, refers to the Qur'ān, and therefore striving with the Qur'ān, or taking the message of the Qur'ān to distant corners of the world, is the greatest *jihād* of Islām. And the item of expenditure *fī sabīli-llāh* therefore refers to both these paramount needs of national existence, that is, wars to defend religion and the propagation of Islām, the latter being the greatest need of this age. Hence it will be seen that the institution of *zakāt*, while chiefly aiming at the amelioration of the condition of the poor, has also in view the defence and advancement of the Muslim community as a whole.

Other national charitable institutions

Zakāt, though the most important, is not, however, the only national institution of charity set up by Islām. There are two others of a similar nature, both connected with the 'Īd festivals, whereby into every Muslim heart is instilled the idea that even when in his happiest mood, he must never forget the distress of his poorer brethren. The first of these institutions is the *ṣadaqāt al-Fiṭr* or *zakāt al-Fiṭr, i.e.*, charity connected with the *'Īd al-Fiṭr*. Every Muslim on that occasion is required to give away in charity a certain measure of food, or its equivalent in money. This sum must be collected by every Muslim community and then distributed among those who deserve it.[24] The second institution is connected with the *'Īd al-Aḏẕḥā*, on which occasion not only are the poor members of the community fed with the meat of the sacrificed animals, but the skins of those animals (and also dried or preserved meat, in case the supply is greater than the demand) are sold, and the sum thus realized spent on some charitable object of national value, such as the propagation of Islām.

[24] It has already been shown, in the chapter on 'Īd prayers, that the *Fiṭr* charity was collected and then distributed; and here too the choice was not with the individual but with the community.

CHAPTER III

ṢAUM OR FASTING

Ṣaum

The primary signification of *ṣaum* is *abstaining*, in an absolute sense.[1] In the technical language of the Islamic law, *ṣaum* and *siyām* signify *fasting* or abstaining from food and drink and sexual intercourse from dawn till sunset.

Institution of fasting in Islām

The institution of fasting in Islām came after the institution of prayer. It was in Madīnah in the second year of Hijrah that fasting was made obligatory, and the month of Ramadzān was set apart for this purpose. Before that the Prophet used to fast, as an optional devotion, on the tenth day of Muḥarram, and he also ordered his followers to fast on that day, it being a fasting day for the Quraish as well, according to 'Ā'ishah (Bu. 30 : 1). The origin of fasting in Islām may thus be traced to the time when the Prophet was still at Makkah; but, according to Ibn 'Abbās, it was after his flight to Madīnah that he saw the Jews fasting on the tenth day of Muḥarram; and being told that Moses had kept a fast on that day in commemoration of the delivery of the Israelites from Pharaoh, he remarked that they (Muslims) were nearer to Moses than the Jews and ordered that day to be observed as a day of fasting (Bu. 30 : 69).

A universal institution

In the Qur'ān, the subject of fasting is dealt with only in one place, that is, in the 23rd section of the second chapter; though there is mention on other occasions of fasting by way of expiation (*fidyah*) in certain cases.

[1] *Al-imsāku 'ani-l-fi'l*, which includes abstaining from eating or speaking or moving about. Thus a horse that abstains from moving about, or from fodder, is said to be *ṣa'īm*, and wind is said to be *ṣaum* when it abates, and the day when it reaches the midpoint (R.). In the sense of abstaining from speech, the word is used in the Qur'ān in an early Makkah revelation: "Say, I have vowed a fast to the Beneficent God, so I shall not speak to any man to-day" (19 : 26).

This section opens with the remark that the institution of fasting is a universal one. "O you who believe! Fasting is prescribed for you as it was prescribed for those before you, so that you may guard against evil" (2 : 183). The truth of the statement made here — that fasting "was prescribed for those before you" — is borne out by a reference to religious history. The practice of fasting has been recognized well-nigh universally in all the higher, revealed religions, though the same stress is not laid on it in all, and the forms and motives vary. "Its modes and motives vary considerably according to climate, race, civilization and other circumstances; but it would be difficult to name any religious system of any description in which it is wholly unrecognized" (*En. Br.*, art. *Fasting*). Confucianism, according to the writer in the *Encyclopaedia Britannica*, is the only exception. Zoroastrianism, which is sometimes mentioned as another exception, is stated as enjoining, "Upon the priesthood at least, no fewer than five yearly fasts." Present-day Christianity may not attach much value to religious devotions of this sort, but not only did the Founder of Christianity himself keep a fast for forty days and observe fasting on the Day of Atonement like a true Jew, but also commended fasting to his disciples: "Moreover, when ye fast, be not as the hypocrites, of a sad countenance...But thou, when thou fastest, anoint thine head, and wash thy face" (Mt. 6 : 16, 17). It appears that his disciples did fast, but not as often as did those of the Baptist, and when questioned on that point, his reply was that they would fast more frequently when he was taken away (Lk. 5 : 33-35). The early Christians are also spoken of as fasting.[2] Even St. Paul fasted.[3]

New meaning introduced by Islām

Cruden's remark in his *Bible Concordance* that fasting in all nations was resorted to "in times of mourning, sorrow and afflictions" is borne out by the facts. Among the Jews, generally, fasting was observed as a sign of grief or mourning. Thus, David is mentioned as fasting for seven days during the illness of his infant son (II Sam. 12 : 16-18); and, as a sign of mourning, fasting is mentioned in I Sam. 31 : 13 and elsewhere. Besides the Day of Atonement, which was prescribed by the Mosaic law as a day of fasting (Lev. 16 : 29) — the people being required to "afflict"

[2] Acts 13 : 2, 3; 14 : 23.

[3] II Cor. 6 : 5; 11: 27.

their souls while the priest made an atonement for them to cleanse them of their sins—various other fast-days came into vogue after the Exile "in sorrowful commemoration of the various sad events which had issued in the downfall of the kingdom of Judah" (*En. Br.*). Four of these became regular fasting-days, "commemorating the beginning of the siege of Jerusalem, the capture of the city, the destruction of the temple and the assassination of Gedaliah" (*ibid.*). Thus it was generally some trouble or sad event of which the memory was kept up by a fast. Moses's fasting for forty days — which example was later followed by Jesus Christ — seems to be the only exception, and the fast, in this case, was kept preparatory to receiving a revelation. Christianity did not introduce any new meaning into the fast; Christ's words that his disciples would fast oftener when he was taken away from their midst, only lend support to the Jewish conception of the fast, as connected with national grief or mourning.

The idea underlying this voluntary suffering in the form of a fast in times of sorrow and affliction seems to have been to propitiate an angry Deity and excite compassion in Him. The idea that fasting was an act of penitence seems gradually to have developed from this as an affliction or calamity was considered to be due to sin, and fasting thus became an outward expression of the change of heart brought about by repentance. It was in Islām that the practice received a highly developed significance. It rejected *in toto* the idea of appeasing Divine wrath, or exciting Divine compassion through voluntary suffering and introduced in its place regular and continuous fasting, irrespective of the condition of the individual or the nation, as a means, like prayer, to the development of the inner faculties of man. Though the Qur'ān speaks of expiatory or compensatory fasts in certain cases of violation of the Divine law, yet these are quite distinct from the obligatory fasting in the month of Ramadzān, and are mentioned only as an alternative to an act of charity, such as the feeding of the poor or freeing of a slave. Fasting, as an institution, is here made a spiritual, moral and physical discipline of the highest order, and this is made clear by changing both the form and the motive. By making the institution permanent, all ideas of distress, affliction and sin are dissociated from it, while its true object is made plain, which is "that you may guard (*tattaqūn*)." The word *ittiqā* from which *tattaqūn* is derived, means *the guarding of a thing from what harms or injures it*, or *the guarding of self against that of which the evil consequences may be feared* (R.). But besides this, the word has been freely used in the Qur'ān in the sense of fulfilment of duties, as in 4 : 1 where *arḥām* (ties of relationship) occurs as an object of *ittaqū*, or, as generally in *ittaqu-llāh* where Allāh is the object of *ittaqū*, and therefore the significance of *ittiqā* in all these cases is a fulfilment of obligations. In fact, in the language of the Qur'ān, to be a *muttaqī* is to attain to the highest stage of spiritual development. "Allāh is the friend of the *muttaqīn*" (45 : 19); "Allāh loves the *muttaqīn*" (3 : 75; 9 : 4, 7); "Allāh is with the *muttaqīn*" (2 : 194; 9 : 36, 123); "The good end is for the *muttaqīn*" (7 : 128; 11 : 49; 28 : 83); "For the *muttaqīn* is an excellent resort" (38 : 49) — these and numerous similar passages show clearly that the *muttaqī*, according to the Qur'ān, is the man who has attained to the highest stage of spiritual development. And as the object of fasting is to be a *muttaqī*, the conclusion is evident that the Qur'ān enjoins fasting with the object of making man ascend the spiritual heights.

A spiritual discipline

Fasting, according to Islām, is primarily a spiritual discipline: On two occasions in the Qur'ān,[4] those who fast are called *sā'iḥ* (from *sāḥa* meaning *he travelled*) or spiritual wayfarers; and according to one authority, when a person refrains, not only from food and drink but from all kinds of evil, he is called a *sā'iḥ* (R.). While speaking of Ramadzān, the month in which fasting is ordained, the Qur'ān specially refers to nearness to God, as if its attainment were an aim in fasting, and then adds: "So they should hear My call (by fasting) and believe in Me, that they may walk in the right way" (2 : 186). In Tradition too, special stress is laid on the fact that the seeking of Divine pleasure should be the ultimate object in fasting: "Whoever fasts during Ramadzān, having faith in Me and seeking My pleasure" (Bu.2 : 28). The Prophet said, "Fasting is a shield, so the faster should not indulge in foul speech ... and surely the breath of a fasting man is pleasanter to Allāh than the odour of musk; he refrains from food and drink and other desires to seek My pleasure: fasting is for Me only" (Bu.30 : 2). No temptation is greater than the temptation of satisfying one's thirst and hunger when drink and food are in one's possession, yet this temptation is overcome not once or twice, as if it were by chance, but day after day regularly for a whole month, with a set purpose of drawing closer and closer to the Divine Being. A man can avail himself of the best diet, yet he prefers to remain hungry;

[4] 9 : 112; 66 : 5.

he has the cool drink in his possession, yet he is parching with thirst; he touches neither food nor drink, simply because he thinks that it is the commandment of God that he should not do so. In the inner recesses, there is none to see him if he pours down his dry and burning throat a glass of delicious drink, yet there has developed in him the sense of the nearness to God to such an extent that he would not put a drop of it on his tongue. Whenever a new temptation comes before him, he overcomes it, because, just at the critical moment, there is an inner voice, "God is with me," "God sees me." Not the deepest devotion can of itself develop that sense of the nearness to God and of His presence everywhere, which fasting day after day for a whole month does. The Divine presence, which may be a matter of faith to others, becomes a reality for him, and this is made possible by the spiritual discipline underlying fasting. A new consciousness of a higher life, a life above that which is maintained by eating and drinking, has been awakened in him, and this is the life spiritual.

A moral discipline

There is also a moral discipline underlying fasting, for it is the training ground where man is taught the greatest moral lesson of his life—the lesson that he should be prepared to suffer the greatest privation and undergo the hardest trial rather than indulge in that which is not permitted to him. That lesson is repeated from day to day for a whole month, and just as physical exercise strengthens man physically, moral exercise through fasting, the exercise of abstaining from everything that is not allowed, strengthens the moral side of his life. The idea that everything unlawful must be eschewed and that evil must be hated is thus developed through fasting. Another aspect of the moral development of man by this means is that he is thus taught to conquer his physical desires. He takes his food at regular intervals and that is no doubt a desirable rule of life, but fasting for one month in the year teaches him the higher lesson that, instead of being the slave of his appetites and desires, he should be their master, being able to change the course of his life if he so wills it. The man who is able to rule his desires, to make them work as he likes, in whom willpower is so developed that he can command himself, is the man who has attained to true moral greatness.

Social value of fasting

In addition to its spiritual and moral values, fasting as prescribed in the Qur'ān has also a social value, more effective than that which is realized through prayer. Rich and poor, great and small, residents of the same vicinity are brought together five times daily in the mosque on terms of perfect equality, and thus healthy social relations are established through prayer. But the commencement of the month of Ramadzān is a signal for a mass movement towards equality which is not limited to one vicinity or even one country but affects the whole Muslim world. The rich and the poor may stand shoulder to shoulder in one row in the mosque, but in their homes they live in different environments. The rich sit down on tables laden with dainties and with these they load their stomachs four, even six, times daily; while the poor cannot find sufficient food with which to satisfy their hunger even twice a day. The latter often feel the pangs of hunger to which the former are utter strangers; how can the one feel for the other and sympathize with him? A great social barrier thus exists between the two classes in their homes, and this barrier is removed only when the rich are made to feel the pangs of hunger like their poorer brethren and go without food throughout the day, and this experience has to be gone through, not for a day or two, but for a whole month. The rich and the poor are thus, throughout the Muslim world, brought on the same level in that they are both allowed only two meals a day, and though these meals may not be exactly the same, the rich have perforce to shorten their menu and to adopt a simpler fare and thus come closer to their poorer brethren. This course undoubtedly awakens sympathy for the poor in the hearts of the rich, and it is for this reason that the helping of the poor is specially enjoined in the month of Ramadzān.

Physical value of fasting

Refraining from food during stated intervals does no physical harm to a healthy person. On the contrary, it does some good. But fasting has yet another, and a more important, physical value. The man who cannot face the hardships of life, who is not able to live, at times, without his usual comforts, cannot be said to be even physically fit for life on this earth. The moment such a man is involved in difficulty or distress, as he must be every now and again, his strength is liable to give way. Fasting accustoms him to face the hardships of life, being in itself a practical lesson to that end, and increases his powers of resistance.

The month of Ramadzān

With some exceptions, which will be mentioned later on, Muslims are required to fast for 29 or 30 days of the month of Ramadzān. The exact number depends on the appearance of the moon which may be after 29 or 30 days. Fasting commences with the new moon of Ramadzān and ends on the appearance of the new moon of Shawwāl. The Prophet is reported to have said: "We are a people who neither write nor do we keep account; the month is thus and thus, showing (by his fingers) once twenty-nine and again thirty" (Bu. 30 : 13). Another tradition says: "The Prophet mentioned Ramadzān and said, "Do not fast until you see the new moon and do not break fasting until you see it (again), and if it is cloudy, calculate its appearance" (Bu. 30 : 11; M. 13 : 2). Another says that if it is cloudy, thirty days should be completed (Bu. 30 : 11). To begin and end by the actual appearance of the new moon[5] was the easier method for a "people who did not know writing, and did not keep account," and it is still the easier method for the vast masses living in villages and distant places, but the tradition quoted above also allows that the appearance of the moon may be judged by computation. There is however an express prohibition against fasting when the appearance of the moon is doubtful (*yaum al-shakk*) (AD. 14 : 10).

Choice of Ramadzān

The injunction laid down in the Qur'ān, relating to fasting in the month of Ramadzān, runs as follows: "The month of Ramadzān is that in which the Qur'ān was revealed, a guidance to men and clear proofs of guidance and the Criterion. So whoever of you is present in the month, he shall fast therein" (2 : 185). It will be seen from the words of the

[5] The actual appearance of the moon may be established by the evidence of a single man if he be trustworthy. It is related that on a certain occasion the people of Madīnah were doubtful about the appearance of the new moon of Ramadzān and they had decided not to fast, when a man came from the desert and gave evidence that he had seen the new moon. And the Prophet accepted his evidence and directed the people to fast (AD. 14 : 14).

injunction that the choice of this particular month for fasting is not without a reason. It has been chosen because it is the month in which the Qur'ān was revealed. It is well-known that the Qur'ān was revealed piecemeal during a period of twenty-three years; therefore by its revelation in the month of Ramadzān is meant that its revelation first began in that month. And this is historically true. The first revelation came to the Prophet on the 24th night of the month of Ramadzān when he was in the cave of Ḥira (IJ-C. 2 : 185). It was therefore in Ramadzān that the first ray of Divine light fell on the Prophet's mind, and the angel Gabriel made his appearance with the great Divine message. The month which witnessed the greatest spiritual experience of the Prophet was thus considered to be the most suitable month for the spiritual discipline of the Muslim community, which was to be effected through fasting.

There are evident reasons for choosing a lunar month. The advantages and disadvantages of the particular season in which it falls are shared by the whole world. A solar month would have given the advantages of shorter days and cooler weather to one part of the world, and burdened the other with the disadvantages of longer days and hotter weather. The lunar month is more in consonance with the universal nature of teachings of Islām, and all people have the advantages and disadvantages equally distributed. On the other hand, if a particular time had not been specified the discipline would have lost all its value. It is due to the choice of a particular month, that with its advent the whole Muslim world is, as it were, moved by one current from one end to the other. The movement effected by the advent of Ramadzān in the Muslim world is the greatest mass movement on the face of the earth. The rich and the poor, the high and the low, the master and the servant, the ruler and the ruled, the black and the white, the Eastern and the Western, from one end of the earth to the other, suddenly change the course of their lives when they witness the tiny crescent of Ramadzān making its appearance on the western horizon. There is no other example of a mass movement on this scale on the face of the earth, and this is due to the specification of a particular month.

Persons who may not fast

The injunction to fast is laid down only for those who *witness* the coming of the month, *man shahida min-kum alshahra*. The verb *shahida* is from the infinitive *shahada*, which means *the bearing of witness*; so the injunction to fast is laid upon those only who witness the coming of the month.

Evidently all people who live in places where the division into twelve months does not exist, are excluded from the purview of the injunction. Fasting is not compulsory in their case.

People who are exempted are specially mentioned either in the Qur'ān or in the Tradition. The Qur'ān mentions the sick and those on journey in the following words: "But whoever among you is sick or on a journey, (he shall fast) a like number of other days. And those who find it extremely hard[6] may effect redemption by feeding a poor man" (2 : 184). This is not an absolute exemption for the sick man and the traveller; they are required to fast afterwards, when the sickness has gone or when the journey ends, but there may be cases of protracted illness or constant journeying, and such people are allowed to effect a redemption by feeding a poor man for every fast missed. Tradition makes a further extension and gives relaxation to certain classes of people who, on account of some physical disability, are not able to fast. It is related of Anas that he used to feed a poor man when he grew too old to fast (Bu. 65, sūrah 2, ch. 25), and Ibn 'Abbās is reported to have held that the words "those who find it hard to do so may effect a redemption" relate to the old man and old woman and the pregnant woman and the woman that suckles a child, and that all of them are allowed to break the fast, — the latter two, only if they fear for the child—and feed a poor man instead (AD. 14 : 3). This view was also held by Ḥasan and Ibrāhīm (Bu. 65, sūrah 2, ch. 25). It will be seen that the underlying idea is that a burden should not be placed on any one, which he is unable to bear. The case of old people who have become enfeebled by age is very clear while in the case of pregnant and nursing women, the permission to effect a redemption is due to the fact that fasting may cause harm to the unborn baby, or the baby that is being nursed, as well as to the woman herself; and as she is likely to remain in this condition for a sufficiently long time, she is given the benefit of the relaxation. Sickly people and those who are too weak to bear the burden would be dealt with as sick. Ibn Taimiyah further extends the principle

[6] The Arabic word is *yuṭīqūna-hū*, which is generally interpreted as meaning *those who are able to do it*. If this interpretation be adopted, the significance would be that invalids and travellers may either fast afterwards when they are not under such disability, or they may effect a redemption by feeding a poor man for every day of fasting. But I prefer the other interpretation which some commentators have accepted, *viz.*, that *yuṭīqūna-hū* means *those who find it hard to keep* the fast even afterwards; only such persons are allowed to effect a redemption by feeding a poor man. This interpretation is supported by a different reading *yuṭayaqūna-hū* which means *those on whom a hard task is imposed*. Ibn 'Abbās' reading *yuṭawwaqūna-hū* (Bu. 65 : sūrah 2, ch. 25) carries a similar significance, and he interprets these words as relating to very old people who are unable to fast.

that the fast may be deferred in cases of hardship, and holds that those engaged in war may not fast, though they may not be journeying, for, he adds, the hardships of war are greater than the hardships of travel (ZM. I. pp. 165, 166). From this it may be argued that, in unavoidable cases of very hard labour, the choice of postponing the fast may be given to those who are engaged in such labour.

To define the limits of sickness or travel is rather difficult. 'Aṭā was of opinion that whatever the ailment, great or small, it entitled a person to the benefit of the exception (Bu. 65, sūrah 2, ch. 25). But generally it has been held that only such sickness as is likely to cause harm comes under the exception. As regards travel, there is nothing on record from the Prophet as to its limit (Zm. I, p. 166). A certain Companion, Diḥyā, is reported to have travelled to a village which was about three miles distant from his own place and to have broken the fast, and some people followed his example but others did not (AD. 14 : 46). But it has been held that the proposed journey must be one that extends over more than a day, *i.e.*, twenty-four hours; according to others, it must extend over two days; and others still think it necessary that it should extend over three days at least. But when the journey is actually started, the fast may be broken, whatever the distance travelled over may be. Thus of Abū Baṣra Ghifārī, a Companion of the Prophet, it is related that he took a boat from Fusṭāṭ to Alexandria, and broke the fast while yet the buildings of Fusṭāṭ had not disappeared (AD. 14 : 45). I would interpret the exception relating to sickness and travel as meaning a sickness or journey which causes inconvenience to the subject of it, as the exception is followed by the words, "Allāh desires ease for you, and He desires not hardship for you" (2 : 185).

The permission to break the fast for sickness or journey is meant for the convenience of the person who is under an obligation to keep the fast, as the words quoted above show. There is, however, a strong opinion that the permission granted by God must be made use of, just as in the case of prayer the traveller must shorten his prayer. The case of prayer and fasting do not, however, stand on a par, because, if the fasts are broken, the number of days must be completed afterwards, while in the case of prayer, there remains no obligation upon the traveller when the journey is over. The sick person and the traveller have therefore the option of keeping the fast if they do not find it hard, or of availing themselves of the permission and breaking the fast. The permissive nature of the words of the Qur'ān is reflected in many of the most reliable traditions. There are reports showing that the Prophet himself kept a fast while on a journey

(Bu. 30 : 33). In one tradition it is stated that on a certain journey on a very hot day, only the Prophet and Ibn Rawāhah kept the fast (Bu. 30 : 35). There are other traditions showing that when a certain person questioned the Prophet whether he should or should not break the fast, when on a journey, his own inclination being for fasting, the Prophet replied: "Keep the fast if thou likest, and break it if thou likest" (Bu. 30 : 33). Anas relates that they used to travel with the Prophet, and those who kept the fast did not find fault with those who broke it, nor did those who broke the fast find fault with those who kept it (Bu. 30 : 37). There is no doubt, a saying of the Prophet to the effect that "it is not a virtue to fast when journeying," but these words were spoken to a person who was in severe distress on account of the fast, and around whom people had gathered to provide shade for him (Bu. 30 : 36). *Bukhārī's* heading of this chapter is significant: "The Prophet's saying to him who was protected with a shade and the heat was severe. It is not a virtue to fast when journeying," the meaning evidently being that one should not fast when one finds it hard. There is a very large number of traditions on this subject, and some of these seem to contradict others, but the weight of evidence lies on the side that one is given the option of keeping the fast or breaking it.

Who is bound to fast?

The commandments of the Qur'ān are meant for those who are full-grown, and so is the injunction relating to fasts. According to Imām Mālik, minors should not fast, but the Caliph 'Umar is quoted as saying: "Even our children are fasting" (Bu. 30 : 47). Probably this may have been done when the weather was not too hot, and the object may have been to habituate the children to fasting. From what has been stated above, it would further appear that only such people are bound to fast as are physically fit. The jurists lay down three conditions, *viz.*, that of being *bāligh* (one who has reached the age of majority), *qādir* (physically fit) and *'āqil* (sane). Women are bound to fast if they are free from menstruation (Bu. 30 : 41). But while the woman who has the menstruation on is freed from the obligation of prayer completely, she is bound to make good the fasts that she has not kept and complete the mumber of days after Ramadzān, being treated in this respect like a sick person. The bleeding of childbirth is considered as menstruation with this difference, that if the mother is nursing the baby, she can effect a redemption by feeding a poor man. In all cases in which fasts have to be recovered, whether it is the case of a sick person or a traveller or a menstruating woman, a person is at liberty to do it when he or she likes, before the coming of the next Ramadzān (Bu. 30 : 40).

Voluntary fasts

In all the four principal ordinances of Islām — prayer, charity, fasting and pilgrimage — there is an obligatory part (*fardz*) and a voluntary part (*nafl*). But there are some restrictions imposed on voluntary fasting, for, if carried to an extreme, it would weaken the constitution. The following tradition is illustrative of how far voluntary fasting may be resorted to: "Ibn 'Umar says that the Prophet was informed of my resolve to fast in the day and keep awake in the night so long as I lived. (On being questioned) I admitted that I had said so. The Prophet said, Thou canst not bear this, therefore keep the fast and break it and keep awake and have sleep, and keep (voluntary) fast for three days in the month, for virtue has a tenfold reward, and this would be like your fasting every day. I said, I can bear more than this. The Prophet said, Then fast for one day and break the fast for two days. I said, I can bear more than this. He said, Then keep the fast for one day and break it for one day, and such was the fasting of David, on whom be peace, and this is the best of voluntary fasts. I said, I can bear more than this. The Prophet said, There is nothing better than this" (Bu. 30 : 56). This tradition shows that what the Prophet really recommended was voluntary fasting for three days in the month, but on no account should the voluntary fast be continuous. There are traditions in which it is stated that the Prophet especially recommended for voluntary fasting the last days of Sha'bān[7] or the *ayyām al-bidz*, that is the 13th, 14th and 15th of the lunar month[8] or Monday and Thursday[9] or the 'Arafah day, that is, one day before the *'Īd al-Adzḥā*,[10] or the first six days of Shawwāl,[11] or Muḥarram[12] or the

[7] Bu. 30 : 62; AD. 14 : 56.

[8] Bu. 30 : 60; Ah. IV, p. 165.

[9] AD. 14 : 59.

[10] (Tr. 8 : 45). There is a ḥadith showing that a cup of milk was sent to the Prophet on the 'Arafa day by Umm al-Faḍl to settle the question, and the Prophet drank it (Bu. 30 : 65).

[11] AD. 14 : 57.

[12] AD. 14 : 55.

Tas͟hrīq days, that is, 11th, 12th and 13th of Ḏhu-l-Ḥijja,[13] or the 'As͟hūra', that is, 10th Muḥarram;[14] but his own practice was that he never specified any particular day or days for voluntary fasting, as the following tradition shows: "'Ā'is͟hah was asked, Did the Holy Prophet, peace and blessings of Allāh be on him, specify any days (for fasting). Ṣhe said, No" (Bu. 30 : 64).

Restrictions on voluntary fasting

Voluntary fasting is particularly prohibited on the two 'Ịd days (Bu. 30 : 66). It is also forbidden that Friday should be specially chosen for voluntary fasting (Bu. 30 : 63). Nor should a day or two before Ramad͟zān be specially selected (Bu. 30 : 14). Other restrictions are that it should not be resorted to if it is likely to interfere with other duties. There is no asceticism in Islām, and no one is allowed to go to the length of neglecting his worldly duties for the sake of religious exercises. Religion is meant to enable a man to live a better life, and voluntary fasting should be undertaken only if the aim is to enable a man to achieve this objective. This is made clear in the story of Abū Dardā' and Salman, between whom brotherhood had been established by the Prophet. Salmān paid a visit to Abū Dardā' and saw his wife in a neglected condition (*mutabad͟hd͟hila*). Being asked the reason she replied that Abū Dardā' had become an ascetic. When Abū Dardā' came home and the meals were served, Abū Dardā' refused to eat because he was fasting. Salmān said that he would not take any food until Abū Dardā' took it, so he ate (and broke the fast). When the night came Abū Dardā' woke up after a little rest, Salmān asked him to remain sleeping, and when it was the latter part of the night, they both said their *Tahajjud* prayers. Then Salmān said to Abū Dardā': "Verily thou owest a duty to thy Lord, and thou owest a duty to thyself, and thou owest a duty to thy wife and children." When this was mentioned to the Prophet, he approved of what Salmān had said and done (Bu. 30 : 51). Here, therefore the husband

[13] Bu. 30 : 68.

[14] Bu. 30 : 69. The tenth of Muḥarram was particularly observed as a fasting day before the fasting of Ramad͟zān was made obligatory, but afterwards it was voluntary (Bu. 30 : 1).

was forbidden to fast, for the sake of the wife. Similarly the wife should not resort to voluntary fasting without the permission of her husband (Bu. 67 : 85). And as the host in the instance cited above broke the fast on account of his guest, there is a tradition stating that the guest should not undertake a voluntary fast, without the permission of the host (Tr. 8 : 69).

Expiatory fasts

Fasts are also recommended as an expiation for breaking certain commandments. The expiatory fasts mentioned in the Qur'ān are, (1) two months' successive fasting when a Muslim has killed a Muslim by mistake and the killer has not the means sufficient to free a slave (4 : 92); (2) two months' successive fasting when the husband resorts to the practice called *zihār* (putting away of the wife by saying, Thou art to me as the back of my mother), and he has not the means to free a slave (58 : 3, 4); (3) three days' fasting as an expiation for taking an oath by which one deprives oneself of something lawful when one is unable to free a slave or feed ten poor men (5 : 89); (4) fasting as decided on by two judges, as an expiation for killing game while one is on pilgrimage as an alternative to feeding the poor (5 : 95).

Tradition mentions two months' successive fasting by way of expiation when a fast during Ramadzān is broken intentionally (Bu.30 : 30). This was the case of a man who had sexual intercourse with his wife while fasting in Ramadzān, and the prophet told him to free a slave. On being told that he was too poor for that, he was asked if he could fast for two months successively, and he replied in the negative. Then he was asked if he could feed sixty poor men, and he again said, No. Thereupon the Prophet waited till there came a sack of dates to be given in charity, and the Prophet gave this away to the breaker of the fast, telling him to give it in charity. He said that there was no one in Madīnah poorer than himself, upon which the Prophet laughed heartily and allowed him to take away the sack of dates for his own use. This would show that the keeping of expiatory fasts for two months was only meant to make the violator feel contrite for his offence. Abū Hurairah was, however, of opinion that the act of not fasting for one day in Ramadzān cannot be expiated, even if the man fasts all his life; others (Sha'bī, Ibn Jubair, Qatāda, etc.) have held that the expiation for not fasting for one day is simply one day's fast to be kept afterwards (Bu. 30 : 29.).

Compensatory fasts

Fasting is also mentioned as being resorted to by way of effecting redemption (*fidya*, that is to say, as a compensation for not being able to do some act. Thus in the case of pilgrims who, for some reason, cannot observe fully the requirements of *iḥrām*, compensatory fasting (for three days) is mentioned as an alternative to giving away something in charity and sacrificing an animal (2 : 196); and in the case of pilgrims who may in combining *'umra* with *ḥajj* (*tamattu'*) get out of the condition of *iḥrām* in the interval between the two, three days' fasting during the pilgrimage and seven days' after returning from the pilgrimage (2 : 196).

Fasting in fulfilment of a vow

An instance of a vow to take a fast is mentioned in the Qur'ān where Mary the mother of Jesus says: "Surely I have vowed a fast to the Beneficent God, so I shall not speak to any man to-day" (19 : 26). This however appears to be only a fast to keep silent and not to talk with any person; a similar fast of silence is spoken of in the case of Zacharias: "Thy sign is that thou shouldst not speak to men for three days except by signs, and remember thy Lord much and glorify Him in the evening and the morning" (3 : 40). The case of Zacharias shows that the object of the fast of silence was the remembrance of God. From certain traditions it appears that if one has vowed to keep a fast, the vow must be fulfilled (Bu.30 : 42), while in one report it is stated that a woman came to the Prophet and spoke of her mother who died; and she had taken a vow to fast for a certain number of days and the Prophet told her to fulfil the vow (*ibid.*). But there is no tradition recommending the taking of such vows.

Limits of the fast

The limits of a fast are clearly laid down in the Qur'ān: "And eat and drink until the whiteness of the day becomes distinct from the blackness of the night at dawn (*al-fajr*), then complete the fast till night (*al lail*)" (2 : 187). *Lail* (night) begins when the sun sets, and hence the fast in the terminology of Islām is kept from the first appearance of dawn, which is generally about an hour and a half before sunrise, till sunset. *Wiṣāl* (lit., *joining together*) is fasting, or continuing the fast throughout the night and then the next day so that there is no break, is definitely prohibited (Bu. 30 : 48, 49). But one tradition permits continuity of fast till daybreak (Bu. 30 : 50). This would mean that a man may not, if he chooses, break the fast at sunset but must take the morning meal for fasting for the next day; in other words, he must take a meal once in twenty-four hours at least. *Wiṣāl* was prohibited lest people should, in trying continuous fast, impair their health or make themselves unfit for worldly work, for it appears that the Prophet himself sometimes kept a continuous fast (Bu. 30 : 48, 49); but, for how many days, is not definitely known. Only on one occasion, when some of the Companions joined with the Prophet in keeping a continuous fast, it was continued for three successive days, and being the close of the month, the moon appeared on the evening of the third day, the Prophet adding that if the moon had not appeared he would have continued the fast. When some one asked him, why he forbade *wiṣāl* to others, when he himself kept continuous fasts, he replied: "I pass the night while my Lord gives me food and makes me drink" (Bu. 30 : 49). He referred of course to the spiritual food which sometimes makes a man bear hunger and thirst in an extraordinary way, thus, in a sense, taking the place of food and drink. But all men had not the same spiritual sustenance, and, moreover, continuity of fast, if allowed generally, would have given rise to ascetic practices which Islām does not encourage. It should be noted in this connection that fasting, according to the Qur'ān, meant abstaining from food as well as from drink, and three days' continual suffering of hunger and thirst, in a hot country like Arabia, shows the extraordinary power of endurance which the Companions of the Prophet had developed, while his own power of endurance was much greater. This endurance was no doubt due to extraordinary spiritual powers.

In this connection it may be further noted that, though the taking of a morning meal is not made obligatory, yet special stress is laid on it, and it is said to be a source of blessing, because it enables a man the better to cope with the hardship of the fast. The Prophet is reported to have said: "Take the morning meal, for there is blessing in the morning meal (*suḥūr*)" (Bu. 30 : 20). This meal was taken very near the break of dawn. One Companion relates that, after taking the morning meal, he hastened to the mosque so that he might be able to join the morning prayer. Another says that the interval between the finishing of the morning meal and the beginning of prayer in congregation was such that hardly fifty verses could be recited in it (Bu. 9 : 27). It is even recommended that the morning meal should be taken as near the break of dawn as possible (Ah.V, p. 147). In one tradition it is stated that the *adhān*[15] of Bilāl should not lead you to give up the morning meal, for, it is added, he utters the *adhān* while yet it is night, so that the man who is saying his *Tahajjud* prayers may finish his prayers and the one who is sleeping may get up from his sleep (Bu.10 : 13). And according to another, the morning meal was to be continued till Ibn Umm Maktūm gave the call to prayer, for he was a blind man and he did not give the call till (dawn became so clear and well established that) "people called out to him, the dawn has broken, the dawn has broken" (Bu. 10 : 11). And even if the *adhān* is called out when the dawn has fully appeared, and a man has a cup in his hand ready to drink, he need not put it away and may drink it up (AD. 14 : 18).

As it is recommended in the case of the morning meal that it should be as late as possible, it is recommended that the breaking of the fast should be as early as possible. The Prophet is reported to have said that when the sun is set, the fast should be broken (Bu. 30 : 45). And according to another tradition: "People will have the good so long as they hasten in breaking the fast" (Bu. 30 : 45). Some wait to break the fast till they see the stars, thinking that the night does not set in till darkness is spread, but there is no authority for this.

The niyyah

A good deal of misunderstanding prevails on the question of *niyyah* in the observance of fasts. The *niyyah* really means *intention, aim* or *purpose* in the doing of a thing; but it is wrongly supposed that the *niyyah* consists in the repetition of certain words stating that one intends to do so and so. Bukhārī shows the true significance of *niyyah* when he gives as the heading to one of his chapters: "He who fasts during Ramadzān having faith (in God) (*imān-an*) and seeking His pleasure (*iḥtisāb-an*) and having an aim or purpose (*niyyat-an*)" (Bu. 30 : 6). And he adds a portion of a tradition reported by 'Āishah in which it is stated that "people will be raised up (on the Judgment Day) according to their aims (*'alā niyyāti-him*)." The very first tradition with which Bukhārī opens his book is an example of what *niyyah* means: "(Good) actions shall be

[15] Call for morning prayers, signifying the break of dawn.

judged only by their aims[16] — *innama-l-a'mālu bi-l-niyyāt.*'' Hence if a good action is done with a bad aim, it shall not benefit the doer. Exactly the same object is in view in the statement that there must be a *niyyah* in fasting, as Bukhārī says: that is, the man who fasts must have an aim or purpose before him. The aim or purpose of fasting has already been stated, being, according to the Qur'ān, the attainment of *taqwā*, to make the fast a spiritual discipline, to attain nearness to God and to seek His pleasure in all one's actions, and to make it a moral discipline, to shun all evil. It is in this sense alone that the *niyyah* is of the essence of fasting, as it is in fact of the essence of all good actions.

''Formulating the *niyyah,*'' or the expression of one's intention in set words, is unknown to the Qur'ān and the Tradition, and is in fact meaningless, for a man will not fast unless he intends to do it. Only in the case of voluntary fasting, it is stated in a tradition, that the Prophet sent a crier to inform the people on the day of 'Āshūra', in daytime that people who had not eaten anything up to that time may fast. And of Abū Dardā', it is related that he used to ask his wife if there was any food, and if none was found, he used to keep the fast (Bu. 30 : 21). According to 'Āishah, the Prophet used to ask if there was any food in the house, and when none was found he would fast (AD. 14 : 70). In the case of voluntary fasts one can understand the making up of mind in daytime, but there is no question of such intention in the month of Ramadzān, when every body knows that he must fast.

What breaks the fast

The word for breaking the fast is *ifṭār*, from *faṭr* meaning *to cleave* or *split* a thing *lengthwise* (R.), and the things which break a fast are called *mufṭirāt*, pl. of *mufṭir*. The three things which one should abstain from in fasting being eating, drinking and having sexual intercourse, these three, if resorted to of free will[17] and intentionally, between day-break and

[16] I have translated the word *a'māl* as meaning *good actions*. A reference to what follows in the report makes it clear, for the example of actions given there is *hijra*, the flight of a man for the sake of his principles which is an action of the highest value, but as the report tells us, if the *hijra* is undertaken with a bad aim in view, to attain worldly wealth or for the love of a woman, it loses all its value. That there can be no question of a good aim in evil actions is self-evident, and hence by *a'māl* in this report are meant *good actions*.

[17] Therefore anything done under compulsion or involuntarily does not break the fast.

sunset, would break the fast, but if done through forgetfulness or inadvertently, the fast remains and must be completed (Bu. 30 : 26). Rinsing the mouth with water or with a toothbrush, gargling or sniffing the water into the nostrils, even if a little water passes into the throat unintentionally, does not break the fast (Bu. 30 : 25, 26, 27, 28). Nor does taking a bath or keeping a wet cloth on the head or pouring water on the head break the fast, even though done intentionally to relieve the severity of thirst (Bu. 30 : 25; MM. 7 : 4-ii). Cupping and vomiting also do not break the fast, for as Ibn 'Abbās and 'Ikrama say, a fast is broken by that which goes into the body, not by that which comes out[18] (Bu. 30 : 32). It is related that the Prophet would kiss his wife when fasting (Bu. 30 : 23). There is a difference of opinion regarding the punishment for breaking a fast intentionally before its time, as shown under the heading "Expiatory fasts." The Qur'ān is silent on this point, while Tradition only shows that it is sufficient that the violator should be sincerely repentant. If fast is broken on a cloudy day, under the impression that the sun has set, and the sun then appears, then the fast should be completed (Bu. 30 : 46). If a man is fasting and then undertakes a journey, the fast may be broken (Bu. 30 : 34). The same rule may be followed in the case of sickness. In the case of voluntary fast, a man is at liberty to break the fast on account of a guest or the persistence of a friend (Bu. 30 : 51).

Ethical side of fasting

What has been said hitherto relates only to the external side of the fast but, as stated in the beginning, the essence of the fast is its moral and spiritual value, and the Qur'ān and Tradition have laid special stress on this. "Whoever does not give up," says one tradition "lying and acting falsely, Allāh does not stand in need of his giving up food and drink" (Bu. 30 : 8). This is true of all the Islamic injunctions. A man who says his prayers and does not keep in view their inner meaning, the object of prayer, is condemned in clear words: "Woe to the praying ones, who are unmindful of (the object of) their prayers" (107 : 4, 5). In another tradition, the ethical side of the fast is shown in the following words: "Fasting is a shield, so let the man who fasts not indulge in any foul speech or do any evil deed (*lā yajhal*), and if any one fights or quarrels with

[18] There is a difference of opinion on some of these minor points, but what has been said here is based on weightier authority.

him or abuses him, he should say, I am fasting. By Him Who holds my soul in His hand, the breath of the faster is pleasanter with Allāh than the scent of musk'' (Bu. 30 : 2). It is not refraining from food that makes the breath of the faster so sweet; it is refraining from foul speech and abuse and evil words and deeds of all kinds, so much so that he does not even utter an offensive word by way of retaliation. Thus a fasting person undergoes not only a physical discipline by curbing his carnal desires, the craving for food and drink, and the sex appetite, but he is actually required to undergo a direct moral discipline by avoiding all kinds of evil words and evil deeds. It is not only a training on the physical side, which has a moral value; it is a direct training on the spiritual side as well. In the sight of God, as plainly stated in these traditions, the fast loses its value not only by taking food or drink but also by telling a lie, using foul language, acting unfaithfully, or doing an evil deed.

The moral value of the fasting discipline is further enhanced by laying stress on the doing of good to humanity in the month of Ramadzān. The example of the Prophet is quoted in this connection in a tradition. ''The Prophet, may peace and the blessings of Allāh be upon him, was the most bountiful of all people, and he exceeded his own bounty in the month of Ramadzān'' (Bu. 30 : 7). Another tradition describes the month of Ramadzān as ''a month in which the sufferings of the poor and the hungry must be attended to '' (MM. 7 : I-iii).

These injunctions make clear the significance of the tradition which says that when the month of Ramadzān commences, ''the doors of Heaven are opened and the doors of Hell are closed and the devils are put into chains'' (Bu. 30 : 5). This is true of the man who keeps the fast, both physically and morally. The devils are chained in his case because he curbs and conquers the lower passions, by exciting which the devil makes a man fall into evil. The doors of Hell are closed on him because he shuns all evil which is man's hell. The doors of Heaven are opened for him because he rises above physical desires and devotes himself to the service of humanity. In one tradition, fasting is described as bringing about a forgiveness of sins ''for him who fasts having faith (in God) and to seek His pleasure and having an aim or purpose'' (Bu.2 : 28; 30 : 6). There is not the least doubt that fasting as qualified here, that is, when it is kept having true faith in God and when the person fasting resorts to it as a discipline for seeking the pleasure of God, is practical repentance of the highest value; and when a man sincerely repents of sins, his previous sins are forgiven, because the course of his life has been changed.

There is, however, yet another sense in which the doors of Heaven are opened to a fasting person in the month of Ramadzan. It is specially suited for spiritual advancement, for attaining nearness to God. Speaking of Ramadzān, the Qur'ān says: "And when My servants ask thee concerning Me, surely I am nigh; I answer the prayer of the suppliant when he calls on Me" (2 : 186). The ways of attaining nearness to God are here spoken of as being specially opened in Ramadzān, and this nearness is to be sought through prayer. It is for this reason that the Prophet used to have special regard for *Tahajjud* prayers in the month of Ramadzān. And he also recommended that his followers should, during this month, awake at night for prayers (Bu. 2 : 27).

I'tikāf

I'tikāf[19] means literally *to stay in a place*; technically it is staying in a mosque for a certain number of days, especially the last ten days of the month of Ramadzān. Bukhārī has devoted a whole book to *I'tikāf* (book 33), showing the practice of the Prophet in this connection. During these days, the man who enters the state of *I'tikāf* (*mu'takif*) dissociates himself from all worldly affairs, and he does not leave the mosque unless there is necessity (*ḥājah*), such as evacuation, or having a bath, etc. (Bu. 33 : 3, 4). Usually a tent was pitched for the Prophet in the yard of the mosque (Bu. 33 : 7). Women are also allowed to enter a state of *I'tikāf* (Bu. 33 : 6). The *mu'takif* may be visited by other people or by his wife (Bu. 33 : 11). According to one tradition, he may visit a sick person[20] (AD. 14 : 78). An *I'tikāf* may be performed in other days (AD. 15 : 75), but the last ten days of Ramadzān are specially mentioned in traditions and *I'tikāf* is spoken of in the Qur'ān in connection with Ramadzān.

Lailat al-Qadr

One of the last ten nights of the month of Ramadzān is called *Lailat al-Qadr, the night of grandeur* or *majesty*. In the Qur'ān, it is spoken of in two places. In ch.97, it is mentioned thrice as *lailat al-Qadr*: "Surely

[19] *I'tikāf* is derived from *'akafa 'alai-hi*, meaning *he kept,* or *clove, to it constantly* or *perseveringly* (LL.).

[20] There are other traditions showing that he should not visit the sick, nor assist at a burial, but evidently such deeds fall within the meaning of *ḥājah*.

We revealed it on *lailat al-Qadr*. And what will make thee comprehend what *lailat al-Qadr* is? *Lailat al-Qadr* is better than a thousand months. The angels and the Spirit descend in it by the permission of their Lord — for every affair — Peace! it is till the break of the morning.'' Here this night is spoken of as the night in which the Qur'ān was revealed, and it is further stated that it is the night on which angels and the Spirit descend. It is also mentioned in ch.44 where it is called a blessed night (*laila mubāraka*): ''By the Book that makes manifest (the truth)! We revealed it on a blessed night — truly We are ever-warning. Therein is made clear every affair — full of wisdom — a command from Us'' (44 : 2-5). It will be seen that, in both places, the Qur'ān is spoken of as having been revealed on this night, and elsewhere it is stated that the Qur'ān was revealed in the month of Rama<u>dz</u>ān, which shows that this night occurs in the month of Rama<u>dz</u>ān. The revelation of the Qur'ān on this night means that its revelation began on that night; in other words, the first revelation came to the Prophet on this night. It is called a blessed night or the grand night because in it was laid the basis of a new revelation to the world which contains every commandment (*amr*) full of wisdom and knowledge (*ḥakīm*). The *lailat al-Qadr* is, therefore, as it were, the anniversary of the revelation of the Qur'ān.

As shown above, the last ten days of Rama<u>dz</u>ān are specially observed as days of devotion, so much so that, though Islām discourages asceticism, yet in these ten days, a Muslim is allowed to lead an ascetic life, by keeping himself to the mosque and giving up all worldly affairs. There are various traditions showing that the Muslims should look for this night as one of the odd nights in the last ten nights of Rama<u>dz</u>ān (Bu. 32 : 3) or in the last seven nights (Bu. 32 : 2). According to some traditions it is the twenty-fifth or twenty-seventh or twenty-ninth night of Rama<u>dz</u>ān. One tradition says that some of the Companions of the Prophet were shown *lailat al-Qadr* in their dreams in the last seven nights (MM. 7 : 9—i). It should be borne in mind that *lailat al-Qadr* is a spiritual experience, as it was the spiritual, not the physical, experience of the Prophet, and as the last-quoted tradition shows, it was the spiritual experience of the Companions, and therefore it is an error to think that it can be beheld as a physical experience, or that any physical change is witnessed on that night. It is the spiritual experience of the man who exerts himself in Rama<u>dz</u>ān to seek nearness to the Divine Being.

Chapter IV

ḤAJJ OR PILGRIMAGE

European views on adoption of pilgrimage by Islām

As an institution *ḥajj*[1] existed, before the advent of Islām, from a very remote antiquity. Modern European criticism takes the view that its adoption by Islām, with certain reforms, of course, was due to several causes which sprang up after the Prophet's flight to Madīnah. Chief among these causes are said to be the victory won by Islām at Badr which, it is opined, made the Prophet look forward to the conquest of Makkah, and the final rupture with the Jews, whom the Prophet had, at first, hoped to win over to his cause. Hughes advances this theory in his *Dictionary of Islam* under the heading "Ka'bah":

> "When Muhammad found himself established in al-Madīnah, with a very good prospect of his obtaining possession of Makkah, and its historic associations, he seems to have withdrawn his thoughts from Jerusalem and its Sacred Rock and to fix them on the house at Bakkah as the home founded for mankind... The Jews proving obdurate and there being little chance of his succeeding in establishing his claim as their prophet, spoken of by Moses, he changes the qiblah, or direction for prayer, from Jerusalem to Makkah. The house at Makkah is made "a place of resort unto men and a sanctuary."

Other European writers have advanced the same theory, and recently A.J. Wensinck has incorporated it into the *Encyclopaedia of Islam*. Writing under "Hadjdj", he says:

> "Muhammad's interest in the Hadjdj was first aroused in al-Medina. Several causes contributed to this, as Snouck Hurgronje has shown in his *Mekkaansche Feest*. The brilliant

[1] The word *ḥajj* means, literally, *repairing to a thing for the sake of a visit (al-qasd li-l-ziyāra)* (R.), and in the technicality of law *the repairing to Bait-Allāh* (the House of Allāh) to observe the necessary devotions (*iqāmat-an li-l-nusuk*) (R.). Bait-Allāh is one of the names by which the Ka'bah is known; and *nusuk* means *'ibādah* (worship or devotion), or *ṭā'a* (obedience); it is also the plural of *nasīkah* meaning *dhabīḥah* (the animal that is sacrificed) (N.). From the same root and carrying the significance of' *ibādah*, is *mansik*, and its plural *manāsik* is particularly used to signify the acts of devotion prescribed in ḥajj. It is generally under the head *manāsik* that injunctions relating to ḥajj are mentioned in collections of Tradition.

> success of the battle of Badr had aroused in him thoughts of a conquest of Mecca. The preparations for such a step would naturally be more successful if the secular as well as the religious interests of his companions were aroused. Muḥammad had been deceived in his expectations regarding the Jewish community in Medina and the disagreements with the Jews had made a religious breach with them inevitable. To this period belongs the origin of doctrine of the religion of Abraham, the alleged original type of Judaism and Islam. The Ka'ba now gradually advances into the centre of religious worship, the father of monotheism built it with his son Isma'il and it was to be a 'place of assembly for mankind.' ... In this period also the Ka'ba was made a kibla — This is the position of affairs in the year 2 of the Hidjra."

On the face of it, it appears to be a very plausible theory but it is in flat contradiction to historical facts. The battle of Badr was fought in the month of Ramadzān, in the second year of Hijrah, and the final rupture with the Jews came in the third year after the battle of Uḥud; while the Ka'bah was made a *qiblah* sixteen months after the Hijrah (Bu. 8 : 31), that is to say, about three months before the battle of Badr. The structure which, according to Hughes, Wensinck and Hurgronje, was built on the victory of Badr and the rupture with the Jews, the idea of formulating a doctrine of the religion of Abraham, the father of monotheism, as a prototype of Islām, Judaism and Christianity; of the sacredness of the Ka'bah and its connection with the names of Abraham and Ishmael; of the Ka'bah being made a *qiblah* and of the institution of ḥajj with prospects of conquering Makkah; all this existed not only long before the battle of Badr but even before the Prophet's flight to Madīnah. The religion of Abraham as pure monotheism is mentioned in a chapter of the Qur'ān (*sūrah*) belonging to the middle Makkah period, where Abraham is also called a *ḥanīf*: "Surely Abraham was a model of virtue, obedient to Allāh, upright (*ḥanīf*)...Then we revealed to thee: Follow the faith (*milla*) of Abraham, the upright one (*ḥanīf*), and he was not of the polytheists" (16 : 120-123). And again in a chapter belonging to the last Makkah period: "My Lord has guided me to the right path — a right religion, the faith (*milla*) of Abraham, the upright one (*ḥanīf*), and he was not of the polytheists" (6 : 162). It is surprising to find Orientalists so learned ignoring such broad facts of history for the sake of a pet theory.

Sacredness of Makkah and the Ka'bah recognized in earliest revelations

Similarly, the sacredness of Makkah and its connection with the names of Abraham and Ishmael, finds clear mention in the early Makkah revelations. In one of the earliest chapters, Makkah is described as "this city made secure" (95 : 3). In another equally early revelation, it is referred to simply as the City: "Nay! I call to witness this City — and thou wilt be made free from obligation in this City — and the begetter and he whom he begot" (90 : 1-3); where, in the last words, Abraham and Ishmael are referred to. The Ka'bah is called *al-Bait al-ma'mūr*, or *the House that is visited* in a revelation of the same period (52 : 4), while another revelation of the early Makkah period speaks of *al-Masjid al-Ḥarām* or the Sacred Mosque (17 : 1). The sacredness of Makkah is spoken of in still clearer words in revelations belonging to the middle Makkah period: "I am commanded only to serve the Lord of this City, Who has made it sacred, and His are all things" (27 : 91). The names of Abraham and Ishmael in connection with Makkah, its sacredness and the fact of its being a place of resort for men, also find mention in the middle Makkah revelations: "And when Abraham said: My Lord, Make this City secure, and save me and my sons from worshipping idols ... Our Lord, I have settled a part of my offspring in a valley unproductive of fruit near Thy Sacred House, our Lord, that they may keep up prayer; therefore make the hearts of some people yearn towards them and provide them with fruits" (14 : 35-37).

Why Ka'bah was not made qiblah *earlier*

The theory thus built up by European savants has no foundation whatever. The sacredness of Makkah and its great Mosque, the connection therewith of the names of Abraham and Ishmael, and the fact of Makkah being made a resort for men, are all themes of the earliest as well as the later revelations. It is true that the various commandments and prohibitions were revealed gradually, and that the command to make the Ka'bah a *qiblah* was revealed at Madīnah, but even this happened before the battle of Badr. Notwithstanding all that was said in the Qur'ān with regard to the sacredness of Makkah and of the Ka'bah, notwithstanding the fact that pilgrimage to Makkah had been ordained as a duty of the Muslims towards the close of the Prophet's stay at Makkah, as shown later, notwithstanding even the fact that it was the Prophet's own desire that the Ka'bah should be made his *qiblah* (Bu. 2 : 30; 8 : 31; 65, sura 2, ch.18), he continued to follow the *qiblah* of the last prophet that had passed away before him, that is, Jerusalem, and awaited the Divine direction. The Qur'ān recognized the truth of all the prophets, including the prophets of Israel, and as Jesus was the last of those prophets and his *qiblah* the same as that of the Israelite prophets,[2] namely, the temple at Jerusalem, which place was honoured by the Qur'ān (17 : 1) as *al-Masjid al-Aqṣā* (lit., *the Remote Mosque*), he retained it as his *qiblah* until he received an express revelation to turn towards the Sacred Mosque. Moreover, he did not receive that commandment when he was at Makkah among the polytheists when it might have been said that he was scheming to win over the Arabs; but it was after his coming to Madīnah, at a time when relations with the Jews were still friendly, when the prospects of winning over the Arabs were as distant as ever, and when war with the Quraish at Makkah had become inevitable, that the Prophet received a revelation to turn to the Ka'bah as the future *qiblah* of the Muslim world. For sixteen long months at Madīnah, he had continued to pray with his back to Makkah, the avowedly sacred territory, because he would not do anything of his own desire. As soon as he came to Madīnah, he felt the difficulty that he could no more, as at Makkah, turn his face to both places, to the Holy temple at Jerusalem and to the Sacred Mosque at Makkah; he realized that in turning his face to one he must turn his back on the other; and however much he desired that the Sacred Mosque at Makkah should be his *qiblah*, still he would not turn his back to the *qiblah* of the last prophet before him, until he received a Divine commandment to that effect.

When was pilgrimage first instituted

The ḥajj was a recognized institution in the first and second years of Hijrah before the commencement of the war with the Quraish. The second chapter which was, in the main, revealed in the first and second years of Hijrah, is full of directions relating to ḥajj, the context whereof shows clearly that fighting had not actually taken place, though prospects of a war were in sight. The months in which ḥajj is to be performed are thus spoken of: "They ask thee concerning the new moons; say, They are times appointed for men and for the pilgrimage" (2 : 189). And again:

[2] It should be noted that the Christians themselves ceased to follow the *qiblah* of Christ.

"The months of the pilgrimage are well-known" (2 : 197). Between these two verses, which speak of the months of ḥajj, occur the verses by which the Muslims were permitted to take up the sword to defend themselves: "And fight in the way of Allāh against those who fight against you" (2 : 190); from which it will be seen that the details of ḥajj were being given when fighting was as yet only permitted, and it was after that that the actual fighting began. The details of ḥajj were, therefore, revealed before the battle of Badr. The rules of conduct to be observed when proceeding on ḥajj are also stated in the same context: "Whoever determines the performance of the pilgrimage therein, there shall be no immodest speech, nor abusing, nor altercation in the pilgrimage" (2 : 197). The running between the hills of Ṣafā and Marwah (*sa'y*) is spoken of in still earlier verses: "The Ṣafā and the Marwah are truly among the signs of Allāh, so whoever makes a pilgrimage to the House or pays a visit[3] to it, there is no blame on him if he goes round them" (2 : 158). This permission was specifically granted because at the time there were two idols on the Ṣafā and the Marwah. The going to 'Arafāt and Muzdalifah is also spoken of: "So when you press on from 'Arafāt, remember Allāh near the Holy Monument" (2 : 198); and there is a clear injunction to accomplish the ḥajj: "And accomplish the hajj and the 'umrah for Allāh" (2 : 196).

The mention of these details of ḥajj is a proof that the institution of ḥajj had already been recognized as part of the laws of Islām. In fact, we find a Muslim, here and there, performing the ḥajj in the earliest days when, on account of some alliance, he deemed himself secure, it being impossible, of course, for the generality of the Muslims. Thus it is related of Sa'd ibn Mu'ādh that on account of his friendship with Umayya ibn Khalf, a Quraish chief, he went to Makkah to perform an *'umrah* after the Hijrah and before the battle of Badr — that is, in the first year of Hijrah — and had an altercation with Abū Jahl, whom he threatened with cutting off the Quraish trade with Syria (Bu. 64 : 2). He would not have done so unless the institution of ḥajj had been adopted by Islām. Hence it is clear that ḥajj was a recognized institution of Islām in the first year of Hijrah. In fact, ḥajj was instituted before the Hijrah took place, and

[3] Ḥajj and 'umrah, the latter of which is translated as the *minor pilgrimage* but which may more correctly be rendered as a *visit*, differ slightly. The 'umrah may be performed at any time, while the ḥajj or the pilgrimage proper, can only be performed at a particular time. Of the ceremonies connected with the pilgrimage proper, the staying in the plain of 'Arafāt is dispensed with in the case of 'umrah.

while the Prophet was still in Makkah. The chapter entitled *al-Ḥajj* was revealed towards the close of the Prophet's career at Makkah[4] and it was in this chapter that ḥajj was proclaimed to be an institution of Islām: "And proclaim to men the hajj:[5] they will come to thee on foot and on every lean camel, coming from every remote path, that they may witness benefits provided for them and mention the name of Allāh on appointed days over what He has given them of the cattle quadruped, then eat of them and feed the distressed one, the needy. Then let them accomplish their needful acts of cleansing, and let them fulfil their vows and go round the Ancient House" (22 : 27-29). These verses leave not the least doubt that ḥajj was ordained as an Islamic institution before the Hijrah.

Description of the Ka'bah

As the chief features of the ḥajj centre round the Ka'bah, something must be said about this building and its name. The root-word *Ka'ba* means *it swelled* or *became prominent* (LL.), or *it became high* and *exalted ('alā-wa-rtafa'a)* (N.) and the Sacred House is called Ka'bah on account of its glory and exaltation (N.). The Ka'bah is a rectangular building, almost in the centre of the Sacred Mosque (*Masjid al-Ḥarām*), whereof

[4] Rodwell is certainly wrong in placing this chapter among the latest Madīnah revelations. The best authorities are agreed that it was revealed at Makkah, though some are of opinion that some of its verses were revealed in the early days at Madīnah, but even this view is untenable. The verses relating to ḥajj, however, are not placed in this category. Muir puts this chapter at the close of the Makkah *sūras* of the fifth period, and internal as well as external evidence shows this to be correct. A recent writer concludes his discussion as to the date of revelation of this chapter with the following words: "To conclude: Sūrah 22 is thoroughly homogeneous, containing no elements from the Madīnah period. And (as was said a moment ago) much stronger evidence than has thus far been offered must be produced before it can be maintained that Makkan *sūras* were freely interpolated after the Hijrah." (C.C. Torrey, *The Jewish Foundation of Islam,* p.100).

[5] This verse is preceded by one in which Abraham is spoken of: "And when We pointed to Abraham the place of the House, saying: Associate naught with Me, and purify My House for those who make circuits and stand to pray and bow and prostrate themselves." The words "Proclaim among men the ḥajj" are, therefore, generally understood to have been addressed to Abraham. Even if this view is accepted, it is equally an address to the Holy Prophet, for, as the context shows, the mention of Abraham is only by way of parenthesis; and inasmuch as the pilgrimage is an ordinance common to both the Abrahamic and the Islamic faiths, the address is equally to both prophets.

the front and back walls (north-east and south-west) are each 40 feet in length, and the two side-walls 35 feet each, the height being 50 feet, the four walls running north-west, north-east, south-west and south-east.

The four corners of the building are known by four different names, the north corner as *al-rukn al-'Irāqī* (after 'Irāq), the south corner as *al-rukn al-Yamanī* (after Yemen), the west corner as *al-rukn al-Shāmī* (after Shām or Syria) and the east corner as *al-rukn al-Aswad* (after the Ḥajar al-Aswad, or the Black Stone). The four walls of the Ka'bah are covered with a black curtain called Kiswa (lit., *clothing*). The door of the Ka'bah is in the north-east wall, about seven feet from the ground, not in the middle of the wall but nearer the Black Stone. When the Ka'bah is opened, a stair-case is placed in front of it to enable the visitors to reach the entrance. Outside the building is an open space, called al-Ḥijr (lit., *prohibited*), marked by a semi-circular wall three feet high, running opposite the north-west wall of the Ka'bah, the two ends of this wall being about six feet distant from the north and west corners of the Ka'bah, and the central part about 37 feet from the wall. This part is also called al-Ḥaṭim (from *ḥāṭama* meaning *it crushed*), though Ibn 'Abbās is reported as saying that it should not be called by that name, as this name was given to it in the days of Ignorance and carried with it the superstitious association of throwing there one's whip or shoe at the time of taking an oath (Bu. 63 : 27). For the purpose of making circuits, the Hijr is included in the building. There are traditions showing that the Ḥijr was considered by the Prophet to be part of the building of the Ka'bah (Bu. 25 : 42; M. 15 : 66). It was for this reason that 'Abd Allāh ibn Zubair included it in the building proper, but it was again left an open space when the Ka'bah was rebuilt after him by Ḥajjāj.

In the east corner at the height of about five feet is the Ḥajar al-Aswad (lit., *the Black Stone*) built into the wall. It is of a reddish black colour about eight inches in diameter, and is now broken into pieces held together by a silver band. The Maqām Ibrāhīm must also be mentioned in connection with the Ka'bah. It means "the place of Abraham," and the name is given to a very small building within the Sacred Mosque, about five feet square, supported on six columns eight feet high. This name, handed down from antiquity from one generation to another, is a decided proof of the connection of Abraham with the Ka'bah, and attention is drawn to this in the Qur'ān in 3 : 96. But in 2 : 125, the words *Maqām Ibrāhīm* are used for the Sacred House itself.

History of the Ka'bah

The Ka'bah is stated in the Qur'ān to be "the first House (of Divine worship) appointed for men" (3 : 95). In one place it is called *al-Bait al-'Atīq* or the Ancient House (22 : 29). It is also called *al-Bait al-Ḥarām* (5 : 97), or *al-Muḥarram* (14 : 37) which carries the same significance as *al-Ḥarām*, both meaning originally *al-mamnū' min-hu* or *that which is forbidden*; in other words, a place whereof the sanctity must not be violated. There is nothing in the Qur'ān, or the Tradition to show when and by whom the Ka'bah was first built; but it is said to have been rebuilt by Abraham and Ishmael: "And when Abraham and Ishmael raised the foundations of the House: Our Lord! Accept from us" (2 : 127). An earlier revelation makes it clear that the Ka'bah was already there when Abraham left Ishmael in the wilderness of Arabia: "Our Lord! I have settled a part of my offspring in a valley unproductive of fruit near Thy Sacred House" (14 : 37). It appears from this that Ishmael had been purposely left near the Sacred House; it was, in fact, under a Divine commandment that Abraham took this step (Bu.60 : 9). It would seem that the Ka'bah was then in a demolished condition and was afterwards, when Ishmael grew to manhood, rebuilt by Abraham and Ishmael as stated in 2 : 127. In a long tradition of Ibn 'Abbās, speaking of Abraham leaving Ishmael and his mother near the Ka'bah, it is said: "And the House was then rising above the surface of the earth like a mound, the flood waters passing to its right and to its left" (Bu. 60 : 9). The tradition then goes on to narrate how long after this, when Ishmael had grown to manhood and was a married man, Abraham came to pay a visit to him and told him that Almighty God had commanded him to build a house at the place where the mound was, and how the father and the son built the Ka'bah. Besides being in a ruined condition, it seems to have had idols placed in it and Abraham was required to purify it of these. "And We enjoined Abraham and Ishmael, saying: Purify My House for those who visit it and those who abide in it for devotion and those who bow down and those who prostrate themselves" (2 : 125). Nearly the same words occur in an earlier revelation (22 : 26).

The Ka'bah was again rebuilt by the Quraish[6] when the Prophet was a young man, and he personally took part in its building, carrying stones on his shoulders. During the construction a dispute arose as to who should

[6] The leading tribe of Makkah.

place the Black Stone in its place. Every tribe was desirous of having this honour accorded to its representative. Finally a settlement was arrived at, namely that the decision of the man who made his appearance first in the Ka'bah should be accepted by all. Fortunately, the man who appeared first was Muhammad, peace and blessings of Allāh be upon him, and there was an outcry that *al-Amīn* (the Faithful one) had come. The Prophet decided this dispute with his usual sagacity, placing the stone in a cloth with his own hands, and then asking a representative of each of the tribes to hold a corner of that cloth and lift the stone to its position, the Prophet himself fixing it in position. The Ka'bah remained as it was built by the Quraish until the time of 'Abd Allāh ibn Zubair, when the building having been damaged by the Umayyad army which had besieged Makkah, 'Abd Allāh decided to rebuild it, instead of repairing it, including the open space of Ḥijr in the building itself. But after the fall of 'Abd Allāh, Ḥajjāj again rebuilt it on the foundations of the structure erected by the Quraish. And the building to-day rests on the same foundations.

Al-Masjid al-Ḥarām

The Ka'bah stands in the centre of a parallelogram whose dimensions, as given in the *Encyclopaedia of Islam,* are as follows: N.-W.side 545 ft., S.-E. side 553 ft., N.-E. side 360 ft., S.-W. side 364 ft. This area is known as al-Masjid al-Ḥarām or the Sacred Mosque, the famous mosque of Makkah. The name is met with in pre-Islamic literature (*En. Is.*). In the Qur'ān this name occurs in revelations of the early Makkah period, as in 17 : 1. The area of the Sacred Mosque contains, besides the Ka'bah, the Maqām Ibrāhīm and the building over the fountain of Zamzam. The Sacred Mosque was the centre of all administrative activities before Islām, as within it was situated the Makkan Council Hall (*Dār al-Nadwah*) where all important matters regarding the weal or woe of the people were settled. Since the advent of Islām, the Sacred Mosque has been the pivot of the intellectual activities of Makkah, and the whole Muslim world looks upon it as its central point.

Historical evidence of antiquity of Ka'bah

The Qur'ān claims the Ka'bah as the first house of Divine worship on earth, and all available historical evidence upholds this claim. It is sufficient to quote Muir.[7] "A very high antiquity must be assigned to the main features of the religion of Mecca ... Diodorus Siculus, writing about half a century before our era, says of Arabia washed by the Red Sea, 'there is, in this country, a temple greatly revered by the Arabs.' These words must refer to the Holy House of Mecca, for we know of no other which ever commanded such universal homage ... Tradition represents the Ka'bah as from time immemorial the scene of pilgrimage from all quarters of Arabia: — from Yemen and Hadhramaut, from the shores of the Persian Gulf, the deserts of Syria, and the distant environs of Hira and Mesopotamia, men nearly flocked to Mecca. So extensive a homage must have had its beginnings in an extremely remote age".

Abrahamic origin of chief features of the Pilgrimage

Not only does Muir recognize "a very high antiquity" for the Ka'bah but also for "the main features of the religion of Mecca," that is to say for the main features of ḥajj. In fact, as he says, the sacredness of the territory around Makkah and the fact of its being a centre of pilgrimage, can only have come down from time immemorial, for there is no tradition or record showing that it was introduced at any time within historical memory. Some of the ceremonial is undoubtedly due to Abraham as for instance the running between Ṣafā and Marwah (*Sa'y*) which is in commemoration of Hagar's running to and fro to seek water for the baby Ishmael, or the sacrifice which is in commemoration of Abraham's endeavour to obey the Divine commandment which, he thought, meant the sacrifice of Ishmael. The circumambulation (*tawāf*) of the Ka'bah, however, must have existed before Abraham. But all the main features of the ḥajj, as existing at the advent of Prophet Muḥammad, were undoubtedly based on the authority of Abraham. Such at any rate was the tradition, and such is the statement of the Qur'ān, for the order was given to Abraham and Ishmael: "And when We pointed to Abraham the place of the House, saying: Associate naught with Me, and purify My House for those who make circuits and stand to pray and bow and prostrate themselves. And proclaim to men the pilgrimage (ḥajj)" (22 : 26, 27). Thus Abraham not only rebuilt the Ka'bah and purified it of all traces

[7] *Life of Mahomet*, p. xc.

of idolatry, but he also enjoined ḥajj with its main features which were therefore based on Divine revelation. Elsewhere, Abraham and Ishmael are spoken of as praying to God: "And show us our ways of devotion" (2 : 128). The Arabic word for *ways of devotion* is *manāsik*, the very word which throughout the collections of Tradition, is adopted for the devotional acts of ḥajj. And it was by Divine revelation that Prophet Muḥammad was led to adopt them.

The only change introduced into the features of ḥajj, after Abraham, seems to have been the placing of idols in the Ka'bah and other important places of the ḥajj. Thus two idols, the Usāf and the Nā'ilah, were placed on the hills of Ṣafā and the Marwah, respectively (IJ-C. II, pp. 26, 27). The Ka'bah itself had within it 360 idols, all of which were thrown out by the Prophet at the conquest of Makkah. Some other minor changes were introduced. For instance, the tribes of Quraish and Kanānah, who styled themselves the Ḥumṣ, as a mark of their strength and vehemence, used to stay at Muzdalifah, thinking it beneath their dignity to join other pilgrims in going forth to the plain of 'Arafāt. This distinction was evidently an innovation on the part of the more powerful tribes; and as Islām tolerated no distinctions, they were ordered to go forth to 'Arafāt along with the others. Another change was the prohibition to go naked while making circuits round the Ka'bah (Bu. 25 : 66). Another tradition shows that before Islām people did not leave Muzdalifah, where the night was passed, until they saw the sun shining. The Prophet abolished this practice and ordered the march form Muzdalifah to begin before sunrise. It may be that the polytheists of Arabia connected it in some way with the worship of the sun and the change may have been ordered to destroy "a solar rite;" but evidently it was to facilitate matters for the pilgrims to enable them to start immediately after saying their morning prayers, that time being more suitable for moving from one place to another as the heat of the sun was avoided. This also seems to be the reason why the march from 'Arafāt was deferred till after sunset.

Asceticism combined with secularism

Islām discourages asceticism in all its aspects. It condemns monkery outright, and speaking of the Christian practice, the Qur'ān says: "And as for monkery, they innovated it — We did not prescribe it to them" (57 : 27). Yet Islām lays the greatest stress upon the spiritual development of man, and in its four main institutions — prayer, *zakāt*, fasting and ḥajj — introduces workable ascetic formulae into the daily life of man — an asceticism which is quite in keeping with the secular side of life. The five daily prayers require the sacrifice of a small part of his time and, without in any way interfering with his everyday life, enable him to realize the Divine that is within him. The institution of *zakāt* demands the giving up of a small portion of his wealth without interfering with his right to property. Fasting requires the giving up of food and drink but not in such a manner as to make him unfit for carrying on his regular work or business. It is only in ḥajj that asceticism assumes a marked form, for the pilgrim is required not only to give up his regular work for a number of days for the sake of the journey of Makkah, but he must, in addition, give up many other amenities of life, and live more or less, the life of an ascetic. The ḥajj is however, a function which generally comes only once in a lifetime, and, therefore, while leading a man through the highest spiritual experience, it does not interfere in any appreciable degree with the regular course of his life. Thus does Islām make a man pass through an ascetic course of life without neglecting his secular duties.

Levelling influence of the Pilgrimage

No other institution in the world has the wonderful influence of the ḥajj in levelling all distinctions of race, colour and rank. Not only do people of all races and all countries meet together before the Holy House of God as His servants, as members of one Divine family, but they are clad in one dress — in two white sheets — and there remains nothing to distinguish the high from the low. There is a vast concourse of human beings, all clad in one dress, all moving in one way, all having but one word to speak, *labbaika Allāh-umma labbaika*, meaning *here are we, O Allāh! here are we in Thy Presence*. It is ḥajj alone that brings into the domain of practicality what would otherwise seem impossible, namely, that all people, to whatever class or country they belong, should speak one language and wear one dress. Thus is every Muslim made to pass once in his life through that narrow gate of equality which leads to broad brotherhood. All men are equal in birth and death; they come into life and pass out of it in the same way, but ḥajj is the only occasion on which they are taught how to live alike, how to act alike and how to feel alike.

A higher spiritual experience

The description of ḥajj by European writers takes notice only of its outward actions and has never tried to discover their real significance and inner value. The details of ḥajj will be discussed later on, but looking broadly at the scene at Makkah during the ḥajj days, one is struck in the first place by the unity which is achieved among the discordant elements of humanity. Deeper than that, however, lies another value of ḥajj, and this is the higher spiritual experience which is made possible by this unique assemblage of men, the experience of drawing nearer and nearer to God till man feels that all those veils which keep him away from God are entirely removed and he is standing in the Divine presence. It is true that God does not live in Makkah, nor is the Ka'bah the House of God in a material sense; true, too, that a Muslim is taught to hold communion with God in a remote corner, in solitude, in the dead of nights, and thus all alone he goes through the experience of drawing nearer to God; but there is yet a higher spiritual experience to which he can attain in that vast concourse of men assembled in the plain of 'Arafāt. Every member of this great assemblage sets out from his home with that object in view. He discards all those comforts of life which act as a veil against the inner sight. He is required to put on the simplest dress, to avoid all talk of an amorous nature and all kinds of disputes, and to undergo all the privations entailed by a journey to a barren land like Arabia, so that he may be able to concentrate all his meditation on the Divine Being. The comforts of life are undoubtedly a veil which shut out the other world from human sight, and sufferings and privations certainly make a man turn to God. To concentrate all one's ideas on God, not in solitude but in the company of others, is thus the object of ḥajj. A man may have the company of his wife and yet he must not have amorous talk with her; he may be in the company of his adversary, yet he is not allowed to have any quarrel with him; and all this that he may have a higher spiritual experience, the spiritual experience not of the hermit who is cut off from the world, not of the devotee holding communion with God in the corner of solitude, but of the man living in the world, in the company of his wife, his friends and his foes.

The higher significance of a man's spiritual experience in an assemblage is evident from another point of view as well. That there is a mysterious communion from one heart to another is an undeniable truth; it is recognized even by the materialist. Therefore the company of a man who is inspired by similar feelings and who is undergoing a similar experience would undoubtedly give additional force to the spiritual experience of each one of such companions. Take the case of hundreds of thousands of people, all inspired by the one idea of feeling the presence of the Divine Being, all concentrating their minds on the One Supreme Being Who for the time is their sole object; and add to this the mighty effect of the outward unity of them all clad in the same two sheets, crying in one language what is understood by all, *labbaika Allāh-umma labbaika* — "Here we are, O Allāh! here are we in Thy august presence." Their appearance, as well as the words which are on their lips, show that they are standing in the Divine presence, and are so engrossed in the contemplation of the Divine Being that they have lost all ideas of self. Europeans who have observed this wonderful scene, but who have yet not gone deep enough into its inner significance, have wondered that, in this vast concourse of humanity, there are sobbings on every side, there are tears flowing from every eye, but perhaps they have never given a thought to the inner change which thus affects them outwardly. So engrossing is the Divine presence in which they feel themselves to be that they quite forget that they are in the midst of an assemblage; they forget even themselves, and the Divine presence is all in all to them. God is surely not in Makkah to the exclusion of other places, yet that vast assemblage at Makkah sees Him and feels His presence as if He is actually there in their very midst. Such is the higher spiritual experience of the pilgrims to Makkah, the experience not of the hermit shut up in his closet, cut off from the world, but the experience of a mighty concourse gathered together in one place.

On whom is pilgrimage obligatory?

Ḥajj is obligatory on every adult, only once in his life, and its performance oftener is voluntary (AD. 11 : 1). The obligation to perform the ḥajj is further subject to the condition that one is able to undertake a journey to Makkah: "And pilgrimage to the House is a duty which men owe to Allāh — whoever can find a way to it" (3 : 96). The ability to undertake the journey depends on various circumstances. There may be a physical disability, such as renders a man unable to bear the hardships of the long journey. For instance, a very aged man was deemed to be exempt from the obligation (Bu. 25 : 1). Or, the disability may be due to financial reasons, as when a man has not got sufficient provisions for the journey as well as for the dependents whom he leaves behind. The condition of taking sufficient provisions for the journey is laid down in the Qur'ān: "And make provision for yourself, the best provision being to keep one's duty'' (2 : 197). It is related that people from Yaman used to come for pilgrimage without any provisions with them, saying that they were *mutawakkil* (people trusting in God), and when they came to Makkah, they resorted to begging (Bu. 25 : 6).

There is also an express prohibition against vowing to go for pilgrimage on foot. When the Prophet saw such a man performing the journey in distress, and was told that he had vowed to make the pilgrimage on foot, he said, Allāh does not need that this man should punish himself thus, and ordered him to get on the back of an animal (Bu. 28 : 27). Similarly a vow to walk barefooted to Makkah was annulled by the Prophet (AD. 21 : 19). This shows that a man must have sufficient provisions to reach Makkah comfortably. Danger to life may also be a reason for freeing a man from the obligation of ḥajj. The Prophet himself and many of his Companions could not perform a pilgrimage after the flight to Madīnah, because their lives would not have been safe at Makkah. And when ultimately the Prophet undertook a pilgrimage ('umrah) with about 1,400 Companions in the sixth year of Hijrah, he was not allowed to proceed beyond Ḥudaibiyah which was outside the limits of the Ḥaram, and had to come back without performing a pilgrimage.

'Umrah

The word *'umrah* is derived from *'amara* meaning *he inhabited a place* or *paid a visit* to it, and in the terminology of Islām 'umrah means a visit to the Ka'bah. It differs from ḥajj in two respects. In the first place, ḥajj cannot be performed except at the fixed time, while 'umrah may be performed at any time; Shawwāl, Dhī-qa'd[8] and ten days of Dhi-l-Ḥijjah[9] are particularly spoken of as months of ḥajj (2 : 197; Bu. 25 : 33), so that a man can enter into the state of iḥrām[10] for ḥajj only in these months, while the actual devotions of ḥajj are limited from the 8th to the 13th Dhi-l-Ḥijjah. Secondly, the going to 'Arafāt and the assembling there is dispensed with in the case of 'umrah, while it is an essential part of ḥajj. Another difference is that the sacrifice of an animal as the concluding act is essential to ḥajj but not so in the case of 'umrah. The 'umrah may be performed separately, or along with ḥajj, when it is like a

[8] The two lunar months immediately preceding the month in which Ḥajj is performed.

[9] The lunar month in which Ḥajj is performed.

[10] For a complete description of the state of iḥrām see page 392.

parallel devotion to the latter. Though ḥajj is spoken of oftener in the Qur'ān, yet there is an express injunction to accomplish both: "And accomplish the ḥajj and the 'umrah for Allāh" (2 : 196). Tradition also speaks of *wujūb al-'umarh*, or the obligatory nature of the 'umrah, and Ibn 'Umar is quoted as saying: "There is no man but on him rests the obligation of the ḥajj and the 'umrah", while Ibn 'Abbās said that the 'umrah is the companion of ḥajj in the Book of Allāh (Bu. 26 : 1). In one tradition it is said that 'umrah in Ramadzān is equivalent to ḥajj (Bu.26 : 4). According to another, 'umrah is not obligatory (Tr. 9 : 86). But any one who performs the ḥajj can easily perform the 'umrah.

There are two ways in which ḥajj may be combined with 'umrah, *tamattu'* and *qirān*. *Tamattu'* (lit., *profiting*) consists in combining the ḥajj and the 'umrah in such a manner that the pilgrim should enter a state of iḥrām in the months of ḥajj with the intention of performing an 'umrah, and get out of that state after the performance of the 'umrah, again entering into a state of iḥrām in the days of ḥajj. Thus between the 'umrah and the ḥajj, the pilgrim profits by living in his ordinary condition and is not bound by the strict rules of iḥrām, and for this he is required to make a sacrifice, or fast for three days in the ḥajj and seven days after returning from ḥajj (2 : 196).[11] The *qirān* (lit., *uniting together*) consists

[11] Snouck Hurgronje's theory regarding *tamattu'* has been incorporated into the *Encyclopaedia of Islam* by A.J.Wensinck under the heading *Iḥrām*: "According to Snouck Hurgronje's suggestion ... the restrictions which were imposed by the *iḥrām* became too severe for Muḥammad, so that during his stay in Mecca before the *hadjdj* he conducted himself in a secular fashion. As his followers looked askance at him for this, the revelation in Surah 2 : 192 is said to have been given." The authority referred to in the concluding words is not stated, but as a matter of fact there is no such early authority. It must have been some other critic of the same type. The Prophet performed ḥajj, after coming to Madīnah, only once, and this was also his last ḥajj, and it was only about eighty days after this that he died. There is not the flimsiest ground for supposing that the verse speaking of *tamattu'* was revealed on that occasion. On the other hand, there is the clearest evidence that this verse had been revealed prior to the battle of Badr, more than eight years before the last Pilgrimage.

There is also evidence to show that the Holy Prophet did not on this occasion break the continuity of the iḥrām. Thus the long ḥadith which speaks of the Prophet having entered into a state of iḥrām for 'umrah and ḥajj, says, after speaking of the performances of his 'umrah: "Then nothing which was forbidden to him became lawful to him until he performed his ḥajj and sacrificed his offering (*hady*, or the animal brought for sacrifice) on the day of sacrifices, then he returned and made circuits of the House, then everything which was forbidden to him became lawful to him, and the people who had brought their offerings with them as the Prophet had done, did the same as was done by the Prophet". (Bu. 25 : 104). The restrictions of iḥrām becoming too severe for the Prophet, the looking askance of his Companions and the revelation of 2 : 192 (2 : 196, according to our computation) on this occasion, are all inventions of an ingenious brain, which, instead

in entering into a state of iḥrām in the months of ḥajj with the intention of performing both ḥajj and 'umrah, and not getting out of that state until both have been performed, or entering into a state of iḥrām in the months of ḥajj with the intention of performing an 'umrah, and remaining in the same state until the ḥajj is also performed. Thus the difference between *tamattu'* and *qirān* is that in *tamattu'* there is a break in the state of iḥrām, while in *qirān* that state is continuous. When ḥajj alone is performed, it is called *ifrād* (lit., to *isolate* a thing). With the two differences pointed out earlier, whatever is said below concerning ḥajj applies also to 'umrah.

Iḥrām

The state into which the pilgrim is required to put himself on the occasion of ḥajj or 'umrah is called iḥrām (from *haram* meaning *prevention* or *forbidding*), or entering upon a state in which a particular dress is put on and certain acts, ordinarily lawful, are forbidden. When the Prophet was asked as to what dress the *muḥrim* (the man entering into a state of iḥrām) should put on, he replied: "He should not put on a shirt or a turban or trousers or a cap, nor a dress coloured by *wars* (red) or saffron (yellow); and if he does not find shoes, let him put on leather stockings (*khuffain*)" (Bu. 3 : 53). Another tradition describes his own dress in the state of iḥrām as follows: "He wore his unsewed waist-wrapper (*izār*) and his unsewed outer garment covering the upper part of the body (*ridā'*)" (Bu. 25 : 23). The iḥrām dress, therefore, consists of two seamless sheets, a sheet reaching from the navel to below the knees and a sheet which covers the upper part of the body. Both these sheets must preferably be white. As regards women, they can wear their ordinary clothes, and 'Āishah held that there was no harm if a woman pilgrim wore cloth dyed black or red or wore boots (*khuff*). She further held that a woman should not cover her face or wear a veil in iḥrām (Bu. 25 : 23). Change of clothes during iḥrām is not forbidden, according to one authority (*ibid.*). But even women must wear simple dress. The object is to remove all distinctions of rank, and this is done, in the case of men, by making

of being exposed by Wensinck have been gladly incorporated into a standard work like the *Encyclopaedia of Islam,* and yet the same learned writer in his index of Ḥadīth, *Handbook of Tradition*, admits, under the heading *Iḥrām*, that the Prophet did not give up the state of iḥrām in combining ḥajj and 'umrah: "Muḥammad makes use of *tamattu'* but does not abandon the sacred state at Makkah."

them all wear two seamless sheets, and in the case of women by requiring them to give up the veil, which was a sign of rank. Probably the iḥrām dress of two seamless sheets dates back from Abraham, and the simple patriarchal dress has been preserved in ḥajj to give men a practical lesson in simple living.

Before donning the iḥrām dress, the pilgrim must take a bath and utter *talbiyah*, facing the Qiblah. The practice is also to say two *rak'ahs* of prayer, but all that is related of the Prophet is that he entered a state of iḥrām after saying two *rak'ahs* of the early afternoon prayer. During the state of iḥrām, and even before that, from the beginning of the journey to Makkah, no amorous discourse is allowed and sexual intercourse is therefore also forbidden: "So whoever determines to perform the pilgrimage therein, there shall be no amorous speech, nor abusing nor altercation in ḥajj" (2 : 197); nor is the use of scent allowed in the state of iḥrām, nor shaving, nor the paring of nails. The cares of the body are sacrificed for a few days to devote greater attention to the cares of the soul, and this is a practical lesson which serves a useful purpose on many occasions in one's life.

Mīqāt *or* muhill

The state of iḥrām, as described above, may be entered upon at any time during the months of ḥajj, after the journey is undertaken; but as it would be too inconvenient to remain in this state for a long time, the law has fixed certain places on the different routes to Makkah, on reaching which the pilgrims enter upon a state of iḥrām. Such a place is called *mīqāt* (from *waqt* meaning *time*) meaning *an appointed time*, or a *place in which a certain action is appointed to be performed*. The *mīqāt* is also called a *muhill* (from *ahalla* meaning *he raised his voice*), which signifies *the place of raising voices with talbiyah*. The *talbiyah* consists in saying aloud *labbaika Allāh-umma labbaika,* meaning "Here am I, O Allāh! here am I in Thy august presence."[12] As soon as the state

[12] The full *talbiyah* runs thus: *Labbaika Allāh-umma labbaika, lā sharīka la-ka labbaika; inn-al-ḥamda w-al-ni'mata la-ka w-al-mulka la-ka lā sharīka la-ka*, which means "Here am I, O Allāh, here am I in Thy presence; there is no associate with Thee, here am I; surely all praise is Thine and all favours are Thine and the kingdom is Thine, there is no associate with Thee" (Bu. 25 : 26).

of iḥrām is entered upon, with the determination to devote as little attention to the cares of the body as possible, the spiritual aspect of ḥajj is brought to mind by all the pilgrims crying aloud that they are in the august Divine presence. The place where iḥrām is entered upon is, therefore, also the place where voices are raised aloud for the remembrance of God, and the *mīqāt*, is, for that reason, also called the *muhill*. The several places appointed for iḥrām are: Dhu-l-Hulaifa for pilgrims coming from the direction of Madīnah, Juhfa for those coming from Syria and Egypt, Qarn al-Manāzil for those from Najd, Yalamlam for those from Yaman (among which are included all pilgrims from India, Pakistan, Indonesia and other countries, proceeding by boats *via* Aden) and Dhāt 'Irq for those from Iraq (Bu. 25 : 7-13). For all places within these limits, the *mīqāt* is the place from which the pilgrim starts, and for the people of Makkah, the *mīqāt* is Makkah itself (Bu. 25 : 7).

Ṭawāf

The word *ṭawāf* is derived from *ṭafā (he went round* a thing), and in the technical language of Islām it means *making circumambulation of the Ka'bah.* The command to perform the ṭawāf of the house is contained in the Qur'ān in a Makkah revelation: "And let them go round the Ancient House" (22 : 29). In the devotional acts of ḥajj, ṭawāf occupies the most important place, being the first act of the pilgrim on his arrival at Makkah and his last act when he leaves the holy place. Bukhārī heads one of his chapters as follows: "He who makes circumambulations of the House on his arrival in Makkah before he goes to his abode, then offers two *rak'ahs* of prayer, then goes out to Safa" (Bu. 25 : 62). Under this heading he reports the tradition of Ibn 'Umar, which says "that the Prophet made circumambulations on his first arrival in ḥajj and 'umrah, then offered two *rak'ahs*, then went to and fro (*ṭāfa*) between Ṣafā and Marwah." The pavement on which the ṭawāf is made is called the maṭāf. The ṭawāf is performed by going round the Ka'bah, as near the walls of the sacred building as possible, but on the north-western side, keeping close to the small semicircular wall, as the Ḥijr is included in the matāf. Before the ṭawāf, it is necessary to make ablutions (Bu. 25 : 77), if possible to take a bath. Men and women perform ṭawāf, together, the women keeping apart from the men, but women are not allowed to go inside the Ka'bah until it is emptied of men (Bu. 25 : 63). Before Islām, some people used to make ṭawāf naked; but

Islām forbade it (Bu.25 : 66). The ṭawāf made on arrival is called *ṭawāf al-qudūm* (the ṭawāf of arrival), the ṭawāf made on departure is called *ṭawāf al-wadā'* (the ṭawāf of departure), and the ṭawāf on the day of sacrifices (*yaum al-naḥr*, or the tenth of Dhi-l-Ḥijjah) is called *ṭawāf al-ziyārah* (the ṭawāf of visit), this last being one of the necessary devotional acts of ḥajj (Bu. 25 : 129), while the first two are not obligatory though they are generally resorted to.

The ṭawāf begins at the Ḥajar al-Aswad (the Black Stone) which is kissed (Bu. 25 : 55), but even the making of a sign over it is sufficient (Bu. 25 : 59,60). The Prophet used to kiss both the rukn al-yamānī and the Ḥajar al-Aswad, but many Companions are reported as kissing all the four corners of the Ka'bah (Bu. 25 : 58). In going round, the Ka'bah is kept to the left, and seven rounds are made in all. The first three rounds are made at a fast pace (*raml*), and the remaining four at an ordinary pace (Bu. 25 : 62). But, if necessary, the ṭawāf may be performed while one is riding on the back of an animal. The Prophet performed the ṭawāf in his Farewell Pilgrimage on the back of a camel, and allowed Umm Salma to do the same on account of her illness (Bu. 25 : 73). The doing of an act or speaking, if there is necessity for it, is not forbidden in ṭawāf (Bu. 25 : 64, 65). Prayers or supplications may be addressed to God in the course of ṭawāf. The Prophet is reported to have prayed thus: "Our Lord! grant us good in this life and good in the Hereafter and save us from the punishment of the fire"[13] (AD.11 : 49). Menstruating women should postpone the ṭawāf, and the *sa'y* between Ṣafā and Marwah, for the duration of the menses. For those who enter upon iḥrām for both ḥajj and 'umrah' at the same time (*ḥajj qārin*), the first ṭawāf (*ṭawāf al-qudūm*) is sufficient (Bu. 64 : 79; AD.11 : 51). But in the case of *tamattu'*, a second ṭawāf must be performed when the iḥrām for ḥajj is entered upon.

The Black Stone

Reference has already been made to the Ḥajar al-Aswad (lit., *black stone*), in the history of Ka'bah, where its description is given, and under the heading "Ṭawāf," where it is stated that it is kissed by the pilgrims as they pass by it in their circumambulations. There is not the least indication to show where this stone came from and when it was placed there,

[13] *Rabba-nā āti-nā fi-l-dunyā ḥasanat-an wa fil-ākhirati ḥasanat-an wa qi-nā 'adhāb al-nār*.

but as it was there before the advent of Islām and was even kissed, it must have been there at least from the time of Abraham, as the main features of the ḥajj are traceable to that patriarch. Yet it is remarkable that though the Ka'bah had 360 idols within its walls before the coming of Islām, the Black Stone was never regarded as an idol by the pre-Islamic Arabs, nor was it ever worshipped by them like the idols of the Ka'bah. The fact that the practice of kissing it in the course of circumambulations has been retained, has been turned by Western critics of Islām into an argument that Islām retains remnants of pre-Islamic idolatry. There are even critics who are of opinion that the ṭawāf of the Ka'bah itself is an idolatrous practice. But a cursory glance at facts is enough to show the absurdity of this view. Among the innumerable objects which were taken for gods by the pre-Islamic Arabs, the Ka'bah and the Black Stone are the only two which are conspicuous by their absence, notwithstanding the reverence which the Arab mind had for them before Islām. The Ka'bah was known by the name *Bait Allāh* or House of God, and there was a belief prevalent among them that no enemy could destroy it. It was due to this belief that when Abrahah[14] attacked Makkah, 'its people took to the surrounding hills, offering no resistance, and when Abrahah asked 'Abd al-Muṭṭalib[15] why he did not request him to spare the Ka'bah, his reply was that the Ka'bah was the House of God and He would take care of it. Yet, notwithstanding all this reverence, the Ka'bah was never worshipped. It, no doubt, contained idols, yet it was the idols that were worshipped, and not the Ka'bah; and the same is true of the Black Stone. It was kissed but it was never taken for a god, though the Arabs worshipped even unhewn stones, trees and heaps of sand. And the Muslims, to say nothing of the Prophet, were so averse to idolatry that when they saw two idols, the Usāf and the Nā'ilah, on the hills of Ṣafā and the Marwah respectively, they refused to make the *sa'y* between these two mountains, until a verse was revealed: "The Ṣafā and the Marwah are truly among the signs of Allāh, so whoever makes a pilgrimage to the House or pays a visit to it, there is no blame on him if he goes round them both (2 : 158). The words used here "there is no blame on him" clearly show that the Muslims thought that there was a *sin* in going round places wherein idols had been set. Evidently they had not the same scruples about the Ka'bah as the idols in the Ka'bah were shut up in the building,

[14] Governor of Yaman.

[15] Grandfather of the Prophet.

while those on the Ṣafā and the Marwah were not only exposed to view but even touched by the pilgrims. The Muslims so hated idolatry that they could not brook the thought of idols being connected in any way with their religious practices. How could they think of worshipping the Ka'bah and the Black Stone, which even the idolaters had never worshipped? Had the idea of idolatry been connected in the least with the circuits round the Ka'bah and the kissing of the Black Stone, the Muslims would never have resorted to those practices. They had no hesitation in turning their backs to the Ka'bah when on reaching Madīnah they were required to take Jerusalem for their *qiblah* of prayer. And it has just been shown that the Prophet once made circuits of the Ka'bah on the back of a camel; he also touched the Black Stone with the rod in his hand; all of which goes to show that the Muslims never entertained the idea of the worship of these things, nor was their attitude towards them at any time that of the worshipper towards the object of his worship. The Black Stone was not kissed alone; the Prophet kissed both the Black Stone, which is in the Eastern corner, and the Yaman corner, while some of the Companions kissed all the four corners of the Ka'bah.

Significance underlying ṭawāf of the Ka'bah

To say that ṭawāf of the Ka'bah is a remnant of idolatry is to force a meaning on idolatry which it has never borne. Circumambulation of an object which is considered sacred is met with in the history of the Israelites, "where the altar is circumambulated once on the first six days and sometimes on the seventh" (*En. Is.*, art. *Ṭawāf*), yet no critic has ever asserted that the altar was worshipped by the Israelites. And, of all men, the Muslim would be the farthest from the idea of idol-worship in his ṭawāf of the Ka'bah, when he feels himself in the presence of the One God, crying aloud, *labbaika Allāh-umma labbaika, la sharīka la-ka labbaika*, "Here am I, O Allāh! here am I in Thy presence, there is no associate with Thee, here am I." From the time when he is still at a distance of several miles from Makkah, to the time when he leaves the Holy City, there is but one phrase on his tongue, one idea in his heart, *there is no associate with God*. How could he at the same time entertain the idea of idol-worship? And what is ṭawāf itself? It is going round about the House which is an emblem of Divine Unity, the place from which sprang the idea of Divine Unity, the place which would always be the centre for all believers in Divine Unity. All ideas of the pilgrim at that time are concentrated upon one theme, the theme of Divine Unity. The pilgrim forgets everything and remembers only the One God. He forgets even his own presence, and to him the august Divine presence is all in all. That is the ṭawāf.

Significance underlying kissing of the Black Stone

That the Ka'bah was rebuilt by Abraham is an historical fact. The Black Stone has been there ever since the Ka'bah has been known to exist, there is not the least reason to doubt. That it was a stone sent down from Paradise, or that it was originally white and became black on account of the sins of men, there is no reliable tradition to indicate. The Black Stone is, in fact, the corner-stone of the Ka'bah, and stands there only as an emblem, a token that that part of the progeny of Abraham which was rejected by the Israelites was to become the corner-stone of the Kingdom of God. The Psalms contain a clear reference to it: "The stone which the builders refused is become the head-stone of the corner" (Ps. 118 : 22). Ishmael was looked upon as rejected and the Divine covenant was considered to have been made with the children of Isaac only. That was the Jewish view, and it was due to the fact that Ishmael was placed by Abraham near the Ka'bah. And again while prophet after prophet appeared among the Israelites, no prophet appeared of the progeny of Ishmael, and hence the Jewish belief that Ishmael was rejected became stronger. Yet it was from the progeny of Ishmael that the Last Prophet, "the head-stone of the corner" in the words of the Psalmist, was to arise, and the Black Stone, whencesoever brought, was placed as the corner-stone of the Ka'bah, as a sign that the rejected Ishmaelites were the real inheritors of the Divine Kingdom. And while David referred to it as "the stone which the builders refused," Jesus spoke of it more plainly in the parable of the husbandman, telling the Israelites that the vineyard, which in the parable stands for the Kingdom of God, would be taken away from them and given to "other husbandmen;" that is, to a non-Israelite people: "Did ye never read in the Scriptures, the stone which the builders rejected, the same is become the head of the corner?" (Mt. 21 : 42); "The Kingdom of God shall be taken from you, and given to a nation bringing forth the fruits thereof" (Mt. 21 : 43). That by the rejected stone in the prophecy was meant a rejected nation is made clear by Jesus Christ. That that rejected nation was no other than the Ishmaelites is borne out by history. And in the whole world there is only this unhewn stone, the stone "cut out of the mountain without hands,'' (Dan. 2 : 45), that is the corner-stone of a building which in point of importance stands unique in the world.

The Sa'y

Sa'y means *running*, and in the Islamic terminology it signifies the running of the pilgrims between the two little hills situated near Makkah, called the Ṣafā and the Marwah. In the devotional acts of ḥajj, it occupies a place next to the ṭawāf. In fact, in the case of 'umrah, the minor pilgrimage as it is called, ṭawāf and sa'y are the only functions of importance, and the 'umrah therefore ends with the *sa'y* unless of course there is an animal to be sacrificed when 'umrah alone is to be performed. The *sa'y* is spoken of in the Qur'ān: ''The Ṣafā and the Marwah are truly among the signs of Allāh, so whoever makes a pilgrimage to the House or pays a visit to it, there is no blame on him if he goes round about them'' (2 : 158). The word used in the Qur'ān is not *sa'y* but a derivative of ṭawāf (*yaṭṭawwafa*). These two hills were the scene of Hagar's running to and fro in quest of water for her baby Ishmael, when she was left there by Abraham (Bu. 60 : 9). They have thus become monuments of patience under the hardest trials, and it is in connection with the teaching of patience that the ṭawāf of Ṣafā and Marwah is spoken of in the Qur'ān, as the context of 2 : 158 would show. Between these two hills there is now a street with houses and shops on both sides.

The ḥajj proper—march to Minā

Ṭawāf and *sa'y* are the individual acts of every pilgrim when he first arrives at Makkah, whether he intends to perform the 'umrah or the ḥajj, or unites ḥajj with 'umrah (*qirān*) or combines the two (*tamattu'*). In case it is simply an 'umrah or in case of *tamattu'*, the pilgrim emerges from the state of iḥrām after performing the 'umrah, the ḥajj proper beginning on the 8th of Dhi-l-Ḥijjah when the whole body of pilgrims moves together. It is called the *yaum al-tarwiyah*.[16] The pilgrims who have got out of the state of iḥrām on account of *tamattu'*, again enter into iḥrām on the morning of the 8th, and so also do the residents of Makkah who

[16] Lit., *the day of watering* or *satisfying the thirst*, because on that day the pilgrims provide themselves with water for the following days (N.), or because the commencement of the ḥajj proper means the satisfaction of spiritual thirst.

wish to perform the pilgrimage (Bu. 25 : 81). The whole body of pilgrims then moves to Minā, a plain which is midway between 'Arafāt and Makkah, about four miles distant from the Holy City. The way into this plain which is about a mile long goes over a hill which is called the 'Aqabah famous in the history of Islām because of the two pledges taken there by the Prophet from the Madīnah Muslims. To the north side rises Mount Thabīr. During the ḥajj proper, pilgrims' longest, and in fact the only, stay, is in Minā. Minā must be reached before noon, so that the early afternoon prayer, *Zuhr*, may be said there. The night is also passed in Minā, and next day, the 9th Dhi-l-Ḥijjah, at midday the pilgrims move to the plain of 'Arafāt.

'Arafāt and the wuqūf

'Arafa or 'Arafāt is the name of the plain which is situated to the east of Makkah at a distance of about nine miles. It is derived from *'arf* or *ma'rifah*, which means *knowledge of a thing*, and *ma'rifah* especially means *the knowledge of God*. The name given to this plain seems to be based on the fact that here men assembled together, as equals in all respects, are best able to *know* their God. This plain is bounded on the east by the lofty mountains of Ṭā'if, while northward rises a small hill of the same name, 'Arafāt, about 200 feet above the level of the plain. The *Jabal al Raḥmah* (lit., the mountain of mercy), on which is the pulpit from which the sermon is delivered, is situated to the east, sixty steps of stone leading to the top. Leaving Minā at noon on the ninth Dhi-l-Ḥijjah, the pilgrims reach 'Arafāt in time to say the *Ẓuhr* and *'Aṣr* prayers combined, after which the Imām delivers a sermon (*Khuṭbah*) from the pulpit on the *Jabal al-Raḥmah*. The pilgrims' stay in 'Arafāt lasts only from afternoon till sunset and is known as *wuqūf* (lit., *halting* or *standing still*), but so important is the place it occupies in the devotional acts of ḥajj, that ḥajj is considered to have been performed if the pilgrim reaches 'Arafāt in time on the 9th Dhi-l-Ḥijjah, but if he is unable to join in the *wuqūf*, the ḥajj is not performed. The whole time of the pilgrims, from afternoon till sunset, is passed in glorifying God and crying aloud *labbaika Allāh-umma labbaika*. Before the advent of Islām, the Quraish and certain other tribes, who claimed superiority over the other Arab tribes, did not go to 'Arafāt, hence the injunction in the Qur'ān levelling down this distinction: "Then hasten on from where people hasten on" (2 : 199).

Muzdalifah

After sunset the pilgrims leave 'Arafāt, and stop at Muzdalifah (from *zalf* meaning *nearness*), which is so called because by staying there nearness to God is sought (N.). In the Qur'ān it is called *al-Mash'ar al-Ḥarām* (lit., *the Sacred Monument*), and the remembrance of God at that place is specially enjoined: "So when you press on from 'Arafāt, remember Allāh near the Holy Monument, and remember Him as He has guided you, though before that you were certainly of the erring ones" (2 : 198). It has also received the name of *al-Jam'* (lit., *the place of gathering together*). On reaching Muzdalifah, the pilgrims say their *Maghrib* and *Ishā'* prayers, combining the two (Bu. 25 : 96). There the night is passed, and then after saying the morning prayer at an early hour the pilgrims leave for Minā. Those who are infirm are allowed to leave even before the morning prayer (Bu. 25 : 98). Before Islām the pilgrims did not leave until the sun shone on the Mount Thabīr (Bu. 25 : 99). It may be that the idea of sun-worship was in some way connected with this custom.

Yaum al-naḥr in Minā

Thus the pilgrims again reach Minā on the morning of 10th Dhi-l-Ḥijjah, which is called *yaum al-nahr* (lit., *the day of sacrifices*), being the day which is celebrated as the *'Īd al-Adzḥā* all over the Muslim world. After saying the 'Īd prayers in Minā, the animals are sacrificed,[17] the pilgrims then return and perform the *ṭawāf* of the Ka'bah. This is called *ṭawāf al-ifādzā* and with it, the pilgrim emerges from the state of *iḥrām*, by having his head shaven or his hair clipped. But before the sacrifice there is another small act of devotion called the *ramy al-jimār*, which will be described presently. Though the pilgrim leaves the state of *iḥrām* after the *ṭawāf al-ifādza*, yet he must return to Minā again, for it is in Minā that the ḥajj ends.

[17] The subject of sacrifices has been fully dealt with in the chapter on Prayer, Section 8.

Ayyām al-tashrīq

The pilgrims are required to stay in Minā for three or at least two days after the *yaum al-naḥr*, that is, on the 11th, 12th and 13th Dhi-l-Ḥijjah. This stay is required by an express injunction of the Qur'ān, where the ending of the devotional acts of ḥajj is thus spoken of: — "And remember Allāh during the appointed days. Then whoever hastens off in two days, it is no sin for him, and whoever stays behind, it is no sin for him, for one who keeps his duty. And keep your duty to Allāh, and know that you shall be gathered together to Him" (2 : 203).

The "numbered days" referred to here are the two or three days that are spent in Minā after the *yaum al-naḥr*, and they are known by the name of *ayyām al-tashrīq* or the days of *tashrīq*. The word *tashrīq* is derived from *sharq* signifying *east*; but, according to some, these three days of pilgrimage are given the name *tashrīq* because one of its meanings is spreading out flesh in the sun for the purpose of drying it, and the flesh of the sacrificed animals was dried during these days to form part of provision for the journey (N.). Another explanation is that they were so named because the animals were sacrificed after the rising of the sun, which is also one of the meanings of *tashrīq* (N.). But, again, *tashrīq* also means *going east* (LL.), and Minā lies to the east of Makkah; or it may have a deeper spiritual significance in that it also means *being beautiful and shining in the face* (LL.). In pre-Islamic days, after the performance of ḥajj, men used to boast of the greatness of their fathers when they gathered together in 'Ukāẓ and other markets. Islām discontinued this and set apart these days for the glorification of God.

Ramy al-jimār

During the last day of ḥajj, the 10th Dhi-l-Ḥijjah and the three *tashrīq* days, the pilgrims are required to cast stones at certain fixed places. This is known as *ramy al-jimār (ramy* meaning *throwing,* and *jimār,* pl. of *jamrah,* meaning *small stones*). Each of the three places in Minā, where stones are thrown, is also called Jamrah, because of the *throwing* or the *collection of stones* there. Of the three Jamrahs, that nearest to Makkah is called Jamrah 'Aqabah, being situated on the 'Aqabāh; the second Jamrah *wusṭā* or the middle Jamrah, is near the Mosque of Minā; and a little further on is the third, the Jamrah *ṣughra*, or the smallest Jamrah. The practice of the Prophet is thus described. On the *yaum al-naḥr* he threw stones in the forenoon, and in *tas͟hrīq* days in the afternoon (Bu. 25 : 134). Again, while a start was made with Jamrah 'Aqabah on the *yaum al-naḥr*, the order was reversed in the *tas͟hrīq* days. The number of stones thrown at each Jamrah was seven, and every stone thrown was accompanied with *takbīr* (Bu. 25 : 138). It is also related that after throwing stones at the first Jamrah he proceeded a little further, and then stood for a long time raising both hands for prayer and facing the Qiblah; then he went to the second Jamrah and after throwing stones there again proceeded a little further, then stood for a long time raising both hands for prayer facing the Qiblah, and last of all he came to the last Jamrah and departed after throwing stones there (Bu. 25 : 142). It is true that in the ḥajj many pre-Islamic practices were retained, but as has been shown above, the origin of these practices is traceable to Abraham, and every one of them carries with it a spiritual significance. The whole atmosphere of ḥajj is a demonstration of the greatness of God and the equality of man. The ḥajj is, as it were, the final stage in man's spiritual progress. Yet in spiritual advancement the temptations of real life must not be forgotten, and the throwing of stones draws attention to the temptations of the Evil one. To live in perfect peace is the message of Islām, but there is no peace of mind for the man who is tempted by evil. The throwing of stones teaches the lesson that man must learn to hate evil and that the Evil one should be kept distant a stone's throw. The nearer a man gets to temptations, the more likely he is to yield, and the best way of avoiding them is to keep them at a distance. The throwing of stones is, moreover, a reminder of the spiritual fight which man must wage against evil.

Other activities allowed in pilgrimage

Though ḥajj is meant to bring about an ascetic experience in man's practical life, yet so closely combined are the ascetic and secular experience in Islām, that the utilizing of the pilgrimage to Makkah for secular purposes is not excluded. The Qur'ān, while enjoining the making of sufficient provision for the ḥajj journey, adds: "It is no sin for you that you seek the bounty of your Lord" (2 : 198). The seeking of bounty is accepted here by all commentators as meaning the seeking of increase in one's wealth by means of trade in the pilgrimage season. Explaining this verse, Ibn 'Abbās says that D͟hu-l-Majāz and 'Ukāẓ were markets for trade in the pre-Islamic times. The Muslims however did not like the idea of mixing up the spiritual lessons of Pilgrimage with material advantages, until this verse was revealed which allowed the carrying on of trade in the pilgrimage season (Bu. 25 : 150). These markets were held in or near 'Arafāt, from the beginning of Dhi-Qa'd till the 8th Dhi-l-Ḥijjah, when pilgrimage began. The Qur'ān thus not only allows the carrying on of trade in the pilgrimage season, but in a way recommends it by calling it a "bounty of your Lord." It is easy to see that, even if trading is allowed in the pilgrimage season, this great assemblage of Muslims from all quarters of the world may also be made the occasion of other advantages of a material or cultural nature, and it should serve the purpose of unifying the Muslim world and removing misunderstanding between nation and nation. World-wide conferences are held on many occasions, and this should, in the new conditions of the world, be a regular feature of the ḥajj, and the best minds among the various nations should on this occasion discuss all problems affecting the Muslim world, not the least important of which is the advancement of Islām itself.

Chapter V

JIHĀD

Significance of jihād

A very great misconception prevails with regard to the duty of *jihād* in Islām, by assuming that the word *jihād* is supposed to be synonymous with *war*; and even the greatest research scholars in Europe have not taken the pains to consult any dictionary of the Arabic language, or to refer to the Qur'ān, to find out the true meaning of the word. So widespread is the misunderstanding that a scholar of the fame of A. J. Wensinck, when preparing his concordance of Ḥadīth, *A Handbook of Early Muhammadan Tradition*, gives not a single reference under the word *jihād*, referring the reader to the word *war*, as if the two were synonymous terms. The *Encyclopaedia of Islam* goes even further, beginning the article on *Djihād* thus: "The spread of Islām by arms is a religious duty upon Muslims in general;" as if *jihād* meant not only *war* but *war undertaken for the propagation of Islām.* Klein in *The Religion of Islām* makes a similar statement: "*Jihād* — The fighting against unbelievers with the object of either winning them over to Islām, or subduing and exterminating them in case they refuse to become Muslims, and the causing of Islām to spread and triumph over all religions is considered a sacred duty of the Muslim nation." If any of these learned scholars had taken the trouble to consult an ordinary dictionary of the Arabic language, he could never have made such a glaring misstatement. The word *jihād* is derived from *jahd* or *juhd* meaning *ability, exertion* or *power,* and *jihād* and *mujāhida* mean *the exerting of one's power in repelling the enemy* (R.). The same authority then goes on to say: "*Jihād* is of three kinds; *viz.*, the carrying on of a struggle: 1. against a visible enemy, 2. against the devil, and 3. against self (*nafs*). According to another authority, *jihād* means *fighting with unbelievers and that is an intensive form (mubālaghah)*, and *exerting one's self to the extent of one's ability and power whether it is by word (qaul) or deed (fi'l)* (N.). A third authority gives the following significance: "*Jihād,* inf. n. of *jāhada,* properly signifies *the using* or *exerting of one's utmost power, efforts, endeavours* or *ability, in contending with an object of disapprobation;* and this is of three kinds, namely a visible enemy, the devil, and one's self; all of which are included in the term as used in the Kur. xxii. 77" (LL.). *Jihād* is therefore far from being synonymous with *war*, while the meaning of ''war undertaken for the propagation of Islām'', which is supposed by European writers to be the significance of *jihād*, is unknown equally to the Arabic language and the teachings of the Qur'ān.

Use of the word **jihād** *in Makkah revelations*

Equally, or even more important is the consideration of the sense in which the word is used in the Qur'ān. It is an admitted fact that permission to fight was given to the Muslims when they had moved to Madīnah, or, at the earliest, when they were on the eve of leaving Makkah. But the injunction relating to *jihād* is contained in the earlier as well as in the later Makkah revelations. The 29th chapter of the Qur'ān is one of a group which was undoubtedly revealed in the fifth and sixth years of the Call of the Prophet; yet there the word *jihād* is freely used in the sense of *exerting one's power and ability*, without implying any war. In one place it is said: ''And those who *strive hard (jāhadū)* for Us, We shall certainly guide them in Our ways, and Allāh is surely with the doers of good'' (29 : 69). The Arabic word *jāhadū* is derived from *jihād* or *mujāhadah,* and the addition of *fī-nā* (for Us) shows, if anything further is needed to show it, that the *jihād*, in this case, is the spiritual striving to attain nearness to God, and the result of this *jihād* is stated to be God's guidance of those striving in His ways. The word is used precisely in the same sense twice in a previous verse in the same chapter: ''And whoever *strives hard (jāhada) strives (yujāhidu)* for his self,'' that is, for his own benefit, ''for Allāh is Self-Sufficient, above need of the worlds'' (29 : 6). In the same chapter, the word is used in the sense of a contention carried on in words: ''And We have enjoined on man goodness to his parents, and if *they content (jāhadā)* with thee to associate others with Me, of which thou hast no knowledge, obey them not'' (29 : 8).

Among the later revelations may be mentioned *al-Naḥl,* the 16th chapter, where it is said, towards the close: ''Then surely thy Lord, with respect to those who flee after they are persecuted then *struggle hard (jāhadū)* and are patient (*ṣabarū*), surely thy Lord after that is Protecting, Merciful (16 : 110). There is another prevalent misconception, namely, that at Makkah the Qur'ān enjoined patience (*ṣabr*) and at Madīnah it enjoined *jihād*, as if patience and *jihād* were two contradictory things. The error of this view is shown by the verse quoted, since it enjoins *jihād* and patience in one breath.

Two more examples may be quoted of the use of the word *jihād* in the Makkah revelations. In one place it is said: "And *strive hard (jāhidū)* for Allāh with due *striving (jihād)*" (22 : 78). And in the other: "So obey not the unbelievers and *strive (jāhid)* against them a mighty *striving (jihād-an)* with it" (25 : 52), where the personal pronoun *it* refers clearly to the Qur'ān, as the context shows. In both these cases, the carrying on of a *jihād* is clearly enjoined, but in the first case it is a *jihād* to attain nearness to God, and in the second it is a *jihād* which is to be carried on against the unbelievers, but a *jihād* not of the sword but of the Qur'ān. The struggle made to attain nearness to God and to subdue one's passions, and the struggle made to win over the unbelievers, not with the sword but with the Qur'ān is, therefore, a *jihād* in the terminology of the Qur'ān, and the injunctions to carry on these two kinds of *jihād* were given long before the command to take up the sword in self-defence.

Jihād in Madīnah revelations

A struggle for national existence was forced on the Muslims when they reached Madīnah, and they had to take up the sword in self-defence. This struggle went, and rightly, under the name of *jihād*; but even in the Madīnah chapters the word is used in the wider sense of a struggle carried on by words or deeds of any kind. As a very clear example of this use, the following verse may be quoted which occurs twice: "O Prophet! *Strive hard (jāhid* from *jihād)* against the disbelievers and the hypocrites, and be firm against them; and their abode is Hell; and evil is the destination" (9 : 73; 66 : 9). Here the Prophet is bidden to carry on a *jihād* against both unbelievers and hypocrites. The hypocrites were those who were outwardly Muslims and lived among, and were treated like, Muslims in all respects. They came to the mosque and prayed with the Muslims. They even paid the *zakāt*. A war against them was unthinkable, and none was ever undertaken. On the other hand, they sometimes fought along with the Muslims against the unbelievers. Therefore the injunction to carry on a *jihād* against both unbelievers and hypocrites could not mean the waging of war against them. It was a *jihād* carried on by means of the Qur'ān as expressly stated in 25 : 52, a striving hard to win them over to Islām. In fact, on other occasions as well, it is a mistake to think that *jihād* means only fighting; the word is almost always used in the general sense of striving hard, including fighting where the context so requires. "Those who believe and those who fled (their homes) and strive hard in the way of Allāh" (2 : 218; 8 : 74), is a description which applies as much to the fighters as to those who carry on the struggle against unbelief and evil in other ways. And the *sābirīn* (those who are steadfast or patient), and the *mujāhidīn* (those who struggle hard), are again spoken of together in a Madīnah revelation as they are in a Makkah revelation: "Do you think you will enter the Garden while Allāh has not yet known those from among you who strive hard (nor) known the steadfast?" (3 : 141).

Jihād in Ḥadīth

Even in the traditions the word *jihād* is not used exclusively for *fighting*. For example, *ḥajj* is called a *jihād:* "The Holy Prophet said, The ḥajj is the most excellent of all *jihāds*" (Bu. 25 : 4). Of all the collections of Tradition, *Bukhārī* is the most explicit on this point. In *I'tiṣām bi-l-Kitāb wa-l-Sunnah,* the 4th chapter is thus headed: "The saying of the Holy Prophet, A party of my community shall not cease to be triumphant being upholders of Truth," to which are added the words, "And these are the men of learning (*ahl al-'ilm*)" (Bu. 97 : 10).[1] Thus Bukhārī's view is that the triumphant party of the Prophet's community does not consist of fighters, but of the men of learning who disseminate the truth and are engaged in the propagation of Islām. Again, in his *Book of Jihād* Bukhārī has several chapters speaking of simple invitation to Islām. For instance, the heading of 56 : 99 is: "May the Muslim guide the followers of the Book to a right course, or may he teach them the Book." The heading of 56 : 100: "To pray for the guidance of the polytheists so as to develop relations of friendship with them"; that of 56 : 102: "The invitation (to the unbelievers) by the Holy Prophet to Islām and prophethood, and that they may not take for gods others besides Allāh"; that of 56 : 143: "The excellence of him at whose hands another man accepts Islām"; that of 56 : 145: "The excellence of him who accepts Islām from among the followers of the Book"; and that of 56 : 178: "How should Islām be presented to a child".

[1] The Prophet's saying, as reported in other traditions, contains the additional word *yuqātilūn,* as in AD. 15 : 4.

These headings show that up to the time of Bukhārī, the word *jihād* was used in the wider sense in which it is used in the Qur'ān, invitation to Islām being looked upon as *jihād.* Other books of Tradition contain similar references. Thus Abū Dāwūd (AD. 15 : 4) quotes under the heading "The continuity of *jihād*" a tradition to the effect that "a party of my community will not cease fighting for truth and it will be triumphant over its opponents", which words are thus explained in the *'Aun al-Ma'būd*, a commentary of Abū Dāwūd, on the authority of Nawavī: "this party consists of different classes of the faithful, of them being the brave fighters, and the *faqīhs* (jurists), and the *muḥaddithūn* (collectors of Tradition), and the *zāhids* (those who abstain from worldly pleasures and devote themselves to the service of God), and those who command the doing of good and prohibit evil, and a variety of other people who do other good deeds". This shows that *jihād* in Tradition includes the service of Islām in any form.

Use of the word **jihād** *by jurists*

It is only among the jurists that the word *jihād* lost its original wider significance and began to be used in the narrower sense of *qitāl* (fighting). The reason is not far to seek. The books of jurisprudence (*fiqh*) codified the Muslim law, and in the classification of the various subjects with which the law dealt, *qitāl* (fighting) found a necesary place, but invitation to Islām, though a primary meaning of the word *jihād*, being a matter of free individual choice, did not form part of the law. The jurists who had to deal with *qitāl*, therefore, used the word *jihād* as synonymus with *qitāl*, and, by and by, the wider significance of *jihād* was lost sight of though the commentators of the Qur'ān accepted this significance when dealing with verses such as 25 : 52. But that was not the only misuse of the word. Together with this narrowing of the significance of *jihād*, the further idea was developed that the Muslims were to carry on a war against unbelieving nations and countries, whether they were attacked or not, an idea quite foreign to the Qur'ān.

The spread of Islām by force

The propagation of Islām is no doubt a religious duty of every true Muslim, who must follow the example of the Prophet, but "the spread of Islām by force", is a thing of which no trace can be found in the Qur'ān. On the other hand, the Holy Book lays down the opposite doctrine in clear words. "There is no compulsion in religion", and the reason is added: "The right way is clearly distinct from error" (2 : 256). This verse was revealed after the permission for war had been given, and it is therefore certain that the permission to fight has no connection with the preaching of religion. That the Qur'ān never taught such a doctrine, nor did the Prophet ever think of it, is a fact which is now being gradually appreciated by the Western mind. After beginning his article on *Djihād* with the statement that "the spread of Islām by arms is a religious duty upon Muslims in general", D. B. Macdonald, the writer of the article in the *Encyclopaedia of Islām*, in a way questions the correctness of his own allegation, by adding that there is nothing in the Qur'ān to corroborate it, and that the idea was not present even to the mind of the Prophet:

> "In the Meccan Surās of the Kur'ān patience under attack is taught; no other attitude was possible. But at Medīna the right to repel attack appears, and gradually it became a prescribed duty to fight against and subdue the hostile Meccans. Whether Muhammad himself recognized that his position implied steady and unprovoked war against the unbelieving world until it was subdued to Islām may be in doubt. Traditions are explicit on the point;[2] but the Kur'ānic passages speak always of the unbelievers who are to be subdued as dangerous or faithless."

Here is a clear confession that the Qur'ān does not enjoin the waging of war against all unbelievers so as to subdue them to Islām, nor was the idea present to the mind of the Prophet. The logical consequence of this confession is that genuine traditions cannot inculcate such a doctrine, for Tradition (ḥadīth) reports the saying of the Prophet. And if the Qur'ān and the Prophet never taught such a doctrine, how could it be said to be the religious duty of the Muslims? There is obviously a struggle here in the writer's mind between preconceived ideas and an actual knowledge of facts.

[2] It will be shown later on that even Tradition does not teach propagation of Islām by force.

Circumstances under which war was permitted

It is a misstatement of facts to say that patience under attack was taught at Makkah, because there was no other alternative, and that the right to repel attack came at Madīnah. The attitude was no doubt changed but that change was due to the change of circumstances. At Makkah there was individual persecution and patience was taught. If the conditions had remained the same at Madīnah, the Muslim attitude would have been the same. But individual persecution could no more be resorted to by the Quraish of Makkah, as the Muslims were living out of their reach. This very circumstance fanned the fire of their wrath, and they now planned the extinction of the Muslims as a nation. The sword was taken up to annihilate the Muslim community or to compel it to return to unbelief. That was the challenge thrown at them, and the Prophet had to meet it. The Qur'ān bears the clearest testimony to it. The earliest permission to repel attack is conveyed in words which show that the enemy had already taken up the sword or decided to do so: "Permission (to fight) is given to those on whom war is made, because they are oppressed. And surely Allāh is able to assist them — Those who are driven from their homes without a just cause except that they say: Our Lord is Allāh. And if Allāh did not repel some people by others, cloisters and churches and synagogues and mosques, in which Allāh's name is much remembered would have been pulled down. And surely Allāh will help him who helps His cause" (22 : 39, 40). The very words of this verse show that it is the earliest on the subject of fighting, as it speaks of a permission being given now which evidently had not been given up to this time. This permission was given to a people upon whom war was made by their enemies (*yuqātalūna*); and it was not a permission to make war with people in general but only with the people who made war on them, and the reason is stated plainly "because they are oppressed" and "have been expelled from their homes without a just cause". It was clearly an aggressive war on the part of the enemies of Islām who thus sought to exterminate the Muslims or to compel them to forsake their religion: "And they will not cease fighting with you until they turn you back from your religion if they can" (2 : 217). It was a holy war in the truest sense because, as stated further on, if war had not been allowed under these circumstances, there would be no peace on earth, no religious liberty, and all houses for the worship of God would be destroyed. Indeed there could be no war holier than the one which was needed as much for the religious liberty of the Muslims as for the principle of religious liberty itself, as much to save the mosques as to save the cloisters and the synagogues and churches. If there had ever been a just cause for war in this world, it was for the war that had been permitted to the Muslims. And undoubtedly war with such pure motives was a *jihād*, a struggle carried on simply with the object that truth may prosper and that freedom of conscience may be maintained.

The second verse giving to the Muslims permission to fight runs as follows: "And fight in the way of Allāh against those who fight against you, and be not aggressive; surely Allāh loves not the aggressors" (2 : 190). Here again the condition is plainly laid down that the Muslims shall not be the first to attack, they had to fight — it had now become a duty — but only against those who fought against them; aggression was expressly prohibited. And this fighting in self-defence is called fighting *in the way of Allāh (fī sabīli-llāh),* because fighting in defence is the noblest and justest of all causes. It was the cause Divine, because if the Muslims had not fought they would have been swept out of existence, and there would have been none to establish Divine Unity on earth. These were the very words in which the Prophet prayed in the field of Badr: "O Allāh! I beseech Thee to fulfil Thy covenant and Thy promise; O Allāh! if Thou wilt (otherwise), Thou wilt not be worshipped any more" (Bu. 56 : 89). The words *fī sabīli-llāh* are misinterpreted by most European writers as meaning the *propagation of Islām.* Nothing could be farther from the truth. The Muslims were not fighting to force Islām on others; rather they were being fought to force them to renounce Islām, as shown by 2 : 217 quoted above. What a travesty of facts to say that war was undertaken by the Muslims for the propagation of Islām!

It is sometimes asserted that these injunctions, relating to defensive fighting, were abrogated by a later revelation in ch. 9. Yet any one who reads that chapter cannot fail to note that it does not make the slightest change in the principles laid down earlier. Fighting with idolaters is enjoined in the ninth chapter, but not with all of them. In the very first verse of that chapter, the declaration of immunity is directed towards only "those of the idolaters with whom you made an agreement" not all the idolaters — and even in their case an exception is made. "Except those of the idolaters with whom you made an agreement, then they have not failed you in anything and have not backed up anyone against you, so fulfil their agreement to the end of their terms; for Allāh loves those who keep their duty" (9 : 4). This shows that there were idolatrous tribes on friendly terms with the Muslims, and the Muslims were not allowed to fight with them; it was only the hostile tribes who broke their agreements and attacked the Muslims that were to be fought against. And individual idolaters, even if belonging to hostile tribes, could still have safety, if they wanted to enquire about Islām, and were given a safe conduct back home even if they did not accept Islām: ''And if anyone of the idolaters seek protection by thee, protect him till he hears the word of Allāh, then convey him to his place of safety. This is because they are a people who know not'' (9 : 6). The idolater who stood in need of protection evidently belonged to a hostile tribe, because the friendly tribes, being in alliance with the Muslims, had no need of seeking protection of the Muslim government. Thus even a hostile idolator was to be sent back safely to his own tribe and not molested in any way, as the words of the verse show. The idolaters with whom fighting was enjoined were those who had violated treaties and were foremost in attacking Muslims, as the words that follow show: ''If they prevail against you, they respect neither ties of relationship, nor of covenant in your case'' (9 : 8). ''Will you not fight a people who broke their oaths and aimed at the expulsion of the Messenger and they attacked you first'' (9 : 13). Thus chapter 9, which is supposed to abrogate the earlier verses, still speaks of fighting only against those idolaters who ''attacked you first'', and this is the very condition laid down in earlier verses, such as 2 : 190.

So-called ''verse of the sword''

Notwithstanding that ch. 9, as shown above, does not go beyond what is contained in the earliest revelations on the subject of war, the fifth verse of that chapter is called by some people ''the verse of the sword'', as if it inculcated the indiscriminate massacre of all idolators or unbelievers. The misconception is due to the fact that the words are taken out of their context, and a significance is forced on them which the context cannot bear. The following words occur in the 5th verse: ''So when the sacred months have passed away, slay the idolators wherever you find them'' (9 : 5). But similar words occur also in the earliest revelation on the subject: ''And kill them wherever you find them'' (2 : 191). In both places it is the context which makes it clear as to the identity of the persons regarding whom the order is given. In both cases those against whom the order is given are the people who have taken up the sword and attacked the Muslims first. It has already been shown that the injunction to fight against the idolaters, as contained in the opening verses of the 9th chapter, relates only to such idolatrous tribes as had made agreements with the Muslims and then broken them and had attacked the Muslims, and not to all idolatrous people, wherever they may be found in the world. If only we read the verse that precedes the fifth verse, not the shadow of a doubt will remain that *all* idolaters are not spoken of here. For the fourth verse, as quoted already, states that those idolators were not within the purview of the order who had remained faithful to their agreements. The order was therefore directed against specified idolatrous tribes, the tribes that had made agreements with the Muslims and broken them repeatedly, as expressly stated in 8 : 56. It is a mistake to regard the order as including all idolatrous people living anywhere in the world or even in Arabia. And if the verse preceding the so-called "verse of the sword" makes a clear exception in case of all friendly idolatrous tribes, that following it immediately makes a clear exception in favour of such members of idolatrous hostile tribes as ask the protection of the Muslims (see v. 6, quoted in the preceding paragraph). And then continuing the subject, it is further laid down that the order relates only to people "who broke their oaths and aimed at the expulsion of the Prophet and they attacked you first" (9 : 13). With such a clear explanation of the fifth verse contained in the preceding and following verses, no sane person would interpret it as meaning the killing of all idolaters or the carrying on of unprovoked war against all idolatrous tribes.

When shall war cease

It is thus clear that the Muslims were allowed to fight only in self-defence, to preserve their national existence, and they were forbidden to be aggressive. The Qur'ān nowhere gives them permission to enter on an unprovoked war against the whole world. Conditions were also laid down as to when war should cease: "And fight with them until there is no persecution, and religion should be only for Allāh. But if they desist, then there should be no hostility except against the oppressors" (2 : 193). The words *religion should be only for Allāh* are sometimes misinterpreted as meaning that all people should accept Islām, a significance utterly opposed to the very next words: "But if they *desist*, there should be no hostility except against the oppressor". The *desisting* plainly refers to desisting from persecution. Similar words occur in another early Madīnah revelation: "And fight with them until there is no more persecution and all religions are for Allāh. But if they desist, then surely Allāh sees what they do" (8 : 39). Both expressions, "religion should be only for Allāh" and "all religions are for Allāh" carry one and the same significance, namely that religion is treated as a matter between man and his God, a matter of conscience, in which nobody has a right to interfere. It may be added that if the words had the meaning which it is sought to give them the Prophet would have been the first man to translate that teaching into practice, while as a matter of fact he made peace with the enemy on numerous occasions, and stopped fighting with idolatrous tribes when they wanted peace. Even when he subjugated a people, he gave them full liberty in their religion as it happened in the conquest of Makkah.

Peace recommended

Notwithstanding what has been said above, the Muslims were told to accept peace in the middle of war if the enemy wanted peace: "And if they incline to peace, incline thou also to it and trust in Allāh; surely He is the Hearer, the Knower. And if they intend to deceive thee — then surely Allāh is sufficient for thee" (8: 61, 62). It should be noted that peace is here recommended even though the enemy's sincerity may be doubtful. And there were reasons to doubt the good intentions of the enemy, for the Arab tribes did not attach much value to their treaty agreements: "Those with whom thou makest an agreement, then they break their agreement every time and they keep not their duty" (8 : 56). None could carry those precepts into practice better than the Prophet, and he was so prone to make peace whenever the enemy showed the least desire towards it, that on the occasion of the Ḥudaibiyah truce he did not hesitate to accept the position of the defeated party, though he had never been defeated on the field of battle, and his Companions had sworn to lay down their lives one and all if the worst had come to the worst. Yet he made peace and accepted terms which his own followers looked upon as humiliating for Islām. He accepted the condition that he would go back without performing a pilgrimage and also that if a resident of Makkah embraced Islām and came to him for protection, he would not give him protection. Thus the injunction contained in the Qur'ān to make peace with the idolators if they desired peace, combined with the practice of the Prophet in concluding peace on any terms, is a clear proof that the theory of preaching Islām by the sword is a pure myth so far as the Qur'ān is concerned.

To sum up, neither in the earlier revelations nor in the later is there the slightest indicataion of any injunction to propagate Islām by the sword.

On the other hand, war was clearly allowed as a defensive measure up to the last. It was to be continued only so long as religious persecution lasted, and when that ceased, war was to cease *ipso facto*. And there was the additional condition that if a tribe, against whom the Muslims were fighting because of its aggressive and repeated violation of treaties, embraced Islām, it then and there became a part of the Muslim body politic, and its subjugation by arms was therefore foregone, and war with it came to an end. Such remained the practice of the Prophet during his lifetime. And there is not a single instance in history in which he offered the alternative of the sword or Islām to any tribe or individual, nor did he ever lead an aggressive attack. The last of his expeditions was that of Tabūk, in which he led an army of thirty thousand against the Roman Empire, but when he found, on reaching the frontier, after a very long and tedious journey, that the Romans did not contemplate an offensive, he returned without attacking them. His action on this occasion also throws light on the fact that the permission to fight against the Christians contained in 9 : 29 was also subject to the condition laid down in 2 : 190 that the Muslims not be aggressive in war.

The opinion now held among the more enlightened European critics of Islām is, that though the Prophet did not make use of force in the propagation of Islām, and that though he did not lead an aggressive attack against an enemy, in the whole of his life, yet this position was adopted by his immediate successors, and was therefore a natural development of his teaching. This opinion is also due to a misconception of the historical facts which led to the wars of the early Caliphate with the Persian and Roman empires. After the death of the Prophet, when Arabia rose in insurrection and Abū Bakr, the first Caliph, was engaged in suppressing the revolt, both Persia and Rome openly helped the insurgents with men and money. It is difficult to go into details of history in a book which does not deal with the historical aspect of the question,[3] but it would not be inappropriate to quote a modern writer who is in no way friendly to Islām:

> "Chaldaea and southern Syria belong properly to Arabia. The tribes inhabiting this region, partly heathen but chiefly (at least in name) Christian, formed an integral part of the Arab race and as such fell within the immediate scope of the new

[3] I have dealt with this subject fully in my book *The Early Caliphate*.

> Dispensation. When, however, these came into collision with the Muslim columns on the frontier, *they were supported by their respective sovereigns*,[4] — the western by the Kaiser, and the eastern by the Chosroes. Thus the struggle widened."[5]

There is actual historical evidence that Persia landed her forces in Bahrain to help the insurgents of that Arabian province, and a Christian woman, Sajāh, marched at the head of Christian tribes, from her home on the frontier of Persia, against Madīnah, the capital of Islām, and traversed the country right up to the central part. Persia and Rome were thus the aggressors, and the Muslims, in sheer self-defence, came into conflict with those mighty empires. The idea of spreading Islām by the sword was as far away from their minds as it was from that of the great Master whom they followed. Thus even Muir admits that, as late as the conquest of Mesopotamia by 'Umar, the Muslims were strangers to the idea of making converts to Islām by means of the sword: "The thought of a world-wide mission was yet in embryo; obligation to enforce Islām by a universal Crusade had not yet dawned upon the Muslim mind."[6] This remark relates to the year 16 of Hijrah, when more than half the battles of the early Caliphate had already been fought. According to Muir, even the conquest of the whole of Persia was a measure of self-defence, and not of aggression, on the part of the Muslims: "The truth began to dawn on 'Omar that necessity was laid upon him to withdraw the ban against advance. In self-defence, nothing was left but to crush the Chosroes and take entire possession of his realm."[7] And if the wars with the Persian and Roman empires were begun and carried on for five years without any idea of the propagation of Islām by arms, surely there was no occasion for the idea to creep in at a subsequent stage.

Ḥadīth on the object of war

As already stated, Tradition (*Ḥadīth*) cannot go against the Qur'ān. Being only an explanation of the Holy Book, it must be rejected if it contains anything against the plain teachings of the Qur'ān. Yet Macdonald,

[4] Italics are mine.

[5] Sir W. Muir, *The Caliphate*, p. 46.

[6] *Ibid.*, p. 120.

[7] Op. cit., p. 172.

in the *Encyclopaedia of Islām*,[8] advances a very strange view. The Qur'ān, he admits, does not sanction unprovoked war against non-Muslims. Even the Prophet had no idea that his teachings would develop into such a position. Yet Tradition, he says, is explicit on the point: "Whether Muḥammad himself recognized that his position implied steady and unprovoked war against the unbelieving world until it was subdued to Islām may be in doubt. Traditions are explicit on the point... Still, the story of his writing to the powers around him shows that such a universal position was implicit in his mind." Now Tradition is nothing but a collection of what the Prophet said or did. How could it be then that a thing of which the Prophet had no idea, as admitted in the above quotation, is met with in Tradition? He could not say or do that of which he had no idea. The propagation of Islām by force is neither contained in the Qur'ān nor did the Prophet ever entertain such an idea, yet Tradition, which is an explanation of the Qur'ān and a record of what the Prophet said or did, explicitly states that Islām must be enforced at the point of a sword until the whole world is converted to Islām! These remarks are obviously due to carelessness on the part of the writer.

The only tradition referred to in the article is "the story of the Prophet's writing to the powers around him". But that letter does not contain a single word about the enforcement of Islām at the point of a sword. The wording of one of these letters addressed to the king of the Copts — and all these letters were addressed in similar words — is as follows: "I invite thee with the invitation of Islām; become a Muslim, and thou wilt have entered security; Allāh will give thee a double reward. But if thou turnest back,then on thee is the sin of the Copts. O followers of the Book! come to an equitable proposition between us and you that we shall not serve any but Allāh and that we shall not associate aught with Him and that some of us shall not take others for lords besides Allāh, but if they turn back, then say, Bear witness that we are Muslims". The mere writing of these letters to all the kings is undoubtedly an evidence of the universality of Islām, but by not stretch of imagination can it be made to yield the conclusion that Islām was to be spread by force of arms. The letter is simply an invitation, combined with an appeal to the followers of all revealed religions to accept the common principle of worship of one God.

There is one tradition, however, which has sometimes been misconstrued, as meaning that the Prophet was fighting people to make them

[8] Art. *Djihād*.

believe in the Unity of God. It runs thus: "Ibn 'Umar says, The Holy Prophet said, I have been commanded to fight people until they bear witness that there is no god but Allāh and that Muḥammad is the messenger of Allāh and keep up prayer and pay the *zakāt*. When they have done this, their lives and their properties are protected unless there is obligation of Islām, and their account is with Allāh" (Bu. 2 : 17). It has already been shown that the principles of Islām are one and all taken from the Qur'ān, not from Tradition, and that the Qur'an lays down in express words that no force shall be used in religion. The report begins with the words *I am commanded to fight*, and surely the commandments of the Prophet were given through Divine revelation and are therefore all of them contained in the Qur'ān. The reference in the report is thus undoubtedly to a Quranic verse. In fact, such a verse is met with in the second section of the chapter entitled "Immunity": "But if they repent and keep up prayer and pay the *zakāt,* they are your brethren in faith" (9 : 11). The subject-matter of the report is exactly the same, and clearly the commandment referred to in it is that contained in this verse. One has only to read the context to find out the purport of these words. Some of these verses have already been quoted but, on account of the importance of the subject, four of these are repeated below:

V. 10. "They respect neither ties of relationship nor covenant, in the case of a believer; and these are they who go beyond the limits".

V. 11. "But if they repent and keep up prayer and pay the poor-rate, they are your brethren in faith; and We make the message clear for a people who know."

V. 12. "And if they break their oaths after their agreement and openly revile your religion, then fight the leaders of disbelief — surely their oaths are nothing — so that they may desist."

V. 13. "Will you not fight a people who broke their oaths and aimed at the expulsion of the Messenger and they attacked you first? Do you fear them?"

No comment is needed. The context clearly shows that there were certain tribes that had no regard for ties of relationships or for agreements entered into, and they were the first to attack the Muslims and made plans to expel the Prophet. These were the people to be fought against. The 9th chapter was revealed in the year 9 of Hijrah and this was the time when tribe after tribe was coming over to Islām, and so the condition was laid down that if one of the tribes, that had been hostile to Islām, and had broken its agreements, and was at war with the Muslims, came over to Islām, all hostilities against it were to be stopped immediately, because those people became brethren in faith with Muslims. Old wrongs and iniquities had to be forgotten and not one individual of it was to be harmed, however guilty he may have been, unless in the words of the tradition an obligation of Islām rendered punishment necessary. It does not mean that the Prophet was commanded to *wage* war against people until they accepted Islām; it simply means, as a reference to the Qur'ān shows, that he was commanded to *cease* fighting with the Muslims if they of their own accord embraced Islām. Even people who had been guilty of the murder of a Muslim were not to be put to death if they accepted Islām afterwards, and examples of this are mentioned in Tradition (Bu. 56 : 28).

One such case may be cited here. "Miqdād ibn 'Amr al-Kindī referred the following case to the Prophet: I meet in battle a man from among the unbelievers and we two fight against each other; he cuts off one of my hands with his sword, then he takes the shelter of a tree and says, I submit (*aslamtu*) to Allāh; can I kill him, O Messenger of Allāh, after he has spoken those words? The Prophet said, Do not kill him. But, I said, he has cut off one of my hands, O Prophet! and then he says this after he has cut it off. The Prophet said, Do not kill him, for if thou killest him, he is in thy place before thou didst kill him, and thou art in his place before he uttered those words which he spoke" (Bu. 64 : 12). This shows that the Prophet had given definite orders, which were known to his Companions, that fighting should immediately cease when the person or tribe fighting declared Islām. It is in this light that the tradition under discussion has to be read, *viz.*, that the Prophet had been commanded to *cease* war when an enemy at war with him professed Islām. Numerous examples of this are met with in the history of the Prophet's wars, but there is not a single instance in which he declared war against a peaceful neighbour because that neighbour was not a believer in Islām.

The fact that treaties and agreements were entered into by the Prophet with polytheists (mushrikīn) and the Jews and the Christians is proof that the word *people* used in the tradition stands for particular tribes which, as the the Qur'ān shows, violated their treaties again and again. If there had been any commandment like that which it is sought to deduce from this tradition, the Prophet would have been the first man to act on it. But he always made peace and entered into agreements with his enemies; not once in his whole life did he demand that a people vanquished in battle should accept Islām. The injunction to make peace with a nation inclined to peace (8 : 16), and the fact of the Prophet's repeatedly making treaties with unbelievers, are clear negations of the impossible construction which it is sought to put upon the words of the tradition namely, that the Prophet was commanded to wage war against people until they embraced Islām.

Other traditions which are sometimes misinterpreted are of a similar nature. For instance, in one it is stated that when the Prophet went out to fight with a people he did not attack them till morning, and if he then heard the *adhạn* being called out he refrained from attacking the people (Bu. 10 : 6). This tradition evidently refers to such people as are spoken of in the ninth chapter as breaking their agreements repeatedly and attacking the Muslims. At this very time, that is, in the ninth and tenth years of Hijrah, the time to which the 9th chapter relates, tribe after tribe came over to Islām, deputations from different tribes coming to Madīnah and going back to their people to convert them to the new faith. Therefore, when an expedition had to be sent for the punishment of a tribe which proved unfaithful to its agreement, it had to be ascertained that it had not in the meanwhile accepted Islām, and therefore the precaution spoken of in the tradition was taken.

In another tradition occur the words, "He who fights that the word of Allāh may be exalted," which being severed from the context are sometimes construed as meaning fighting for the propagation of Islām, but when read with the context, their meaning is clear. The tradition runs thus: "A man came to the Prophet and said: There is a man who fights for gain of riches and another man who fights that his exploits may be seen, which of these is the way of Allāh? The Prophet said, The man who fights that the word of Allāh may be exalted, that is in the way of Allāh" (Bu. 56 : 15). It is clear that these words only mean that a man who fights in the way of Allāh (which, as shown from the Qur'ān, means only *in defence of the faith*) should have his motives free from all taint of personal gain or reputation. The unbelievers sought to annihilate the faith of Islām, and the defence of the faith was, therefore, equivalent to the exaltation of the word of Allāh. In the Qur'ān these words are used on the occasion of the Prophet's flight to Madīnah. The Prophet's safe flight is spoken of as making the word of the disbelievers lowest, and the word of Allāh highest: "... So (Allāh) made lowest the word of those who disbelieved. — And the word of Allāh, that is the uppermost" (9 : 40).

There are many traditions which speak of the excellence of *jihād* or of the excellence of fighting, and these are sometimes misconstrued, as showing that a Muslim must always be fighting with other people. It is in a tradition that a Muslim is defined as being "one from whose hand and tongue Muslims — or, according to another account, people — are secure'' (Bu. 2 : 4; FB. I, p. 51); and a Muslim literally means ''one who has entered into peace''. According to another tradition, a *mu'min* (believer) is ''one from whom people are secure concerning their lives and their properties'' (MM. I—ii). But war is undoubtedly a necessity of life, and there are times when fighting becomes the highest of duties. Fighting in the cause of justice, fighting to help the oppressed, fighting in self-defence, fighting for national existence are all truly the highest and noblest of deeds, because in all these cases a man lays down his life in the cause of truth and justice, and that is, no doubt, the highest sacrifice that a man can make. Fighting, in itself, is neither good nor bad; it is the occasion which makes it either the best of deeds or the worst of them.

The question is simply this, What was the object for which the Prophet fought? There is not the least doubt about it, as the Qur'ān is clear on the point: ''Permission to fight is given to those on whom war is made, because they are oppressed'' (22 : 39); ''And if Allāh did not repel some people by others, cloisters and churches and synagogues and mosques in which Allāh's name is much remembered, would have been pulled down'' (22 : 40); ''And what reason have you not to fight in the way of Allāh and of the weak among the men and the women and the children who say, Our Lord, take us out of this town, whose people are oppressors, and grant us from Thee a friend and grant us from Thee a helper'' (4 : 75); ''Will you not fight a people who broke their oaths and aimed at the expulsion of the Messenger, and they attacked you first'' (9 : 13); and so on. If then there are traditions which speak of the excellence of keeping a horse (Bu. 56 : 45), or of keeping horses ready on the frontier of the enemy (Bu. 56 : 73), or traditions recommending the learning of shooting (*ramy*) (Bu. 56 : 78), or practising with implements of war (Bu. 56 : 79), or traditions of speaking of swords and shields and armour and so on, they show, not that the Muslims were spreading Islām by force of arms, not even that they were waging aggressive war against peaceful neighbours, but that they had to fight, and hence all deeds done to carry on a successful war are praised. Indeed in one tradition it is stated that ''Paradise (*al-Jannah*) is under the shadow of swords'' (Bu. 56 : 22). All this is true as long as the sword is used in a right cause.

Jurists' wrong notion of **jihād**

The wrong notion of *jihād*, introduced by the jurists, was owing to a misconception of certain verses of the Qur'ān, due, in the first place, to the fact that no regard had been paid to the context, and, in the second place, to a disregard of the circumstances under which the Prophet fought. It has already been shown that the fifth verse of the ninth chapter contains nothing that is not contained in the earlier revelation, and that it is simply a reassertion of the original injunction to fight against tribes that were first to attack the Muslims and that broke their agreements; but reading it out of its context, a significance was given to it that was never comtemplated, and it received the name of *ayāt al-ṣaif* (the verse of the sword), which is assuredly a misnomer. Another verse, which the *Hidāyah* brings in support of this wrong conception of *jihād*, is the 36th verse of the ninth chapter which runs as follows: "And fight the polytheists all together as they fight you all together" (9 : 36). Now this is, in fact, only an injunction to the Muslims to remain united in the war against polytheists, as they, the polytheists, were united in their war against the Muslims. It does not mean that there were no polytheist tribes that did not fight against the Muslims, for this is not only historically untrue, but is also contradicted by the Qur'ān itself: "Except those of the idolaters with whom you make an agreement, then they have not failed you in anything and have not backed up any one against you" (9 : 4). A reference to history would show that there were idolatrous tribes that never fought against the Muslims, but, on the other hand, were in alliance with them, and the Muslims fought in their behalf. Such alliances are met with not only in the lifetime of the Prophet but also in wars of the Early Caliphate.[9] Nor does the verse mean that there should be no Muslim on the face of the earth who should not be engaged in war against the polytheists. Even the supporters of unprovoked war hardly go as far as that. The *Hidāyah*, after quoting this verse in support of a war against all polytheists, adds that this is a *fardz kifāyah*, an obligation which if performed by some Muslims relieves others of the duty. Now the word *kāffa* (meaning *all together*) occurs in this verse twice, once in connection with the Muslims and again in connection with the idolaters, so that if *all* polytheists, without any exception, are to be fought against, *all* Muslims without any exception must fight against them. As this is impossible, it follows that the verse only enjoins unification in the ranks of the Muslims, in like manner as

[9] The Khuzā'a were an idolatrous tribe that entered into an alliance with Muslims after the truce of Ḥudaibiyah and when they were attacked by the allies of the Quraish with the latter's help, the Prophet led an attack on Makkah to punish the Quraish for their breach of agreement. There were many other tribes in similar alliance with the Muslims. In the early Caliphate wards, Christian soldiers fought side by side with the Muslims, and so also some of the Magian tribes.

there was unification in the ranks of the idolaters, and there is nothing said here as to the conditions under which fighting is to be carried on. These conditions are expressly laid down in other verses and can on no account be dispensed with: "And fight in the way of Allāh against those who fight against you and be not aggressive. Surely Allāh loves not the aggressors" (2 : 190).

The jurists themselves have challenged the accuracy of the principle on which their wrong notion of *jihād* is based. For instance, the *Hidāyah* gives the following reason for *jihād* being a *fardz kifāyah*: "It is not made obligatory for its own self (*il 'aini-hī*), for in itself it is the causing of mischief (*ifsād*), and it is made obligatory for the strengthening of the religion of Allāh and for the repelling of evil (*daf' al-sharr*) from His servants" (H.I, p. 537). The use here of the words *daf' al-sharr* shows that, even according to the jurists, *jihād* in its origin is only for repelling evil and is therefore defensive, not offensive. Again, when discussing the reasons for the prohibition of killing women and children and old men and those who refrain from fighting (*muq'id*) and blind men, the *Hidāyah* says: "For what makes the killing lawful (*mubīḥ li-l-qatl*) according to us, is the fighting (*ḥirāb*), and this is not true in their case, and therefore the man whose one side is withered (*yābis al-shiqq*) and the man whose right hand is cut off and a man whose hand and foot are cut off cannot be killed" (H. I, p. 540). Here it is admitted that what makes the killing of a man lawful is not his unbelief (*kufr*) but his fighting (ḥirāb), for, if men could be killed for unbelief, even women, children, and old and incapacitated men would not be spared. That is indeed a sound basis. But if the reason given on this occasion is true, and it is unlawful to kill any one merely on account of unbelief, it is also unlawful to undertake war against a people because they are unbelievers or idolaters, as in such a war people would be killed for mere unbelief.

In still more plain words, the *Hidāya* recognizes, in its discussion on the making of peace with unbelievers, that the real object of *jihād* is the repelling of the enemy's mischief: "And when the Imām is of opinion that he should make peace with those who are fighting (against the Muslims) (*ahl al-ḥarb*), or with a party of them, and it is in the interests of the Muslims, there is no harm in peace, on account of what Allāh says, "And if they incline to peace, do thou incline to it and trust in Allāh; and the Holy Prophet entered into agreement with the people of Makkah in the year of Ḥudaibiyah, that there shall be no war between him and them for ten years; and because entering into agreement is *jihād* in spirit, when it is for the good of the Muslims, as the object, which is the repelling of mischief (*daf‘ al-sharr*), is attained thereby'' (H. I, p. 541). Here again it is admitted that the real object of *jihād* is *the repelling of the enemy's mischief*, and it is on this basis alone that peace can be made with the unbelievers. The annotator of the *Hidāyah* does not conceal the fact that it is a plain contradiction of what is said elsewhere[10] as to the object of *jihād*. But the question is, how can peace with unbelievers and idolaters be justified? If the object of *jihād* is the enforcing of Islām at the point of a sword, peace with unbelievers is simply a contradiction of this object. But peace with unbelievers is not only a matter of choice; it is an injunction which must be carried out when the enemy is inclined to peace: ''And if they incline to peace, do thou incline to it'' (8 : 61).

The above quotations from the *Hidāyah* will show that even the jurists felt that their exposition of *jihād* was opposed to its basic principles laid down in the Qur'ān. Probably the new doctrine grew up slowly. It is clear that the earlier jurists did not go as far as their later annotators. Notwithstanding the wrong conception which was introduced into the meaning of *jihād,* by not paying proper attention to the context of the Qur'ān and the circumstances under which the Prophet fought, they still recognized that the basic principle of *jihād* was the repelling of the enemy's mischief, and that hence peace with the unbelievers was *jihād* in spirit. But the later generation would not tolerate even this much. Some of them have gone to the length of holding that no permanent peace but only peace for a limited period can be concluded with the unbelievers, an opinion flatly contradicting the Quranic injunction in 8 : 61. It must however be repeated — and it would bear repetition a hundred times — that, essentially, the Qur'ān is opposed to taking the life of a man for unbelief. It gives full liberty of conscience by stating that there is no compulsion in religion (2 : 256); it establishes religious freedom by enjoining war to cease when there is no religious persecution, and religion becomes a matter between man and his God (2 : 193); it plainly says that the life of a man cannot be taken for any reason except that he kills a man or causes mischief (*fasād*) in the land (5 : 32).

[10] The annotator's note on *daf‘ al-sharr* (repelling of the enemy's mischief) as the object of *jihād* runs thus: ''In many places it has been stated that the object of *jihād* is the exaltation of the word of Allāh and this contradicts what is stated here.''

Dār al-ḥarb *and* Dār al-Islām

With the new notion introduced into the word *jihād*, the jurists artificially divided the whole word into *dār al-ḥarb* and *dār al-Islām*. *Dār al-ḥarb* literally means *the abode* or *seat of war*, and *dār al-Islām, the abode of Islām*. The words are not used in the Qur'ān, nor are they traceable in any tradition. Bukhārī uses the word *dār al-ḥarb* in the heading of one of his chapters: "When a people embrace Islām in *dār al-ḥarb*" (Bu. 56 : 180). Two traditions are mentioned under this heading, in neither of which do the words *dār al-ḥarb* occur. The first speaks of Makkah, and its subject-matter is that when, after the conquest of Makkah, the unbelieving Quraish accepted Islām; they were recognized as owners of property of which they had become masters, though it originally belonged to those Muslims who had fled to Madīnah. The second speaks of Rabdhah, a place at a distance of about three days' journey from Madīnah, the lands near which were turned into pasture by 'Umar and, on the owners' protest, made over to them. Both Makkah and Rabdhah were at one time at war with the Muslims and on this account Bukhārī speaks of them as *dār al-ḥarb*. *Dār al-Islām* is evidently a place where the laws of Islām prevail and which is under a Muslim ruler. The use of *dār al-ḥarb* in the sense of a place actually at war with the Muslims, is unobjectionable. But the jurists apply the word to all states and countries which are not *dār al-Islām* or under the Muslim rule, though they may not be at war with the Muslims, and thus look upon a Muslim state as being always in a state of war with the whole of the non-Muslim world. This position is not only inconsistent with the very basic principles of Islām but actually it has never been accepted by any Muslim state that has ever existed in the world. The difficulty has been met by some jurists by bringing a third class, called *dār al-ṣulḥ* or *dār al-'ahd,* or a country which has an agreement with the Muslims. But even this does not exhaust the whole world. Many of the laws relating to war are based on this fictitious division of the world, for which there is not the least authority either in the Qur'ān or in Tradition.

Jizyah

The word *jizyah* is explained as meaning *the tax that is taken from the free non-Muslim subjects of a Muslim government, whereby they ratify the compact that ensures them protection, or a tax that is paid by the owner of land,* being derived from *jazā* which means *he gave satisfaction* or *he compensated* him for a certain thing, or for what he had done (LL.). In the Qur'ān, *jizyah* is spoken of only in one place, and there in connection with wars with the people of the Book: "Fight those who believe not in Allāh... out of those who have been given the Book, until they pay the *jizyah* in acknowledgement of superiority and they are in a state of subjection" (9 : 29). The Prophet made treaties subject to the condition of payment of *jizyah* with the Magians of Bahrain (Bu. 58 : 1), with Ukaidar, the Christian chief of Dūmah (AD. 19 : 29; IH), with the Christian ruler of Ayla (IJ-H. III, p. 146), with the Jews of Jarbā' and Adhruḥ[11] (*ibid.*), and with the Christians of Najrān (IS. T. I-ii, p. 35). But in all these cases, the *jizyah* was a tribute paid by the state and not a poll-tax. Bukhārī opens his book of *jizyah* with a chapter headed as follows: "*Jizyah* and concluding of peace with *ahl al-ḥarb* (those at war with the Muslims)" (Bu. 58 : 1). Continuing, he is more explicit, remarking under the same heading: "And what is related in the matter of taking *jizyah* from the Jews and the Christians and the Magians (*Majūs*) and the non-Arabs (*'Ajam*). " The rule of the *jizyah* was thus applicable to all enemy people, and the Prophet's own action shows that treaties subject to the payment of *jizyah* were concluded, not only with the Jews and the Christians but also with Magians. It would be seen from this that the words *ahl al-Kitāb* used in 9 : 29, quoted above, must be taken in the wider sense of followers of any other religion. But *jizyah*, which was originally a tribute paid by a subject state, took the form of a poll-tax later on in the time of 'Umar; and the word also applied to the land-tax which was levied on Muslim owners of agricultural land. The jurists, however, made a distinction between the poll-tax and the land-tax by giving the name of *kharāj* to the latter. Both together formed one of the two chief sources of the revenue of the Muslim state, the *zakāt* paid by the Muslims being the other source.

Jizyāh was not a religious tax

European writers on Islām have generally assumed that, while the Qur'ān offered only one of the two alternatives, Islām or death, to other non-Muslims, the Jews and the Christians were given a somewhat better

[11] Dūmah, Ayla, Jarbā' and Adhruḥ are all places situated on the Syrian frontier, and these treaties were made during the expedition to Tabūk, in the ninth year of Hijrah.

position, since they could save their lives by the payment of *jizyah*. This conception of *jizyah* as a kind of religous tax whose payment entitled certain non-Muslims to security of life under the Muslim rule, is as entirely opposed to the fundamental teachings of Islām as the myth that the Muslims were required to carry on an aggressive war against all non-Muslims till they accepted Islām. Tributes and taxes were levied before Islām, and are levied to this day, by Muslim as well as non-Muslim states, yet they have nothing to do with the religion of the people affected. The Muslim state was as much in need of finance to maintain itself as any other state on the face of this earth, and it resorted to exactly the same methods as those employed by other states. All that happened in the time of the Prophet was that certain small non-Muslim states were, when subjugated, given the right to administer their own affairs, but only if they would pay a small sum by way of tribute towards the maintenance of the central government at Madīnah. It was an act of great magnanimity on the part of the Prophet to confer complete autonomy on a people after conquering them, and a paltry sum of tribute (*jizyah*) in such conditions was not a hardship but a boon. There was no military occupation of their territories, no interference at all with their administration, their laws, their customs and usages, or their religion; and, for the tribute paid, the Muslim state undertook the responsibility of protecting these small states against all enemies. In the later conquests of Islām, while it became necessary for the Muslims to establish their own administration in the conquered territories, there was still as little interference with the usages and religion of the conquered people as was possible, and for enjoying complete protection and the benefits of a settled rule they had to pay a very mild tax, the *jizyah*.

It may, however, be said that the Muslim state made a discrimination between the Muslim and the non-Muslim and that it was this feature of *jizyah* which gave it a religious colouring. A discrimination was indeed made, but it was not in favour of the Muslim but that of the non-Muslim. The Muslim had to do compulsory military service and to fight the battles of the state, not only at home but also in foreign countries, and in addition had to pay a tax heavier than that which the non-Muslim was required to pay, as will be shown presently. The non-Muslim was entirely exempt from military service on account of the *jizyah* he paid, and half a guinea or a dīnār a year is certainly cheap for exemption from military service. So the Muslim had to pay the *zakāt*, a far heavier tax than *jizyah*, and do military service, while the non-Muslim had only to pay a small tax for the privilege of enjoying all the benefits of a settled rule.

The very name *ahl al-dhimmah* (lit., *people under protection*) given to the non-Muslim subjects of a Muslim state, or to a non-Muslim state under the protection of Muslim rule, shows that the *jizyah* was paid as a compensation for the protection afforded; in other words, it was a contribution of the non-Muslims towards the military organization of the Muslim state. There are cases on record in which the Muslim state returned the *jizyah*, when it was unable to afford protection to the people under its care. Thus, when the Muslim forces under Abū 'Ubaida were engaged in a struggle with the Roman Empire, they were compelled to beat a retreat, at Ḥimṣ, which they had previously conquered. When the decision was taken to evacuate Ḥimṣ, Abū 'Ubaida sent for the chiefs of the place and returned to them the whole amount which he had realized at *jizyah* saying that as the Muslims could no longer protect them, they were not entitled to the *jizyah*.

Further it appears that exemption from military service was granted only to such non-Muslims as wanted it, for where a non-Muslim people offered to fight the battles of the country, they were exempted from *jizyah*. The Banī Taghlib and the people of Najrān, both Christians, did not pay the *jizyah (En. Is.)*. Indeed the Banī Taghlib fought alongside the Muslim forces in the battle of Buwaib in 13 A.H. Later on in the year 17 A.H., they wrote to the Caliph 'Umar offering to pay the *zakāt*, which was a heavier burden, instead of the *jizyah*. "The liberality of 'Omar," says Muir in his *Caliphate*,[12] "allowed the concession; and the Banī Taghlib enjoyed the singular privilege of being assessed as Christians at a 'double *Tithe*', instead of paying the obnoxious badge of subjugation". Military service was also accepted, in place of *jizyah*, in the time of 'Umar, from Jurjān. Shahbarāz, an Armenian chief, also concluded peace with the Muslims on the same terms.

Incidence of the **Jizyah**

The manner in which the *jizyah* was levied also shows that it was a tax for exemption from military service. The following classes were exempt from *jizyah*: all females, males who had not attained majority, old people, people whom disease had crippled (*zamin*), the paralyzed, the blind, the poor (*faqīr*) who could not work for themselves (*ghair mu'tamil*), the slaves, slaves who were working for their freedom *(mudbir)*, and the monks

[12] Sir W. Muir, *The Caliphate*, p. 142.

(H.I., pp. 571, 572). And besides this, "in the first century ... many persons were entirely exempt from taxation, though we do not know why" (*En. Is.*). It has already been shown that certain non-Muslim tribes that had agreed to do military service, were also exempted from *jizyah*, and these two facts — the exemption of non-Muslims unfit for military service and of the able-bodied who agreed to military service — taken together lead to but one conclusion, namely, that the *jizyah* was a tax paid by such *Dh͟immīs* as could fight, for exemption from military service.

A study of the items of the expenditure of *jizyah* leads to the same conclusion, for the *jizyah* was spent for strengthening of the frontiers or obstructing the frontier approaches (*sadd al-th͟agh͟ūr*), for the building of bridges, payment to judges and governors and the maintenance of the fighting forces and their children (H. I, p. 576).

In spite of exemptions on so vast a scale, the rate of *jizyah* was very low, being originally one dinār[13] per head for a whole year. Later on, the rate was raised in the case of rich people, who had to pay four dinārs or forty-eight dirhams annually, or four dirhams monthly; next came those who paid two dinārs annually, or two dirhams per month; the lowest rate being one dinār, at which all were originally assessed. This is according to Ḥanafī law, while Shafi'ī retained the original rate of one dinār per head in all cases (H.). The three grades are defined thus: (1) the rich man (*al-ẓahir al-gh͟inā*, or he whose wealth is manifest) who owns abundant property, so that he need not work for his livelihood; (2) the middle class man who owns property, but in addition thereto needs to earn money to make a living; and (3) the poor man who has no property, but earns more than is necessary to maintain himself. The Muslim was, apparently, more heavily taxed, for he had to pay at the rate of 2½ per cent of his savings, and, in addition, to perform military service. The *jizyah* was levied in a very sympathetic spirit, as the following anecdote will show. Caliph 'Umar once saw a blind *Dh͟immī* (non-Muslim) begging, and finding on enquiry that he had to pay *jizyah*, he not only exempted him but, in addition, ordered that he be paid a stipend from the state-treasury, issuing further orders at the same time that all *Dh͟immīs* in similar circumstances should be paid stipends.

[13] The dīnār was a gold coin the original weight of which was 65.4 grains troy.

Islām, **jizyah** *or the sword*

Another myth concerning the early Caliphate wars may be removed in connection with the discussion of *jizyah.* It is generally thought that the Muslims were out to impose their religion at the point of a sword, and that the Muslim hosts were over-running all lands with the message of Islām, *jizyah* or the sword. This is, of course, quite a distorted picture of what really happened. If the Muslims had really been abroad with the message, and in this spirit, how was it possible for non-Muslims to fight in their ranks? The fact that there were people who never became Muslims at all, nor ever paid *jizyah*, and yet were living in the midst of the Muslims, even fighting their battles, explodes the whole theory of the Muslims offering Islām or *jizyah* or the sword. The truth of the matter is that the Muslims finding the Roman Empire and Persia bent upon the subjugation of Arabia and the extirpation of Islām, refused to accept terms of peace without a safeguard against a repetition of the aggression; and this safeguard was demanded in the form of *jizyah*, or a tribute, which would be an admission of defeat on their part. No war was ever *started* by the Muslims by sending this message to a peaceful neighbour; history belies such an assertion. But when a war was undertaken on account of the enemy's aggression — his advance on Muslim territory or help rendered to the enemies of the Muslim state — it was only natural that the Muslims did not terminate the war before bringing it to a successful conclusion. They were willing to avoid further bloodshed after inflicting a defeat on the enemy, only if he admitted defeat and agreed to pay a tribute, which was only a token tribute as compared with the crushing war indemnities of the present day. The offer to terminate hostilities on payment of *jizyah* was thus an act of mercy towards a vanquished foe. But if the payment of a token tribute was unacceptable to the vanquished power, the Muslims could do nothing but have recourse to the sword, until the enemy was completely subdued.

The only question that remains is whether the Muslim soldiers invited their enemies to accept Islām; and whether it was an offence if they did so? Islām was a missionary religion from its very inception, and every Muslim deemed it his birthright to invite other people to embrace Islām. The envoys of Islām, wherever they went, looked upon it as their first duty to deliver the message of Islām, because they felt that Islām imparted a new life and vigour to humanity, and offered a real solution to the problems of every nation. Islām was offered, no doubt, even to the fighting enemy, but it is a distortion of facts to say that it was offered at the point of the sword, when there is not a single instance on record of Islām being enforced upon a prisoner of war; nor of Muslims sending a message to a peaceful neighbouring state to the effect that it would be invaded if it did not embrace Islām. All that is recorded is that, in the midst of war and after defeat had been inflicted on the enemy in several battles, when there were negotiations for peace, the Muslims in their zeal for the faith related their own experience before the enemy chiefs. They stated how they themselves had been deadly foes to Islām and how, ultimately, they saw the truth and found Islām to be a blessing and a power that had raised the Arab race from the depths of degradation to great moral and spiritual heights, and had welded their warring elements into a solid nation. In such words did the Muslim envoys invite the Persians and the Romans to Islām, not before the declaration of war, but at the time of the negotiations for peace. If the enemy then accepted Islām, there would be no conditions for peace, and the two nations would live as equals and brethren. It was not offering Islām at the point of a sword, but offering it as a harbinger of peace, of equality and of brotherhood. Not once in the wars of the early Caliphate did the Muslims send a message to a peaceful neighbour that, if it did not accept Islām, the Muslim forces would carry fire and sword into its territory. Wars they had to wage, but these wars were due to reasons other than zeal for the propagation of Islām. And they could not do a thing which their Master never did, and which their only guide in life, the Qur'ān, never taught them.

Directions relating to war

The directions given to his soldiers by the Prophet also show that his wars were not due to any desire to enforce religion. " 'Abd Allāh ibn 'Umar reports that, in a certain battle fought by the Prophet, a woman was discovered among the slain. On this, the Prophet forbade the killing of women and children (in wars)" (Bu. 56 : 147, 148). Traditions relating to this prohibition are repeated very often in all collections (AD. 15 : 112; Tr. 20 : 18; Ah. I, p. 256; II, pp. 22, 23; III, p. 488; M. 32 : 7). Now if the wars of Islām had been undertaken with the object of forcing Islām upon a people, why should women and children have been excepted? It would rather have been easier to win them over to Islām, by holding the sword over their heads, because women and children naturally do not have the power to resist, like men who can fight. The fact that there is an express direction against killing three-fourths of the population, as women and children must be in every community, shows that the propagation of religion was far from being the object of these wars. In some traditions the word *'asīf* is added to *women* and *children*, showing that there was also a prohibition against killing people who were taken along with the army as "labour units" (Ah. III, p. 488; IV, p. 178; AD. 15 : 112). There is yet another tradition prohibiting the killing of *shaikh fānī* (very old man) who is unable to fight (MM. 18 : 5-ii). Monks were also not to be molested (Ah. I, p. 300). It was only in a night attack that the Prophet excused the chance killing of a woman or child saying, "They are among them" (Bu. 56 : 146); what he meant was that it was a thing which could not be avoided, for at night children and women could not be distinguished from the soldiers.

The above examples may be supplemented by some others taken from Sayyid Amīr 'Alī's *Spirit of Islam*. The following instructions were given to the troops dispatched against the Byzantines by the Prophet: "In avenging the injuries inflicted upon us, molest not the harmless inmates of domestic seclusion; spare the weakness of the female sex; injure not the infant at the breast, or those who are ill in bed. Abstain from demolishing the dwellings of the unresisting inhabitants; destroy not the means of their subsistence, nor their fruit trees; and touch not the palm" (p. 81). Abū Bakr gave the following instructions to the commander of an army in the Syrian battle: "When you meet your enemies acquit yourselves like men, and do not turn your backs; and if you gain the victory, kill not the little children, nor old people, nor women. Destroy no palm trees, nor burn any fields of corn. Cut down no fruit trees, nor do any mischief to cattle, only such as you kill for the necessity of subsistence. When you make any covenant or article, stand to it, and be as good as your word. As you go on, you will find some religious persons that live retired in monasteries, who propose themselves to serve God that way. Let them alone, and neither kill them nor destroy their monasteries" (p. 81).

Prisoners of war

The treatment of prisoners of war, as laid down in the Qur'ān and Tradition, also bears evidence of the fact that the idea of enforcement of Islām by the sword is entirely foreign to the conception of Islamic warfare. If the wars, during the time of the Prophet or early Caliphate, had been prompted by the desire of propagating Islām by force, this object could easily have been attained by forcing Islām upon prisoners of war who fell into the hands of the Muslims. Yet this the Qur'ān does not allow, expressly laying down that they must be set free: "So when you meet in battle those who disbelieve, smite the necks; then when you have overcome them, make them prisoners, and afterwards set them free as a favour or for ransom until the war lays down its burdens" (47 : 4). It will be seen from this that the taking of prisoners was allowed only as long as war conditions prevailed; and even when the prisoners are taken they cannot be kept so permanently, but must be set free either as favour or at the utmost by taking ransom. The Prophet carried this injunction into practice in his lifetime.[14] In the battle of Ḥunain, six thousand prisoners of the Ḥawāzin tribe were taken, and they were all set free simply as an act of favour (Bu. 40 : 7; IJ-H. III, p. 132). A hundred families of Banī Mustaliq were taken as prisoners in the battle of Muraisī', and they were also set at liberty without ransom being paid (IJ-H. III, p. 66). Seventy prisoners were taken in the battle of Badr, and it was only in this case that ransom was exacted, but the prisoners were granted their freedom while war with the Quraish was yet in progress (AD. 15 : 122; Ah. I, p. 30). The form of ransom adopted in the case of some of these prisoners was that they should be entrusted with some work connected with teaching (Ah. I, p. 247; ZI, p. 534). When war ceased and peace was established, all war-prisoners would have to be set free, according to the verse quoted above.

Slavery abolished

This verse also abolishes slavery for ever. Slavery was generally brought about through raids by stronger tribes upon weaker ones. Islām did not allow raids or the making of prisoners by means of raids. Prisoners could only be taken after a regular battle, and even then could not be retained for ever. It was obligatory to set them free, either as favour or after taking ransom. This state of things could last only as long as war conditions existed. When war was over, no prisoners could be taken.

The name applied to prisoners of war is *mā malakat aimānu-kum*, lit.,

[14] In spite of the clear injunction of the Qur'ān to set free all prisoners, and the practice of the Prophet who never killed a single prisoner of war and generally set them free as an act of favour, the Rev. Klein writes in *The Religion of Islam*: "Unbelievers taken in war, except idolaters of Arabia and apostates who must be killed, who do not embrace Islām may either be killed, or made captive... or be granted their liberty on condition of their becoming Zimmīs" (p. 179). This is an entirely baseless statement.

what your right hands possess. What one's right hand possesses means that which one has obtained by superior power, and prisoners of war were given this name because it was by superior power in war that they were reduced to subjection. The name *'abd* (slave) was also applied to them, because they had lost their freedom. The treatment accorded to prisoners of war or slaves in Islām is unparalleled. No other nation or society can show a similar treatment even of its own members when they are placed in the relative position of a master and a servant. The slave or the prisoner was, no doubt, required to do a certain amount of work, but the condition, in which it was ordained that he should be kept, freed him of all abject feelings. The golden rule of treating the slave like a brother was laid down by the Prophet in clear words: "Ma'rūr says, I met Abū Dharr in Rabdha and he wore a dress and his slave wore a similar dress. I questioned him about it. He said, I abused a man (*i.e.,* his slave) and found fault with him on account of his mother (addressing him as son of a Negress). The Prophet said to me, O Abū Dḥarr! Thou findest fault with him on account of his mother, surely thou art an ignorant man; your slaves are your brethren, Allāh has placed them under your hands; so whoever has his brother under his hand, let him give him to eat whereof he himself eats, and let him give to wear what he himself wears, and impose not on them a work which they are not able to do, and if you give them such a work, then help them in the execution of it" (Bu. 2 : 22). The prisoners were distributed among the various Muslim families because no arrangements for their maintenance by the state existed at the time, but they were treated honourably. A prisoner of war states that he was kept in a family whose people gave him bread while they themselves had to live on dates (IJ-H. II, p. 287). Prisoners of war were therefore not only set free but, as long as they were kept prisoners, they were kept honourably.

War as a struggle to be carried on honestly

It will be seen from what has been stated above, concerning the injunctions relating to war and peace, that war is recognized by Islām as a struggle between nations — though a terrible struggle — which is sometimes necessitated by the conditions of human life; and when that struggle comes, a nation is bound to acquit itself of its responsbility in the matter in an honourable manner, and fight it to the bitter end whatever it is. Islām does not allow its followers to provoke war, nor does it allow them to be aggressors, but it commands them to put their whole force into the struggle when war is forced on them. If the enemy wants peace after the struggle has begun, the Muslims should not refuse, even though there is doubt about the honesty of his purpose. But the struggle, as long as it lasts, must be carried on to the end. In this struggle, honest dealing is enjoined even with the enemy, throughout the Qur'ān: "And let not hatred of a people — because they hindered you from the Sacred Mosque — incite you to transgress; and help one another in righteousness and piety, and help not one another in sin and aggression" (5 : 2); "And let not hatred of a people incite you not to act equitably. Be just, that is nearer to observance of duty" (5 : 8). This is in a chapter which was revealed towards the close of the Prophet's life. Tradition too enjoins honest dealing in war: "Fight and do not exceed the limits and be not unfaithful and do not mutilate bodies and do not kill children" (M. 32 : 2). Such are some of the directions given which purify war of the elements of barbarity and dishonesty in which warring nations generally indulge. Neither inhuman nor immoral practices are allowed.

A tradition is sometimes cited as allowing deceit in war. This is due to a misinterpretation of its words. Deceit and lying are not allowed under any circumstances. The tradition runs thus: "The Holy Prophet said, The Chosroes shall perish and there shall be no Chosroes after him, and the Caesar shall perish and there shall be no Caesar after him, and their treasures shall be distributed in the way of Allāh, and he called war a deception (*khad'at-an*)" (Bu. 56 : 157). These words were uttered by the Prophet, when he received the news that the Chosroes had torn his letter to pieces and ordered his arrest; and the words contain a clear prophecy that the power of both the Chosroes and the Caesar shall depart in their wars with the Muslims, so that there shall be neither a Persian empire under the Chosroes, nor a Roman empire under the Caesar. Evidently the concluding words "and he called war a deception" explain how the Chosroes and the Caesar will perish.

War is a deception, in the sense that sometimes a great power makes war upon a weaker power thinking that it will soon crush it, but such war proves a deception and leads to the destruction of the great aggressive power itself. This was what happened in the case of the wars of Persia and Rome against the Muslims. They both had entered upon an aggressive war against the Arabs, thinking that they would crush the rising power of Arabia in a little time. They began by helping the tribes on the frontier of Arabia to overthrow the Muslim power, and were thus drawn into a war with the Muslims which ultimately crushed their own power. This is the explanation given in *Bukhārī's* famous commentary, the *'Ainī*: "Whoever is deceived in it once (*i.e.* overthrown or defeated), he is exhausted and perished and is unable to return to his former condition" (Ai. VII, p. 66). Ibn Athīr gives three explanations, according as the word is read *khad'ah* or *khud'ah* or *khuda'ah,* and in all three cases the meaning is almost the same as given in *'Ainī*. Taking the first reading which it calls the most correct and the best, the significance is thus explained: "In the first case the meaning is that the affair of the war is deceived with an overthrow; when the fighter is overthrown once, then he finds no respite" (N.). In the case of the third reading "the meaning is that the war deceives people; it gives them hope but does not fulfil them" (N.). It is only imperfect knowledge of the Arabic language which has led some people to think that this tradition means that it is lawful to practise deception in war. The Islamic wars were in fact purified of all that is unworthy when the Muslims were plainly told that a war fought for any gain (which includes acquisition of wealth or territory) was not in the way of Allāh (Bu. 56 : 15). The Qur'ān puts it still more clearly: "Let those fight in the way of Allāh who sell this world's life for the Hereafter" (4 : 74).

Apostasy

The word *irtidād* is the measure of *ifti'āl* from *radd* which means *turning back. Ridda* and *irtidād* both signify *turning back to the way from which one has come,* but *ridda* is specially used for *going back to unbelief,* while *irtidād* is used in this sense as well as in other senses (R.), and the person going back to unbelief from Islām is called *murtadd* (apostate). There is as great a misconception on the subject of apostasy as on the subject of *jihād*, the general impression among both Muslims and non-Muslims being that Islām punishes apostasy with death. If Islām does not allow the taking of the life of a person on the score of religion, and this has already been shown to be the basic principle of Islām, it is immaterial whether unbelief has been adopted after being a Muslim or not, and therefore as far as the sacredness of life is concerned, the unbeliever (*kāfir*) and the apostate (*murtadd*) are at par.

Apostasy in the Qur'ān

The Qur'ān is the primary source of Islamic laws and therefore we shall take it first. In the first place, it nowhere speaks of a *murtadd* by implication. *Irtidād* consists in the expression of unbelief or in the plain denial of Islām, and it is not to be assumed because a person who professes Islām, expresses an opinion or does an act which, in the opinion of a learned man or a legist, is un-Islamic. Abuse of a prophet or disrespect to the Qur'ān are very often made false excuses for treating a person as *murtadd*, though he may avow in the strongest terms that he is a believer in the Qur'ān and the Prophet. Secondly, the general impression that Islām condemns an apostate to death does not find the least support from the Qur'ān. Heffeming begins his article on *murtadd*, in the *Encyclopaedia of Islam*, with the following words: "In the Qur'ān the apostate is threatened with punishment in the next world only." There is mention of *irtidād* in one of the late Makkah revelations: "Whoso disbelieves in Allāh after his belief — not he who is compelled while his heart is content with faith, but he who opens his breast for disbelief — on them is the wrath of Allāh, and for them is a grievous chastisement" (16 : 106). Clearly the *murtadd* is here threatened with punishment in the next life, and there is not the least change in this attitude in later revelations, when Islamic government had been established immediately after the Prophet reached Madīnah. In one of the early Madīnah revelations, apostasy is spoken of in connection with the war which the unbelievers had waged to make the Muslims apostates by force: "And they will not cease fighting you until they turn you back from your religion, if they can. And whoever of you turns back from his religion (*yartadda* from *irtidād*), then he dies while an unbeliever — these it is whose works go for nothing in this world and the Hereafter, and they are the companions of the fire; therein they will abide"[15] (2 : 217). So if a man becomes

[15] In their zeal to find a death sentence for apostates in the Qur'ān, some Christian writers have not hesitated to give an entirely wrong translation of the word *fa-yamut (then he dies)* as meaning *then he is put to death. Fa-yamut* is the active voice and *yamūtu* means *he dies*. The use of this word shows clearly that apostates were *not* put to death. Some interpreters have drawn a wrong inference from the words "whose works go for nothing". These words do not mean that he is to be treated as an outlaw. By his "works" are meant the good deeds which he did when he was a Muslim, and these in fact go for nothing even in this life, when a man afterwards adopts unbelief and evil courses. Good works are only useful if they continue to lead a man on to better things, and develop in him the consciousness of a higher life. Elsewhere the deeds of a people are spoken of

apostate, he will be punished — not in this life, but in the Hereafter — on account of the evil deeds to which he has reverted, and his good works, done while he was yet a Muslim, become null because of the evil course of life which he has adopted.

The third chapter, revealed in the third year of Hijrah, speaks again and again of people who had resorted to unbelief after becoming Muslims, but always speaks of their punishment in the Hereafter: "How shall Allāh guide a people who disbelieved after their believing and after they had born witness that the Messenger was true" (3 : 85); "Their reward is that on them is the curse of Allāh" (3 : 86); "Except those who repent after that and amend" (3 : 88); "Those who disbelieve after their believing, then increase in disbelief, their repentance is not accepted" (3 : 89).

The most convincing argument that death was not the punishment for apostasy is contained in the Jewish plans, conceived while they were living under the Muslim rule in Madīnah: "And a party of the People of the Book say, Avow belief in that which has been revealed to those who believe, in the first part of the day, and disbelieve in the latter part of it" (3 : 71). How could people living under a Muslim government conceive of such a plan to throw discredit on Islām, if apostasy was punishable with death? The fifth chapter *Mā'idah*, is one of those revealed towards the close of the Prophet's life, and even in this chapter no worldly punishment is mentioned for the apostates: "O you who believe! Should one of you turn back from his religion, then Allāh will bring a people whom He loves and who love Him" (5 : 54). Therefore so far as the Qur'ān is concerned, there is not only no mention of a death-sentence for apostates but such a sentence is negatived by the verses speaking of apostasy, as well as by that *magna charta* of religious freedom, the 256th verse of the second chapter, *la ikrāha fi-l-dīn,* "There is no compulsion in religion."

as going for nothing, when they work solely for this life and neglect the higher: "They whose labour is lost in this world's life and they think that they are well-versed in skill of the work of their hands. These are they who disbelieve in the communications of their Lord and His meeting, so their deeds become null, and therefore We will not set up a balance for them on the Day of Resurrection" (18 : 104, 105). In this case *ḥabṭ* of the works of this life means their being useless so far as the higher life is concerned.

Ḥadīth on apostasy

Let us now turn to Tradition, for it is on this authority that the *Fiqh* books have based their death-sentence for apostates. The words in certain traditions have undoubtedly the reflex of a later age, but still a careful study leads to the conclusion that apostasy was not punishable unless combined with other circumstances which called for punishment of offenders. Bukhārī, who is undoubtedly the most careful of all collectors of traditions is explicit on the point. He has two "books" dealing with the apostates, one of which is called *Kitāb al-muḥāribīn min ahl al-kufr wa-l-ridda,* or "the Book of those who fight (against the Muslims) from among the unbelivers and the apostates," and the other is called *Kitāb istitābat al-mu'ānidīn wa-l-murtaddīn wa qitāli-him,* or "the Book of calling to repentance of the enemies and the apostates and fighting with them." Both these headings speak for themselves. The heading of the first book clearly shows that only such apostates are dealt with in it as fight against the Muslims, and that of the second associates the apostates with the enemies of Islām. That is really the crux of the whole question, and it is due to a misunderstanding on this point that a doctrine was formulated which is quite contrary to the plain teachings of the Qur'ān. At a time when war was in progress between the Muslims and the unbelievers, it often happened that a person who apostatized went over to the enemy and joined hands with him in fighting against the Muslims. He was treated as an enemey, not because he had changed his religion but because he had changed sides. Even then there were tribes that were not at war with the Muslims and, if an apostate went over to them, he was not touched. Such people are expressly spoken of in the Qur'ān: "Except those who join a people between whom and you there is an alliance, or who come to you, their hearts shrinking from fighting you, or fighting their own people; and if Allāh had pleased He would have given them power over you so that they would have fought you; so if they withdraw from you and fight not you and offer you peace, then Allāh has not given you a way against them" (4 : 90).

The only case of the punishment of apostates, mentioned in trustworthy traditions, is that of a party of the tribe of 'Ukul, who accepted Islām and came to Madīnah. They found that the climate of the town did not agree with them, and the Prophet sent them to a place outside Madīnah where the state milch-camels were kept, so that they might live in the open air and drink of milk. They got well and then killed the keeper of the camels and drove away the animals. This being brought to the knowledge of the Prophet, a party was sent in pursuit of them and they were put to death[16] (Bu. 56 : 152). The report is clear on the point that they were put to death, not because of their apostasy but because they had killed the keeper of the camels.

Much stress is laid on a tradition which says: "Whoever changes his religion, kill him" (Bu. 89 : 2). But in view of what the *Bukhārī* itself has indicated by describing apostates as fighters or by associating their name with the name of the enemies of Islām, it is clear that this refers only to those apostates who join hands with the enemies of Islām and fight with the Muslims. It is only by placing this limitation on the meaning of the tradition that it can be reconciled with other traditions or with the principles laid down in the Qur'ān. In fact, its words are so comprehensive that they include every change of faith, from one religion to any other whatsoever; thus even a non-Muslim who becomes a Muslim, or a Jew becomes a Christian, must be killed. Evidently, such a statement cannot be ascribed to the Prophet. So the tradition cannot be accepted, without placing a limitation upon its meaning.

Another tradition relating to the same subject throws further light on the significance of that quoted above. In this it is stated that the life of a Muslim may only be taken in three cases, one of which is that "he forsakes his religion and separates himself (*al-tārik*) from his community (*li-l-jama'ah*) (Bu. 88 : 6). According to another version, the words are "who forsakes (*al-mufāriq*) his community". Evidently separation from the community or the forsaking of it, which is here added as a necessary condition, means that the man leaves the Muslims and joins the enemy camp. Thus the words of the tradition show that it relates to wartime;

[16] It is stated in some traditions that they were tortured to death. If it ever happened, it was only by way of retaliation, as before the revelation of the penal laws of Islām, retaliation was the prevailing rule. In some reports it is stated that this party of the tribe of 'Ukul put out the eyes of the keeper of the camels and threw him on hot stones to die a slow death of torture, and that they were put to death in a similar manner (Ai. VII, p. 58). But others have denied that the law of retaliation was applied in this case. According to these reports, the Prophet had intended to put them to death by torture in the same way as they had put to death the keeper of the camels, but before they were executed he received the revelation dealing with the punishment of such offenders: "The only punishment of those who wage war against Allāh and His Messenger and strive to make mischief in the land is this, that they should be killed or crucified or their hands and their feet should be cut off on opposite sides or they should be imprisoned" (5 : 33) (IJ-C. VI, p. 121). The apostates are thus spoken of here as waging war against God and His Messenger. The punsihment varies according to the nature of the crime; it may be death or even crucifixion where the culprit has caused terror in the land or it may be simply imprisonment.

and the apostate forfeited his life not for changing his religion, but for desertion.

An instance of a simple change of religion is also contained in the *Bukhārī*. "An Arab of the desert came to the Prophet and accepted Islām at his hand; then fever overtook him while he was still in Madīnah; so he came to the Prophet and said, Give back my pledge; and the Prophet refused; then he came again and said, Give me back my pledge; and the Prophet refused; then he came again and said, Give me back my pledge; and the Prophet refused; then he went away" (Bu. 94 : 47). This tradition shows that the man first accepted Islām, and the next day on getting fever he thought that it was due to his becoming a Muslim, and so he came and threw back the pledge. This was a clear case of apostasy, yet it is nowhere related that anyone killed him. On the other hand, the tradition says that he went away unharmed.

Another example of a simple change of religion is that of a Christian who became a Muslim and then apostatized and went over to Christianity, and yet he was not put to death: "Anas says, there was a Christian who became a Muslim and read the *Baqarah* and the *Āl 'Imrān* (2nd and 3rd chapters of the Qur'ān), and he used to write (the Qur'ān) for the Prophet. He then went over to Christianity again, and he used to say, Muḥammad does not know anything except what I wrote for him. Then Allāh caused him to die and they buried him" (Bu. 61 : 25). The tradition goes on to say how his body was thrown out by the earth. This was evidently at Madīnah after the revelation of the second and third chapters of the Qur'ān, when a Muslim state was well-established, and yet the man who apostatized was not even molested, though he spoke of the Prophet in extremely derogatory terms and gave him out to be an imposter who knew nothing except what he (the apostate) wrote for him.

It has already been shown that the Qur'ān speaks of apostates joining a tribe on friendly terms with the Muslims, and of others who withdrew from fighting altogether, siding neither with the Muslims nor with their enemies, and it states that they were left alone (4 : 90). All these cases show that the tradition relating to the killing of those who change their religion applied only to those who fought against the Muslims.

Apostasy and **Fiqh**

Turning to *Fiqh*, we find that the jurists first lay down a principle quite opposed to the Qur'ān, namely that the life of a man may be taken on account of his apostasy. Thus in the *Hidāyah*: "The *murtadd* (apostate) shall have Islām presented to him whether he is a free man or a slave; if he refuses, he must be killed" (H.I, p. 576). But this principle is contradicted immediately afterwards when the apostate is called "an unbeliever at war (*kāfir-un ḥarabiyy-un*) whom the invitation of Islām has already reached" (H.I, p. 577). This shows that even in *Fiqh*, the apostate forfeits his life because he is considered to be an enemy at war with the Muslims. And in the case of the apostate woman, the rule is laid down that she shall not be put to death, and the following argument is given: "Our reason for this is that the Holy Prophet forbade the killing of women, and because originally rewards (for belief or unbelief) are deferred to the latter abode, and their hastening (in this life) brings disorder, and a departure from this (principle) is allowed only on account of an immediate mischief and that is *ḥirāb* (war), and this cannot be expected from women on account of the unfitness of their constitution" (H. I, p. 577). And the annotator adds: "The killing for apostasy is obligatory in order to prevent the mischief of war, and it is not a punishment for the act of unbelief" (*ibid.*). And again: "For mere unbelief does not legalize the killing of a man" (*ibid.*). It will be seen that, as in the case of war against unbelievers, the legists are labouring under a misconception, and a struggle is clearly seen going on between the principles as established in the Qur'ān and the misconceptions which had somehow or other found their way into the minds of the legists. It is clearly laid down that the apostate is killed, not on account of his unbelief but on account of *ḥirāb* or of his being in a state of war, and the argument is plainly given that killing for unbelief is against the accepted principles of Islām. But the misconception is that the mere ability to fight is taken as a war condition, which is quite illogical. If it is meant that the apostate possesses the potentiality to fight, then potentially even a child may be called a *ḥarabiyy* (one at war), because he will grow up to be a man and have the ability to fight; even woman apostates cannot be excepted because they also possess the potentiality to fight. The law of punishment is based not on potentialities but on facts. Thus, even the *Fiqh* recognizes the principle that the life of a man cannot be taken for mere change of religion and that, unless the apostate is in a state of war, he cannot be killed. It is quite a different matter that the legists should have made a mistake in defining *ḥirāḅ* or a state of war.

CHAPTER VI

MARRIAGE

SEC. 1 — SIGNIFICANCE OF MARRIAGE

'Ibādāt *and* mu'āmalāt

In the foregoing five chapters we have dealt with laws relating to the self-development of the community as a whole, or, as they are generally called, the laws governing the relations of man to God — the religious duties of man in a stricter sense. In the terminology of *Fiqh*, these are classed as *'ibādāt.*[1] They undoubtedly relate not only to the spiritual growth of man but also to the growth of the community, or rather humanity, as a whole. But the scope of the religion of Islām is, as already stated, very wide and covers the whole field of the relations of man to man, as well as that of man to God. The object of the laws relating to this part of human life is to teach man his duties and obligations to others, and to show him how to lead a happy life in this world in his relations with others. Technically, these are called *mu'āmalāt* or *transactions*,[2] and include the laws relating to home life, civic life and the political life of man. In the *Fiqh* terminology, the *mu'āmalāt* are either contracts and agreements, to which the mutual consent of the contracting parties is required, or matters depending on the will of a single person, or general laws and regulations.

Ḥudūd *or restrictions*

In all these matters the Islamic law imposes certain restrictions, for the benefit of society, upon the free acts of men as members of that society. The Arabic word for these restrictions is *ḥudūd.*[3] In the Qur'ān, the expression *ḥudūd Allāh* (limits of God) is used in connection with the

[1] Pl. of *'ibādat* meaning *the service of God*.

[2] Pl. of *mu'āmalah*, from *'aml* meaning *work*.

[3] Pl. of *ḥadd*, which means *prevention, restraint, prohibition* and the like, and hence *a restrictive ordinance*, or *statute, of God respecting things lawful and things unlawful* (LL.).

Divine ordinances on various subjects, such as matters relating to marriage and divorce and good treatment of women[4], fasting[5] and laws of inheritance[6], and also in a general sense relating to all kinds of restrictive ordinances[7], but never with regard to punishments inflicted for the infringement of certain laws, that being the sense in which this word has been used in the Tradition (*Ḥadīth*) and jurisprudence (*Fiqh*).

Everything is lawful unless prohibited

The basic principle in the matter of all restrictive ordinances is that a thing which is not disallowed is deemed to be lawful, as the well-known juridical dictum has it: *Al-ibāḥa aṣl-un fi-l-ashyā'*[8] *i.e.*, "Lawfulness is a recognized principle in all things." In other words, everything (in which is included every free act of man) is presumed to be lawful, unless it is definitely prohibited by law. This dictum is in fact based on the plain words of the Qur'ān: "He it is Who created for you all that is in the earth" (2 : 29). There are some jurists who have held the contrary view that everything is unlawful unless the law declares it to be lawful, but this view is, on the face of it, absurd and impossible; moreoever it is against the clear principle laid down in the Qur'ān, that everything has been created for the benefit of man, which leads to the only possible presumption that everything can be made use of by him, unless a limitation is placed, by law, on that use.

Importance of the marriage institution

The most important of the restrictive regulations of Islām are those relating to marriage, which institution is, in fact, the basic principle of human civilization. The Arabic word for marriage is *nikāḥ* which originally means *'aqd* or *uniting*. Marriage in Islām is a sacred contract which every Muslim must enter into, unless there are special reasons why

[4] 2 : 229, 230; 58 : 4; 65 : 1.

[5] 2 : 187.

[6] 4 : 13, 14.

[7] 9 : 97, 112.

[8] NA. p. 197.

he should not. Thus in the Qur'ān it is said: "And marry those among you who are single and those who are fit among your male slaves and your female slaves; if they are needy, Allāh will make them free from want out of His grace;[9] and Allāh is Ample-giving, Knowing. And let those who do not find a match keep chaste until Allāh makes them free from want out of His grace" (24: 32, 33). In another verse, marriage relationship is given the same importance as blood-relationship: "And He it is Who has created man from water, then He has made for him blood-relationship and marriage-relationship" (25: 54). Tradition also lays stress upon living in a married state. The Prophet is reported to have said to certain people who talked of fasting in the day-time and keeping awake during the night, praying to God and keeping away from marriage: "I keep a fast and I break it, and I pray and I sleep, and I am married, so whoever inclines to any other way than my Sunnah, he is not of me." (Bu. 67 : 1). Another saying of the Prophet laying stress upon marriage is worded thus: "O assembly of young people! Whoever of you has the means to support a wife *(al-bā'ah)*, he should get married, for this *(i.e.*, marriage) is the best means of keeping the looks cast down and guarding the chastity; and he who has not the means, let him keep fast, for this will act as castration"(Bu. 67 : 2). Celibacy *(tabattul)* was expressly forbidden by the Prophet (Bu. 67 :8). According to one tradition, "the man who marries perfects half his religion" (MM.13 : I-iii). Another says: "Matrimonial alliances increase friendship more than anything else" *(ibid.)*.

Marriage as the union of two natures which are one in their essence

The Qur'ān repeatedly speaks of the two mates, man and woman, as being created from each other: "O people, keep your duty to your Lord, Who created you from a single being and created its mate of the same (kind) and spread from these two many men and women"(4 : 1); "He it is Who created you from a single soul and of the same did He make his mate that he might find comfort in her"(7 : 189). Both these verses are generally understood as referring to the creation of the first man and

[9] Merely being poor is not sufficient excuse for not marrying because the needy are told that if they marry, Allāh will make them free from want out of His grace. The Prophet is reported to have performed the marriage of a man who did not possess so much as a ring of iron (Bu. 67 : 16).

the first woman,[10] but that they signify the relation of man to woman in general is obvious from other verses: ''And Allāh has made wives for you from among yourselves (*min unfusi-kum*), and has given you sons and daughters from your wives'' (16 : 72); ''And of His signs is this, that He created mates for you from yourselves (*min unfusi-kum*), that you may find quiet of mind in them'' (30 : 21). And thus, in a Makkah revelation of the middle period: ''The Originator of the heavens and the earth; He has made for you pairs from among yourselves ... multiplying you thereby'' (42 : 11). Thus marriage is, according to the Qur'ān, the union of two souls which are one in their essence.

Multiplication of the human race through marriage

It will be noted that, in the above verses, the multiplication of the human race is mentioned as one of the objects of marriage. But it may be said that the multiplication of the race can be brought about without marriage, as with the lower animals; that is to say, without uniting one man with one woman for their whole life. This would be only true if man lived upon earth like other animals, if there was nothing to distinguish him from the brute creation, if there were no such thing as civilization, no society, no sense of respect for one's own obligations and the rights of others, no sense of property and ownership. Deprived of its civilization there would be no human race at all, but a race of brutes in human form. The family, which is the real unit of the human race and the first cohesive force which makes civilization possible, owes its existence solely to marriage. If there is no marriage, then there can be no family, no ties of kinship, no force uniting the different elements of humanity and consequently, no civilization. It is through the family that humanity is held together and civilization made possible.

[10] Nowhere in the Qur'ān or in any reliable tradition is there any mention of the woman being created from the rib of man or of Eve being created from the rib of Adam. The allegation made is that God created all men from a single being (*nafs-in wāḥidat-in*) and created the *zauj* (mate) of that being from the same. The word *wāḥidah* as well as the personal pronoun *hā,* used twice, are all in the feminine gender, and three renderings are possible; the male being created from the female, or the female being created from the male, or both being created from the same essence.

Feelings of love and service developed through marriage

The institution of marriage is also responsible to a very great extent for the development of those feelings of love and service which are the pride of humanity to-day. The mutual love of husband and wife — a love based not on momentary passion but lifelong connection — and the consequent parental love for offspring leads to a very high development of the feeling of love of man for man as such, and thus to the disinterested service of humanity. This love is described as a sign of God in the Qur'ān: "And of His signs is this, that He created mates for you from yourselves that you may find quiet of mind in them, and He put between you love and compassion" (30 : 21). The natural inclination of the male to the female and of the female to the male finds expansion through marriage and is developed, first, into a love for the children, then a love for one's kith and kin, and ultimately into a disinterested love for the whole of humanity. The home, or the family, is in fact the first training ground of love and service. Here man finds real pleasure in the service of humanity, and the sense of service is thus gradually developed and broadened. It is in fact a training ground for every kind of morality, for it is in the home that a man learns to have a sense of his own obligation and responsibilities, to have a respect for others' rights and, above all, to have a real pleasure in suffering for the sake of others. The Prophet is reported to have said: "The best of you is he who treats his wife best" (IM. 9 : 50).

Marriage and "free love"

The Western world is undoubtedly leaning more and more to "free love" in the place of marriage, but "free love" will certianly prove the ruin of Western civilization. Marriage is being discarded, not on account of any inherent defect in it, but simply because it entails certain responsibilities on both parties to the marriage contract, and it is really these responsibilities that are shirked in avoiding marriage. Marriage undoubtedly strengthens the ties of the natural love of the two mates, but it also requires them to share each other's cares and sorrows; for human life has its cares and sorrows as well as its pleasures. "Free love" makes each of the mates selfish in the extreme because, while the male and the female become each other's partners in happiness, each is free to leave the other, uncared for, in his or her sorrow. Marriage again makes the two mates jointly responsible for the welfare of the children, but in "free love," either the procreation of children is altogether avoided, and thus the end which nature has in view in the union of the male and the female is defeated, or when either of the parents has had his or her satisfaction of the other, the children may be left without a shelter. The institution of marriage is found in all countries and all nations, has been practised in every age for thousands of years and has worked to the advancement and welfare of humanity on the whole. Free love, if practised on so large a scale for half a century, would either put an end to the human race altogether, or bring such chaos in society as would destroy its very foundations. It may suit a few irresponsible, selfish persons who are the slaves of their passions, but there can be no spark of true love in a union which may end abruptly at the whim of either, and it can serve no useful purpose for humanity in general.

SEC. 2 — LEGAL DISABILITIES

Mut'ah or *temporary marriage disallowed*

A marriage for a fixed period was recognized before Islām. It went under the name of *mut'ah*, meaning *profiting by* or enjoying a thing. Besides the temporary marriage, four kinds of union of man and woman were recognized by the pre-Islamic Arabs (Bu. 67 : 37). The first of these was the permanent marriage tie which, in a modified form, was recognized by Islām. The second was known as the *istibdzā'*.[11] The following explanation of this word is given in *Bukhārī* and other authorities: "A man would say to his wife, Send for such a one and have cohabitation with him; and the husband would remain aloof from her and would not touch her until her pregnancy was clear" (Bu. 67 : 37; N.). This is exactly the form which goes under the name of *niyoga* in the reformed Hindu sect, Ārya Samāj. The third form was that in which any number of men, less than ten, would gather together and have cohabitation with a woman, and when she became pregnant and gave birth to a child, she would call for all those men and would say that the child belonged to such a one from among them, and he was bound by her word to accept the

[11] From *bidz'* meaning *a portion* or *a large portion of wealth, sufficient to carry on a trade* (R.).

responsibility. Fourthly, there were prostitutes who were entered upon promiscuously and when one of them bore a child, a man known as *qā'if* (lit., *one who recognized*) was invited and his decision, based on similarity of features, was final as to who was the father of the child. The last three forms only legalized adultery in one form or another and Islām did not recognize any of them, nor was any such practice resorted to by any Muslim at any time.

Temporary marriage stood on a different basis, and reform in this matter was brought about gradually. Recently the idea has appealed to the Western mind which is seeking in temporary marriage, by way of experiment, a remedy for the rigidity of the Christian marriage laws. Islām, however, discarded the idea of temporariness in marriage, because it opens the way to loose relations of the sexes, and entails no responsibility of any kind on the father for the care and bringing up of the children, who, with the mother, might thus be left quite destitute. Occasions may arise for the dissolution of a permanent marriage, and will continue to arise as long as human nature is what it is, but the remedy for this is divorce and not temporary marriage. The moment the idea of temporariness is introduced into marriage, it loses its whole sanctity, and all responsibilities which are consequent on it are thrown off. According to the Qur'ān, the union of the two sexes is only lawful because of the acceptance of the responsibilities consequent thereupon, and the idea of a temporary marriage is not in accordance with it. A union of the sexes with the acceptance of the consequent responsibilities is called *iḥṣān* (marriage), and without such acceptance it is called *safāḥ*[12] (fornication), and the Qur'ān allows the first while it forbids the second (4 : 24).

There is some confusion in Tradition about the *mut'ah*. *Bukhārī* has the following as the heading of the chapter on *Mut'ah*: "The prohibition by the Holy Prophet of *mut'ah* finally." Under this heading he cites first a tradition which says that 'Alī (the reporter) said to Ibn 'Abbās that the Prophet prohibited *mut'ah* and the eating of the flesh of domestic asses at the time of the Khaibar (expedition) (Bu. 67 : 32). It is then related that Ibn'Abbās being asked if the permission to practise *mut'ah* related to the time of distress and when the number of women was very small,

[12] *Iḥṣān* is derived from *ḥaṣuna* meaning *it was* or *became inaccessible*, or *it was fortified* or *protected against attack*, and *safāḥ* is derived from *safḥ*, meaning *pouring out of water* or *shedding of blood* (LL.). The first word carries the idea of a permanent strengthening through marriage and the second that of satisfying a passion. It is clear that *mut'ah* or temporary marriage of any kind, falls within the second category. Ibn 'Umar is reported to have spoken of *mut'ah* or temporary marriage as *safāḥ* (AM.—AD. II, p. 186).

replied in the affirmative (*ibid.*) The third tradition is that of Salmah ibn Akwa' who says that they were in an expedition when a messenger of the Prophet came and said that they were permitted to contract temporary marriages, at the end of which Bukhārī adds "and 'Alī has made it clear, reporting from the Prophet, that this was abrogated" (*ibid.*). Abū Dāwūd has two traditions from Sabrah, the first stating that the Prophet prohibited *mut'ah* in the year of the Farwell Pilgrimage (10 A.H.), and the second simply that he prohibited *mut'ah* (AD. 12 : 13). There is no mention of *mut'ah* having ever been allowed. *Muslim* has several contradictory traditions. But even there it is admitted that though *mut'ah* was permitted on certain occasions, it was finally prohibited (M. 16 : 3).

A consideration of the various traditions shows that the orders against *mut'ah* were issued on several occasions: first on the occasion of the Khaibar expedition, according to 'Alī; secondly on the occasion of the 'umrah known as *al-Qadzā*; thirdly at the conquest of Makkah; fourthly in the Auṭās expedition; fifthly in the Tabūk expedition; sixthly in the Farewell Pilgrimage. The earliest occasion is thus the Khaibar expedition, which took place in the beginning of the seventh year of Hijrah. The 'umrah *al-Qadzā* also relates to the 7th year, the other occasions to the 8th, 9th and 10th years. If *mut'ah* was prohibited in the 7th year, as Bukhārī states on the authority of 'Alī, and this tradition is repeated four times,[13] and is also accpeted by Muslim and others, it could not have been permitted by the Prophet after this. But as the only occasions on which it is reported to have been permitted relate to the 8th year, it seems that there must have been some misconception. The explanation given by some authorities, that it may have been prohibited on the earliest occasion only as a temporary measure, and that the final and decisive prohibition may have come later, is not only repugnant to reason but goes against the whole course of the history of reform, as brought about by Islām. The evils that prevailed in Arabia were not touched until the Prophet received a Divine revelation, but when a reform was introduced after a Divine revelation, it was impossible that the Prophet himself should have allowed the evil again. It is very probable that the first or a later reporter laboured under a misconception; or, if the traditions which speak of temporary marriages having been contracted are accepted as true, the right explanation seems to be that the practice of *mut'ah* was a deep-rooted one, and

[13] Bu. 64 : 40; 67 : 32; 72 : 27; 90 : 4.

that repeated injunctions had to be given by the Prophet, or that all people were not at once apprised of the order of its prohibition.

At any rate the report that the Prophet had sent a message to inform people of the legality of temporary marriages in the battle of Auṭās, in the 8th year of Hijrah, clearly seems to have been due to a misconception. It may be that someone who had not, up to that time, been informed of the illegality of a temporary marriage, told his companions that it was allowed, but the Prophet could not have said so after having declared its prohibition at Khaibar. Notwithstanding its clear prohibition in the time of the Prophet, it is stated that some men remained under a misconception even up to the time of 'Umar, who had again to make a public declaration that temporary marriage was not allowed in Islām (M. 16 : 3). It may be further added that even those who legalized it, considered its legality to be dependent on *idztirār* (compulsion), and as on the same level as the permission to use prohibited food when driven by necessity (Bu. 67 : 32; M. 16 : 3).[14] But even this position is unacceptable, as being quite opposed to the Qur'ān and to the clear injunctions of the Prophet prohibiting it. All the Muslim sects agree in holding temporary marriage to be unlawful, with the exception of Akhbārī Shī'ahs, but even according to them it is not a very honourable transaction.[15]

Prohibitions to marry

The Qur'ān forbids certain marriage relations: "Forbidden to you are your mothers, and your daughters, and your sisters, and your paternal aunts, and your maternal aunts, and brother's daughters and sister's daughters, and your mothers that have suckled you, and your foster-sisters, and mothers of your wives, and your step-daughters who are in your guardianship, born of your wives to whom you have gone in — but if you have not gone in to them, there is no blame on you — and the wives of your sons who are of your own loins, and that you should have two sisters together, except what has already passed" (4 : 23).

[14] The words in *Muslim* are: *Kānat rukhuṣat-an fī awwali-l-Islāmi liman-idzturra ilai-hi ka-l-maitati wa-l-dami wa laḥmi-l-khinzīr;* and in *Bukhārī: Innamā dhālika fi-l-ḥāli-l-shadīd.*

[15] Thus Sayyid Amīr 'Alī writes in his *Muhammadan Law:* "It is declared to be abominable, though not actually prohibited, to marry in the *mut'ah* form a virgin girl who has no father ... the reason being that, as such a marriage is to her prejudice, and she has had no paternal advice or guidance in the matter, she should not be subject to the degradation of a temporary union.

It will be seen that these prohibitions arise either from consanguinity, as in the cases of mother, daughter, sister, brother's daughter, sister's daughter, father's sister and mother's sister; or from fosterage, such as in the case of foster-mother and foster-sister; or from affinity, such as in the case of wife's mother, wife's daughter and son's wife. Jurists have enlarged the conception of certain relations, and the *Hidāyah* thus expands these prohibitions:

1. Mother includes all female ascendants both on the male, *i.e.* the father's, and the female *i.e.* the mother's side.
2. Daughter includes daughter of son or daughter, *i.e.* all female descendants how low soever.
3. Father's sister and mother's sister do not include the daughters of the paternal and maternal aunts but include grandfather's sister and grandmother's sister and so on.

The second class of prohibitions relates to fosterage, but while the Qur'ān mentions only the foster mother and the foster-sister, Tradition is clear on the point that all those relations that are prohibited in marriage on account of consanguinity are prohibited also on account of fosterage[16] (Bu. 67 : 21). Thus the foster-uncle of Ḥafṣah was declared to fall within the prohibitions of the Qur'ān, and a daughter of Ḥamzah who, though an uncle of the Prophet, was also his foster-brother, was regarded as forbidden for the Prophet (Bu. 67 : 21). Certain foster-relations may, however, be complete strangers, though they would not be so in the case of blood relations. For instance, the brother's mother is either the mother or step-mother of a man, and in both cases she is among the prohibited relations, but the foster-brother's mother may be quite a stranger and in that case is not prohibited.

As to what constitutes fosterage (*radẕā'ah* or giving suck), there is a very slight difference of opinion. A child is recognized as a suckling only up to the age of two years, in the Qur'ān (2 : 233), and there is no

[16] Sayyid Amīr 'Alī mentions the following exceptions to this rule as recognized by the Ahl Sunnah: *(i)* The marriage of the father of the child with the mother of his child's foster-mother; *(ii)* with her daughter; *(iii)* the marriage of the foster-mother with the brother of the child whom she has fostered; *(iv)* the marriage with foster-mother of an uncle or aunt. And he adds: "According to the *Durr al-Mukhtār* there are twenty-one exceptions to this rule. For example, the foster-mother of a child and her mother are lawful to the child's grandfather. Similarly a man may marry his brother's or sister's foster-mother; his son's foster-sister; paternal or maternal uncle's foster mother; son's paternal aunt by fosterage, etc. The husband of the foster-mother may marry the natural mother or sister of his wife's foster-child." The Shī'ahs recognize no exception.

difference on this point. Tradition lays down that foster-relationship is not established unless the child is suckled when hungry (Bu. 67 : 22). Imām Abū Ḥanīfah, however, considers the child's being given suck only once as sufficient to establish foster-relationship; Imām Shāfi'ī is of opinion that he must have been suckled four times, while the Shi'ahs consider it necessary that he should have been suckled at least for twenty-four hours.

The third class of prohibitions is that which arises from affinity, and here, too, the Jurists have expanded the conception of relationship in the same manner as in the case of consanguinity. Thus wife's mother includes wife's mother's mother, and so on; wife's daughter includes her daughter's daughter;[17] son's wife[18] includes son's son's wife. Step-mothers are expressly prohibited in the Qur'ān: "And marry not women whom your fathers married" (4 : 22). Jurists also lay down that a man's unlawful connection with a woman included her in the category of a wife so far as prohibitions arising from the wife's connection are concerned.

The last prohibition relates to the gathering together of two sisters as co-wives. Tradition expands this conception and prohibits the gathering together of a woman with her paternal aunt or her maternal aunt (Bu. 67 : 27, 28). *Fiqh* expands the conception further and includes the wife's brother's and sister's daughter in the same category. The rule is in fact laid down in the *Ḥidāyah* that it is prohibited to have as wives at one time two women so related to each other that, if one of them were a man, their marriage would be prohibited.

Marriage relations betwen Muslims and non-Muslims

The only other ground on which marriage is prohibited in the Qur'ān is *shirk* or associating gods with God: "And marry not the idolatresses (*al-mushrikāt*) until they believe, and certainly a believing maid is better than an idolatress even though she pleases you; nor give (believing women) in marriage to idolaters until they believe, and certainly a believing slave is better than an idolater even though he pleases you" (2 : 221). Along with this, it is necessary to read another verse which allows

[17] The wife's mother is prohibited unconditionally while the wife's daughter is prohibited only in case a man has gone in to his wife; see 4 : 23 quoted above.

[18] It is expressly laid down in the Qur'ān that the son whose wife is forbidden is one from one's own loins. The adopted son who is really not a son at all, is thus excluded.

marriage with women who profess one of the revealed religions: "This day all good things are made lawful for you. And the food of those who have been given the Book is lawful for you and your food is lawful for them. And so are the chaste from among the believing women and the chaste from among those who have been given the Book before you when you have given them their dowries, taking them in marriage, not fornicating nor taking them paramours in secret" (5 : 5). Thus it will be seen that while there is a clear prohibition to marry idolaters or idolatresses, there is an express permission to marry women who profess a revealed religion (*Ahl al-kitāb*). And, as the Qur'ān states that revelation was granted to all nations of the world,[19] and that it was only the Arab idolaters who had not been warned,[20] the conclusion is evident that it was only with Arab idolaters that marriage relations were prohibited, and that it was lawful for a Muslim to marry a woman belonging to any other nation of the world that follows a revealed religion. The Christians, the Jews, the Parsīs, the Buddhists and the Hindūs all fall within this category; and it would be seen that, though the Christian doctrine of calling Jesus Christ a God or son of God is denounced as *shirk*, still the Christians are treated as followers of a revealed religion and not as *mushrikīn*, and matrimonial relations with them are allowed. The case of all those people who have originally been given a revealed religion, though at present they may be guilty of *shirk*, would be treated in like manner, and Parsī and Hindū women may be taken in marriage, as also may those who follow the religion of Confucius or of Buddha or of Tao. *Fiqh*, however, recognizes only the legality of marriage with women belonging to the Jewish and Christian faith, and this is due to the narrow conception of the word *Ahl al-Kitāb* adopted by the jurists. It is strange, however, that while the Majūs or Parsīs are not accepted as *Ahl al-Kitāb*, the Sabians are expressly spoken of in the *Hidāyah* as being *Ahl al-Kitāb*. "And it is lawful to marry Sabian women (*Ṣābiyāt*) if they profess a religion and accept a revealed book, for they are among *Ahl al-Kitāb*." If the Sabians are *Ahl al-Kitāb* simply for the reason that they profess a religion and accept a revealed book, there is no reason why the Magians, the Hindūs and others who profess a religion and accept a revealed book, should not be treated as such.

It may be noted here that, while there is an express mention of a Muslim man marrying a non-Muslim woman who professes a revealed religion,

[19] 35 : 24; 42 : 3.

[20] 32 : 3; 36 : 6.

there is no mention of the legality or illegality of a marriage between a Muslim woman and a non-Muslim man.[21] The mere fact however that the Qur'ān speaks of the one and not of the other is sufficient to show that marriage between a Muslim woman and a non-Muslim man is not allowed.

A marriage which is otherwise legal may be illegal because it does not fulfil a requirement of the law. For instance, the divorced woman and the widow have both to observe a waiting period (*'iddah*), and marriage during this period is illegal. A woman who has been divorced thrice is not allowed to remarry her first husband. As the pregnant woman is required to observe *'iddah* till delivery (65 : 4), marriage during pregnancy is not allowed. But if a woman is pregnant by fornication, her marriage with either the fornicator or somebody else is allowed by Imām Abū Ḥanīfah and Imām Muḥammad, only in the latter case sexual intercourse is forbidden till delivery (H.I. p. 292). According to other Imāms, including Imām Abū Yūsuf, this is illegal. The Shī'ah law follows Imām Abū Ḥanīfah.

SEC. 3 — FORM AND VALIDITY OF MARRIAGE

Preliminaries of marriage

The very fact that marriage is looked upon as a contract in Islām, shows that before marriage both parties must satisfy themselves that each will have a desirable partner for life in the other. The Qur'ān lays down expressly: "Marry such women as seem good to you (*mā ṭāba la-kum*)" (4 : 3). The Prophet is reported to have given an injunction to this effect: "When one of you makes a proposal of marriage to a woman, then if he can, he should look at what attracts him to marry her" (AD. 12 : 18), the heading of this chapter being: "A man should look at the woman whom he intends to marry." *Bukhārī* also has a chapter, headed "To look at the woman before marriage" (Bu. 67 : 36). *Muslim* has a similar chapter:

[21] The Jewish law does not allow marriage with non-Jews in any case: "Neither shalt thou make marriages with them; thy daughter thou shalt not give unto his son, nor his daughter shalt thou take unto thy son" (Deut. 7 : 3). Paul follows the Jewish law: "Be ye not unequally yoked together with unbelievers: for what fellowship hath righteousness with unrighteousness? and what communion hath light with darkness? (II, cor. 6 : 14). The Hindu law is even stricter, and allows marriage of a member of one caste of Hindūs only within that caste.

"Inviting a man who intends to marry a woman to have a look at her face and hands" (M. 16 : 12). In this chapter is cited the case of a man who came to the Prophet and said that he was marrying a woman from among the Anṣār, and the Prophet said to him, Hast thou looked at her? On his replying in the negative, the Prophet said, Then go and look at her, for there is a defect in the eyes of (some) Anṣār. In another tradition, it is reported that when Mughīrā ibn Shu'ba made a proposal of marriage to a woman, the Prophet asked him if he had seen her and on his replying in the negative, he enjoined him to see her, because "it was likely to bring about greater love and concord between them" (MM.13 : 2-ii). The jurists are almost all agreed upon the *istīḥbāb* (approval) of looking at the woman whom one intends to marry. And since the contract is effected by the consent of two parties, the man and the woman, and one of them is expressly told to satisfy himself about the other by looking at her, it would seem that the woman has the same right to satisfy herself before giving her assent. The consent of both the man and the woman is an essential of marriage, and the Qur'ān lays down expressly that the two must agree: "Prevent them not from marrying their husbands when they agree among themselves in a lawful manner" (2 : 232). In this respect, however, much will depend upon the customs prevailing among a people. Aḥmad Shukrī, quoting an earlier authority ('Abd al-Qādir, *al-Nahr*, p. 218), says: "The time for seeing her should precede the betrothal ... The woman is recommended to have a look at the man, if she wants to marry him; because anything that would please her with him will please him with her ... (ASh., p. 43).

Proposal of Marriage

The word *khaṭaba* which means *he addressed* (another) also signifies *he made a proposal of marriage*. The infinitive noun *khuṭbah* means *an address and khiṭbah* means *proposal of marriage*. When a man, who wants to marry, has satisfied himself about a woman, he makes a proposal of marriage either to the woman in question or to her parents or guardians. When a man has made a proposal of marriage to a woman, others are forbidden to propose to the same woman, till the first suitor has given up the matter, or has been rejected (Bu. 67 : 46). A woman may also make a proposal of marriage to a man (Bu. 67 : 33), or a man may propose the marriage of his daughter or sister to a man (Bu. 67 : 34); generally, however, it is the man who makes the proposal. When assent has been given to the proposal of marriage, it becomes an engagement, and usually a certain time is allowed to pass before the marriage (*nikāḥ*) is performed. This period allows the parties to study each other further, so that if there be anything undesirable in the union, the engagement may be broken off by either party; it is only after the *nikāḥ* has been performed that the two parties are bound to each other.

Age of marriage

No particular age has been specified for marriage in the Islamic law; in fact, with the difference of climatic conditions, there would be a difference as to the marriageable age in different countries. But the Qur'ān does speak of an age of marriage which it identifies with the age of majority: "And test the orphans until they reach the age of marriage (*nikāḥ*). Then if you find in them maturity of intellect, make over to them their property, and consume it not extravagantly and hastily, against their growing up" (4 : 6). Thus it will be seen that the age of marriage and the age of maturity of intellect are identified with full age or the age of majority. And as marriage is a contract the assent to which depends on personal liking, as already shown on the basis of the Qur'ān and Tradition, and since this function cannot be performed by any one but the party who makes the contract, it is clear that the age of marriage is the age of majority, when a person is capable of exercising his choice in matters of sexual liking or disliking. A man or a woman who has not attained puberty is unable to exercise his or her choice in sexual matters and unable to decide whether he or she will like or dislike a certain woman or man as wife or husband.

It is true that Jurisprudence, following the general law of contracts, recognizes, in the case of a marriage contract, the legality of the consent of a guardian on behalf of his ward, but there is no case on record showing that the marriage of a minor through his or her guardian was allowed by the Prophet after details of the law were revealed to him at Madīnah. His own marriage with 'Ā'ishah which took place when she was nine years of age, is sometimes looked upon as sanctioning the marriage of a minor through his guardian, but there are two points worth consideration in this matter. In the first place, 'Ā'ishah's *nikāḥ* at nine was tantamount only to an engagement, because the consummation of marriage was postponed for five years, to allow her, no doubt, to attain majority.[22] In the second place, 'Ā'i<u>sh</u>ah's *nikāḥ* was performed in Makkah long before the details of the Islamic law were revealed to the Prophet, and therefore her marriage at nine can be no argument for the marriage of a minor. There is no reliable tradition showing that marriages were contracted by minors through their guardians in the time of the Prophet, af-ter the revelation of the fourth chapter which identifies the age of marriage with the age of majority. In the chapter headed "The giving in marriage by a man of his minor children" (Bu. 67 :39), two arguments are brought forward, first, the report relating to 'Ā'i<u>sh</u>ah's marriage which has just been dealt with; and, secondly, a verse of the Qur'ān (65 : 4), whereon light is thrown in the next paragraph. Similar chapters in other books[23] mention simply the case of 'Ā'i<u>sh</u>ah.

Support is sometimes sought for the marriage of minors from the verse which speaks of women not having their course as being divorced: "And those of your women who despair of menstruation, if you have a doubt, the prescribed time shall be three months, and of those too who have not had their courses" (65 : 4). But it is wrong to identify women who have not had their courses with minors, for there may be cases in which a woman reaches the age of majority though she has not had her courses and it is with such exceptional case that this verse deals. At any rate, there is no mention anywhere in the Qur'ān or Tradition of minors being married or divorced. In Jurisprudence, however, the legality of the marriage of a minor when contracted by a lawful guardian is recognized. This subject is further discussed under the heading "Guardianship in marriage."

Essentials in the contract

Marriage is called a covenant (*mīthāq*) in the Qur'ān, a covenant between the husband and the wife: "And how can you take it (*i.e.*, the dowry) when one of you has already gone in to the other and they have taken from you a strong covenant (*mīthāq-an <u>gh</u>alīzan*)" (4 : 21). The marriage contract is entered into by mutual consent expressed by the two parties, the husband and the wife, in the presence of witnesses, and that is the only essential. This mutual consent is technically called *affirmation*

---

[22] I have discussed the question of the age of 'Ā'i<u>sh</u>ah fully, in my *Early Caliphate*.

[23] M. 16 : 10; AD. 12 : 33.

or *declaration* (*ījāb*) and *acceptance* or *consent* (*qabūl*) in Jurisprudence. The marriage is made complete by the expression of mutual consent in the presence of witnesses[24], but it was the practice of the Prophet to deliver a sermon (*khuṭbah*), before the declaration of marriage was made, to give it the character of a sacred contract. A dowry (*mahr*) must also be settled on the woman, according to the Qur'ān, but the marriage is valid even if *mahr* is not mentioned, or even if the amount of *mahr* is not agreed upon. The expression of the consent is in the preterite form according to the *Hidāyah*; for instance, the parties would say, *qabiltu* (I have accepted) or *zawwajtu* (I have taken as my mate or partner), but no particular form or particular words are essential; any expression which conveys the intention of the parties in clear words is sufficient. It is not necessary that the proposal should come from one side and the acceptance from the other, or that the one should precede the other. The words of mutual consent may be addressed to each other by the two parties, but generally it is the man who delivers the sermon (khaṭīb) who puts the proposal before each party, the latter giving consent to the proposal.

Mahr *or the nuptial gift*

The second most important thing in marriage is *mahr* or dowry. The word generally used for dowry in the Qur'ān is *ajr* (pl. *ujūr*), meaning *reward* and *a gift that is given to the bride* (LL.).[25] The word *ṣaduqāt* (pl. of *ṣaduqāh*)[26] is also once used in the Qur'ān to signify the nuptial gift (4 : 4). Another word sometimes used in the Qur'ān to indicate the nuptial gift is *farīdzah,* literally *what has been made obligatory* or *an appointed portion*. The word *mahr* is used in Tradition to signify dowry, or the nuptial gift. According to the Qur'ān, the *mahr* is given as a free gift by the husband to the wife at the time of contracting the marriage: "And give women their dowries as a free gift" (4 : 4). The payment of

[24] Sayyid Amīr 'Alī says in his *Muhammadan Law* that according to the Shī'ahs, the marriage is valid without the presence of witnesses, but this doctrine cannot hold in the presence of what is clearly stated to be the practice of the Prophet. Moreover, when there is a clear direction in the Qur'ān as to the necessity of witnesses at the time of divorce, it stands to reason that the presence of witnesses at marriage should be equally necessary.

[25] In fact, *ajr is that in which there is gain but no loss* (R.).

[26] Other words from the same root signifying dowry are *ṣudāq* and *ṣidāq*. The root word *ṣadaqa* (verb) means *he was truthful,* and an obligatory deed is called a *ṣadaqa* (noun) when the doer of it aims thereby at truthfulness (R.).

the *mahr* on the part of the husband is an admission of the independence of the wife, for she becomes the owner of property immediately on her marriage, though before it she may not have owned anything. The settling of a dowry on the woman at the marriage is obligatory; "And lawful for you are all women besides those, provided that you seek them with your property, taking them in marriage, not committing fornication. Then as to those whom you profit by (by marrying), give them their dowries as appointed" (4 : 24). The payment of dowry is also necessary in the case of marriage with a slave-girl: "So marry them with the permission of their masters and give them their dowries justly" (4 : 25); and also in the case of a Muslim marrying a non-Muslim woman: "And the chaste from among the believing women and the chaste from among those who have been given the Book before you, when you have given them their dowries, taking them in marriage" (5 : 5).

It would appear from this that the Qur'ān renders the payment of dowry necessary at the time of marriage. Tradition leads to the same conclusion. The payment of the dowry was necessary even though it might be a very small sum (Bu. 67 : 51,52; AD. 12 : 29, 30, 31). In exceptional cases, marriage is legal even though the amount of *mahr* has not been specified, but it is obligatory and must be paid afterwards. Thus the Qur'ān says, speaking of divorce: "There is no blame on you if you divorce women when you have not touched them, or appointed for them a dowry" (2 : 236). This shows that marriage is valid without specifying a dowry. Tradition also speaks of the validity of a marriage, even though dowry has not been named (AD. 12 : 31). But the dowry must be paid, either at the time of the consummation of marriage or afterwards. The amount of dowry in this case would depend upon the circumstances of the husband and the position of the wife. The Qur'ān makes this clear by requiring the provision for wife to depend upon the circumstances of the husband, "the wealthy according to his means and the strained according to his means" (2 : 236). In a tradition it is related that the case of a woman, whose husband had died before fixing a dowry and consummating marriage, was referred to 'Abd Allāh ibn Mas'ūd, who decided that she should be paid a dowry according to the dowry of the women of like status with herself, and his decision was afterwards found to be in accordance with the decision of the Prophet in a similar case (AD. 12 : 31). In Jurisprudence, it is called customary dower (*mahr mithl*, lit., *the mahr of those like her* or *her equals*). It is determined by the *mahr* of her sisters and paternal aunts and uncles' daughters (H.I, p. 304); that is to say, with reference to the social position of her father's family. Therefore even if the dowry has not been specified at the marriage, it is to be determined and paid afterwards, and if unpaid in the husband's lifetime, it is a charge on his property after his death. The plain words of the Qur'ān require its payment at marriage, barring exceptional cases when it may be determined or paid afterwards. Imām Mālik follows this rule and renders payment necessary at marriage, while the Ḥanafī law treats it more or less as a debt.

No limits have been placed on the amount of *mahr*. The words used in the Qur'ān show that any amount of dowry may be settled on the wife: "And you have given one of them a heap of gold" (4 : 20). Thus no maximum or minimum amount has been laid down. The Prophet paid varying amounts, to his wives; in one case when the Negus paid the amount to Umm Ḥabībah (Abū Sufyān's daughter), who was then in Abyssinia, where the marriage took place, it was four thousand dirhams, while in the case of the other wives it was generally five hundred dirhams.(AD.12 : 28). The *mahr* of his daughter Fāṭimah was four hundred dirhams. The lowest amount mentioned in Tradition is a ring of iron (Bu. 67 : 52), and a man who could not procure even that was told to teach the Qur'ān to his wife (Bu. 67 : 51). In some traditions two handfuls of meal or dates are also mentioned (AD.12 : 29). The amount of the dowry may, however, be increased or decreased by the mutual consent of husband and wife, at any time after marriage; and this is plainly laid down in the Qur'ān: "Then as to those whom you profit by (by marrying), give them their dowries as appointed. And there is no blame on you about what you mutually agree after what is appointed of dowry" (4 : 24).

Generally, however, *mahr* is treated simply as a check upon the husband's power of divorce, and very high and extravagant sums are sometimes specified as *mahr*. This practice is foreign to the spirit of the institution, as laid down by Islām; for, *mahr* is an amount which should be handed over to the wife at marriage or as early afterwards as possible; and if this rule were kept in view, extravagant *mahr* would disappear of itself. The later jurists divide *mahr* into two equal portions, one of which they call prompt (*mu'ajjal*, lit., *that which is hastened*) and the other deferred (*mu'ajjal*). The payment of the first part must be made immediately on the wife's demand, while the other half becomes due on the death of either party, or on the dissolution of marriage.

Shighār

Among the pre-Islamic Arabs, *shighār* was a recognized form of marriage, a marriage by exchange, in which one man would give his daughter or sister or other ward in exchange for taking in marriage the other man's daughter or sister or ward, neither paying the dowry. Such a marriage was expressly forbidden by the Prophet because it deprived the woman of her right of dowry (Bu. 67 : 29); which shows that the woman's right of dowry is a right of which the wife cannot be deprived under any circumstances, and that it is her property and not the property of her guardians.

Publicity of the marriage

When the Qur'ān speaks of marriage, it at the same time excludes clandestine sexual relations, " taking them in marriage, not fornicating, nor taking them for paramours in secret (4 : 24, 25; 5 : 5). Thus the one fact distinguishing marriage from fornication and clandestine relations is its publicity. The mutual consent of two parties to live as husband and wife does not constitute a marriage unless that consent is expressed publicly and in the presence of witnesses. An essential feature of the Islamic marriage is therefore the publication of the news by gathering together, preferably in a public place. There are traditions showing that marriage must be made publicly known, even with the beat of drums (Tr. 11 : 5; Ns. 26 : 72; IM. 9 : 20; Ah, IV, pp. 5, 77). With the same object in view music is allowed at marriage gatherings. On such an occasion, girls sang with the beating of drum (*dzarb al-duff*)[27] in the presence of the Prophet (Bu. 67 : 49). The following tradition on this subject may be quoted: "Make public this marriage and perform it in the mosques and beat drums for it." "The difference between the lawful and the unlawful (*i.e.* marriage and fornication) is proclamation and the beating of drums." " 'Ā'ishah had with her a girl from among the Anṣār whom she got married. The Prophet came and said, Have you sent the young girl to her husband? And on receiving a reply in the affirmative, he said, Have you sent with her those who would sing? 'Ā'ishah said, No. Said the Prophet, The Anṣār are a people who love singing, and it would have

[27] *Duff* or *daff*, the former more approved, and the latter now more common, is *tambourine* or *a certain thing which one beats* or *with which one plays* (LL.).

been better if you had sent with her someone to sing thus and thus'' (MM. 13 : 4—ii). The presence of witnesses, when so much stress is laid on proclamation, is a foregone conclusion.

Marriage sermon

The delivery of a sermon before the announcement of marriage is another factor which helps the publicity of the marriage, and, at the same time, serves the double purpose of giving it a sacred character and making it an occasion for the education of the community. When the friends and relatives of both parties have assembled, a sermon is delivered by someone from among the party, or by the Imām, before announcing the marriage itself. The text of this sermon, as reported from the Prophet by Ibn Mas‘ūd, consists of tashahhud, with which every sermon generally opens, and of three verses of the Qur’ān. Tashahhud, literally, means the act of bearing witness, and technically the bearing of witness to the Unity of God and the prophethood of Muḥammad, and the tashahhud of the marriage sermon consists of the following words:

الْحَمْدُ لِلّهِ نَحْمَدُهُ وَنَسْتَعِينُهُ
وَنَسْتَغْفِرُهُ وَنَعُوذُ بِاللّهِ مِنْ شُرُورِ
أَنْفُسِنَا وَمِنْ سَيِّئَاتِ أَعْمَالِنَا مَنْ
يَهْدِهِ اللّهُ فَلَا مُضِلَّ لَهُ وَمَنْ
يُضْلِلْ فَلَا هَادِيَ لَهُ وَأَشْهَدُ أَنْ
لَا إِلَهَ إِلَّا اللّهُ وَأَشْهَدُ أَنَّ
مُحَمَّدًا عَبْدُهُ وَرَسُولُهُ

Al-ḥamdu li-llāhi naḥ madu-hū wa nasta‘inu-hū wa nastaghfiru-hū wa na-‘ūdhu bi-llāhi min shurūri anfusi-nā wa min sayyi’āti a‘māli-nā, man yahdi-hi-llāhu fa-lā mudzilla la-hū wa man yudzlil fa-lā hādiya la-hū, wa ashhadu an lā ilā ha ill-Allāhu wa ashhadu anna Muḥammad-an ‘abdu-hū wa rasūlu-hū.

All praise is due to Allāh; we praise Him and we beseech Him for help and we ask for His protection and we seek refuge in Allāh from the mischiefs of our souls, and from the evil of our deeds; whomsoever Allāh guides there is none who can lead him astray and whom Allāh finds in error, there is none to guide him; and I bear witness that there is no god but Allāh and that Muḥammad is his servant and His Messenger.

After the tashahhud, the Prophet would take as his text the following three verses of the Qur’ān, viz., 3 : 101; 4 : 1; 33 : 70, 71 (MM. 13 : 4—ii). All three verses remind man of his responsibilities in general, and the middle one lays particular stress on the obligations towards women. I quote the three verses, as they form an essential part of the marriage sermon:

يَٰٓأَيُّهَا ٱلَّذِينَ ءَامَنُوا ٱتَّقُوا ٱللَّهَ حَقَّ تُقَاتِهِۦ وَلَا تَمُوتُنَّ إِلَّا وَأَنتُم مُّسْلِمُونَ ○	Yā ayyuha-lladhina āmanu-ttaqu-llāha ḥaqqa tuqāti-hī wa lā tamūtunna illā wa antum Muslimūn (3 : 101).	O ye who believe! Keep your duty to Allāh, as it ought to be kept, and die not unless you are Muslims.
يَٰٓأَيُّهَا ٱلنَّاسُ ٱتَّقُوا رَبَّكُمُ ٱلَّذِى خَلَقَكُم مِّن نَّفْسٍ وَٰحِدَةٍ وَخَلَقَ مِنْهَا زَوْجَهَا وَبَثَّ مِنْهُمَا رِجَالًا كَثِيرًا وَنِسَآءً وَٱتَّقُوا ٱللَّهَ ٱلَّذِى تَسَآءَلُونَ بِهِۦ وَٱلْأَرْحَامَ إِنَّ ٱللَّهَ كَانَ عَلَيْكُمْ رَقِيبًا ○	Yā-ayyuha-n-nāsu-ttaqū Rabba-kumu-lladhī khalaqa-kum min naf-sin wāḥidat-in wa khalaqa min-hā zauja-hā wa baththa min-humā rijāl-an kathīr-an wa nisā'a; wa-ttaqullāha-lladhī tasā'alūna bi-hī wa-l-arḥām; inn-Allāha kāna ‘alai-kum raq-ība (4 : 1).	O people! keep your duty to your Lord, Who created you from a single being and created its mate of the same (kind), and spread from these two many men and women. And keep your duty to Allāh, by Whom you demand one of another (your rights) and to the ties of relationship; surely Allāh watches over you.
يَٰٓأَيُّهَا ٱلَّذِينَ ءَامَنُوا ٱتَّقُوا ٱللَّهَ وَقُولُوا قَوْلًا سَدِيدًا ○ يُصْلِحْ لَكُمْ أَعْمَٰلَكُمْ وَيَغْفِرْ لَكُمْ ذُنُوبَكُمْ وَمَن يُطِعِ ٱللَّهَ وَرَسُولَهُۥ فَقَدْ فَازَ فَوْزًا عَظِيمًا ○	Yā-ayyuha-lladhīna āmanu-ttaqu-llāha wa qūlū qaul-an sadīd-an yuṣliḥ la-kum a‘māla kum wa yaghfir la-kum dhunūba-kum wa man yuṭi‘i-llāha wa rasūla-hū fa-qad fāza fauz-an ‘azīmā (33 : 70, 71).	O you who believe keep your duty to Allāh and speak straight words. He would put your deeds into a right state for you and forgive your sins; and whoever obeys Allāh and His Messenger he indeed achieves a mighty success.

The sermon of course must expatiate on these verses and explain to the audience the mutual rights and duties of husband and wife. At the conclusion of the sermon is made the announcement that such and such a man and such and such a woman have accepted each other as husband and wife, and the dowry is also announced at the time. The man and the woman are then asked if they accept this new relationship and on the reply being given in the affirmative, the marriage ceremony proper is concluded. The consent of the woman is generally obtained through her father or other guardian or relation. After the expression of consent by both parties, the whole audience raises its hands and prays for the blessings of God on the newly wedded couple. Generally some dates or sweets are distributed before the audience disperses. The words of prayer in one tradition are *bārak-Allāhu la-ka*, or may Allāh shower His blessings on thee (Bu. 67 : 57). In another, the words are, *bārak-Allāhu wa bāraka 'alai-ka wa jam'a baina-kumā fī khair-in* (Tr. 11 : 6) — which means, "May Allāh shower His blessings (on the union) and may He bless you and unite you two in goodness."

Evidence of marriage

That there should be witnesses of marriage is clear enough from what has already been stated. The Qur'ān requires witnesses even for ordinary contracts and business transactions (2 : 282), and marriage is a contract of the highest importance, a contract affecting the lives of two persons to an extent to which no other contract affects them. It further requires witnesses even in the case of the dissolution of marriage by divorce (65 : 2). The Ḥanafī law rightly lays special stress on this point, so that marriage is not valid if at least two witnesses are not there (H.I, p. 286). To procure the best testimony, and one free from doubt of all kinds, it is quite in accordance with the law of Islām that all marriages should be registered.

Walīmah *or marriage feast*

After *nikāḥ* is over, the bride is conducted to the husband's house, and this is followed by the marriage-feast called *walīmah*. This feast is another step in the publicity of the marriage, and hence the Prophet laid stress on it. It is related of 'Abd al-Raḥmān ibn 'Auf that the Prophet, on being told of his marriage, prayed for him and told him to arrange for a feast though there be only one goat to feed the guests (Bu. 34 : 1; 67 : 7, 57). On the occasion of his own marriage with Ṣafīyyah, when returning from Khaibar, he gave a feast in which every one was required to bring his food with him (Bu. 8 : 12). Of course this was on a journey, but at the same time it shows the great importance given to the marriage-feast. He also invited his friends to a *walīmah* feast on the occasion of his marriage with Zainab, which is said to have been the most sumptuous of all his *walīmah* feasts, and yet he slaughtered only one goat (M.

16 : 15). Bukhārī devoted several chapters to *walīmah* in particular, in addition to numerous stray references.[28]

Guardianship in marriage

The essence of marriage being then, according to Islām, the consent of two parties, after they have satisfied themselves about each other, to live together as husband and wife permanently and accepting their respective responsibilities and obligations in the married state, it follows from its very nature that the marrige contract requires the contracting parties to have attained puberty and the age of discretion. The Qur'ān has already been quoted on this point, and *fiqh* also recognizes this principle. Thus, according to the *Fatāwa 'Ālamgīrī*, "among the conditions which are requisite for the validity of a contract of marriage are understanding (*'aql*), puberty (*bulūghah*) and freedom (*ḥurriyyah*) in the contracting parties" (Ft.A.II, p.1). A distinction is, however, made between a minor who is possessed of understanding and one who is not so possessed, and while a marriage contracted by the latter is recognized as a mere nullity, one contracted by the former can have its invalidity removed by the consent of his guardian. As regards those who have attained majority, there is no difference of opinion in the case of the man, who can give his consent to marriage without the approval of a guardian, but some difference exists in the case of the woman, whether she can give such consent without the approval of her father or guardian. The Ḥanafī view of the law of Islām answers this question in the affirmative: "The marriage contract of a free woman who has reached the age of majority, and is possessed of understanding, is complete with her own consent, whether she is a virgin or has been married before, though it may not have been confirmed by her guardian" (H. I, p. 293). The Shī'ah view is exactly the same: "In the marriage of a discreet female (*rāshidah*, or one who is adult), no guardian is required" (AA.). Both Mālik and Shāfi'ī hold that the consent of the guardian is essential. Bukhārī inclines to the same view as that of Mālik and Shāfi'ī, the heading of one of his chapters being, "Who says that there is no marriage except with the consent of a guardian"

[28] I quote a few headings: "The *walīmah* is necessary" (Bu. 67 : 68); "The *walīmah* (is necessary) though there be only one goat to feed the guests" (Bu. 67 : 69); "He who entertains in *walīmah* with less than a goat" (Bu. 67 : 71); "It is necessary to accept an invitation to *walīmah*" (Bu. 67 : 72).

(Bu. 67 : 37); though he adds another, "The father or any other guardian cannot give in marriage a virgin or one who has been married before without her consent" (Bu. 67 : 42). At the same time, he extends the meaning of the word guardian, saying that "the king is a guardian" (Bu. 67 : 41), and cites under this heading the case of a woman who came to the Prophet and offered herself for marriage, and she was then and there married to a person who could not even settle any dowry on her on account of his poverty. It does not appear whether or not she had a natural guardian (father or other near relative). Some Quranic verses are quoted which however do not speak of a guardian in express words. Thus: "And when you divorce women and they end their term, prevent them not from marrying their husbands if they agree among themselves in a lawful manner" (2 : 232). From this it is probably concluded that the injunction against preventing women from marrying husbands who have divorced them presupposes a right of the guardian. This argument is, however, defective, as the guardians are here prohibited from exercising any such right, in the case at least of a *thayyibah* (a woman who has seen a husband). The other verse quoted is: "...Nor give believing women in marriage to idolaters until they believe" (2 : 221). The argument is that the verse is addressed to the guardian, who have therefore the right to give in marriage. But this is also doubtful as the verse may just as well be addressed to the Muslim community as a whole, as on so many other occasions.

Among the traditions cited by Bukhārī, the first is that in which 'Ā'ishah speaks of four kinds of marriage, and the first of these which was the only form sanctioned by Islām is stated to be that in which "one man makes a proposal to another regarding his ward or his daughter, then he settles a dowry on her and marries her." But that describes the general practice, and does not lead to the conclusion that a woman cannot marry without the consent of a guardian. The second tradition is also from 'Ā'ishah and in it she speaks of the guardian of an orphan girl marrying her himself. That however is only 'Ā'ishah's interpretation of a certain verse of the Qur'ān and there is no reference in it to any particular incident that might have occurred. The third speaks of 'Umar proposing his widowed daughter Ḥafṣah to Abū Bakr. This, too, does not establish that marriage is invalid without the consent of a guardian. It only shows that the father of a widow may exert himself to procure a match for his daughter. None of the other three traditions mentioned in this chapter has any bearing on this subject.

On the other hand, the Qur'ān, as well as Tradition, recognizes a woman's right to marry the man she pleases. Thus the verse quoted above says plainly: "Prevent them not from marrying in a lawful manner" (2 : 232). This is the case of a divorced woman. And of a widow the Qur'ān says: "Then if they themselves go away, there is no blame on you for what they do of lawful deeds concerning themselves " (2 : 240). This recognizes the widow's right to marry herself. These two verses clearly recognize the right of the *thayyibah* (the divorced woman or the widow) to give herself in marriage, and prohibit the guardian from interference when the woman herself is satisfied. This is quite in accordance with a tradition: "*Al-ayyim* (the widow and the divorced woman) has greater right to dispose of herself (in marriage) than her guardian" (AD. 12 : 25). The words of another tradition are: "The guardian has no business in the matter of a *thayyibah" (ibid)*.

In view of the verses and traditions quoted above, it seems clear that the widow and the divorced woman are allowed complete freedom in the choice of their husbands. Does the same rule apply to virgins? The Imām Abū Ḥanifah answers this question in the affirmative. His principle is that, since a woman who has attained the age of majority can dispose of her property without reference to a guardian, so she is also entitled to dispose of her person. But at the same time it cannot be denied that there is a natural bashfulness about the virgin, and, moreover, she has not the same experience of men and affairs as has a widow or a divorced woman, and it is therefore in the fitness of things that her choice of a husband should be subject to the check of a father or other guardian, who would also settle the terms, and guard her against being misled by unscrupulous people. But as the contract, after all depends on her consent and not on the consent of her guardian, which in fact is only needed to protect her, her will must ultimately prevail and the opinion of Imām Abū Ḥanīfah is more in accordance with the essentials of marriage as expressed by the Qur'ān. He says: "Her's is the right of marrying, and the guardian is only sought lest it (the contraction of marriage) should be attributed to *waqāhah* (want of shame)". (H.I,p.294); and again: "It is not lawful for the guardian to compel a virgin who has attained majority to marry according to his wishes" (*ibid.*). Tradition also supports this view, for the Prophet is reported to have said: "The widow and the divorced woman shall not be married until her order is obtained, and the virgin shall not be married until her permission is obtained" (Bu.67 : 42). And *Bukhārī's* next chapter is headed thus: "When a man gives his daughter in marriage and she dislikes it, the marriage shall be repudiated" (Bu.

67 : 43), and a tradition is quoted showing that the Prophet repudiated such a marriage.

The jurists have also dealt with cases of the marriage of minors. According to Ḥanafī interpretation of the Muslim law, "the marriage of a minor boy or girl is lawful, whether the minor girl is a virgin or a *thayyibah*, provided the guardian is one of the *'aṣabah* (relations on the father's side) (H.I, p. 295). Mālik recognizes such marriage only when the guardian is a father, and Shāfi'ī when the guardian is a father or a grandfather (*ibid.*). Again in the Ḥanafī law, if the minor has been given in marriage by a guardian who is not the father or the grandfather, the minor has the opinion, on attaining majority, of repudiating the marriage. But, as a tradition already quoted shows, even if the father gives away his daughter in marriage against her wishes, and she is of age, the marriage must be repudiated if the girl desires, and so in the case of a minor too if, on coming of age, she finds the match unsuitable. Bukhārī speaks only of a *thayyibah* (a widow or a divorced woman), but another tradition is reported from Ibn 'Abbās, stating that a virgin girl came to the Prophet and said that her father had married her against her wishes, and the Prophet gave her the right to repudiate the marriage (AD. 12 : 25). He also mentions the case of a *thayyibah* (AD. 12 : 27).

Marriage in **Akfā'**

Akfā' is the plural of *kuf'* which means *an equal* or *one alike*. For example, the Arabs are the *akfā'* of the Arabs and the Quraish are the *akfā'* of the Quraish. Thus the people of one tribe or one family would be *akfā'* among themselves, and people of one race would be *akfā'* among themselves. There is nothing in the Qur'ān or in the Tradition to show that a marriage relation can only be established among the *akfā'*. It is quite a different thing that, generally, people should seek such relations among the *akfā'*, but Islām came to level all distinctions, whether social, tribal or racial, and therefore it does not limit the marriage relationship to *akfā'*. The principle that tribes and families have no special value with God is clearly established: "O mankind, surely We have created you from a male and female, and made you tribes and families that you may know each other. Surely the noblest of you with Allāh is the most dutiful of you" (49 : 13). The way is opened for establishing all kinds of relationships between Muslims to whatever country or tribe they may belong by declaring that "the believers are brethren" (49 : 10), and "the believers, men and women, are friends (*auliyā'*) of each other'' (9 : 71). The Prophet interpreted these verses by saying: ''The Arab has no precedence over the non-Arab, nor the non-Arab over the Arab, nor the white man over the black one, nor the black man over the white one except by excelling in righteousness.''

When speaking of contracting marriage-relationships, the Qur'ān speaks only of certain forbidden relations and then adds: ''And lawful for you are all women besides those'' (4 : 24). And again it goes so far as to allow marital relations with non-Muslims: ''And so are the chaste from among the believing women and the chaste from among those who have been given the Book before you'' (5 : 5). The Prophet recommended the marriage of a lady of the tribe of Quraish of the noblest family, his aunt's daughter, Zainab, to Zaid who was a liberated slave; and Bilāl, a negro, was married to the sister of 'Abd al-Raḥmān ibn 'Auf. There are other examples of the same kind in the early history of Islām. In one tradition it is stated that the Prophet recommended a certain man, called Abū Hind, to the tribe of Banī Bayādz, to whom he stood in the relation of a *maulā* (a liberated slave), and followed the profession of *ḥajāmah* (the craft of the cupper), saying: ''O Banī Bayādz! Give (your daughters) to Abū Hind in marriage and take in marriage his daughters'' (AD. 12 : 26). This tradition cuts at the root of the limitation of marriage to *akfā'*; yet the jurists have insisted on it. Imām Mālik, in this respect, differs from others, saying that *kafā'ah* (equality) is brought about by religion, that is to say, all Muslims are alike or equal. The majority of the jurists require equality in four things—religion, freedom, descent and profession. Imām Shāfi'ī says that he could not declare a marriage outside the *akfā'* to be illegal (*ḥarām*); it is a disability which is removed by the consent of the women and her guardians.

Conditions imposed at the time of marriage

It is lawful to impose and accept conditions, which are not illegal, at the time of marriage, and the parties are bound by such conditions. The Prophet is reported to have said: ''The best entitled to fulfilment of all conditions that you may fulfil, are the conditions by which sexual union is legalized'' (Bu. 67 : 53; AD. 12 : 39). It is also related that the Prophet spoke of a son-in-law of his (an unbeliever), in high terms, saying: ''He spoke to me and he spoke the truth, and he made promises with me and he fulfilled those promises'' (Bu. 67 : 53). Illegal conditions are those which are opposed to the law of Islām or to public morality, for instance, that the wife shall have the right to frequent immoral places or that she shall not be entitled to any dower or maintenance or that the husband and the wife shall not inherit from each other. If such a condition be imposed the condition is void while the marriage is valid. Examples of legal conditions are that the wife shall not be compelled to leave her *dār* (conjugal domicile), that the husband shall not contract a second marriage during the existence of the first, that the husband and the wife or one of them shall live in a specified place, that a certain portion of the dower shall be paid immediately and the remainder on death or divorce, that the husband shall pay the wife a certain amount by way of maintenance, that he shall not prevent her from receiving visits from her relatives, that the wife shall have the right to divorce for a specified reason or for any reasonable cause, and so on (AA.).

Polygamy

As a rule, Islām recognizes only the union of one man and one woman as a valid form of marriage. Under exceptional circumstances it allows the man more wives than one, but does not allow the woman more husbands than one. Thus while a married woman cannot contract a valid marriage, a married man can do it. There is no difficulty in understanding this differentiation, if the natural duties of man and woman in the preservation and upbringing of the human species are kept in view. Nature has so divided the duties of man and woman, in this respect, that while one man can raise children from more wives than one, one woman can have children only from one husband. Therefore while polygamy may at times be a help in the welfare of society and the preservation of the human race, polyandry has no conceivable use for man.

Polygamy is an exception

In the first place it must be borne in mind that polygamy is allowed in Islām only as an exception. It is expressly so stated in the Qur'ān: "And if you fear that you cannot do justice to orphans, marry such women as seem good to you, two or three or four; but if you fear that you will not do justice (between them), then (marry) only one" (4 : 3). This is the only passage in the Qur'ān that speaks of polygamy, and it will be seen that it does not enjoin polygamy; it only permits it and that, too, conditionally. Before we consider the significance of this verse, it must be understood clearly that polygamy is here allowed only when there are orphans to be dealt with, and it is feared that they will not be dealt with justly. This condition relates more to the welfare of society than to the needs of the individual.

The traditional interpretation put upon this verse is that of 'Ā'ishah, as contained in the *Bukhārī*. She is reported to have said: "This is the orphan girl who is under the care of her guardian and is his partner in property, and her property and her beauty please him, so her guardian wishes to marry her without being just in regard to her *mahr*, so that he should give her what another man would give; so they were forbidden to marry them unless they would do justice to them and give them their dowries according to their usage, and therefore they were commanded to marry other women that seemed good to them" (Bu. 65, sūrah 4, ch. I). It will be seen that this explanation introduces into the passage words and phrases of which there is no trace, nor is this significance traceable to the Prophet. It is unacceptable for another reason too. Verse 127 of this very chapter, which is admittedly a further explanation of the verse under discussion, is thus explained by 'Ā'ishah: "It is the man who has got an orphan girl of whom he is a guardian and an inheritor, so she becomes his partner in his property, even in the palm trees, and he is disinclined to marry her, nor does he like that she should marry another person who would thus become his partner in his property on account of her partnership and therefore prevents her from marrying" (*ibid.*). Admittedly the latter verse explains the previous one, but 'Ā'ishah's explanation of the latter is just the opposite of her explanation of the former. The guardian is described as desiring to marry his girl ward in the first case, and the first verse is said to be a prohibition against it, while in the case of the latter verse he is said to be disinclined to marry her himself or to anybody else.

Hence it is that the commentators have suggested three other explanations. The first of these is that this verse (4 : 3) is only meant to prohibit the marrying of more wives than four, so that not having too many wives they may not be tempted to embezzle the property of the orphans, when their own proved insufficient. The second is that if you fear that you cannot be just to orphans, you should also fear that you cannot be just to too many wives. The third is that if you fear that you cannot be just to orphans, you should also fear the great sin of adultery, and to shun it you are allowed up to four wives.

It will be seen that these explanations are even less satisfactory than the one given in the *Bukhārī*. The meaning of this verse is really explained by 4 : 127: "And they ask thee a decision about women. Say: Allāh makes known to you His decision concerning them; and that which is recited to you in the Book is concerning widowed women whom you give not what is appointed for them, while you are not inclined to marry them, nor to the weak among children, and that you should deal justly with orphans." The reference to "that which is recited in the Book" is admittedly to 4 : 3. And the reference in "whom you give not what is appointed for them ... nor to the weak among children" is to the Arab custom, according to which women and minor children did not get a share of inheritance, the recognized usage being that only he could inherit who could ride on the back of a horse and take the field against the enemy. The position was therefore this, that when a widow was left with orphans to bring up, she and her children would get no share of the inheritance, nor were people inclined to marry widows who had children. In 4 : 3, the Qur'ān has therefore enjoined that if you cannot be otherwise just to orphans, marry the mothers of such orphans so that you may thus be interested in their welfare, and for this purpose you are allowed to contract other marriages.

A consideration of the historical circumstances of the time when this chapter was revealed corroborates this conclusion. It was a time when the Muslims were compelled to carry on incessant war against an enemy bent upon their extirpation. The breadwinners had all to take the field against the enemy, and many had been lost in the unequal battles that were being fought by the small Muslim band against overwhelming forces. Women had lost their affectionate husbands and young children their loving fathers, and these widows and orphans had to be provided for. If they had been left to the mercy of circumstances, they would have perished, and the community would have been weakened to such an extent that it would have been impossible to maintain the struggle for life. It was under these circumstances that the fourth chapter was revealed, allowing the taking of more wives than one, so that the widows and orphans may find a shelter. If you fear, says the revelation, that you will not be able to do justice to orphans, marry women (the mothers of the orphans) up to four, but only on condition that you are just to all of them. That by *women* here are meant *the mothers of orphans* is made clear by v.127, as already shown.

It might be said that other arrangements could be made for the maintenance of widows and orphans. But a home-life could not be given to them in any other manner, and home-life is the real source whence all those good qualities of love and affection spring, which are the greatest asset of social life and civilization. Islām bases its civilization on home-life; and under exceptional circumstances, where monogamy fails to provide a home for widows and orphans, it allows polygamy to extend to them that advantage. Even if it be half a home that the women and children find in a polygamous family, it is better than no home at all. Moreover, a community the ranks of whose fighting men were daily dwindling stood in urgent need of increasing its numbers by all possible means, and hence also it was necessary to provide a home for the widows so that they might be helpful in strengthening the numerical position of the community. The moral aspect of the question is not the least important. The war had decimated the male population and the number of women exceeded that of men. This excess, if not provided with a home, would have led to moral depravity, which is the greatest danger to a civilization like that of Islā m, which is based on morality.

The question of war is not peculiar to one age or one country. It is a question which affects the whole of humanity for all ages to come. War must always be a source of decrease in the number of males, bringing about a corresponding increase in the number of females and a solution will have to be sought by all well-wishers of humanity for the problem of the excess of women over men. Monogamy is undoubtedly a right rule of life under normal conditions, but when abnormal conditions are brought about by the excess of females over males, monogamy fails, and it is only through a limited polygamy that this difficulty can be solved. Europe is to-day confronted with that question, independently of war, and war only aggravates its seriousness. Professions may be opened up for women to enable them to earn bread, and Islām has never closed the door of any profession against women. But the crux of the question is not the provision of bread but the provision of a home-life and that question cannot be solved without polygamy.

It may be added here that polygamy in Islām is, both in theory and in practice, an exception, not a rule, and as an exception it is a remedy for many of the evils of modern civilization. It is not only the preponderance of females over males that necessitates polygamy in certain cases, but there is a variety of other circumstances which require polygamy to be adopted under exceptional circumstances, not only for the moral but also the physical welfare of society. Prostitution, which is on the increase with the advancement of 'civilization', and which is eating into it like a canker, with its concomitant increase of bastardy, is practically unknown to countries where polygamy is allowed as a remedial measure.

It may be further stated that the institution of polygamy, which was allowed by Islām only as a remedy, has largely been abused by sensual people, but then there are people in every society who would abuse any institution, however necessary it may be to the right growth of human society. In countries where polygamy is not allowed, the sensuality of man has invented a hundred other ways of giving vent to his carnal passions, and these are a far greater curse to society than the abuse of polygamy. Indeed that abuse can be easily remedied by the state by placing legal limitations upon its practice, while the state is quite helpless against the evils which result from its entire rejection.

SEC. 4 — RIGHTS AND OBLIGATIONS OF HUSBAND AND WIFE

Woman's position in general

From a material as well as a spiritual point of view, Islām recognizes the position of woman to be the same as that of man. Good works bring the same reward, whether to a male or a female: "I will not suffer the work of a worker among you to be lost, whether male or female, the one of you being from the other" (3 : 194). Paradise and its blessings are equally for both: "And whoever does good whether male or female, and he (or she) is a believer — these shall enter the Garden" (40 : 40; 4 : 124). Both shall enjoy the higher life: "Whoever does good, whether male or female, and is a believer, We shall certainly make him (or her) live a good life" (16 : 97). Revelation which is God's greatest spiritual gift in this life is granted to men as well as to women: "And when the angels said: O Mary, surely, Allāh has chosen thee and purified thee" (3 : 41); "And We revealed to Moses'mother, saying: Give him suck;then when thou fearest for him, cast him into the river and fear not nor grieve" (28 : 7). From a material point of view, woman is recognized as on a par with man. She can earn money and own property just as man can do and therefore she may, if she feels the need, follow any profession. "For men is the benefit of what they earn. And for women is the benefit of what they earn" (4 : 32). She has full control over her property and can dispose of it as she likes: "But if they (the women) of themselves be pleased to give you a portion thereof (*i.e.*, of their property), consume it with enjoyment'' (4 : 4). Women can also inherit property as men can: ''For men is a share of what the parents and the near relatives leave, and for woman a share of what the parents and the near relatives leave'' (4 : 7).

Woman's position as wife

By entering the married state, woman does not lose any of the rights which she possesses as an individual member of society. She is still free to carry on any work she likes, to make any contract she desires, to dispose of her property as she wishes; nor is her individuality merged in that of her husband. But she is at the same time recognized as undertaking new responsibilities of life, which carry with them new rights. The Qur'ān settles the principle: ''And women have rights similar to their obligations, in a just manner'' (2 : 228). These are the rights and responsibilities of the home. Tradition describes her position in the home as that of a *rā'īyah* or ruler: ''Every one of you is a ruler and every one shall be questioned about his subjects; the Amīr (the King) is a ruler, and the man is a ruler over the people of his house, and the woman is a ruler over the house of her husband and his children, so every one of you is a ruler and every one shall be questioned about his subjects'' (Bu. 67 : 91). Thus so far as the home is concerned, the wife has the position of a ruler in it, the home being her territory. By marriage she is at once raised to a higher dignity and acquires new rights, though at the same time she incurs new responsibilities. Her rights as regards her husband are also affirmed in Tradition, as the Prophet said to 'Abd Allāh ibn 'Umar: ''Thy body has a right over thee and thy soul has a right over thee and thy wife has a right over thee'' (Bu. 67 : 90).

Mutual relation of husband and wife

As already stated the mutual relation of husband and wife is described in the Qur'ān as one of a single soul in two bodies: ''And of His signs is this, that He created mates for you from yourselves that you might find quiet of mind in them, and He put between you love and compassion'' (30 : 21); ''He it is Who created you from a single soul, and of the same did He make his mate, that he might find comfort in her'' (7 : 189). The same idea is elsewhere very beautifully described in different words: ''They (your wives) are an apparel for you and you are an apparel for them''(2

: 187). The closest union of two souls could not be described more aptly; yet Islām is a practical religion and it does not shut its eyes to the hard realities of life. It describes the home as a unit in the greater organization of a nation as a whole, and just as in the vaster national organization there is somebody to exercise the final authority in certain cases, so the smaller organization of the home cannot be maintained without a similar arrangement. Hence the husband is first spoken of as being "a ruler over the people of the house" and the wife is then described as "a ruler over the house of her husband and his children." The home is thus a kingdom in miniature, where authority is exercised by both the husband and the wife. But unless one of them is given a higher authority, there would be chaos in this kingdom. The reason for giving the higher authority to the male parent is thus stated in the Qur'ān: "Men are the maintainers of women, with what Allāh has made some of them to excel others, and with what they spend out of their property" (4 : 34). The Arabic word for *maintainers* is *qawwāmūn*, pl. of *qawwām*, derived from *qāma*, meaning *he stood up*, but when used with a *bā* or *'alā*, *qāma* carries the significance of *maintaining* or *managing*. Thus *qāma bi-l-yatīm* means *he maintained the orphan*, and *qāma' alai-hā* means *he maintained the woman and managed her affair* (LL.). The word *qawwāmūn* (maintainers) carries a double significance. It means that the husband provides maintenance for the wife, and also that he has final charge of the affairs of the home, thus exercising authority over the wife when there is need for it. The reason for giving a higher authority to man is contained in the word *qawwāmūn* itself. It is the man who can be entrusted with the maintenance of the family, and therefore it is he who must hold the higher authority.

A division of work

The function of the husband and the wife are quite distinct, and each is entrusted with the functions which are best suited for his or her nature. The Qur'ān says that God has made man and woman to excel each other in certain respects. The man excels the woman in constitution and physique, which is capable of bearing greater hardships and facing greater dangers than the physique of woman. On the other hand, the woman excels the man in the qualities of love and affection. Nature, for her own purpose of helping in the growth of creation, has endowed the female among men, as well as the lower animals, with the quality of love to a much higher degree than the male. Hence there is a natural division as between man and woman of the main work which is to be carried on for the progress of humanity. Man is suited to face the hard struggles of life on account of his stronger physique; woman is suited to bring up the children because of the preponderance of the quality of love in her. The duty of the maintenance of the family has therefore been entrusted to the man, and the duty of bringing up the children to the woman. And each is vested with authority suited to the function with which he or she is entrusted. Hence it is that men are spoken of as being the maintainers of women, and women as "rulers over the household and the children."

Woman not excluded from any activity in the sphere of life

This division of work is only the general rule; it does not mean that woman has entirely been excluded from other kinds of activity. A study of the Tradition literature shows that, notwithstanding her rightful position in the home, as the bringer up of children and manager of the household, women took interest in all the national activities of the Muslim community. The care of the children did not prevent her from repairing to the mosque to join the congregational prayers,[29] nor was this care an obstacle in her way to join the soldiers in the field of battle, to perform a large number of duties, such as the carrying of provisions,[30] taking care of the sick and the wounded,[31] removing the wounded and the slain from the battlefield,[32] or taking part in actual fighting when necessary.[33] One of the Prophet's wives, Zainab, used to prepare hides and to devote the proceeds of the sale to charitable work.[34] Women also helped their husbands in the labour of the field,[35] served the male guests at a feast[36] and

29 Bu. 10 : 162, 164.

30 Bu. 56 : 66.

31 Bu.56 : 67.

32 Bu. 56 : 68.

33 Bu. 56 : 62, 63, 65.

34 Is. VIII, p. 93.

35 Bu. 67 : 108.

36 Bu. 67 : 78.

carried on business,[37] they could sell to and purchase from men, and men could sell to and purchase from them.[38] A woman was appointed by the Caliph 'Umar as superintendent of the market of Madīnah. But these were exceptions. The proper sphere of the woman was the house and care of the children.

Rights of husband and wife

The family concern must be kept going by husband and wife in mutual co-operation. The husband is mainly required to earn for the maintenance of the family, and the wife is responsible for the management of the household and the bringing up of the children. The rights of each against the other are therefore centred in these two points. The husband is bound to maintain the wife according to his means, as the Qur'ān says: "Let him who has abundance spend out of his abundance, and whoever has his means of subsistence straitened to him, let him spend out of that which Allāh has given him. Allāh lays not on any soul a burden beyond that which He has given it." (65 : 7).

He must also provide for her a lodging: "Lodge them where you live, according to your means" (65 : 6). The wife is bound to keep company with her husband, to preserve the husband's property from loss or waste, and to refrain from doing anything which should disturb the peace of the family. She is required not to admit any one into the house whom the husband does not like, and not to incur expenditure of which the husband disapproves (Bu. 67 : 87). She is not bound to render personal service such as the cooking of food, but the respective duties of the husband and wife are such that each must always be ready to help the other. The wife must help the husband even in the field of labour if she can do it, and the husband must help the wife in the household duties. Of the Prophet himself, it is related that he used to help his wives in many small works of the household, such as the milking of the goats, patching his clothes, mending his shoes, cleansing the utensils, and so on.

[37] Bu. 11 : 40.

[38] Bu. 34 : 67.

Stress laid on kind treatment towards wife

The Qur'ān lays the greatest possible stress on kindly and good treatment towards the wife. "Keep them in good fellowship" and "treat them kindly" is the oft-recurring advice of the Qur'ān (2 : 229, 231; 4 : 19, etc.). So much so that kindness is recommended even when a man dislikes his wife, for "it may be that you dislike a thing while Allāh has placed abundant good in it" (4 : 19). The Prophet laid equally great stress upon good treatment of a wife. "The most excellent of you," he is reported to have said," is he who is best in his treatment of his wife" (MM.13 : II-ii). "Accept my advice in the matter of doing good to women," is another tradition (Bu.67 : 81). In his famous address at the Farewell Pilgrimage, he again laid particular stress on the good treatment of women: "O my people! you have certain rights over your wives and so have your wives over you...They are the trust of Allāh in your hands. So you must treat them with all kindness" (M.16 : 17).

In one tradition which enjoins kindness to women, the woman is compared to a rib: "The woman is like a rib, if you try to straighten it, you will break it"[39] (Bu. 67 : 80). The rib is bent in its make and not straight, and it serves best its purpose in the state in which it is created, and so of the woman it is said that being like a rib she serves her purpose best in the state in which she has been created; to straighten her, *i.e.*, to make her work just as the man pleases, or to try to make her possess the sterner qualities of man, is to break her down. As already pointed out, the temperament of man differs from that of woman in one respect. Man is stern and harsh, therefore largely unyielding; it was necessary that he should be so, so that he might be able to face the hard struggles of life. The woman who is meant to bring up the children has been so created that the quality of love preponderates in her and she is devoid of the sternness of man; she is therefore inclined to one side sooner than the man, and on account

[39] In another ḥadīth (Bu. 60 : 1; 67 : 81), instead of *like a rib* the words are *khuliqat min dzil'-in, i.e.* "she has been created of a rib." The meaning is still the same, that is to say, her *nature* or temperament may be compared to a rib. It is the woman in general, not Eve, that is spoken of here nor is it said that woman has been created of the rib of man. In Arabic, we often say a certain thing has been created of so and so, meaning that the temperament of that thing is so. Thus the Qur'ān says: "Man has been created of haste (*min 'ajal*)" (21 : 37), the significance being that the characteristic of haste is prominent in him.

of this quality she is compared to the rib. Her being bent like the rib is adduced as an argument for being kind to her and for leaving her in that state.

Sterner measures allowed in case of immoral conduct

While, however, great stress is laid on the kind treatment of woman, and it is even recommended that she may be allowed to work in any way she likes, the husband is permitted to take stern measures in case of her immoral conduct. Islām places the highest value upon the chastity of the woman, and therefore if there is a falling off from the high standard of morality, the woman is not entitled to that honour and kindly treatment which is accorded to her otherwise. The Qur'ān allows stern measures in the case of *nushūz*, which means *the rising of the wife against her husband* or *her revolt* and includes *resisting the husband*, and *hating*, and *deserting him* (LL.). Some commentators explain *nushūz* as meaning *her leaving the husband's place and taking up an abode which he does not like* (AH.). Apparently the word covers a wide range of meaning and, therefore the remedy suggested in such cases is of three kinds. "And as to those on whose part you fear desertion (*nushūz*) admonish them and leave them alone in the beds, and chastise them" (4 : 34). When the *nushūz* is very ordinary and there is nothing serious about it, for instance, when it is a mere resistance of the husband's authority, the remedy suggested is simple admonition. If hatred is combined with resistance of authority, a stronger remedy is suggested, and the husband is allowed, in that case, to show his disapproval of her conduct by keeping her separated from himself. But if the wife goes beyond that and deserts the husband, and her conduct becomes suspicious, then, as a last resort, chastisement is permitted. It cannot be denied that cases do happen when this extreme step becomes necessary, but these are exceptional cases and their occurrence is generally limited to the rougher strata of society where the remedy of slight corporal punishment is not only unobjectionable but necessary.

There are traditions showing that the infliction of slight corporal punishment was permitted only when the conduct of the wife became objectionable, and she was as it were in open revolt against the husband. Thus a tradition in *Muslim* says: "And be careful of your duty to Allāh in the matter of women, for you have taken them as the trust of Allāh...and they owe to you this obligation that they will not allow any one to come into your house when you do not like. If they do, then give them (slight) corporal punishment which may not leave any effect on their bodies'' (M. 15 : 19). This shows that the infliction of slight corporal punishment is limited only to the extreme cases. Another tradition shows that such conduct on the part of the wife, or such treatment on the part of the husband, would not be expected in any good family. When certain women complained to the Prophet of the ill-treatement of their husbands, he is reported to have admonished the men in the following words: 'Many women have come to the house of Muḥammad complaining about their husbands; such husbands are by no means the good ones among you'' (AD. 12 : 42). Bukhārī also refers to the tradition of Muslim quoted above and gives another under the heading ''What is disliked in the matter of giving corporal punishment to women,'' according to which the Prophet is reported to have said: ''Let not one of you inflict corporal punishment upon his wife as he would inflict it upon his slave, for he will be having amorous relations with her soon afterwards'' (Bu. 67 : 94).

On another occasion too, the husband is allowed to exercise his authority against the wife, and this too is an occasion where the wife's conduct is openly immoral: ''And as for those of your women who are guilty of an indecency (*fāḥishāh*), call to witness against them four witnesses from among you; then if they bear witness, confine them to the houses until death takes them away or Allāh opens some way for them'' (4 : 15); Allāh's opening a way for them means that they show sincere repentance. The *fāḥishah* spoken of here is clearly immoral conduct, and the punishment is a restriction on the woman's movements so that she is deprived of the liberty to move freely in society. Reading this verse along with 4 : 34, relating to the infliction of corporal punishment it appears that confining to the house is the first step, and it is when they repeat their evil deeds in the house, or do not submit to the authority of the husband and desert him, that permission is given to inflict corporal punishment which is the last resort. And if even this step does not make them mend their ways, matrimonial relations may be ended.

Seclusion of women

It has already been shown that women are not forbidden to take part in any activity when necessary, nor is there any injunction in the Qur'ān or the tradition shutting them up within the four walls of their houses. On the other hand, the Holy Book speaks of a Muslim society in which man and woman had often to meet each other: "Say to the believing men that they lower their gaze and restrain their sexual passions. That is purer for them... And say to the believing women that they lower their gaze and restrain their sexual passions and not display their adornment except what appears thereof" (24 : 30, 31). A later revelation supports the same conclusion: "O Prophet, tell thy wives and thy daughters and the women of the believers to let down upon themselves their over-garments. This is more proper, so that they may be known, and not be given trouble" (33 : 59). If women did not go out of their houses, where was the necessity of asking them to wear a distinctive dress, and where was the occasion for their being troubled? According to Tradition, the Prophet is reported to have said to women: "It is permitted to you to go out for your needs (*ḥājah*) (Bu. 4 : 13; 67 : 116). The injunction to the Prophet's wives in a verse of the Qur'ān does not mean that they were not to go out for their needs. The verse in question runs thus: "And stay in your houses and display not your beauty like the displaying of the ignorance of yore" (33 : 33). This is evidently an injunction against the parading of finery and display of beauty and thus exciting the uncontrolled passions of youth. It cannot and does not mean, as explained by the Prophet himself that the women are not allowed to go out for their needs. Display of beauty and going out for one's need are quite different things. There is, therefore, no seclusion in Islām in the sense that women are shut up within their houses for they are as free to move about for their needs, or the transaction of their affairs, as men. Only their needs outside the home are generally fewer, and their duties are to a large extent limited to the home.

The veil

The next question is whether women are commanded to veil themselves when they have to go out for their needs. These needs may be either religious or secular. Two prominent instances of the former are taking part in public prayers, and the performance of pilgrimage. If it had been necessary for women to wear veils, an injunction should have been given to wear them on these two sacred occasions, since these are the occasions on which men's sentiments should be purest, and when, therefore, all those things that excite the passions must be avoided. There is, however, not only no such injunction but it was a recognized practice that women came into the congregation of men in mosques unveiled (IJ-C. XVIII, p. 84).

It is even admitted by the jurists that women should not veil themselves at prayers, and on pilgrimage. In the conditions of prayers it is laid down that the body of the women must be covered entirely except her face and her hands (H.I, p. 88, *Shurūṭ al-Ṣalāṭ*). The exception of these two parts, it is added, is due to the fact that they must of necessity be left exposed. As regards pilgrimage, there is an express injunction in Tradition that no woman shall put on a veil during the pilgrimage (Bu. 25 : 23). It is also a well-established fact that the mosques in the Prophet's time contained no screens to keep the two sexes separate. The only separation between the men and the women was that women stood in separate rows behind the men. Otherwise they were in the same room or in the same yard, and the two sexes had to intermingle. In the pilgrimage there was a much greater intermingling of the sexes, women performing circumambulations of the Ka'bah, running between Ṣafā and Marwah, staying in the plain of 'Arafāt and going from place to place, along with men, and yet they were enjoined not to wear a veil.

If then, as admitted on all hands, women did not wear a veil when the two sexes intermingled on religious occasions, when the very sacredness of the occasion called for a veil, if ever the veil was a necessity, it is a foregone conclusion that they could not be required to veil themselves when going out for their secular needs whose very performance would be hampered by the veil. And there is no such injunction either in the Qur'ān or Tradition. In fact, no such injunction could be given when there existed an injunction that women shall remain unveiled in pilgrimage. This injunction rather shows that the veil was adopted simply as a mark of rank or greatness, and the unveiling was required in order to bring all on a level of equality. However that may be, the order to remain unveiled in the pilgrimage is a clear proof that wearing the veil is not an Islamic injunction or practice. And the verses requiring both men and women to keep their looks cast down[40] show clearly that, when the two sexes had to intermingle as a matter of necessity, the women were not veiled, for otherwise there would have been no need for the men to keep their looks cast down. And to make the matter clearer still, it is added that they should "not display their adornment, except what appears thereof." The part that necessarily appears is the face and the hands, and this is also the view of the vast majority of commentators (IJ—C. XVIII,

[40] See vv. 24 : 30, 31 quoted earlier.

p. 84; RM. VI, p. 52).[41] There is also a tradition according to which the Prophet is reported to have excepted the face and the hands from the parts which were required to be covered: "Asmā', daughter of Abū Bakr, came to the Prophet, and she was wearing very thin clothes (through which the body could be seen). The Prophet turned away his face from her and said, O Asmā'! when the woman attains her majority, it is not proper that any part of her body should be seen except this and this, pointing to his face and his hands" (AD. 31 : 30).

Decent dress

All that the Qur'ān requires is that women should be decently dressed when they go out and that they should not uncover their bosoms. This is made clear in 24 : 31: "And say to the believing women that they ... should not display their adornment except what appears thereof. And let them wear their head-coverings over their bosoms." The practice in Arabia, in pre-Islamic times, of displaying beauty, included the uncovering of the bosom, and hence the injunction relating to its covering. A difference was thus made between the dress of women within their houses and when they appeared in public; in the former case they were allowed to be more at ease in the matter of their dress, but in public they had to be particular so that their very appearance should be indicative of modesty. On another occasion, the Muslim women are required to wear a dress whose very appearance should distinguish them from such women as did

[41] Ibn Jarīr quotes three different explanations of *illā mā ẓahara min-hā* (except what appears thereof); 1.The view of Ibn Mas'ūd that these words mean the adornment of dress; 2. The view of Ibn'Abbās, Sa'īd, Dzaḥāk, 'Aṭā, Qatādah, Mujāhid and others that they mean the adornment which it is lawful for the woman to show, *i.e.*, collyrium, ring, bangles and face; 3. The view of Ḥasan that they mean the face and the clothes; and then adds his own view in the following words:

"The most correct explanation of these words is that they mean the face and hands and include collyrium, ring, bangles and dyeing of hands. We say it is the most correct explanation because there is a consensus of opinion (*ijmā'*) that it is obligatory for him who says his prayers that he should cover all those parts of the body which it is necessary to cover, and for the woman it is obligatory that she should uncover her hands and face in prayers and cover the rest of the body, except that it is reported from the Prophet that he allowed the uncovering of half of her wrist. When there is a consensus of opinion on this, it follows as a matter of course that she can keep uncovered that part of the body which is not included in *'aurāt* (the part which it is necessary to cover), for it is not unlawful to uncover that which is not the *'aurāt*. And as she can keep it uncovered, it follows that this is what is meant by *illā mā ẓahara min-hā* (IJ—C. XVIII, p. 84).

not have a good reputation: "O Prophet! tell thy wives and thy daughters and the women of the believers to let down upon them their over-garments; this is more proper, so that they may be known, and not be given trouble" (33 : 59). It seems that this injunction was required by the special circumstances which then prevailed at Madīnah, where the hypocrites would molest a good Muslim woman who went out to transact her affairs and then offer the excuse that they thought her to be a woman of ill repute. This is plainly hinted in the verse that follows: "If the hypocrites and those in whose hearts is a disease and the agitators in Madīnah desist not, We shall certainly urge thee on against them, then they shall not be thy neighbours in it but for a little while" (33 : 60). The Arabic word for over-garment is *jilbāb* and it means *a garment with which the woman covers her other garments* or *a woman's head-covering,* or *a garment with which she covers her head and bosom* (LL.). It may be part of an ordinary dress or it may be a kind of overcoat. Nor is the wearing of it compulsory under all circumstances; it is rather a kind of protection when there is fear of trouble, and in the case of older women it is dispensed with altogether as stated elsewhere: "And as for women past childbearing who hope not for marriage, it is no sin for them if they put off their cloaks without displaying their adornments" (24 : 60).

Privacy

Islām sets great value on the privacy of home-life. In the first place going into houses without permission is strictly forbidden: "O you who believe, enter not houses other than your own houses, until you have asked permission and saluted their inmates" (24 : 27). And again: "O you who believe, let those whom your right hands possess and those of you who have not attained to puberty ask permission of you three times; before the morning prayer, and when you put off your clothes for the heat of noon, and after the prayer of night. These are three times of privacy for you" (24 : 58). The Prophet's privacy was also to be respected: "O you who believe, enter not the houses of the Prophet unless permission is given to you for a meal, not waiting for its cooking being finished — but when you are invited, enter, and when you have taken food, disperse ... And when you ask of them (the women) any goods, ask of them from behind a curtain (*ḥijāb*)" (33 : 53). The concluding words of the verse aim not only at privacy but also afford a rule of guidance for the maintenance of better relations between the husband and the wife. In fact, all the above rules relating to privacy aim at creating a better atmosphere of sexual morality.

Intermingling of the two sexes

In the struggle of life the intermingling of the two sexes cannot be avoided, and Islām allows such intermingling even for religious purposes, as in prayers and pilgrimage. On all such occasions, when intermingling is necessary, the Qur'ān requires the women to appear in their simplest dress, or to wear an over-garment which should cover their ornaments, at the same time requiring both sexes to keep their looks cast down. Unnecessary mingling of the sexes is discouraged. Some traditions prohibit a woman being alone in private with a man who is not her *dhū maḥram* (*i.e.*, a near relative with whom marriage is prohibited) unless a *dhū maḥram* is present (Bu. 67 : 112); but when other people are also present, or one is exposed to public view, there is no harm in being alone with a woman (Bu. 67 : 113). The intermingling of the sexes in social functions generally cannot be traced in the early history of Islām, though there are examples in which a woman entertained the male guests of her husband (Bu. 67 : 78). This was a case of a marriage-feast (*walīmah*) in which the bride served the guests, but it cannot be said whether this was before the revelation of the 24th chapter or after it. In fact, much would depend, in these matters, on the social customs of the people, and no hard and fast rules can be laid down as to the limits to which the intermingling of the sexes may be allowed. The great object before Islām is to raise the moral status of society and to minimize the chances of illicit sexual relations growing up between the sexes, so that the home may be a haven of peace for the husband, the wife and the children.

SEC. 5. — MARRIAGE OF SLAVES

Prostitution abolished and marriage introduced

Slavery was an institution recognized by all people before Islām. To Islām belongs the credit of laying down principles which, if developed on the right lines, would have brought about its ultimate extinction. But it was not the work of a day, and therefore, as long as the institution remained, provision had to be made for slaves which should make them as good citizens as the free men. Before Islām, slave-girls served the purpose of either satisfying the master's carnal passions or earning money for him through prostitution. To both these evil practices an end was put immediately, and order was given that both free men and slaves, males as well as females, should remain in a married state: "And marry those among you who are single and those who are fit among your male slaves and your female slaves; ... and compel not your slave-girls to prostitution when[42] they desire to keep chaste, in order to seek the frail goods of this world's life" (24 : 32,33). The order to keep the male as well as female slaves in a married state is here combined with the order which puts an end to prostitution, and thus the two evil practices of pre-Islamic Arabia, which were the result of keeping slave-girls in an unmarried state, were put an end to by the one clear injunction that they shall be married. To this order there is no exception either in the Qur'ān or in Tradition. The injunction could be carried out in one of the three ways: by marriage, 1. between two slaves; 2. between a free person and a slave; and 3. between the master and the slave. There is no fourth alternative. At the present day, when the institution of slavery has been abolished in the whole of the civilized world, there is no need of going into the details of the marriages of the first two classes. The third class of marrying may however be dealt with briefly, as there exists a great misunderstanding to the effect that Islām allows concubinage.

[42] The Arabic word for *when* is *in*, which is generally translated as meaning *if*, but *in* in Arabic conveys both senses, *if* as well as *when*. The rendering *if* here is not allowed by the context, for the significance would then be that if the slave-girls desire to keep chaste, they may not be compelled to prostitution. This would lead to the evident conclusion that if they do not desire to keep chaste, they may be compelled to prostitution which is self-contradictory. Hence the rendering adopted here, the meaning being that, as it is the nature of woman, whether free or slave, that she would remain chaste, slave-girls who are under the control of their masters, should not be compelled to prostitution by not allowing them to marry. A modern writer is of opinion that in Arabia "prostitution was too firmly established to be at once removed" (*Sociology of Islam* by Levy, vol. I). This opinion is due to a misinterpretation of the Quranic words. The significance of this verse is further clarified by traditions as there is a very large number of these stating that prostitution and its wages were expressly forbidden by the Prophet (Bu. 34 : 113; 37 : 20; 68 : 51; AD. 22 : 39, etc.).

There is no concubinage in Islam

Concubinage is regular sexual connection with a female who does not hold the legal status of a wife; in other words, keeping a woman in the position of a wife without marrying her. There is a general impression that Islām gives an unlimited license to have as many concubines as one likes, so long as the concubine is a slave or a prisoner of war and not a free woman. Concubinage was undoubtedly practised in Arabia before Islām, and it may have been practised by some Muslims until the revelation of the verse quoted above. By this revelation, however, concubinage was put an end to. A plain injunction had been received that all male and female slaves must be married. If any master of a female slave kept her as a concubine after that, it was against the Quranic injunction. The Qur'ān does not make any exception in favour of the master; on the other hand, it lays the responsibility, of having the slaves married, on the masters. No master of a slave-girl could keep her as a concubine when the Qur'ān enjoined him to have her married, and if he did so keep her, his deed, whether due to his ignorance of the Quranic injunction or to intentional violation of it, had no validity in law.

The legality of concubinage has been inferred from certain expressions used in the Qur'ān. The most important of these are the following words: "And who restrain their sexual passions except in the presence of their mates or those whom their right hands possess, for such surely are not blamable" (23 : 5, 6; 70 : 29, 30). These verses are a part of a detailed description of true believers, and are preceded and followed by other verses describing the many attributes of true believers. They apply equally to men as well as women, the latter being clearly described as possessing all the good and great qualities which are possessed by men (33 : 35). If therefore the above description of the faithful, which occurs twice in the Qur'ān, and no more, can justify a man having sexual relations with his female slaves, it can also justify similar relations of a woman with her male slaves. But no one has ever drawn such an absurd conclusion from these words. The Arabic word for *sexual passions* as used here, is *furūj,* (pl. of *farj*) which means the *part of a person which it is indecent to expose* (LL.). *Ḥifẓ al-farj* therefore signifies not only refraining from actual sexual intercourse but also refraining from exposing certain parts of the body which it is indecent to expose. But a certain degree of freedom in this latter sense is allowed, to both men and women, in the presence of their slaves who had to wait upon them on all occasions. Ideas of decency may differ, so much so that there are people in all civilized countries who think that it is not indecent to be nude in the presence of others; on the other hand, they take pride in remaining naked even in public and sometimes try to take out processions of naked people, both men and women. Such practices are revolting to Islamic ideas of decency. But even if, for the sake of argument, the inference drawn from these words, to wit, that Muslims are allowed to have concubines, were accepted as true, that inference loses all its value when it is borne in mind that the two chapters in which this expression occurs are early Makkah revelations, when Islām had not yet introduced its reforms, and that the permission, if ever there was any, to keep concubines was taken away by the reforms introduced at Madīnah, when a clear injunction was given that all female slaves should be kept in a married state. If the female slave must be married, the master certainly has no right to sexual enjoyment with her.

It must be further borne in mind that neither the Qur'ān nor the Tradition anywhere speaks of the right of the master to have sexual intercourse with a slave. In other words, ownership is nowhere recognized as legalizing sexual relationship. The only thing that legalizes sexual intercourse is a contract, duly witnessed, between the two parties to undertake the responsibilities accruing from that contract, with a dowry settled upon the woman, and thus marriage, whether with a free person or a slave, is the only means of legalizing sexual connection.

Evidently, then the master could have sexual connection with his female slave under the rules laid down in the Qur'ān, relating to the marriage of a free man with a slave girl: "And whoever among you cannot afford to marry free believing women, (let him marry) such of your believing maidens as your right hands possess. And Allāh knows best your faith: you are (sprung) the one from the other. So marry them with the permission of their masters, and give them their dowries justly, they being chaste, not fornicating, nor receiving paramours ... This is for him among you who fears falling into evil" (4 : 25). The conditions of marriage, as laid down in this case, are the same as those in the case of a free woman, with one addition, *viz.*, that the consent of the master of the slave must be obtained, in addition to the consent of the girl herself. The dowry (*mahr*) must be paid as in the case of the free woman, though the burden would be lighter. In 4 : 3 again, the taking of a slave as wife is permitted, but still it is through proper marriage that she can become a wife,[43] as explained further on in 4 : 25.

There is only one more verse of the Qur'ān which has a bearing on this subject. It runs thus: "O Prophet, We have made lawful to thee thy wives whom thou hast given their dowries, and those whom thy right hand possesses, out of those whom Allāh has given thee as prisoners of war ... specially for thee, not for the rest of the believers. We know what We have ordained for them concerning their wives and those whom their right hands possess" (33 : 50). Here it is stated that all his wives and all those whom his right hand possessed, out of the prisoners of war, were made lawful to the Prophet specially. These words must be read along with 4 : 3, which lays down that the permission of plurality of wives was limited to four. Those of the believers who had more than four wives were thus required to divorce the excess number, but a special permission was given to the Prophet to retain all his wives, and those whom his right hand possessed, out of the prisoners of war, though their number was more than four. This phrase *mā malakat aimānu-ka* (what thy right hand possesses) is the same as *mā malakat aimānu-kum* (what your hands possess), the former speaking of one person and the latter of many. Now the question is, who were the women that fell in the category of "what thy right hand possesses?" Were they women to whom the Prophet had gone in simply because they had fallen into his hands as captives of war? In other words, were these concubines with whom sexual relations were legalized because of the right of ownership? There was none such in the Prophet's household. The Prophet had taken only two women as wives out of the prisoners of war, *viz.*, Safiyyah from among the Jews, and Juwairiyah from among the Banī Muṣṭalaq. They were not concubines but lawfully married wives, taken as wives in as honourable a manner as any of the others. If there was any difference, it was this that their freedom was considered as their dowry (*mahr*). This verse, read along with the history of the Prophet's life, sets at rest the question as to the meaning of *mā malakat aimānu-kum* (what your right hands possess) in the Qur'ān. Such women were from among the prisoners of war, but

[43] The verse states first that a man may marry up to four wives under exceptional circumstances and then adds that if he fears that he will not be able to do justice, then (he should marry) only *one* or (if he cannot find a free woman as wife, then he may marry) *that which your right hands possess*. A reference to the original would show that both *wāḥidat-an* (one) and *mā malakat aimānu-kum* (that which your right hands possess) are objects of *ankiḥū* (marry).

they were lawfully married wives. Hence the only difference between *azwāj* (wives) and *mā malakat yamīnuka* (those whom thy right hand possesses) is that the former were free women at the time of marriage while the latter were captives, but both were lawfully married.

In the same verse, the words *mā malakat aimānukum* have again been used regarding the believers generally: "We know what We have ordained for them concerning their wives and those whom their right hands possess." It shows that there already existed some ordinance in the Qur'ān both as regards wives and as regards those "whom your right hands possess." Now the ordinance as regards wives is contained in 4 : 3 and elsewhere, but the only ordinance as regards *mā malakat aimānu-kum* is that contained in 4 : 25, where conditions are laid down, under which prisoners of war can be taken in marriage. There is no ordinance with regard to them anywhere else in the Qur'ān except of course that contained in 24 : 32, which lays an obligation upon all owners of slaves or prisoners of war to have them married. Therefore prisoners of war or slaves could only be taken in marriage, and no other form of sexual relations was permitted.

The case of the master of a female slave who would himself have sexual relations with her differs only in one respect, *viz.*, that he, being himself her master, does not stand in need of permission from anybody else. But there must still be a legal marriage. The Prophet's example, however, shows that when a prisoner of war was elevated to the dignity of wifehood, she was also set free. It was in this manner that he took two ladies, who were prisoners of war, as wives. He set an example in this matter, and the faithful were enjoined to take him for an exemplar (33 : 21) and imitate him. His acting in this manner was undoubtedly based on his interpretation of the Quranic revelation, and that interpretation, of which the proof exists in his act, must be followed by all Muslims. He was divinely guided to act in this manner, and a Muslim who does not follow his example follows his own desire, instead of following the Divine guidance. But more than this, the Prophet most emphatically laid it down that the master of a slave-girl should educate her, set her free and marry her: "The Holy Prophet said, There are three people for whom there is a double reward; a person belonging to the Ahl al-Kitāb who believes in his own prophet and believes in Muḥammad, and the slave owned by another when he performs his obligation towards Allāh and his obligations towards his master, and the man who has a slave-girl with him,[44] then he teaches her good manner and instructs her well in polite accomplishment, and he educates her and gives her a good education, then he sets her free and marries her; he has a double reward'' (Bu.3 : 31; 49 : 14,16; 56 : 145, 60 : 48; 67 : 13; M.16 : 14; AD.12 : 5, etc.). This tradition which is repeated in the *Bukhārī* no less than six times, and is accepted by all the six reliable collections of Traditions, claims a very high degree of reliability. If its words were only recommendatory, they would still show what reform the Prophet desired to bring about, and combined with his own practice they lead to certain conclusion that his ultimate object was to raise slave-girls to a status of perfect equality with free women. But the recommendation is really of an imperative nature. It is not meant that the man who believes in his own prophet may reject the Prophet Muḥammad, nor that the slave who performs his obligations towards his master may not care for his obligations towards God. The double reward is rather due to the fact that he overcomes a great temptation. A man who believes in one prophet thinks that it is sufficient for him, but this is not actually the case; a belief in the Prophet Muḥammad is a greater necessity, as the man who believes in him believes in other prophets as well. Similarly, it is not sufficient for the slave to do his duty to his master; to bear in mind his obligations towards the Great Master is a greater necessity still. And thus, even if the master treats his slave-girl well, and gives her the best of education, it is not sufficient; he must set her free and raise her to the status of a wife, if he desires to have sexual relations with her.

The Qur'ān, the Prophet's practice and Tradition are thus all agreed that slave-girls must be married; there is no exception to that rule whether her husband is a slave or a free man or the master himself. It is only in Jurisprudence (*fiqh*) that the rule has been laid down that a master may have sexual relations with his slave-girl simply because of the right of ownership which he has in her. But even *fiqh* maintains that cohabitation with a slave-girl is only allowed if all those conditions are fulfilled which

[44] In only one report of this tradition (Bu. 3 : 31), some copies of *Bukhārī* add the words *kāna yaṭa'u-hā* after *amat* (slave-girl), in which case the meaning would be that he had a slave-girl with whom he used to have sexual relations, but the more authoritative copies do not contain these words. That this addition is a later interpolation is clear from the fact that Bukhārī narrates this ḥadīth five times again through different channels, and these words do not occur in any copy in all these places, nor is this addition met with in *Muslim* and *Abū Dāwūd*. But even if the Prophet spoke them, he was referring to the conditions that prevailed before this reform was introduced.

must be fulfilled if she were to be taken in marriage as a wife. For instance, it is necessary that such a slave-girl should be either a Muslim or one following a revealed religion, and that she is not already married. Both these are also necessary conditions of marriage. Again, just as a man cannot have two sisters as wives at one and the same time, a master, according to *fiqh*, cannot cohabit with two slave-girls who are sisters or who stand to each other in such relationship that their being taken as wives together is prohibited. This shows that even the *fiqh,* though allowing cohabitation on the ground of ownership, recognizes such cohabitation as the equivalent of marriage.

SEC. 6 — DIVORCE

Marriage and Divorce

Though marriage, according to Islām, is only a civil contract, yet the rights and responsibilities consequent upon it are of such importance to the welfare of humanity that a high degree of sanctity is attached to it. But in spite of the sacredness of the character of the marriage tie, Islām recognizes the necessity, in exceptional circumstances of keeping the way open for its dissolution. With the exception, perhaps, of the Hindu law, the necessity of divorce has been recognized by all people. The right of divorce according to the Jewish law belongs to the husband who can exercise it at his will. The Roman Catholic law recognizes the right of divorce only when there is faithlessness on the part of either of the parties but the divorced parties are precluded from marrying again. According to Hindu law marriage once performed can never be dissolved. Islām effected several reforms in divorce. It restricted the husband's right to divorce while recognizing the wife's right to it.

Divorce is permitted under exceptional circumstances

The Arabic word for divorce is *ṭalāq* which carries the literal significance of *freeing* or *the undoing of a knot* (R.). In the terminology of the jurists, the *ṭalāq* is called a *k͟hul'* (meaning literally *the putting* or *taking off* a thing), when it is claimed by the wife. Both from the Qur'ān and the Traditions it appears that, though divorce was permitted, yet the right could be exercised only under exceptional circumstances.

The Prophet is reported to have said: "Never did Allāh allow anything more hateful to Him than divorce" (AD. 13 : 3). According to a report of Ibn 'Umar, he said: "With Allāh the most detestable of all things permitted is divorce" (*ibid.*). The Qur'ān also approves of the Prophet insisting that Zaid should not divorce his wife, notwithstanding a dissension of a sufficiently long standing. The incident is spoken of thus: "And when thou didst say to him to whom Allāh had shown favour and to whom thou hadst shown a favour. Keep thy wife to thyself (*i.e.*, do not divorce her) and keep thy duty to Allāh" (33 : 37). Refraining from divorce is spoken of here as *taqwā* or righteousness. Elsewhere divorce is thus discouraged: "If you hate them (*i.e.*, your wives), it may be that you dislike a thing while Allāh has placed abundant good in it" (4 : 19). Remedies are also suggested to avoid divorce as long as possible. "And if you fear a breach between the two (*i.e.*, the husband and the wife), appoint an arbiter from his people and an arbiter from her people. If they both desire agreement, Allāh will effect harmony between them," (4 : 35). It was due to such teachings of the Qur'ān that the Prophet declared divorce to be the most hateful of all permitted things. And it is due to this that, in spite of the facility with which it may be effected, divorce takes place only rarely among the Muslims, compared with the large number of divorces in Christian countries. The mentality of the Muslim is to face the difficulties of the married life along with its comforts, and to avoid disturbing the disruption of the family relations as long as possible, turning to divorce only as a last resort.

Principle of divorce

From what has been said above, it is clear that not only must there be a good cause for divorce, but that all means to effect reconciliation must have been exhausted before resort is had to this extreme measure. The impression that a Muslim husband may put away his wife at a mere caprice, is a grave distortion of the Islamic institution of divorce. But though the Qur'ān, refers to several causes when divorce may become necessary, it does not enumerate all of them, nor does it strictly limit them to specified cases. These causes must vary with changing conditions of humanity and society.

The principle of divorce spoken of in the Qur'ān, and which in fact includes to a greater or less extent all causes, is the decision no longer to live together as husband and wife. In fact, marriage itself is nothing but an agreement to live together as husband and wife, and when either of the parties finds itself unable to agree to such a life, divorce must follow. It is not, of course, meant that every disagreement between them would lead to divorce; it is only the disagreement to live any more as husband and wife. In the Qur'ān such disagreement is called *shiqāq* (from *shaqq* meaning *breaking into two*). But not even the *shiqāq* entitles either party to a divorce, unless all possibilities of agreement have been exhausted. The principle of divorce is, therefore, described in the Qur'ān thus: "And if you fear a breach (*shiqāq*) between the two, then appoint an arbiter from his people and an arbiter from her people. If they both desire agreement, Allāh will effect harmony between them; surely Allāh is ever Knowing, Aware" (4 : 35). And further on it is added: "And if they separate, Allāh will render them both free from want out of His ampleness, and Allāh is ever Ample-giving, Wise" (4 : 130).

This verse gives us not only the principle of divorce, which is *shiqāq* or a disagreement to live together as husband and wife, but also the process to be adopted when a rupture of marital relations is feared. The two sexes are here placed on a level of perfect equality. A "breach between the two" would imply that either the husband or the wife wants to break off the marriage agreement, and hence either may claim a divorce when the parties can no longer pull on in agreement. In the process to be adopted, both husband and wife are to be represented on a status of equality; an arbiter has to be appointed from his people and another from her people. The two are told to try to remove the differences and reconcile the parties to each other. If agreement cannot be brought about, a divorce will follow.

It will be seen that the principle advanced here in the matter of divorce is an all-inclusive one. All causes of divorce are subject to the condition that one of the parties cannot pull on with the other. If both are willing to live in marital agreement, no power on earth can effect a divorce; but if one party finds that she or he is unable to live in marital agreement with the other, it would be a case of *shiqāq* or breach of the marriage agreement.

This breach of the marriage agreement may arise from many causes or from the conduct of either party; for instance, if either of them misconducts himself or herself or either of them is consistently cruel to the other, as may sometimes happen, there is incompatibility of temperament to such an extent that they cannot live together in marital agreement. At first sight it may look like giving too much latitude to the parties to allow them to end the marriage contract, even if there is no reason other than incompatibility of temperament, but this much is certain that if there is such disagreement that the husband and the wife cannot pull on together, it is better for themselves, for their offspring and for society in general that they should be separated rather than that they should be compelled to live together. No home is worth the name wherein instead of peace there is wrangling; and marriage is meaningless if there is no spark of love left between the husband and the wife. It is an error to suppose that such latitude tends to destroy the stability of marriage, because marriage, is entered into as a permanent and sacred relation based on love between a man and a woman, and divorce is only a remedy when marriage fails to fulfil its object.

Wife's right of divorce

It will have been seen that the Qur'ān places the two parties on a perfect level of equality in the matter of divorce. Tradition makes it clearer still. The Prophet is related to have married a woman called Umaima or Ibnat al-Jaun, and when he went into her, she said that she sought refuge in God from him, that is to say, wanted a divorce; and he granted her a divorce, and sent her off with some presents (Bu. 68 : 3). Another case is that Ṭhābit ibn Qais whose wife is reported to have come to the Prophet and said: "O Messenger of Allāh! I do not find fault in Ṭhābit ibn Qais regarding his morals or faith but I cannot pull on with him."[45] The Prophet said: "Wilt thou return to him his orchard (which he had settled upon her as a dowry)?" On receiving a reply in the affirmative, the Prophet sent for Ṭhābit and ordered him to take back his orchard and divorce his wife (Bu. 68 : 11). These two examples are sufficient to show that the wife had the right to claim divorce on those very grounds on which the husband could divorce his wife.

The right of the wife to claim a divorce is not only recognized by the Qur'ān and Tradition but also in Jurisprudence (*fiqh*). The technical term for the wife's right to divorce by returning her dowry is called khul', and it is based on the tradition already quoted, and on the following verse of the Qur'ān: "Divorce may be pronounced twice; then keep them in good fellowship or let them go with kindness. And it is not lawful for

[45] The words in one report are: "I hate *kufr* (ungratefulness) in Islām," and in another: "I cannot bear him (*lā uṭīqu-hū*)."

you to take any part of what you have given them, unless both fear that they cannot keep within the limits of Allāh. Then if you fear that they cannot keep within the limits of Allāh, there is no blame on them for what she gives up to become free thereby'' (2 : 229). By keeeping ''within the limits of Allāh''here is clearly meant the fulfilment of the object of marriage or performance of the duties imposed by conjugal relationship. The dowry is thus a check on the party who wants the divorce; if the husband wants to divorce the wife, the wife shall have the dowry; if the wife wants the divorce, the husband is entitled to dowry. But it is the arbiters spoken of in 4 : 35, and referred to here in the words ''if you fear that they cannot keep within the limits of Allāh,'' that shall decide whether the husband or the wife is responsible for the breach and which of them is entitled to the dowry.

The wife is also entitled to a divorce if the husband is missing, or *mafqūd al-khabar*, which means that he has disappeared and cannot be communicated with; because, though there is no *shiqāq* in this case, yet the husband is unable to fulfil his marital obligations. There is no definite statement in the Qur'ān, or Tradition, to show how long the wife should wait in such a case. The Ḥanafī law on this point is very unreasonable, requiring the wife to wait for 120 to 100 years, according to the opinions of Imām Abū Ḥanīfah and Abū Yūsuf respectively (H.I, pp. 598, 599). The Shāfi'ī law requires seven years' waiting, while according to Imām Mālik she should wait for four years (H.I, p. 597). The view of Imām Aḥmad ibn Ḥanbal and the Shī'ah view agree with Mālik. This is a more reasonable view. Bukhārī has a chapter on the *Mafqūd* (Bu. 68 : 22), in which there is no tradition of the Prophet relating to the subject proper, but the view of Ibn al-Musayyab is quoted, according to which when a person becomes *mafqūd* in the course of fighting, his wife shall wait for at least a year; and a report is added relating to Ibn Mas'ūd who searched for the husband of a maid-servant of his for one year and then treated him as *mafqūd*, and this was not the case of a man lost in fighting. Under present conditions when communication is so easy, one year would be a sufficient period of waiting for the *mafqūd*.

Husband's right of pronouncement of divorce

Though the Qur'ān speaks of the divorce being pronounced by the husband, yet a limitation is placed upon the exercise of this right. The following procedure is laid down in clear words: ''And if you fear a breach between the two, then appoint an arbiter from his people and an arbiter from her people. If they desire agreement, Allāh will effect harmony between them'' (4 : 35). ''And if they separate, Allāh will render them both free from want out of His ampleness'' (4 : 130). It will be seen that in all disputes between the husband and the wife, which it is feared will lead to a breach, two arbiters are to be appointed from the respective people of the two parties. They are required first to try to reconcile the parties to each other, failing which divorce is to be effected. Therefore, though it is the husband who pronounces the divorce, he is as much bound by the decision of the arbiters as is the wife. This shows that the husband cannot repudiate the marriage at will. The case must first be referred to two arbiters and their decision is binding. The Caliph 'Alī is reported to have told a husband, who thought he had the sole right to divorce, that he would have to abide by the judgement of the arbiters appointed under this verse (Rz. III, p. 320). The Prophet is reported to have intervened and disallowed a divorce pronounced by a husband, restoring the marital relations (Bu. 68 : 1, 2). It was no doubt a matter of procedure, but it shows that the authority constituted by law has the right to interfere in matters of divorce. The only question is as to the procedure to be adopted when the Muslims are living under non-Muslim rule. In such a case, if no judge, has been appointed by the authorities, the appointment of the judges shall be in the hands of the Muslim community, and it may exercise that right in any way it likes. If, therefore, a Muslim government or the Muslim community makes any rules laying down the procedure of divorce and placing such limitations upon the husband in matters of divorce as are not inconsistent with the principles laid down by the Qur'ān, it would be quite Islamic.

Divorce during menstruation

The menstrual discharge is looked upon as pollution in many religions, and the woman who has her courses on is segregated, as among the Hindūs and the Jews. In the Qur'ān, the subject of menstruation is dealt with as a preliminary to that of divorce, and sexual intercourse is prohibited when the courses are on, as it is said to be ''harmful'' (2 : 222). It is owing to this temporary cessation of the sexual relations between the husband and the wife that divorce is prohibited during the period when the menstrual discharge is on. It was brought to the notice of the Prophet that Ibn 'Umar had divorced his wife while she was menstruating. The divorce was declared to be illegal by the Prophet, and Ibn 'Umar was asked to take back his wife (Bu. 68 : 1). Thus divorce is only permitted in the state of *ṭuhr* (when the woman is clear from the menstrual discharge), there being a further condition that the husband and the wife should not have copulated during that *ṭuhr*. Evidently this is meant as a sort of check upon the freedom of divorce.

The 'iddah or *waiting period*

The final breaking off of marital relations is discouraged in many other ways and every chance is afforded to the parties to maintain the conjugal tie, even after differences have arisen leading to divorce. Every divorce must be followed by a period of waiting called the *'iddah*: "O Prophet! when you divorce women, divorce them for their *'iddah (prescribed* or *waiting time*)" (65 : 1). The *'iddah* is about three months: "And the divorced women should keep themselves in waiting for three courses (*qurū'*)" (2 : 228). A *qar'*(pl.*qurū'*) is the entering from the state of *ṭuhr* (cleanness) into the state of menstruation. In normal cases it is about four weeks, but there are variations in the case of different women. In the case of women who do not menstruate as well as those whose courses have stopped, the *'iddah* is three months (65 : 4), and in the case of pregnant women, the waiting period is till delivery (*ibid.*). The *'iddah* among other purposes serves the purpose of affording the parties a chance of reconciliation. Though they are divorced, yet they still live in the same house, the husband being plainly told not to expel the wife from the house in which she has been living unless she is guilty of misconduct, and a similar advice is given to the wife not to leave the house (65 : 1). This injunction clearly aims at restoring amicable relations between the parties. If there is any love in the union, its pangs would assert themselves during the period of waiting and bring about a reconciliation.

Divorce is revocable

In fact, reconciliation is recommended in plain words when, speaking of the *'iddah*, the Qur'ān says: "And their husbands have a better right to take them back in the meanwhile if they wish for reconciliation" (2 : 228). Every divorce is thus an experimental temporary separation during its initial stages, and by making the parties live together, every chance is afforded to them to re-establish conjugal relations. Even after the period of waiting has passed away, the two parties are allowed, even encouraged, to remarry: "And when you have divorced women and they have ended their term of waiting, prevent them not from marrying their husbands, if they agree among themselves, in a lawful manner. With this is admonished he among you who believes in Allāh and the Last Day. This is more profitable and purer of you. And Allāh knows while you do not know" (2 : 232). Remarraige of the divorced parties is thus encouraged and recommended as being more profitable and purer for the parties. The condition is also laid down that such a revocable divorce, allowing reunion of the parties, can be pronounced twice: "Divorce may be pronounced twice: then keep them in good fellowship or let them go with kindness" (2 : 229). Thus the revocable divorce, the *ṭalāq raj'ī* in the terminology of the jurists, can be pronounced twice.

Irrevocable divorce

After the first divorce, the parties have the right to reassert their conjugal relations within the period of waiting, or to remarry after the waiting period is over. A similar right is given to them after a second divorce, but not after a third. Before Islām, however, while the wife had no right of divorce, the husband had an unchecked licence to divorce the wife and to reassert his conjugal rights during *'iddah* as many times as he pleased (Rz. II, p. 372). Thus women were looked upon as mere chattel which could be discarded and taken at will. This had demoralized the whole institution of marriage. Islām not only gave the wife a right of divorce but also checked the husband's licence to divorce as often as he liked, by declaring that revocable divorce could be given only twice: "Divorce may be pronounced twice: then keep them in good fellowship or let them go with kindness" (2 : 229). It was thus laid down that, after the second revocation or remarriage, the parties must make their choice either to live together as husband and wife for ever, or to separate for ever, never thinking of reunion. Hence if even the second experiment failed and the parties were separated by a divorce for the third time, this was an irrevocable divorce, or *ṭalāq bā'in*, in the terminology of the jurists.

Pronouncement of divorce in three forms

The jurists have recognized divorce in three forms. A man would sometimes pronounce divorce thrice on one and the same occasion, and this would be understood as meaning that divorce had been given thrice. This is called *ṭalāq bid'ī* (or an innovation in divorce after the Prophet's time). Or a man would divorce his wife for the first time in one *ṭuhr*, following on with a second divorce in the second *ṭuhr* and with a third divorce in the third, thus divorcing thrice in one *'iddah* or one period of waiting. This method of *ṭalāq* is called *ṭalāq ḥasan* (a good way of divorcing) in the terminology of the jurists. The name *ṭalāq aḥsan* (or the best method of divorcing) is given to the form in which *ṭalāq* is pronounced in a *ṭuhr* only once, and this is followed by the period of waiting (H.I, p. 333). This last method is the only method recognized by the Qur'ān. It is plainly laid down: "O Prophet! When you divorce women, divorce them for their prescribed period (*'iddah*), and calculate the period and keep your duty to Allāh, your Lord" (65 : 1). The divorce is thus to be pronounced only once and when it has been pronounced, the *'iddah*, or waiting period, follows, and during this time the parties have a right to revocation of the divorce. All other forms of divorce are against the Qur'ān and the practice of the Prophet (*Sunnah*).

Subterfuges to make the revocable divorce irrevocable

Thus the Qur'ān recognizes *ṭalāq* only in one form, the *ṭalāq al-sunnah*, or the *ṭalāq aḥsan* of the Ḥanafī jurists. There is no mention at all of the other two forms, either in the Qur'ān or in Tradition. These two forms are, in fact, only subterfuges to make the revocable divorce an irrevocable one. The tendency to resort to these subterfuges is noticeable even in the lifetime of the Prophet. The pronouncing of three divorces without an interval seems to have been a remnant of pre-Islamic days. The Prophet is reported to have shown indignation when it was brought to his notice that a certain person had pronounced three divorces together (Ns. 27 : 6), and a divorce thus pronounced was annulled by him (Ah.I, p. 265). Another report shows that, until the time of 'Umar, people used to pronounce three divorces together, but that these counted as a single divorce (Ah.I, p. 314). 'Umar, in order to restrain people from such an un-Islamic procedure, ordered three divorces given at one time to be reckoned as three separate acts of divorce, taking place at intervals, but this order had the opposite effect to that intended. It became a general practice to pronounce divorce three times on one occasion, and this was supposed to have the effect of three separate acts of divorce, thus making a revocable divorce irrevocable. This is really a negation of the very principle underlying the institution of divorce in Islām. It is true that divorce is allowed, but as it disturbs the normal family relations, it is looked upon with disfavour and is permitted only in extreme cases when the carrying on of marital obligations by the husband or the wife becomes impossible. But even after this extreme step has been taken, not only are the parties still free to resume conjugal relations within the waiting period, or to remarry after that period has expired, but they are actually encouraged to do so. The two forms of divorce, called *bid'ī* and *ḥasan*, take away the freedom to reunite which the Qur'ān has conferred upon the two parties, and they are therefore against the teachings of the Qur'ān and must be discarded. The revocable divorce of the Qur'ān cannot be made irrevocable as, by this change, a death-blow is dealt to the beneficial spirit underlying the institution of divorce in Islām. Hence, whether divorce is pronounced once or thrice or a hundred times during one waiting period, it is only a single divorce, and it is revocable during that period.

Effect of irrevocable divorce

It is clear from what has been stated that irrevocable divorce is the very rarest of things that can happen among Muslims, and it can only occur if the two un-Quranic forms of divorce, to make revocable divorces irrevocable, are brought in. When a man and a woman have found by two experiments that they cannot live together as husband and wife, it is absurd on their part to think of remarriage again. Hence the Qur'ān lays down that they shall not remarry after the second failure of the union, except in one case: "So if he divorces her (for the third time), she shall not be lawful to him afterwards until she marries another husband. If he (the second husband) divorces her, there is no blame on them both if they return to each other (by marriage), if they think that they can keep within the limits of Allāh" (2 : 230). Thus the one case in which marriage with the first husband is allowed, after being divorced for the third time, is that in which a marriage has been contracted with a second husband and that too has proved a failure. If there be such a rare case, the parties to the marriage have probably learned a lesson, through another marital union, to the effect that they should behave better towards each other. An irrevocable divorce, being in itself a rarity according to the teachings of the Qur'ān, a case, like the one spoken of in the verse quoted above, would be a still greater rarity, but still if such a case should arise, the parties are allowed to remarry even after an irrevocable divorce.

Taḥlīl *or* ḥalālah

Taḥlīl or *ḥalālah*, which means *legalizing* or making a thing *lawful*, was a pre-Islamic practice. When the wife was divorced irrevocably, by thrice pronouncing the divorce formula, and the husband wanted to take her back again, she had first to marry a third person on condition that he would divorce her after having sexual connection with her. This was called *ḥalālah*. It is a mistake to confound the *ḥalālah* with the marriage spoken of in the verse quoted under the previous headings, since *ḥalālah* was a kind of punishment for the woman who had to undergo the disgrace of sexual connection amounting practically to adultery, while the marriage spoken of in the previous paragraph is a perpetual marital tie, and the divorce in that case may not follow at all; in fact, in the normal course of things it would not follow at all. It is for this reason that the Prophet cursed those who resorted to this practice, his words being: "The curse of Allāh be on the man who commits *ḥalālah* and the man for whom the *ḥalālah* is committed " (Tr. 9 : 25). The Caliph 'Umar is reported to have said that if there were brought to him two men who took part in the practice of *ḥalālah*, he would treat them as adulterous people. The three divorces, as allowed in the Qur'ān, of which the third is irrevocable, were of very rare occurrence, as such divorces naturally occurred at long intervals. The case of Rukānah is mentioned in the reports; he first divorced his wife in the time of the Prophet, then remarried her and divorced her a second time in the reign of 'Umar, and finally in the caliphate of 'Uthmān (ZM. II, p. 258).

Procedure of divorce

Divorce may be given orally, or in writing, but it must take place in the presence of witnesses: "So when they have reached their prescribed time, retain them with kindness or dismiss them with kindness, and call to witness two just ones from among you, and give upright testimony for Allāh" (65 : 2). Whatever the actual words used, they must expressly convey the intention that the marrige tie is being dissolved. As to whether a divorce would be effective under certain circumstances, there are differences among the various schools of jurists. Evidently, intention is as necessary a factor in the dissolution of marriage as in the marriage itself; but while some recognize that divorce is ineffective if given under compulsion or influence, or in a state of intoxication, or in anger or jest, or by mistake or inadvertence, others hold it to be ineffective in some of these cases and effective in others. The Ḥanafī law recognizes that divorce is effective whether the words be uttered in sport or jest or in a state of drunkenness and whether a person utters them willingly or under compulsion, but Imām Shāfi'ī takes the opposite view (H.I, p. 337). Evidently the Ḥanafī views are against the spirit of the teachings of the Qur'ān which declares divorce to be a very serious matter, and lays down special procedure to be gone through before it is resorted to.

Ilā'

Ilā' and *ẓihār* were two practices of the pre-Islamic days by which the wife was kept in a state of suspense, sometimes for the whole of her life. *Ilā'*, which means literally *swearing*, signifies technically *the taking of an oath that one shall not go into one's wife.* In the pre-Islamic days the Arabs used to take such oaths frequently, and as the period of suspension was not limited, the wife had sometimes to pass her whole life in bondage, having neither the position of a wife nor that of a divorced woman free to marry elsewhere. The Qur'ān reformed this state of things by commanding that if the husband did not reassert conjugal relations within four months, the wife should be divorced: "Those who swear that they will not go into their wives, should wait four months; then if they go back, Allāh is surely Forgiving, Merciful. And if they resolve on a divorce, then Allāh is surely Hearing, Knowing" (2 : 226, 227).

Ẓihār

The word *ẓihār* is derived from ẓahr meaning *back*. An Arab in the days of ignorance would say to his wife *antī 'alayya ka-ẓahrī ummī, i.e.* thou art to me as the back of my mother. This was technically called *ẓihār*. No sooner were these words pronounced than the relation between husband and wife ended as by a divorce, but the woman was not at liberty to leave the husband's house, and remained as a deserted wife. One of the Muslims, Aus ibn Ṣāmit, treated his wife Khaula in a similar manner. The wronged woman came to the Prophet and complained of her husband's ill-treatment. The Prophet told her that he was unable to interfere. She went back disappointed and it was then that he received the following revelation: "Allāh indeed has heard the plea of her who pleads with thee about her husband and complains to Allāh, and Allāh hears the contentions of both of you; surely Allāh is Hearing, Seeing. As for those of you who put away their wives by calling them their mothers — they are not their mothers. None are their mothers save those who gave them birth; and they utter indeed a hateful word and a lie" (58 : 1, 2). The man who resorted to this practice was ordered as a punishment to free a slave; or if he could not find one, then to fast for two successive months, and if unable to do that, to feed sixty poor people (58 : 3, 4).

Li'ān

The word *li'ān* is derived from *la'na* meaning *curse*. *Li'ān* and *mulā 'ana* signify literally *mutual cursing*. Technically, however, the two words indicate that particular form of bringing about separation between the husband and the wife in which the husband accuses the wife of adultery but has no evidence to support the accusation, while she denies it. The Qur'ān makes adultery a severely punishable crime, since it aims at the destruction of the whole social fabric. At the same time it makes an accusation of adultery an equally serious crime, punishable like adultery if strong evidence of adultery be not forthcoming. This is to stop the tongue of slander, which is generally very busy, and does not spare even the most innocent persons. One man has no concern with another's private affairs, but if a man has strong reasons to believe that his own wife is adulterous, the case is quite different. The *li'ān* is suggested in this case, as the means of bringing about separation between husband and wife, for, whether the accusation is right or wrong, it is in the interests of both to get separated. The following verses deal with this subject: "And those who accuse their wives and have no witnesses except themselves let one of them testify four times, bearing Allāh to witness that he is of those who speak the truth. And the fifth time that the curse of Allāh be on him if he is of those who lie. And it shall avert the chastisement from her if she testify four times, bearing Allāh to witness, that he is of those who lie. And the fifth time that the wrath of Allāh be on her if he is of those who speak the truth'' (24 : 6-9). After the parties have thus borne witness, they are separated for ever. It will be noticed that there is no mutual cursing in this case; only each of the parties, while bearing witness of his or her own truthfulness, calls for the curse or wrath of God on himself or herself if he or she tells a lie.

Charitable views of divorce

Divorce is looked upon as a necessity in marital relations, under the varying human conditions, irrespective of moral turpitude on the part of husband or wife. The Qur'ān takes the most charitable view of the necessity for divorce, and therefore recommends as much kindness towards women in the case of divorce as in that of marriage. Again and again stress is laid on this point: ''Divorce may be pronounced twice; then keep them in good fellowship or let them go with kindness (*iḥsān*)'' (2 : 229); ''And when you divorce women and they reach their prescribed time, then retain them with kindness or set them free with kindness'' (2 : 231); ''So when they have reached their prescribed limit, retain them with kindness or dismiss them with kindness (65 : 2). Thus woman is to be treated with equal kindness and generosity, whether she is a sharer in a man's weal or woe as wife, or one from whom he has been compelled to part company. Marital differences, like other differences, may be as often honest as not, but the Qur'ān recommends that the most charitable view of them should be taken.

CHAPTER VII

ACQUISITION AND DISPOSAL OF PROPERTY

Acquisition of individual property

Property may be acquired in three ways, by earning *(iktisạb),* by inheritance *(warāt͟hah)* and by gift *(ḥibah).* Of these, inheritance, on account of its importance, is dealt with in a separate chapter. Acquisition of property by the individual, whether male or female, is recognized by Islām as one of the basic laws regulating human society: "For men is the benefit of what they earn. And for women is the benefit of what they earn" (4 : 32). Both sexes have also an equal right to inheritance of property: "For men is a share of what the parents and the near relatives leave, and for women a share of what the parents and the relatives leave" (4 : 7). No limitation is placed upon the property or wealth which an individual may acquire or give away. The Qur'ān speaks even of heaps of gold being in the possession of a man which he may give away to a woman as her dowry: "And (if) you have given one of them a heap of gold, take nothing from it" (4 :20). Islām is thus opposed to Bolshevism, which recognizes no individual right of property; but it is at the same time socialistic in its tendencies, inasmuch as it tries to bring about a more or less equal distribution of wealth.

Unlawful means of acquiring wealth

All unlawful means of acquiring property are denounced: "O you who believe, devour not your property among yourselves by illegal methods except that it be trading by your mutual consent" (4 : 29); "And swallow not up your property among yourselves by false means, nor seek to gain access thereby to the judges, so that you may swallow up a part of the property of men wrongfully while you know" (2 : 188). The latter verse alludes to bribery. Dacoity and theft are spoken of elsewhere as punishable crimes (5 : 33, 38). Misappropriation is forbidden: "Allāh commands you to make over trusts to those worthy of them" (4 : 58). Gambling is prohibited as being a false or dishonest means of acquiring property: "They ask thee about intoxicants and games of chance. Say, In both of these is great sin and some advantage for men, and their sin is greater than their advantage'' (2 : 219) ''Intoxicants and games of chance ... are only an uncleanness, the devil's work; so shun it that you may succeed'' (5 : 90). Intoxicating liquors and gambling are mentioned together in both places, and one of the reasons for their prohibition is that they are an aid to creating mischief and enmity between members of the same society: ''The devil desires only to cause enmity and hatred among you by means of intoxicants and games of chance'' (5 : 91). All kinds of lotteries and card games etc., involving a stake, however small the sum involved, fall within the definition of games of chance, and are therefore prohibited by Islām. They not only promote habits of indolence and are thus a negation of honest labour, but also reduce some members of society to penury while others prosper at their expense. Usury, which is dealt with later on, is also prohibited for the same reason.

The Qur'ān on the exercise of property rights

The Qur'ān gives full rights of disposal of property to its owner, whether male or female, but at the same time, it requires the owner to be most careful in spending it. There are many injunctions of a general nature to that effect. Thus, speaking of the righteous servants of God (*'ibād al-Raḥmān*) it says: ''And they who, when they spend, are neither extravagant nor parsimonious, and the just mean is ever between these'' (25 : 67). And elsewhere: ''And make not thy hand to be shackled to thy neck, nor stretch it forth to the utmost limit of its stretching forth, lest thou sit down blamed, stripped off'' (17 : 29). But it does not content itself with these general directions, and gives society or the state a right to interfere when money is being squandered by its owner: ''And make not over your property, which Allāh has made a (means of) support (*qiyām*) for you, to the weak of understanding (*sufahā'*), and maintain them out of it, and clothe them and give them a good education'' (4 : 5). Here certain owners of property are called *sufahā'*, and the community or the state is enjoined not to give such people control of their property, which is here described as *your property*, because Allāh has made it ''for you a means of suppport''; and the rule is laid down that these owners of property should be maintained out of the profits of the property, the management being clearly in other hands. Thus wealth, though possessed by individuals, is recognized as a national asset, and a check placed upon the rights of the individual if money in his possession is being wasted. *Sufahā'* is the plural of *safīh* which means *a person deficient* or *unsound in intellect* or *understanding* or *having little or no understanding* (TA., LL.). The commentators make various suggestions as to what is here meant by this word, some saying that it applies to women or children, but Ibn Jarīr rightly points out that this view is wrong, and the word conveys a general significance (IJ-C. IV, p. 153). In fact, minors are not spoken of in this verse at all, since they are mentioned separately in the verse that follows, and the *sufahā'* of this verse are persons who, on account of deficiency or unsoundness in intellect, are unable to manage their own property.

This conclusion is further corroborated by the use of the word *safīh* in connection with the contracting of debts: "But if he who owes the debt is unsound in understanding (*safīh*) or weak (*dza'īf*), or if he is not able to dictate himself, let his guardian dictate with fairness" (2 : 282). Here the *safīh* and the *dza'īf* are mentioned separately; the former signifying the weak in understanding whether male or females, and the latter minors. Thus the Qur'ān requires that persons who, on account of weakness of intellect, mismanage their property and squander their wealth should be deprived of the control of their property and maintained out of its profits, the control being handed over to some peron who is called a *waliyy (guardian)* in 2 : 282.

Ḥajr *or restrictions on disposal of property*

This restriction on the exercise of rights of property by individual owners is spoken of in Tradition collections as *ḥajr* (Bu. 43 : 19), which literally means *what is forbidden*, that being also the terminology of the jurists. Tradition lays great stress on saving wealth from being wasted. Bukhā rī has the following heading for one of his chapters: "There is no charity unless a man has sufficient to give, and whoever spends in charity and he is himself in want or his family is in want or he has a debt to pay, it is more in the fitness of things that the debt should be paid than that he should spend in charity or free a slave or make a gift, and such a gift or charity shall be annulled, for he has no right to waste the wealth of the people (*amwāl al-nās*); and the Holy Prophet has said, "Whoever takes the wealth of the people that he may waste it, Allāh will destroy him, unless he is a man well-known for his patience (ṣabr) so that he prefers others before himself, though poverty may afflict him" (Bu. 24 : 18). Here, the individual property of a man is called the wealth of the people, and a man is prohibited from making even charitable gifts when he does not have sufficient to support those dependent on him. According to tradition the Prophet is reported to have said: "Allāh hates three things in you: useless talk and wasting of wealth and asking or begging (*su'āl*) frequently" (Bu. 24 : 53). This tradition is repeated frequently in the *Bukhārī* and other collections, and forms the basis of restrictions[1] which may rightly be laid on owners of property for their benefit. The State is therefore entitled to make laws for the benefit of owners of property, placing restrictions on them as to the disposal of that property.

Guardian of minor

A guardian is also appointed to deal with the property of minors. The Quranic injunction on this point is as follows : "And test the orphans until they reach the age of marriage. Then if you find in them maturity of intellect, make over to them their property, and consume it not extravagantly and hastily against their growing up. And whoever is rich, let him abstain, and whoever is poor, let him consume reasonably. And when you make over to them their property, call witnesses in their presence; and Allāh is enough as a Reckoner" (4 : 6). A minor is thus not allowed to manage his own property which must be made over to a guardian. If the guardian is rich, he is required to do the work of guardianship honorarily, and if he is poor, his wages would be a charge on the property. The age of majority is eighteen years, according to Abū Ḥanīfah, in the case of males and seventeen in the case of females (H. II, p. 341), but according to Shāfi'ī and Aḥmad, it is fifteen in both cases (H. II, p. 342). In a tradition it is stated that 'Ibn 'Umar was not enlisted in the army when he was fourteen years old but was taken when he was fifteen (Bu. 52 : 18), but this by no means shows that maturity of intellect is attained at fifteen, for at that time there were so few Muslims that could take the field against overwhelming numbers, that boys and old men had to be enlisted perforce.

[1] For example the laws placing restrictions on disposal of agricultural property fall within the definition of *ḥajr*. In this case, the owners of agricultural land are prevented from selling their lands in certain cases, except with the permission of the State: and this measure is in their own interest, for otherwise all agricultural land would gradually pass out of their hands and they would be left without any means of support.

Honest dealing in Business

Subject to what has been stated above and what will be stated further on, the owner of movable property, whether a male or a female, has the right to sell or barter it. The Qur'ān lays stress on honest and straight dealing in the very earliest revelation: "Woe to the cheaters! who, when they take the measure (of their dues) from men, take it fully; and when they measure out to others or weigh out for them, they give less than is due" (83 : 1-3); "And give full measure when you measure out and weigh with a true balance. This is fair and better in the end" (17 : 35); "Give full measure and be not of those who diminish; and weigh things with a true balance, and wrong not men of their dues and act not corruptly in the earth making mischief" (26 : 181-183). Tradition also lays stress on honest dealing, so much so that if there is any defect in a thing it must be pointed out to the intending buyer (Bu. 34 : 19; Ah. III, p. 491). The Prophet himself is reported to have written to 'Addā' ibn Khālid as follows: "This is the writing by which Muḥammad, the Messenger of Allāh, has made a purchase from 'Addā' ibn Khālid, the barter of a Muslim with a Muslim, there is no defect in it nor any deception or an evil" (Bu. 34 : 19). According to another tradition he is reported to have said: "If the two parties speak the truth and make it manifest, their transaction shall be blessed, and if they conceal and tell a lie, the blessing of their transaction shall be obliterated" (Bu. 34 : 19). Honesty and *bona fides* in matters of sale are stressed in a large number of traditions.

General directions relating to sale transactions

The many other details that are met with in Tradition need not be stated here, being but of minor importance; a few only which are of a general nature are briefly noted. Men and women are expressly mentioned as selling to and buying from one another, so that there is not the least sex disqualification in this respect (Bu. 34 : 67). While a transaction is being carried on with a man, another should not intervene (Bu. 34 : 58), but auction is allowed (Bu. 34 : 59). There is no restriction as to whom a man may sell his property, but the withholding of food-stuffs so that they may become dear (*iḥtikār*) is prohibited (Bu. 34 : 54), and so is the inflation of prices in general. The seller of cattle is prohibited from leaving them unmilked some days before selling, so that they may fetch a higher price (Bu. 34 : 64). Sale of fruits or crops before they are in a fit condition to be reaped is deprecated, because it gives rise to disputes (Bu. 34 : 85). In the tradition narrated in this chapter, it is expressly stated that it was not an injunction but an advice. If the fruits on trees are valued, they may be sold (Bu. 34 : 75, 82, 83). Imaginary sales, when there are no goods to deliver, are prohibited (Bu. 34 : 61); neither should one sell what one does not possess (Ah. II, pp. 189, 190). The sale of land is not favoured, and it is recommended that one should not sell his land or house unless he intends to purchase other land or another house with the money (Ah. I, p. 190; III, p. 467). The taking of oaths in sale transactions is expressly forbidden (Ah. V, p. 297).

Mortgage

Mortgage of property, or giving it as security for debt, is also allowed. The Qur'ān expressly allows the giving or taking of a security of which possession is taken by the mortgagee (*rihān-un maqbūdzah*) (2 : 283); and though this case is mentioned in connection with a journey, the words have been taken by all commentators as conveying a general permission, and reliable traditions corroborate this conclusion. It is related that the Prophet himself left his shield as security with a Jew when borrowing some barley from him (Bu. 48 : 1, 2). When a horse was given as a security, the mortgagee was allowed to use it for riding as a compensation for feeding it. Similarly a milch-animal's milk was allowed to the mortgagee when he fed the animal (Bu. 48 : 4). Hence it is evident that when agricultural land or a house is mortgaged with possession, the mortgagee can derive benefit from it when he pays land-revenue or house-tax, or spends money on the upkeep of the property.

Bequest

An owner of property is also allowed to bequeath his property for a charitable object or to anyone excepting a legal heir. This is called *waṣiy-yah*, and the making of a will is specially recommended. The Qur'ān speaks of the making of a will as a duty incumbent upon a Muslim when he leaves sufficient property for his heirs: "It is prescribed for you, when death approaches one of you, if he leaves behind wealth for his parents and near relatives, to make a bequest in a kindly manner; it is incumbent upon the dutiful" (2 : 180). And the Prophet is reported to have said: "It is not right for a Muslim, who has property to bequeath, that he should pass two nights without having a written will with him'' (Bu. 55 : 1). But this duty, or right, is subject to certain limitations. In the first place, not more than one-third of the property can be disposed of by will (Bu. 55 : 2, 3); and secondly, no will can be made in favour of an heir (AD. 17 : 6; Ah. IV, p. 186). But, as expressly stated in the Qur'ān, the making of a will is incumbent only on well-to-do people. This is also mentioned in Traditions (D. 22 : 5). The reason for limiting the bequest to one-third is clearly stated in a tradition: ''That one should leave his heirs free from want is better than that they should be begging of other people'' (Bu. 55 : 2). And the reason for excluding the heirs is that no injustice may be done to certain heirs at the expense of others. A *waṣiyyat* which is against these principles would be ineffective to that extent. It may be added that if a property in respect of which a bequest is made is encumbered with a debt, the debt is payable before the will is executed.[2]

Gift

An owner of property has also the right to dispose of his property by gift (*hibah*). The giving and accepting of gifts is recommended very strongly, and even the smallest gift is not to be despised (Bu. 51 : 1). A gift is allowed in favour of a son, but it is recommended that similar gifts should be made in favour of other sons (Bu. 51 : 12). The husband can make a gift to his wife, and the wife to her husband, or others than husband (Bu. 51 : 14, 15). Gifts from, and in favour of, non-Muslims are allowed (Bu. 51 : 28, 29). A gift may also be compensated (Bu. 51 : 11). The jurists allow a *hibah bi-l-'iwadz*, or gift for a consideration, and also *hibah bi-sharṭi-l-'iwadz*, or a gift made on the condition that the donee shall give the donor some determinate thing in return for the gift (AA.). The gift transaction (*hibah*) is complete when the donee has accepted it and taken possession of the gift. It is not allowed to a person to revoke the *hibah* when it has been accepted by the donee (Bu. 51 : 30). While a will is allowed only to the extent of one-third of the property, no such limitation exists on *hibah*, because in this case the owner divests himself of all rights in the property immediately, while in the case of a will, not the owner but the heirs are deprived.

2 See Chapter VIII for a complete discussion on Inheritance.

Waqf

Waqafa means literally *he was,* or *became, still* or *stationary* or *he continued standing* (LL.), and in law *waqf* is "the settlement in perpetuity of the usufruct of any property for the benefit of individuals or for a religious or charitable purpose" (AA.). Subject to conditions already noted, and those which follow, an owner of property has a right to make his property waqf, or dedicate it to a particular purpose. In *Bukhārī* the traditions relating to *waqf* are given in the book of *Waṣāya* (Wills), though the two differ in many respects. *Waqf,* like gift, takes effect immediately while the will takes effect after the death of the testator, and it differs from both, gift and will, inasmuch as the property which is dedicated remains untouched, not being the property of a particular person, and it is only the income drawn from it that is spent on the particular objects specified in the *waqf* deed. Many cases of *waqf* are reported in Tradition. Abū Ṭalḥah created a *waqf,* the income from which was to be spent on his poor relatives (*aqārib*), and this was done under the Prophet's direction (Bu. 55 : 10). From this it is evident that a man can create a *waqf* for the benefit of his own relatives. It is made clear in another tradition that a man's son or his wife falls within the definition of his relatives (Bu. 55 : 11). The man who creates a *waqf* is allowed to draw from it, for he himself may be its manager (*mutawalli*) as well as anybody else, even though this be not stated in the *waqf* deed (Bu. 55 : 12). Another tradition states that 'Umar created a *waqf* in accordance with the directions of the Prophet in favour of the poor as well as his rich relatives (Bu. 55 : 29). There are other instances on record in which a *waqf* was created for the benefit of the poor as well as the near relatives (*aqrabīn*) (Bu. 55 : 29). The person who creates the *waqf* may also include himself among the beneficiaries of the trust (Bu. 55 : 33).

CHAPTER VIII

INHERITANCE

Reform introduced by Islām

The reform introduced by Islām into the rules relating to inheritance is twofold: it makes the female a co-sharer with the male, and divides the property of the deceased person amongst the heirs on a democratic basis, instead of handing it all over to the eldest son, as is done by the law of primogeniture. The Arabs had a very strong tradition that he alone could inherit who smites with the spear, and therefore they did not give any portion of inheritance to such of the heirs as were not capable of meeting the enemy and fighting in battles (IJC, IV, p. 171). Owing to this tradition, which strongly appealed to people among whom tribal fighting was carried on day and night, not only were all females — daughters, widows and mothers — excluded, but even male minors had no right to inheritance. Woman, in fact was looked upon as part of the property of the deceased (4 : 19), and therefore her right to property by inheritance was out of the question. Even in the Jewish law she had no better position; "There could have been no question in those days of a widow inheriting from her husband, since she was regarded as part of the property which went over to the heirs... Nor could there have been a question about daughters inheriting from their father, since daughters were given in marriage either by their father, or by their brothers or other relatives after the father's death, thus becoming the property of the family into which they married." (*En. J.*, p. 583).

Islām came as the defender of the weaker sex and the orphans, and just when a defensive war against the whole of Arabia was being carried on by a handful of Muslims, the prevailing law of inheritance, which gave the whole of the property to those members of the family who bore arms, was declared to be unjust, and a new law was given which put widows and orphans on a level of equality with those who fought for the defence of the tribe and the country. When the change was first introduced, some of the Companions thought it very hard and complained to the Prophet, saying that they were required to make over half the property to a daughter who did not ride on horseback or fight with the enemy (IJ-C IV, p. 171). The general principle of inheritance is first laid down in the following words: "For men is a share of what the parents and the near relatives leave, and for women a share of what the parents and the near relatives leave, whether it be little or much" (4 : 7).

Inheritance law as contained in the Qur'ān

The law of inheritance is then stated in the following words: "Allāh enjoins you concerning your children: for the male is the equal of the portion of two females; but if there be more than two females, two-thirds of what the deceased leaves is theirs, and if there be one, for her is the half. And as for his parents, for each of them is the sixth of what he leaves if he has a child; but if he has no child and only his two parents inherit him, for his mother is the third; but if he has brothers, for mother is the sixth, after the payment of any bequest he may have bequeathed, or a debt... And yours is half of what your wives leave if they have no child, but if they have a child, your share is a fourth of what they leave after payment of any bequest they may have bequeathed or a debt; and theirs is the fourth of what you leave if you have no child, but if you have a child, their share is the eighth of what you leave after payment of any bequest you may have bequeathed or a debt. And if a man and a woman having no children, leaves property to be inherited and he (or she) has a brother or a sister, then for each of these is the sixth, but if they are more than that, they shall be sharers in the third after payment of a bequest that may have been bequeathed or a debt not injuring others" (4 : 11, 12). "Allāh gives you decision concerning the person who has neither parents nor children. If a man dies and he has no son, and he has a sister, hers is half of what he leaves, and he shall be her heir if she has no son; but if there be two sisters, they shall have two-thirds of what he leaves. And if there are brethren, men and women, then for the male is the like of the portion of two-females" (4 : 177).

The persons spoken of in these verses, as inheriting the property of the deceased, may be divided into two groups, the first group consisting of children, parents and husband or wife, and the second consisting of brothers and sisters. All the persons mentioned in the first group are immediate sharers, and if all three of them are living, all of them have a right in the property, while the members of the second group inherit only if all or some of the members of the first group are wanting. Both groups are capable of further extention: as for instance grand-children, or still lower descendants, taking the place of children; grandparents, or still higher ascendants, taking the place of parents; and uncles, aunts and other distant relatives taking the place of brothers and sisters.

Among the members of the first group, children are mentioned first, then parents, and then husband or wife, and that is the natural order. In the case of children, only a broad principle is laid down — the male shall have double the share of the female. Thus, all sons and all daughters would be equal sharers, the son however having double the share of the daughter. Another example of apparent inequality of treatment of the two sexes is that in which a man leaves only female issue. If there is only one daughter, she takes half the property; if there are two[1] or more daughters, they take two-thirds of the whole, the residue going to the nearest male members, according to a tradition quoted further on. The reason for this is not far to seek. Man is generally recognized as the bread-winner of the family, and that is the position assigned to him in the Qur'ān. Keeping in view his greater responsibilities, it is easy to see that he is entitled to a greater share, and therefore the Qur'ān has assigned to him double the share of the female. In fact, if the responsibilities of the two sexes are kept in view, there is real justice and real equality beneath this apparent inequality.

If there are no members of the first group besides the children, the whole property will be divided among the latter, but if there are other members, then evidently the children take the residue, because the shares of the other members are fixed, one-sixth in the case of each parent and one-fourth or one-eighth in the case of the husband or wife.

Children's children and lower descendants are, as is usual in the language of the Qur'ān, included among the children, but the basis of division will be the immediate descendants. Thus if there are grandsons, they will take the shares of their respective fathers. The case in which there are sons and grandsons should be treated on a similar basis, but here the jurists make a distinction, treating the grandsons as the remoter relatives and therefore not entitled to any inheritance, as long as there is a son. Again a son's daughters, where there is no son, are treated by the jurists not as taking the place of that son who, if alone, would have taken all the property, but as the daughters of the deceased, taking one half in case of a single daughter and two-thirds in the case there are two or more.

[1] The words in the Qur'ān are *fauq ithnatain* which literally mean *above two*, but as the other case mentioned is that of only one daughter, two are included in *fauq ithnatain*. It may be noted that in 4 : 177 only *two* sisters are spoken of and *more than two* are included therein. Thus the two verses read together explain each other — *above two*, in the one case including *two*, and *two* in the other including *more than two*.

But curiously enough, a son's daughter when co-existing with one daughter of the deceased is considered as a sharer in inheritance, the two being treated together as two daughters of the deceased.

The words of the Qur'ān may however be interpreted in a manner which will avoid all such inconsistencies. The issue of a deceased son or daughter would take the place of their father or mother, and would take what their father or mother would have taken if alive. Suppose a person has one daughter only, who dies before her father, but who has got children; then her children would take the share their mother would have got, *ie.,* one-half of the property. Again, where there are several children, some of whom are dead and have left issue behind them, while others are alive, then it is only an equitable principle that the issue of the dead offspring should take the place of their parents, and that is also the natural interpretation of the words of the Qur'ān. Moreover if this interpretation is adopted, the law of inheritance becomes very simple and free from all the complications and inconsistencies which juristic reasoning has in some cases introduced into it. All that is traceable to the Prophet in this case is only a broad principle: "Give the fixed portions (*farā'idz*) to those who are entitled to them, and what remains should go to the nearest male" (Bu. 85 : 6). This tradition does not show at all that the grandson is not entitled to inheritance, if there is a son living; though it is on this that the juristic principle of excluding grandsons is based. The application of the tradition may be illustrated by an example. A man dies leaving two parents and one daughter. The parents will get one-third; one half of the residue will go to the daughter and the remaining half will revert to the father who is the nearest male relative. The selection of the nearest male relative is based on a principle of equity, because it is he who is required to maintain the family.

The case of parents is taken after that of children, each of the parents taking a sixth, if the deceased has children. It is clear from this statement that after the parents have taken one-sixth each, the residue will go to the children and this residue will be divided among them, as laid down above, equally, the son taking double the share of the daughter. If however the deceased leaves only daughters, one-half of the residue shall go to a single daughter, and two-thirds to two or more than two daughters, and what remains shall go to the nearest male relative, according to the tradition quoted above. If the father or the mother is not alive, the grandfather or grandmother shall take his or her place.

The second case in which parents inherit from a deceased person is that in which the deceased leaves no issue. In this case it is said that if the parents are the only heirs, that is there is neither a husband or wife, nor brothers and sisters, the mother takes one-third, the remaining two-thirds evidently going to the father. But if the deceased has no issue but has brothers (or sisters), the mother shall receive only one-sixth. It is not stated here what the father shall get or what the brothers' and sisters' share shall be. The prevalent view is that the presence of the brothers reduces only the mother's share; the remaining five-sixths going to the father. Though, even in this case, the brothers and sisters, if dependent on the father, will benefit by the father's increased share, yet it seems more reasonable that when the share of the mother is decreased on account of the presence of brothers and sisters, the latter should be entitled to a share in the property in their individual capacity.

The latter part of 4 : 12 lends support to this view, where, after specifying portions of the husband and the wife, it is added: "And if a man or a woman having no children (*kalālah*) leaves property to be inherited, and he (or she) has a brother or a sister, then for each of them is the sixth, but if they are more than that, they shall be sharers in the third." The *kalālah* is spoken of here as well as in 4 : 177, where the brothers and sisters take the whole property. The explanation generally adopted is that the brothers and sisters spoken of in 4 : 12 are uterine, while those spoken of in 4 : 177 are full or consanguine. But there are strong reasons for the view that the *kalālah* spoken of in the two places carries a different significance; for while *kalālah* is generally explained by lexicologists as meaning *one who has neither children nor parents*, according to the Caliph 'Umar and Ibn 'Abbās it also means simply *one who has no children* (IJ-C, IV, p. 177; VI, p. 25). Now in 4 : 11, the Qur'ān speaks of an issueless person who has parents as well as brothers or sisters, but it does not there speak of the shares of these brothers or sisters. The conclusion is evident that the share of these brothers and sisters have been mentioned elsewhere. In fact what has been left unexplained in v. 11 has been fully explained in v. 12, and the case of *kalālah* there is the case of inheritance of a person who has no children but who has parents as well as brothers or sisters. According to v. 11, the mother gets one-third if a person has no issue, nor brothers or sisters, and she gets one-sixth if the issueless person has brothers or sisters. This reduction of her share is evidently due to the presence of brothers or sisters, and it is these brothers or sisters, that are spoken of in v. 12, so that the *kalālah* of that verse is the issueless person who has parents. Thus when a person dies without issue but leaves parents, brothers and sisters, according to 4 : 12, get a share which is one-sixth of the deceased's property if there is only one brother or sister, and one-third of it if there are two or more brothers and sisters. And according to 4 : 177, a single sister (of a male deceased) or brother (of a female deceased) is entitled to one-half, two or more sisters to two-thirds, brothers and sisters to the whole property, the male having double the share of the female. This evidently is the case in which the deceased leaves neither issue nor parents.

The case of husband or wife is also dealt with in v. 12. The husband gets one-half if the deceased wife has no issue, and one-fourth if she leaves issue. The wife gets one-fourth if the deceased husband has no issue, and one-eighth if he leaves issue. The share of the husband or the wife, being fixed like that of the portions of the parents, must be taken out first, and the rest of the property will go to the children, or in case there are no children, to brothers and sisters.

Briefly, the inheritance law as laid down in the Qur'ān is this. After the payment of debts and execution of the will, if any, the shares of the parents and husband or wife shall be first taken out; after that the rest of the property shall go to the children, the son having double the portion of the daughter; if there are no children and there are brothers and sisters one-sixth if there is only one brother or sister, and one-third if there are more than one, shall go to them; if the deceased leaves neither children nor parents, the whole of the property, after the husband's or the wife's share has been taken out, shall go to brothers and sisters; if there is a single female, daughter or sister, she shall take one-half of the property, a single brother following the same rule, and if there are two or more daughters or sisters they shall take two-thirds, the residue going to the nearest male relative according to Tradition; if a person entitled to inheritance is dead but leaves behind offspring, that offspring shall take his place, if the father or the mother is dead, the grandfather or grandmother shall take his or her place; all brothers and sisters, whether uterine or consanguine or full, shall be treated equally; if there are no brothers or sisters, the nearest relatives after them, such as father's brothers or father's sisters, shall take their place.

The inheritance law as explained above, on the basis of the Qur'ān, is very simple, and not the least complication arises in its application. It is when the spirit underlying that law is neglected that complication arises. For instance, it is clear that when there are parents and a husband or wife along with the children, the parents and the husband or wife would get their shares first and the rest of the property would go to the children. In case there are two or more daughters only among the children, two-thirds of the residue ought to go to them, the remaining one-third going to the nearest male relative. But the jurists in this case adopt a peculiar course. They allot two-thirds of the whole to the daughters, one-third to the parents and one-fourth or one-eighth to the husband or the wife, as the case may be. This evidently leads to a complication, as the daughter gets two-thirds, parents one-third, husband or wife one-fourth or one-eighth, the total amount of shares being 5/4 or 9/8. This difficulty has been solved by dividing the property into fifteen parts in the first case, and giving 8/15 to the daughters, 4/15 to the parents and 3/15 to the husband, and into 27 parts in the second case, giving 16/27 to the daughters, and 8/27 to the parents and 3/27 to the wife. These are not the shares specified in the Qur'ān, and this is due to neglect of the spirit of the ordinance which, while allowing the whole of the residue, after taking away the shares of the parents and the husband or wife, to the children if they are all sons or sons and daughters mixed, allows them only two-thirds of the residue if they are only daughters, the rest going to the nearest male relative according to Tradition. The jurists' convention goes under the name of *'aul.* The introduction of the *'aul* is, however, due only to an infringement of the real essence of the ordinance relating to the two-thirds share of the daughters.

Similary, the jurists treat a grandson, when the son is dead, as belonging to the second group of inheritors, whereas he really belongs to the same category as the son, because he takes the dead son's share. Suppose a man has three sons, one of whom is dead at the time of the death of his father, but has left children. To deprive these children is to go against all rules of equity, but the jurists are of opinion that the grandsons are excluded by the living sons and are not entitled to their father's share. In fact, if the rule were generally adopted that when a person entitled to a share in an inheritance is dead, his children shall take his place, many of the complications which are the result of juristic reasoning, would disappear. The third point on which, in my opinion, the jurists have gone against the spirit of the Qur'ān, is the distinction between uterine and consanguine and full brothers which is the result of a misconception about the word *kalālah* and which has been fully explained above.

Ḥanafī view of inheritance law

In the Ḥanafī law of inheritance, the heirs are divided into two groups.[2] The first group goes under the name *aṣhāb al-farā'idz* or

[2] See next page.

dhawi-l-furūdz, i.e., those whose shares are specified.[3] These sharers are twelve in number; four males, the father, the grandfather, the uterine brothers and the husband; the eight females, wife, daughter, son's daughter, mother, grandmother, full sister, consanguine sister, uterine sister. The father's share is one-sixth when the deceased leaves a son or a grandson, but he sometimes takes a simple residuary and sometimes both as a sharer and a residuary, the former being the case when he co-exists with a simple sharer such as a husband, a mother or a grandmother, and the latter being the case when he co-exists with a daughter or a son's daughter. The grandfather takes the same share as the father when the father is not living. The uterine brother, if one, takes one-sixth; if there are more than one, they are sharers in one-third. The husband takes one-half when the deceased leaves no children, otherwise one-fourth.

Among the female sharers, the widow takes one-fourth if the deceased leaves no children, otherwise one-eighth. The daughter, when only one, takes one-half; if there are two or more daughters, they are equal sharers in two-thirds. The son's daughter takes one-half, if she is the only one and there is no lineal male descendant; if there are two or more in a similar position, they take two-thirds; co-existing with one daughter only, she takes one sixth. The mother takes one-sixth, if there are children, or two or more brothers or sisters; otherwise one-third. The grandmother takes the mother's share when there is no mother. The full sister or the consanguine sister takes one-half, if she is only one; two or more than two take two-thirds. The uterine sister's share is the same as the uterine brother's.

The second group of inheritors goes under the name of *ahl al-mīrāth* or the heirs who take a residuary interest. The most imporant of these are the *'aṣābah*, or relations on the male side, as the lineal male descendants, the lineal male ascendants, the direct collaterals such as full or consanguine brothers or their sons, or indirect collaterals such as full or consanguine uncles or their sons, or full or consanguine uncles of the father and their sons and so on; and the *dhawi-l-arḥām* or relations connected through females, such as (*a*) the sons and daughters of daughters, (*b*) the father of the paternal grandmother or mother of the paternal grandfather, *(c)* the children of sisters, daughters of full and consqnguine brothers,

[2] For this summarization of the Ḥanafī law of inheritance, I am indebted to Sayyid Ameer 'Alī's *Muhammadan Law.*

[3] *Farā'idz* or *furūdz* being the plural of *farīdza* (lit., *anything made obligatory*) meaning a *portion* or *share made obligatory*. For this reason, the law of inheritance is generally spoken of as *'ilm al-farā'idz*.

sons of uterine brothers and (*d*) paternal aunts and their children, maternal uncles and their children, maternal aunts and their children and uterine paternal uncles and aunts and their children.

Besides, these are recognized (*a*) residuaries for special cause to which class belongs the emancipator of a slave, (*b*) the patron of the deceased, (*c*) heirs by acknowledgement, (*d*) the universal legatee (one to whom the deceased has bequeathed the whole of his property), and lastly the *bait al-māl* or public treasury. The subject is too technical and complicated to be dealt with in a book intended for the layman; and the bare outlines of the law of inheritance according to the jurists, as given above, is sufficient for the purpose of this book. If however the law is applied in its simplicity, as given in the Qur'ān, even the layman will find no difficulty in its application as shown above.

Debts

It will be seen that debts are the first charge on the property of the deceased, as the words "or a debt" in verses 11 and 12 show. The expenses relating to burial are also regarded as a debt which must be paid out of the property of the deceased. The wife's dower, if unpaid, is also a debt and must be paid out of the property before it is divided. In the case of a person who leaves no issue, the words are "or a debt that does not harm others", the implication evidently being that a person who has no children may contract a debt simply to deprive his heirs. The jurists divide debts into three kinds: (*a*) those contracted in health; (*b*) those contracted during illness which ends in death; and (*c*) those contracted partly in health and partly in illness (AA.). All wages due to servants are also included in debts.

Bequest

The legality of a bequest is clearly admitted in both the verses dealing with the law of inheritance. The property left is to be divided "after payment of a bequest that may have been made or a debt" (4 : 11, 12). There is a further injunction, of an earlier date, relating to bequests: "It is prescribed for you, when death approaches one of you, if he leaves behind wealth for parents and near relatives[4], to make a bequest in a kindly

[4] See next page.

manner; it is incumbent upon the dutiful'' (2 : 180). There is also mention of a bequest in a verse which was decidedly revealed later than 4: 11, 12: ''O you who believe, call to witness between you, when death draws nigh to one of you, at the time of making the will, two just persons from among you'' (5 : 106). All these verses afford clear proof that a person can make a will with regard to his property.

There are, however, reliable traditions which place a certain limitation upon the right to make a bequest and, in fact, if no limitations were placed, the injunctions contained in 4 : 11, 12 would be nullified, for there would be no property to be divided among the legal heirs. Sa'd ibn Abī Waqās is said to have made the following report: ''I fell ill in the year in which Makkah was conquered, being almost on the brink of death when the Prophet paid me a visit. I said to him, O Messenger of Allāh! I possess much wealth and my only heir is a single daughter; may I therefore make a will with regard to the whole of my property? The Prophet said, No. I then enquired about two-thirds of it, and he again said, No. I then asked him, if I may give away one-third of my property by will, and he approved of one-third, adding: A bequest of one-third is much, for if thou leavest thine heirs rich, it is better than that thou dost shouldst leave them poor, begging of other people, and thou dost not spend anything with which thou seekest the pleasure of Allāh but thou art rewarded for it, even for the morsel that thou puttest into thy wife's mouth'' (Bu. 85 : 6; M. 26 : 0; Tr. 29 : 1). The same tradition is reported somewhat differently through another channel and, according to this report Sa'd ibn Abī Waqās said: ''The Holy Prophet paid me a visit when I was ill, and he asked me if I had made a will. I said, Yes. He then asked, How much. I said, I have bequeathed the whole of my property to be spent in the way of Allāh. He said, And what hast thou left for thy children? I said, They are in sufficiently good circumstances. He said, Better make a will about one-tenth of thy property. I then continued to ask him for less and less (for the heirs), until he said, Make a will of one-third of property and one-third is much'' (MM. 12 : 20-ii). These reports make it clear that the will spoken of on various occasions in the Qur'ān is a charitable

[4] Generally the words ''for parents and near relatives'' are supposed to be connected with the injunction to make a bequest, the import of the passage thus being that a man who leaves wealth should bequeath it to parents and kindred, and owing to this interpretation the verse is looked upon as being abrogated by 4 : 11, 12. But as already shown, both these verses expressly speak of the bequest and require the property to be divided only after payment of bequest or debt. The interpretation I have adopted makes it consistent with the other verses of the Qur'ān.

bequest, and not a will for the heirs, and that this bequest was to be limited to one-third of the property, so that the heirs might not be deprived of their share of inheritance, the well-being of the heirs being as good a consideration with the law-giver as charity. It may also be added that, according to another tradition, a bequest is not allowed in favour of an heir: "There is no bequest for an heir" (AD. 17 : 6; Tr. 29 : 4; IM. 23 : 6). To this are added in some reports the words "unless the heirs wish it" (MM. 12 : 20-ii). Thus while generally a will can be made only for charitable objects, and not for heirs, it is permissible to make a will in favour of heirs, if they wish it; so that if they have no objection, any arrangement may be made for the disposal of the property by will. Hence if the heirs agree, a man may either divide the whole property by will, or he may leave the property undivided, fixing the shares of the heirs in the income.

Chapter IX

DEBTS

Writing of Debts

The writing down of debts is an ordinance of the Qur'ān: "O you who believe, When you contract a debt for a fixed time, write it down. And let a scribe write down between you with fairness; nor should the scribe refuse to write as Allāh has taught him, so let him write. And let him who owes the debt dictate, and he should observe his duty to Allāh, his Lord, and not diminish anything from it. But if he who owes the debt is unsound in understanding or weak, or if (he) is not able to dictate himself, let his guardian dictate with fairness. And call to witness from among your men two witnesses... And be not averse to writing it whether it is small or large along with the time of its falling due. This is more equitable in the sight of Allāh and makes testimony surer and the best way to keep away from doubts" (2 : 282).

Debtors should be dealt with most leniently: "And if the debtor is in straitness, let there be postponement until (he is in) ease. And that you remit (it) as alms is better for you, if you only knew" (2 : 280).

Leniency towards debtors recommended

These two regulations, the writing down of debts according to the dictation of the debtor in the presence of witnesses and lenient dealing with those in straitened circumstances, are the basis of Islamic regulations on debts and are supplemented by a large variety of detailed directions and recommendations contained in Tradition. The concern of the Prophet for the debtors is reflected in his sayings on this point, of which only a few are as follows: "May Allāh have mercy on the man who is generous when he sells and when he buys and when he demands payment of debt" (Bu. 34 : 16). "The angels received the soul of a person from among those who were before you and asked him if he had done any good. He said, I used to deal leniently with the well-to-do debtor and to remit the debt to one who was in straitened circumstances, so he was forgiven" (Bu. 34 : 17). "Allāh will give shelter to His servant who gives respite to one in straitness or remits to a debtor" (Ah. I, p. 73). "Whoever gives respite to one in straitness or makes a remission in his favour, Allāh will save him from the vehement raging of the heat of Hell'' (Ah. I, p. 327). ''There is no believer but I am nearest to him in this world and the Hereafter ... so any believer who leaves behind him property, his relatives shall inherit whoever they may be, but if he leaves a debt, or a family for whom there is none to care, I am his *maulā* (guardian)'' (Bu. 65, sūra 33, ch. 1). ''I am nearer to the believers than themselves, so whoever of the believers dies and leaves a debt, its payment is on me, and whoever leaves property, it is for his heirs'' (Bu. 69 : 15). These traditions show that the debts of a debtor who is in straitened circumstances and unable to pay must either be remitted or paid by the state.

Insistence laid on payment of debts

While the lender is advised in numerous traditions to be lenient and not to exert undue pressure, and to remit, if the debtor is in straitened circumstances, part, or even the whole, of a debt, the debtor is also told to repay the debt in a goodly and liberal manner (Bu. 40 : 5, 6). In the tradition narrated in these chapters, the Prophet is reported to have said: ''Among the best of you are those who are good in payment of debt.'' The rich, especially, are told not to postpone payment of debt. Postponement in their case is called injustice (*zulm*) (Bu. 38 : 1, 2). The man who contracts a debt intending not to pay it back is condemned (Ah. II, p. 417). The tradition has already been quoted which shows that the payment of debt has preference over spending in charity. In the case of an inheritance, the heirs do not take their shares until all debts have been paid (Ah. IV, p. 136); and when there is a will, the debts must be paid before its execution (Ah. I, p. 79).

Warning against indebtedness

Though the necessity of contracting debts at time is recognised, and the Prophet himself is reported to have done so on occasion, yet he, at the same time, gave warning against being in a state of indebtedness. It is related in a tradition that ''he used to pray very frequently, O Allāh! I seek refuge from faults and debts. A man said to him, O Messenger of Allāh, it is very frequently that thou prayest against being in debt; and he replied, A man when he is in debt speaks and tells lies and makes promises and fails to fulfil them'' (Bu. 43 : 10). According to another tradition, "Anas said that he heard the Prophet often praying, O Allāh! I seek Thy refuge from anxiety and grief, and from lack of strength and indolence, and from niggardliness and cowardice, and from being overcome by debt and the oppression of men" (Bu. 56 : 74). It is also related that when a bier was brought to him, he would enquire if the dead man was in debt, and if so, he would tell his Companions to say funeral prayers over him; and if he was told that he had left something to pay his debts, he would personally lead his funeral prayers (Bu. 69 : 15).

Usury prohibited

It would be seen from what has been stated above that helping those in distress forms the basic outlook of Islām on human society. The prohibition of usury rests on the same basis. Even the earlier revelation at Makkah denounced usury, yet without prohibiting it: "And whatever you lay out at usury, so that it may increase in the property of men, it shall not increase with Allāh; and whatever you give in charity desiring Allāh's pleasure, it is these that shall get manifold" (30 : 39). Prohibition came later, and is contained in the following verses which are among the latest revelations: "Those who swallow usury (*ribā*) cannot arise except as he arises whom the devil prostrates by his touch. That is because they say, Trading is only like usury; and Allāh has allowed trading and forbidden usury" (2 : 275). "Allāh will blot out usury and He causes charity to prosper. And Allāh loves not any ungrateful sinner" (2 : 276). "O you who believe, keep your duty to Allāh and relinquish what remains due from usury, if you are believers. But if you do it not, then be apprised of war from Allāh and His Messenger; and if you repent, then you shall have your capital. Wrong not, and you shall not be wronged" (2 : 278, 279). To these may be added an earlier revelation: "O you who believe, devour not usury, doubling and redoubling, and keep your duty to Allāh that you may be successful" (3 : 129).

Reasons for prohibition

The prohibition of usury is clearly associated in these Quranic verses with charity, for inasmuch as charity is the broad basis of human sympathy, usury annihilates all sympathetic affections. The usurer is compared to one whom the devil has prostrated by his touch, so that he is unable to rise. Such is, in fact, the usurer who would not hesitate to reduce the debtor to the last straits if thereby he might add to his wealth. He grows in selfishness until he is divested of all sympathetic feelings. Usury, moreover, promotes habits of idleness, since the usurer, instead of doing any hard work or manual labour, becomes like a parasite living on others. In the great struggle that is going on between capital and labour, Islām sides with labour, and by its prohibition of usury tries to restore the balance between the two, not allowing capital to enthral labour. It is in reference to the honourable place that Islām gives to labour that the Qur'ān says that "Allāh has allowed trading and forbidden usury," for while trading requires the use of labour and skill, usury does not. To help the distressed one who is in straits is the object of Islām and to reduce him to further straits is the aim of usury, and hence it is that usury is called "war" with Allāh and His Apostle.

Tradition on usury

Tradition is equally emphatic against usury. It condemns not only the usurer but also the man who pays the usury[1] because he helps the cause of usury; and, according to one tradition, the witnesses and the scribe in a usurious transaction are equally blamable.[2] Certain details are also added, describing the exchange of gold with gold and wheat with wheat, and dates with dates, as *ribā'* (usury), unless it is a hand to hand transaction.[3] Another report makes it more clear. Usāma reports that the Prophet said, "There is no *ribā'* unless there is postponement in payment." (Bu. 34 : 79). This shows that only those cases were treated as usury (*ribā'*) in which there was a barter only in name, the transaction being really usurious. Gold was given to a man on condition that he would pay a greater quantity of the same after some time, or wheat was delivered on condition that he would repay a larger quantity of the same. This is clearly a usurious transaction though it was given the apparent form of a sale. It may be added that a case in which the debtor, of his own free-

[1] Bu. 34 : 25.

[2] Ibid., 34 : 24.

[3] Ibid., 34 : 54.

will, paid to the creditor a certain sum over and above the original debt, was not considered a case of *ribā'*.[4] This was a case in which the Prophet himself was the debtor, and when he paid back the debt, he paid something in addition. Such excess is in fact a gift made by the debtor of his own free-will and is not prohibited.

Interest

The basis of the prohibition of usury is undoubtedly sympathetic feelings towards those in distress, but the word used is *ribā'* (lit. *an excess* or *addition)* which means *an addition over and above the principal sum lent* (TA., LL.); and, therefore, though the word is considered by some modern writers to apply only to usurious transactions, it apparently includes all kinds of interest, whether the rate be high or low, and whether the interest is or is not added to the principal sum, after fixed periods. In fact, it would be difficult to discriminate between interest and usury, and indeed all interest has a tendency to assume, ultimately, the form of usury, and becomes oppressive for the debtor, a fact which is borne out by the history of indebtedness in all countries. It is sometimes argued that the prohibition of interest would be a serious drawback in the carrying on of trade and business transactions and also in the execution of important national schemes. It is true that this prohibition, if taken in a broad sense, does not fit in the frame of the modern world conditions, but the high ideal which Islām places before itself is not unworkable, and the great Muslim nation of early days, spread over vast territories, the vanguard of the great nations of the world in the march of civilization, carried the Quranic injunction regarding *ribā'* faithfully into practice. The material civilization of Europe has, however, given rise to conditions in which usury and interest seem to be unavoidable, and so the Muslims were told thirteen centuries before: "The Holy Prophet said, A time will come over people when not a single person will remain who does not swallow down *ribā'* and if there is any one who refrains from it, still its vapour (or dust) will overtake him" (AD. 22 : 3).

[4] AD. 22 : 11.

Deposits in banks or Government treasuries

Such is the time in which we are living, and until a new civilization is evolved which is based on morality and the sympathy of man for man, some solution has to be sought for the great economic questions which confront the Muslim nations. In the forefront of all these questions is the modern banking system. Is this system in conformity with Quranic law which prohibits *ribā'*? Usury is undoubtedly universally condemned today, though it is still rampant in some places and has demoralized both the lenders and the borrowers, but the banking system with its legalization of interest is looked upon as a necesary condition of economic life and in the prevailing conditions this seems to be unavoidable. Not only Muslims living under non-Muslim governments cannot avoid it but even Muslim states seem to be driven to the necessity of employing it. Take only the question of trade, which is, today, no longer a national but an international concern, and it will be found that it is entirely dependent on the banking system. Now the banking system, if it had to be evolved anew, could have been based on a co-operative system in which capital and labour should be sharers in profit as well as in loss; but, as it is, the modern banking system favours capitalism and the amassing of wealth instead of its distribution. For whatever its defects, it is there, and the dust of *ribā'* overtakes the man who does not swallow it, as the tradition says.

Bank deposits

The question of deposits in banks, on which interest is payable, seems to be more or less like the question of trade, a necessity of modern world conditions, which cannot bc avoided. The bank receives the deposits not as a borrower but as a trustee, where money is safe and may be withdrawn in need. But at the same time it does not allow the money to lie idle, and draws some profit from it, the major portion of which again comes in the shape of interest. Out of this profit, the bank pays a certain amount to the depositors, the rate of which depends generally on the economic conditions prevailing in the country concerned, or in the world at large. It does not make over the entire profit either to the shareholders or the the depositors, but carries a certain amount to a reserve fund which it can fall back upon in less profitable years, or in case of loss. So far, therefore, as it is a part of the profits earned by the bank, there is nothing objectionable in it, but that profit itself being largely income from interest, the question of *ribā'* comes in indirectly.

To be on the safe side, a depositor may spend the excess amount which he receives as interest on his deposit for a charitable object.[5] In fact, if the depositor deposits his money with the intent that he would not receive the interest for his personal use, and, on receiving the amount from the bank, he actually makes it over to some charitable institution, he has relinquished the *ribā'*, as commanded by the Qur'ān. The only difference is that he relinquishes it, not in favour of the bank, which takes the place of the borrower in the case of a debt, but in favour of some charity. But still the depositor, who takes the place of the creditor, does relinquish the interest. A little thought will show that, in this case, the person in whose favour the interest should be relinquished is not the bank, or a Government treasury, which does not stand in need of such help, but only charitable institutions which are working for the welfare of the Muslim community as a whole.

Co-operative banks

The co-operative banks are more in consonance with the spirit of the teaching of Islām, as the idea underlying them is the amelioration of the lot of the poor who are thus saved from the clutches of the usurious money-lenders. There is, moreover, this difference between an ordinary bank and a co-operative bank, that the former is generally for the benefit of the rich and the capitalists, and the latter for that of the poor and the labourers. In the co-operative bank, moreover, the shareholders are also the depositors as well as the borrowers of money, and that interest paid to the bank is, more or less, in the nature of a contribution by which the borrower of money is also ultimately benefited.

[5] It was the founder of the Aḥmadiyyah movement who first suggested this course. On account of his great anxiety for the propagation of Islām, he directed that the interest on bank deposits should be spent for the propagation of Islām. He particularly laid stress on the point that insistence on receiving the *ribā'* was called a "war with Allāh and His Messenger" (2 : 27), and that therefore the money so received should be spent on the struggle which was being carried on for the defence and propagation of Islām. The opinion that the amount of interest on bank deposits should be spent on charitable objects was also adopted by the *Jamī'at al-Ulamā'*, a representative body of Muslim theologians in India.

Interest on business capital

Interest on the capital with which a business is run differs a little from ordinary debt. It is in fact a case in which capital and labour are sharers. Islām does not prohibit a partnership in which one person supplies the capital and the other labour. But it requires that both capital and labour shall be sharers in profit as well as in loss. The payment of interest at a fixed rate means that capital shall always have a profit, even though the business may be running at a loss. It is true that when the business is profitable, the rate of interest may be much less than the profit earned, but in all such uncertainties the view-point of Islām is that neither side should have undue advantage or be made to suffer undue loss. If the business is run at a profit, let capital have its due share of the profit, but if it is being run at a loss, let capital also share in the loss. It is sometimes urged that the keeping of an account of profit and loss is impracticable, but this is really not the case, as every businessman must keep an account of profit and loss, if only for the purpose of taxation. Similar accounts are also kept by all joint-stock companies, and there is not the least difficulty in keeping them. This method is more advantageous for the general welfare of the community than the method of charging interest on capital, which promotes capitalism and is unjust to labour.

State borrowings

Borrowing by a state or a company for the purpose of executing large-scale projects stand on a different basis. In such cases the shareholders who supply the capital are generally paid a dividend, which is caluculated on the basis of profits. But sometimes the shareholders are paid a fixed rate of interest. The question is whether these cases would come under the Quranic prohibition of *ribā'*? The rate of interest is no doubt fixed, but still this interest is paid out of the profits and is generally a part of the profits. Occasionally the profits of the concern may be less than the amount of interest paid, or there may even be a loss, but in such cases there is a reserve fund to fall back upon. It cannot, however, be denied that the payment of a varying dividend is more in accord with the spirit of the teachings of Islām than the payment of a fixed rate of interest.

Chapter X

GENERAL REGULATIONS

SEC. 1 — FOODS

Islām promotes cleanliness

In addition to rules and regulations for the perfection of self and for the better relations of man with man, there are certain restrictive regulations of a general nature the object of which is to teach man the ways of clean living. These regulations relate to foods, drinks, dress and a number of other things, and have both a physical and a moral value. It is a recognized fact that the food which a man eats, or even his dress, affects not only his constitution but also the building up of his character, and hence in a complete code of life it was necessary that men should be taught ways of clean eating, clean drinking, clean dressing, clean appearance and clean habits of all kinds. These regulations are sometimes obligatory but very often of a recommendatory nature.

General rules regarding food

The first general rule regarding foods, and which applies to drink as well, is laid down in the following words in the Qur'ān: "O men, eat the lawful and good things from what is in the earth" (2 : 168).[1] The first condition therefore is that the food and drink should be lawful. Lawful things are not only those which the law has not declared to be forbidden, but even unforbidden things become unlawful if they are acquired unlawfully, *e.g.*, by theft, cheating, bribery, etc. The other condition is that it should be good (*ṭayyib*).[2] The word *ṭayyib* carries the significance of *pleasant, delightful, delicious* or *sweet,* and *pure* or *clean* (LL.). An

[1] The Arabic word for lawful is *ḥalāl,* and that for good things *ṭayyib. Ḥalla* means *he untied* or *undid a thing,* and hence *ḥill* or *ḥalāl* means *being free* or *allowable.*

[2] This word is derived from *ṭāba* which means *it was good, pleasant, delightful, delicious* or *sweet,* or *it was considered to be so,* or *it was* or *became pure* or *clean.*

impure or unclean thing or a thing which offends good taste should, therefore, not be used as an eatable. The same rule applies to drinks.

Moderation recommended

The above rule, to avoid unlawful and unclean things, is supplemented by two other equally important directions of a general nature. The first is an interdiction against excess "And eat and drink and be not prodigal; surely He loves not the prodigals" (7 : 31). Immoderation may either be in the taking of diet, when one over-loads the stomach with food, or may be in the taking of particular kinds of food. Any food, however good, is injurious to health if taken in excess. Moderation in eating is a guarantee of health. And just as overfeeding spoils the system, underfeeding undermines the health. Hence the direction is given: "O you who believe, forbid not the good things which Allāh has made lawful for you and exceed not the limits" (5 : 87). In these words, all self-denying practices, by which a man either deprives himself of the necessary quantity of food or of certain kinds of food are denounced. Good things which are helpful in building up the system should not be denied.

Prohibited foods

Four things are expressly prohibited in the Qur'ān: "O you who believe, eat of the good things that We have provided you with, and give thanks to Allāh, if He it is Whom you serve. He has forbidden you only that which dies of itself, and blood and the flesh of swine, and that over which any other name than that of Allāh has been invoked. Then whoever is driven to necessity, not desiring nor exceeding the limit, no sin is upon him; surely Allāh is Forgiving, Merciful" (2 : 172, 173). The same prohibition had already been revealed in 16 : 115, while the Prophet was yet at Makkah, in nearly the same words, whereas in 6 : 146, another Makkah revelation, reasons are added for the prohibition, and 5 : 3, which is the latest revelation on the point, adds several things by way of explanation.

The prohibited foods thus are:

1. That which dies of itself.[3] According to 5 : 3, the following are included: "The strangled animal, and that beaten to death and that killed by a fall and that killed by goring with the horn, and that which wild beasts have eaten."[4]

2. Blood, explained as "blood poured forth" in 6 : 146.[5]

3. Flesh of swine: This was also forbidden by the law of Moses (Lev. 11 : 7). Jesus Christ, like a true Jew seems to have held the swine in abhorrence: "Neither cast ye your pearls before swine" (Mt. 7 : 6). He is also reported to have cast out a number of unclean spirits which he then allowed to go into a herd of swine, causing it to perish thereby (Mt. 8 : 30 - 32; Mk. 5 : 11-13). This shows that he looked upon the animal as unclean. St. Peter compares sinners who relapse into evil to swine who go again to wallow in the mire after they are washed (2 Pet. 2 : 22).

4. The fourth kind of forbidden food is that over which any other name than that of Allāh has been invoked at the time of slaughtering it. In 5 : 3 "what is sacrificed on stones set up (for idols)" is added, and it evidently comes under this description.

The Qur'ān speaks of the first three forbidden foods, carrion, blood and pork, as unclean things, while the fourth the invocation of other than Allāh's name at the time of slaughtering an animal, is called *fisq* or a transgression of the Divine commandment. The reason for this distinction is that there is uncleanness in the case of first three, since they have a pernicious effect upon the intellectual, the physical or the moral system; while in the fourth case, the spiritual side is affected, as the invocation of other than Allāh's name, or sacrificing for idols, associates one with idolatry. In this case the thing is not unclean in itself, like blood or carrion or pork; it is forbidden because the use of such food associates a man with idolatry.

[3] The flesh is prohibited, but the skin may be used. The Prophet saw a dead goat of which the skin had not been removed and said that what was unlawful thereof was the flesh, and that there was no harm in profiting by its skin (Bu. 72 : 30). From this may be concluded that other parts, such as bones, may, also be made use of.

[4] "That which died of itself and that which was torn by beasts" were forbidden by the law of Moses also (Lev. 17 : 15).

[5] This was also forbidden by the law of Moses (Lev. 7 : 26).

Slaughtering of an animal

According to the law of Islām, all animals that are allowed as food must be slaughtered[6] in such a manner that blood flows out. The approved method is to cut off the *windpipe*, the *oesophagus* and the *two external jugular veins.*[7] The idea underlying this particular manner of slaughter is causing the blood to flow so that the poisons contained in it should not form part of food.[8] The same appears to be the reason for prohibition of blood as food. Fish, or other watergame does not require to be slaughtered,[9] and it is allowed irrespective of who has caught it; so also fish which has been thrown out by the sea or river on dry land or which has been left by the water having receded from it,[10] and which has therefore died before it is caught, provided it is not spoiled.

Invoking the name of God on slaughtered animal

It should be further noted that, when an animal is slaughtered, it is necessary that the name of God should be invoked. The Qur'ān lays down plainly: "And eat not of that on which Allah's name has not been mentioned, and that is surely a transgression" (6 : 122). Hence it is necessary that at the time of slaughtering an animal, the following words should

[6] The Arabic word for slaughter is *dhabaḥa* which means originally *he cut* or *divided lengthwise: in a general sense, he killed* or slaughtered, and technically *he slaughtered* an animal *in the manner prescribed by law* i.e., *by cutting the two external jugular veins,* or by *cutting the throat from beneath, at the part next to the head* (LL.). In the Qur'ān however, this word is used in a general sense, while the technical word for slaughtering an animal for food in a particular manner is *tadhkiyah* which occurs in 5 : 3. *Tadhkiyah* is the intensive form of *dhak-an* or *dhakā'* which is originally applied to the *burning* or *flaming of fire, and dhakka-l-nār* means *he made the fire to burn* (LL.). According to the same authority, the proper significance of *tadhkiyah* (the infinitive form of *dhakkā*) *is the causing of the natural heat to pass forth,* but it is used peculiarly in the law to signify *the destroying of life in a particular manner,* being the same as *dhabḥ*.

[7] The Arabic equivalent for these are *ḥulqūm, mārī'* and *wadajān* respectively. See H. II, p. 421.

[8] *Jhatkā* or killing the animal by one stroke does not allow the blood to flow forth, and it is therefore not allowed to the Muslims. Similar is the case with all other methods of killing in which blood does not flow out completely.

[9] Bu. 72 : 12.

[10] "Lawful to you is the game of the sea and its food" (5 : 96), where "food" as distinguished from "game" is explained in traditions (Bu. 72 : 11) as fish thrown out on dry land or found after the water has receded, provided it is not spoiled (Bu. 72 : 11, 12).

be pronounced: *Bismillāh Allāhu Akbar* — In the name of Allāh, Allāh is the Greatest of all. This practice is traceable to the Prophet.[11] If the man who slaughters the animal forgets to pronounce these words, the flesh of the animal is allowed,[12] but if he omits the words intentionally, there is a difference of opinion. Imām Shāfi'ī *allows it even in this case against the Ḥanafī view.*[13] In slaughtering an animal, any sharp instrument may be used which causes the blood to flow, and the flesh of an animal which was slaughtered by a maid with a stone was allowed.[14] The food of the followers of the Book is expressly allowed in the Qur'ān: "And the food of those who have been given the Book is lawful for you, and your food is lawful for them" (5 : 5). A Muslim may therefore invite the followers of the Book to his own table and he may eat at their table. But Tradition makes it further clear that the animal slaughtered by the followers of the Book (*Ahl al-Kitāb*) is allowed in this verse. Zuhrī adds the condition that, if the slaughterer is heard uttering a name other than that of God, the flesh is not be be eaten, but if he is not so heard then it is lawful for the Muslims to eat it.[15] An animal slaughtered by an uncircumcised person is also allowed.[16] As stated elsewhere, the words *Ahl al-Kitāb* are applicable to followers of all revealed religions, including the Magi, the Hindūs, etc. A certain food (cheese) prepared by the Māgi was allowed by the Prophet, though he was told that in its preparation use had been made of what died of itself; and he only said: "Mention the name of Allāh over it.[17] *Dhabīḥat al-A'rab* — Animals slaughtered by desert Arabs — is the heading of one of Bukhārī's chapters, and under this is mentioned a tradition from 'Ā'ishah, according to which certain people came to the Prophet and enquired of him about meat which was brought to them by other people, about which they did not know whether the name of God had been mentioned over it or not. The Prophet's

[11] Bu. 72 : 16; Ah. III, pp. 115, 183. Aḥmad speaks of both *tasmiyah* (saying *bismillāh*) and *takbīr* (saying *Allāhu Akbar*), while Bukhārī speaks only of mentioning the name of Allāh, which in fact includes both *tasmiyah* and *takbīr*.

[12] Bu. 72 : 15.

[13] H. II, p. 419.

[14] Bu. 72 : 18.

[15] Bu. 72 : 21.

[16] Ibid.

[17] Ah. I, p. 302.

reply was: "Mention the name of Allāh over it and eat it" (Bu. 72 : 21). This gives a wide latitude in doubtful and difficult cases where a Muslim must depend on food provided or prepared by other people.

Game

The Qur'ān expressly allows game: "The good things are allowed to you and what you have taught the beasts and birds of prey, training them to hunt — you teach them of what Allāh has taught you; so eat of that which they catch for you, and mention the name of Allāh over it" (5 : 4). Tradition[18] makes it clear that the name of Allāh is to be mentioned when letting off the beast or bird of prey. The animal caught may be eaten even though it is killed by the beast or bird of prey. The killing of game by throwing pebbles and hazel-nuts is however forbidden. Killing it by arrow is allowed, since the arrow causes the blood to flow. Game shot with a gun must follow the same rule, but in both cases the *bismillāh* must be uttered before letting off the arrow or firing the gun, and if the game is killed before it is caught and slaughtered, there is no harm. As regards the game of sea or water, it is all to be taken as slaughtered.

Prohibitions in Tradition and Jurisprudence

According to Tradition, the Prophet prohibited all beasts of prey with a *nāb* (the canine tooth) and all birds of prey with a claw.[19] The tame ass is also prohibited, but not the wild ass which is allowed,[20] the mule is prohibited but not the horse.[21] Dhabb (lizard) is not prohibited, but the Prophet did not eat it when it was brought before him.[22] In one tradition it is said that the Prophet did not eat the hare, though he did not prohibit it,[23] as if he did not like it personally, but this is the view of 'Abd Allāh ibn 'Umar and some others as against the universal view; and Bukhārī has a clear report that when the hare was hunted by Abū Ṭalḥah and he sent a part of it to the Prophet, it was accepted by him,[24] and therefore there is no reason to suppose that he disliked it. To the list of prohibitions

18 See Bu. 72 : 1, 4, 5, 8 and 12 for the contents of this paragraph.

19 72 : 28; AD. 26 : 32.

20 Bu. 56 : 130; 28 : 3.

21 AD. 26 : 25.

22 Bu. 51 : 7.

23 AD. 26 : 26.

24 Bu. 72 : 32.

mentioned in Tradition, the jurists add hyenas, foxes, elephants, weasels, pelicans, kites, carrion-crows, ravens, crocodiles, otters, asses, mules, wasps and all insects.[25] As shown at the very outset of this section, among things which are allowed much depends on personal likes and dislikes; a thing which may be good (*ṭayyib*) as food for one man or one people may not be so for another. Certain things may be good and even useful as food, but their use might be offensive to others; it was due to this that the Prophet said that whoever ate raw onions and garlic, he should not approach the mosque,[26] because the odour would be offensive to others; but there is no harm in taking them in a cooked form,[27] or in some other form in which it may not give an offensive odour, or on occasions when one is not likely to appear in public.

Good manners in eating

It is recommended[28] that hands should be washed before the taking of food and after finishing it, and that when one begins a meal, he should do so with the pronouncement of *bismillāh*, and that when he finishes it he should give thanks to God or say *al-ḥamdu li-llāh*.

In another tradition,[29] the man who gives thanks to God after taking a meal is compared to the man who fasts and is patient in suffering. It was the Prophet's practice to cleanse the mouth with water after taking food.[30] There is also a direction that a man should eat with the right hand.[31] To blow on food or drink is prohibited.[32] Taking of food when in a reclining posture is not recommended,[33] nor eating and drinking while standing,[34] but Bukhārī reports that 'Alī intentionally drank water while standing, and added that people did not like it but he had seen the Prophet drinking water while standing.[35] It is also regarded as good manners in eating that a man should take only so much in his plate as not to leave anything on it after eating,[36] and that he should take a morsel from what lies near his

[25] H. II, p. 424.
[26] Bu. 10 : 160.
[27] Tr. 24 : 14, Ah. I, p. 15.
[28] AD. 26 : 11; Bu. 70 : 2, 54.
[29] Bu. 70 : 56.
[30] Bu. 70 : 52.
[31] Bu. 70 : 2.
[32] Bu. 70 : 24; Ah. I, 309, 357.
[33] Bu. 70 : 13.
[34] Ah. III, p. 199.
[35] Bu. 74 : 15.
[36] Ah. III, p. 177.

hand.[37] Of the Prophet it is related that he would never find fault with the food which he was offered; if he liked it he would eat of it, and if he disliked it he would leave it.[38] There is nothing to show that helping oneself with a spoon or a knife is disapproved of. On the contrary, the Prophet is spoken of as helping himself with a knife to cut cooked meat.[39] Feeding the hungry when one sits at a meal is also regarded as good manners in eating.[40] Eating and drinking in vessels of silver and gold was prohibited,[41] because it is a luxury which can be enjoyed by the rich at the expense of the poor, and is against the democratic spirit of Islām.

Entertainments

For fostering good relations it is recommended that a man should have no hesitation in eating at the house of his relatives or friends: "There is no blame ... that you eat at your houses or your fathers' houses or your mothers' houses or your brothers' houses, or your sisters' houses, or your paternal uncles' houses, or your paternal aunts' houses, or your maternal uncles' houses, or your maternal aunts' houses, or houses whereof you possess the keys, or your friends' houses" (24 : 61). Apparently, it is meant that among near relatives and close friends, one may eat at another's house if the time has arrived for a meal, though he may not have been invited beforehand. Stress is laid on the acceptance of an invitation to a feast: "The Prophet said, When a person is invited and he does not accept (or reply), he disobeys Allāh and His Messenger".[42] Entertainment of guests is also emphasized.[43] It is stated that when the Prophet came to Madīnah, he sacrificed a camel or a cow (to feast his friends);[44] from this it is concluded that when a person comes home from a journey, he should entertain his friends at meals. Inviting the followers of other religions, and accepting their invitation, is expressly spoken of in the Qur'ān: "And the food of those who have been given the Book is lawful for you, and your food is lawful for them" (5 : 5). The Qur'ān speaks of eating together or separately as one likes: "It is no sin in you

[37] Bu. 70 : 3.
[38] Bu. 70 : 21.
[39] Bu. 10 : 43; Tr. 24 : 32.
[40] Bu. 70 : 1, 11.
[41] Bu. 70 : 29; 74 : 26, 27.
[42] AD. 26 : 1.
[43] AD. 26 : 4.
[44] AD. 26 : 3.

that you eat together or separately" (24 : 61). Tradition recommends social functions in which people should eat together: "Gather together at your meals, you will be blessed therein".[45] The levelling influence of Islām asserts itself even in eating, and it is recommended that a servant may be seated at the same table as his master, or at least he should be given a part of the food which the master eats.[46] Islām therefore allows no distinction between superiors and subordinates in sitting at the same table at meals, as in standing in the same row at prayers. In its physical as well as spiritul aspects, it is essentially the religion of democracy.

SEC. 2 — DRINKS

Intoxicating liquors

The drink prohibited in the Qur'ān is described under the name *khamr.*[47] *Khamr* is differently explained as meaning *what intoxicates, of the expressed juice of grapes,* or *the juice of grapes when it has effervesced and thrown up froth, and become freed therefrom and still*, or it has common application to *intoxicating expressed juice of anything*, or *any intoxicating thing that clouds* or *obscures the intellect* (LL.). And it is added: "The general application is the more correct, because *khamr* was forbidden when there was not any *khamr* of grapes, the beverage of its inhabitants being prepared only from dates in Madīnah... it is sometimes prepared from grains" *(ibid.)*. The wider sense of *khamr*, as prepared from other things besides grapes, is borne out by the Qur'ān as quoted in the next paragraph. According to 'Umar, wine, when prohibited, was made of five things, grapes, dates, wheat, barley and honey.[48] Hence *khamr* is intoxicating liquor prepared from anything.

Intoxicating liquors are first spoken of in deprecatory terms towards the close of the Makkah period: "And of the fruits of the palms and the grapes, you obtain from them intoxicants and goodly provision"

[45] AD. 26 : 15.

[46] Bu. 70 : 55.

[47] *Khamara* originally means *it veiled* or *covered*,or *concealed a thing* from the same root as *khimār* which means a *woman's head-covering* and wine is called *khamr* because *it veils the intellect*.

[48] Bu. 74 : 4.

(16 : 67). Intoxicants are here spoken of in contrast to goodly provision. The prohibition against their use, however, belongs to the Madīnah period and the earliest revelation on this point is that contained in the first long chapter revealed at Madīnah: "They ask thee about intoxicants and games of chance. Say: In both of them is great sin and some advantage for men, and their sin is greater than their advantage" (2 : 219). This was the first stage in the prohibition of wine, but it was more of a recommendatory nature as it only says that the disadvantages of the use of intoxicating liquors preponderate over their advantages. The next stage was that in which the Muslims were prohibited from coming to mosques while intoxicated: "O you who believe, Go not near prayer when you are intoxicated until you know what you say" (4 : 43). Finally, intoxicating liquors were definitely forbidden: "O you who believe, intoxicants and games of chance and sacrificing to stones set up and dividing by arrows are only an uncleanness, the devil's work; so shun it that you may succeed" (5 : 90). These three stages of the prohibition of wine are clearly mentioned in a tradition.[49] On the last of these occasions, a proclamation was made by command of the Prophet that wine was prohibited, and people who heard the proclamation emptied their stores of wine immediately,[50] so that wine flowed in the streets of Madīnah.[51]

As wine is prohibited on account of its intoxication, it is stated in tradition that every intoxicant is prohibited (*kullu muskir-in ḥarām-un*) (Bu. 64 : 62). Herbs and drugs taken for their intoxicating effect and all other intoxicating things are therefore also forbidden; only a drink that does not intoxicate is allowed. The Prophet was questioned about *bit' — an intoxicating beverage made of honey* (LL.) — and he replied, "Every drink that intoxicates is prohibited" (Bu. 74 : 3). It is further related that Abū Usaid invited the Prophet to a wedding feast at which his wife, the bride herself, served food, and at this feast a beverage of dried dates, over which only one night has passed, was used and there was no objection,[52] because it had not become intoxicant. Mālik ibn Anas was asked about *fuqqā' — a beverage made of barley* or *a kind of beer* (LL.) ... and he said: "So long as it does not intoxicate there is no harm" (Bu. 74 : 3). *Nabīdh*, or fresh juice of grapes over which not more than a night or a day had passed, is also allowed. Thus certain people are spoken of as

49 Ah. II, p. 351.

50 Bu. 74 : 2; 46 : 21.

51 Ah. III, p. 217.

52 Bu. 74 : 8.

having come to the Prophet and asked him what to do with their grapes, and he told them to dry them and then make use of their juice in the evening if they were wet in the morning, and in the morning if they were wet in the evening.[53] But when a beverage becomes intoxicant, even a small quantity of it, that could not intoxicate, is not allowed: "That of which a large quantity intoxicates, even a small quantity of it is prohibited" (AD. 25 : 5). The question whether a very small quantity may be given as a medicine is quite different. It is true that there is a tradition according to which one, Ṭāriq ibn Suwaid, was ordered by the Prophet not to make wine, and when he said that he made it to be used as a medicine, the Holy Prophet replied that it was not a medicine (*dawā'*) but a disease (*dā'*).[54] But this prohibition was, in all likelihood, directed only against the making of wine; and as Navawī, the famous commentator of *Muslim*, explains, in a serious case, when life was in danger, wine could be used to save life, for even carrion and flesh of swine could be used in such a case. It may be added here that trading in wine was also prohibited by the Prophet,[55] and indeed it was necessary to prohibit both the preparing of wine and trading in it when the use of it was no longer permitted.

SEC. 3 — TOILET

Toilet and cleanliness recommended

The Qur'ān lays down a general rule on toilet as follows: "Say, who has prohibited the adornment (*zīnat*) of Allāh, which He has brought forth for His servants, and the good provisions?" (7 : 32). The word *zīnat*, in this verse, has generally been understood to mean apparel, but it has really a wider significance including both the dress and make-up of person. *Zīnat* has further been explained as including spiritual adornment, such as knowledge and good beliefs; bodily adornment, such as strength and tallness of stature; and extrinsic adornment such as wealth and dignity (R.). A good toilet is recommended even when going to a

[53] AD. 25 : 10.

[54] M. 36 : 3.

[55] Bu. 34 : 24.

mosque: "O children of Adam, Attend to your adornment at every time of prayer" (7 : 31). The Qur'ān lays the greatest stress on cleanliness and literally gives it a place next to godliness when it says in one of the earliest revelations: "O thou who wrappest thyself up, arise and warn, and thy Lord do magnify, and thy garments do purify and uncleanness do shun" (74 : 1 -5). Great stress is laid on outward as well as on inward purity throughout the Qur'ān.

Clothing

No limitations are placed upon the form or quality of clothing, either in the Qur'ān or in Traditions. The Prophet is reported to have said: "Eat and drink and wear clothes and be charitable, not being extravagant or self-conceited" (Bu. 77 : 1). Ibn 'Abbas said: "Eat what you like and wear what you like, so long as you avoid two things, extravagance and vanity" (*ibid.*). Thus Islām requires no particular dress. A man may choose what he eats and what he wears. The only thing required is that the clothes should be clean and good.[56] Anything which may serve as a covering for the body is allowed. A simple sheet or trousers or shorts may serve the purpose, and so a shirt or a coat or a loose coat,[57] so long as it covers the *'aurah* (the parts which it is necessary to cover). The *'aurah* is defined thus: "The part or parts of the person which it is indecent to expose; in a man, what is between the navel and the knee, and in a free woman, all the person except the face and the hands as far as the wrists" (LL., TA.). Silk is forbidden to men but women are permitted to wear it,[58] which shows that silk is not discarded for men on account of any impurity attaching to it, but because the wearing of it is not in consonance with the hard life which men have to lead to earn their living, and also because it is a luxury, and the money thus wasted would be better spent on the amelioration of the condition of the poor. In some cases even men were allowed to wear silk. Thus, a Companion of the Prophet is reported as wearing *khazz*,[59] which is explained as being a *cloth woven of wool*

[56] AD. 31 : 13.

[57] Bu. 8 : 9.

[58] Bu. 23 : 2; 34 : 40; 77 : 12; 77 : 30.

[59] Ah. IV, p. 233.

and silk and *also a cloth woven entirely of silk.*[60] The same is related of another Companion, who at the same time remarked that the Prophet had said that on whomsoever God bestowed a favour, He also loved to see the effect of that favour on him.[61] To 'Abd al-Raḥmān and Zubair the wearing of silk was allowed on account of itching.[62] Once a silk garment was presented to the Prophet and he wore it and said his prayers in it; but afterwards he took it off, as though he did not like it.[63] Those who wear long garments or trail the train of the garment, in order to be looked at or for vanity, are censured.[64]

The make-up of a man or a woman, like his or her clothes, is a matter of choice. Very long hair, in the case of men, was not approved.[65] There is an injunction to cut off the hair after the pilgrimage is over, and therefore there is no sin in keeping the hair cut. One may have his head shaved or keep his hair long or short. The Prophet is himself reported to have worn his hair in different ways.[66] Trimming of the beard and clipping short the moustaches is, however, recommended,[67] as also the removal of superfluous hair under the navel or in the armpits.[68] The use of perfumes is recommended in many traditions,[69], especially on Fridays when there is an assemblage of people,[70] and to women in particular.[71] While women may make use of any ornaments they like,[72] men are allowed only the wearing of a seal-ring, the Prophet himself wearing one which was made of silver and was used to seal letters.[73]

60 LL., TA.
61 Ah. IV, p. 438.
62 Bu. 77 : 29.
63 Bu. 77 : 12.
64 Bu. 77 : 4, 5.
65 Ah. IV, p. 180.
66 AD. 32 : 8, 9.
67 Bu. 77 : 65.
68 Bu. 77 : 64.
69 Bu. 77 : 74, 78, 79, 80, 81.
70 Bu. 11 : 3, 6.
71 Bu. 6 : 12, 14.
72 Ah. IV, p. 392; AD. 33 : 8.
73 Bu. 3 : 7.

CHAPTER XI

PENAL LAWS

Ḥudūd

The penal laws of Islām are called *ḥudūd*[1] in the Tradition and Jurisprudence books. In the parlance of jurists, the word *ḥudūd* is limited to punishment for crimes mentioned in the Qur'ān or the Tradition, while other punishments left to the discretion of the Imām or the ruler are spoken of as *ta'zīr* (lit., *chastisement*).[2]

It should be pointed out at the very beginning of a discussion on the penal laws of Islām, that all violations of Divine limits *in a general sense* are not punishable by the state; punishment is inflicted only in those cases in which there is violation of other people's rights. For instance, neglect of prayer, or omission to keep fasts or perform pilgrimage is not punishable; but in the case of zakāt there is difference. Zakāt is a charity as well as a tax, and the Prophet appointed official collectors to collect the zakāt, which was received in the state treasury (*bait al-māl*), thus showing that its collection was a duty of the Muslim state. Hence it was that when, after the death of the Prophet, certain Arab tribes refused to pay, Abū Bakr the first Caliph sent out troops against them, this step being taken because the withholding of zakāt on the part of an entire tribe was tantamount to rebellion.

General law of punishment

The punishable crimes in Islamic law are those which affect society; and those spoken of in the Qur'ān are murder, dacoity or highway

[1] This word is the plural of *ḥadd*, which means *prevention, hindrance, restraint, prohibition* and hence a *restrictive ordinance*, or *statute of God, respecting things lawful and things unlawful* (LL.). The same authority then goes on to add: "*Ḥudūd* of God are of two kinds: first, *those ordinances prescribed to men respecting eatables and drinkables and marriages*, etc., *what are lawful thereof and what are unlawful; the* second kind, *castigations*, or *punishments, prescribed*, or *appointed, to be inflicted upon him who does that which he has been forbidden to do.*

[2] The general word for punishment is *'uqūbah* (from *'aqb* meaning *one thing coming after another*), being so called because punishment follows transgression.

robbery, theft, adultery or fornication (*zinā*) and accusation of adultery. Before discussing in detail the various punishments prescribed in these cases, it may be stated that the Qur'ān lays down a general law for the punishment of offences in the following words: "And the recompense of evil (*sayyi'ah*) is punishment (*sayyi'ah*) like it, but whoever forgives and amends, he shall have his reward from Allāh" (42 : 40). This golden rule is of very wide application, since it applies both to individual wrong done by one person to another and to offences of a less particular nature: offences against society. Similar instructions as to the punishment of offenders are given elsewhere in the Qur'ān: "And if you take your turn (*'āqabt-um*), then punish (*'āqibū*) with the like of that with which you were afflicted. But if you show patience, it is certainly best for the patient" (16 : 126); "And whoever retaliates (*'āqaba*) with the like of that with which he is afflicted (*'ūqiba*) and he is oppressed, Allāh will certainly help him" (22 : 60); "Whoever acts aggressively (*i'tadā*) against you, inflict injury (*i'tadū*) on him according to the injury he has afflicted on you" (2 : 194).

While in the verses quoted above and similar other verses, a golden rule is laid down for the individual wronged, that he should in the first instance forgive the offender provided the latter amends by forgiveness, the basis also is ordained of penal laws in general for the protection of society, and that basis, according to all these verses, is that the punishment of evil should be proportionate thereto. Every civilized code of penal laws is based on that principle, and by enunciating this general rule, ample scope is given to Muslim peoples and states to formulate their own penal laws. It is for this reason that the Qur'ān does not go into many details, and speaks of punishment only in cases of the most glaring offences against person and property. It should be further noted that the Qur'ān generally adopts the same word for punishment as for the crime. Thus in 42 : 40, both evil and its punishment are called *sayyi'ah* (evil); in 16 : 126 and 22 : 60, it is a derivative of *'uqūbah* (punishment); and in 2 : 194, it is *i'tidā'* (aggression). The adoption of the same word *evil* for the crime and its punishment indicates that punishment itself, though justified by the circumstances, is a necessary evil.

Punishment for murder

Undoubtedly the greatest crime known to society is taking away of the life of another man (*qatl*). It is a crime denounced in the earliest revelations: "And kill not the soul which Allāh has forbidden except for a just cause" (17 : 33; 6 : 152)."And they who ... slay not the soul which Allāh has forbidden except in the cause of justice ... and he who does this shall meet a requital of sin—the chastisement shall be doubled to him on the day of Resurrection, and he shall abide therein in abasement" (25 : 68-69).

The punishment of murder is, however, prescribed in a Madīnah revelation: "O you who believe, retaliation (*qiṣāṣ*) is prescribed for you in the matter of the slain; the free for the free, and the slave for the slave and the female for the female. But if remission is made to any one by his (aggrieved) brother, prosecution (for bloodwit) should be according to usage, and payment to him in a good manner. This is an alleviation from your Lord and a mercy. Whoever exceeds the limit after this, will have a painful chastisement. And there is life for you in (the law of) retaliation, O men of understanding, that you may guard yourselves" (2 : 178, 179).

The word *qiṣāṣ* rendered as *retaliation*, is derived from *qaṣṣa* meaning *he cut it* or *he followed his track in pursuit* and it comes therefore to mean retaliation by *slaying for slaying, wounding for wounding* and *mutilating for mutilating* (LL.). The law of *qiṣāṣ* among the Israelites extended to all these cases, but the Qur'ān has expressly limited it to cases of murder (*fil-qatlā*). It speaks of retaliation in wounds as being an ordinance of the Mosaic law (5 : 45), but it is nowhere prescribed as a law for the Muslims, who are required to observe retaliation only in the case of the slain (2 : 178). In some traditions it is no doubt mentioned that the Prophet ordered retaliation in some cases of wounds, but this was in all likelihood due to the fact that he followed the earlier law until he received an express commandment to the contrary.

The law of retaliation in murder cases is followed by the words"the free for the free, the slave for the slave and the woman for the woman," which have sometimes been misunderstood as meaning that if a free man has been murdered, a free man should be murdered in his place and so on. This is falsified by the very word *qiṣāṣ* which requires that the murderer should be killed and not an innocent man. The words were meant to abolish an old Arab custom, for the Arabs before Islām used to insist, when the person killed was of noble descent, upon the execution of others besides the murderer. So it was made clear that whoever it might be, a free man or a slave or a woman, the murderer himself was to be slain.

An alleviation is, however, allowed in case the person who suffers from the death of the murdered person makes a remission and is satisfied with *diyah* or blood-money. Another case in which blood-money takes the place of a death sentence is that of unintentional killing. The Qur'ān says: "And a believer would not kill a believer except by mistake. And he who kills a believer by mistake should free a believing slave, and blood-money should be paid to his people unless they remit it as alms. But if he be from a tribe hostile to you and he is a believer, the freeing of a believing slave suffices; and if he is from a tribe between whom and you there is a covenant, the blood-money should be paid to his people along with the freeing of a believing slave" (4 : 92).

Murder of a non-Muslim

It may be noted here that by the hostile tribe, spoken of in the above quotation, is meant a tribe at war with the Muslim state. The murder of a non-Muslim living under a Muslim state or in a friendly non-Muslim state, is punishable in exactly the same way as the murder of a Muslim. The Prophet is reported to have said: "Whoever kills a *mu'āhad* (a non-Muslim living under the protection of a Muslim state), he shall not perceive the odour of Paradise, and its odour is perceivable from a distance of forty years' journey" (Bu. 88 : 30; Tr. 15 : 11; Ah. II, p. 186). Thus, even from a purely religious point of view, not the least distinction is made between the murder of a Muslim and a non-Muslim, and therefore any distinction in their temporal punishments is out of the question. And where the Qur'ān speaks of a murderer, it always speaks of the murderer of a *nafs* (person) and not of a Muslim: "Whoever kills *a person* unless it be for manslaughter or for mischief in the land, it is as though he had killed all men" (5 : 32). It is true that 'Alī is stated to have with him a written paper, according to which a Muslim was not to be killed for an unbeliever,[3] but evidently this related to a state of war and not a state of peace; the latter is expressly spoken of in the tradition already quoted. In fact, the rights of non-Muslims in a Muslim state are in all respects at par with those of Muslims, so much so that Muslims are required even to fight in their defence[4], and the Prophet is reported to have said: "Their property is like our property and their blood is like our blood." According to another report: "The property of the *mu'āhads* is not lawful for the Muslims" (Ah. IV, p. 89).

[3] Bu. 88 : 31.

[4] Bu. 56 : 174.

Alleviation of punishment in murder cases

Tradition speaks of cases of murder in which the murderer's intention is doubtful and, in these cases too, blood-money is to be paid.[5] And where the murderer could not be discovered, blood-money was paid from the state treasury.[6] There does not appear to be any reported case in which the murderer may have been imprisoned in case of unintentional murder, but the *alleviation* of punishment in such cases is clearly provided for in the Qur'ān. The form of alleviation spoken of in the Holy Book is the payment of blood-money, but the right of the state to give that alleviation any other form is not negatived.

Punishment for dacoity

Another crime for which capital punishment may be awarded is dacoity. In the Qur'ān, dacoity is spoken of as waging war against God and His Apostle: "The only punishment of those who wage war against Allāh and His Messenger and strive to make mischief (*fasād*) in the land is only this, that they should be put to death or crucified, or their hands and their feet should be cut off on opposite sides,[7] or they should be imprisoned;[8] this shall be as a disgrace for them in this world and in the Hereafter they shall have a grievous chastisement" (5 : 33). It has been accepted by the commentators, by a consensus of opinion, that dacoits and murderers who create disorder in a settled state of society are referred to in this verse. The punishment prescribed is of four kinds, which shows that the punishment to be inflicted in any particular case would depend upon the circumstances of the case. If murder has been committed in the course

5 AD. 38 : 18; Ah. II, p. 36.

6 Bu. 88 : 22.

7 The original words for "on opposite sides" are *min khilāf*, which might as well mean *on account of opposition,* referring to their creation of mischief in the land, while God and His Apostle want to establish peace in which the life and property of every man shall be secure. The word *khilāf* originally means *opposition.*

8 The Arabic words are *yunfau min-al-ardz* and *nafā-hu* means *he drove away* or expelled or *banished him* (LL). Therefore the words may mean either transportation or imprisonment, because in imprisonment, too, a man is banished from his usual place of habitation. Both Imām Abū Ḥanīfah and Aḥmad take the words here as meaning imprisonment.

of dacoity, the punishment would be the execution of the culprit, which may take the form of crucifixion if the offence is so heinous or the culprit has caused such terror in the land that the leaving of his body on the cross is necessary as a deterrent. Where the dacoits have committed excesses, one of their hands and feet may be cut off. In less serious cases of dacoity, the punishment may be only imprisonment.

Punishment of theft

Theft is the next punishable crime spoken of in the Qur'ān: "And as for the man and the woman addicted to theft, cut off their hands as a punishment for what they have earned, an exemplary punishment from Allāh, and Allāh is Mighty, Wise. But whoever repents after his wrong-doing and reforms, Allāh will turn to him mercifully. Surely Allāh is Forgiving, Merciful" (5 : 38, 39). The cutting off of hands may be taken metaphorically, as in *qata'a lisāna-hū* (lit., *he cut off his tongue*) which means *he silenced him* (LA.). But even if taken literally, it is not necessary to cut off the hands for every type of theft, and this is a fact which all jurists have recognized. As stated above, in the case of dacoity four grades of punishment are mentioned, ranging from death or crucifixion to mere imprisonment. It is evident that theft is not as serious a crime as dacoity, and hence the minimum punishment for it could not be severer than the minimum punishment for dacoity, which is imprisonment, the next higher being the cutting off of hands. Evidently what is meant is that whereas the maximum punishment, for dacoity is death, the maximum punishment for theft is the cutting off of the hand. Therefore it is for the judge to decide which punishment will suit a particular case. The state of society may sometimes demand the maximum punishment, even in less serious cases, but there are several circumstances which go to show that the maximum punishment of the cutting off of hands may ordinarily be reserved for habitual thieves. Firstly, the minimum punishment for dacoity, having already been mentioned in v. 33, may also be taken as the minimum punishment for the much less serious offence of theft, and this would meet the ends of justice. Secondly, the cutting off of hands, being a punishment for the more serious offences falling under dacoity, should also be reserved for the more serious offences falling under theft, and the offence of theft generally becomes more serious when it becomes habitual. Thirdly, the punishment of cutting off of hands, in cases of theft, is called an exemplary punishment and such punishment could only be given in very serious cases, or when the offender is addicted thereto and the milder punishment of imprisonment has no deterrent effect upon him. Lastly, v. 39 shows that the object of the punishment is *reform*, and an occasion to reform can only be given if the punishment for a first or second offence is less severe.

It is true that the cutting off of the hand, for even a first crime, is reported in Tradition but this may be due to the particular circumstances of society at the time, and it is for the judge to decide which punishment will suit the circumstances. For instance, according to some traditions, the hand was cut off when the amount stolen was one-quarter of a dīnār or more; according to others when it was one dīnār or more[9]. According to another report the hand of the thief was not to be cut off at all when a theft was committed in the course of a journey or on an expedition[10]. The words in *Abū Dāwūd* are: "I heard the Messenger of Allāh say, Hands shall not be cut off in the course of a journey." Probably some other punishment was given in such cases. There are also traditions showing that the hand was not to be cut off for stealing fruit on a tree[11]. The cutting off of the hand is also prohibited in the case of criminal misappropriation.[12] When Marwān was Governor of Madīnah, a certain slave stole young palm trees from the garden of a man, and being caught was imprisoned by Marwān, who intended to cut off his hand. The master of the slave went to Rafī' ibn Khudaij who said that he had heard the Prophet say that there was to be no cutting off of the hand in the case of theft of fruit, and when Rafī' related this to Marwān, the slave was let off. It is further related, however, that Marwān had him flogged[13]. In another tradition it is stated that when a certain person stole another's mantle valued at thirty dirhams from underneath his head, the owner of the mantle offered that he would sell the same to the person who had stolen it, without demanding immediate payment, and the Prophet approved of this arrangement[14]. These examples show that great latitude was allowed to the judge in the choice of the punishment.

[9] AD. 37 : 12; Ns. 46 : 7.

[10] AD. 37 : 19; Tr. 16 : 20; Ns. 46 : 13.

[11] AD. 37 : 13.

[12] AD. 37 : 14.

[13] AD. 37 : 13.

[14] AD. 37 : 15.

Punishment for adultery

Adultery, and false accusation of adultery, are both punishable according to the Qur'ān: "The adulteress and the adulterer, flog each of them (with) a hundred stripes, and let not pity for them detain you from obedience to Allāh if you believe in Allāh and the last day, and let a party of believers witness their chastisement" (24 : 2). In the case of slave-girls, who are guilty of adultery, the punishment is half of this: "Then if they (the slave-girls) are guilty of adultery when they are taken in marriage, they shall suffer half the punishment for free married women" (4 : 25).

These are the only verses speaking of punishment for adultery, and they clearly show that flogging, and not death or stoning to death, is the punishment for adultery. In fact 4 : 25 precludes all possibility of death having ever been looked upon by the Qur'ān as a punishment for adultery. It speaks clearly of the punishment of adultery in the case of married slave-girls, and says further that punishment for them is half the punishment of adultery in the case of free married women. It is generally thought that while the Qur'ān prescribes flogging as a punishment for fornication, *i.e.*, when the guilty person is not married, stoning to death is the punishment for adultery, and that this is allegedly based on the Prophet's practice. But the Qur'ān plainly speaks of the punishment for adultery in the case of married slave-girls as being half the punishment of adultery in the case of free married women (*muḥsanāt*), and therefore death or stoning to death cannot be conceived of as possible punishment in case of adultery as it cannot be halved, while imprisonment or flogging may be. Thus the Qur'ān not only speaks of flogging and not death, as punishment for adultery, but it positively excludes death or stoning to death.

Flogging

A few words may be added as to the method of flogging. The Arabic word for flogging is *jald* which means *skin*, and *jalada* signifies *he hit* or *hurt his skin* (LL.). *Jald* (flogging) was therefore a punishment which should be felt by the skin, and it aimed more at disgracing the culprit than torturing him. In the time of the Prophet, and even for some time after him, there was no whip, and flogging was carried out by beating with a stick or with the hand or with shoes.[15] It is further stated by the same authority that the culprit was not stripped naked for the infliction of the punishment of flogging; he was only required to take off thick clothes such as would ward off the stroke altogether. According to a report of Ibn Mas'ūd, baring the back for flogging is forbidden among the Muslims, and according to Shāfi'ī and Aḥmad, a shirt or two must be left over the body.[16] It is further related that it is preferable to give the strokes on different parts of the body so that no harm should result to any one part, but the face and the private parts must be avoided.[17]

Stoning to death in Jewish law

As already shown, stoning to death, as a punishment for adultery, is nowhere spoken of in the Qur'ān; on the other hand, the injunction to halve the punishment in certain cases is a clear indication that stoning to death was never contemplated as the punishment of adultery in the Holy Book. In Tradition, however, cases are met with in which adultery was punished with stoning to death. One of these cases is expressly mentioned as that of a Jew couple: "The Jews came to the Prophet with a man and a woman from among them who had committed adultery; and by his order they were stoned to death near the place where funeral services were held" (Bu. 23 : 61). Further explanation of this incident is given in another report where it is stated that when the Jews referred the case to him, he enquired of them what punishment the Torah prescribed in case of adultery. The Jews tried at first to conceal the fact that it was stoning to death, but on 'Abd Allāh ibn Salām giving the reference,[18] they admitted it, and the guilty persons were dealt with as prescribed in Torah (Bu. 61 : 26). According to a third version, which is the most detailed, the Jews who desired to avoid the severer punishment of stoning for adultery said one

15 RM. VI, p. 4.

16 *Ibid.*, p. 5.

17 *Ibid.*

18 That the present Torah does not give stoning as the punishment for adultery is clear proof that the text has been altered. The Gospels show that such was the punishment up to the time of Jesus. "And the scribes and the Pharisees brought unto him a woman taken in adultery; and when they had set her in the midst, they say unto him, Master, this woman was taken in adultery, in the very act. Now Moses in the law commanded us, that such should be stoned: but what sayest thou? (Jn. 8 : 3-5).

to another: "Let us go to this Prophet, for he has been raised with milder teaching; so if he gives his decision for a milder punishment than stoning, we will accept it." It is then related that the Prophet went with them to their *midrās* (the house in which the Torah was read), and asked them what punishment was prescribed in their sacred book. They tried to conceal it at first but the truth had to be admitted at last, and the Prophet gave his decision saying: "I give my judgment according to what is in the Torah" (AD. 37 : 26).

Jewish practice followed by the Prophet at first

These reports leave not the shadow of a doubt that stoning was the punishment of adultery in the Jewish law, and that it was in the case of Jewish offenders that this punishment was first resorted to by the Prophet when he came to Madīnah. There are other reports which show that the same punishment was given in certain cases when the offenders were Muslims, but apparently this was before the revelation of the verse (24 : 2) which speaks of flogging as the punishment for both the adulterer and the adulteress, it being the practice of the Prophet to follow the earlier revealed law until he received a definite revelation on a point. A suggestion to that effect is contained in a tradition: "Shaibānī says, I asked 'Abd Allāh ibn Abī Aufā, Did the Holy Prophet stone to death? He said, Yes. I said, Was it before the chapter entitled *the Light* (the 24th chapter) was revealed or after it? The reply was, I do not know" (Bu. 87 : 6). The chapter referred to is that which speaks of flogging as a punishment for adultery, and the question shows clearly that the practice of stoning for adultery was recognized as being against the plain injunction contained in that chapter. It is likely that some misunderstanding arose from the incidents which happened before the Qur'ānic revelation on the point, and that that practice was taken as the Sunnah of the Prophet. The Khwārij, the earliest Muslim sect, entirely rejected stoning to death (*rajm*) as a punishment in Islam[19].

The question seems to have arisen early as to how an adulterer could be stoned, when the Qur'ān prescribed flogging as the only punishment for adultery. 'Umar is reported to have said that "there are people who say, What about stoning, for the punishment prescribed in the Book of

[19] RM. VI, p. 6.

Allāh is flogging''[20]. To such objectors 'Umar's reply was: ''In what Allāh revealed, there was the verse of *rajm* (stoning); we read it and we understood it and we guarded it; the Prophet did stone (adulterers to death) and we also stoned after him, but I fear that when more time passes away, a sayer would say, We do not find the verse of *rajm* in the Book of Allāh''.[21] According to another version he is reported to have added: ''Were it not that people would say that 'Umar has added in the Book of Allāh that which is not in it, I would have written it''.[22] The argument attributed to 'Umar is very unsound. He admitted that the Qur'ān did not contain any verse prescribing the punishment of stoning for adulterers, and at the same time he is reported as stating that there was such a verse in what Allāh revealed. In all probability what 'Umar meant, if he ever spoke those words, was that the verse of stoning was to be found in the Jewish sacred book, the Torah, which was undoubtedly a Divine revelation, and that the Prophet stoned adulterers to death. The use of words ''Book of God'' (*Kitāb Allāh*) for the Torah is common in the Qur'ān itself, the Torah being again and again spoken of as *Kitāb Allāh* or the Book of God, or *al-Kitāb, i.e.*, the Book.[23] In all likelihood 'Umar only spoke of *rajm* as the punishment of adultery in the Mosaic law and he was misunderstood. At any rate he could not have spoken the words attributed to him. Had there been such a verse of the Qur'ān, he would have brought it to the notice of other Companions of the Prophet, when a complete written copy was first prepared in the time of Abū Bakr at his own suggestion. The words, as attributed to him in some of these reports, are simply meaningless. How could he say that there was a verse of the Qur'ān which he would have written down in the Qur'ān, but he feared that people would say that he had made an addition to the Qur'ān, that is to say, added to it what was not a part of it? A verse could not be said to be a part of the Qur'ān and not a part of the Qur'ān at one and the same time.

There is further evidence in tradition itself that 'Umar himself, at least in one reported case (and it is a reliable report), punished adultery with flogging as laid down in the Qur'ān in 24 : 2, and not with stoning to death. According to Bukhārī, one of 'Umar's collectors, Ḥamzah by name, found that a married man who had committed adultery with his wife's slave-girl had been punished by 'Umar with a hundred stripes, and

20 Ah. I, p. 50.

21 Bu. 87 : 16.

22 AD. 37 : 24.

23 2 : 213, etc.

he referred the case to 'Umar, and 'Umar upheld his first decision.[24] His own action therefore negatives the report which attributes to him the statement that stoning to death as a punishment for adultery was an ordinance contained in a Quranic verse. An explanation is sometimes offered, that such a verse had been revealed but that it was abrogated afterwards, though the ordinance contained in it remained effective. There is no sense at all in this explanation. If the words of the verse were abrogated, the ordinance contained in those words went along with them. No ordinance can be given except in words, and if the words are abrogated, the ordinance is also abrogated. If therefore such a verse was ever revealed (for which there is no testimony worth the name), the admission that it was abrogated leaves the matter where it was before its revelation[25].

Accusation of adultery

A false accusation of adultery is punished almost as severely as adultery itself: "And those who accuse free women and bring not four witnesses, flog them (with) eighty stripes and never accept their evidence, and these are the transgressors — Except those who afterwards repent and act aright; surely Allāh is Forgiving, Merciful" (24 : 4, 5).

It may be added here that while in ordinary matters two witnesses are required,[26] in the case of an accusation of adultery four witnesses must be produced. Thus a case of adultery can be established only on the strongest possible evidence. That circumstantial evidence is accepted is shown by the Qur'ān itself in Joseph's case who, when accused of an assault on the chief's wife, was declared free of the charge on circumstantial evidence.[27] There are also a number of traditions showing that circumstantial evidence was accepted when it led to the establishment of a certain fact.

Drunkenness

The Qur'ān does not speak of any punishment for the man who drinks intoxicating liquors, but there are traditions showing that the Prophet inflicted punishment in such cases. This punishment seems to have been of a very mild type and it appears that it was inflicted only in cases when

[24] Bu. 39 : 1.

[25] Also see pp. 37-46.

[26] 2 : 282.

[27] 12 : 26-28.

a man was intoxicated with drink. Thus it is related that a certain person called Nu'aimān or Ibn Nu'aimān was brought to the Prophet in a state of intoxication, and it distressed the Prophet, so he ordered those who were in the house to give him a beating, and he was beaten with shoes and sticks.[28] Another incident is related in which the person who had drunk wine was beaten with hands and with shoes and with garments (*thaub*).[29] Such remained the practice in the time of the Prophet and that of Abū Bakr, and for some time during the caliphate of 'Umar, and very mild punishment was inflicted with hands or shoes or *ardiya* (pl. of *ridā'*, being the wrapping garment covering the upper half of the body), but 'Umar then introduced flogging, giving forty stripes, raising the punishment to eighty stripes, it is added, when people behaved inordinately (*'atau*) and transgressed limits (*fasaqū*).[30] It is very likely that this punishment, or at any rate the severer punishment, was inflicted for disturbing the public peace by drunkards.

General directions for execution of punishment

Punishment must be inflicted without respect of persons, nor should mediation be accepted in such cases. When, in the case of a certain woman who was guilty of theft, some people sought to intercede on her behalf through Usāmah, since she came of a good family, the Prophet was enraged and said, Dost thou intercede in the matter of a *ḥadd* (punishment)? and then addressed the people in general, saying, "Those before you went astray, for, when one of them committed a crime and he was a great man, they would not punish him, and when he was a poor man they would execute the punishment" (Bu. 86 : 12). But leniency was shown in the execution of punishment when the guilty person showed signs of repentance[31]. It is strictly forbidden that one man should be punished for the crime of another.[32] Nor is any punishment to be inflicted on a mad man or a minor.[33] The punishment of the pregnant woman is to be deferred until she has delivered her child.[34]

28 Bu. 86 : 4.

29 Bu. 86 : 5.

30 86 : 4

31 Bu. 86 : 12; AD. 37 : 9.

32 AD. 38 : 2.

33 Bu. 86 : 22; AD. 37 : 17.

34 IM. 21 : 22.

Chapter XII

THE STATE[1]

All modern conceptions of state have one thing in common; material benefits have so obsessed the views of the civilized world that God and religion have been relegated to the corner of oblivion and the higher values of life are utterly neglected even in countries which nominally still owe allegiance to Christ and Christianity. The modern states may not be one in their lip professions so far as the supreme authority of God is concerned, but, strangely enough, they are one in worshipping the two new gods which Western civilization has created in place of the One God Whom it has dismissed as a thing of the past. The Nation and the State are the new idols before which the civilized man has fallen prostrate. And along with the old — perhaps the oldest-living — god Mammon, a new Trinity has emerged in place of the Trinity of the Church. The gain of economic advantages or the acquisition of wealth being the sole consideration of the civilized man, he is prepared to make any sacrifice that is required of him to gain this end, in the name of the State and for the love of the Nation. Wealth, Nation and State have thus the highest place of honour in the heart of the civilized man and he worships these idols. The desire to bow is there in human nature, and if men will not bow before their Maker, they must bow before things of their own making. Objects unworthy of worship have, however, always led humanity to ruin, and the worship of Mammon and its two associates, the Nation and the State is even now leading civilization to sure destruction. The State in the West whether it is labelled as a democracy or a Fascist or a Communist state, stands for expansion, aggression and exploiting the weak. It is not Machiavelli alone with whom "consideration of justice or injustice" carries no weight, and with whom "every scruple must be set aside" when the safety of the State is at stake. Even those who condemn him are following in his footsteps. With the gold of the world in their possession and with their bombs and bombers, they claim that they have an additional right of controlling the destinies of others to bring more and more economic

[1] The chapters on *The State* and *Ethics* did not form a part of the book as originally published. Material for these chapters has been taken from two later works of the author, *Living Thoughts of the Prophet Muhammad* (first published in 1947) and *The New World Order* (first published in 1944).

advantages to their own people. Aggression in one form or another is the very essence of the civilized state. The weak have no rights; the right belongs only to those who have the might, who have the strength to command respect and attention. This mentality has been developed by Western nations, resulting in states striving to outvie others in armies and armaments. And the result is a deadly conflict of the different states and the desire to destroy one another.

The responsibility for this state of things rests entirely with the materialistic concept of the state. Every state must necessarily be invested with power, with which it may stop aggression and protect the weak, dealing out fair justice to all. The advance of science has increased this Power a thousandfold. On the other hand, materialistic outlook on life has made man more unscrupulous in the use of his power against fellow man, and with advancement in the conquest of nature, the conquest of self which alone serves as a check on the tyranny of man against man, has been retarded and thrown to the background. The result is that the increased powers of the state, which must necessarily be exercised through individuals, are being used more for the enslavement and destruction of man than for his deliverance from tyranny and upholding the cause of truth and justice. It has been rightly remarked that while science has given man powers fit for the gods, to their use the civilized man brings the mentality of a savage. The state, instead of being helpful in increasing human happiness for which it was originally meant, has become a menace to human happiness, the individual, being so enthralled by this idol that, willingly or unwillingly, he is working as a part of the machinery for the destruction of humanity.

It is to remedy this evil that Islām requires the vesting of state authority in the hands of men who are God-fearing before all. The state which the Prophet founded was invested with physical force, as every state must necessarily be, but it was a unique service which he rendered to humanity that he spiritualized the greatest of all human physical forces. The head of the state in Islām is called both an *Amīr* (lit., *one who commands*) and an *Imām* (lit., *a person whose example is followed*), *i.e.*, a person who stands on a very high moral plane. On his deathbed the Prophet gave an indication as to who should succeed him as the head of the Muslim state by appointing Abū Bakr, admittedly the fittest man, to lead prayers in his absence. For a long time this practice was continued, and the head of the state led the prayers. Righteousness — fear of God and regard for other people's rights — was as necessary a qualification for the ruler as fitness to rule. Spiritual force alone could enable a man to control the powers which temporal authority gives him and which, in the absence of such force, are often in danger of being abused. The early Islamic state organisation, which combined the office of the spiritual and the temporal head of the community, was, therefore, the most perfect which the history of statecraft can show. The head of the state considered himself responsible to God, in the first place, for the exercise of his temporal authority.

The foundations of the state laid down by the Prophet were thus spiritual. They were at the same time democratic in the truest sense of the word. There exists a misconception in some quarters that the Islamic state was a theocracy. The head of the Muslim state never considered himself a representative of God on earth but as a representative of men who had chosen him to serve them; nonetheless, he certainly considered himself responsible to God for every act that he did in the exercise of his authority. All people, including the ruler, had equal rights and obligations and were subject to the same law. The Prophet himself did not claim any rights beyond those which other Muslims had. In the actual working of the state organisation, of which he was the founder and the head, there was nothing to distinguish him from the others. Outsiders came and asked: which of you is Muḥammad? He lived in thc simplest possible manner, and never claimed any superiority on account of his being a ruler. When his soldiers were digging a ditch for the defence of Madīnah, he was there with his pick-axe, and when they were removing heaps of dust and stones, he was one of the labourers who were covered with dust. If ever there was a democracy free from all differences of heredity, rank or privilege, it was the democratic state of which foundations were laid by the Prophet. Perhaps history cannot show a greater conqueror than ‘Umar, the second successor of the Prophet, a conqueror and an administrator at one and the same time. Yet he would not stop even his lowest subjects from rebuking him in the public. It is reported that an ordinary citizen once interrupted him repeatedly. ‘‘Fear God, O ‘Umar!’’ said the man; and when others wanted to stop him, ‘Umar himself intervened, saying: ‘‘Let him say so; of what use are these people if they do not tell me such things?’’This monarch of four kingdoms visited a famine-stricken camp at night incognito, and finding a woman with no food to give to her children, he rushed back to Madīnah, a distance of three miles, and took a sack of flour on his back to feed the distressed woman and her children. When a servant offered his services to carry the load, he said: ‘‘In this life you might carry my burden, but who will carry my burden on the day of Judgement?’’ Yet when this great servant of the people was lying on his death-bed and a young man lauded his great services, he said: "Enough, young fellow! It is sufficient if the evil I may have done in the exercise of authority is neutralised by any good that I have done". It is such a mental attitude alone which can make men fit for ruling their fellow beings. But such a mentality is created only by a strong faith in God and a feeling of one's responsibility to God.

It was such a responsible Government that Islām created, a government by men who realised that above all other things they were responsible to God for everything they did. The men to be honoured—and entrusting a man with command was certainly doing him honour—were those who paid the greatest regard to their duties. It was such men that were to be placed in authority over others. "Allāh commands you to make over (positions of) trust to those worthy of them" (4 : 58).[2] Every one who was entrusted with any authority was told that he was a ruler in his own sphere and that he was responsible to God for those placed under his trust: "Everyone of you is a ruler and everyone shall be questioned about his subjects; the king is a ruler and he shall be questioned about his subjects; and the man is a ruler over the people of his house and he shall be questioned about those under his care; and the woman is a ruler over the house of her husband and she shall be questioned about those under her care; and the servant is a ruler so far as the property of the master is concerned and he shall be questioned about that which is entrusted to him" (Bu. 11 : 11). The ruler or head of the state is, thus, along with all those persons who hold any authority over others, placed in the same category as a servant. Just as a servant is entrusted with a certain property for which he is responsible to his master, those entrusted with authority of the state, in whatever position they may be, are entrusted with the care of the people and guarding their rights, and for the proper discharge of their duties they are responsible, in the first place, to the Real Master, Who is God,

[2] The whole section of ch.4, in which this verse appears, deals with granting of kingdom to Muslims, who are here required to entrust the affairs of State to people who are worthy of this responsibility. The words that follow—"and that when you judge between people, you judge with justice"—corroborate this significance of the word *amānāt* "(positions of) trust", the whole verse stating the reciprocal duties of the governed and the governors. Explaining the word *amānāt*, I'Ab said that it meant *duties*. The Prophet himself has explained the word *amānat*(sing.of *amānāt*) as meaning *Government* or *affairs of State*. The Prophet said: When the *amānat* is wasted, wait for the doom. It was said: "How will the *amānat* be wasted, O Messenger of Allāh? He said: when Government is entrusted to those unworthy of it, then wait for the doom" (Bu. 81 : 35).

and then to the people who have entrusted him with this charge. The first necessity of a good state organization is this mentality on the part of each one of its members, and the greatest stress is, therefore, laid on this in the Islamic concept of state.

The verses and traditions quoted above also show that hereditary kingship is foreign to the concept of the State in Islām. Nor is the Islamic state an autocracy, as uncontrolled authority is not vested in the head of the state. It has already been stated that the law was one for all, and all were one in the eye of the law including the man entrusted with the highest command, and including the Prophet himself who was as much subject to law[3] as any of his followers. Speaking of the most prominent qualities of the Muslims, the Qur'ān mentions an equally prominent quality: "And whose affairs are (decided) by counsel among themselves" (42 : 38). The chapter in which this verse occurs is entitled *shūrā* or *counsel* on account of the great democratic principle of counsel laid down here as the basis of the future state of Islām. This is one of the early revelations, when the Prophet was still leading the life of a helpless and persecuted reformer, and shows how the two ideas of democratizing and spiritualizing the state were blended: "And those who respond to their Lord and keep up prayer and whose affairs are (decided) by counsel among themselves and who spend out of what We have given them" (42 : 38).[4] The verse gives prominence to the great acts which are needed to spiritualize man, answering the call of God, praying to God and devoting oneself to the service of humanity, while laying down the principle for conducting the affairs of state. The verses that follow also show that the Prophet wanted his followers to be trained on spiritual lines while preparing them for conducting the affairs of the state: "And those who, when great wrong afflicts them, defend themselves. And the recompense of evil is

[3] "I follow naught but what is revealed to me. Indeed I fear the chastisement of a grievous day if I disobey my Lord" (10 : 15).

[4] In this verse the Muslims are enjoined as usual to observe prayer and to spend out of what Allāh has given them. Yet between these two injunctions, which always go together in the Qur'ān and which are the basis of a true Islamic life, is placed a third: *And their affairs are decided by counsel among themselves.* This injunction at such an early period clearly meant to prepare Muslims for transacting the momentous affairs of state and all matters connected with national weal or woe. In fact the word *amr*, translated as *affairs* meant *command,* and *amr Allāh*, or *Allāh's command* often signifies the establishment of the kingdom of God, which stands for an Islamic Kingdom. The use of the word *amr*, therefore, here refers to the Islamic kingdom, the affairs of which must be transacted by counsel.

punishment like it, but whoever forgives and amends (matters thereby), his reward is with Allāh; surely He loves not the wrong-doers. And whoever defends himself after his being oppressed, these it is against whom there is no way of blame. The way of blame is only against those who oppress men and revolt in the earth unjustly. For such there is a painful chastisement. And whoever is patient and forgives — that surely is an affair of great resolution'' (42 : 39-43). These excellent rules for the defence of the Muslim community which was being oppressed and persecuted at that time, and for the forgiveness of the enemy that was bent upon its extirpation, clearly show that the basis was herein being laid of the Muslim State, because forgiveness could only be exercised towards a vanquished enemy. It was in their sufferings that the Muslims were being told to exercise forgiveness when their turn should come to take revenge upon a fallen enemy. The passion for revenge was thus being obliterated from their hearts from the very beginning and the physical force of the state was spiritualized by making it subject to moral considerations.

The Islamic State is a democracy in the truest sense of the word. The first successor to Prophet was Abū Bakr, who was elected the head of the state by the agreement of all parties, and so were the three successors that followed him. Why the state organisation was needed and what the constitutional position of the head of the state was, was explained by Abū Bakr in his very first address: ''You have elected me as *Khalīfah*, but I claim no superiority over you. The strongest among you shall be the weakest with me until I get the right of others from him, and the weakest among you shall be the strongest with me until I get all his rights ... Help me if I act rightly and correct me if I take a wrong course ... Obey me so long as I obey God and His Messenger. In case I disobey God and His Messenger, I have no right to obedience from you''.

The head of the state was a servant of the state who was paid a fixed salary for maintenance out of the public treasury, like all other public servants. It was Abū Bakr, the very first successor of the Prophet, who acted on this rule (Bu. 34 : 15). The head had no special privileges and in his private capacity he could be sued in the court like any other member of the community. The great 'Umar appeared as a defendant in the court of a judge. Some of the orders given by him to his provincial governors were that they should be accessible at all hours of the day to those who had a complaint to make and that they should not keep a door-keeper who should prohibit people from approaching them. And further that they should accustom themselves to lead hard lives. The head of state carried on the administration with the help of ministers, all important state affairs being decided by a council.

Those entrusted with the work of government, including the head, were required to work for the good of the people: "There is not a man whom Allāh grants to rule people, then he does not manage their affairs for their good but he will not smell the sweet odour of paradise" (Bu. 94 : 8). They were required to be gentle to the people and were forbidden to do anything which might cause aversion (Bu. 64 : 62). They were enjoined to lead simple lives and to be easily accessible to those who needed their services (MM. 17 : 1), to be Godfearing, (Bu. 94 : 16), to tax the different classes of people according to their capacity, to provide for those who could not earn and to have as much regard for the rights of the non-Muslims as for those of the Muslims (Bu. 62 : 8). The state was not only required to maintain uncared for families but also to pay the unpaid debts which were contracted for a lawful need (Bu. 43 : 11).

The people's responsibility to the state is to respect its laws and obey its orders as long as they do not involve disobedience to God and His Messenger. The first successor of the Prophet, Abū Bakr, in his first address to those who had sworn allegiance to him, said: "Help me if I am in the right, set me right if I am in the wrong". And again: "Obey me as long as I obey Allāh and His Messenger: in case I disobey Allāh and His Messenger, I have no right to obedience from you". The law of the Qur'ān was to be held supreme and it was the Prophet who had laid down this rule of the supremacy of the law: "To hear and obey the authorities is binding, so long as one is not commanded to disobey God; when one is commanded to disobey God, he should not hear or obey"[5] (Bu. 56 : 108). Thus while it was considered an act of great merit, "an excellent *Jihād*", to speak out the truth in the presence of an unjust ruler

[5] This was in accordance with the Quranic injunction in which, immediately after laying down the principle of rule by counsel, it is stated: "O you who believe, obey Allāh and obey the Messenger and those in authority from among you; then if you quarrel about anything, refer it to Allāh and the Messenger, if you believe in Allāh and the Last Day. This is best and more suitable to (achieve) the end" (4 : 59). This verse lays down three important rules of guidance in matters relating to the welfare of the Muslim Community, particularly in those relating to affairs of State. These are obedience to God and His Messenger in the first place; secondly, obedience to those in authority from among the Muslims; and thirdly, referring matters to God and His Messenger in cases of dispute with those in authority. God and His Messenger are thus the final authority.

The words *those in authority* have a wide significance, so that in different matters relating to the life of man different persons would be in authority. Thus the commander of a section of the army was considered as one in authority (Bu. 65 : iv, 11).

(MM. 17), active opposition to constituted authority or rebellion against it was not allowed because the Prophet had laid down the condition to hear and obey "whether we liked or disliked, and whether we were in adversity or ease, even if our rights were not granted," and "the authority of the head could only be disputed if he committed open acts of disbelief in which you have a clear ordinance from Allāh (Bu. 93 : 2).

The law of the Qur'ān was supreme indeed, but there was no ban to making laws according to the needs of the people so long as they did not go against the spirit of the revealed law. On being appointed Governor of Yemen, Mu'ādh was asked by the Prophet as to the rule by which he would abide. "By the law of the Qur'ān," was the reply. "But if you do not find any direction therein," asked the Prophet. "Then I will act according to the Sunnah of the Prophet," was the reply. "But if you do not find any direction in the Sunnah of the Prophet," he was again asked. "Then I will exercise my judgement and act on that," came the reply. The Prophet raised his hands and said: "Praise be to Allāh Who guides the messenger of His Messenger as He pleases" (Bu. 23 : 11).

The necessary laws were, however, to be made by consultation in accordance with the general command: "And whose affairs are (decided) by counsel among themselves" (42 : 38). In reply to 'Alī who enquired as to how to proceed in cases where there was no definite direction in the Qur'ān, the Prophet is reported to have said: "Gather together the righteous from among my community and decide the matter by their counsel and do not decide it by one man's opinion". Counsel was freely resorted to by the Prophet himself in all important matters. Madīnah was attacked thrice by the Quraish of Makkah, and every time the Prophet held a consultation with his followers as to how to meet the enemy. On one of these occasions he acted upon the opinion of the majority and marched out of Madīnah to meet the enemy, although his own opinion was that the Muslim army should not leave the town. He definitely directed his followers to take counsel whenever an important matter was to be decided: "Never do a people take counsel but they are guided to the right course in their affair." When some people disobeyed his orders in one of the battles and this act of theirs caused heavy loss to the Muslim army, he was still commanded to take counsel with them. "Pardon them and ask Divine protection for them, and consult them in (important) matters" (3 : 158).

It appears from the Qur'ān that people were gathered together for counsel on many important occasions: "Only those are believers who believe in Allāh and His Messenger and, when they are with him on a momentous affair, they go not away till they ask his permission" (24 : 62).

It was due to these clear directions to make laws for themselves and to decide other important matters by counsel that the first successors of the Prophet had councils to help them in all such matters. It was also in the early history of Islām that the great Imāms, such as Imām Abū Ḥanīfah, freely resorted to analogical reasoning in legislation, and *Ijtihād* was recognized as a source of Islamic law along with the Qur'ān and the Sunnah. The two principles of democracy, the supremacy of the law and the taking of counsel in making new laws and deciding other important affairs, were thus laid down by the Prophet himself. The third principle of democracy, the election of the head of the state, was also recognized by him. He went so far as to say that even a Negro could be appointed to rule over the Arabs and that obedience was due to him as to any other head (Bu. 10 : 54). It was due to such teachings of his that the election of a head was the first act of his companions after his death.

When the news of his death spread, the Muslims gathered together and freely discussed the question as to who should succeed the Prophet as the head of the state. The Anṣār, the residents of Madīnah, were of the opinion that there should be two heads, one from among the Quraish and one from among themselves, but the error of this view was pointed out by Abū Bakr who made it clear in an eloquent speech that the state could have only one head (Bu. 62 : 6). And so Abū Bakr was elected, being as 'Umar stated,'' the best''of them and ''the fittest of the Muslims to control their affairs'' (Bu. 93 : 2). Fitness to rule was the only criterion to decide the election, as indeed in the Qur'ānic injunction: ''Allāh commands you to make over (positions of) trust to those worthy of them'' (4 : 58).

Justice was declared to be the corner-stone of the State which the Prophet founded; in dealing equitably no distinction was to be made between friend and foe, between people whom one loved and those whom one hated: ''O you who believe! be upright for Allāh, bearers of witness with justice; and let not the hatred of a people incite you not to act equitably: act equitably that is nearer to piety; and be careful of your duty to Allāh, for Allāh is aware of what you do'' (5 : 8) ''O you who believe! Be maintainers of justice, bearers of witness for Allāh even though it be against your own selves or your parents or near relatives—whether he be rich or poor, Allāh has a better right over them both. So follow not your low desires lest you deviate. And if you distort or turn away from truth, surely Allāh is Aware of what you do'' (4 : 135). In a state, some men have necessarily to be placed in authority over others, but those placed in authority have been repeatedly warned that they would be answerable to God, first of all, for what they did in the exercise of authority. The warning to David is a warning to every true believer: ''O David, surely We have made thee a ruler in the land; so judge between men justly and follow not desire, lest it lead thee astray from the path of Allāh. Those who go astray from the path of Allāh, for them is surely a severe chastisement because they forgot the day of Reckoning'' (38 : 26).

Chapter XIII

ETHICS

Service of humanity

Even in the earliest revelations to the Prophet as much stress was laid on prayer to God as on service to humanity, perhaps more on the latter. In fact, prayer to him was meaningless if it was not accompanied with service to humanity. It would then be a mere show, severely condemnable. One of the short earlier chapters is devoted entirely to this: "Hast thou seen him who belies religion? That is the one who is rough to the orphan. And urges not the feeding of the needy. So woe to the praying ones, who are unmindful of their prayers! who do good to be seen, and refrain from acts of kindness" (107 : 1-7). Prayer, therefore, had no value if it did not lead to the service of humanity. Of the two, prayer to God and service of humanity, the latter was the more difficult task. It was an uphill road: "And (have We not) pointed out to him (man) the two conspicuous ways? But he attempts not the uphill road. And what will make thee comprehend what the uphill road is? It is to free a slave, or to feed in a day of hunger, an orphan nearly related, or the poor man lying in the dust" (90 : 10-16). The orphan and the needy were not only to be helped; they were to be honoured: "Nay! But you honour not the orphan; nor do you urge one another to feed the poor; and you devour heritage, devouring all; and you love wealth with exceeding love" (89 : 17-20). Elsewhere the Qur'ān states: "Righteous is the one who believes in Allāh ... and gives away wealth out of love for Him to the near of kin and the orphans and the needy and the wayfarers and to those who ask and to set slaves free" (2 : 177). The Qur'ān lays great stress on the point that wealth was not given to man for amassing; the needy have a right in the wealth of the rich: "And in their wealth is a due share for the beggar and for the one who is denied (good)" (51 : 19). In other revelations the possessors of wealth who do not help the poor are threatened with destruction (*e.g.* 68 : 17-27).

From his earliest life the Prophet was a staunch supporter of the cause of the weak and oppressed. When deputation after deputation of his opponents, the Quraish of Makkah, went to his uncle, Abū Ṭālib to persuade him to deliver the Prophet to them to be put to death, Abū Ṭālib sang his praises in the memorable words which have come down to us in one of his poems: What! said he, shall I make over to you one "who is the refuge of the orphans and the protector of the widows?" And when, on receiving the Call, the Prophet trembled for fear that he might not be able to achieve the grand task of the reformation of humanity, his wife consoled him in these words ... Allāh will never bring thee to disgrace, for thou unitest the ties of relationship and bearest the burden of the weak and earnest for the destitute and honourest the guest and helpest people in real distress" (Bu. 1 : 1).

That service of humanity was a great goal of life was repeatedly impressed upon his hearers by the Prophet. He once likened the Muslims to a body; when a part of it ails, the entire body ails (Bu. 78 : 27). He placed the person who faithfully manages the affairs of the widows and the needy at par with one who performs *Jihād* in the way of Allāh or with one who stands up for prayer in the night and fasts during the day (Bu. 69 : 1). He described the man who brings up an orphan as closest to him in Paradise (Bu. 78 : 24). And he clearly stated that "he is not of us who does not show mercy to our little ones and respect to our great ones (MM. 24 : 15). He had a tender heart even for animals and specifically forbade acts of cruelty to animals; stating that doing good to the animals had its rewards (MM. 6 : 6).

Charity

The Prophet's charity was proverbial. "He was the most charitable of men" was the description of him given by his companions to the later generations. Along with the theme of obedience to God, great stress has been laid in the Qur'ān and in the sayings of the Prophet on charity to man. It has been emphasized that love of God should be the basis for charity. It is said in one of the earliest revelations: "And they give food, out of love for Him, to the poor and the orphan and the captive. We feed you for Allāh's pleasure only — we desire from you neither reward nor thanks" (76 : 8, 9). And in a later revelation: "...Righteous is the one who believes in Allāh, and the Last Day, and the angels, and the Book and the prophets, and gives away wealth out of love for Him to the near of kin and the orphans and the needy and the wayfarer and to those who ask and to set slaves free..." (2 : 177). Charity proceeding from such a pure motive brought about increase of wealth: "...And whatever you give in charity, desiring Allāh's pleasure — these will get manifold" (30 : 39). The increase which charity brought in its wake is likened to the seed which multiplies a large number of times: "The parable of those who spend their wealth in the way of Allāh is as the parable of a grain growing seven ears, in every ear a hundred grains. And Allāh multiplies (further) for whom He pleases..." (2 : 261).

The exercise of charity must be free from show and from all sordid motives such as any personal gain or even placing the recipient of charity under an obligation: "Those who spend their wealth in the way of Allāh, then follow not up what they have spent with reproach or injury, their reward is with their Lord, and they shall have no fear, nor shall they grieve. A kind word with forgiveness is better than charity followed by injury. And Allāh is Self-Sufficient, Forbearing. O you who believe, make not your charity worthless by reproach and injury, like him who spends his wealth to be seen of men and believes not in Allāh and the Last Day...." (2 : 262-264).

Charity must be given out of good things, out of things which a man loves for himself: "O you who believe, spend of the good things that you earn and of that which We bring forth for you out of the earth, and aim not at the bad to spend thereof, while you would not take it yourselves..." (2 : 267). And elsewhere it is stated "you cannot attain righteousness unless you spend out of what you love" (3 : 91). Charity may be exercised openly, as for some national good, or secretly, as for helping the poor: "If you manifest[1] charity, how excellent it is! And if you hide it and give it to the poor, it is good for you..." (2 : 271). The charity of a Muslim is not limited to his co-religionist (2 : 272). Charity must be exercised specially towards those who abstain from begging (2 : 273). Above all, Islām wishes its followers to acquire a new mentality altogether about possession of wealth, by doing away with love for wealth and its hoarding, and by stating plainly that the poor have a due share in the wealth of the rich. Describing the existence of the true Muslims in the hereafter, their qualities in this life are stated to be: "They used to sleep but little at night. And in the morning they asked (Divine) protection. And in their wealth there was a due share for the beggar and for one who is denied (good)" (51 : 17-19). Elsewhere the true Muslims are described as "Those who are constant at their prayer, and in whose wealth there is a known right for the beggar and the destitute" (70 : 23-25).

[1] Exercising charity openly is quite different from exercising it "to be seen of men"(2 : 264). It means spending money for works of public utility and advancement of national welfare and for organized efforts for dealing with the poor, without which national growth is impossible.

Prayer and charity were thus the two essential conditions of righteousness. The "due share"or "known right" mentioned here is different from Zakāt which, being obligatory and leviable at a fixed rate and being the due of the state, is a kind of tax. The Prophet himself made this clear: "In one's wealth there is a due besides Zakāt" (Bu. 24 : 31). All the wealth a man earned was not his own. A part of it should go to charity, however stringent the circumstances in which a man lives. "Charity is incumbent on every Muslim" were the clear orders of the Prophet (Bu. 56 : 72). But what about him who has not got anything? asked his Companions. He replied: "he should work with his hands and profit himself and give in charity." They again asked, if he has nothing in spite of this? The reply was: "He should help the distressed one who is in need". And if he is unable to do that? they said again. He said: "He should do good deeds and refrain from doing evil—this is charity on his part" (Bu. 46 : 2).

The Prophet's conception of charity was the broadest possible: "On every bone of the finger, charity is incumbent every day. One assists a man in riding his beast or in lifting his provisions to the back of the animals, this is charity; and a good word and every step which one takes in walking over to prayer is charity" (MM. 6 : 6). "Removal from the way of that which is harmful is charity" (Bu. 46 : 2). Even to meet a fellow-being with a cheerful countenance was charity: "Every good deed is charity, and it is a good deed that thou meet thy brother with a cheerful countenance and that thou pour water from thy bucket into the vessel of thy brother" (MM. 6 : 6).

The Prophet thus wanted to make men realize that to be charitable was to be a man. To make men prayer-minded and to make them charity-minded for the services of humanity are the two distinctive characteristics of the religious system which he established.

Character-building

One of the earliest works to which the Prophet applied himself, as can be seen from the earliest revelations, was the building up of character. Long before any reforms were introduced about social relations or state policy, emphasis was being placed in the revelations on the moral uplift of man, and very correctly too, because even good laws could benefit humanity only when they were worked out by men standing on a high moral plane.

The Prophet was recognized by friends and foes as the most truthful of men. On repeated occasions, his bitterest enemies had to acknowledge his eminent truthfulness, on account of which he was called *al-Amīn* (the Faithful one). Himself so eminently truthful, he laid stress on truth as the basis of a high character: "Surely truth leads to virtue, and virtue leads to paradise, and a man continues to speak the truth until he becomes thoroughly truthful; and surely falsehood leads to vice and vice leads to the fire, and a man continues to tell lies until he is written down a great liar with Allāh (Bu. 78 : 69). The Qur'ān mentions truthfulness as one of the most prominent qualities of true Muslims: "... And the truthful men and the truthful women ... Allāh has prepared for them forgiveness and a mighty reward" (33 : 35). Speaking of the great transformation which the Prophet had brought about, the Qur'ān bears testimony to the truthfulness of the Muslims by stating that they do not bear witness to what is false (25 : 72). The Qur'ān also lays down the basis of a society in which everyone is required to enjoin truth upon those with whom he comes into contact (103 : 2, 3), and states repeatedly that it is with truth that falsehood can be challenged and vanquished. It exhorts again and again that truth is to be adhered to at all costs, even if it goes against one's own interest or interest of one's friends and relatives: "O you who believe, be maintainers of justice, bearers of witness for Allāh, even though it be against your own selves or your parents or near relatives ... Follow not your low desires lest you deviate. And if you distort or turn away from truth, surely Allāh is aware of what you do" (4 : 135). The principle of truth was not to be deviated from even if it went in favour of the enemy: "O you who believe be upright for Allāh, bearers of witness with justice; and let not hatred of a people incite you not to act equitably. Be just; that is nearer to observance of duty..." (5 : 8). And even if one was called upon to speak the truth in the face of a tyrant, he must do it: "The most excellent *jihād* is the uttering of truth in the presence of an unjust ruler" (MM. 17). Only truth shall benefit in the final judgment: "...This is the day when their truth shall profit the truthful ones. For them are Gardens wherein flow rivers, abiding therein ever. Allāh is well pleased with them and they are well pleased with Allāh. This is the mighty achievement" (5 : 119).

The Prophet enjoys the distinction that he made people walk in the ways which he pointed out. The quality of truth was so ingrained in the heart of his followers that they not only loved it but underwent severest hardship for the sake of truth. When about two centuries later, the critics laid down certain canons to judge the truthfulness of the transmitters of

Tradition (Ḥadīth) they all agreed on one point, that no companion of the Prophet had uttered a deliberate falsehood. In fact one of the latest revelations of the Qur'ān itself bears witness to this: "...Allāh has endeared the faith to you and has made it seemly in your hearts, and He has made hateful to you disbelief and transgression and disobedience" (49 : 7). Faith includes all virtues taught by the Prophet and truthfulness was one of the most prominent of these.

Perseverance was another characteristic on which great emphasis is laid in the Qur'ān and which shone prominently in the life of the Prophet and those inspired by him. Persecuted on all sides, suffering the severest hardships, with no apparent prospects of success, the Prophet stood adamant when threatened with death. He was equally firm when offered worldly temptations. During the flight to Madīnah, hidden in a cave with a search party at its mouth, he consoled his single companion, Abū Bakr, with these words: "Grieve not, surely Allāh is with us" (9 : 40). The Qur'ān states clearly that the perseverance in the cause of truth brings down angels from heaven to console a man (41 : 30, 31). Patience and perseverance were inculcated again and again in the early revelations as well as in the later ones (*e.g.* 14 : 12; 42 : 15; 11 : 112, 113; 11 : 49; 3 : 199). Patience and prayers are said to be the two doors through which Divine help is received: "O you who believe, seek assistance through patience and prayer; surely Allāh is with the patient" (2 : 153).

Courage was another great quality on which stress was laid. The heart in which there was fear of God could not entertain fears of others than God, and this makes a Muslim fearless in the face of severest opposition: "Those to whom men said: Surely people have gathered against you, so fear them; but this increased their faith, and they said: Allāh is sufficient for us and He is an excellent Guardian.... (So) no evil touched them and they followed the pleasure of Allāh... It is the devil who only frightens his friends, but fear them not and fear Me, if you are believers" (3 : 172-174). "Fear not, surely I am with you — I do hear and see" (20 : 46). "Those who deliver the messages of Allāh and fear Him, and fear none but Allāh, and Allāh is Sufficient to take account" (33 : 39). "Surely those who say, Our Lord is Allāh, then continue on the right way, on them is no fear, nor shall they grieve" (46 : 13). "Now surely the friends of Allāh, they have no fear, nor do they grieve" (10 : 62). It was on account of their fearlessness and great moral courage that the Muslims, in the Prophet's time, defended themselves in battles against three to ten times their numbers and won on all occasions. Later, in the battles they had to fight against Persia and the Roman Empire, their numbers bore no comparison with the enemy forces, and they were almost always victorious. The courage which they showed on the battle-fields was in fact due to their firm faith.

But while facing so boldly all opposition to the cause of truth, the Muslims were required to develop the quality of humility: "And go not about in the land exultingly..." (17 : 37); "And turn not thy face away from people in contempt, nor go about in the land exultingly. Surely Allāh loves not any self-conceited boaster" (31 : 18); "Surely He loves not the proud" (16 : 23). Humility, in fact, should be deeply rooted in a Muslim's heart because of the five daily prayers when all standing on terms of perfect equality bow down and prostrate themselves before their Lord as one body. The Prophet's own example is a beacon-light in this respect. In his dealings with others he was humble and never placed himself on a higher pedestal. And along with humility, selflessness is another great quality with which Islām arms every Muslim to fight the battle of life. There are repeated injunctions in the Qur'ān that God's pleasure is to be the only motive for one's actions and not one's personal gains or losses.

Great stress has been laid in Islām on faithfulness to agreements and trusts: "Those who are faithful to their trusts and their covenants" is a twice repeated description of the true believers (23 : 8; 70 : 32). Elsewhere too, it is enjoined: "And fulfil the promise; surely the promise will be enquired into" (17 : 34); "O you who believe, fulfil the obligations (*'uqūd*)" (5 : 1), where *'uqūd* (sing. *'aqd*, a tie) stands not only for *covenants, contracts, agreements, leagues, treaties* and *engagements* but also for *Divine ordinances* (LL.). The obligation to fulfil both the covenant of Allāh and covenants between man and man, particularly between nations, is again mentioned together in 16 : 91, 92. Thus respect for law, both religious as well as temporal, has been placed on equal footing. True to this teaching the Prophet and his followers stood firmly by their agreements under the most trying circumstances.

There is not a single instance on record in which they broke their agreement with any other nation. A typical example of this, in the Prophet's time, is that of the truce of Ḥudaibiyah, under which Abū Jandal, a refugee convert to Islām, who had been tortured by the enemy, had to be returned under the terms of the truce. In the time of 'Umar, the Muslim general Abū 'Ubaidah was obliged to evacuate the occupied territory of Ḥimṣ, which the enemy was going to occupy, and he ordered that the tax received from the people as a condition for their protection should be paid back to them as Muslims could protect them no longer. Another example of such scrupulous honesty and regard for agreements can hardly be met with elsewhere.

Hypocrisy has been condemned in the Qur'ān in the severest terms. The hypocrites have been described as "in the lowest stage of fire" (4 : 145) and uttering words from the mouth which are not in the heart has been condemned again and again.

All qualities which make man stand on a high moral plane were inculcated one after another. Thankfulness was one of them. "If you are grateful, I will give you more; and if you are ungrateful My chastisement is truly severe" (14 : 7). "Eat of the good things that We have provided you with, and give thanks to Allāh if He it is Whom you serve" (2 : 172). "If you are ungrateful, then surely Allāh is above need of you. And he likes not ungratefulness in His servants. And if you are grateful, He likes it in you" (39 : 7). One was required to be grateful to fellow-men as well. The Prophet said: "Whoever is not thankful to men is not thankful to Allāh". Thankfulness to men meant repaying their kindness: "Is the reward of goodness aught but goodness (55 : 60).

The high morals depicted in the Qur'ān were the morals of the Prophet, and it was in this shape that he wanted to mould the character of his followers. Even a cursory glance at the lives of his Companions and his first four successors, who were the rulers of a vast empire, would show that the Prophet achieved a mighty success in this respect. One of the many descriptions of the high moral plane on which the Prophet's Companions stood occurs in the Qur'ān as follows: "And the servants of the Beneficent God are they who walk on the earth in humility, and when the ignorant address them, they say, Peace! And they who pass the night prostrating themselves before their Lord and standing... And they who, when they spend, are neither extravagant nor parsimonious, and the just mean is ever between these. And they who call not upon another god with Allāh and slay not the soul which Allāh has forbidden except in the cause of justice, nor commit fornication ... And they who witness no falsehood, and when they pass by what is vain, they pass by nobly. And they who, when reminded of the messages of their Lord, fall not down thereat deaf and blind. And they who say, our Lord, grant us in our wives and our offspring the joy of our eyes, and make us leaders for those who guard against evil. These are rewarded with high places because they are patient, and are met therein with greetings and salutation" (25 : 63-75).

Social conduct

Good morals and good manners are, according to the Qur'ān and Tradition, the real test of a man's excellence. "The noblest of you in the sight of Allāh is the best of you in conduct" (49 : 13). The Prophet used to say: "The best of you are those who have the most excellent morals" (Bu. 61 : 23). In the moral code of Islām respect of and kindness to the parents occupies a very high place. "And do good to your parents. If either of them or both of them reach old age with thee, say not to them, fie; nor chide them; and speak to them a generous word. And make thyself submissively gentle to them with compassion, and say, My Lord! Have mercy on them as they brought me up when I was little" (17 : 23-24). The great stress which the Qur'ān lays on the duty of obedience to parents is also apparent from two other verses: "And We have enjoined on man concerning his parents ... saying: Give thanks to Me and to thy parents. To Me is the Eventual coming. And if they strive with thee to make thee associate with Me that of which thou hast no knowledge, obey them not, and keep kindly company with them in this world, and follow the ways of him who turns to Me..." (31 : 14, 15). Here disobedience to parents is permitted only if there is a clash with one's duty to one's Maker. Even then kind behaviour towards them is enjoined. Special emphasis was placed by the Prophet on showing consideration to one's mother, so much so that paradise was described by him to be beneath her two feet. It is reported in a tradition that a companion of the Prophet came to him and consulted him about enlistment in the fighting forces. The Prophet asked him if he had a mother living. On receiving the reply in the affirmative the Prophet said: "Then stick to her for paradise is beneath her two feet" (Ns. 25 : 6). Another companion once asked the Prophet: "Who has the greatest right that I should keep company with him with goodness?" The Prophet said: "Thy mother". The man asked: "Who next?" The Prophet said: "Thy mother". The man asked: "Who next" The Prophet said: "Then thy father."

Parents on the other hand were required to be kind and gentle towards their children. The suffering of parents in providing for and protecting their children was described by the Prophet as "a screen from the fire" for the parents (Bu. 24 : 10). In one tradition the Prophet is reported to have said: "He is not one of us who does not show mercy to our little ones and respect to our great ones" (MM. 24 : 15). The words of this tradition are general and apply not only to those younger or older in age but also to degrees of position and authority.

Unity and brotherhood of all mankind is a fundamental conception of Islām. The Muslims were, however, particularly exhorted to be kind to one another and to help one another. Believers are frequently described in the Qur'ān as brethren, and the quality of being "merciful among themselves" (48 : 29) is expressly mentioned. Muslims have been specifically prohibited from deriding others or looking down upon other Muslims with contempt, seeking faults in and being unduly suspicious of one another, etc: "O you who believe, let not people laugh at people, perchance they may be better than they. Neither find fault with your own people, nor call one another by nicknames. Evil is a bad name after faith ... O you who believe, avoid most of suspicion, for surely suspicion in some cases is sin; and spy not, nor let some of you backbite others. Does one of you like to eat the flesh of his dead brother? You abhor it! And keep your duty to Allāh, surely Allāh is oft-returning (to mercy), Merciful" (49 : 11, 12). Tradition describes Muslims as parts of one structure and compares them to a human body; when one member of it ails, the entire body ails. The Prophet said: "Thou wilt recognize the believers in their having mercy for one another and in their love for one another and in their kindness towards one another like the body; when one member of it ails, the entire body ails, one part calling out the other with sleeplessness and fever (Bu. 78 : 27). Books of Tradition are full of reports of a similar nature, some of which are given below:

"A Muslim is the brother of a Muslim; he does him no injustice, nor does he leave him alone (to be the victim of another's injustice); and whoever fulfils the need of his brother, Allāh fulfils his need; and whoever removes the distress of a Muslim, Allāh removes from him a distress out of the distresses of the Day of Resurrection; and whoever covers (the fault of) a Muslim, Allāh will cover his sins on the Day of Resurrection" (Bu. 46 : 3).

"Help thy brother whether he does wrong or wrong is done to him". The Companions said, "O Messenger of Allāh! We can help a man to whom wrong is done, but how can we help him, when he himself does wrong?" The Prophet said, "Take hold of his hand from doing wrong" (Bu. 46 : 4).

"Believers are in relation to one another as (parts of) a structure, one part of which strengthens another", and he inserted the fingers of one hand amid those of the other (so as to conjoin his two hands)" (Bu. 8 : 88).

"Do not hate one another and do not be jealous of one another and do not boycott one another, and be servants of Allāh as brethren; and it is not lawful for a Muslim that he should sever his relations with his brother for more than three days'' (Bu. 78 : 57).

Finally, in his last pilgrimage sermon at Minā, the Prophet said: ''Surely Allāh has made sacred to you your blood and your property and your honour as this day of yours is sacred in this month of yours in this city of yours'' (Bu. 25 : 132).

Kindness and good relations with one's neighbours are separately mentioned in a number of traditions. The Prophet said: ''Whoever believes in Allāh and the Last Day should not harm his neighbour and whoever believes in Allāh and the Last Day should honour his guests'' (Bu. 78 : 31). According to another report the Prophet said: ''Gabriel continued to enjoin me with good treatment towards the neighbour until I thought he would make him heir of the property (of the deceased neighbour)'' (Bu. 78 : 28). Kindness and generosity towards one's servants and employees is also separately mentioned in a number of traditions (*e.g.*, Bu. 2 : 21, 78 : 39) with the injunction to treat them on a basis of equality. But most of all, emphasis has been placed on kind and good behaviour towards the widows and orphans, as explained earlier in this chapter.

Home life

The home is the unit of human society and the human happiness and stability of the society depends to a large extent on the stability of the home and the happiness which prevails in it. As the male and the female together make the home, it was necessary to bring about a right understanding of their positions and relations. Women, before the time of the Prophet, were regarded as property of their husbands. They could not themselves own property nor carry out transactions in their own names. It was a perfect revolution in the existing social order which Islām brought about. Even in the earliest revelations of the Prophet men and women were spoken of as standing on the same level in the sight of God[2] and it is mentioned that both male and female were made perfect.[3] It was also in the earlier revelations that it was made clear that spiritually the woman stood on the same level with the man.[4] Women were also spoken of as receiving Divine revelation,[5] the greatest spiritual gift. They were

[2] 92 : 1-3; 53 : 44-46.
[3] 75 : 37-39.
[4] 40 : 40; 16 : 97.
[5] 28 : 7.

chosen by God and purified as men were chosen and purified.[6] And generally women are spoken of as equal to men in all spiritual aspects.[7]

The Prophet, however, went further and introduced a reform by which woman became a free person in the fullest sense of the word. She could earn, inherit and own propety. "For men is the benefit of what they earn and for women is the benefit of what they earn" (4 : 32). This direction opened for her all vocations, and though her maintenance was a condition of marriage, she could support herself and even become the breadwinner of the family, if she stood in need of it. Further, the Arabs had a very strong tradition against inheritance by women. Islām had a new message for her: "... for women is a share of what the parents and the near relatives leave ... an appointed share ..." (4 : 7). Every woman was, in fact, made the owner of some property at her marriage, and there was no limitation to the amount of dowry.[8] This was a practical step to raise the status of the woman. The status of a woman even before marriage was recognized by laying down that a woman could be taken in marriage only with her permission or consent.[9] In fact marriage has been described in the Qur'ān as a sacred contract[10] (*mīthāq*) and there would be no contract without the consent of the two parties.

For the stabilization of society every one was required to live in a married condition. There is a clear injunction to this effect: "And marry those among you who are single" (24 : 32). The Prophet is reported to have said that "the man who marries perfects half his religion". Marriage was thus recognized as a means to the moral uplift of man, and such it is in fact. Mutual love between husband and wife and parental love for offspring lead to a very high development to the feeling of love of man for man as such, and this in turn leads to the disinterested service of humanity. Through marriage the home is made a training ground for the development of the feeling of love and service. Here a man finds a real pleasure in suffering for the sake of others, and the sense of service is thus gradually developed and broadened.

Special emphasis has been laid in Islām on the mutual rights and responsibilities of husbands and wives. The position of the wife in the family was, according to the Prophet, that of a ruler (Bu. 67 : 91), and in a number of traditions the Prophet has emphasized the rights of women.

[6] 3 : 41; 33 : 33.

[7] 33 : 35.

[8] 5 : 5; 4 : 20.

[9] 4 : 19; Bu. 67 : 42, 43.

[10] 4 : 21.

The husband was required to provide for the maintenance of the wife and for her lodging according to his means.[11] The wife was bound to keep company with her husband, to preserve the husband's property from loss or waste and to refrain from doing anything which should disturb the peace of the family.[12] Stress was laid on kindly and good treatment of the wife. "Keep them in good fellowship" (2 : 229), "Treat them kindly" (4 : 19) is the oft-recurring advice, so much so that kindness was recommended even if a man disliked his wife (4 : 19). Good treatment towards the wife was a criterion of good morals: "The most excellent of you is he who is best in the treatment of his wife" (MM. 13 : 11-ii). While imparting advice to his followers at the Farewell Pilgrimage, the Holy Prophet said: "O my people! you have certain rights over your wives and so have your wives over you...They are the trust of Allāh in your hands. So you must treat them with all kindness".[13]

Work and Labour

Islām places great emphasis on the necessity for hard work and the dignity of labour. The principle was laid down in the earliest revelations in unequivocal terms that no one who does not work shall hope to reap any fruit and that the worker should have his full reward: "That man can have nothing but what he strives for; and that his striving will soon be seen. Then he will be rewarded for it the fullest reward" (53 : 39-41); "So whoever does good deeds and is a believer, there is no rejection of his effort, and We surely write it down for him" (21 : 94). Equal stress is laid in the Qur'ān, on faith and work: "those who believe and do good" is the ever-recurring description of the faithful.

The Prophet himself was an indefatigable worker. While he passed half the night, and even two-thirds of it, praying to God, he was doing every kind of work in the day time. No work was too low for him. He would milk his own goats, patch his own clothes and mend his own shoes. In person he would dust his home and assist his wife in her household duties. In person he would do shopping, not only for his own household but also for his neighbours and friends. He worked like a labourer in the

[11] 4 :34; 65 : 7; 4 : 19.

[12] Bu. 67 : 87.

[13] MM. 15 : 19.

construction of the mosque. Again, when a ditch was being dug around Madīnah to fortify it against a heavy attack, he was seen at work among the rank and file. He never despised any work, however humble, notwithstanding the dignity of his position as Prophet, as generalissimo and as king. He thus demonstrated through his personal example that every kind of work dignified man, and that a man's calling, whether high or low, did not constitute the criterion of his status. "No one eats better food than that which he eats out of the work of his own hand", he is reported to have said (Bu. 34 : 15). In his other sayings he has made clear that every work was honourable in comparison with asking for charity. His Companions followed his example and the most honourable of them did not disdain even the work of a porter.

The relations between a labourer and his employer were those of two contracting parties on a term of equality. The Prophet laid down a general law relating to contracts: "Muslims shall be bound by the conditions which they make" (Bu. 37 : 14). The master and the servant were considered two contracting parties, and the master was bound as much by the terms of the contract as the servant. This was made clear by the Prophet: "Allāh says, there are three persons whose adversary in dispute I shall be on the Day of Resurrection: a person who makes a promise in My name and then acts unfaithfully, a person who sells a free person then devours his price and a person who employs a servant and receives fully the labour due from him, then does not pay his remuneration" (Bu. 34 : 106).

The employees of the State, its collectors and executive officers and judges, were all included in the category of servants. They were entitled to a remuneration but they could not accept any gift from the public. Even those who taught the Qur'ān were entitled to remuneration: "The most worthy of things for which you take a remuneration is the Book of Allāh" (Bu. 37 : 16). 'Umar was once appointed a collector by the Prophet, and when offered a remuneration he said that he did not stand in need of it. The Prophet, however, told him to accept it and then give it away in charity if he liked (Bu. 94 : 17). The principle was thus laid down that every employee, every servant, every labourer was entitled to a remuneration.

Trading was one of the most honourable professions and the Prophet had special words of praise for the truthful and honest merchant (Tr. 12 : 4). People were taught to be generous in their dealings with one another, in buying and selling and demanding their dues (Bu. 34 : 16). Honesty was to be the basic principle in all dealings. "If they both speak the truth and make manifest (the defect, if any, in the transaction), their transaction shall be blessed, and if they conceal (the defect) and tell lies, the blessing of their transaction shall be obliterated (Bu. 34 : 19). Speculation, in cereals especially, was strictly prohibited: "Whoever buys cereals, he shall not sell them until he obtains their possession" (Bu. 34 : 54). The cultivation of land and planting of trees was encouraged (Bu. 41 : 1). It was also stated by the Prophet that whoever cultivates land which is not the property of anyone has a better title to it (Bu. 41 : 15). Those who had vast tracts of land, which they could not manage to cultivate for themselves, were advised to allow others to cultivate them free of charge: "If one of you gives it (*i.e.*, cultivable land) as a gift to his brother, it is better for him than that he takes it for a fixed payment" (MM. 12 : 13). But it was allowed that the owner of the land should give it to others to cultivate for a share of the produce or for a fixed sum (Bu. 41 : 8, 11, 19). The ownership of land by individuals was thus recognized, as also their right to buy or sell it or to have it cultivated for them by others. A warning was at the same time given that a people who give themselves up entirely to agriculture, neglecting other lines of development, could not rise to a position of great glory (Bu. 41 : 2).

Transformation wrought by the Prophet

The most outstanding characteristic of the Prophet's life is the amazing success which he achieved in bringing about a complete transformation in the life of his followers in all aspects. And all this came to pass in a short span of a little over 20 years. No other reformer found his people at such a depth of degradation as the Prophet found the Arabs, and no one raised them materially, morally and spiritually to the height to which he raised them. Not only was their deep-rooted love for idols and their superstitions swept away and the nation awakened to a sense of true dignity of humankind based on a rational religion but also there was a complete metamorphosis in their character. The Arab was cleansed of deep-rooted vice and bare-faced immorality; he was inspired with a burning desire for the best and noblest deed in the service of, not a country or nation, but, what is far higher than that, humanity. Old customs which involved injustice to the weak were all swept away and just and reasonable laws took their place. Drunkenness to which Arabia was addicted from time immemorial disappeared completely, gambling became unknown and loose relations between sexes gave place to the highest regard for chastity.

The Arab who prided himself on ignorance became the lover of knowledge, drinking deep at every fountain of learning to which he could get access. The whole character of the nation was changed. And thus from a discordant and disunited people full of vices and superstitions the religion and the Prophet of Islām welded together a united nation full of life, vigour and virtues before whose onward march the greatest kingdoms of the world crumbled. No man ever breathed such a new life into a people on such a wide scale, no other religion brought about such transformation in their lives affecting all branches of human activity — a transformation of the individual, of the family, of the society, of the nation, of the country, an awakening material as well as moral, intellectual as well as spiritual — as did the religion of Islām.

INDEX
OF
ARABIC WORDS AND PHRASES

INDEX

— Jews and Christians called, 146
— the word used in two senses, 143
Jizya, 426-432
— appropriation of, 429
— exemptions from, 428, 429
— non-Muslims exempted from military service on paying, 428
— not a religious tax, 427
— optional, 428
— refund of, 429
— zakāt and, 429
John the Baptist, 135, 172, 197, 343
Joseph, 560
Jurjān, 429
Juwairiyah, 492

K

Ka'b Aḥbār, 59
Ka'bah, 284, 285, 378, 381, 383
— antiquity of, 384
— circumambulation of, see Ṭawāf
— cleared of idols, 385-386
— discription of, 381
— history of, 383
— names of the four corners of, 382
— other names of, 377, 378, 383, 396
— place of security, 285
— rebuilt by Abraham and Ishmael, 285, 383
— reconstructed by Quraish, 384
— sacredness of, 378
— women going in, 394
— and Qiblah, 285, 378
Kāfir, 93, 94
— a Muslim cannot be called a, 94
— dividing line between a Muslim and a, 94
— none of the Ahl Qiblah can be called, 95
— cannot be killed for unbelief, 424
Kāhins, 148-151
Kalimah, belief in, 95
Kalimah Shahādah, 322
Kashf, 155
Khadījah, 20f
Khaibar, 450, 451
Khalīfah, head of a democracy, 74, 563-568
Kharāj, 427
khaulah, 507
Khawārij, 558
— divisions introduced into Islām by, 97
Khidzr, 166
Khul', 498
Khuṭbah, language of, 322
— object of, 322
Khuzā'ah, 423
Killing for unbelief, Qur'ān opposed to, 424
Kingdom of God, the, 398
Kissing, corners of Ka'bah, 395
— the Black Stone, 395
Kiswah, 382
Kufr, 93
Kursī, 117

L

Laḥd, 332
Lailat al-Qadr, 16, 374, 375

U

BOOK REVIEWS

Islamic Culture, Hyderabad Dn., October 1936:

Reviewed by M. Marmaduke Pickthall:

Probably no man living has done longer or more valuable service for the cause of Islamic Revival than Maulana Muḥammad Ali of Lahore. His literary works, with those of the late Khwaja Kamal-ud-Din have given fame and distinction to the Ahmadiyya Movement. In our opinion the present volume is his finest work. It is a description of Al-Islam by one well-versed in the Sunnah who has on his mind the shame of the Muslim decadence of the past five centuries and in his heart the hope of the revival, of which signs can now be seen on every side. Without moving a hair's breadth from the traditional position with regard to worship and religious duties, the author shows a wide field in which changes are lawful and may be desirable because here the rules and practice are not based on an ordinance of the Qur'ān or on an edict of the Prophet (peace be on him), and should be altered when they cease to meet the needs of the community. Such a book is greatly needed at the present day when in many Muslim countries we see persons eager for the reformation and revival of Islām, making mistakes through lack of just this knowledge.

The work is well-printed and handsomely got up, a credit to the Lahore publishers.

We recommend it as a stimulus to Islamic thought. To use an old-fashioned word it is an *edifying* book.

The Islamic Review, May 1937:

The name of Maulana Muḥammad Ali is well known to the English-speaking world of religion and even beyond. His English Translation of the Holy Qur'ān with commentary was the first translation of the Holy Book in a European language by a Muslim. Since then he has been incessantly wielding his pen in expounding the religion of Islām for the benefit of the modern world of science and reasoning.

He assumes the task of old-time Fuqaha in applying the principles of Shariat to the changing needs of human social life. Accordingly, the light of discursive logic which he has thrown on the third part of his work entitled "The laws and regulations of Islām" is not only a courageous, though much needed step, but also one that is likely to commend Islām to the practical West, tired of and almost antagonistic to, the mystical side of religion.

Mushir Hussain Kidwai of Gadia:

Like almost all other works of the Maulana, this also is a classical book exhaustive, bold and authentic. I wish it were translated in other languages, particularly in Turkish, Persian and Arabic.

Chaudhri Muḥammad Zalfrullah Khan, 5th February 1936:

The book is an extremely valuable contribution to the rather meagre literature on Islām in the English language; and of course being compiled by a scholar of your eminence and learning, it must rank as a *standard work on Islām*.

Mr. Justice Abdur Rashid, 5th January 1936:

It reveals great learning, deep research and a thorough mastery of the subject. "The Religion of Islām", its principles, laws and regulations, have all been exhaustively discussed in this comprehensive book. The conclusions of the learned author are amply supported by authority, and every controversial doctrine has been critically examined.

Dr. Muḥammad Iqbal, Lahore, 6th February 1936:

Thank you so much for your kind present to me of your new book, "The Religion of Islām". I very much appreciate the gift. I have glanced through parts of it, and find it an extremely useful work almost indispensable to the students of Islām. You have already written a number of books; one cannot but admire your energy and power of sustained work.